Victimology

Rejani Thudalikunnil Gopalan
Editors

Victimology

A Comprehensive Approach to Forensic, Psychosocial and Legal Perspectives

 Springer

Editor
Rejani Thudalikunnil Gopalan
Department of Clinical Psychology
Mahatma Gandhi Medical College and Hospital
Jaipur, Rajasthan, India

ISBN 978-3-031-12932-2   ISBN 978-3-031-12930-8   (eBook)
https://doi.org/10.1007/978-3-031-12930-8

This Springer imprint is published by the registered company Springer Nature Switzerland AG
The registered company address is: Gewerbestrasse 11, 6330 Cham, Switzerland

The book is dedicated to my beloved father
Late. Mr. T. K. Gopalan

Preface

The last few decades witnessed the fast growth of victimology and its impact on judiciary and policy makings, and this book is an attempt to explore more victims of different crimes. The term victim refers to a person harmed, injured, or killed as a result of a crime, accident, or other event or action, and victimology focuses on the victimization in terms of psychological effects, impact on the criminal justice system, and new policies, and it is a major aspect in the forensic field, especially the branch forensic victimology. Victimization can occur due to abuse, assault, maltreatment, war, terrorism, and crimes which can happen in different settings like home, school, and public places. The attempt to understand victims of various crimes and violence started since beginning of my career, and my work experience with victims of sexual abuse has given me the drive to explore further into this area in the late 1990s. Handling sexually abused males made me think in a different direction, and I understood that gender does not have much importance in the suffering of the victims, in other words, psychological suffering caused by sexual assault or rape is more or less the same for both genders and individuals with different sexual orientations. My clinical and research works with convicted offenders, especially sexual offenders, and the victims enriched my understanding of victimization. I also dealt with intimate partner violence or domestic violence victims and abusers, and my long association with the criminal justice system made me curious about the link between various crimes and violence and its impact on the criminal justice system. All my 20 years of experience in this field enticed me to focus more on victimization and revictimization processes which eventually led to the development of a book on victimization and a thread of new theory which I explain in the sixteenth chapter of this book.

The field of criminology deals with crime, and various theories have developed to explain why crime occurs. In the past, more emphasis was given to perpetrators, and various theories tried to explain the behavior of perpetrator and their offences. Recently, researchers started focusing on different aspects of victimology and explored risk factors for becoming a victim, reasons for repeated victimization, and forensic, psychological, and social dimensions of victims and consequences of victimization. A crime involves perpetrator and victim and not much attention has been given to the victim until recently. What happens to a victim? What are the psychological and social consequences of a harmful act on a victim? Vulnerabilities leading to victimhood are garnering serious attention nowadays and beginning to influence the criminal justice system. The psychological and social impacts of victimization may remain for a short or long duration, but the impacts cannot be ignored. Legal remedies and psychological healing are important aspects of victimization. While considering these factors, the book would be focusing on the origin and scope of victimology, and different types of victimization such as sexual abuse, domestic violence, maltreatment, cybercrimes, war and terrorism, natural calamities, victimization at school and workplace, human trafficking, crime against persons, crime against property, elder abuse, a victim with disabilities, and secondary victim and re-victimization and its psychological impacts and related issues. The book gives more attention to victims and focus on them while mentioning various crimes and forms of violence. This book is an attempt to explore and combine recent development in the area of victimization on different dimensions to impart knowledge mainly to students, researchers, clinicians, and academicians.

The first chapter is introductory and aims to provide the historical development of the field of victimology and its present and future scenario. Specifically, the chapter covers definitions of victimology and the history of the development of victimology as a special area. Types of victimology, various theories, and perspectives of victimology have been elaborated. Also, various risk factors/biopsychosocial factors associated with victimization have been discussed. The chapter mentions the influence of the criminal justice system and related disciplines.

Chapter 2 discusses the psychological assessment of victims and the guidelines for mental health practitioners who deal with them. Psychological assessments are an important part of investigations and treatment which enable the forensic expert to get leads or evidence of the crime. The chapter provides an overview of various assessments and effects on victims, and also provide a horizontal view of the needs and interventions available for mental health professionals working with victims and trauma clients. Professionals dealing with trauma may also go through secondary trauma, vicarious trauma, compassion fatigue, counter transference, and occupational burnout, and thus, the second part of the chapter would focus on it. The authors suggest that seeking effective and appropriate supervision by mental health professionals also aids in dealing with victims and trauma clients.

Chapter 3 deals with sexual abuse, and the chapter throws light on theoretical and etiological frameworks contributing to being a victim or a perpetrator. The authors explain the assessment related to sexual abuse and suggest a holistic approach catering to psychological, medical, and forensic investigations providing a basis for further legal proceedings. The chapter also deals with various treatment and prevention strategies.

Chapter 4 explores victims of sexual abuse in childhood. Children may not understand what is happening to them at that young age due to the developmental limitations in terms of cognitive and emotional aspects. The chapter focuses on the later life problems experienced by sexual abuse victims and the effect on the quality of life. Physiological markers, mental health concerns, interpersonal relationships, socio-economic facets, and issues around disclosure are some of the areas this chapter aims to address. The social and legal issues around the disclosure of the assault, the forensic aspects of sexual assault crimes, and various treatment modalities are also discussed.

Chapter 5 attempts to explore one of the growing crimes in the world called intimate partner violence or domestic violence. This chapter throws light on definition, types, prevalence, theories of intimate partner violence, risk factors, impacts, theories, forensic investigations, preventions, and interventions. It also explores various vulnerability and risk factors for IPV at multiple levels as well as the factors favoring the attitude of IPV at individual, relationship, social, and cultural levels.

Chapter 6 focuses on child maltreatment, and there are four common types of child maltreatment such as physical abuse, sexual abuse including sex trafficking, emotional abuse, and threatening abuse or neglect. One of the most common forms of child maltreatment is exposing a child to sexual abuse. This chapter focuses more on sexual abuse, and in cases of sexual abuse, there are mostly no eyewitness other than the child and the perpetrator, which increases the importance of the child's testimony. They explained very well on forensic interview for sexually abused children and the forensic assessment, interview, and related aspects were explained by giving Turkey model as an example.

Chapter 7 covers on cyberbullying. The purpose of this chapter is to examine cyberbullying among children and adolescents, referred to as "youths" throughout the chapter. An extension of traditional bullying, cyberbullying is a form of bullying which takes place by means of electronic technologies, such as email, instant messaging, social networking websites, and text messaging through mobile devices. Drawing on research from a variety of disciplines, such as psychology, education, social work, sociology, and computer science, this chapter describes the definition of cyberbullying, the electronic technologies used, the prevalence rates, characteristics and risk factors, negative psychosocial and academic difficulties, theoretical frameworks, recommendations, and future directions.

Chapter 8 deals with victims of war and terrorism. War always affects civilians, especially children and women, and it is necessary to rebuild their lives. This impact is long standing and has detrimental effects on the physical and mental health of the victims, which passes on to generations. The first section of the chapter focuses on the psychological process of war victims and their rehabilitation. The second section of the chapter deals in depth with terrorism, its definition, types, causes, psychosocial risk factors, and psychological and sociological theories. This chapter further provides insight into various strategies mental health professionals can use in order to rehabilitate war and terrorism victims and terrorist detainees.

Chapter 9 draws attention to natural calamities like earthquakes; landslides; volcanoes; hurricanes, tornados, and cyclones; floods; extreme temperature; and wildfires, which destroy life and environment. The victims of natural calamities face economic and social crises in addition to the loss of dear ones. This chapter focuses on the psychological reactions through a trauma lens of the victims when facing natural calamities and psychological aids to be provided. The chapter also deals with the stages and reactions of counsellors or volunteers at natural calamity sites, and psychological precautions and interventions to be taken care of to prevent the vicarious trauma, compassion fatigue, and burnout. It also describes the individual and group therapies and rehabilitation at individual and community levels.

Chapter 10 delves into different aspects of bullying at school and work place. Traumas, phobias, fear, and anxiety are commonly manifested mental health conditions for anyone who has experienced bullying. Bullying at school and workplace has become one of the highly researched topics across the globe, and it has been linked with poor mental health and productivity. This chapter compiles research conducted over the years and highlights the aspects, causes, and impact of victimization at school and workplace across the globe.

Chapter 11 covers human trafficking, and major theories from a psychosocial perspective are discussed, which support formulating a better understanding of human trafficking. This chapter also discusses the impact of trafficking, victims' sufferings, profile of offenders, forensic and psychiatric protocols for evaluating the victim, and prevention and interventions.

Chapter 12 aims to draw attention to different crimes that are committed against individuals. Examples of such crimes are homicide, assault, harassment, sexual violence, threat and abduction, and hate crimes, to name a few. These atrocities directly impact another person regardless of whether intentional or non-intentional. The principal focus areas of the chapter are on the types, causes, and theories of crime that explain criminal behavior targeted at persons. It also identifies the risk factors that make an individual or a group of individuals susceptible to becoming a potential victim of a crime. The chapter thus looks into theories of victim experiences and risk factors, personality traits, and associated psychosocial factors that explain crime and criminal behavior. Additionally, it covers the legal and social implications of crimes against persons, victimization, and preventive methods and intervention for victims and perpetrators along with the associated methods of investigation.

Chapter 13 focuses on crimes against property such as extortion, robbery, or arson that may be with or without force. It can involve cheating, destruction, and taking of property, such as stealing money. This chapter explains different types of crimes in general as well as against property and the causes. The risk factors, personality traits of the person executing the crime, the vulnerabilities of victims, and psychological reactions of victims are discussed. The prevention methods, as well as interventions, are described at length, which include actions to be taken at the individual level and society at large.

Chapter 14 explores elder abuse which has received increasing attention worldwide as a common problem with serious consequences for older people. This chapter has two sections, the first section deals with elder abuse and the second section focuses on elder victims with disabilities. Many different forms of elder abuse are reported, with a consensus regarding physical abuse, psychological/emotional abuse, sexual abuse, neglect, self-neglect, abandonment, and financial/material exploitation, which are described in detail. The cases and risk factors, victim experiences, and the social and policy impacts are discussed. The second section is about elder victims with physical and intellectual disabilities and other related disabilities who are also very vulnerable to crimes. Risk factors and victim experiences, prevention, intervention, and rehabilitation methods are described.

Chapter 15 deals with secondary victimization. Secondary victimization not only pushes the victim into deeper psychological trauma effects but in some way encourages possible offenders to "show" their supremacy, given by gender and tradition, by violence and sexual attacks. In this chapter, different forms of secondary victimization are explained and analyzed through historical and societal perspectives, as well as through different theoretical and research approaches.

Chapter 16 explores re-victimization. The concept of revictimization has been defined in many different ways, but the common theme that arises is the repetition of the victimization of the same person which can be physical, sexual, emotional, or any form of abuse. This chapter explores the factors associated with the revictimization of sexual abuse and intimate partner violence (IPV) to delineate the common factors in both violations. From the background of ecological and violence perspectives, and clinical and research experiences with different forms of violence and crimes, the author introduces a conceptual framework for revictimization. As it is a thread of conceptual formulation of theory, empirical studies are required to validate it.

Chapter 17 deals with early childhood violence exposure and subsequent antisocial behavior, which is explained in terms of intergenerational trauma by describing the aboriginal youth among Canadian young offenders, and this is a well written and interesting chapter. The Indian residential schools (IRS) policy and practice have caused severe historical trans-generational trauma among Canadian Indigenous people. The chapter attempts to correlate criminal intentions and a cascade of trauma among this population to grasp the connection between trauma, violence exposure, and subsequent juvenile delinquency and related antisocial behaviors.

Chapter 18 provides a conceptual lens around adolescent behavior with an understanding of victimization of youth through Bronfenbrenner's framework, and it is another well-written chapter. The author has comprehensively written about all risk factors at various levels described in Bronfenbrenner's theory. Recommendations are offered on how to best support this growing population with an understanding of trauma-informed instruction and supports offered in settings from school, community, agency, and religious institutions.

Chapter 19 covers psychological assessment of the victims. The first part of the chapter focuses on the bio-psycho-social impacts of stress and trauma while considering the field of victimology and emphasizes the theoretical-practical considerations. The second part of the chapter focuses on the various psychological tests used for the evaluations with detailed descriptions of each test. It is concluded that a comprehensive psychological assessment is required for the victims by a trained psychologist who has expertise in dealing with victims to give a clear picture of the psychological process of the victims.

Chapter 20 focuses on forensic investigations, and it briefly described the important forensic investigations such as medical analysis and investigations, criminal profiling, psychological autopsy, fingerprint matching, and ballistic analysis. Criminal profiling is a technique to identify the personality and behavior characteristics to predict the offender which assumes an inherent uniformity among the perpetrator's characters, personality and mode of Operandi and required knowledge and skill to produce each offender profiling and to make common characteristics of the offenders committing similar crimes and the chapter dealt with various aspects of criminal profiling. The current trends in psychological autopsy, fingerprint examination, and ballistic analysis are described. One section deals with the report writing of forensic investigations and court proceedings and focuses on the guidelines. The chapter also describes the guidelines and policies to be followed for investigations, especially in special cases of sexual abuse.

Finally, Chap. 21 deals with the mental health consequences of criminal victimization and its intervention. General guidelines for working with victims of violent crime are discussed in the context of the "Declaration of Basic Principles of Justice for Victims of Crime and Abuse of Power" adopted by the General Assembly of the United Nations in 1985. Mental health interventions for victims of violent crime in the immediate aftermath of victimization, including debriefing and psychological first aid, are evaluated with research evidence. This chapter also discusses various therapies such as trauma-focused approaches, including prolonged exposure therapy, cognitive processing therapy, trauma-focused CBT, and eye movement desensitization and reprocessing.

Jaipur, Rajasthan, India   Rejani Thudalikunnil Gopalan

Acknowledgments

I express my gratitude to all who have contributed and joined with me in the process of writing this book, especially York Williams, Michelle F. Wright, Claude R. Shema, and Vaitsa Giannouli, whose immense support and encouragement meant a lot to me all these years, and I hope to continue our mutual support in future too. I thank my son Hari Krishnan for his patience, sacrifices, and motivation for completing this book. I extend my thanks to family members, friends, and colleagues for their understanding and support. My heartfelt thanks to the publisher for their continuous support and suggestions.

Contents

Contributors

Namitha Babu THRIVE, Wayanad, India

Huseyin Batman Sandıklı School of Applied Sciences, Afyon Kocatepe University, Afyonkarahisar, Turkey

Milica Boskovic Faculty of Diplomacy and Security, Belgrade, Serbia

Dorothy Bhandari Deka Sarvodaya Healthcare, Guwahati, India

Vaitsa Giannouli Aristotle University of Thessaloniki, Thessaloniki, Greece

Rejani Thudalikunnil Gopalan Mahatma Gandhi Medical College and Hospital, Jaipur, India

Aarzoo Gupta Government Medical College & Hospital, Chandigarh, India

Afreen A. Hussain Forensic Psychology Division of the Central Forensic Science Laboratory, Guwahati, India

Avinash G. Kamath Department of Psychiatry, KMC Manipal Academy of Higher Education, Manipal, Karnataka, India

Archana Kashyap Government Medical College & Hospital, Chandigarh, India

Cagatay Serkan Kaya Sandıklı School of Applied Sciences, Afyon Kocatepe Üniversitesi, Afyonkarahisar, Turkey

Smriti Maini IILM University, Gurgaon, India

Mahak Mathur Mahatma Gandhi Medical College and Hospital, Jaipur, India

Gargi Chauhan Mehta Mahatma Gandhi Medical College and Hospital, Jaipur, India

Gordana Misev Center for Multidisciplinary Research and Communication, Belgrade, Serbia

Ashwini Deshpande Nagarhalli Little Pods, Mumbai, India

Kalpana Raman Auckland University of Technology, Auckland, New Zealand

Vikas Singh Rawat Mahatma Gandhi Medical College and Hospital, Jaipur, India

Sheeba Shamsudeen Central Institute of Psychiatry, Ranchi, India

Claude R. Shema Lancaster University, Lancaster, UK

Mauro Siri University of Genoa, Genoa, Italy

Nitha Thomas Private Practice, Udupi, Karnataka, India

York Williams West Chester University, West Chester, PA, USA

Michelle F. Wright DePaul University, Chicago, IL, USA

Chapter 1
Recent Updates on Victimology and Its Influence on Criminal Justice System

Rejani Thudalikunnil Gopalan

Introduction

Victimology, a branch of criminology, is a growing field, and many studies have been conducted on victims and perpetrators to understand the crime in a better way. The evolution of this branch has been subjected to many changes, mainly the definition, and its focus depends on social changes and legal understanding of the terms and viewpoints, and the influence of victimology on the current justice system is very remarkable. As the term victimology indicates, it is related to the victim, and it is important to understand the concept of victim and the emergence of the branch of victimology.

Definition of Victim

The definition of victim evolved as society progressed and the changes in the legal perspectives over time. The word victim originated from the Latin word *victima* which is used to describe animals sacrificed in religious ceremonies, and thus, the word is used in a spiritual context (Nash, 2008). According to Van Dijk (2009), in no language was the word victim first introduced as a technical, legal term, and the first use of the word victim for human beings in Western languages was as a special name for Jesus Christ, and thereafter, the word victim has in modern times come into use as a label to indicate suffering of fellow human being; and if it is viewed from a Christian background, victims are expected to show compassion, meekness and forgiveness, and in most languages, the first citations of the word in its broader sense do not even necessarily refer to victims of crimes but victims of disasters

R. T. Gopalan (✉)
Mahatma Gandhi Medical College and Hospital, Jaipur, India

R. T. Gopalan (ed.), *Victimology*, https://doi.org/10.1007/978-3-031-12930-8_1

generally. Later victims were considered in a legal context and considered as innocent and thus to be eligible for mercy. The term victim is defined by the World Society of Victimology as 'persons who, individually or collectively, have suffered harm, including physical or mental injury, emotional suffering or economic loss or substantial impairment of their fundamental rights through acts or omissions that violate criminal laws, including those proscribing abuses of power' (Van Dijk, 1997). Related to the concept of victims, victimhood is also another important concept that has both personal and cultural meanings. According to Mythen (2007), victimhood is defined as acquiring the status of a victim involving being party to a range of interactions and processes, including identification, labelling and recognition. By labelling as a victim, an individual or group needs to face lots of negative and positive consequences. On the positive side, victims may receive sympathy and support both from their social environment and official organizations, but on the negative side, they need to carry social and psychological stereotypical qualities of a victim such as weakness, vulnerability, frailty and fear. Moreover, passivity and helplessness may be perceived by victims as therapeutically unhelpful and even as stigmatizing, and sometimes, situation of the victim may be like disqualified from full social acceptance and may force them to refuse the services due to their distaste for the label 'victim' and the kind of stereotypes it elicits (Van Dijk & Groenhuijsen, 2009; Römkens & Diekstra, 1966; Goffman, 1963a: 9; Spalek, 2017). Victim status reflected socially constructed cultural values associated with notions of the 'ideal victim', and in Western culture, the ideal victim was considered as someone who suffers in silence. In addition to that, crime victims were confronted with a set of preconceived ideas about their emotions and behaviour, including a set of moral imperatives or role expectations, and hence, victim labelling is a process activated by the victims'social environment wherein victims must either accept a status limiting their freedom of behaviour or actively engage in renegotiating their identity (Walklate, 2006). According to Fohring (2018), such social construction, combined with the continued politicization of victimhood and victim's rights, has reinforced the dichotomy not only between victim and offender but also between victims and survivors, and deserving and undeserving victims. Research also confirmed that victims' perceptions and labelling of an incident on their subsequent response to the incident – that is, whether or not they perceived an incident as a crime (and thus themselves as victims) – affected their involvement with the criminal justice system by doing underreporting of crime and low uptake of victim support services (Fohring, 2015).

Definition of Victimology as It Evolves and History

As mentioned earlier, victimology is a branch related to victims, and it was used to describe the study of individuals harmed by criminals. The term appeared in 1949 in a book by Fredric Wertham (Karman, 2007). The definition of victimology has undergone changes and modifications from the victim's contribution to the crime, and in recent times, it is defined as the scientific study of victims and victimization, including the relationships between victims and offenders, investigators, courts, corrections, media, and social movements (Karmen, 1990). According to Van Dijk (1999), there are two types of victimology, one is general victimology which is defined as the study of victims generally harmed by accidents, natural disasters, war, etc., and the second one is interactionist (or penal) victimology, which studies the causation of crimes with those relating to the victim's role in the criminal proceedings. Initially, victimology research often hinged on the attribution of blame towards victims despite a lack of conceptual agreement on the definition and measure of the construct (Cramer et al., 2013), and it can be noted from the recent definitions that focus shifted to victim contribution or victim blame to interaction or relationship between victim and offender.

History of Victimology in Legal and Social Perspectives

Identifying as a victim of crime is a complex process involving both social and personal motivations, and the word victim originated from the Latin word victim, which was more related to sacrifice, individuals or animals to be sacrificed to please a deity. Later, the word victim was used to refer to harm or loss. According to Christie (1986), any individual, group or entity that has been injured or has lost their livelihood as a result of criminal activity is referred to as a 'crime victim'. How a victim identifies themselves suggests an acknowledgement of the incident as wrong and illegal, and one of the core characteristics of victims is weakness (Fohring, 2018; Spalek, 2017; Christie, 1986).

The definition of crime, victim and offender changed over the legal and social changes, and the way the victim was viewed from innocent to contributor to some extent of crime reflected the same changes. Based on victims'role in justice systems, three distinct historical eras were described as the golden age, the dark age and the re-emergence of the victim (Jerin & Moriarty, 1998, 6). During earlier times, victim-driven approaches prevailed especially in tribal law time which is considered to be the golden age because personal retribution was the solution for the crime happened, and victims had the right to seek revenge or compensation for their losses directly from those who wronged them (Jerin & Moriarty, 1998, 6; Karman, 2007; Shichor & Tibbetts, 2002; Shichor & Tibbetts, 2002, p. 3; Doerner & Lab, 2011), and such kinds of laws still exist in some countries where the tribal system is predominant. Even the revenge runs into families and thus resulted in re-victimization or punishing people who weren't directly involved (Shichor & Tibbetts, 2002).

During the dark age, the offences were considered to be against the laws of the king or state; hence, more emphasis was given to punishing the individual or groups that initiated the crime, and punishing the offender was the major focus, and gradually the victim's suffering and rights were almost forgotten (Doerner & Lab, 2002; Karman, 2007).

During the period from 1950 to 1960, insight related to the victims' rights and needs in the judicial system that victims were mainly considered as a source of information did not emphasize their rights or needs which eventually led to another movement, and focus shifted away from offender to victim rights and their relationship with the offender. This is considered as the period of the re-emergence of the victim, and lots of empirical studies also facilitated this movement studies (Karman, 2007; Petherick & Sinnamon, 2013). Between the 1960s and 1970s, the victims' rights movement had been started in the United States and emphasized enhancing victims' participation in criminal adjudications and improving social services for victims because victims lacked any right to confer with prosecutors or influence sentencing decisions. The plight of the victim, forgotten person, was dominant during the 1980s, and the political context of victims' rights also began to change (Nash, 2008; Slavin & Sorin, 1984).

There was a growing understanding that justice to victims means when society and the state are resorting to every possible measure of correction and rehabilitation of offenders, equal concern must be shown for the victims by at least providing compensation to them for their loss, agony, and physical and mental torture. So, it is important to gain knowledge about victims of crime, the struggles faced by such people in coping with the adverse effects of a criminal act, and how could the Justice System compensate and rehabilitate such victims, and the crime victims became central relevance to the subject of victimology apart from being a sad product of the activity (Randhawa, 2011; Williams, 2001).

There were pioneers of victimology named Hans von Hentig, Benjamin Mendelsohn, Stephen Schafer and Marvin Wolfgang whose interest and attempts to understand victim contribution to a crime laid the foundation of the branch of victimology in the middle of the twentieth century (Doerner & Lab, 2011; Ferguson & Turvey, 2009). In his curiosity regarding the causes of becoming a victim, Hans von Hentig, a criminologist from Germany, classified victims into one of 13 categories based on victims' characteristics which might cause increased victimization. According to him, being young, female, old, mentally defective and deranged, immigrants, minorities, dull normal, depressed, acquisitive, wanton, lonesome or heartbroken, tormentor, blocked, exempted or fighting has increased the victim's vulnerability or exposure to danger and thus contributed a role in their victimization (Von Hentig, 1948; Doerner and Lab 2005; Menkel-Meadow 2007). Similar to this, the contribution of victims was studied by a French-Israeli lawyer named Benjamin Mendelsohn in 1947 who created the term victimology and was considered to be the father of victimology by proposing a typology based on situational factors such as completely innocent victim, victim due to ignorance, voluntary victim, victim more guilty than the offender, most guilty victim and simulating or imaginary victim. He observed a strong interpersonal relationship between the victim and offender which might have invited their victimization (victim precipitation). He emphasized victim proneness and that many victims shared an unconscious capacity for being victimized (Menkel-Meadow, 2007; Doerner & Lab, 2011; Ferguson & Turvey, 2009; Wilson, 2009). Another attempt to make a typology based on victim culpability was done by Dr. Stephen Schafer who was a professor of sociology and proposed seven types of victim responsibility such as unrelated victims, provocative victims, precipitative victims, biologically weak victims, socially weak victims, self-victimizing and political victims (Doerner & Lab, 2002; Petherick & Sinnamon, 2013). In his empirical studies on homicides from 1948 to 1952 on victim contribution and participation, Dr. Marvin Wolfgang (1958), a professor of criminology, described victim-precipitated homicide in which the victim initiated the physical violence or threat (Doerner & Lab, 2005; Shichor & Tibbetts, 2002; Doerner & Lab, 2011; Pesta, 2011). The typologies they made may not be relevant today, but their vision contributed to a shift from the offender to the victim and victim–offender interaction in the occurrence of crime, especially before, during and after the crime which laid pathways for future studies on this domain.

As noted by Van Dijk (1999), early victimologists have indeed often exhibited precious little sensitivity for victims and studied less on the experiences or needs of victims and were more interested in offenders, and the research on the needs of the victims started in the middle of the 1970s (e.g. Knudten, 1976; Dumig & van Dijk, 1975; Waller & Okihiro, 1978; Shapland et al., 1985). The second wave of victimological studies was characterized by not much emphasis on guilt, emotional problems and needs of the victim related to the crime and mainly centred around the clinical concept of post-traumatic stress syndrome (PTSD) and highlighted the stereotypical nature of the common notion that individuals with PTSD are full of helplessness and fear, but not of anger and hostility, and even the treatment model reproduced and reinforced the stereotypical image of the victim as weak and passive rather than as angry and action-oriented (Horowitz, 1986; Winkel, 2007). The victim movement towards criminal justice system resulted in more services to reduce the pain and suffering of victims due to victimization experience such as crisis intervention, individual and group counselling, and so forth, and some studies found it as effective in the improvement of the psychological functioning of crime victims, while some studies did not (Sims et al., 2006). Also, the suggestions emerged that victimology should focus on ways to nurture the strengths of victims and to assist them in benefitting from their negative experiences and/or transforming their suffering into social or political action to prevent crimes or assist victims, in addition to focus on possible disorders and needs of the victim for treatment or services (Van Dijk, 2009). The process of victimization also includes the process of coping and healing, one that may take many years to complete. The criminal justice system is a major component of this process and should seek to aid rather than hinder or hamper the healing process and should support and assist rather than add to the burden of victimization. There is a complex interaction between individuals and society inherent in crime and victimization, apparent in the interlinking of patterns across the process. Although it has been evidenced that variation in risk, reporting and service use is largely due to variation at the individual level, significant variation across neighbourhoods does exist (Fohring, 2012). The seriousness of the offence is still the most important factor influencing victims'decisions, and property crime is less likely to be reported, whereas violent crime is more likely to be reported (Tarling & Morris, 2010).

Theories of Victimization

Theories of victimization mainly focus on what made a person become a victim or why the person was victimized, and various factors are being proposed to explain victimization such as demographic, personal vulnerabilities, biopsychosocial factors and cultural factors. Accordingly, many theories have emerged in the last few decades, and the current section will focus on major theories of victimization.

Victim Precipitation Theory

Victimology originated with the victim precipitation theory, and this first theory of victimization states that characteristics of the victim precipitate the crime which harms them, either through victim facilitation or through victim provocation, and accordingly, typologies were developed also (Lasky et al., 2022). Although scientific evidence supports the fact that precipitation is useful within the disciplines of criminology and victimology, it always remains a controversial theory, but it cannot be denied that some victims can also be offenders, and some offenders can also be victims (Petherick, 2017; Muftić & Hunt, 2013). Timmer and Norman (1984) opined that the ideology of victim precipitation has no place in progressive criminology or progressive criminal justice system that attempts to identify how crime is generated and prevented structurally. According to Petherick (2017), this theory provides a deeper understanding of victimization, dynamics between offender and victims, and risk for re-victimization. However controversial it is, the theory is still relevant now.

Lifestyle and Exposure Theory

To explain victimization, Hindelang, Gottfredson, and Garofalo (1978) put forward the lifestyle and exposure theory which mainly focused on the contribution of victim lifestyle to victimization. Lifestyle involves daily activities done on a routine basis which is influenced by age, gender or income, role expectations and structural constraints that may increase the risk to get victimized and emphasized that victim–offender (targeted victim and motivated offender) contact is essential for the crime to happen (Meier & Miethe, 1993; Wilson, 2009, p. 158; Averdijk, 2011). This first systematic theory has substantial empirical backups in explaining various types of crimes (Miethe et al., 1987; Kennedy & Forde, 1990; Valan & Srinivasan, 2021).

Routine Activity Theory

Routine activity theory, as proposed by Cohen and Felson (2010), is inspired by lifestyle theory that motivated offenders, suitable targets and lack of capable guardianship are essential for the occurrence of crime, and crime actually happens when these factors occur on a convergence of time and space (Cohen & Felson, 2010 p. 589) and proposed that a person's routine activities or daily routine patterns may risk him to be in contact with motivated offenders. According to routine activity theory, crime can only be committed if a likely offender thinks that a target is suitable and a capable guardian is absent which presents a clear-cut explanation of why crimes occur, and the theory was used to explain changes in crime trends over time. But it also found a useful tool for crime reduction or prevention practitioners to evaluate crime problems, especially property crime, and also take routine precautions and measures that reduce crime opportunities in people's daily activities (Argun & Dağlar, 2016). Though this theory provides a simple and powerful insight into the causes of crime problems, it contributed a time dimension to the crime–space relationship and proposed the idea that offenders will prey upon attractive targets in the absence of effective controls. It has been criticized for crime displacement, its failure to explain the circumstances to cause motivated offenders and suitable targets to converge in the absence of capable guardians, why some people are more prone than others to seek out places where deviant behaviour is likely to occur, and why it failed to identify what distinguishes individuals who develop delinquent behaviour from those who do not in the availability of same opportunities (Argun & Dağlar, 2016; Dolu, 2010; Brunet, 2002:75–76; Wilcox et al., 2003; Bratt, 2018).

Deviant Place Theory

This theory states that victimization happens when an individual is in a bad or risky environment which is conducive to crimes and thus to avoid such places to avoid the victimization, and now, this theory is known as ecology theory. Social disorganization, which involves high crime areas, lack of parental control, high population in a small geographic area, poverty, or drug sale, and being in such areas, would increase the likelihood of victimization (Leading Theories of Victimization Risk, 2020). In his research regarding crime and deviant places, Stark (1987) focused on urban places and urban traits such as density, poverty, mixed-use, transience and dilapidation (five-place traits) and four individual traits (moral cynicism, increased opportunities for crime and deviance, increased motivation, and diminished control) to explain crime risk through 30 propositions and noticed that density was one of the biggest risk factors of deviance and crime. It is well known that high rates of crime and deviance can persist in specific neighbourhoods despite repeated, complete turnovers in the composition of their population. Studies have confirmed that place and age were significant factors to the occurrence of crime, and metropolitan principal cities have the strongest relationship to crime victimization and victimization sex gaps (Stark, 1987; Helle, 2014).

Social Learning Theory

Two theorists, Edwin Sutherland and Ronald Akers who build on symbolic interactionism, are key to understanding social learning theories of crime, and it argues that some people learn to commit crimes through the same process through which others learn to conform (Triplett & Upton, 2015). As noted by Jensen (2015), Robert Burgess and Ronald Akers reformulated differential association theory in terms of operant learning theory in 1966, and Akers and colleagues elaborated on a more general social learning theory in later works (1979). The four fundamental premises of social learning theory are differential association, definitions, differential reinforcement and imitation (Akers & Sellers, 2004). When applying this theory to victimization, it was noticed that those who engage in modelling behaviours, differential association, differential reinforcement and who adopt favourable definitions are more inclined to become victims of criminal activities (Gover & Wells, 2022). Much empirical research has been done regarding the relation with social learning theory on crime; perhaps, this is one of the most researched theories on crime and consistently proved the link with crime, especially in interpersonal violence and stalking.

Control Balance Theory

Charles R. Tittle (1995) developed the control balance theory and refined it in 2004 which proposes that control ratio imbalances are associated with deviance because they will lead to an imbalance between motivation towards deviance and constraints on deviance behaviour, and there are two types of control imbalances such as control deficits, which occur when the control that individuals can exercise is exceeded by the amount of control to which they are subject, and control surpluses, which indicate that the controls that individuals can exercise surpass the controls they experience. Perceived control ratio imbalances may produce feelings of disrespect or humiliation, thus promoting contemplations of how to extend control of people, events and circumstances without stimulating counter control, and more controlled or bonded individuals may not get into deviance while opposite dimensions attract deviance (Tittle, 1995; Tittle & Dollar, 2019; Piquero & Hickman, 1999). This theory opens up the potential for a more productive integration of explanatory and normative theory in criminology, and it was able to predict deviant behaviours in adults and adolescents, and many different forms of crime and both control surpluses and control deficits were associated with the probability of both general and predative victimization (Braithwaite, 1997; Piquero & Hickman, 2003).

General Theory of Crime

According to the general theory of crime as proposed by Gottfredson and Hirschi (1993), crime happens because of poor self-control of individuals due to poor parenting, and those who are having poor self-control exhibit characteristics like risk-taking behaviour, insensitiveness to others, problems in social relationships, and use of drugs and alcohol, and this theory is used to explain offending behaviours mainly and received empirical supports. It is also applied to explain victimization, and studies found that higher self-control does directly decrease victimization and that self-control also affects victimization indirectly through opportunities (peer deviance) among juveniles (Nofziger, 2009), and women who displayed low levels of self-control had a higher risk of violent victimization, even after controlling for demographic and lifestyle correlates of victimization (Stewart et al., 2004).

Though many different theories tried to explain crime and victims, and the interaction of victim and offender, a comprehensive explanation for different crimes is yet to happen. Most of the theories are limited with a focus on one or few aspects of crime, victims and offender. As the crime itself is complicated with multifactorial aspects, future studies can focus on the same to explain and propose theories more comprehensively.

Risk Factors/Biopsychosocial Factors Associated with Victimization

There are risk factors associated with crime and victimization such as genetics, neurotransmitters, mental disorders, alcohol and social factors like the neighbourhood, peer group/spending time with delinquent/ personal interaction, family factors, adult social bond, immigration, social interaction perspective and age-graded theory of adult social bond.

Genetic

Association between genetic factors and criminal behaviours is well established, and recent studies have been focussing on the genetic origins of victimization. Studies have noticed gene X environment interaction in the creation of victimization, especially interaction of DRD2 to predict victimization (Beaver et al., 2007), the interaction of DRD4 and environment for verbal victimization and child-reported externalizing behaviours, specifically DRD4 7-repeat allele to verbal victimization environment (DiLalla et al., 2015). The presence of the A1 allele of DRD2 among females showed more vulnerability to the negative effects of violent victimization (Vaske et al., 2009), and more studies are required to have a better understanding of the gene X environment interaction for victimization.

Neurotransmitters

Studies on the link between neurotransmitter functioning and violent crime have suggested that monoamine (i.e. serotonin, dopamine, and norepinephrine) neurotransmitter functioning is related to human aggressive behaviour, especially violent criminal behaviour and dysfunctional interactions between serotonin and dopamine systems in the prefrontal cortex play important role in impulsive aggression and its comorbid disorders. It is also argued that serotonin hypofunction may represent a biochemical trait that predisposes individuals to impulsive aggression, but both genetics and the environment act collaboratively in the expression of violent behaviour (Berman & Coccaro, 1998; Seo et al., 2008; Karalis & Kleisiari-Karalis, 2019).

Mental Disorders

Victimization is related to mental disorders, and patients with serious mental disorders present a higher risk of victimization when compared to the general population with an estimation of 11.8 times more chances for violent crimes (Passos et al., 2013; Teplin et al., 2005). It was observed that diagnosis of anxiety disorders was associated with more sexual assaults, schizophreniform disorders risked more threatened and completed physical assaults, alcohol dependence disorders were associated with more completed physical assaults, while marijuana dependence disorders were paired with more attempted physical assaults (Silver et al., 2005). The main factors associated with victimization among people with mental disorders were substance use, young age, severe symptomatology, a recent history of violence perpetration, criminal history, male gender and homelessness (Passos et al., 2013) and that for inside the mental health care system were psychotic disorder, victimization in childhood and youth, female gender, number of hospitalizations and duration of illness (Rossa-Roccor et al., 2020).

Alcohol

Alcohol is a double-edge sword related to victimization, as it can initiate victimization or can lead to becoming a victim, and many studies have noticed that alcohol intoxication is involved for both victims and perpetrators of sexual victimization, and a reciprocal relationship was observed between heavy alcohol use and sexual victimization (Kehayes et al., 2019; Kilpatrick et al., 1997). Women's heavy episodic drinking can be a proximal risk factor or in another way alcohol use increases a woman's vulnerability to sexual victimization, and the majority of rapes in college occur when the victim is too intoxicated to resist ('incapacitated rape'), and the impact of victimization for both male and female can be different in terms of coping methods or is experiencing depression or anxiety. For example, female victims may drink more to cope with victimization, and males who were victimized by someone drinking displayed increased anxiety (Testa & Livingston, 2009; Parks et al., 2014; Kehayes et al., 2019).

Social Factors

Neighbourhood

Like alcohol, the neighbourhood also plays a double-edge impact on crime and victimization. Neighbourhood contexts such as disorder, leisure opportunities, perceived safety, female-headed families, residential mobility and structural density have the strongest effects on victimization rates, and poverty, inequality, percentage of black, residential mobility, structural density, and economic and social decay within neighbourhoods were related with victimization (Sampson, 1983, 1985; Holt et al., 2014).

Peer Group/Spending Time with Delinquent/ Personal Interaction

Studies have noticed that delinquent peer affiliation is a potential link between peer victimization and aggressive behaviour (Lin et al., 2018), and victimization is predicted to increase externalizing, attention dysregulation and immature/dependent behaviour as the child grows (Schwartz et al., 1998).

Family Factors

The risk for victimization and family factors are closely related such as family structure, high parental conflict, drug or alcohol problems, family adversity, community disorder, single-parent families and exposure to multiple forms of victimization within the family, and such victimization exposure was significantly related with parental dysfunction, family adversity, residential instability and problematic parenting practices (Hartinger-Saunders et al., 2012; Turner et al., 2012, 2013; Lauritsen and Rezey, 2013).

Immigration

Immigrants have a high risk for victimization as indicated by many studies. Sela-Shayovitz (2021) reported that immigration plays a key role in both femicide and femicide-suicide, and femicide-suicide rates were significantly higher among immigrants than among Israeli-native Jews and Arabs. As observed by Rashad (2020), there has been a considerable amount of research examining the potential connection between immigration and the risk of victimization, and the results generated from this body of research have produced somewhat mixed results and found no association between being an immigrant and being victimized during adolescence and adulthood. Other studies too reported less victimization among immigrants, and a person's foreign-born status confers protection against victimization (Sabina, Cuevas, & Schally, 2013; Xie & Baumer, 2021). Homicide victimization rates were substantially lower for foreign-born persons (Freemon et al., 2022). According to Papadopoulos (2012), immigrants face a lower risk of violent victimization because of lifestyles associated with lower exposure to crime.

Cultural and Feminist View Points on Victimology Theories

Feminists' viewpoints largely influenced the criminal justice system, especially during the second wave of feminism, and major contributions have been made especially to the understanding of sexual violence. Radical feminism challenges men's sexual power over women and argues for the foregrounding of women's knowledge, and socialist feminism dwells on the interplay between patriarchy and capitalism insisting on the interaction of class, race, sex and gender age in terms of getting justice. Post-modern feminism accommodates different standpoints and gives voice to diversity (Davies et al., 2007). Radical feminists greatly developed female victimology, and particularly sex and gender relations are established issues in the form of deviance, conformity and social control that archetypical masculinist concepts of crime and justice have either been disregarded or neglected (Chesney-Lind & Daly, 1986). The feminist movement has sought to change these issues surrounding victimology, interlinking the feminist perspective and a change to the theories of criminology as a whole (UKEssays. November, 2018; Rennison, 2014). The mostly feminist theory looks into the crime among women. However, there is a growing body of literature related to feminist victimization theory and/or examining victimization through a feminist lens (Crittenden & Policastro, 2018).

Influence of Criminal Justice System and Related Disciplines

Every crime produces a victim, and as providing justice to the victim is mandatory, the importance of the criminal justice system is established. It is the governmental and commercial organization network that manages offenders charged with conviction, and academics, law enforcement, forensic, judicial and corrective measures are its different pillars, and it aimed to defend human and state rights from the deliberate violation of offenders who breach society's fundamental rules and security. In the Modern Criminal Justice System, mainstream victimology continues to focus solely on the study of crime victims which resulted in increased awareness and understanding of not only victims of crime, but the way crime is measured and the role victims play. Also, society as a whole has a moral responsibility because the crime is a result of certain undesired conditions existing in the society, and the importance of restorative justice is very significant here. Restorative justice is an umbrella concept under which various concrete projects, such as victim–offender mediation and conferencing, fall, and it overtly recognizes the victim and the harm suffered as a result of the crime (Kumar & Verma, 2020; Wemmers, 2009). To provide justice to the victim, it is important to consider the impact of crime on the victim which can be in physical, psychological, financial and social areas and to consider both short-term and long-term impacts. These factors point out the needs of the victims and how to meet these needs and also provide justice to the victim. Many crimes, especially violent crimes, involve physical injuries which can be serious enough to make bedridden, handicapped or lose the cognitive functions where the victims need financial support to undergo treatment and sustain their livelihood. The psychological scar of crime on victims is another important need to address. Many victims undergo severe emotional reactions such as fear, sadness and anger, which may lead to psychological issues or mental disorders in long term and will again affect them financially. Many may have limited financial resources to undergo treatment for mental agonies caused by the crime or make them incapable of doing their work. The crime itself can cause financial loss such as property crime, theft and destruction of properties, and legal battling also cost financially. It is also important to notice that the legal battle to get justice for their loss of dignity, property, and physical and psychological damages involves time and money which also cause emotional turmoil to the victims. In addition to all these, victims may also face social stigma, isolation, embarrassment and the negative connotations attached to the term victim, especially the rape victims. More delays in the court proceedings and investigations further add to the victims' suffering. The criminal justice system always addressed the needs of the victims on different levels and tried to rectify or modify the laws to provide maximum justice to the victims in terms of compensation and restoration, and the efforts are continuing.

The field of victimology extends its support to the criminal justice system in many ways to deliver justice to the victim. According to Szabo (1981), offender-oriented criminal policy depends primarily on the medical model (treatment, rehabilitation), and victimology suggests policies using the preventive model (public education, citizen crime prevention) and the justice model (restitution, compensation programs). Victimology is an essential component in the crime scene analysis and related criminal profiling process which may assist with modus operandi analysis, case linkage or motivational analysis or simply to offer an opinion regarding the victim's risk or exposure to various kinds of harm or loss (Turvey, 2011, 2014). The field of victimology can assist in crime prevention mainly by providing information regarding the risk of crime and high-risk groups, law enforcement, corrections by providing the relationships or interaction between offender and victim, and the psychological impact of crime, which can help them provide more effective feedback and, ultimately, reduce recidivism. This field also can help in criminal prosecution by providing accuracy of testimony and helping attorneys choose effective cross-examination questions (Morgan et al., 2006).

Future Directions

While looking into history, victims initially had an active participatory role in the criminal justice process. The less active role of victims fuelled initiatives with restorative justice that claim to more fully include victims than conventional criminal justice (Wemmers, 2009). The emergence of forensic victimology is a new development to deeply understand the victim and the relationship between victim and offender in the crime, and the field is growing fast. The definition of victims always links with innocents, suffering and loss, and in most cases, it is true. Traditionally, the victim accuses or points out to someone or a group (the offender) that he or she did a crime. But many cases gave the clue that victim accuses some one as an offender though victim knows that he is innocent and the victim is doing it intentionally to damage his reputation or to take revenge. This scenario is very important in the case of sexual abuse. In India, the law is more favourable to women and children, especially related to sexual abuse. But some misuse the law and falsely or intentionally accuse males in order to destroy their reputation as the repercussion of being an offender is very damaging to him and their family in the society. It is the turn of the accused to prove his innocents and may take long years meanwhile he may lose his job and family and face humiliation in the society in addition to the mental agony. In many cases, the accused may end their life to end the turmoil. My argument is that the accused is the actual victim in this scenario, so the definition of victim is applicable here for the accused. In the above-mentioned case scenario, strict punitive is required to be given for false accusations. Though they are similar but the definitions and criteria of crime are different which has to be a major concern in forensic victimology. The field can rectify the existing loop poles of the law and can provide suggestions to improve it. In a brief span of a few decades, victimology has evolved from a subject studied by a few scattered researchers to one that generates worldwide interest and has become an academic branch. The academic discipline of victimology has a critical role to play in the future, and more studies are required for the growth of the victimology such as victimization surveys, studies to explore offender–victim relationships, impacts of psychological victimization, benefits of victim assistance and crime prevention policies, and comparative studies of the victim's role and function in society and the criminal justice system added to that research are to be conducted with conviction, compassion, commitment and courage (Lehner-Zimmerer, 2011; Szabo, 1981). It is important to continue to develop and implement standard international protocols on the rights of victims and abuse of power and to influence the criminal justice system across the world.

References

Akers, R. L. (1979). Theory and ideology in Marxist criminology: Comments on Turk, Quinney, Toby, and Klockars. *Criminology, 16(4), 527–544.*

Akers, R., & Sellers, C. (2004). *Criminological theories: Introduction, evaluation, and application* (4th ed.). Roxbury Publishing, Los Angeles.

Argun, U., & Dağlar, M. (2016). Examination of Routine Activities Theory by the property crime. *Journal of Human Sciences, 13*(1), 1188–1198. https://doi.org/10.14687/ijhs.v13i1.3665

Averdijk, M. (2011). Reciprocal effects of victimization and routine activities. *Journal of Quantitative Criminology, 27*(2), 125–149. https://doi.org/10.1007/s10940-010-9106-6

Beaver, K. M., Wright, J. P., DeLisi, M., Daigle, L. E., Swatt, M. L., & Gibson, C. L. (2007). Evidence of a gene X environment interaction in the creation of victimization: Results from a longitudinal sample of adolescents. *International Journal of Offender Therapy and Comparative Criminology, 51*(6), 620–645. https://doi.org/10.1177/0306624X07304157

Berman, M. E., & Coccaro, E. F. (1998). Neurobiologic correlates of violence: Relevance to criminal responsibility. *Behavioral Sciences & the Law, 16*(3), 303–318. https://doi.org/10.1002/(SICI)1099-0798(199822)16:3<303::AID-BSL309>3.0.CO;2-C

Braithwaite, J. (1997). Charles Tittle's control balance and criminological theory. *Theoretical Criminology, 1(1), 77–97.* https://doi.org/10.1177/1362480697001001005

Bratt, D. (2018). Implementing the Reform Party agenda: the roots of Stephen Harper's foreign policy. *Canadian Foreign Policy Journal, 24*(1), 1–17.

Brunet, J. R. (2002). Discouragement of crime through civil remedies: An application of a reformulated routine activities theory. *Western Criminology Review, 4, 68.*

Chesney-Lind, M., & Lind, I. Y. (1986). Visitors as victims crimes against tourists in Hawaii. *Annals of Tourism Research, 13*(2), 167–191.

Christie, N. (1986). Ideal victim. In E. A. Fattah (Ed.), Crime policy to victim policy (pp. 17–30), NCJ-102547. National Criminal Justice Reference Service (NCJRS), New York.

Cohen, L. E., & Felson, M. (2010). Social change and crime rate trends: A routine activity approach (1979). In Classics in environmental criminology (pp. 203–232). American Sociological Association, New York.

Cramer, R. J., Nobles, M. R., Amacker, A. M., & Dovoedo, L. (2013). Defining and evaluating perceptions of victim blame in antigay hate crimes. *Journal of Interpersonal Violence, 28*(14), 2894–2914. https://doi.org/10.1177/0886260513488687

Crittenden, C., & Policastro, C. (2018). *Feminist victimization theories. Last modified: 11 Jan.* https://doi.org/10.1093/OBO/9780195396607-0231.

Davies, K., Block, C. R., & Campbell, J. (2007). Seeking help from the police: Battered women's decisions and experiences. *Criminal Justice Studies, 20*(1), 15–41.

DiLalla, L. F., Bersted, K., & John, S. G. (2015). Peer victimization and DRD4 genotype influence problem behaviors in young children. *Journal of Youth and Adolescence, 44*, 1478–1493. https://doi.org/10.1007/s10964-015-0282-4

Doerner, W., & Lab, S. (2002). *Victimology* (4th ed.). Andersen Publishing.

Doerner, W. G., & Lab, S. P. (2005). *Victimology.* Cincinnati, OH: Lexis Nexis.

Doerner, W. G., & Lab, S. P. (2011). *Victimology* (6th ed.). Lexis Nexis/Anderson Publishing Company.

Dolu, O. (2010). *Theories of crime: Criminology in theory, research and practice*. Distinguished.

Dumig, A. G., & van Dijk, J. J. M. (1975). Actions and reactions of victims of violence: Some results of a victimological investigation. *Journal of Criminology, 17*(2), 63–73.

European Union law. In Handbook of victims and victimology (pp. 363–379), Willan, Cullompton.

Ferguson, C., & Turvey, B. E. (2009). Victimology: A brief history with an introduction to forensic victimology. In *Forensic victimology: Examining violent crime victims in investigative and legal contexts* (pp. 1–32).

Fohring, S. J. (2012). *Process of victimisation: investigating risk, reporting and service use*. http://hdl.handle.net/1842/6436

Fohring, S. (2015). An integrated model of victimization as an explanation of non-involvement with the criminal justice system. *International Review of Victimology, 21*(1), 45–70. https://doi.org/10.1177/0269758014547993

Fohring, S. (2018). Introduction to the special issue: Victim identities and hierarchies. *International Review of Victimology, 24*(2), 147–149. https://doi.org/10.1177/0269758018755152

Freemon, K. R., Gutierrez, M. A., Huff, J., Cheon, H., Choate, D., Cox, T., & Katz, C. M. (2022). Violent victimization among immigrants: Using the National Violent Death Reporting System to examine foreign-born homicide victimization in the United States. *Preventive Medicine Reports, 26, 101714*.

Garland, J., Spalek, B., & Chakraborti, N. (2006). Hearing lost voices: Issues in researching 'hidden' minority ethnic communities. *British journal of criminology, 46*(3), 423–437.

Goffman, E. (1963a). *Stigma: Notes on the management of spoiled identity*. Simon & Shuster.

Goffman, E. (1963b). *Stigma*. Penguin.

Gover, A. R., & Wells, K. S. (2022). Social learning theory of victimization. In F. P. Bernat & K. Frailing (Eds.), *The Encyclopedia of Women and Crime*. https://doi.org/10.1002/9781118929803.ewac0474

Hartinger-Saunders, R. M., Rine, C. M., Wieczorek, W., & Nochajski, T. (2012). Family level predictors of victimization and offending among young men: Rethinking the role of parents in prevention and interventions models. *Children and Youth Services Review, 34*(12), 2423–2432. https://doi.org/10.1016/j.childyouth.2012.08.017

Helle, K. (2014). *Significance of place and gender an Ohio violent crime victimization study (Doctoral dissertation)*. http://hdl.handle.net/1989/11374

Hindelang, M. J., Gottfredson, M. R., & Garofalo, J. (1978). Victims of personal crime: An empirical foundation for a theory of personal victimization. Cambridge, MA: Ballinger.

Hirschi, T., & Gottfredson, M. (1993). Commentary: Testing the general theory of crime. *Journal of research in crime and delinquency, 30*(1), 47–54.

Holt, T. J., Turner, M. G., & Exum, M. L. (2014). The impact of self-control and neighborhood disorder on bullying victimization. *Journal of Criminal Justice, 42*(4), 347–355. https://doi.org/10.1016/j.jcrimjus.2014.04.004

Horowitz, M. J. (1986). *Stress response syndromes*. Jason Aronson. https://doi.org/10.1111/1745-9125.12278

Jensen, G. F. (2015). *International encyclopedia of the social & behavioral sciences (second edition)*. Elsevier.

Jerin, R. A., & Moriarty, L. J. (1998). *Victims of crime*. Nelson-Hall Publishers.

Karalis, D., & Kleisiari-Karalis, A. (2019). Biology and criminal behavior: Neurotransmitters, neurohormones and brain damages. *Encephalos, 56*, 60–66.

Karmen, A. (1990). *Crime, victims. An introduction to victimology*. Pacific Grove.

Karman, A. (2007). Crime victims, Belmont, CA: Thomson-Wadsworth.

Kehayes, I. L. L., Hudson, A., Thompson, K., Wekerle, C., Stuart, H., Dobson, K., ... & Stewart, S. H. (2019). The consequences of alcohol-involved sexual victimization in male and female college students. *Canadian Journal of Community Mental Health, 37*(3), 127–143.

Kennedy, L. W., & Forde, D. R. (1990). Routine activities and crime: An analysis of victimization in Canada. *Criminology, 28*(1), 137–152. https://doi.org/10.1111/j.1745-9125.1990.tb01321.x

Kilpatrick, D. G., Acierno, R., Resnick, H. S., Saunders, B. E., & Best, C. L. (1997). A 2-year longitudinal analysis of the relationships between violent assault and substance use in women. *Journal of Consulting and Clinical Psychology, 65*(5), 834.

Knudten, R. D. (1976). *Victims and witnesses: The impact of crime and their experience with the criminal justice system.* Marquette.

Kumar, A., & Verma, A. (2020). Status and position of victim in criminal justice system. *Journal of Advances and Scholarly Researches in Allied Education, 17*(1), 395–400. https://doi.org/10.29070/JASRAE

Lasky, T., Richmond, B. K., Samanta, D., & Annie, F. (2022). A 10-year review of spatio-temporal patterns of firearm injury in a rural setting. *The American Surgeon, 88*(5), 834–839.

Lauritsen, J. L., & Rezey, M. L. (2013). Measuring the prevalence of crime with the national crime victimization survey. Washington, DC: US Department of Justice, Office of Justice Programs, Bureau of Justice Statistics.

Leading Theories of Victimization Risk. (2020, May 9). Retrieved from https://study.com/academy/lesson/leading-theories-of-victimization-risk.html

Lehner-Zimmerer, M. (2011). Future challenges of international victimology. *African Journal of Criminology and Justice Studies, 4*, 13–27.

Lin, S., Yu, C., Chen, W., Tian, Y., & Zhang, W. (2018). Peer victimization and aggressive behavior among Chinese adolescents: Delinquent peer affiliation as a mediator and parental knowledge as a moderator. *Frontiers in Psychology, 9*, 1036.10.3389/fpsyg.2018.01036.

Meier, R. F., & Miethe, T. D. (1993). Understanding theories of criminal victimization. *Crime and Justice, 17*, 459–499.

Menkel-Meadow, C. (2007). Restorative justice: What is it and does it work?. Georgetown Public Law Research Paper, (1005485).

Miethe, T. D., Stafford, M. C., & Long, J. S. (1987). Social differentiation in criminal victimization: A test of routine activities/lifestyle theories. *American Sociological Review, 184–194.* https://doi.org/10.2307/2095447

Morgan, E., Johnson, I., & Sigler, R. (2006). Public definitions and endorsement of the criminalization of elder abuse. *Journal of Criminal Justice, 34(3), 275–283.*

Muftić, L. R., & Hunt, D. E. (2013). Victim precipitation: Further understanding the linkage between victimization and offending in homicide. *Homicide Studies, 17*(3), 239–254.

Mythen, G. (2007). Reappraising the risk society thesis: Telescopic sight or myopic vision?. *Current Sociology, 55*(6), 793–813.

Nash, A. (2008). Victims by definition. *Washington University Law Review, 85*, 1419. Available at: https://openscholarship.wustl.edu/law_lawreview/vol85/iss6/5

Nofziger, S. (2009). Victimization and the general theory of crime. *Violence and Victims, 24*(3), 337–350. https://doi.org/10.1891/0886-6708.24.3.337

Papadopoulos, G. (2012). Immigration status and victimisation: Evidence from the British Crime Survey. *Applied and Financial Economics Working Papers Series.*

Parks, K. A., Hsieh, Y. P., Taggart, C., & Bradizza, C. M. (2014). A longitudinal analysis of drinking and victimization in college women: Is there a reciprocal relationship? *Psychology of Addictive Behaviors, 28*(4), 943. https://doi.org/10.1037/a0036283

Passos, A. F., Stumpf, B. P., & Rocha, F. L. (2013). Victimization of the mentally ill. *The Revista de Psiquiatria Clínica, 40*(5), 191–196.

Pesta, R. E. (2011). *Provocation and the point of no return: An analysis of victim-precipitated homicide* (Doctoral dissertation, Youngstown State University). http://rave.ohiolink.edu/etdc/view?acc_num=ysu1320413987

Petherick, W. (2017). Victim precipitation: Why we need to expand upon the theory. *Forensic Research & Criminology International Journal, 5*(2), 263–264. https://doi.org/10.15406/frcij.2017.05.00148

Petherick, W., & Sinnamon, G. (2013). Motivations: Offender and victim perspectives. In *Profiling and serial crime: Theoretical and practical issues* (pp. 393–430). Elsevier. https://doi.org/10.1016/B978-1-4557-3174-9.00018-5

Piquero, A. R., & Hickman, M. (1999). An empirical test of Tittle's control balance theory. *Criminology, 37*(2), 319–342. https://doi.org/10.1111/j.1745-9125.1999.tb00488.x

Piquero, A. R., & Hickman, M. (2003). Extending Tittle's control balance theory to account for victimization. *Criminal Justice and Behavior, 30(3), 282–301.* https://doi.org/10.1177/0093854803030003002

Randhawa, G. S. (2011). *Victimology and compensatory jurisprudence* (1st ed., p. 123). Central Law Publications.

Rashad, S. M. (2020). African Climate Refugees: Environmental Injustice and Recognition. *Open Journal of Political Science, 10*(03), 546.

Rennison, C. M. (2014). Feminist theory in the context of sexual violence. In *Encyclopedia of criminology and criminal justice* (pp. 1617–1627). https://doi.org/10.1007/978-1-4614-5690-2_70

Römkens, R., & Diekstra, S. (Eds) (1966). *Het Controversiele Slachtoffer, Geweld van Vrouwen en Mannen.* (The Controversial Victim, Violence of Women and Men.) (In Dutch) Ambo; Baarn.

Rossa-Roccor, V., Schmid, P., & Steinert, T. (2020). Victimization of people with severe mental illness outside and within the mental health care system: Results on prevalence and risk factors from a multicenter study. *Frontiers in Psychiatry, 932.* https://doi.org/10.3389/fpsyt.2020.563860

Sabina, C., Cuevas, C. A., & Schally, J. L. (2013). The effect of immigration and acculturation on victimization among a national sample of Latino women. *Cultural Diversity and Ethnic Minority Psychology, 19*(1), 13.

Sampson, R. J. (1983). *The neighborhood context of criminal victimization* (Doctoral dissertation). State University of New York at Albany.

Sampson, R. J. (1985). Neighborhood and crime: The structural determinants of personal victimization. *Journal of Research in Crime and Delinquency, 22*(1), 7–40. https://doi.org/10.1177/0022427885022001002

Schwartz, D., Mcfadyen-Ketchum, S. A., Dodge, K. A., Pettit, G. S., & Bates, J. E. (1998). Peer group victimization as a predictor of children's behavior problems at home and in school. *Development and Psychopathology, 10*(1), 87–99. https://doi.org/10.1017/s095457949800131x

Sela-Shayovitz, R. (2021). Femicide and femicide-suicide in Israel: The role of immigration and the cultural context. *Violence and Victims, 36*(3), 347–362. https://doi.org/10.1891/VV-D-19-00087

Seo, D., Patrick, C. J., & Kennealy, P. J. (2008). Role of serotonin and dopamine system interactions in the neurobiology of impulsive aggression and its comorbidity with other clinical disorders. *Aggression and Violent Behavior, 13*(5), 383–395. https://doi.org/10.1016/j.avb.2008.06.003

Shapland, J., Willmore, J., & Duff, P. (1985). *Victims in the criminal justice system* (pp. 176–178). Gower.

Shichor, D., & Tibbetts, S. (2002). *Victims and victimizations: Essential readings.*

Silver, E., Arseneault, L., Langley, J., Caspi, A., & Moffitt, T. E. (2005). Mental disorder and violent victimization in a total birth cohort. *American Journal of Public Health, 95*(11), 2015–2021. https://doi.org/10.2105/AJPH.2003.021436

Sims, B., Yost, B., & Abbott, C. (2006). The efficacy of victim services programs: Alleviating the psychological suffering of crime victims? *Criminal Justice Policy Review, 17*(4), 387–406. https://doi.org/10.1177/0887403406290656

Slavin, L., & Sorin, D. J. (1984). Congress opens a Pandora's box-the restitution provisions of the Victim and Witness Protection Act of 1982. *Fordham Law Review, 52*(4), 507.

Spalek, B. (2017). Crime victims: Theory, policy and practice. Bloomsbury Publishing.

Stark, R. (1987). Deviant places: A theory of the ecology of crime. *Criminology, 25*(4), 893–910.

Stewart, E. A., Kirk, W., Elifson, K. W., Claire, E., & Sterk, C. E. (2004). Integrating the general theory of crime into an explanation of violent victimization among female offenders. *Justice Quarterly, 21*(1), 159–181. https://doi.org/10.1080/07418820400095771

Szabo, D. (1981). Who are the criminals. *Revue internationale de criminologie et de police technique, 34,* 343–352.

Tarling, R., & Morris, K. (2010). Reporting crime to the police. *The British Journal of Criminology, 50*(3), 474–490. https://doi.org/10.1093/bjc/azq011

Teplin, L. A., McClelland, G. M., Abram, K. M., & Weiner, D. A. (2005). Crime victimization in adults with severe mental illness: Comparison with the National Crime Victimization Survey. *Archives of General Psychiatry, 62*(8), 911–921. https://doi.org/10.1001/archpsyc.62.8.911

Testa, M., & Livingston, J. A. (2009). Alcohol consumption and women's vulnerability to sexual victimization: Can reducing women's drinking prevent rape? *Substance Use & Misuse, 44*(9–10), 1349–1376. https://doi.org/10.1080/10826080902961468

Timmer, D. A., & Norman, W. H. (1984). The ideology of victim precipitation. *Criminal Justice Review, 9*(2), 63–68. https://doi.org/10.1177/073401688400900209

Tittle, C. R. (1995). Control Balance: Toward a General Theory of Deviance. Boulder, Colorada: Westview Press.

Tittle, C. R., & Dollar, C. B. (2019). Control balance theory of deviance. In *Handbook on crime and deviance* (pp. 243–257). Springer. https://doi.org/10.1007/978-3-030-20779-3_13

Triplett, R., & Upton, L. (2015). Labeling theory: Past, present, and future. *Handbook of Criminological Theory*, 271–289.

Turner, H. A., Finkelhor, D., Ormrod, R., Hamby, S., Leeb, R. T., Mercy, J. A., & Holt, M. (2012). Family context, victimization, and child trauma symptoms: Variations in safe, stable, and nurturing relationships during early and middle childhood. *American Journal of Orthopsychiatry, 82*(2), 209. https://doi.org/10.1111/j.1939-0025.2012.01147.x

Turner, H. A., Finkelhor, D., Hamby, S. L., & Shattuck, A. (2013). Family structure, victimization, and child mental health in a nationally representative sample. *Social Science & Medicine, 87*, 39–51. https://doi.org/10.1016/j.socscimed.2013.02.034

Turvey, B. E. (2011). Crime scene analysis. In Criminal profiling: An introduction to behavioral evidence analysis (pp. 187–222). Academic Press, Amsterdam.

Turvey, B. E. (2014). Victimology: A brief history with an introduction to forensic victimology. In *Forensic victimology: Examining violent crime victims in investigative and legal contexts* (pp. 1–28).

UKEssays. (2018, November). *Contributions of feminism to the study of victimology*. Retrieved from https://www.ukessays.com/essays/criminology/contributions-of-feminism-to-the-study-of-victimology-8903.php?vref=1

Valan, M. L., & Srinivasan, M. (2021). The application of routine activity theory in explaining victimization of child marriage. *International Review of Victimology, 27*(2), 211–226. https://doi.org/10.1177/0269758020988218

Van Dijk, J. (2009). Free the victim: A critique of the western conception of victimhood. *International Review of Victimology, 16*(1), 1–33. https://doi.org/10.1177/026975800901600101

Van Dijk, J. J. (1999). Introducing victimology. *Caring for crime victims*, 1–13.

Vaske, J., Makarios, M., Boisvert, D., Beaver, K. M., & Wright, J. P. (2009). The interaction of DRD2 and violent victimization on depression: An analysis by gender and race. *Journal of Affective Disorders, 112*(1–3), 120–125.

Von Hentig, H. (1948). The criminal & his victim: Studies in the sociobiology of crime. Yale University Press.

Walklate, S. (2006). *Imagining the victim of crime*. McGraw-Hill Education.

Waller, I., & Okihiro, N. R. (1978). *Burglary: The victim and the public*. Centre of Criminology, University of Toronto by University of Toronto Press.

Wemmers, J. A. (2009). Where do they belong? Giving victims a place in the criminal justice process. In *Criminal law forum* (Vol. 20, No. 4, pp. 395–416). Springer Netherlands. https://doi.org/10.1007/s10609-009-9107-z

Wilcox, P., Quisenberry, N., & Jones, S. (2003). The built environment and community crime risk interpretation. *Journal of Research in Crime and Delinquency, 40*(3), 322–345.

Williams, T. (2001). Racism in justice: The report of the Commission on Systemic Racism in the Ontario criminal justice system.

Wilson, J. K. (Ed.). (2009). *The Praeger handbook of victimology. ABC-CLIO*.

Winkel, F. W. (2007). Post traumatic anger. *Missing link in the wheel of misfortune*.

Wolfgang, M. E. (1958). Delinquency and crime as part of a course of social studies. *The Social Studies, 49*(1), 20–24.

Xie, M., & Baumer, E. P. (2021). Immigrant status, citizenship, and victimization risk in the United States: New findings from the National Crime Victimization Survey (NCVS). *Criminology, 59*(4), 610–644.

Chapter 2
Working with Victims: Psychological Assessment of Victims and Mental Health of Professionals

Smriti Maini and Kalpana Raman

Introduction

Victimology has been defined as the '...study of victimization, offender relationship, victim criminal justice system relationship, victim and media, victim and the cost of crime, and victim and social movements' (Karmen, 1990, p. 307). As per the definition, a victim can be anyone, and any event can result in one or many victims. Thus, it is the scientific study of 'crime victims', a sub-discipline of criminology that aims to investigate the interaction between victims and criminals, as well as the victim's placement in the criminal justice system (Siddique, 1993). The concept of victim may be traced back into the ancient culture and civilisation. Initially, the definitions were based on the concept of sacrifice, defined as the death of a man or an animal for the satisfaction of a deity (Karmen, 1990). Victimologists such as Mendelshon, Von Hentig, and Wolfgang in the early 1940s described victims as weak dupes who cause their own victimisation during the creation of victimology.

The identification and definition of a victim has evolved since then, and in the recent times, they are defined as someone who suffers harm, loss, or difficulty as a result of any cause (Collins English Dictionary, 2010). Any individual, group, or entities that have been injured or have lost their livelihood as a result of criminal action are referred to as a 'crime victim' (Christie, 1986). The injury might be an outcome precipitating from various reasons such as physical, psychological, or financial; hence, the term 'victim of crime' is usable in a broad and inclusive meaning rather than in a restrictive fashion. It contains a collectively made-up group, a class, or a community of people from many backgrounds, including racial,

S. Maini
IILM University, Gurgaon, India

K. Raman (✉)
Auckland University of Technology, Auckland, New Zealand

economic, political, and religious groups, who have witnessed and felt suffering, loss, or injury, both physical and psychological (Batten, 2010).

Victimisation may make a person feel vulnerable or powerless, as well as change their perspective of the world and/or self-perception. The psychological impact of victimisation has been well-researched as much as the physiological impact. The most common psychological symptoms and disorders are neurotic such as depression, anxiety, and post-traumatic stress disorder (PTSD). One of the nuances associated with observing the symptoms is that although not always, the psychological symptoms that are disruptive to a person's life may match the diagnostic criteria for a specific condition, but they may be present at a certain degree which might still require intervention from the mental health professionals (Kilpatrick et al., 1985). Withdrawal, avoidance, and nightmares are certain symptoms that may be part of one or the other diagnostic disorders but may occur in a lesser or more isolated form but not in the severity, frequency or intensity as required to diagnose a specific disorder which does not deny the need for assessment or intervention for the specific vulnerable section of the society (Krakow & Neidhardt, 1992). The following paragraphs assist in classifying the victims according to various aspects and underline the needs of the victims and the commonly used assessment tools by the mental health professionals in identifying and diagnosing the victims.

Types of Victims

With the conceptual clarity about victimology and victims, it is vital to know and develop our understanding towards the various ways victims have been classified. Victims are those who have been harmed by an event such as a criminal act, a disaster, or an accident creating an impact either physically and/or psychologically/emotionally as a result of being exposed to such a traumatic experience. As mentioned in the above paragraph, victims tend to experience various emotional, cognitive, and/or behavioural issues and thus, they can be classified under various categories as outlined in the figure below (Fig. 2.1).

Firstly, on the basis *of crime and situation*, victims can be classified as (Victim Services of S.D.G. & A):

- *Directly* involved in the events like the death of someone in any situation and/or injury caused to someone or the victim.
- *Eyewitnesses*, rescuers, and converging rescuers, i.e., observers of immediate traumatic consequences on main victims.
- Victims harmed as a result of coming into *contact* with a primary or secondary victim, such as neighbours, community members, or former victims.

Secondly, on the basis of *vulnerable sections* requiring utmost attention, such as:

- *Child victims/younger victims* refer to children and adolescents under the age of 18 who are victims of crime (Tiwari, 2012).

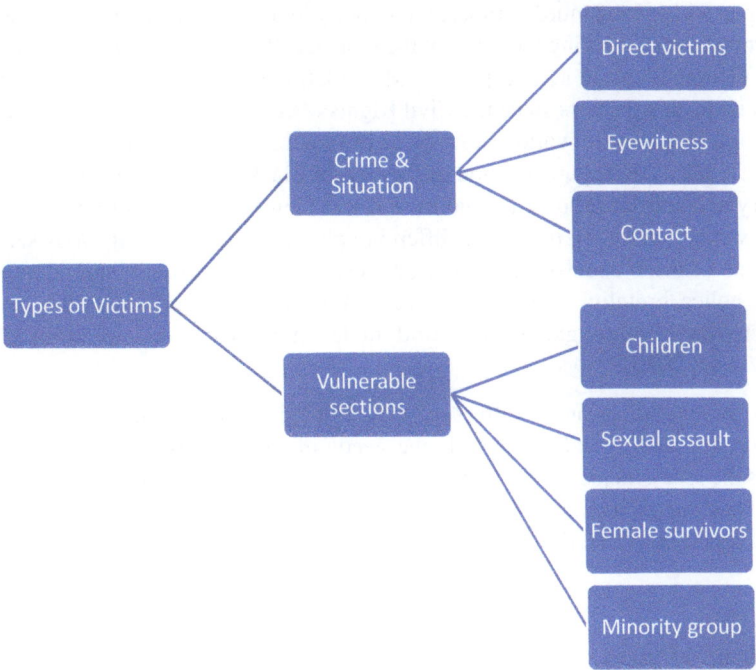

Fig. 2.1 Type of victims

- *Sexual assault victims*: alludes to the casualties who have been affected/hurt by physical/sexual maltreatment, attack, or assault. Because of the emotional, psychological, and human issues involved, this group of victims, regardless of age, may be deserving of special attention (Tiwari, 2012).
- *Female survivors*: In western civilisation, criminality against women is usually limited to sexual offences. The Southeast Asia, particularly Cambodia, is linked to acid throwing/attack. The Middle East and South Asia are also accounted for honour killings. Presently in Africa, Middle East, and some regions of Asia, female genital mutilation is present. Kidnapping the women and marrying them forcefully as well as women and child trafficking are quite common in the certain regions of East and South Africa and Central Asia (Muthegheki et al., 2012). Women are exposed to assault by individuals from the prevailing station, sati, spouse beating, prostitution, and, surprisingly, intermittent witch-hunting in India. Legislation is in place, but it is not being enforced effectively. Settlement passing is much of the time given the shade of self-destruction by the spouse and parents in law of weak ladies who can't satisfy their better halves or parents in law's interest in view of insatiability (Tiwari, 2012).
- *Section that is less strong*: In diverse communities, 'members of ethnic, religious, or linguistic minorities' (Tiwari, 2012, p. 93) may be more exposed to crime and violence as a result of socioeconomic inequity and political reasons. Every year, a number of caste and sectarian riots erupt across the nation, result-

ing in widespread murder, rape, and property looting, with minorities and weaker groups clearly bearing the brunt of the violence (Tiwari, 2012). The assassination of George Floyd in Minneapolis in May 2020 ignited the country's (US) largest racial justice protests since the Civil Rights Movement and attracted attention of people in the entire world. The footage of Floyd's violent death in police custody on 25 May 2020 sparked some of the largest Black Lives Matter protests in history in countries all over the world as it was viewed as mark of unjust and racist acts experienced by people of different colour, origin and indigenous sections. Some of these countries had their own George Floyd, a Black individual killed by police brutality or racial violence who sparked anger across the country. Activists all throughout the world understood there was no turning back (Warren, 2020).

As the classification of different types of victims is clearer, we also need to develop our understanding towards the needs of the victims to be able to better access the assessments and provide timely and appropriate comprehensive intervention. Thus, the following section briefly mentions the needs of the victims that we must keep in consideration.

Needs of Victims

The victim's requirement undergoes constant changes temporally which is also considered to be an integral aspect in general. Some requirements occur right after/ immediately after the offence, the other needs include during the criminal justice process, other demands emerge, such as the need to have one's voice heard during criminal proceedings. These casualties' necessities are met by the United Nations Declaration, which incorporates the option to regard and acknowledgment, the right to insurance, admittance to equity and fair treatment, help and backing, and review for the adverse results of wrongdoing as restitution and compensation (UNODC-United Nations Office Drugs and Crime).

The victims experience serious mental or emotional health consequences, including feelings of severe guilt, post-traumatic stress disorder, depression, anxiety, abuse (alcohol or narcotics), and eating disorders. Victims of trafficking often need psychological care as a part of comprehensive medical treatment. Providing culturally appropriate and trauma-informed mental state treatment is challenging. A number of the commonly reported barriers and challenges to helping victims with their trauma include: There is a scarcity of competent mental health services and access to them. Establishing trusting relationships with survivors is difficult. When engaging with victims, mandated therapy initiatives may be harmful. This is especially important in places where the only way to get mental health care is to be locked up in a treatment centre. Trauma, recognised mental health disorders and substance misuse or addiction all occur together. Poly victimisation also has been into the talk since a long time, and it has a long history among victims (Ford & Wilson, 2012), wherein the victims experience multiple layers of trauma caused by various sources. After identifying the type of victim and their specific needs, a mental health professional is in a sound position to anchor their assessments and provide adequate and appropriate intervention.

Assessment

In the study of victimology and to aid the mental health professionals dealing with various victims as outlined above, many tools and assessments have been developed. In this section, based on the developmental years of human life, the needs, symptoms, and assessment tools have been mentioned below. An attempt has also been made wherever possible to cluster these assessment tools under the predominant categories of tools assessing cognitive functions (intelligence quotient, understanding, problem solving, etc.), personality (diagnostic, trait, type oriented), and psychopathology.

The foremost clusters of assessments are designed to be utilised with children and adolescents' victims. According to the World Health Organization (WHO), children and adolescents are those '…children age span ranges from birth to puberty and adolescents as those people between 10 and 19 years of age'. The great majority of adolescents are, therefore, included in the age-based definition of 'child', adopted by the Convention on the (Rights of the Child United Nations General Assembly, 1989, p. 3). Mental health is especially important during childhood and adolescence due to the developmental nature of brain, physiology and emotionality. It is marked as a period of fast growth and development. Children and adolescents develop cognitive and social-emotional skills that influence their mental health in the future and are necessary for them to take on adult roles in society.

As the nature–nurture debate has been on-going in all the major scientific realms, it has also been talked about while assessing the impact on children and adolescents. Thus, keeping the debate in view, the environment (sociocultural, political, natural surroundings etc.) in which the children and adolescents grow up also has a significant impact along with the heredity component on their well-being and development. Early bad experiences in homes, schools, or digital environments, such as violence, a parent's or caregiver's mental illness, bullying, and poverty, all tends to increase the likelihood of mental illness. Childhood epilepsy, developmental impairments, depression, anxiety, and behavioural problems are all common causes of sickness and disability in children and adolescents (Banger et al., 2012). The needs and requirements for assessment and intervention for this category of victims might be different and requires more intense efforts and skills by the mental health professionals.

Child victims require an accurate evaluation of how the crime has affected their life and what will help them heal in a timely and professional manner. The initial, also known as the first clinical evaluation serves as the foundation for building a successful crime-related treatment plan. Child and adolescent crime victims, presents unique obstacles to the mental health assessor. A traumatic occurrence is generally the catalyst for the initial referral, rather than specific symptoms in the children. In this group of individuals, clinicians most typically diagnose post-traumatic stress disorder (PTSD), which is marked by symptoms of re-experiencing, numbness, and avoidance, as well as hyper-arousal (Diagnostic and Statistical Manual Fourth edition DSM-IV, APA, 1994). Avoidant symptoms, cognitive distortions, emotional discomfort, diminished sense of self, academic challenges, and interpersonal difficulties can all occur in children who have been traumatised by crime (Briere & Elliot, 1994).

Commonly used assessment tools for assessing cognitive functions during childhood and adolescence are:

- *Wechsler Intelligence Scale for Children (WISC-IV)* developed by Wechsler (2003) who defined intelligence as '...the aggregate or global capacity of the individual to act purposefully, to think rationally and to deal effectively with his environment' (Wechsler, 1949, p. 3). In most intelligence assessments, there are two types of intelligence: verbal intelligence, i.e., the capacity to grasp and solve language-based difficulties, and non-verbal intelligence, i.e., the capacity to grasp and solve sequential and spatial difficulties (Grondhuis et al., 2018). It can be used with children between the ages 6–16 years old and it produces a full-scale IQ score as well as four index scores: Verbal Comprehension index includes tests on similarities, vocabulary, comprehension, information and word-reasoning; Perceptual Reasoning index includes tests on matrix reasoning, block design, picture concepts and picture completion; Processing Speed index includes tests on coding, cancellation, and symbol search; and Working Memory index includes tests on letter-number sequencing, digit-span, and arithmetic (Wechsler, 2003).
- *The Kaufman Assessment Battery for Children (K-ABC,* Kaufman, 1983) is a standardised test that evaluates children's intelligence and accomplishment between the ages of 2 and 6 months and 12 years and 6 months. A revised version was brought in the year 2002 to broaden its age range (to include children aged 3–18) and improve its use. New subtests were also created, and old subtests were updated (Sattler, 1992). The K-ABC takes between 35 and 85 minutes to administer. The longer the test takes to administer, the older the child is. Sequential processing scales, simultaneous processing scales, accomplishment scales, and mental processing composite are the four worldwide test scores. A non-verbal scale is also available that permits eligible subtests to be administered via gestures.
- *Bhatia's Intelligence Performance Tests Battery (*Bhatia, 1955*)*: Bhatia's intelligence exam, often known as Bhatia's battery, is a famous intelligence test in India. Five subtests make up the battery of tests. Some examples include Kohs' Block Design (BD), Alexander's Pass-along (PA), Pattern Drawing (PD), Picture Construction (PC), and Immediate Memory (IM) Tests. In the 1950s, the battery was standardised on Indian males aged 11–16. The above test gives two overall quotient's – Intelligence Quotient (IQ) and Performance Quotient (PQ) – which

are based on the above-mentioned subtest. The test's IQ and PQ ranges are relatively narrow, ranging from 69 to 131 (Bhatia, 1955). It is likely one of the first IQ tests to focus solely on performance subtests/items. It can be utilised in some circumstances with children who are suspected of having a Specific Learning Disability (SLD), when the examiner is confident that the child has average intellect but wishes to objectively confirm it. It takes about 30–45 minutes, which is relatively short.

- *Malin's Intelligence Scale for Indian Children (MISIC*, Malin, 1969*)*: This test has been derived from Dr. David Wechsler's WISC test in the United States. Dr. Arthur J. Malin of Nagpur is the creator of the Indian version of the WISC adaptable for Indian children/population. The test had to be virtually completely rewritten during adaptation, notably the culturally biased language items. This test is notably known as ISIC or MISIC (Intelligence Scale for Indian Children). As India is a country characterised by several regional languages, it was afterwards adapted in Hindi and Marathi. MISIC is an intelligence test designed for children aged 6–15 years and 11 months. It takes about 2–3 hours to administer separately. There are 12 subtests in total, divided into two categories: verbal and performance. The verbal scale has six subtests, while the performance scale has five: Information Test, General Comprehension Test, Arithmetic Test, Vocabulary Test, Digit Span Test, and Analogy and Similarity Test are part of verbal scale, whereas the performance scale includes tests on picture completion test, block design test, object assembly, coding, and mazes (Malin, 1969).

- *The Seguin Form Board Test (SFBT)* is a speed and accuracy test based on the single component theory of intelligence. Two French physicians, Edouard Seguin (1812–1880) and J.E.D. Esquirol (1772–1840), altered the way people with mental retardation were thought about. It can be used to assess a child's eye-hand coordination, shape perception, visual perception, and cognitive abilities. It can be used for age group 3–15 years. The test is mostly used to evaluate visuo-motor abilities. It has Gesell figures, which require the kid to copy ten geometrical figures in order to assess visuo-motor skills. Ten varied shaped wooden blocks and a huge form board with recessed equivalent shapes make up the test materials (Bharatraj, 1971).

Some commonly used tools for assessing personality in childhood and adolescents are as follows:

- *The Personality Inventory for Children* is a test that evaluates a child's emotional, behavioural, cognitive, and interpersonal adjustment from Some of the commonly used tools for assessing psychopathology in children and adolescents are kindergarten to grade 12 (Lachar & Gruber, 2007). It's a set of assertions about the child that the parent or guardian assesses as true or untrue. This clinical assessment tool's objective is to learn more about the children and his or her difficulties so that therapeutic treatment may be recommended (Sattler & Hoge, 2006). It is employed in both therapeutic and educational settings.

- *Children Personality Questionnaire (CPQ, Porter & Cattell,* 1956) is a self-report inventory which can be used to assess their personal, social, and academic growth, as well as personality traits that influence school performance and social adjustment both inside and outside the classroom. The test assesses 14 aspects of a child's personality. R.B. Cattell identified the 14 personality dimensions that are being tested, noting that they are objectively determined source attributes. The CPQ test is available in four different formats (A, B, C, and D). Each form contains 140 items, with 10 items per factor every form. Each form is divided into two sections. As a result, Form A is made up of Parts A1 and A2, each of which has 70 items. Forms B, C, and D are divided in the same way. Each item has a forced-choice 'yes' or 'no' response (with the exception of the factor B, intellect, items). In terms of social desirability, the products were designed to be as 'neutral' as feasible. It is supposed to simply require average eight-year-standard reading vocabulary skills. The test is not timed, and for younger students, the testing period can be divided into two portions for each form; however, one test session should not go longer than 50 minutes. Separate stencils are provided for scoring the answer sheet, and two stencils are required to obtain the 14 raw scores from each of the test forms. Separate norms tables are provided for boys and girls (Porter & Cattell, 1985).

To assess trauma in childhood and adolescents:

- *Childhood trauma interview (CTI,* Fink et al., 1995) consists of 49 screening items, as well as additional follow-up probes for those things that are found to be positive. Childhood separation and loss, physical neglect, emotional abuse or assault, physical abuse or assault, exposure to violence, and sexual abuse or assaults are the six kinds of events that the CTI assesses. Depending on the amount of early trauma events, CTI takes approximately 30–90 minutes to be administered. The tool is considered excellent for gathering thorough information about a variety of childhood traumatic incidents and assessing their occurrence, length, and intensity. CTI entails questions regarding the people involved, the events themselves, the kind of the events, the age of the participants at the time of the events, the frequency of the events, threats during the events, the clients' comments on the events, and the outcome of the events (Carlson et al., 1997).

Some commonly used tools for assessing Psychopathology in children and adolescents are as follows:

- *Beck's Youth Inventory (BYI, Beck et al.,* 2001) – This psychological testing tool is a quick self-report that is used to assess the level of distress in children and adolescents (Flanagan & Henington, 2005). Five self-administered scales are used in the Beck Youth Inventory. The Beck Depression Inventory, Beck Anxiety Inventory, Beck Anger Inventory, Beck Disruptive Inventory, and Beck Self-Concept Inventory are among the five exams. These exams can be given to children separately or in combination. The target audience for this test is children aged 7–14. (Flanagan & Henington, 2005). This test is intended to evaluate sadness, anxiety, anger, disruptive behaviour, and self-esteem problems (Beck, 2001).

- *The Children's Apperception Test (CAT)* is a projective personality test that assesses individual contrasts in children's reactions to standardised stimuli in the form of photographs of animals (CAT-A) or humans (CAT-H) in common social situations. Leopold Bellak and Sonya Sorel Bellak and first published in 1949 is based on the Thematic Apperception Test, a picture-story test (TAT). It can be used with age range of 3–11 years. Pictures of children in frequent family scenarios, such as protracted illnesses, births, deaths, and separations from parental figures, are included in a supplement to the CAT called the CAT-S. The CAT is used to evaluate personality, maturity, and, in many cases, psychological health. According to the notion, a child's reactions to a sequence of drawings of animals or humans in familiar scenarios will disclose important characteristics of their personality. The CAT is administered in a clinical, research, or educational setting by a skilled professional psychiatrist, psychologist, social worker, teacher, or particularly qualified paediatrician and takes 20–45 minutes. The exam can be utilised in a variety of settings, including therapy and play. After carefully establishing rapport with the child, the examiner shows the child one card after another in a specific sequence (although the examiner may use fewer than ten cards at his or her discretion) and encourages the child to tell a story about the characters (with a beginning, middle, and end). The examiner may question the youngster to describe what happened before the incident was presented, the characters' feelings, and what might happen in the future (Paul, 2004). There is no right or wrong answer on a projective test such as the CAT. As a result, the test does not have a numerical or scaled score. The test administrator writes down the main points of each storey and checks off whether or not certain thematic components are included on the form. Each tale is meticulously examined, just like the TAT, to identify the child's underlying needs, conflicts, emotions, attitudes, and response patterns. When analysing the results, the CAT's developers suggest taking into account a series of ten variables. The fundamental theme of the narrative, the demands, impulses, anxieties, conflicts, fears, and the child's understanding of the external world are all variables to consider (Paul, 2004).

When interviewing older adults' vs. younger adults, there are two important considerations to keep in mind. Firstly, the older adults are typically found to be more hesitant to discuss previous or current psychological and interpersonal issues. Secondly, the physical issues and difficulties/impairments (e.g. weariness, hearing problems) have a greater impact on their spoken reports (Ouslander, 1984; Patterson & Dupree, 1994). Deficits in cognitive functioning, hearing loss, greater susceptibility to tiredness, difficulty to sit for long periods of time (e.g. arthritis), and the effects of medicine on attention and memory are all physical health obstacles to reporting victimisation occurrences. Ageism, interview stress, higher bodily presentations that may reflect psychopathological symptoms, greater time needed to create trust and rapport, and increased medication use are all considerations to consider while diagnosing older persons. 'A personal repulsion to, and hatred for, becoming old, as well as a dread of impotence, uselessness, and death' is according to ageism (Patterson & Dupree, 1994, p. 373).

In addition, determining the optimum method of violence assessment, as well as whether or not testing of the older adult is even suitable, requires some assessment of cognitive functioning. Because of the increased risk of weariness and attention issues associated with the exposure of highly intimate information, it's best to keep stress to a minimum during interviews (Gurland et al., 1978).

Some commonly used tools for assessing cognitive functioning in adults and elderly are as follows:

- *The Mini-mental state examination (MMSE,* Folstein et al., 1975) is used to assess cognitive impairment in older adults. It can be used to screen for cognitive impairment, quantify the severity of cognitive impairment at a specific point in time, track the course of cognitive changes in an individual over time, and document an individual's response to treatment, according to Folstein et al. It evaluates various aspects of cognitive functioning, such as attention, language, memory, orientation, and visuo-spatial ability. It has also been recommended for the examination of cognition in depressed patients (Palmqvist et al., 2009). The patented mini-mental state evaluation takes about 10–15 minutes to administer. Alternatives to the Mini-Mental State Examination for dementia include the Mini-Cog and the improved Addenbrooke's Cognitive Examination (ACE). Many revisions have been developed for the above-mentioned assessment tools.

Some commonly used tools for assessing trauma in adults and elderly are as follows:

- *Trauma Assessment for Adults (TAA,* Resnick et al., 1996) is a 17-item self-report that inquiries about numerous potentially traumatic events that an individual may have experienced and/or different types of stressful life events using a yes/no format. It is a 10- to 15-minute test.
- *The Hwalek–Sengstock Elder Abuse Screening Test (HSEAST,* Neale et al., 1991) is a paper-and-pencil measure of elder mistreatment that has been evaluated psychometrically. The 15-item test was verified by Neale et al. (1991), who discovered that 9 of the items indicated abused or exploited individuals Abuse, neglect, financial exploitation, and abandonment are all examples of how elderly people are mistreated. Most states require professionals to report suspected mistreatment, but many have little or no training in spotting the signs of mistreatment, hence most incidents go unreported. Abuse, neglect, financial exploitation, and abandonment are all examples of how elderly people are mistreated. Most states require professionals to report suspected mistreatment, but many have little or no training in spotting the signs of mistreatment, hence most incidents go unreported.
- *The Elder Assessment Instrument (EAI):* used in most clinical settings, allows nurses to examine older persons for suspected abuse (Fulmer et al., 2004). The EAI is a 41-item evaluation instrument that was initially published in 1984 and has since been modified and customised for certain clinical and research situations. It will undoubtedly continue to evolve as care professionals gain a better understanding of how to assess elder maltreatment. Elder abuse is a problem that occurs when age and gender collide. There is growing evidence of high rates of depression among elder abuse victims, with nearly one-third reporting major

depressive symptoms (Sirey et al., 2015), and older women victims are especially vulnerable.

- *The Vulnerability to Abuse Screening Scale (VASS)* was validated in 2003. Through a self-report tool, VASS is designed to help identify women over the age of 70 who may be at risk of elder abuse (Schofield & Mishra, 2003). VASS was created with the goal of being a self-reporting tool; the authors believe that self-reporting provides more accurate information regarding the danger of elder abuse since it removes the embarrassment that some adults feel when dealing with medical personnel. The VASS comprises of 12 yes or no questions that ask whether the respondent is fearful, feeling harm, sad, or being compelled to do something they don't want to do.

   The above assessment tools cater to specific age groups. Along with them, there are some commonly used assessment tools for all age groups which have been highlighted below:

For cognitive functioning:

- *The Stanford–Binet Intelligence Scales*, Fifth Edition is a self-administered intelligence and cognitive skills test for people aged 2–5. The SB5 can be used in early childhood assessments, psychoeducational evaluations for special education services, and later career development planning to detect a wide range of developmental disorders.
- *Raven's Progressive Matrices* (RPM, Raven, 1936) is a non-verbal exam that is commonly used to assess general human intellect and abstract reasoning. It is regarded as a non-verbal assessment of fluid intelligence (Bilker et al., 2012). It is one of the most common tests given to both groups and individuals ranging in age from 5 to 80 years old. The exams were created in 1936 by John C. Raven. The respondent is asked to identify the missing element that completes a pattern in each test item. And the matrices are designed to move from easy to difficult pattern completion. Standard Progressive Matrices (SPM), Coloured Progressive Matrices (CPM), and Advanced Progressive Matrices (APM) are the three types of matrices accessible for participants of various abilities (Raven, 2000).

Personality tests:

- *House-Tree-Person (H-T-P, Buck, 1948 & Hammer, 1958)* is most commonly used projective assessments for children and adults. It is suitable for people aged 3 and above and is virtually fully unstructured. The respondent is merely directed to draw a home, a tree, and a person freehand (Buck, 1948). Test takers are instructed to draw illustrations of a home, a tree, and a person with a crayon during the first section of the test. Each drawing is done on its own sheet of paper, and the test taker is encouraged to be as exact as possible. They are given questions regarding the drawings once they have completed them. Buck has designed a total of 60 questions that examiners can ask. Examiners can also ask unscripted follow-up questions or construct their own queries. Test takers are instructed to sketch the same drawings using a pencil during the second portion of the test. The questions that follow this phase are identical to those that came before it.

Some examiners merely administer one of the two stages, selecting a crayon, pencil, or other writing tool. One method of administering the test is to have the participant sketch two distinct people, one of each gender. Another option is to have test takers compile all of the drawings onto a single sheet.

- *The Sixteen Personality Factor Questionnaire (16PF*, Cattell & Mead, 1949) is a self-report personality test. The paper-and-pencil version of the test takes roughly 35–50 minutes to administer, whereas the computer version takes about 30 minutes. The test instructions are short and straightforward, and the test is not timed; as a result, the test is generally self-administrable and can be utilised in an individual or group situation. The 16PF test was created for adults who are at least 18 years old. The 16PF exam was created for people aged 16 and over, although there are other tests for children in various age groups (Schuerger, 2001).

- *Million Clinical Multiaxial Inventory–Fourth Edition (MCMI-IV):* It is a psychological assessment tool that focuses on personality traits and psychopathology, including particular psychiatric disorders as defined by the DSM-5. It is designed for people above 18 years of age who are currently seeking mental health care and have a reading level of at least fifth grade (Millon et al., 2015). The MCMI was created and standardised with clinical populations in mind (i.e. patients in clinical settings or people with mental health issues), and the authors are clear that it should not be utilised with the general public or teenagers. Hence psychologists may occasionally administer the test to members of the general public with caution. It is unsuited for anyone with below average intelligence or reading ability due to the concepts involved in the questions and their presentation. The fourth version contains 195 true–false questions that should take about 25–30 minutes to complete. Theodore Millon, Seth Grossman, and Carrie Millon invented it (Millon et al., 2015). The test is based on four different scales: 15 scales of personality patterns, the Clinical Syndrome Scales (CSS) are a set of 10 scales, 3 modifying indices, 2 random response indicators; 5 validity scales, and 45 Grossman personality facet scales (based on Seth Grossman's psychopathology and personality theories).

- *The Minnesota Multiphasic Personality Inventory (MMPI)* is a standardised personality and psychopathology examination for adults (Camara et al., 2000). Different versions of the MMPI are used by psychologists and other mental health professionals to develop treatment plans, assist with differential diagnosis, and answer legal questions (forensic psychology). The original MMPI was created by University of Minnesota teachers Starke R. Hathaway and J. C. McKinley and published by the University of Minnesota Press in 1943. Butcher et al., 1989, replaced it with an upgraded version, the MMPI-2. In 1992, the MMPI-A, a version for adolescents, was released. The MMPI-2 Restructured Form is an alternative version of the test. In 1992, the MMPI-A, a version for adolescents, was released. The MMPI-2 Restructured Form (MMPI-2-RF), launched in 2008, is an alternate version of the test that keeps some characteristics of the classic MMPI assessment technique while taking a new theoretical approach to personality test development. MMPI development ostensibly allowed the test to capture recognised and significant components of human psychopathology despite changes in clinical beliefs. The MMPI, on the other hand, had validity issues that were quickly apparent and could not be overlooked indefinitely. For its first testing, a small group of people, largely young, white, and married men and women from rural areas of the Midwest, served as the control group. The MMPI also has issues with language and its lack of relevance to the demographic it was supposed to measure. The MMPI needed to be expanded to include a broader range of potential mental health issues, such as suicidal tendencies, drug abuse and treatment related behaviours (Gregory, 2007).

- *The Big Five Inventory (BFI, John & Robins, 1998)* is a self-report questionnaire that assesses the big five personality characteristics (extraversion, agreeableness, conscientiousness, neuroticism, and openness). The BFI comprises of 44 items that are scored on a five-point Likert scale ranging from 1 (strong disagreement) to 5 (strong agreement) (agree a lot). There are five basic scales produced by the BFI. It is suitable for people aged 10–65 years. The scales' descriptions and item loadings are mentioned below. The sum of the individual components is used to determine scale scores. Items marked with an asterisk (*) are scored in the opposite direction (John & Srivastava, 1999).

For psychopathology:

- *The Depression Anxiety Stress Scales (DASS)* is a set of three self-report scales designed to measure the negative emotional states of depression, anxiety and stress (Lovibond & Lovibond, 1995). The 'Depression scale assesses dysphoria, hopelessness, devaluation of life, self-deprecation, lack of interest/involvement, anhedonia, and inertia. The Anxiety scale assesses autonomic arousal, skeletal muscle effects, situational anxiety, and subjective experience of anxious affect. The Stress scale assesses difficulty in relaxing, nervous arousal, and being easily upset/agitated, irritable/over-reactive and impatient' (Lovibond & Lovibond, 1995, p. 2). DASS was originally developed as 42 items version which was revised as 21-items version and has also been adapted to different regional languages such as Hindi and Tamil. Each subscale, i.e., depression, anxiety and stress has a range mentioned to be interpreted within normal, mild, moderate, severe and extremely severe.
- *The Thematic Apperception Test (TAT, Morgan & Murray, 1935)* is a projective psychological exam. It has long been one of the most commonly studied, taught, and used of such assessments. The TAT, according to its proponents, taps into a person's unconscious to uncover repressed personality traits, motivations and demands for achievement, power and intimacy, and problem-solving talents. It is suitable for age range 5–79 years (Harrison, 1965). Because it uses a regular series of enticing yet ambiguous photos about which the subject is asked to describe a storey, the TAT is also known as the picture interpretation technique For each photo exhibited, the subject is requested to give as dramatic a tale as they can, including: what led up to the action shown, what is happening right now, what the characters are feeling and thinking, and what the story's outcome was. If these elements are missing, the evaluator may ask the subject about them directly, especially if the subject is a kid or has low cognitive capacities. In the TAT's regular format, there are 31 picture cards. Male figures, female figures,

male and female figures, unclear gender figures, adults, children, and no human beings are depicted on some of the cards.

- *The Beck Depression Inventory (BDI, Beck*, 1961) is a self-report questionnaire with 21 multiple-choice questions. It is one of the most commonly used tools for determining the severity of depression. The most recent edition of the questionnaire is for people of age group between 13 to 80 years and it includes things like despondency and irritation, as well as cognitions like guilt or emotions of being punished, and bodily symptoms like weariness, weight loss, and a lack of interest in sex (Beck, 1972).
- *The Beck Anxiety Inventory (BAI, Beck* et al., 1996) is a 21-question self-report inventory that is used to assess the degree of an individual's anxiety (Osman et al., 2003). It can be used with age range of 17–80 years. The BAI consists of questions on how the person has felt in the previous week. Every question has the same set of four answer options.
- *The Psychopathy Checklist-Revised (PCL-R*, Hare & Neumann, 2006) is the psychodiagnostic tool used to assess Psychopathy. It can be utilised with age scope of 18 years or more. Notwithstanding way of life and criminal conduct the agenda surveys chatty and shallow appeal, self-importance, need for feeling, neurotic lying, clever and controlling, absence of regret, hardness, poor social controls, impulsivity, recklessness, and inability to acknowledge liability regarding one's own activity.
- *Aggression Questionnaire (AQ*, Buss & Perry, 1992) is a self-report questionnaire which makes it feasible to screen children and adults for aggressive tendencies on a regular basis. It assesses a person's aggressive reactions as well as his or her ability to channel such reactions in a healthy, constructive manner. It can be used with age range of 9–88 years. It takes 10 minutes to do this inventory. Physical aggressiveness, verbal aggression, hostility, anger, and indirect aggression are among the 34 items that are assessed on the following scales: physical aggression, verbal aggression, hostility, rage, and indirect aggression (Arnold et al., 2005).

Assessing and providing adequate and appropriate interventions requires sound knowledge, skills and expertise in the relevant field such as clinical psychology, forensic psychology, behavioural study, counselling, psychometric etc. Because there is a lot of overplay of feelings and emotions while dealing with victims and trauma. The following section provides a brief about the effects and needs of professionals providing support to various kinds of victims.

Professionals Working in Trauma Settings

Mental health practitioners are increasingly being asked to assist clients who are faced with one or more multiple traumatic events (Trippany et al., 2004). School violence, terrorist attacks, pandemics and natural disasters have raised the clinicians' awareness and sharpened the mental state to treat clients who have encountered crisis and trauma all around the world. These occurrences, along with the abundance of media images, have raised public awareness and exposed a wider number of individuals to pain through vicariously experiencing it. Despite the actual fact that these well-publicised and large-scale events have focused attention on crisis and trauma counselling, people are suffering from unexpected loss, accidents, and tragedies on a daily basis.

Because psychology practitioners are getting more aware and awake to the character of trauma, its impact on those that have experienced it, and also the significance of treating traumatised clients. It's also becoming increasingly important to address variables that both reduce and complicate the impact of trauma work on counsellors' quality of life. Providing required assistance for these professionals, protects not just their well-being, but also their capacity to continue serving as crisis and trauma counsellors (Clukey, 2010). There are certain professional and personal characteristics of mental health practitioners that works as assets and protective factors while working with trauma clients and victims, such as, certain person-centred and supportive techniques like empathy, unconditional positive regard, mindful awareness and observation, non-judging, calmness, confidentiality along with the professional and technical expertise and skills to work with crisis and trauma. This kind of work has the potential to be both strenuous and rewarding simultaneously (Figley, 1995; Munroe et al., 1995). Strenuousness leads to compassion fatigue which is characterised by negative behaviours and emotions that arise as a result of assisting someone else who has been through a painful situation (Figley, 1993). Many researchers have also identified the positive and benefitting aspects of working with trauma and victim clients. These concepts are labelled in literature alternately as compassion satisfaction (Stamm et al., 2002) and vicarious post-traumatic growth (Arnold et al., 2005).

Vicarious traumatisation (VT) (McCann & Pearlman, 1990) is a concept used to explain how trauma therapists deal with traumatised clients and the impact it has on them. Dr. Charles Figley invented the term 'secondary traumatic stress' to describe the phenomena. Secondary traumatic stress (STS) (Figley, 1995; Stamm, 1999) is a condition that arises in mental health professionals and other professionals dealing with trauma clients and is similar to post-traumatic stress disorder (PTSD). Because of the constant exposure to victims of trauma and violence, those working and volunteering in victim services, police enforcement, emergency medical services, fire services, and other associated professions face vicarious trauma. Hearing about or responding to the aftermath of violence and other traumatic events day after day; and responding to mass violent situations that have resulted in multiple injuries and fatalities can all lead to work-related trauma exposure (Arvay & Uhlemann, 1996).

It is caused by exposure to other people's painful experiences. The premise behind vicarious trauma is that the connection of sympathetic bonding with a client causes the therapist to have a significant world shift and is permanently transformed (Hesse, 2002). Empathic involvement and exposure to violent and distressing content, the therapist being exposed to human cruelty, and recreation of trauma within the treatment process are regarded to be three precondition criteria for this development. This shift might affect a therapist's faith, worldview, and sense of self-identity. The consequences of vicarious trauma affect anti-violence profession-als in all aspects of their life, and they are cumulative, inevitable, and unique to each individual. Changes in attitudes and values, as well as the way one looks/perceives the world, intrusive images, and bodily effects, are all common outcomes of the practise. Different elements influence what causes a personal reaction, as well as how restricted or amplified the effect is. Personal features or attributes, past experi-ence, a personal history of abuse, and the organisation's culture and policies are some of these influences or precursors that make the professional vulnerable towards vicarious trauma, compassion fatigue, and countertransference (Crothers, 1995).

Countertransference is linked to psychodynamic approach and appears to be the therapist's emotional reaction to a client. Although there are numerous definitions, in psychotherapy, countertransference is the therapist's distortion as a result of her or his life experiences and related with her or his unconscious, neurotic reaction to the client's transference (Freud, 1959). Countertransference was recently character-ised by Corey (1991) as the process of seeing oneself in the client, over-identifying with the client, or compassion fatigue satisfying needs through the client. It is addressed in a number of ways by therapists. Surveillance or consultation with other therapists is one of the most popular ways therapists cope with countertransference. Because it can be difficult for therapists to recognise when countertransference is occurring, discussing the situation with other experts can assist the therapist in iden-tifying and modifying countertransference behaviours. Experience might also lead to countertransference. Supervision is vital to deal with countertransference issues and feelings. When a therapist is experiencing countertransference, their supervisor can frequently identify it and assist them control it so that the client is not harmed (Joyce & Piper, 1993). Therapists can also cope with countertransference by seek-ing their own treatment to assist them deal with the conditions that cause it. Similarly, burnout is also evident in professionals. It is a reaction to the demands of one's employment and surroundings, rather than being exclusive to individuals who work with trauma victims. It is defined as 'a state of physical, emotional, and mental weariness brought on by prolonged engagement in emotionally challenging events' (Pines & Aronson, 1998, p. 9).

Healthy recruiting procedures are required, as well as periodic sensitivity train-ing. Staff members must reflect on their own actions and attitudes, as well as be committed to continuing learning and challenges from the rest of the team (Cooper & Cartwright, 1994). The cumulative effect of these stories might become quite intrusive. Intrusive visions or nightmares are clear indications. After intensive, pain-ful sessions, timely debriefing might help to lessen the consequences of vicari-ous trauma.

Thus, there are various ways to help the professionals cope effectively and deal better with self, environment, and others. The first technique relates to physical body relaxation via various treatments which may aid in the absorption of trauma material by offering a physical release. Professionals can use a variety of wellness measures to deal with the symptoms of burnout (Shanafelt et al., 2003). Second technique is social support and relationships as the pillars to provide nurturance and sustenance to the individual. It's about appreciating the value of spending quality time with family, friends, and significant others. This technique also entails actively cultivating relationships with colleagues in order to discuss and reflect on the emotional and existential elements of being a doctor with them. Third technique is religious belief and/or spiritual practise that appear to boost happiness in certain people. This refers to a personal commitment to cultivating one's own spiritual well-being that assists in coping.

The other major component or the fourth technique to deal with professional's feelings and emotions is to gauge work attitudes. There are two aspects while discussing work attitudes. The first refers to finding meaning and fulfilment in one's work, while the second refers to actively choosing and limiting the type of medical practise one engages in, such as working part-time, participating in education and/or research, scheduling, and discontinuing unfulfilling aspects of practise. Self-care activities are fifth technique, in which a person deliberately cultivates personal interests and self-awareness in addition to career and familial obligations. This also entails aggressively seeking expert assistance in the event of personal bodily or mental issues or sickness. Exercise, self-expression activities, sufficient diet and sleep, regular medical care, professional counselling, and other practises are examples of such behaviours. Finally, adopting a definite life philosophy is the sixth component which entails cultivating a philosophical view on life that is founded on a positive attitude, in which one recognises one's own values and acts in accordance with them, with a focus on maintaining a balance between personal and professional life. Such tactics are likely to be the specified instruments to be used in the prevention of the development of burnout (Linzer et al., 2001).

The usefulness of mental health services for crime victims is occasionally questioned, particularly during the investigation and prosecution phases of their cases. Questions concerning discovery requirements and beliefs about how mental health services would alter the victims'recollections and perceptions about the crime arise in reaction to the use of mental health services during investigations and subsequent prosecutions (Herman, 2003). Victims and their families might be devastated by crimes, and they may require assistance in coping with the consequences. The following are some of the signs and symptoms to keep an eye out for: Physical symptoms include eating disturbances (more/less than usual), sleep disturbances (more/less than usual), sexual dysfunction, low energy, gastrointestinal distress, and chronic, unexplained pain. Emotional symptoms include depression, anxiety, panic attacks, feeling out of control, emotional numbness, distress irritability, and anger, and cognitive symptoms include memory lapses, difficulty making decisions, decreased concentration, feeling distracted, and guilt/blaming (Potter & Brewer, 1999).

Various mental health professionals are involved at various degrees and levels while working with trauma and victim clients such as psychiatrists with degree of Medical Doctor (MD), clinical psychologist with either a Masters in Philosophy (M.Phil.) in certain countries and/or Doctor of Philosophy (PhD) or Doctor of Psychology (PsyD). Other professionals involved are psychiatric social workers, occupational therapist, marriage and family therapist, counsellors, etc., and each professional has a licensing or registration system that regulates their practice in each region/country. With reference to the above-listed professionals, there are series of mental health services – psychological first aid (PFA) is unquestionably important in aiding patients' mental and emotional recovery following stressful events such as catastrophes and pandemics by using several techniques such as psychoeducation through factual information, supportive techniques assisting in limiting the lasting effects of PTSD (Horn et al., 2019).

Psychological therapies are required to promote catastrophe survivors' resiliency and rehabilitation by decreasing mental breakdown. Crisis intervention although is immediate and short-term management method but a powerful tool aiding in inhibiting the long-lasting effects of trauma and crisis. These techniques help restore one's mental state immediately after a crisis and prevent trauma. Crisis intervention has also been proposed as a therapy option for people suffering from serious mental health issues/difficulties (Murphy and Cherney, 2012).

Similarly, cognitive behavioural therapy (CBT) focuses on the relationship between ideas, feelings, and behaviours; it targets current issues and symptoms; and it focuses on modifying patterns of behaviour, thoughts, and feelings that lead to functional difficulties (Ehlers, 2013). To help clients reduce symptoms and improve functioning, therapists employ a range of strategies. CBT therapists ask clients to reassess their thought patterns and maladaptive assumptions to identify patterns and directing the clients to adopt more balanced and adaptive thinking patterns instead (Monson & Shnaider, 2014). These are meant to assist the person rethink their perceptions of traumatic events, as well as their perceptions of themselves and their abilities to cope.

Counselling is widely acknowledged as an emotionally challenging profession. Therapists are expected to be empathetic, compassionate, and kind, but they must also manage their own emotional demands and responsiveness when working with clients. Clinicians are at danger of experiencing emotional, mental, and physical tiredness while empathically dealing with a traumatised adult or child (Figley, 1995; McCann & Pearlman, 1990; Pearlman & Saakvitne, 1995; Pearlman & MacIan, 1995). Empirical research backs up the hypothesis that counsellors who work with other people's trauma are more likely to experience changes in their own psychological functioning (Chrestman, 1995). Some of the aspects noticed in the psychological shift in mental health professionals assisting trauma clients are destructive coping strategies such as avoidance of the trauma, intense fear or feelings of terror, shame, fury, grief, detachment, if chronic or increasing levels can lead to burnout and countertransference. These reactions might also have an impact on the therapeutic relationship. If counsellors aren't aware of this stress response, they may send the message to clients that they don't want to hear the details of their trauma, or they may be less likely to ask questions to stimulate discourse about it.

Individuals who often have restricted circumstances in which speaking their narrative is safe and acceptable may be re-victimised as a result of this (McCann & Pearlman, 1990). Compassion fatigue symptoms can be avoided if a counsellor's psychological well-being is maintained, according to research (Figley, 1995). When it comes to determining what constitutes psychological well-being, spirituality is a major consideration. According to Graham et al. (2001), spirituality is an important component of mental health for counsellors, according to a survey performed by the American Counselling Association. These researchers performed more research into the role of religion and spirituality in stress management and discovered a link between spiritual health and resilience to stressful situations (Graham et al., 2001). Self-care is a term that advocates use to describe proactive measures for reducing the negative impacts of working with trauma (Morrison, 2007). When an advocate practises self-care, he or she employs cathartic and integrative techniques. These strategies can be used in a variety of ways, including cognitive, physical, spiritual, social/recreational, and linguistic.

The various methods towards supporting mental health professionals working with trauma and victim clients include Cognitive methods: altering one's perspective on a subject, recognising that one has made a difference, or acknowledging that one has done everything potentially they could; Physical ways: exercising, listening to music, or taking self-defence training are examples of physical methods; Spiritual methods: praying or believing in a higher force, as well as relying on religion or spirituality for assistance; Social/recreational methods include interaction with friends and family, as well as the use of creative outlets. Watching movies, travelling, buying, and being surrounded by social circle who keeps the environment positive and happy are also some of these tactics. Verbal methods include the act of putting one's ideas and feelings into words, such as journaling or being able to communicate with others.

In numerous ways, a trauma lens informs our understanding of supervision. Staff should be able to get help, debrief about their job, and enhance their skills and knowledge through supervision. Supervisors should support professional growth and learning opportunities while functioning with a trauma lens. Organisations must offer safe venues for important and sometimes difficult dialogues, as well as reduce the effects of vicarious trauma (Walsh et al., 2017).

Also, supervision becomes vital during these times for mental health professionals. A definitive objective of oversight is to assist staff with giving the most elevated level of administration to their clients (Edwards & Chen, 1999). Supervisors use a combination of administration, instruction, and support to achieve this purpose (Tsui, 2005). In most cases, supervision is considered as a collaborative effort between the supervisor and the supervisee. Supervision is something that is done with a person rather than something that is done to a person. Both the supervisor and the supervisee must be actively involved. People who work with trauma sufferers frequently experience vicarious trauma (VT). Working with trauma survivors over time can have a transforming influence on an advocate's identity and view on the world, which is known as vicarious trauma (Pearlman & Saakvitne, 1995). Without regular supervision, advocates are more prone to develop VT, which can lead to burnout and turnover (Cyr & Dowrick, 1991; Killian, 2008; Neumann & Gamble, 1995; Pearlman & Saakvitne, 1995). Many advocates and volunteers have stated that having a supportive work environment and supervision are important aspects in minimising work stress and weariness, both of which contribute to burnout (Cyr & Dowrick, 1991; Killian, 2008).

Overall, the chapter provides the overview of various assessments available to study victimology, effects on victims and also provide a horizontal view about the needs and interventions available for the mental health professionals working with victims and trauma clients.

Acknowledgement This chapter received no specific grant from any funding agency in the public, commercial, or not-for-profit sectors. The access to books, journal articles, and research articles was supported by the online library facilities of the Auckland University of Technology.

References

American Psychiatric Association. (1994). *Diagnostic and Statistical manual of mental disorders (4th ed.).* American Psychiatric Publishing, Inc.

Arnold, D., Calhoun, L. G., Tedeschi, R., & Cann, A. (2005). Vicarious Posttraumatic Growth in Psychotherapy. *Journal of Humanistic Psychology, 45*(2), 239–263.

Arvay, M., & Uhlemann, M. R. (1996). Counsellor stress in the field of trauma: A preliminary study. *Canadian Journal of Counselling, 30*(3), 193–210.

Batten, D. (2010). Victims of crime. In *Gale encyclopaedia of American law* (3rd ed.).

Beck, A. T. (1972). *Depression: Causes and treatment.* University of Pennsylvania Press.

Beck, J. (2001). *New scales for children: The beck youth inventory.* The Beck Institute, 1–5.

Beck, J. S., Beck, A. T., & Jolly, J. (2001). *Manual for the Beck Youth Inventories of Emotional and Social Impairment.* San Antonio, TX: The Psychological Corporation.

Beck, A.T., Steer, R.A., & Brown, G.K. (1996). *Manual for the Beck Depression Inventory-II.* San Antonio, TX: Psychological Corporation.

Beck, A.T., Ward, C. H., Mendelson, M., Mock, J., & Erbaugh, J. (1961) An inventory for measuring depression. *Archives of General Psychiatry, 4*, 561–571.

Bharatraj, J. (1971). AIISH norms on Seguin Form Board with Indian children. *The Journal of All India Institute of Speech and Hearing, 2*, 117–127.

Bhatia, C. M. (1955). *Performance tests of intelligence under Indian conditions.* Oxford University Press.

Bilker, W. B., Hansen, J. A., Brensinger, C. M., Richard, J., Gur, R. E., & Gur, R. C. (2012). Development of abbreviated nine-item forms of the Raven's standard progressive matrices test. *Assessment, 19*(3), 354–369.

Briere, J. N., & Elliott, D. M. (1994). Immediate and long-term impacts of child sexual abuse. *The Future of Children, 4*(2), 54–69.

Buck, J. N. (1948). The H-T-P. *Journal of Clinical Psychology, 4*, 151–159.

Buss, A. H., & Perry, M. (1992). The Aggression Questionnaire. *Journal of Personality and Social Psychology, 63*, 452–459.

Butcher, J. N., Dahlstrom, W. G., Graham, J. R., Tellegen, A. M., & Kaemmer, B. (1989). *Minnesota Multiphasic Personality Inventory-2 (MMPI-2): Manual for administration and scoring.* Minneapolis: University of Minnesota Press.

Camara, W. J., Nathan, J. S., & Puente, A. E. (2000). Psychological test usage: Implications in professional psychology. *Professional Psychology: Research and Practice, 31*(2), 141–154.

Cattell, R. B., & Mead, A. D. (1949). *The Sixteen Personality Factor questionnaire (16PF).* Champaign: IPAT.

Carlson, E. B., Armstrong, J., & Loewenstein, R. (1997). Reported amnesia for childhood abuse and other traumatic events in psychiatric inpatients. In J. D. Read & D. S. Lindsay (Eds.), *Recollections of trauma: Scientific evidence and clinical practice* (pp. 395–401). Plenum Press.

Chrestman, K. R. (1995). Secondary exposure to trauma and self-reported distress among therapists. In B. H. Stamm (Ed.), *Secondary traumatic stress: Self-care issues for clinicians, researchers, and educators* (pp. 29–36). TheSidran Press.

Christie, N. (1986). The ideal victim. In E. A. Fattah (Ed.), *From crime policy to victim policy.* Palgrave Macmillan.

Clukey, L. (2010). Transformative experiences for hurricanes Katrina and Rita disaster volunteers. *Disasters, 34*(3), 644–656.

Cooper, L., & Cartwright, S. (1994). Stress management interventions in the workplace: Stress counselling and stress audits. *British Journal of Guidance and Counselling, 22*(1), 65–73.

Collins. (2010) Victim. *Collins English Dictionary.* London.

Corey, G. F. (1991). *Theory and practice of counselling psychotherapy.* Brooks Cole.

Crothers, D. (1995). Vicarious traumatization in the work with survivors of childhood trauma. *Journal of Psychosocial Nursing and Mental Health Services, 33*(4), 9–13.

Cyr, C., & Dowrick, P. W. (1991). Burnout in crisis line volunteers. *Administration and Policy in Mental Health and Mental Health Services Research, 18,* 343–354.

Edwards, J., & Chen, M. (1999). Strength-based supervision: Frameworks, current practice and future directions: A Wu-weiMethod. *The Family Journal, 7*(4), 349–357.

Ehlers, A. (2013). Trauma-focused cognitive behavior therapy for posttraumatic stress disorder and acute stress disorder. In G. Simos & S. G. Hofmann (Eds.), *CBT for anxiety disorders: A practitioner book.* Wiley.

Figley, C. R. (1993). Coping with stressors on the home front. *Journal of Social Issues, 49*(4), 51–71.

Figley, C. R. (1995). *Compassion fatigue: Coping with secondary traumatic stress disorder in those who treat the traumatized.* Brunner/Mazel.

Fink, L. A., Bernstein, D., Handelsman, L., Foote, J., & Lovejoy, M. (1995). Initial reliability and validity of the childhood trauma interview: A new multidimensional measure of childhood interpersonal trauma. *American Journal of Psychiatry, 152*(9), 1329–1335.

Flanagan, R., & Henington, C. (2005). Review of the beck youth inventories for children and adolescents: Second Edition. *Mental Measurements Yearbook, 18.*

Folstein, M. F., Folstein, S. E., & McHugh, P. R. (1975). "Mini-mental state". A practical method for grading the cognitive state of patients for the clinician. *Journal of Psychiatric Research, 12*(3), 189–198.

Ford, J., & Wilson, C. (2012). *SAMHSA's trauma and trauma-informed care experts meeting.*

Freud, S. (1959). Future prospects of psychoanalytic psychotherapy. In J. Strachey (Ed., Trans.), *The standard edition of the complete psychological works of Sigmund Freud* (Vol. 2, pp. 139–151). Hogarth Press. (Original work published 1910.)

Fulmer, T., Guadagno, L., Dyer, B. C., & Connolly, M. T. (2004). Progress in elder abuse screening and assessment instruments. *Journal of the American Geriatric Society, 52,* 297–304.

Graham, S., Furr, S., Flowers, C., & Burke, M. T. (2001). Religion and spirituality in coping with stress. *Counseling and Values, 46*(1), 2–14.

Gregory, R. (2007). *Psychological testing: History, principles, and applications* (pp. 391–398). Pearson.

Grondhuis, S., Lecavalier, L., & Arnold, L. E. (2018). Differences in verbal and nonverbal IQ test scores in children with autism spectrum disorder. *Research in Autism Spectrum Disorders, 49,* 47–55.

Gurland, B., Kuriansky, J., Sharpe, L., Simon, R., Stiller, P. & Birkett, P. (1978). The Comprehensive Assessment and Referral Evaluation (Care)—Rationale, Development and Reliability. *The International Journal of Aging and Human Development, 8*(1), 9–42.

Hammer, E. F. (1958). *The clinical application of projective drawings.* Springfield: Charles Thomas.

Hare, R. D., & Neumann, C. N. (2006). The PCL-R assessment of psychopathy: Development, structural properties, and new directions. In C. Patrick (Ed.), *Handbook of psychopathy* (pp. 58–88). Guilford.

Harrison, R. (1965). Thematic apperception test. In B. Wolman (Ed.), *Handbook of clinical psychology* (pp. 562–620). McGraw-Hill.

Herman, J. L. (2003). The Mental Health of Crime Victims: Impact of Legal Intervention. *Journal of Trauma Stress,16*, 159–166.

Hesse, A. R. (2002). Secondary trauma: How working with trauma survivors affects therapists. *Clinical Social Work Journal, 30*(3), 293–309.

Horn, R., O'May, F., Esliker, R., Gwaikolo, W., Woensdregt, L., & Ruttenberg, L. (2019). The myth of the 1-day training: The effectiveness of psychosocial support capacity-building during the Ebola outbreak in West Africa. *Global Mental Health, 6*(5).

John, O. P., & Robins, R. W. (1998). Recent trends in Big Five research: Development, predictive validity, and personality types. In J. Bermudez et al. (Eds.), *Personality Psychology in Europe, 6*, 6–16.

John, O. P., & Srivastava, S. (1999). The Big-Five trait taxonomy: History, measurement, and theoretical perspectives. In L. A. Pervin & O. P. John (Eds.), *Handbook of personality: Theory and research* (Vol. 2, pp. 102–138). Guilford Press.

Joyce, A. S., & Piper, W. E. (1993). The immediate impact of transference in short-term individual psychotherapy. *American Journal of Psychotherapy, 47*, 508–526.

Karmen, A. (1990). *Crime Victims – An Introduction to victimology (2nd ed)*. Pacific Grov, Calif: Brooks/Cole.

Kaufman, A. S. (1983). Some questions and answers about the Kaufman Assessment Battery for Children (K-ABC). *Journal of Psychoeducational Assessment, 1*(3), 205–218.

Killian, K. D. (2008). Helping till it hurts? A multimethod study of compassion fatigue, burnout, and self-care in clinicians working with trauma survivors. *Traumatology, 14*(2), 32–44.

Kilpatrick, D. G., Best, C. L., Veronen, L. J., Amick, A. E., Villeponteaux, L. A., & Ruff, G. A. (1985). Mental health correlates of criminal victimization: A random community survey. *Journal of Consulting and Clinical Psychology, 53*(6), 866–873.

Krakow, B., & Neidhardt, J. (1992). *Conquering bad dreams and nightmares: A guide to understanding, interpretation, and cure*. Berkley.

Lachar, D., & Gruber, C. P. (2007). *Personality inventory for children*, 2nd Ed.: PIC-2 (W-375). WPS.

Linzer, M., Visser, M. R., Oort, F. J., Smets, E. M., McMurray, J. E., de Haes, H. C., & Society of General Internal Medicine (SGIM) Career Satisfaction Study Group (CSSG) (2001). Predicting and preventing physician burnout: results from the United States and the Netherlands. *The American Journal of Medicine, 111*(2), 170–175.

Lovibond, S. H., & Lovibond, P. F. (1995). *Manual for the depression anxiety stress scales* (2nd ed.). Psychology Foundation.

Malin, A. J. (1969). *Manual for Malin's intelligence scale for Indian children (MISIC)*. Indian Psychological Corporation.

McCann, I. L., & Pearlman, L. A. (1990). Vicarious traumatization: A framework for understanding the psychological effects of working with victims. *Journal of Traumatic Stress, 3*, 131–149.

Millon, T., Grossman, S., & Millon, C. (2015). *MCMI-IV: Millon clinical multiaxial inventory manual* (1st ed.). NCS Pearson.

Monson, C. M., & Shnaider, P. (2014). *Treating PTSD with cognitive-behavioral therapies: Interventions that work*. American Psychological Association.

Morgan, C. D., & Murray, H. A. (1935). A method for investigating fantasies: the thematic apperception test. *Archives of Neurology & Psychiatry, 34*, 289–306.

Morrison, Z. (2007). "Feeling heavy": Vicarious trauma and other issues facing those who work in the sexual assault fled. *Australian Centre for the Study of Sexual Assault Wrap, 4*.

Munroe, J. E., Shay, J., Fisher, L., Makary, C., Rapperport, K., & Zimering, R. (1995). Preventing compassion fatigue: A team treatment model. In C. R. Figley (Ed.), *Compassion fatigue: Secondary traumatic stress disorder from treating the traumatized* (pp. 209–231). New \brk: Brunner/Mazel.

Murphy, K., & Cherney, A. (2012). Understanding cooperation with police in a diverse society. *The British Journal of Criminology, 52*(1), 181–201.

Muthegheki, S. B., Crispus, K. S., & Abrahams, N. (2012). *An exploratory study of bride price and domestic violence in Bundibugyo district, Uganda.* Centre for Human Rights Advancement.

Neale, A.V., Hwalek, M.A., Scott, R.O., Sengstock, M.C., Stahl, C. (1991). Validation of the Hwalek-Sengstock Elder Abuse Screening Test. *Journal of Applied Gerontology, 10*(4), 406–418.

Neumann, D. A., & Gamble, S. J. (1995). Issues in the professional development of psychotherapists: Countertransference and vicarious traumatization in the new trauma therapist. *Psychotherapy: Theory, Research, Practice, Training, 32*(2), 341–347.

Osman, S. L. (2003). Predicting men's rape perceptions based on the belief that "no" really means "yes". *Journal of Applied Social Psychology, 33*(4), 683–692.

Ouslander, J. G. (1984). Psychiatric manifestations of physical illness in the elderly. *Psychiatric Medicine, 1*, 63–388.

Palmqvist, S., Hansson, O., Minthon, L., & Londos, E. (2009). Practical suggestions on how to differentiate dementia with Lewy bodies from Alzheimer's disease with common cognitive tests. *International Journal of Geriatric Psychiatry, 24*(12), 1405–1412.

Patterson, R., & Dupree, L. (1994). Issues in the assessment of older adults. In M. Herson & S. M. Turnur (Eds.), *Diagnostic interviewing* (2nd ed., pp. 373–379). Plenum.

Paul, A. M. (2004). *The cult of personality: How personality tests are leading us to miseducate our children, mismanage our companies, and misunderstand ourselves.* Simon & Schuster.

Pearlman, L. A., & MacIan, P. S. (1995). Vicarious traumatization: An empirical study of the effects of trauma work on trauma therapists. *Professional Psychology: Research and Practice, 26*, 558–565.

Pearlman, L. A., & Saakvitne, K. W. (1995). *Trauma and the therapist: Countertransference and vicarious traumatization in psychotherapy with incest survivors.* W. W. Norton & Company.

Pines, A. M., & Aronson, E. (1998). *Career burnout: Causes and cures.* Free Press.

Porter, A. B., & Cattell, R. B. (1956). *Children's personality questionnaire.* Champaign, Illinois: Institute for Personality and Ability Testing.

Porter, R. B., & Cattell, R. B. (1985). *Handbook for the children's personality questionnaire (CPQ).* IPAT.

Potter, R., & Brewer, N. (1999). Perceptions of witness behavior-accuracy relationships held by police, lawyers and mock-jurors. *Psychiatry, Psychology and Law, 6*(1), 97–103.

Raven, J. C. (1936). *Raven Standard Progressive Matrices (RSPM)* [Database record]. APA PsycTests.

Raven, J. (2000). *The outstanding properties of the standard progressive matrices plus test.*

Resnick, H. S., Falsetti, S. A., Kilpatrick, D. G., & Freedy, J. R. (1996). Assessment of rape and other civilian trauma-related post-traumatic stress disorder: Emphasis on assessment of potentially traumatic events. In T. W. Miller (Ed.), *Stressful life events* (pp. 231–266). Madison, WI: International Universities Press.

Sattler, J. M. (1992). *Assessment of children: WISC—III and WPPSI—R supplement.*

Sattler, J. M., & Hoge, R. D. (2006). Goals of behavioral and clinical assessment. In *Assessment of children: behavioral, social, and clinical foundations* (5th ed., p. 5). J.M. Sattler.

Schofield, M. J., & Mishra, G. D. (2003). Validity of self-report screening scale for elder abuse: Women's Health Australia Study. *The Gerontologist, 43*(1), 110–120.

Schuerger, J. M. (2001). *16PF adolescent personality questionnaire.* IPAT.

Shanafelt, T. D., Sloan, J. A., & Habermann, T. M. (2003). The well-being of physicians. *The American Journal of Medicine, 114*(6), 513–519.

Siddique, A. (1993). *Criminology: Problems and perspectives.* Eastern Book Company.

Sirey, J. A., Berman, J., Salamone, A., DePasquale, A., Halkett, A., Raeifar, E., & Raue, P. J. (2015). Feasibility of integrating mental health screening and services into routine elder abuse practice to improve client outcomes. *Journal of Elder Abuse & Neglect, 27*, 254–269.

Stamm, B. (1999). *Secondary traumatic stress: Self-care issues for clinicians, researchers, andeducators.* Sidran Press.

Stamm, B. H., Varra, E. M., Pearlman, L. A., & Giller, E. (2002). *The Helper's Power to Heal and To Be Hurt- Or Helped-By Trying*. Washington, D.C.: Register Report: A Publication of the National Register of Health Service Providers in Psychology.

Tiwari, P. (2012). Victimology: A sub discipline of criminology. *Dehradun Law Review, 4*(1), 87–97.

Trippany, R. L., White Kress, V. E., & Wilcoxon, S. A. (2004). Preventing vicarious trauma: What counsellor should know when working with trauma survivors. *Journal of Counseling and Development, 82*(1), 31–37.

Tsui, M. (2005). *Social work supervision: Contexts and concepts*. Sage Publications.

United Nations General Assembly. (1989). *Convention on the rights of the child, Treaty Series, 1577:3*. United Nations.

Walsh, C. R., Mathieu, F., & Hendricks, A. (2017). *Report from the Secondary Traumatic Stress San Diego Think Tank.Traumatology, 23*(2), 124–128.

Warren, T. S. (2020, June 18). Prosecutors say officer had knee on George Flyod's neck for 7:46 rather than 8:46. *Los Angeles Times*.

Wechsler, D. (1949). *Manual for the Wechsler intelligence scale for children*. The Psychological Corporation.

Wechsler, D. (2003). *Wechsler intelligence scale for children—4th edition (WISC-IV)*. Harcourt Assessment.

Additional Reading

Ashutosh, A. V. (1983). *Cultural survival quarterly magazine, ethnic and religious conflicts in India*.

Barry, C. T., Kamphaus, R. W., & Frick, P. J. (2009). *Clinical assessment of child and adolescent personality and behavior*. Springer.

Chamberlain, L. (2016). Assessment tools for children's exposure to violence. In *Futures without violence*. USA.

Hersen, M,, & Van Hasselt, V. B. (1998). *Handbook of clinical geropsychology* / edited by Michel Hersen and Vincent B. Van Hasselt. Plenum Press.

Chapter 3
Sexual Abuse

Aarzoo Gupta and Archana Kashyap

Introduction

Abuse simply implies improper use or misuse of something either once or more on one or many occasions. One may misuse one's gender, age, authority, power, or any internal or external resource to ill-treat someone. Abuse is any unwelcomed comment, gesture, or/and action imposed on an individual that threatens one's sense of self or identity, or individuality. The one who receives the abuse is a victim, and the one who imposes it is a perpetrator. The discretion of victim and perpetrator gets more complex as we gain insights into theoretical and etiological frameworks of sexual abuse. Abuse is the result of many cognitive processes as well as cognitive functions responsible for regulating emotions and behaviors in any given situation. The processes and functions are common to all humans so what distinguishes the victims or abusers from the nonabusers. We are not using the word nonvictims, as it's difficult to believe there are any nonvictims. It's not about holding a pessimistic stand but a realistic one, one has to survive in isolation to be a nonvictim, and one could still be a victim of self-imposed seclusion. The onus of improper use of any resource lies on both perpetrators as well as the victims. One may abuse power or discretion or information etc. resulting in a bad effect or for a bad purpose or to treat someone with cruelty. The moment an individual decides not to raise his voice, one becomes a victim. So, it's challenging to identify the perpetrator sometimes, the one who decided to abuse or the one who chose to be abused or both (Fig. 3.1).

Sexual abuse is more common than we think, and the global prevalence of various forms of sexual abuse is reported to be 30% as reported by World Health Organization (WHO, 2021). The countries that rate the highest in rape are Botswana (92.93%), Australia (91.92%), and Lesotho (82.68%) (World Population Review, 2022). The lifetime experience of sexual abuse and sexual assault was by 17 years

A. Gupta (✉) · A. Kashyap
Government Medical College & Hospital, Chandigarh, India

© The Author(s), under exclusive license to Springer Nature
Switzerland AG 2022
R. T. Gopalan (ed.), *Victimology*, https://doi.org/10.1007/978-3-031-12930-8_3

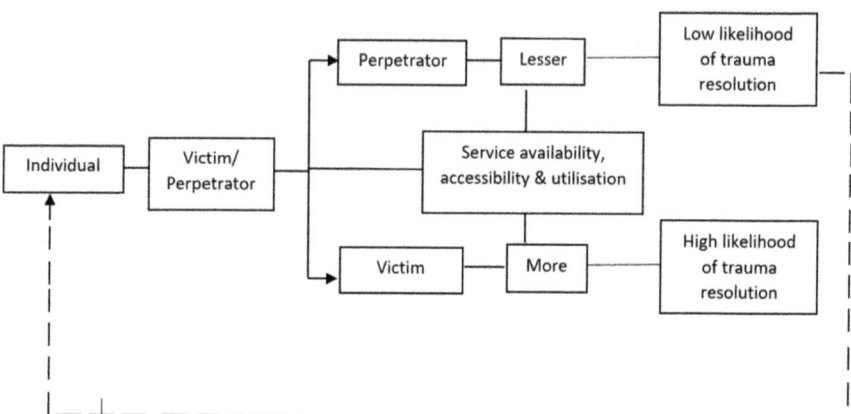

Fig. 3.1 Cycle of a victim to perpetrator

of age; 26.6% for girls and 5.1% for boys and females being higher in number as perpetrators than males (Finkelhor & Hamby, 2014). Over 90% of all respondents to a survey had experienced or observed sexual abuse within their workplace (Legal Service India). The form of sexual abuse varies as per the setting and the victim variables. It is out of ignorance that some forms of sexual abuse such as gender stereotypes and sexist attitudes are completely ignored. In addition, attention needs to be paid to sexual abuse among sexual minorities. According to a Human Rights Campaign report when compared to straight women (35%), lesbian (44%), and bisexual women (61%) are victimized more of rape, physical violence, or stalking by an intimate partner. This campaign further brought out that 29% straight men, 26% gay men, and 37% bisexual men faced similar forms of abuse. The US Transgender survey (2015) reported 47% of transgender people are sexually victimized at some point in their lifetime (James & Anafi, 2016).

There are various forms of abuse manifesting as verbal, physical, sexual, emotional, psychological, etc. Sexual abuse has been macrosized as compared to other forms of abuse while literature says the impact of abuse is not only determined by the type of abuse rather factors related to abuse (Van Der Kolk, 2000). Contrary to this, sexual abuse gained more attention because of its impact and related consequences. This also may be because attention is not paid much to the impact or consequences of the abuse rather mere act of abuse is highlighted. So an act of physical abuse such as hitting someone, depriving someone of any physical need like food, shelter, etc. is perceived as an acceptable act compared to sexually abusing someone like molesting, touching, or raping. This stigmatizes the sexual abuse, and this attached stigma makes the individual hide the sexual abuse, therefore not reaching out. Also, the attached stigma does not let a person come out of it and increases the impact by shamefully perceiving the consequences. Similarly, verbal abuse is normally advised to be ignored; social abuse is interwoven in social phenomena like discrimination, outcasts, etc. Hence, abuse is an integral part of any society and is considered a norm as the society expects the victim to develop tolerance to ignore.

Emotional or psychological abuse is mislabeled as weakness and making assumptions. The authors attempt to convey physical, social, emotional, or psychological abuse is well tolerated and accepted in society, and the victim is not victimized rather victim is perceived as a strong figure who could put all of this behind and move on.

In the case of sexual abuse, the victim of sexual abuse is a victim because society wants you to be the victim. And if society stops stigmatizing may be the victims stop feeling victimized and continue to function and live just as they did either before the act of sexual abuse or like the victims of other forms of abuse. In addition, the victim of sexual abuse is not perceived as strong to sustain the abuse, and also attention is not paid to the contextual factors that precede the act of abuse. This may be because of the moral and social values attached to sex that are often fused with the phenomena of sexual abuse.

Sexual Abuse Stages

Sexual abuse can be traced back to various social and gender-related theories and has its origin in social role theory, gender belief system, gender schema theories (Kalra & Bhugra, 2013). These theories explain the role of stereotypes as part of socialization that puts people in various brackets based on sex and roles including occupation, caste, class, community, etc. This builds a frame to narrow the beliefs about gender-based schemas perpetuating the social system which in turn influences the family and work-related decisions as well as behaviors against certain sex or gender (Davis & Wilson, 2016). Sexual abuse insidiously penetrates any society at a micro level reinforcing gender stereotypes as a sociocultural practice. This lays the foundation for the onset of sexual abuse, and in certain individuals, abuse may take its severe form such as sexual violence. We affiliate with the sexual violence continuum given by feminist scholar Liz Kelly in 1988 (Cowburn, 2011) but we revamp it by categorizing and labeling the sexual abuse into progressive stages taking a gender-neutral stand, given as follows:

1. *Stereotypes*: Sexual abuse originates with stereotypes that are a collective inheritance of any society or community. These stereotypes are intergenerational and communicated through day-to-day conversations via various agencies of socialization. These stereotypes imbibe in concept formation learned during early childhood years. Therefore, it provides a lens to see the differences among humans as discrimination derived out of demographics, roles, responsibilities, actions, illness, authority, power, and so on. Some common examples are community or religion or racist jokes, daughter-in-law and mother-in-law jokes, etc. The list of such examples across the global societies can be infinite, one is usually unaware when the switch from being a listener one becoming a participant, either as a victim or a perpetrator, utilizing these stereotypes in daily communication and decisions.

2. *Sexist attitude*: Based on the impressions formed by the stereotypes an individual now starts developing a sense of superiority or inferiority. The stereotypes are diversifying based on many parameters. An example can be whites are more intelligent than blacks. Similarly, a sexist attitude gets shaped to believe women are bad drivers, men are good in certain skills, gays have HIV, etc. The differentiation of sexes is communicated through discrimination based on certain attributes of male/female/third gender/one's identity. The perception of sexes is based on these underlying beliefs resulting from the stereotypes received through socialization.

3. *Verbal and nonverbal manifestation of sexism*: Sexism is defined as individuals' attitudes, beliefs, behaviors, and organizational, institutional, or cultural practices that either reflect negative evaluations of the individuals based on their gender or support unequal status of women and men (Swim & Hyers, 2009). Some individuals may stop at being only sexist, while others may progress to sexism taking unfair advantage of another sex due to one's position in the social system. The discrimination or prejudices that an individual covertly learns begin to manifest at this stage. The manifestation may vary depending upon the geographical location and sociocultural practices of a particular community or society. The examples may include eve-teasing, taunting, commenting, gesturing, flashing, sending unwelcomed letters, gifts, messages, images, etc. At times, the sexual abuse may stop at this point due to the measures adopted by the victim such as reporting, taking help, revolting, avoiding, etc., but some perpetrators may progress to the next stage in response to fight, flight, or freeze reaction in victims. A fight response may induce threat to ego or fear in perpetrator and freezing may enhance a sense of power, both reinforcing the abuse either at the same stage or progression to the next stage.

4. *Acts of sexual harassment*: This stage involves the misuse of power, authority, or other resources to induce threat or fear or to trade or bargain with the victim. The manifestation at this stage mostly progresses to physically approaching the victim and exerting pressure using nonsexual behaviors coaxing, hitting, etc. These behaviors are usually determined by the penetrator and the victim variables. A child victim may be taken to parks to assess the environment and grooming strategy, a female victim may be stalked in a street; the employer may propose unwelcomed demands or withdraw certain benefits to harass an employee, etc. All of these acts usually are a precursor to sexual behaviors that perpetrator plans to execute either by force or consensually in a conducive environment.

5. *Forced sexual behaviors*: The perpetrator if succeeds to exert pressure in the previous stage, usually now begins to misinterpret the victim's emotional state or verbal or behavioral cues under the light of his illusionary success. This feeling of elated sense of giving them the confidence to execute sexual behaviors including touching, fondling, rubbing either genitals or other body parts or both or rape. A perpetrator may even skip a few stages and reach this stage of abuse directly driven by stereotypes or sexist attitudes. Date rape or marital rape or sexual abuse of gay or transgender, child sexual abuse, harassment, or abuse at the workplace are some common examples of this stage of abuse. In addition, a

perpetrator may victimize many individuals inflicting the same or varied forms of sexual abuse.

6. *Sexual violence*: This is the last stage where forced sexual behaviors may include violence. The extreme form of violence may be identified as either intentional murder or killing the victim or inflicting violence to an extent that the victim dies his course of death.

These stages are not discrete and one may be at one or more stages of being a victim or perpetrator. Also, the victim and perpetrator may or may not be discrete individuals, being a victim in one setting may make him a perpetrator in another setting. Also, the stages may be observed and interpreted neutral to the demographic attributes of the individual who either inflicts or suffers the sexual abuse.

Risk Factors

It's being understood that certain attributes whether inherent or environmental increase the vulnerability of both victims as well as the perpetrator. Some of the factors that play a role are described as follows:

Early Experiences Mother is the source of fulfillment of various needs of infant such as meeting physiological needs of food & nutrition, ensuring safe environment and nurturing their emotional needs. Mother–child bond lays the foundation of future or adult relationships. The mother may be replaced by significant other under certain circumstances which tend to act as a protective factor. The mother–child bond is not limited to the affection that the mother feels or showers on the infant or child but numerous factors necessitate. These factors include the physical and mental health of the mother cognized by her inherent traits or inclinations as well as environmental stressors. These attachment styles moderate and mediate the relationships of adulthood, and insecure attachment style is found to be a predictor of being victimized as well as victimizing others (Wekerle & Wolfe, 1998). If a mother or significant other is a victim or a perpetrator, this too accelerates the risk of victimization as the child may model parental coping strategies or behavioral patterns.

Cognitive Factors Intelligence is an inherent ability that ascertains cognitive functioning and cognitive processes. It's the cognitive processing responsible for sensory input and the corresponding output. The thinking style, appraisal or attribution, fantasies, problem solving, creativity, decision making, calculations, and estimation are numerous abilities that determine how one deals with various situations in one's life. Intellect research concludes that persons with lower intelligence including intellectual disability and borderline intelligence are at a higher risk to be a victim or a perpetrator than those with average or higher intelligence (Henning & Holdford, 2003). In addition, it may also be the problem solving and decision making that clinches the choices and risk assessment of the situation which makes them subject to the abuse (Beauregard & Leclerc, 2007).

Personality Factors Each individual has a set of certain temperamental or personality traits, some traits or types of personality being closely associated with defiant and offensive acts (Giotakos et al., 2004). Those high on sensation seeking usually have multiple sexual partners and may be abused as well as being abusive in intimate relationships (Charnigo et al., 2013). In addition, aggression, passivity, suppression, vengeance, etc. become barriers in the reappraisal of life events and limit the capacity to forgive oneself or others (Birkley & Eckhardt, 2015; Chester & DeWall, 2016). This can extend to carry unresolved trauma that may precipitate sexual abuse.

Emotional Intelligence Emotions render in one's interpersonal dealings. Fear and aggression are the most primitive emotions of the human race and most of our actions are driven by the emotional state (Williams, 2017; Gu et al., 2019). When witnessing domestic violence at home, the child starts fearing if he is going to be the next victim or if he will lose his significant other(s). This sense of insecurity sets in on witnessing the violence or physical abuse. Even experiencing or witnessing emotional abuse triggers these feelings of inadequacy (Oates et al., 1985; Christensen et al., 1994). Indirect or direct victims of such experiences instigate fear and attempt to protect themselves from any hurt or reaction, and this may push them to react with either rage or aggression. This may be due to the learned helplessness of childhood where one feels incapable to fight the perpetrator and vengeance borne against the perpetrator may get displaced and generalized to intimate as well as social relations. Therefore, the ability to tolerate distress and regulate emotions may be grounded in early experiences. The perseveration of negative emotions may extend to poor social skill development resulting in emotional outbursts. Such individuals with severe and frequent outbursts often get caught in the cycle of sexual abuse (Covell & Scalora, 2002).

Psychopathology Multiple forms of psychopathology are known to be either cause or consequences of sexual abuse. The personality disorders most commonly linked with sexual abuse include borderline (De Aquino Ferreira & Aguiar Melo, 2018) and narcissist (Widman & McNulty, 2014). Persons with physical or mental disabilities have higher rates of being victims as well as being perpetrators of sexual abuse in multiple settings (Tomsa & Jenaro, 2021). The relationship between temperament, character, and executive functions revealed certain abilities in persons with higher intelligence may result in being curious, quick-tempered, and easily bored hence seeking novelty; this may be appraised as psychopathic traits (Seidi & Wallinius, 2020). Impulsivity is associated with malfunctions in cognitive functions associated with regulation, logical thinking, and problem solving contributing to law-breaking decisions (Foroozandeh, 2017).

Sexual Profile An individual who has been victimized or bullied due to feminine or masculine attributes usually is at higher risk of being victimized. In addition, such individuals also may become perpetrators and continue to be the victims in another setting. People identifying with sexual minorities were reported to have almost four times higher risk to experience sexual abuse (Friedman & Stall, 2011). Individuals with hypersexuality also indulge in risky sexual behavior; child sexual abuse, male gender, nonheterosexual sexual orientation, less than full-time work, and living in a capital city are some predictors of hypersexuality (Slavin & Kraus, 2020a, b). Sexual exposure at a younger age is the most significant predictor of sexual deviance or unsafe sexual practices.

The mentioned risk factors are informative to infer the track that directs to sexual abuse but these are contributing factors and not definite causes. Additionally, intelligence, coping mechanisms, resilience, and various protective factors interact to determine emotional as well as behavioral outcomes.

Impact of Sexual Abuse

To conceive the impact of abuse it's important to cite the individual variables as well as the role of family, community, and society. The nature of sexual abuse depends upon inter and intrapersonal as well as socioeconomic factors. The nature of abuse including the stage or form of abuse, whether it was a single episode or multiple exposures of short or long duration furnish the impact on the victim as well as the perpetrator. The perpetrator–victim relationship is elementary, whether it was a stranger or an acquaintance. The impact is more detrimental if the perpetrator is an immediate family member which even threatens the sense of a safe place and future risk of abuse in a foster or residential home. A known person may involve confrontations or encounters that trigger the suffering and makes the escape or avoidance more challenging.

The authors have attempted to comprehensively reason that makes the impact of sexual abuse stronger and deeper than other forms of abuse or neglect. First, it's silent; children, adolescents, or even adults are either persuaded not to talk or feel ashamed to talk about it. The silence is not only imposed by the perpetrator, rather a victim may choose to stay silent fearing familial or occupational, or social consequences of it. The fear is mostly rooted in either confusion or dilemma or cost-benefit analysis. And this kind of cognitive processing comes from various beliefs, stereotypes, norms, and perceptions that are translated into actions in a routine living being carried forward from one to another generation. Second, sexual abuse mostly encompasses other forms of abuse and affects multiple domains of one's life. It may be accompanied by verbal or physical abuse. The victims usually react in expressed or controlled manner or shocked state of emotion. Third, other forms of abuse like physical or emotional may come to an end and the protective factors may create resilience to sail through it. Also, the victim may get sympathy against other forms of abuse as it's talked about without any stigma attached to it. Next, a person may continue to experience either stereotypes or sexist attitudes even if sexual abuse may not advance to the verbal and nonverbal manifestation of sexism, acts of sexual harassment, forced sexual behaviors, sexual violence. The initial stages of sexual abuse are interwoven in social communication and are usually not even perceived as abuse, but it's these initial or mild stages that lay a strong foundation of one's self-esteem and self-concept defining one as a male, female, third-gender, or the individual. These also lay protocols for one's roles and responsibilities within families as well as organizations outside the family. Therefore, the perpetrators vary but the victims or even the perpetrators continue to pendulum through various stages or forms of sexual abuse as it does not completely stop. As a result, the affected individual may become either a victim or/and a perpetrator or both. These wounds or scars are constantly triggered and the response to the outer or inner world is affected determining one's personal, occupational, and social functioning.

In addition, it's rare to find an individual who has been a victim or a perpetrator recognized by the first two stages of sexual abuse, and imposing this form of sexual abuse is usually encouraged by the social system. It's only when sexual abuse progresses to stage three, the individual differentiation becomes more evident. Society isolates the perpetrator inflicting advanced stages of sexual abuse; this contradictory communication reinforces the threat to self-esteem and identity of the perpetrator. This further challenges sense of self and induces a feeling of rejection creating confusion and herding the perpetrator to victimize others. Last, the process of safeguarding the victim and punishing or reforming the perpetrator may route to the sequels of victimization. This augments their existing trauma and suffering that may compel them into the vicious cycle of abuse. Sexual abuse at any stage leaves a scar, and the size and depth of the scar are fabricated by several components. However, the repercussions that divulge in clinical observations and research are following (Fig. 3.2):

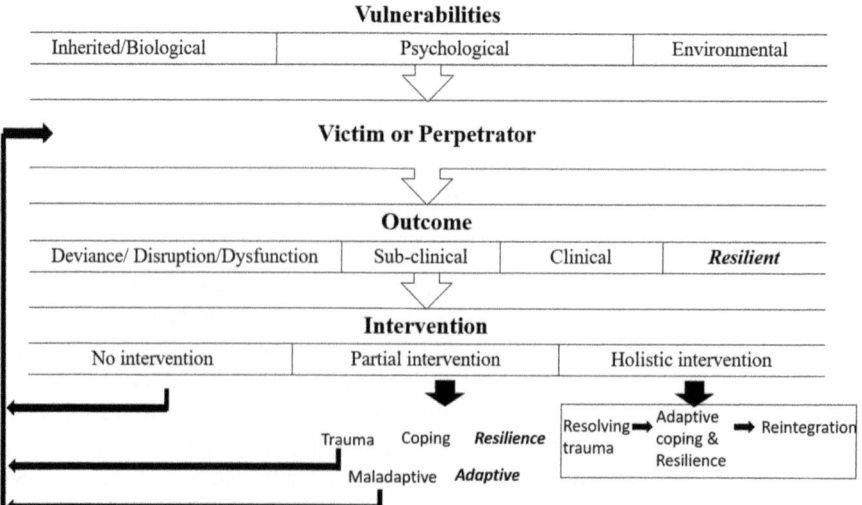

Fig. 3.2 Factors contributing to the sequel of trauma

Physical and Physiological The physical impact on the victim may involve neglect of physical needs. In severe stages of abuse, it may involve mild physical injuries to an extreme form of physical disabilities or even death in extreme cases. The perpetrator may also have a physical injury as a result of inflicting suffering on the victim. It may result in a physical attack by the victim or others or even a mass attack in certain social situations. The physiological impact includes changes in neurobiochemical pathways in the body; exposure to abuse affects the endocrinology including metabolism (Neigh & Nemeroff, 2009), circadian rhythm, heart rate, blood pressure, and body temperature. The changes in the biological pathways may put an individual at risk for various short as well as long-term medical conditions or illnesses (Keeshin & Strawn, 2012). Men are identified as perpetrators more than women due to increased testosterone that may moderate attraction to cruel and violent cues in men (Weierstall & Elbert, 2014).

Neural and Cognitive The studies support the differences in stereotypes on sex-role are rooted in the limbic brain structures as well as generation of social biases, prejudices, and stereotypes related to the amygdala, along with the importance of dorsolateral, ventrolateral, frontal, and inferior parietal and the anterior cingulate cortices, perhaps in regulatory and social roles (Takeuchi & Kawashima, 2015). The brains have been studied and structural differences are found to be based on sex, gender roles, temperament and trait, and offensive versus criminal acts. Also, higher activations in the left lateral and medial superior frontal gyrus in abused are seen. The batterers had an over-activation in the hippocampus, the fusiform gyrus, the PCC, the thalamus, and the occipital cortex; while specific higher activation was observed in the precuneus on exposure to female aggression pictures versus neutral pictures (Noll-Hussong & Guendel, 2010). In addition, the children who have history of abuse show significant cognitive impairments driving them to develop aberrant behaviors and are vulnerable to become perpetrators due to difficult experiences of helplessness and fear in early years (Salter & Skuse, 2003; Burgess & McCormack, 1987). When these adults gain power and authority, they can extend their aggression to unsuspecting innocent victims (Konopka, 2015). The benevolent sexism increases mental intrusions and suppresses working memory to hold the necessary data and ignore task-irrelevant information that induces a state of self-doubt, anxiety, preoccupation, or threatened sense of competence (Benoit & Thierry, 2007).

Psychological and Emotional The emotions and emotional state of both victims, as well as perpetrators, have been a subject of interest to the researchers. The perpetrators usually have low self-esteem and poor self-concept grounded in their early life experiences. They tend to be low on emotion regulation and hounded by aggressive bents. Also, since stereotypes and sexism are part of any society, so perpetrator's beliefs and perceptions to either view oneself as superior or others' as inferior based on sex, age, authority, etc. may appear natural to him. Any threat to this sense of superiority usually leads to victimizing the one viewed as inferior such as abusing children or adolescents at home, a student at school, females in families by spouse or others, an employee at the workplace, individuals in deserted locations as well as in crowds, etc. The perpetrators are often criticized or rejected by a certain segment of the society after the onset of perpetration; this further puts the perpetrator in a negative emotional state challenging his identity as a member of the society. These perceptions and beliefs conclude the interpretation of the emotional cues of others. As a result, poor emotional intelligence may coach the sequel acts of sexual abuse. On the other hand, the victim usually suffers a form of trauma in response to sexual abuse. The impact of abuse may vary across the various stages of sexual abuse. The stereotypes carve one's self-concept and do not necessarily have a negative impact. This may even motivate people to achieve or prove their potential to break the stereotypes. Even after achieving the aspired heights abuse may either continue or rather advance to other stages of sexual abuse or one may indulge in perpetuating others. This sense of either inferiority or superiority colors the self-esteem and self-concept. The victims or perpetrators experience more negative emotions than nonabused individuals. The differences may also be observed among those who suffered sexual abuse or other forms of abuse.

Physical and Mental Health The victims and perpetrators both are known to suffer medical as well as mental health illnesses. It's not the mere act of sexual abuse which brings health issues but it's the cumulative response to stress-causing health issues. The stress may grow insidiously drifting through various life stages and triggered by a certain event that can catalyze the diagnosis of any medical or mental illness. Some of the covert health issues that may go unnoticed include obesity, eating disorders, and body-image disorders. While in other cases disease or disorder may not be evident but personal, occupational, or social functioning may be impaired due to unresolved trauma resulting from sexual abuse. The victims of sexual abuse often suffer from psychosis, mood disorders, anxiety disorders, substance use, and personality disorders with an overall higher prevalence for females (13.5%) than males (2.5%) (Molnar & Kessler, 2001). It's analyzed that 7.83% of victims of child sexual abuse seek mental health help (Cutajar & Spataro, 2010). Also, the victims often report problems in respiratory, gastrointestinal, musculoskeletal, neurological, and gynecological functions, cardio-pulmonary symptoms, and obesity (Lechner & Steibel, 1993; Irish & Delahanty, 2010). It may be firmly understood that sexual abuse disintegrates the individual. The disintegration may induce either disruption or dysfunction in varied individuals depending upon the extent of impact and more significantly the internal and external resources of support. The maximization of these resources can result in minimizing the impact and direct the person on to the path of healing and recovery.

Assessment

An individual in need of help can be identified by a family member, teacher, friend or neighbor, etc. Early intervention usually has promising outcomes and may break the cycle by facilitation of trauma resolution and reintegration. The assessment is more reliable when the funnel approach is followed as it permits rapport building and developing trust. The assessment process usually begins with a standard interview and supporting evidence with the index victim/perpetrator as well as another available informant(s). The assessment and management cannot be separated and go hand-in-hand. Rapport building is the key to generating cooperation and engagement of the participants in assessment as well as management. The professionals, specialists, or nonspecialists involved in assessment and management must be sensitive, and skilled in communication. The use of tests is recommended to maintain objectivity. However, the findings of the tests must be viewed in the light of information collected through observations, interviews, and evidence. The initial point of contact may be a teacher or a psychologist or a clinical psychologist or any other. If abuse has not progressed to the advanced stages then a clinical psychologist (CP) can intervene and disseminate the services. If there are legal implications of abuse in that case CP has to team up with other agencies such as educational or employment agencies, and state legal services. Also if sexual abuse involves physical injuries and rape with or without violence, then an interdisciplinary and multidisciplinary approach is required. In cases where a CP recommends psychiatric referral for pharmacotherapy, a psychiatrist also is involved. Last, if sexual abuse has resulted in any form of social disruption or dysfunction then seeking aid from support groups, NGOs, and advocacy groups to reintegrate with the social system is recommended. If sexual abuse in nature is of stage three or advanced then, the psychological assessment and intervention are secondary to medical and forensic assessment. Whereas if the nature of abuse is limited to stages one, two, or/and three, the intervention may be catered by the CP working with individuals, family, and sometimes with the school as well (Fig. 3.3).

Assessment phase	Management/Intervention phase	Resolution phase

*Rapport
*Introductions
*Purpose of meeting
*Purpose, process and methods of assessment
*Consent or request order or referral
	*Communicate findings
	*Liaison/referral
	  *Pediatrician
	  *General physician
	  *Gynecologist
	  *Psychiatrist
		*Family interventions
		*Social interventions

*Assess crisis *Assess vulnerabilities *Assess impact * Identify extent of abuse *Assess perpetrator variable *Record the sequence of events	* Crisis intervention * Risk management	*Rehabilitate/reintegrate *Liaison services
*Use of psychological tests *Interviewing significant informant(s) *Assess physical/mental health issues	*A viable management plan *Identify stakeholders *Consent for implementation	*Introduce termination *Liaison

*Corroborate, validate, conceptualize
*Conclusion/ diagnosis
	*Dissemination
	  *Psychological aid
	  *Medical aid
	  *Evidence-based psychotherapies
		*Follow-ups to assess
		  *Improvement
		  *Triggers
		  *Relapse/recidivism
		* Feedback

Fig. 3.3 Process of psychological intervention phases

In addition, the legal and forensic; and medical assessment is carried out relying upon the stage, extent, and impact of sexual abuse. The first contact may be established with a helpline or police personnel etc. The collection of samples and evidence in the first 48–72 hours is pivotal to medical and forensic examination or investigation. Any clinician who comes in contact with the victim of the advanced stage of abuse must first make a referral for the same. Time-lapse, collection of evidence, report submission, and confidentiality are of utmost significance in a medical and forensic assessment (Central Forensic Science Lab, 2018; Linden & Jackson, 2016). The legal proceedings themselves can trigger trauma, especially in victims of sexual harassment, domestic violence, and rape. Therefore, being in service of a CP, support groups, NGOs, and social worker facilitates going through the medical and legal procedures. The assessment is complementary to management and goes on until the individual (both victim and perpetrator) rehabilitates or reintegrates into community living. The process of assessment can be exhausting for both the parties, those who are undergoing assessment and those who conduct it. The principles of psychological assessment may be summarized as follows:

Approach and Attitude The interview usually proceeds in a funnel approach from general to specific questions and nondirective to the directive (Wolberg, 2013). The interviewer must adopt a style that is nonjudgmental and communicates empathy, congruence, as well as unconditional positive regard. The use of language should be such that the interviewee must not feel criticized, accused, preached, or judged. Nonverbal communication including posture, gestures, paralinguistic must be cautiously and skillfully utilized in one's communication. The implementation of interviewing techniques and skills can make it appear more like a conversation than an interrogation.

Building Rapport A good working relationship between the interviewer and interviewee facilitates communication required to elicit information, which is elementary to further proceedings. While dealing with young children, an interviewer can use artwork, narrating stories, and joint activities to put the child at ease. This helps to create a nonintimidating, friendly and comforting environment. These techniques may also be used to elicit information in a nondirective manner. While those of other age groups identifying the interests of the interviewee can establish free-flowing communication. The knowledge and skills to use ice-breaking activities strategically with patience are beneficial in establishing rapport.

Functional Analysis (FA) The assessment interviews are designed to identify the trigger, sequence of events, and consequences. The occurrence of single or multiple events is elicited. The interviewer(s) identify the patterns of communication, reactions, coping mechanisms, of the interviewee and significant others(s) (Kazdin, 2002). The reasons effectuating to interviewee's role as victim or perpetrator or both in any given situation are clarified and conceptualized by connecting the dots. The interviews are usually extended to involve available and required family members, peers, educational or employment authorities, neighbors, other social agents, etc. The timeline, driving forces, psychosocial factors, and vulnerabilities must be defined.

Identifying Warning Signs The help-seeking indicators and impact on the interviewee are recognized. It's important to identify the cognitive, emotional, and behavioral changes pointing toward physical or mental health issues. The psychosocial functioning of the interviewee before the occurrence of the sexual abuse is taken as a baseline to label the oddities or dysfunction.

Resources and Barriers The interview with the interviewee and the informants must be able to elicit and identify the internal and external resources as well as barriers. This can be inter or intrapersonal comprising coping, resilience, intelligence, temperament, emotion regulation, and social skills. The family assets both materialistic as well as nonmaterialistic along with practices, beliefs, attitudes can be either resources or a barrier. Other social agents or agencies are also identified that can be the source of support or a risk factor.

Liaison The interviewer by now has conceptualized the genetic and psychosocial factors producing the occurrence of an event or its sequel. The impact of the event(s) is well conceptualized through the various aspects of the interviewee's development, internal and external reactions or responses, personal and sociooccupational functioning, signs and symptoms, resources, and barriers. This translates the plan and liaison with other social agencies including education, employer, legal, medical, mental health, etc. The tests, examinations, and investigations are allowed to maintain objectivity, corroborate findings, and create evidence. Teamwork is the key and inter as well as a multidisciplinary approach to assessment results in holistic intervention or management plan addressing the multidomain needs of the sufferer, be a victim or perpetrator.

Forensic Evaluation

The forensic evaluation begins with reporting the abuse. The referral to the forensic agency may come through various administrative, legal, or judicial agencies. It may also come through nonprofit government organizations, advocacy groups, or other investigating agencies. The forensic evaluation pertains to the acts of sexual harassment and other advanced stages of sexual abuse including forced sexual behaviors and violence or death. Forensic evaluation involves hard as well as soft evidence (Herman, 2009). The forensic evaluation is determined by the victim variables, perpetrator variable, and nature of the sexual abuse. The evaluation begins with consent, seeking consent from the individual(s), and education, work, and health organization (s). There is also a provision to exercise e-consent (Yesodharan et al., 2021). In addition, there are few principles in forensic evaluation (American Academy of Child and Adolescent Psychiatry, 1997).

1. Role definition: The roles of inter-disciplinary members must be well defined and communicated to each other.

2. Clear communication: It's very similar to the introduction, the reason for investigations, the evidence, and sample collection must be explained.
3. Confidentiality: is of prime importance in terms of recording, preserving, and producing the evidence as well as information.
4. Privilege: The right to deny to testify must be discussed. If the victim or the perpetrator are seeking any kind of medical or psychiatric treatment from any Physician or Psychiatrist or seeking any psychotherapy or psychological help from any Clinical Psychologist, in that case, the client can utilize clinician-patient privilege.
5. Awareness of limitation or biases: Any investigating officer or professional may develop bias about the person or situation which may be translated to others involved in the evaluation or judgment. Also, as information keeps getting added to the existing knowledge the opinions may fluctuate. So it's important to stay vigilant for such biases formed on the limited knowledge.
6. Degree of certainty: When submitting the forensic evidence, one must express the level of certainty of that evidence cautiously.
7. Knowledge of law: The investigating officers and professionals involved in the forensic evaluation must be having adequate knowledge of legal issues. For example, if the abuse involves anyone with a disability, lesbian, gay, bisexual, transgender (LGBT), etc., then it's required to know rights and laws related to disability or LGBT.

Hard Evidence It can include the following:

Medical Reports It's a form of hard evidence that may not be present and significant in all forms of sexual abuse. Many times victims of stereotype and sexist attitudes develop physical and mental health problems causing them to seek treatment (Herman, 2009) and may be advised light work or rest but this does not make sufficient evidence to prove the abuse rather emphasis is on strengthening the tolerance, resilience and coping of the victim. Medical reports of injuries, bruises, etc. resulting from self-defense or aggression may be available for the acts of sexual harassment but the most significant evidence of medical reports pertain to the last two stages of sexual abuse that is, forced sexual behavior and sexual violence.

A piece of medical evidence may involve a thorough medical check-up in search of bruises, injuries, or any damage to external body parts, internal organs, and genitals. An examination can further involve the collection of samples, impressions, and traces of the perpetrator from the victim's body, the site where the act occurred, and objects in that surroundings. The perpetrator may also be examined for sample collection to prove or refute the collected samples. In case of rape, samples of the perpetrator's impressions must be collected within 24–72 hours before it's lost or faded. In the case of children and adolescents, inappropriate changes or damage to genitals may be examined and interpreted in the light of age-appropriate sexual development (Niec, 2002). While for adults, history of last consented sexual act and intercourse holds significance to view the contamination of medical samples. In the case of females, menstrual cycle details must be enquired to plan further assessment and management.

Confession of the Perpetrator At times the perpetrator may confess or may not deny when accused of the act. Though this may appear as direct evidence this also needs to be examined. The intent behind the confession may require investigation whether the perpetrator is in remorse or has been forced to accept the blame owing to some threat or pressure. Further investigations may be continued to find the supporting or refuting evidence.

Audio-Video and Photo Evidence This evidence can hold significance owing to all types of sexual abuse. One can even record the verbal remarks conveying the stereotype or discrimination that form the evidence for sexual harassment. These recordings can be audio or video recordings, chats or messages, photographs, etc. The episodes of sexual abuse involving physical behaviors, sexual behaviors, and violence, may hold planned or accidental recording by the victim or some witness. The healthcare professionals usually are the first ones to witness and examine the injuries or damage, and it is significant that photographs of these are clicked by seeking consent to preserve the evidence before starting the treatment. Sometimes, this evidence is also collected by the professional or investigating agencies with prior information. In the case of children and adolescents, either a parent or legal guardian or any significant other must be involved in viewing the best interest of the child. However, the authenticity of the evidence needs to be established.

Normal Sexual Development and Functioning In children (Smith et al., 2019) inappropriate sexual behaviors such as trying to remove clothes of others, excessive preoccupation with sexual acts and discussing it, masturbating with objects, inserting it into private parts, touching others in sexual way, gestures of sexual nature may start surfacing in response to sexual abuse. The clinician can also test the age-appropriate sexual development as per stages given by Tanner to identify signs of abuse (Niec, 2002). For male adults involved in child sexual abuse, the penile plethysmography (PPG) test is carried out to observe if the sexual response is present to children which testify for the pedophilic tendencies. An equivalent test, vaginal photoplethysmography (VPP), is also available, but its utility and interpretation are debatable (Knack et al., 2015).

Soft Evidence Many times hard pieces of evidence may not be either available or lost, soft evidence in such cases becomes more significant. Soft evidence may take precedence over hard evidence. Soft evidence is more subjective than hard evidence but reliability can be enhanced with multiple interviews involving various sources to corroborate the information by different professionals or specialists. The soft evidence includes a list of formal and informal assessment techniques. A few standardized techniques have been developed by various practitioners/researchers that are summarized in Fig. 3.4.

Professionals must gather evidence through interviews, observation and judgments must be aware of the forensic markers in children and elderly as in both

Population	Tool
Children	Child Sexual Behavior Inventory (CSBI)
	Child Behavior Checklist (CBCL)
	Child Trauma Questionnaire-Short Form (CTQ-SF)
	Conflict in Adolescent Dating Relationship Questionnaire (CADRI)
	Trauma and Symptom Checklist for Children (TSCYC)
Adults	Comprehensive Sexual Assault Assessment Tool (CSAAT)
	Screening tools- sexual assault
	Sexual and Physical Abuse History Questionnaire (SPAHQ)
	Sexual Assault Investigation Checklist (SAIC)
	Trauma Symptom Checklist-40 (TSC-40)
	Abuse Assessment Screen (AAS)
	Universal Violence Prevention Screening Protocol (UVPSP)
	Victimization Assessment Tool (VAT)
Elderly	Comprehensive Sexual Assault Assessment Tool - Elder (CSAAT-E)
	Elder Assessment Instrument (EAI)
	Hwalek-Sengstock Elder Abuse Screening Test (H-S/EAST)
	Elder Abuse Questionnaire (EAQ)
	Elder Abuse Suspicion Index (EASI)
Intellectual Disability	Detection of Sexual Abuse Risk Screening Scale (DSARss)
Organization	Organizational Assessment for Agencies Serving Victims of Sexual Violence
	Personal Assessment for Advocates Working with Victims of Sexual Violence

Fig. 3.4 Assessment tools for general and specific evaluation in different populations

populations direct reporting of the abuse may not be found. Children may not comprehend the experience and hence usually feel confused whereas in the elderly it can be the sociocultural values that may become a barrier or the cost of reporting may result in being uprooted from their physical environment, especially if the elderly are dependent on the perpetrator in some sense.

Markers in children (Al Odhayani et al., 2013):

- Academic: His behavior in school may change including incomplete work, memory or concentration issues, decreased participation, a decline in performance etc.
- Peer and play: His peer interaction may decrease, complains of low energy, tiredness, bodily pain, or injury interrupting age-appropriate activities.
- Temperament: The child who has been a victim usually appears timid and withdrawn. He may not appear as his usual self.
- Loss of sense of security: The sense of security is shaken in children as a result of abuse. The normal expectations of being taken care of and comforted are left unfulfilled hence the child does not expect the same anymore.
- Emotional reaction: The child may get startled or react numb to touch rather than feeling comforted. The children may become over vigilant to one's surroundings.
- Behavior in the environment: The child may look for safe spaces or show signs to avoid or escape a certain person or setting. For example, being fearful, timid,

or quiet in some specific person's presence, refusing to go to school, neighbor's house, stay alone with some person.

Markers in the elderly (Teaster et al., 2007):

- Biological: The changes in sleep and appetite may be significant. There may be signs of repetitive urine or vaginal infections, spotting of undergarments, inflicted burns. In addition, laboratory tests may reveal genital scarring, sexually transmitted diseases, sperm in urine.
- Psychological or emotional: There may be an exhibition of negative emotions such as fear, anxiety, mistrust, suspiciousness, etc.
- Behavioral changes: Irritability, change in the day-to-day routine, decreased participation, change in timings of routine activities, change in companionships, etc.

Special Populations Over the decades the sexual abuse of children, adolescents, and females has gained the attention of various disciplines and organizations. However, abuse in the male population is still significantly underreported due to cultural beliefs of masculinity and patriarchy. Likewise, other populations which are more vulnerable to sexual abuse include, institutionalized children in a residential home, elderly in senior citizen homes, prisoners, disabled in a nursing home or facility, underprivileged persons in shelter homes, and migrants in refugee camps. The sexual abuse incidences are suppressed due to the consequences and allegations involving administration and government agencies or agents.

Person(s) with disabilities involved in sexual abuse maybe not be heard or believed as a victim and may escape as perpetrators due to undue sympathy. There are issues and challenges to testify and investigate sexual abuse in LGBT. The limited knowledge, ignorance, and personal biases on part of the investigating officers or professionals can be a barrier in assessment and management. Therefore, sensitivity and gender-neutral attitude are essential when sexual minorities are victims of sexual abuse.

Management

Intervention starts with a help-seeking attitude of the sufferer (authors perceive both victim and perpetrator as a victim) and; empathy and listening provided by the confidant or the service agent. The first contact of the sufferer can be with any confidant in family, friend circle, extended family, neighborhood, educational or workplace setting, etc. Sometimes one may come in contact with a service agent including police personnel, social worker, activist, psychologist, medical professional, mental health professional, legal service representative, etc. to report the sexual abuse. The confidant or the service agent must be sensitive and aware of the subject of sexual abuse to communicate empathy and listen to the sufferer (Fig. 3.5).

Primary level	Secondary level	Tertiary level
• Educate	• Assertive communication	• Reintegration
• *Stereotypes*	• One-stop centers	• Family intervention
• *Attitudes*	• Grievance cell	• Collaboration
• *Boundaries*	• Internal complaint	• *Education*
• *Touch/Sex*	committee	• *Employment*
• Awareness	• Legal aid	• *Health services*
• *Emotions*	• Medical aid	• *Support groups*
• *Feelings*	• *Assessment*	• *Advocacy groups*
• *Sensations*	• *Intervention*	
• *Abuse*	• Mental health aid	
• Programs	• *Assessment*	
• *Educational Institutes*	• *Crisis intervention*	
• *Organizations*	• *Brief intervention*	
• *Public forums*	• *Long term intervention*	

Fig. 3.5 Multilevel interventions

The intervention is directed to prevent the occurrence as well as reoccurrence of the sexual abuse, minimize its impact, and return to the pathway of normal developments, transitions, and functioning. The role of intervention is highlighted in the figure, the victims and perpetrator both require multilevel (Fig. 3.5) interventions to break the cycle of victims turning into perpetrators. Also, the model of intervention is influenced by primary secondary and tertiary prevention in epidemiology or physical illnesses (Institute for Work & Health, 2015). The intervention for sexual abuse has to be multilevel and multidisciplinary.

Primary Intervention These are set to prevent the occurrence of abuse across all the ages and settings. This can be borne by educating individuals as well as institutions or organizations. For this, *children* must be provided age-appropriate sex education containing information of all body parts, genital included, private and public exposure, appropriate versus inappropriate settings, setting boundaries, use, and display of body parts, assertiveness, escape and help-seeking skills, communication, and reporting, grooming pathways to give rise to abuse, risks associated with spaces, places or timings, etc. (Breuner et al., 2016). It's important to educate parents when working with children or adolescents as sex abuse begins with imposing stereotypes translated through socialization. So educating the young ones must be supplemented by involving the parents in sex education, and parents can later continue dissemination of information and mental set to their young ones (Martino & Schuster, 2008). As programs are of limited duration, educating parents or significant others can change the processing of information as well as response to it. In addition, exclusive programs on parenting styles and their consequences can be conducted with the families. These programs begin with information and education; later providing intervention for effective parenting through behavioral principles using techniques such as parent management training, quality time concept to enhance parent–child relationships, etc.

Adolescence is a phase of conflict that is an age-long myth. We perceive it's a phase of independent growth where the plant that was growing under the shadow of a tree has now begun to be a tree as well and starts seeking its light independently. So it's time to realize that the child will make his own choices, and experiences, have inferences and judgments. So, the individuals who acknowledge and permit this independence usually take up the role of guiding and supporting adults or parents, or significant others(s). While individuals who don't accept the idea of independent growth and continue to hold on or cling, then a situation of conflict arises for which the onus cannot be completed on the adolescent. Therefore, working with adolescents continues to develop programs for parents, sex-education programs encompassing various sexual practices, sexual curiosities, appropriate versus inappropriate settings, safe sex practices, consequences of unsafe sex as well as a sexual indulgence at a minor age, legal consequences of sexual abuse, sexual offenses, and sex; sexual orientations and identities, etc. Life-skill training for adolescents is a comprehensive program teaching and preparing youngsters about various aspects of life. It lays a strong foundation for effective problem solving, decision making, emotion regulation, adaptive coping, building resilience, and interpersonal dealing that are essential to carve a pathway for oneself (Bharath & Kumar, 2010).

The interventions bending on *adults* may begin with definitions; personal, legal, and social implications of sexual offenses, discrimination, sexual harassment, sexual behaviors, offenses, unsafe sex, sexual abuse, its types, impact, and consequences to both the victim as well perpetrator. Then education safe-sex practices, a sense of responsibility, and acceptance of consequences. Many adults grow up forming myths on masturbation, sexual orientation, or identities, the sex-education program must address the myths proving clarification on sexual functioning and process in humans (Masters et al., 1986). The education may provide newer insights into the existing stereotypes or sexist attitudes, and facilitate change. In addition, some psychological interventions may include modules of distress tolerance, emotion regulation, interpersonal effectiveness of dialectical behavior therapy (DBT) (Swales & Heard, 2008), diffusion and acceptance processes from acceptance and commitment therapy (ACT) (Hayes, 2004) to create newer ways of cognitive structuring and information-processing. Marital or couple therapy including sex therapies may also be beneficial. The individual having addiction issues must be identified and addiction is a high risk for abuse (Resnick & Self-Brown, 2007), and interventions for alcohol, substance and other behavioral addictions must be disseminated as per the individual needs.

Secondary Intervention The dissemination begins after the sexual abuse has occurred and concentrates on minimizing the impact on the cognitive, emotional, and behavioral responses as well as patterns. The abuse does not only impact an individual rather various micro and macro systems or units of the society. The messages communicated to the sufferer via various social agencies using verbal and nonverbal ways affect the future course of life. To reduce the impact, the protective factors must be identified and enhanced. The interventions may be short-term or long-term.

The most common psychological measures employed in *short-term interventions* are supportive, behavioral, and educational approaches that bear at symptom relief and problem solving.

Crisis Intervention: Crisis is a situation that activates a denial mechanism and failure of coping resources. The emotional reaction can be feeling numb, and detached along with anxiety to manage followed by depressive symptoms. In extreme circumstances, suicidality may be reported with a sense of hopelessness or helplessness. An individual may take 4–6 weeks to resume usual life functioning due to the breaking down of flexibility of ego defenses and ego strength (Wolberg, 2013). The intervention within 24 hours inclines to manage emotional disturbance using relaxation techniques, distraction, and reassurance. Later, triggers and sequences of events causing the disequilibrium or breakdown may be elicited. Such a situation usually disrupts the family system and therefore exploring the unresolved conflicts becomes significant. Once immediate symptoms are addressed, the evaluation of internal and externals resources may invoke the utilization or structuring of the support system. After the restoration of stabilization, usually, 6 sessions or 3 months, the interventions to learn newer behaviors, develop awareness and growth must be continued. The victim and perpetrator-friendly helplines can be instrumental in the initiation of the crisis intervention.

Supportive Therapy: It is another form of short-term therapy and intervention is centered on the problem. The length is usually 6–10 sessions, sometimes extended to 25 sessions (Wolberg, 2013). The individual is permitted free-flowing verbal ventilation with a great sense of empathy and validation communicated by the therapist in establishing faith. The process involves identifying triggers causing reactions or symptoms and relating feelings; making observations of interpersonal dealing, dreams, fantasies, generating insights. The procedures employed in supportive therapy are guidance, tension control and release, environmental manipulation, externalization of interests, reassurance, prestige suggestion, pressure and coercion, persuasion, and inspirational group therapy (Wolberg, 2013). Once the symptoms are relieved, individuals may be motivated to address peripheral issues through long-term interventions that utilize these insights to bring change.

Counseling: The initial phase of that focuses on rapport building, permitting ventilation, prompting, listening, and assessing risks and impact. The counselors use the interviewing skills and approach (Wolberg, 2013) that establish open communication between counselor and counselee. Gradually this stage moves to the next level of elicitation and clarifications, identifying signs and symptoms. The process of counseling then progresses to the middle phase where the techniques are disseminated to integrate oneself, re-establish coping and resilience, provide reassurance and support to minimize suffering. The liaison with other service agents and specialists to intervene may be required in the advanced stages of sexual abuse. The final, and execution of the plan to create a sense of safety for the sufferer. It may involve environmental manipulation to strengthen internal and external support systems. Last, counseling involves follow-ups to monitor as well as to motivate the ongoing intervention process. It provides support to enhance well-being.

On the other hand, *long-term interventions* may continue for months to years concentrating on underlying conflicts, resolving trauma that drives an individual to victimize others as well the trauma of being victimized.

Cognitive-Behavioral Interventions: These interventions debate the erroneous cognitions associated with sexual assault in addition to enhancing behavioral functioning and overwhelming emotions using various relaxation techniques. The sufferer is assisted to identify, label, and then modify the maladaptive thought-content related to the negative experiences (Freeman & Simon, 1990). In a meta-analysis, CBT was cited as the most frequent intervention used for female adults with trauma related to sexual abuse (Foa & Murdock, 1991). The modules with issues related to trauma have been developed (Trauma-focused CBT). It is focused on healing the trauma and incorporates exposure, along with cognitive reprocessing and reframing of traumatic events. TF-CBT focusing on the caregivers of the sufferer has been shown to reduce symptoms of trauma (Ramirez de Arellano & Delphin-Rittmon, 2014). Recent developments in the area have highlighted the cognitive distortions in sexual offenders such as fortune-telling, discounting the positive and cognitive operations such as denial, rationalization, etc. (Ward & Keown, 2006).

Third-Wave Therapies: Third-wave therapies include therapies that highlight the contextual change and place a great deal of emphasis on enhancing functioning. This is the reason why such therapies are often addressed as contextual therapies. Unlike cognitive therapy where the focus is to identify and modify the maladaptive thought content, third-wave therapies mediate the relationship to the maladaptive patterns to promote engagement in value-driven behaviors. It uses principles such as mindfulness, acceptance, committed actions, etc. to enhance the functioning of the sufferer. Therapies that fall under the domain are acceptance and commitment therapy (ACT), dialectical behavior therapy (DBT), functional analytic psychotherapy, integrative behavioral couples therapy (IBCT), mindfulness-based cognitive therapy (MBCT), and metacognitive therapy (MCT) (Dimidjian & Schneider, 2016). A meta-analysis reported the medium to large effect of third-wave therapies in reducing posttraumatic stress (PTS) (Benfer & Bardeen, 2021). ACT even has protocols designed to level this specific population (Walser & Westrup, 2007) and shown results in a reappraisal of trauma resulting from child sexual abuse with acceptance of unwanted internal states and reduction of avoided behavior (Aarzoo & Sidana, 2019). DBT, a manualized treatment designed by Marsha Linehan, attempts to teach emotion regulation skills, interpersonal skills, distress tolerance skills, and mindfulness skills to alleviate the psychiatric symptoms (Swales & Heard, 2008). Similar to CBT it has a prototypic phase-based treatment known as Dialectical behavior therapy for PTSD (DBT-PTSD) developed to bargain the issues related to abuse generating PTSD and personality issues (Bohus & Nat, 2020).

In addition, various principles and techniques of psychology are utilized to relieve the suffering, resolve trauma and grief from early experiences that minimize abuse and its impact (Chivers-Wilson, 2006).

Tertiary Intervention: These tend to accomplish the prevention of retraumatization or recidivism. This can be achieved through the integration of micro, miso, and macro systems considering the welfare of individuals and society at large (Sawatzky et al., 2021; Willging & Verney, 2021). The support must be forwarded to the last phase of follow-up that monitors the individual in process of resuming community living. The assistance of support groups and advocacy groups in working with families, organizations (educational and employment) can facilitate a dignified living. The primary interventions lay the foundation for tertiary care interventions, and the vision of policymakers can implement these mandates. An individual may reintegrate oneself to a fresh start but the discriminatory attitude of families, neighbors, educational and employment organizations can trigger trauma. If victims are provided a voice by letting them share their journey and appreciate their resilience, it may encourage others to come out and talk about their abuse. Talking about abuse can onset many others onto the journey of healing. Similarly, the perpetrators who change the track may be viewed as champions if they decide to change course but those without remorse must be punished for their misdeeds to discourage deviance in society. Going by the learning principles the desired acts must be reinforced while to avoid reoccurrences of undesired behaviors these must be punished. The stereotypes and sexist attitudes are usually encouraged in society and this kind of reinforcement needs to be stopped for the seed of sexual abuse to grow. An act of sexual abuse being reinforced and suddenly an advanced act of sexual abuse gives a contradictory message to society. Therefore, any act of sexual abuse must be denied and discouraged to allow an individual to rebuild his life.

To summarize, there are biopsychosocial factors that determine the vulnerability as well as the occurrence of sexual abuse. The interventions require to be implemented at the individual, organizational, and government levels using interdisciplinary as well as multidisciplinary approaches. These interventions must facilitate integration and rehabilitation of both victims as well as the perpetrator to prevent retraumatization and recidivism. Last, sexual abuse needs to be discouraged from its roots in stereotypes by adopting primary interventions and each individual taking responsibility to change the attitude.

References

Aarzoo, K., & Sidana, A. (2019). Acceptance and commitment therapy in the reappraisal of past events? Report of two cases. *Delhi Psychiatry Journal, 22*(2), 428–430.

Al Odhayani, A., Watson, W. J., & Watson, L. (2013). Behavioral consequences of child abuse. *Canadian family physician Medecin de famille canadien, 59*(8), 831–836.

American Academy of Child and Adolescent Psychiatry. (1997). Practice parameters for the forensic evaluation of children and adolescents who may have been physically or sexually abused. *Journal of the American Academy of Child & Adolescent Psychiatry, 36*(3), 423–442. https://doi.org/10.1097/00004583-199703000-00026

Beauregard, E., & Leclerc, B. (2007). An application of the rational choice approach to the offending process of sex offenders: A closer look at the decision-making. *Sexual Abuse: A Journal of Research and Treatment, 19*(2), 115–133. https://doi.org/10.1007/s11194-007-9043-6

Benfer, N., & Bardeen, J. R. (2021). Efficacy of third-wave cognitive-behavioral therapies in the treatment of posttraumatic stress: A meta-analytic study. *Journal of Anxiety Disorder, 78*(1), 102360. https://doi.org/10.1016/j.janxdis.2021.102360

Benoit, D., & Thierry, B. (2007). Insidious dangers of benevolent sexism: Consequences for women's performance. *Journal of Personality and Social Psychology, 93*(5), 764–779. https://doi.org/10.1037/0022-3514.93.5.764

Bharath, S., & Kumar, K. V. K. (2010). Empowering adolescents with life skill education in schools- School mental health program: Does it actually work? *Indian Journal of Psychiatry, 52*(4), 344–349. https://doi.org/10.4103/0019.5545.74310

Birkley, E. L., & Eckhardt, C. I. (2015). Anger, hostility, internalizing negative emotions, and intimate partner violence perpetration: A meta-analytic review. *Clinical Psychology Review, 37*, 40–56. https://doi.org/10.1016/j.cpr.2015.01.002

Bohus, M., & Nat, R. (2020). Dialectical behavior therapy for posttraumatic stress disorder (DBT-PTSD) compared with cognitive processing therapy (CPT) in complex presentations of PTSD in women survivors of childhood abuse: A randomized clinical trial. *JAMA Psychiatry, 77*(12), 1235–2148. https://doi.org/10.1001/jamapsychiatry.2020.2148

Breuner, C. C., Mattson, G., & Committee on Adolescence, Committee on Psychosocial Aspects of Child and Family Health. (2016). Sexuality education for children and adolescents. *Pediatrics, 138*(2), e1–11. https://doi.org/10.1542/peds.2016-1348

Burgess, A. W., & McCormack, A. (1987). Abused to abuser: Antecedents of socially deviant behaviors. *American Journal of Psychiatry, 144*(11), 1431–1436. https://doi.org/10.1176/ajp.144.11.1431

Central Forensic Science Laboratory. (2018, July). *Guidelines for forensic medical examination in sexual assault cases.* http://cfslchandigarh.gov.in/Uploads/Media/Original/20180627121658_MO-SOP%20Final.pdf

Charnigo, R., Noar, S. M., Garnett, C., Crosby, R., Palmgreen, P., & Zimmerman, R. S. (2013). Sensation seeking and impulsivity: Combined associations with risky sexual behavior in a large sample of young adults. *Journal of Sex Research, 50*(5), 480–488. https://doi.org/10.1080/00224499.2011.652264

Chester, D. S., & DeWall, C. N. (2016). The pleasure of revenge: Retaliatory aggression arises from a neural imbalance toward reward. *Social Cognitive and Affective Neuroscience, 11*(7), 1173–1182. https://doi.org/10.1093/scan/nsv082

Chivers-Wilson, K. A. (2006). Sexual assault and posttraumatic stress disorder: A review of the biological, psychological and sociological factors and treatments. *McGill Journal of Medicine, 9*(2), 111–118.

Christensen, M. J., Brayden, R. M., Dietrich, M. S., McLaughlin, F. J., Sherrod, K. B., & Altemeier, W. A. (1994). The prospective assessment of self-concept in neglectful and physically abusive low income mothers. *Child Abuse & Neglect, 18*(3), 225–232. https://doi.org/10.1016/0145-2134(94)90107-4

Covell, C. N., & Scalora, M. J. (2002). Empathetic deficits in sexual offenders: An integration of affective, social, and cognitive constructs. *Aggression and Violent Behavior, 7*, 251–270.

Cowburn, M. (2011). Perceiving the continuum of sexual harm and the need for varied responses to sexual violence. *International Journal of Offender Therapy and Comparative Criminology, 55*(2), 179–181.

Cutajar, M. C., & Spataro, J. (2010). Psychopathology in a large cohort of sexually abused children followed up to 43 years. *Child Abuse & Neglect, 34*(11), 813–822. https://doi.org/10.1016/j. chiabu.2010.04.004

Davis, T., & Wilson, J. M. (2016). Gender schema theory. In *The Wiley Blackwell encyclopedia of gender and sexualities studies*. Wiley Online Library. https://doi.org/10.1002/9781118663219. wbegss655

De Aquino Ferreira, L. F., & Aguiar Melo, M. C. (2018). Borderline personality disorder and sexual abuse. A systematic review. *Psychiatry Research, 262*, 70–77. https://doi.org/10.1016/j. psychres.2-18.01.043

Dimidjian, S., & Schneider, R. L. (2016). Considering meta-analysis, meaning, and metaphor: A systematic review and critical examination of "third wave" cognitive and behavioral therapies. *Behavior Therapy, 47*(6), 886–905. https://doi.org/10.1016/j.beth.2016.07.002

Finkelhor, D., & Hamby, S. L. (2014). The lifetime prevalence of child sexual abuse and sexual assault assessed in late adolescence. *Journal of Adolescent Health, 55*(3), 329–333. https://doi. org/10.1016/j.jadohealth.2013.12.026

Foa, E. B., & Murdock, T. B. (1991). Treatment of posttraumatic stress disorder in rape victims: A comparison between cognitive-behavioral procedures and counseling. *Journal of Consulting and Clinical Psychology, 59*(5), 715–723. https://doi.org/10.1037//0022-006X.59.5.715

Foroozandeh, E. (2017). Impulsivity and impairment in cognitive functions in criminals. *Forensic Research & Criminology International Journal, 5*(1), 232–233. https://doi.org/10.15406/ frcij.2017.05.00144

Freeman, A., & Simon, K. M. (1990). *Clinical applications of cognitive therapy*. Plenum Press.

Friedman, M. S., & Stall, R. (2011). A meta-analysis of disparities in childhood sexual abuse, parental physical abuse, and peer victimization among sexual minority and sexual nonminority individuals. *American Journal of Public Health, 101*(8), 1481–1494. https://doi.org/10.2105/ AJPH.2009.190009

Giotakos, O., Vaidakis, N., Markianos, M., Spandoni, P., & Christodoulou, G. N. (2004). Temperament and character dimensions of sex offenders in relation to their parental rearing. *Sexual and Relationship Therapy, 19*(2), 141–150. https://doi.org/10.108 0/14681990410001691352

Gu, S., Wang, F., Patel, N. P., Bourgeois, J. A., & Huang, J. H. (2019). A model for basic emotions using observations of behavior in drosophila. *Frontiers in Psychology, 10*, 781–793. https://doi. org/10.3389/fpsyg.2019.00781

Hayes, S. C. (2004). Acceptance and commitment therapy and the new behavior therapies mindfulness, acceptance, and relationship. In S. C. Hayes, V. M. Follette, & M. M. Linehan (Eds.), *Mindfulness and acceptance expanding the cognitive-behavioral tradition* (pp. 5–6). Guilford Press.

Henning, K., & Holdford, R. (2003). Treatment needs of women arrested for domestic violence: A comparison with male offenders. *Journal of Interpersonal Violence, 18*(8), 839–856. https:// doi.org/10.1177/0886205032253876

Herman, S. (2009). Forensic child sexual abuse evaluations. In K. Kuenhle & M. Connell (Eds.), *The evaluations of child sexual abuse allegations: A comprehensive guide to assessment and testimony* (pp. 247–266). Wiley.

Institute for Work & Health. (2015, April). *Primary, secondary, and tertiary intervention*. https:// www.iwh.on.ca/what-researcher-mean-by/primary-secondary-and-tertiary-prevention

Irish, L., & Delahanty, D. L. (2010). Long-term physical health consequences of childhood sexual abuse: A meta-analytic review. *Journal of Pediatric Psychology, 35*(5), 450–461. https://doi. org/10.1093/jpepsy/jsp118

James, S. E., & Anafi, M. (2016). *The report of the 2015 U.S. transgender survey*. National Center for Transgender Equality.

Kalra, G., & Bhugra, D. (2013). Sexual violence against women: Understanding cross-cultural intersections. *Indian Journal of Psychiatry, 55*(3), 244–249. https://doi. org/10.4103/0019-5545.117139

Kazdin, A. E. (2002). Applied behavior analysis. In M. Hersen & W. Sledge (Eds.), *Encyclopedia of psychotherapy* (pp. 71–94). Elsevier Science.

Keeshin, B. R., & Strawn, J. R. (2012). Physiologic changes associated with violence and abuse exposure. *Trauma, Violence & Abuse, 13*(1), 41–56. https://doi.org/10.1177/1524838011426152

Knack, N. M., Murphy, L., Ranger, R., Meston, C., & Fedoroff, J. P. (2015). Assessment of female Sexual arousal in forensic populations. *Current Psychiatry Reports, 17*, 18. https://doi.org/10.1007/s11920-015-0557-1

Konopka, L. M. (2015). The impact of child abuse: Neuroscience perspective. *Croatian Medical Journal, 56*(3), 315–316. https://doi.org/10.3325/cmj.2015.56.315

Lechner, M. E., & Steibel, K. R. (1993). Self-reported medical problems of adult female survivors of childhood sexual abuse. *Journal of Family Practice, 36*(6), 633–638.

Linden, J. A., & Jackson, M. C. (2016, August). *Forensic examination of adult victims and perpetrators of sexual assault.* https://aneskey.com/forensic-examination-of-adult-victims-and-perpetrators-of-sexual-assault

Martino, C. M., & Schuster, M. A. (2008). Beyond the "big talk": The roles of breadth and repetition in parent-adolescent communication about sexual topics. *Pediatrics, 121*(3), e612–e618. https://doi.org/10.1542/peds.2007-2156

Masters, W. H., Johnson, V. E., & Kolodny, R. C. (1986). *Masters & Johnson sex and human loving.* Jaico books.

Molnar, B. E., & Kessler, R. C. (2001). Child sexual abuse and subsequent psychopathology: Results from the national comorbidity survey. *American Journal of Public Health, 91*(5), 753–760. https://doi.org/10.2105/ajph.91.5.753

Neigh, G. N., & Nemeroff, C. B. (2009). The neurobiological toll of child abuse and neglect. *Trauma Violence Abuse, 10*(4), 389–410. https://doi.org/10.1177/1524838009339758

Niec, A. (2002). Forensic issues in the assessment of sexually assaulted adolescents. *Paediatrics & Child Health, 7*(3), 153–159. https://doi.org/10.1093/pch/7.3.153

Noll-Hussong, M., & Guendel, H. (2010). Aftermath of sexual abuse history on adult patients suffering from chronic functional pain syndromes: An fMRI pilot study. *Journal of Psychosomatic Research, 68*(5), 483–487. https://doi.org/10.1016/j.jpsychores.2010.01.020

Oates, R. K., Forrest, D., & Peacock, A. (1985). Self-esteem of abused children. *Child Abuse & Neglect, 9*(2), 159–163. https://doi.org/10.1016/0145-2134(85)90007-9

Ramirez de Arellano, M. A., & Delphin-Rittmon, M. E. (2014). Trauma focussed cognitive behavioral therapy: Assessing the evidence. *Psychiatric Services, 65*(5), 591–602. https://doi.org/10.1176/appi.ps.201300255

Resnick, H. S., & Self-Brown, S. (2007). An acute post-sexual assault intervention to prevent drug abuse: Updated findings. *Addictive Behaviors, 32*(10), 2031–2045. https://doi.org/10.1016/j.addbeh.2007.01.001

Salter, D., & Skuse, D. (2003). Development of sexually abusive behavior in sexually victimized males: A longitudinal study. *The Lancet, 361*(9356), 471–476. https://doi.org/10.1016/S0140-6736(03)12466-X

Sawatzky, R., & the Response Shift-in Sync Working Group. (2021). Implications of response shift for micro-, meso-, and macro-level healthcare decision-making using results of patient-reported outcome measures. *Quality of Life Research, 30*, 3343–3357. https://doi.org/10.1007/s11136-021-02766-9

Seidi, H., & Wallinius, M. (2020). Personality and cognitive functions in violent offenders–implications of character maturity? *Frontiers in Psychology, 11*, 58. https://doi.org/10.3389/fpsyg.2020.00058

Slavin, M. N., & Kraus, S. W. (2020a). Child sexual abuse and compulsive sexual behavior: A systematic literature review. *Current Addiction Reports, 7*(1), 76–88. https://doi.org/10.1007/s40429-020-00298-9

Slavin, M. N., & Kraus, S. W. (2020b). Gender-related differences in associations between sexual abuse and hypersexuality. *The Journal of Sexual Medicine, 17*(10), 2029–2038. https://doi.org/10.1016/j.jsxm.2020.07.008

Smith, T. J., Lindsey, R. A., Bohora, S., & Silovsky, J. F. (2019). Predictors of intrusive sexual behaviors in preschool-aged children. *Journal of Sex Research, 56*(2), 229–238. https://doi.org/10.1080/00224499.2018.1447639

Swales, M. A., & Heard, H. L. (2008). *Dialectical behavior therapy distinctive features*. Routledge.

Swim, J. K., & Hyers, L. L. (2009). Sexism. In T. D. Nelson (Ed.), *Handbook of prejudice, stereotyping, and discrimination* (pp. 407–430). Psychology Press.

Takeuchi, H., & Kawashima, R. (2015). Amygdala and cingulate structure is associated with a stereotype on sex-role. *Scientific Reports, 5*(14220). https://doi.org/10.1038/srep14220

Teaster, P. B., Ramsey-Klawsnik, H., Mendiondo, M. S., Abner, E., Cecil, K., & Tooms, M. (2007). From behind the shadows: A profile of the sexual abuse of older men residing in nursing homes. *Journal of Elder Abuse & Neglect, 19*(1–2), 29–45. https://doi.org/10.1300/J084v19n01_03

Tomsa, R., & Jenaro, C. (2021). Prevalence of sexual abuse in adults with intellectual disability: Systematic review and meta-analysis. *International Journal of Environmental Research and Public Health, 18*(4), 1980. https://doi.org/10.3390/ijerph18041980

Van Der Kolk, B. A. (2000). Physical and sexual abuse of adults. In B. J. Sadock & V. A. Sadock (Eds.), *Kaplan & Sadock's comprehensive textbook of psychiatry* (pp. 4126–4135). Lippincott Williams & Wilkins Publishers.

Walser, R. D., & Westrup, D. (2007). *Acceptance & commitment therapy for the treatment of post-traumatic stress disorder and trauma-related problems: A practitioner's guide to using mindfulness and acceptance strategies*. New Harbinger Publications.

Ward, T., & Keown, K. (2006). Beliefs, values, and action: The judgment model of cognitive distortions in sexual offenders. *Aggression and Violent Behavior, 11*(4), 323–340. https://doi.org/10.1016/j.avb.2005.10.003

Weierstall, R., & Elbert, T. (2014). Testosterone reactivity and identification with a perpetrator or a victim in a story is associated with attraction to violence-related cues. *International Journal of Law and Psychiatry, 37*(3), 304–312. https://doi.org/10.1016/j.ijlp.2013.11.016

Wekerle, C., & Wolfe, D. A. (1998). The role of child maltreatment and attachment style in adolescent relationship violence. *Development and Psychopathology, 10*(3), 571–586. https://doi.org/10.1017/S095457948001758

Widman, L., & McNulty, J. K. (2014). Sexual narcissism and the perpetration of sexual aggression. *Archives of Sexual Behavior, 39*(4), 926–939. https://doi.org/10.1007/s10508-008-9461-7

Willging, C. F., & Verney, S. P. (2021). Macro- and meso-level contextual influences on healthcare inequities among American Indian elders. *BMC Public Health, 21*, 636. https://doi.org/10.1186/s12889-021-10616-z

Williams, R. (2017). Anger as a basic emotion and its role in personality building and pathological growth: The neuroscientific, developmental and clinical perspectives. *Frontiers in Psychology, 8*, 1950. https://doi.org/10.3389/fpsyg.2017.01950

Wolberg, L. R. (2013). *The technique of psychotherapy*. International Psychotherapy Institute E-Books.

World Health Organisation. (2021). *Violence against women*. https://www.who.int/news-room/fact-sheets/detail/violence-against-women

World Population Review. (2022). *Rape statistics by country 2022*. https://worldpopulationreview.com/country-rankings/rape-statistics-by-country

Yesodharan, R., Jose, T. T., Krishnan, M. N., Anitha, S., & Nayak, V. C. (2021). Looking through the lens of a sexual assault examiner: Novel trends and approaches in forensic photography. *Egyptian Journal of Forensic Sciences, 11*, 27. https://doi.org/10.1186/s41935-021-00241-7

Chapter 4
Adult Molested as Child

Namitha Babu

Introduction

Victimology is a multidisciplinary field of research that examines injury, trauma, victimization, victims and survivors of crimes, victims and survivors of noncriminal victimizations such as human rights abuses and societal interactions and responses to victimization (Quinney, 1972). Childhood sexual abuse (CSA) and its long-term effects in the life of an individual are topical public health concerns as well as a human rights issues (Choudhry et al., 2018). It is considered as an activity that provides sexual gratification, pleasure or stimulation to an adult by taking advantage or superiority of a minor (Castro et al., 2019). It includes the involvement of being touched sexually, fondling or inviting the child to touch, exhibitionism, intercourse, causing the child to participate in prostitution or pornography or online persuasion by cyber predators (Putnam, 2003; Wolak et al., 2008).

Adult victims of childhood sexual assault or childhood trauma suffer a slew of setbacks. To mention a few, there is a loss of innocence, a loss of a carefree childhood, a loss of security, and a loss of trust. There could have been a loss of a normal relationship with parental figures, as well as the ability to choose your own sexual experiences and partner, as well as a lack of nurturing (Beitchman et al., 1992). Adults who were abused at younger age, early phases of life may have trouble trusting others. They may believe that if they trust and allow others to approach them, they will be hurt and victimized again. This is a reasonable dread; especially if the person who abused the adult was someone they knew and trusted (Leserman, 2005).

Studies have shown life-long devastating and wide-ranging consequences of child maltreatment on the victim. Exposure to childhood abuse and trauma has cardinal significances on the cognitive, socioemotional, mental, and neurobiological

N. Babu (✉)
THRIVE, Bangalore, India
e-mail: namitha@rewirenthrive.com

aspects of development at later stages of life especially adulthood (Goodman et al., 2010). According to the dictionary of the American Psychological Association (APA n.d.), 'adulthood is the period of human development in which full physical growth and maturity have been achieved and certain biological, cognitive, social, personality, and other changes associated with the aging process occur. Beginning after adolescence, adulthood is sometimes divided into young adulthood (roughly 20–35 years of age); middle adulthood (about 36–64 years); and later adulthood (age 65 and beyond)'.

Adverse childhood events (ACEs) tend to activate a set of biopsychosocial events that can result in various kinds of dysfunctions and disorders in adulthood which leads to poor life situations and health outcomes. During transition in to adulthood, a number of customary changes happen in the physical, mental, social and spiritual aspects of life in the general population. These events and changes can cause a drastic impact on the psychological, emotional, relationship, health and quality of life aspects during adulthood (Daines et al., 2021). Childhood trauma can culminate in to adulthood symptoms in many areas of life. Survivors of early life abuse and trauma may find it difficult to form intimate bonds or create closeness with others. Intimacy necessitates the qualities of trust, respect, love, and sharing. Because of the imagined vulnerability, these things can be frightening. It has also been found that adults who have been molested, abused or witnessed and directly experienced trauma tend to cling too tightly to a connection that makes them feel safe because of the fear of losing that person. Many survivors find it beneficial to speak with a counsellor who can assist them in developing skills and gaining the confidence necessary to engage in a healthy romantic relationship (DiLillo, 2001). Another potential difficulty is the ability to set limits and boundaries as they may have given up hope of having any control over what occurred with them in the past. It is critical, however, that the adult victims recognize that they are no longer a child who is powerless to resist the abuse committed on them by adults in their life. They have greater power today, but more importantly, they have the right to pick their sexual partners and to control what happens to them (DiLillo, 2001; Smedley, 2012; Ensink et al., 2020).

Individuals may be plagued by disturbing memories of the assault. A flashback is a recurrence of a visual recollection that occurs suddenly. One may not only 'see' what happened during a flashback, but you may also 'feel' all of the emotions and feelings you felt at the time of the assault. A flashback might be terrifying and possibly cause a panic attack. Memories and flashbacks might be triggered by sounds, scents, people, and places linked with the assault (Brown & Kulik, 1977). In general, population studies an association between early adverse effects and psychiatric morbidity has been commonly recorded (Breslau, 2002). Early onset trauma is a strong and substantial predictor of adult psychopathology. Although the specific link is unknown, early life trauma has been associated with issues in adulthood such as mood and anxiety disorders, substance abuse disorders, personality disorders, and psychosis (McElroy et al., 2016).

Due to the lack of clarity in CSA definitions and the differences across areas, research has shown major incongruence in the low number of official reports and the rates at which CSA is self-reported (Stoltenborgh et al., 2011). Studies corroborate high prevalence of CSA universally. Even the lowest prevalence involves a huge number of early onset abuse victims. A meta-analysis conducted in '2009 in 22 countries estimated a figure of 7.9% males and 19.7% females who was sexually abused before the age of 18 years' (Singh et al., 2014). According to the data provided by UNICEF, a minimum of 120 million girls under the age of 20 years, i.e., 1 in 10 females have been the victims of sexual violence (UNICEF, 2021). The lack of disclosure and reporting due to many factors such as shame, fear, and guilt makes it very difficult to ascertain that a considerable number of adult psychopathologies are based on early onset abuse or trauma.

The impact of early life trauma and its magnitude tends to differ greatly from person to person and case to case. Reports have shown that a wide majority of sexual abuse happens in childhood and incest is the most distressing and common form of abuse (Hall & Hall, 2011). Extensive abuse, higher number of experiences and younger age increases the form and severity of the impact on the victim. Other factors like the individual perspective as well as internal resources and support also play a role in the degree of damage experienced by the victim (Ron, 2020). Studies have revealed that the adverse outcomes of early trauma during childhood affect all areas of the victim's life. Long-term longitudinal research has also thrown light in to seven areas and these effects are not experienced over short term but can persist throughout the survivor's lifetime (Fisher et al., 2017). Research has shown that childhood victimization is a serious risk factor that leads to adult sexual assault and the prevalence of trauma and distress is twice likely for survivors of early onset trauma (Elliott et al., 2004).

Despite the large number of adults seeking help for multiple symptoms and researches available discussing the effects of childhood abuse and trauma throughout life, the further paragraphs comprehensively expand the lens by outlining the impact and effects of early life abuse and trauma on adult life at multiple layers/facets of life and the various treatment modalities available to effectively deal with the adult trauma clients.

Effects on Physiological Markers

As outlined in the previous paragraphs, early childhood abuse and trauma impacts the livelihood and other important parameters and markers throughout life. Some of the major markers are listed below:

Overall Risk Factors Associated with CSA

Exposure to an adverse life event like Childhood abuse, trauma, and incest etc. can result in problems in physiological aspects in adulthood. Abuse can cause stress-induced alterations in 'cortisol levels, changes in processes of pro-inflammatory substances as well as gene expression which in turn has an adverse effect on a person's health'. Early childhood abuse or trauma is an Adverse Childhood Experience (ACE) which greatly impacts an individual's Health-Related Quality of Life (HRQoF) (Downing et al., 2021). Research shows that adults with a history of childhood trauma and victimization have reported severe negative perceptions of their overall health as well as higher somatization symptoms compared to individuals without any abuse history (Irish et al., 2009). Various studies conducted comparing individuals with and without childhood abuse and trauma history on several health themes such as pain, reproductive or gynaecologic health, gastrointestinal health, obesity, cardiopulmonary health and general health found that individuals with early trauma history indicated concerns in each health outcome (Wegman & Stetler, 2009; Afifi et al., 2007; Lepsy et al., 2022). The impact of childhood abuse, molestation and trauma on adults manifested in higher odds of depression, suicide attempts, alcohol problems, drug abuse and issues in family and relationships (Dube et al., 2005; Felitti et al., 2019).

The lack of clear distinction between the mind and body, due to the interrelatedness of the nervous, endocrine and immune systems, early childhood stressful experiences can cause immune dysregulation throughout the lifespan of an individual. A case study by Sigurdardottir and Halldorsdottir (2018) on a 40-year-old female CSA survivor to understand the lived experience indicated devastating effects of trauma throughout lifespan. Anne's case presented severe and complex nature of trauma that was marked by sexual abuse from her father from a very young age of 2 or 3 years old until she was 9 years old. Anne's physical symptoms were reported to have started around the age of four when her parents got divorced. From the age between 9 and 21, Anne was sexually assaulted by various people inside and out of the family circle. The recurrent retraumatization also leads to a sense of dissociation and disconnection from her body. Through the seven interviews that were conducted, the study revealed widespread consequences on her physical, mental and psychiatric health during adulthood. Concerns of sleep issues, widespread and chronic pain, chronic back pain, vaginal and abdominal infections, fibromyalgia, cervical dysplasia, recurrent urinary tract infections, cervical dysplasia, musculoskeletal problems, menorrhagia, ovarian cysts, ectopic pregnancies, endometrial hyperplasia, chlamydia, ovarian cancer, adhesions and other uterus problems were reported. This study shows the widespread array of potential disorders and difficulties caused to an adult with a history of childhood abuse and trauma. Even though this is reported as a unique case study, the aforementioned problems and the nature of comorbidity reflects the severity of the impact early onset trauma can have across the lifespan in mainly female survivors.

Gastroenterology and Gynaecological Difficulties Associated with Childhood Abuse

A marked difference in adverse physical health was also observed among individuals who reported CSA with intercourse and without intercourse (Felitti et al., 2019). Other physiological markers identified in adults who have experienced trauma and abuse in childhood are related to abdominal discomfort, peptic ulcers, chronic pain, lung disease, arthritis, high levels of cholesterol, low density lipoprotein were reported. And these were adults who reported early onset trauma with more number of doctor and hospital visits compared to those without the history of childhood abuse and trauma (Kamiya et al., 2015).

Studies conducted on gastroenterology patients found that '53% of the population diagnosed with gastro intestinal disorders reported to have experienced CSA compared to the total population' (Fullwood & Drossman, 1995, p. 483–496). Several researches have also reported that individuals with CSA history are twice as likely to experience Irritable Bowel Syndrome (IBS) (Hashemi et al., 2020). There were two types of chronic pain syndromes associated with past abuse – fibromyalgia and irritable bowel syndrome (Kendall-Tackett, 2009). Fibromyalgia syndrome (FMS) is characterized by pervasive musculoskeletal pain, decreased threshold for pain, sleep problems, and marked psychological distress (Boisset-Pioro et al., 1995). Studies have also shown that individuals with an abuse history in the past, primarily during their childhood experienced more severe indications of symptoms and stronger functional disabilities (Taylor et al., 1995). Irritable bowel syndrome (IBS) is a disorder of the lower gastrointestinal tract. Severe abdominal cramping, altered bowel habits with either diarrhoea or constipation, passage of mucus, bloating and abdominal distension are some of the symptoms of IBS (American Gastroenterological Association, 1997). Physicians in the past has written off pain symptoms as neuroticism or somatization without knowing the physiological basis of the symptoms as well as lowered pain threshold in victims and survivors of childhood abuse (Kendall-Tackett, 2009).

Furthering the understanding of effects on physiology, gynaecological studies corroborate strong links between CSA and chronic pelvic pain (CPP) (Walker et al., 2004). Early onset trauma and abuse were also related to higher risks in reproductive characteristics in women which includes early menarche (menstrual period occurring before the age of 11 years) as well as adolescent pregnancy (Wosu et al., 2015). Early life trauma has consistently proven to increase various stressors in childhood that also leads to biological influences on the endocrine development which in turn results in early onset of menarche (Henrichs et al., 2014). Early menarche were also found to be associated with health risks such as metabolic dysfunction, cardiovascular disease, depression and cancer and in some cases late menarche (menstrual periods after the age of 15 years) was associated with depression and low bone mineral density (Boynton-Jarrett et al., 2013). Amid pregnant women, the effect of early trauma was a manifestation of psychiatric disorders, prolonged abuse, and risk behaviours such as smoking and drinking. Research also suggests that early life stress also leads to preterm birth (PTB) which is birth without completing the gestation period of 37 weeks (Wosu et al., 2015).

Orthopaedic and Neurology-Related Issues in Early Onset Trauma

Some of the other known physical consequences of childhood trauma are adult onset arthritis (Newton et al., 2009), long-term fatigue and diabetes (Sigurdardottir & Halldorsdottir, 2018; Romans et al., 2002), circulatory problems (Kendall-Tackett, 2009), digestive and respiratory problems (Wegman & Stetler, 2009; Dube et al., 2009) and neurological problems (Paras et al., 2009). Early abuse survivors can also develop medically unexplained symptoms which were recognized through greater number of hospital outpatient and emergency department visits, speciality and primary care as well as pharmacy visits compared to those without the experience childhood sexual abuse (Bonomi et al., 2008).

Obesity and Body Mass Index (BMI) Problems in Adults with Abuse History

Adult survivors who experienced early life trauma with intercourse were found to have two times the chances of being obese (McCarthy-Jones & McCarthy-Jones, 2014). Body mass index (BMI) is considered to be a significant mediator for heart disease in individuals who has experienced childhood abuse (Williamson et al., 2002; McCarthy-Jones & McCarthy-Jones, 2014). Adults who fall in to the obese range tend to develop physical health problems such as cardiac disease, as a consequence of increased blood pressure, higher probabilities of atherosclerosis and insulin resistance and the occurrences of low grade chronic inflammatory disease (Muntner, 2004; Siervo et al., 2012; Willett, 1995). Studies conducted to explore the causal factors other than the traditional pathways which include smoking, diabetes and the rest of Ischemic heart disease (IHD) strongly indicate that adverse childhood experiences (ACEs), especially CSA is directly linked to a higher risk of IHD. It was also shown that psychological factors which are caused mainly due to ACEs appear to be more significant factors than the traditional risk factors in the increased risk of IHD in adulthood. The study comprised of a cluster of possible mediators which included BMI as a mediator to IHD (Dong et al., 2004). Animal as well as human studies have revealed that ACEs cause inflammatory responses. Chronic stress associated with early trauma also leads to the development of inflammation which reduces the inhibitory effects of cortisol which otherwise has the ability to supress inflammation (Danese et al., 2009; Hennessy et al., 2010; Raison et al., 2006).

Survivors and victims of early life trauma often experience distorted perceptions body and self-image. These include dissatisfaction about body, body shape and appearance due to the disgust and shame caused by the abuse. Many individuals who have experienced early onset trauma also uses these body perceptions and distortions as an escape from the debilitating emotional and cognitive effects of the traumatic event. Body oriented self-harm, binge eating, purging behaviours, reducing or increasing the size of the body which subsequently reduces attractiveness to avoid any future abuse are all coping mechanisms used to gain back the loss of control over oneself and their body as a coping mechanism towards the interpersonal and intrapsychic conflicts which includes shame, guilt and powerlessness (Karr et al., 2012).

Mental Health Concerns

Early onset sexual abuse is considered to be one of the highest risk factor in contributing to psychological trauma in adulthood and is proven to have a negative impact on the brain development and functionality (Heim et al., 2013). Childhood abuse is also a strong determinant in lifetime psychopathology in adults who have experienced early onset trauma (Lev-Wiesel et al., 2018). Depending on the age, the consequences of sexual abuse symptoms can be varied. Some of the symptoms exhibited by children early on can be maladjustment in school, social isolation behaviour, somatic problems like enuresis, developmental delays, neurobiological changes, sexual behaviour problems, PTSD, behavioural concerns, and poor self-esteem (Paolucci et al., 2001). While in adults the symptomatology can be different. Growing up, individuals with the experience of an early onset trauma can exhibit high-risk sexual behaviours, early sexual initiation, unwanted pregnancies, sexually transmitted diseases, PTSD, depression, neurobiological changes, distrust, anxiety, fear, eating disorders, self-harming or self-destructive behaviours, strained relationships, lack of emotional commitments, revictimization, etc. are some of the most commonly reported symptoms (Putnam, 2003).

Neuropsychological Findings (Structural and Functional Changes)

Childhood trauma is a strong forecaster of psychopathology. Studies suggest that adverse early childhood effects like sexual abuse contributes to long lasting and permanent structural brain alterations such as neurohumoral and neurotransmitter effects which manifests in the poor development of the hippocampus, amygdala, corpus callosum, cerebral cortex and the cerebellar vermis These brain alterations explain the difficulties associated with communication, memory retrieval, development of psychiatric disorders, emotional processing and regulation. Childhood trauma, especially sexual abuse trauma is a major contributor to the later development of serious mental health concerns. The change in the structure of the brain along with severe stress and impacts of the trauma causes serious emotional and physical implications in the life of an individual (Lev-Wiesel et al., 2018; Frodl et al., 2010; Rinne-Albers et al., 2013; Tomoda et al., 2009). The abnormalities in the brain that signifies psychological trauma caused by early trauma entails comparable neurobiological pathogenies to the damage caused by traumatic brain injury (TBI) (Hadanny & Efrati, 2016). Depending on an individual's background and social and personal resources, adverse childhood experiences can have detrimental long-term consequences on the mental health of an adult which manifests in various forms of impairments such as anxiety disorders, depression, posttraumatic stress disorder (PTSD), recall and memory problems, dissociative disorders, personality disorders and psychosis (Bremner et al., 1997; Wolf & Nochajski, 2013; Hovens et al., 2015).

Studies have reported consistent findings in the 'structural abnormalities in the development of the corpus callosum, amygdala, hippocampus, cerebral cortex and cerebral vermis of the brain in children and adolescents who have experienced ACEs' (Rinne-Albers et al., 2013, p. 745–755; Lev-Wiesel et al., 2018). Research has also revealed that CSA is associated with changes in brain morphology in the stress-sensitive regions of the brain. It was found that there was a reduction in the grey matter volume due to the exposure to early life trauma which also has a significant influence on the developing mammalian visual cortex (Tomoda et al., 2009). Adults who experienced adverse childhood experiences also displayed higher occurrences of lifetime major depression, substance abuse, sexual dysfunction and somatization (Harrop-Griffiths et al., 1988) and was found to have more than three times the chances of having mental health disorders, more than four times the chances of being alcohol dependent, five times the likelihoods of being drug dependant and more than six times the odds of attempting suicide compare to individuals with no history of childhood abuse (McCarthy-Jones & McCarthy-Jones, 2014).

Posttraumatic Stress Disorder (PTSD) in Adults with Sexual Abuse Trauma

One of the most prominent long-term effects of childhood abuse is posttraumatic stress disorder that carries on in to adulthood (Briggs & Joyce, 1997). Traumatic stress is a mental health condition that is classified under anxiety disorders and is developed as a response to a traumatic situation. 'PTSD is characterised by the symptoms of reliving the traumatic experience(s) called "flashbacks", avoidance of any reminders of the unpleasant event(s), emotional dysregulation, startled responses' (McLean et al., 2014). Posttraumatic stress disorder includes symptoms such as nightmares, flashbacks and re-experiencing the traumatic event. Dissociation which involves losing track of time and place or having experiences of depersonalization and derealization as well as flashback which is primarily emotional which manifests as feeling fearful, distressed and anxious without any apparent reason are also symptoms of PTSD. Some other debilitating effects of traumatic stress disorder are vivid and intrusive memories, altered attention and consciousness, problems in affect regulation, difficulty in making and maintaining interpersonal relationships, distorted belief systems, feeling of being defeated or worthless, strong physical sensations and somatic symptoms and hypervigilance with persistent feelings of threat (Su & Stone, 2020). Self-harm in childhood abuse victims is a form of emotional avoidance and numbing as well as posttraumatic dissociation, and individuals also develop memory issues related to the event. Stress disorder is an alarming factor and is a strong manifestation of sexual abuse trauma. PTSD is the result of re-experiencing the trauma even after a month of the occurrence of the incident. Traumatic events causes dysregulation in the body that can be observed in the major systems of the body such as endocrine, immune and the neural systems (Brunello et al., 2001). For some people, traumatic stress can occur after 3 months of the occurrence of an event and for some after a year or more.

Abuse-related PTSD in children manifests in losing interest in pleasurable activities, regressions to thumb sucking, bedwetting and age inappropriate behaviours, outbursts, emotion dysregulation, unusual fears, attachment issues, learning, attention and concentration problems, inability to talk and disrespectful attitudes (Batchelder et al., 2018). Early onset abuse manifestation in PTSD in adults has been associated with problems in sexuality, emotional dysregulation, lack of self-esteem and boundaries, anxiety, difficulty in relationships, distorted body image and engaging in risky behaviours (The Ranch TN, 2021). Complex trauma which has higher chances of becoming PTSD results in an adult losing core capabilities such as self-regulation, increased impairment in mental, behavioural and emotional functioning, interpersonal relatedness as well as legal, family and vocational problems (Cook et al., 2005).

Attachment-Related Findings with People with Early Onset Trauma

Research also suggests a reciprocal relationship between attachment and trauma in adulthood. Attachment is a subjective sense of security that one may have that other people will react to their needs of support, belonging and comfort. Trauma activates the attachment system and the need to feel protected (Lieberman et al., 1997). Secure attachment patterns can have restorative effects on trauma since the feelings of safety can eliminate the feelings of danger or threat and help in the neurobiological rewiring of the brain after a traumatic experience (Maunder & Hunter, 2001). Studies have also shown that adult CSA survivors with a secure attachment representation were at lower risk of PTSD compared to early life abuse survivors with an insecure attachment pattern.

The attachment pattern becomes very evident in trauma-related symptoms especially because these patterns manifested in considerably more depressive, anxiety, dissociative and somatic symptoms in adults. Those with an insecure attachment style were also found to display more trauma-related anger later in their life (Briere et al., 2008). Research also suggests that maltreatment, especially childhood abuse often co-occurs in adverse family conditions and environments.

Poor parenting and a generally maltreating nature of environment has shown to have reported higher rates of child abuse. Studies have also revealed a strong relation between household instability and parenting variables to increased suicide ideation in adult early onset trauma survivors and victims. There is also a variance in how household instability affects men and women; parenting variables and household instability is seen to have a higher impact on the suicidal ideation and attempts in women than in men (Li et al., 2012). Most victims and survivors of early life abuse trauma, especially men, tend to exhibit an array of externalizing behaviours in their adult life such as addictions, confusion in sexual identity, anger and aggression at themselves and others, self-harm and suicidal ideation as a result of the emotional dysregulation caused by the trauma. These maladaptive coping strategies are considered as a way of relief from distressing emotions and also contribute to a distortion in self-perception (Fisher et al., 2017; Nelson et al., 2011). These destructive coping strategies which includes self-destructive and avoidant behaviours used by survivors are also a result of the availability of social and personal resources available. This link between early life abuse and negative coping strategies increases the likelihood to sexual revictimization in adulthood (Astbury, 2013).

Personality Pathology Among Adults with Sexual Abuse History

A study comparing men's and women's experiences on childhood abuse found that men were more prone to anger, aggression and fear which lead to physical and emotional disconnection. As a result men who experienced early life trauma was reported to be hyperactive, have gone through indisposition and bullying, had learning difficulties, misused alcohol and drugs, addictions and displayed criminal behaviours. They also had poor interpersonal relationships as well as broken self-image and self-identity (Karr et al., 2012). Most men also reported to have endured the pain and trauma silently due to prejudice and were unable to seek help later in life (Sigurdardottir et al., 2012).

In females, CSA trauma had severe consequences on physical and mental health, especially incestuous abuse. A lack of trauma-informed care was also identified in females with the history of early onset abuse. Poor self-identity, body image and self-esteem also lead to revictimization during adulthood in large number of females. Women also reported multiple chronic complaints, mental and physical health comorbidities, pregnancy, and birth-related issues as well as severe relationship concerns (Bachmann et al., 1988a).

Sexual abuse trauma affects many facets of the victim's life and can leave long-term impacts that not only affect the self but people around them. For many victims of early onset trauma, mental health concerns also stem from a lack of trust and inability to create and maintain healthy intra and interpersonal relationships.

Interpersonal Relationships

CSA is correlated to reduced social adjustment and relationship-related problems in adults. It is also associated with violence in intimate relationships, adult sexual assault, disturbed sexual functioning and poor relationship satisfaction (Heiman &

Heard-Davison, 2004; DiLillo, 2001; Messman-Moore & Long, 2003). A large number of early abuse survivors also reported difficulty in maintaining stable and safe intimate relationships in their adulthood due to increased levels of sexually risky behaviours (Testa et al., 2005). A lot of early onset sexual abuse cases have been found to be unreported even during adulthood of the victims. Reporting childhood abuse is also linked to a decline in socioeconomic status, sexual problems, issues with trust and disruption in intimate relationships (Montigny Gauthier et al., 2018).

Early life trauma survivors tend to naturally perceive their partners as controlling and uncaring. The families or couples that reported emotional and physical abuse and violence had childhood abuse as a more common history (Mullen et al., 1994). 'More than one third female victims, which is 35.2% who were victims of early onset abuse and trauma reported rape or sexual assault as adults' (Messman-Moore et al., 2010, p. 967). Intimate partner violence (IPV) is also a common reported problem among childhood abuse victims (Messman-Moore et al., 2010). Risky sexual behaviours, poor risk assessment and recognition, dissociation, and drug and alcohol misuse might act as mediators of early life abuse and adult revictimization. Emotion dysregulation, dissociation, and poor attachment styles lead to problems in interpersonal difficulties which increases the complexity of intimate relationships (Messman-Moore & Long, 2003).

The psychological trauma inflicted by abuse can be categorized in to 'four trauma genic dynamics during adulthood- stigmatization, betrayal, traumatic sexualization and powerlessness' (Finkelhor & Browne, 1985, p. 530). The dynamic of powerlessness results in an inability in saying 'no' (Gelinas, 1983). Along with the learned helplessness, this dynamic of powerlessness is internalized to minimize the injury as a result of which the seriousness of the abuse is denied (Auerbach Walker & Browne, 1985). The stigmatization and betrayal dynamics- both internal and external, leads to shame and self-blame which affects the peer acceptance and friendship and closeness perceptions. This also results in making the victim feel less capable of satisfying relationships with peers and romantic partners (Feiring et al., 2000). This disrupts interpersonal relationships and results in fewer friends and trustworthy relationships in the life of an early life abuse survivor. Due to the impairment in perceptual abilities and the feelings of powerlessness and lack of boundaries, childhood abuse victims often tend to fulfil others' needs at the expense of their wellbeing and have poor understanding of a healthy balance in relationships as adults (Gelinas, 1983).

Issues with relationships flags a number of concerns such as loneliness, isolation, lack of support and vulnerability. This also leads to development of thought and behavioural patterns that can impact the personality of an individual with an early life trauma (Hemmati et al., 2020).

Behavioural and Personality-Related Concerns

Behavioural concerns on adults with the history of early onset abuse manifests as inappropriate and risky sexual behaviours. Research has corroborated the effects of early onset abuse on satisfaction and sexual relationship with intimate partners. In women with the history of early onset abuse, experiencing very intense ambivalent feelings such as devaluation, hostility, disillusionment, idealization and mistrust are common occurrences compared to women without the history of abuse (Briere, 1996).

Research interview data also suggests that a general dissatisfaction in couple relationships, fear of partners, marital and relationship discord is a general pattern due to the trauma caused by the abusive event(s). Revictimization or later life victimization from partner or intimate relationships in the form of sexual or physical assault is also reported in a lot of individuals with the history of childhood abuse due to the disturbed dynamics and perceptions. In many studies, two general patterns of sexual behaviours are observed in victims and survivors of childhood abuse. One reveals the relation of early life sexual abuse to high-risk sexual behaviours and activities such as increased number of relationships and frequencies, taking part in prostitution or commercialized sexual activities and poor use of risk reducing contraceptives. The second reveals a high association with sexual victimization early in life and behavioural symptoms of poor sexual satisfaction. This is generally manifested in the form of copulatory pain, sexual arousal disorders or repressed orgasms (Najman et al., 2005).

Survivors and victims of early onset abuse often experience distorted perceptions body and self-image. These include dissatisfaction about body, body shape and appearance due to the disgust and shame caused by the abuse. Many individuals who have experienced childhood trauma also uses these body perceptions and distortions as an escape from the debilitating emotional and cognitive effects of the traumatic event. Body oriented self-harm, binge eating, purging behaviours, reducing or increasing the size of the body which subsequently reduces attractiveness to avoid any future abuse are all coping mechanisms used to gain back the loss of control over oneself and their body as a coping mechanism towards the interpersonal and intrapsychic conflicts which includes shame, guilt and powerlessness (Karr et al., 2012). Self-harm in childhood sexual abuse victims is a form of emotional avoidance and numbing as well as posttraumatic dissociation, and individuals also develop memory issues related to the event (Jacobs-Kayam & Lev-Wiesel, 2019).

Personality traits of an adult are not the result of genetic predisposition alone. It can also be attributed to an individuals lived personal experiences. Children who have been maltreated and abused continue to show heightened risks in psychiatric comorbidities and personality disorders in adulthood (Fletcher & Schurer, 2017). Many victims of early life trauma experiences complex PTSD which tends to be diagnosed as Borderline Personality Disorder (BPD) because of the crossover of the symptomatology and as a result of which they experience the stigma associated with a personality disorder (Cloitre et al., 2014). PTSD is also comorbid with many other mental health disorders such as substance abuse disorders, personality disorders, major depressive disorder and eating disorders. Bipolar disorder is also an additional mental illness that is associated with CSA. Individuals who have experienced severe physical and sexual abuse in their childhood experience severe manic episodes (Brietzke et al., 2012). The repeated depression that hinders a successful treatment process is later diagnosed as bipolar disorder. Sexual abuse trauma is associated with higher number of mood episodes in individuals with the diagnosis of bipolar disorder (Larsson et al., 2013).

Socioeconomic/Environmental Context

The impact of early onset trauma and abuse significantly extends to other areas of life such as the socioeconomic wellbeing, career, achievements and social status. The functional domains of education is greatly affected which results in underachievement and failure (Boden et al., 2007). Research conducted by Zielinski (2015) found that adults who were physically and sexually abused as children were markedly on the possibility to be living below the poverty line, unemployed compared to adults who did not experience abuse in their life. A study on the gap between early trauma experiences and socioeconomic wellbeing in adulthood indicated growing rates of poor economic productivity, over spending, diminished tax revenue, poor socioeconomic status as well as transmission of violence through generations (Zielinski, 2009). CSA is correlated with poor educational outcomes, unemployment, reduced income and financial instability during adulthood. As a result of this poor socioeconomic backwardness, also causes homelessness in many adult victims of early onset trauma (Henny et al., 2007).

Social Issues of CSA Disclosure

Disclosure of CSA is an extremely difficult and complex process due to the detected and experienced incongruities. '60–70% of childhood abuse survivors fail to disclose the event until they become adults and 27.8% of them do not share the incident at all'. Most of the time, children do not understand what they are being exposed to, since they do not have any preconditioning to the event (Halvorsen et al., 2020, p. 1). This makes disclosure a problem even during adulthood due to the conflicts it can create in their personal and interpersonal lives (Halvorsen et al., 2020, p. 1). The psychological consequences for a someone exposed to a traumatic event includes fear, shock, denial, nervousness and anxiety, confusion, withdrawal, guilt, isolation and grief. These chronic effects can have severe impact on their adjustments and thoughts throughout their adult lives (De Sousa et al., 2017). Most individuals who are exposed to an early life abuse incident tend to feel guilty after the exposure to a traumatic event as they feel responsible for what happened (Paul, 2019). Through disclosure and from the perpetrator being a family member, most familial relationships tend to suffer and the survivors may feel responsible for the changes in the family dynamics.

A disclosed event of sexual abuse has been observed to also affect the parents and close ones of survivors and victims of the trauma since they feel greatly responsible and feel powerless for the inability in protecting the person exposed to the event (IICSA, 2018). There is also an innate urge to keep things normal in victims and survivors due to the negative self-representation caused by early onset abuse as staining. Due to the lack of self-respect and devaluation of one's own needs, individuals fear disclosure due to the feeling that it would take away their identity and be marked as different even as an adult (Halvorsen et al., 2020). Research also throws light in to the fact that victims of an abusive event fail to disclose and seek help and tend to blame themselves for the events and experiences they do not necessarily understand. They try to not put themselves through any trouble by keeping a secret or maintaining silence since their dependence on the perpetrator (Turkus, 1994; Herman, 1998; Alaggia et al., 2017; Solberg et al., 2021).

Early onset abuse disclosure is understood as a reiterative and interactive process rather than an isolated one-time event. Childhood abuse is now recognized as a multidimensional and carefully assessed matter rather than a single event (Alaggia et al., 2017). The revolutionary proposition by Summit (1983), on the Child Sexual Abuse Accommodation Syndrome (CSAA) lead to this understanding of early life abuse which mentioned a five stage model of sexual victimization dynamic. 'The proposed contingencies that are sequential to a sexual assault incident were (1) secrecy (2) helplessness (3) accommodation and entrapment (4) tentative, delayed and unconvincing disclosure (5) denial or recantation'. Although this model was developed to help therapists improve the therapy outcomes as a clinical opinion, this has also served in advanced understanding of the process of disclosure (Summit, 1983, p. 1). Childhood sexual abuse is the most universal public health concern and is the most hidden form of violence that is under reported. The shame and social stigma associated with childhood abuse is why it remains the most underreported crime (Human Rights Watch, 2013). Most newspapers and media fail to report the necessary and crucial details and includes unwarranted details, not maintaining ethical standards. This consequently adds on to the shame and psychological and social burden experienced by the victims (Collings et al., 2005). The International Federation of Journalists (IFJ) and UNICEF has adopted guidelines on maintaining accuracy and sensitivity while reporting on issues that involve children. A lack of knowledge about children's rights along with the sensationalism and news worthiness of early life abuse are major reason in unethical news reporting of sexual abuse which leads to shame in disclosing an incident (Anik et al., 2021).

Studies on early life trauma has shown that some children are able to disclose and report the abuse soon after the event and some are not able to tell anyone and they may remain silent for years and sometimes over their lifetime (Alaggia et al., 2017). Disclosure is also depends greatly on the kind of abuse, the perpetrator being a stranger or a family member or a known person, the age of the child and the availability of a trusted person (Collin-Vézina et al., 2015; Lemaigre et al., 2017). Collin-Vézina et al. (2015) indicates that there are a few barriers that inhibits the reporting of an abusive incident. Barriers with the self like self-blame, attempts of protecting the self, age and maturity at the time of the traumatic event, shame, guilt, poor cognitive development; difficulties related to others such as dysfunctional family dynamics, power dynamics, poor social network, judgements, fear of consequences; factors connecting to the social world such as culture, societal taboo around sexuality, labelling, name calling.

Gender plays an important role in the disclosure (Easton, 2012). Men experience more fear, guilt and embarrassment when it comes to reporting an abusive experience. They also experience a fear of being perceived as a potential perpetrator following the disclosure (Fontes & Plummer, 2010). The social and cultural perceptions of masculinity also impact the disclosure and reporting of early onset abuse. Masculinity equates abuse and victimization as weakness and it leads to anger, shame and withdrawal in male survivors (Easton et al., 2014).

Studies have also identified several cultural factors that prevent disclosure of abuse. These factors include accusation of women for being abused, beliefs that men cannot be victimized, the sexual scripts assigning gender roles, beliefs that virginity affects the dignity of the person and the family as well (Fontes & Plummer, 2010). Existing quantitative and qualitative research shows that several of the aforementioned factors affect the disclosure of an early life traumatic and abusive event (Lemaigre et al., 2017).

One other factor that affects disclosure is intrafamilial abuse (London et al., 2005). In such cases, the perpetrator may or may not be related to the victim. From the child's point of view, if an individual is considered as family, then it is classified under intrafamilial abuse. More than two thirds of childhood abuse reported was found to be involving a perpetrator close to the victim. Research has also recorded majority of perpetrators being males and below the age of 18 years. Intrafamilial abuse has very rarely been an isolated event. The abuse may go on for years with the victim being fearful of the abuser, worrying that the perpetrator might get in to trouble, a sense of responsibility for what happened as well as the dignity of the family being affected. Intrafamilial abuse also involves a great amount of secrecy, stigma and a sense of betrayal (McNeish & Scott, 2018).

Survivors or victims experience a great deal of shame, guilt, shame, fear of stigmatization, fear of the perpetrator, worries about the future, worries about losing dignity and the fear of not being believed. Fear of being unsafe and fear of others' reactions and judgements as well as being neglected at the attempt of disclosure are also major contributing factors to disclosure (or nondisclosure) (Hershkowitz et al., 2007; McElvaney & Culhane, 2015). Another factor that contributes to the rate of disclosure is the time-period when the victim or the survivor grew up. An understanding about how safe it is to discuss and reveal their experience and the listeners being open enough to create a safe space is greatly depended on the time-period and the environment which considers topics alongside sexual activities as a taboo or not (McRobert, 2022).

All of the above-mentioned factors lead to lack of self- respect and devaluation of the self which in turn affects the self-expression and perceptions about oneself. It takes enormous strength and courage to let others and the world know about the incident.

Forensic and Legal Aspects of Sexual Abuse

The forensic focus to aid the conviction of the enforcer has been on the thorough documentation, collection of evidences and the resetting the crime to help with the prosecution of the case. In cases of abuse, forensic examinations play a major role in the court proceedings and the legal management of suspected traumatic abusive incident. A forensic examination is conducted using a forensic kit to collect the biological evidences that is usually only handled by the clinician, nurse or police handling the case. The principles that are followed using and holding the kit throws light at the relevance of the kit at the time the individual decides to press charges against the perpetrator. The collection of forensic evidence is also time bound (Niec, 2002). Due to the possible transfer of secretions in sexual abuse, forensic kits and DNA traces facilitates the identification of the perpetrator (Kaur et al., 2021). A study conducted by Christian et al. (2000), on identifying forensic evidences on prepubertal sexual assault victims found that timely collection of evidences was mandatory such as clothes and linens to be given predominance. All other evidences such as body swab collection, blood and sperm/semen collected after 24 hours were unnecessary. DNA analysis is seen to have an exceptional effect on the criminal justice system due to the high reliance on the validation of a case. Most lawyers and jurors expect DNA evidence to convict a case. This also raises concerns as DNA in sexual assault cases becomes a major part in conviction and the cases without the probatory DNA evidences may lose stance (Waltke et al., 2017). In the medico-legal examinations post assault, forensic samples along with genital examinations are the most important components of assessments. To determine the components of the forensic testing, a standard method of assessment of sexual maturity is also adopted to aid the understanding of the physical maturity of the victim (Niec, 2002).

When collecting forensic evidences, any bruises, bite marks, injury, seminal fluids, pubic hair, any damage to the mouth and oral cavity, nail clippings, finger prints, blood or urine samples, body, breasts, vaginal and anal swabs are some of the best suited components to be included in the kit (Christian et al., 2000; Kaur et al., 2021). Another important factor that aids forensic examination in the case of a sexual assault crime is the informed consent from the victim. The victims must be informed of what can be expected and what procedures will be carried out during the examination. In case of victims younger than 16 years of age, the consent is to be obtained from the parent or guardian accompanying the victim only after the individual agrees to undergo the assessment. In case of a minor who is unaccompanied by an adult, they are usually termed as 'mature minor' and is qualified to provide consent. In any case, the victim should be given ample information about the procedures, protocols and limitations of the examination before the decision to give the consent is made (Niec, 2002).

Science is about facts and it is nonjudgemental. This is the very reason that sexual assault crimes can rely on forensic evidences for case convictions. Hence, criminal justice systems can get great help from DNA and non-DNA samples. Although, identifying, collecting, processing, analysing and preserving the evidences being done in a timely manner is most critical (Waltke et al., 2017). The legal issues around reporting of sexual assault is found to be the lack of testing of the forensic kits as well as the police not submitting the Sexual Assault Kits (SAKs) due to the doubts on the value of evidence these kits provide and the credibility of the people that have been assaulted. This impacts the criminal proceedings as well as the arrest decisions (Campbell et al., 2015).

The other legal and forensic issues in cases of CSA are related to the disclosure discrepancies between the reported, experienced and identified incidents (Stoltenborgh et al., 2014). A major forensic and legal concern of sexual assault cases is the delay in disclosure which has serious implications in the outcomes of these cases. The clarity in remembering incidents and the reality and honesty of the cases disclosed within forensic interviews merits further attention (Alaggia et al., 2017). In forensic interviews that are carried out in courtrooms, the strategies used by the defence lawyers imply lack of credibility and dishonesty from the victims. The nature of questions asked by the defence and the prosecution as well as the tactics used to interview greatly affects the response given by the victim. Most individuals fail to disclose and report and abusive incident due to the shame and fear attached to such a disclosure. Due to the delay in disclosing a traumatic event, the nature of trauma involved and factors like PTSD or dissociation or effects on the memory can affect the clarity with which a person can report the event. From a prosecution standpoint, these aspects greatly influence the indictment or conclusion of the case (Skinner, 2020). Through adult surveys of sexual abuse disclosure, it has been found that delays in disclosure and nondisclosure have great impacts on child protection, social justice and mental and physical health outcomes. Studies conducted on adult survivors as well as adolescents who experienced early life trauma revealed that forensic and interrogatory interactions lead to high nondisclosures in children even in cases with medical evidences. In adults, a disclosure delayed by 20–50 years was found (McElvaney, 2013). While CSA disclosures are delayed, researchers agree that the delay is due to repressed memories due to the traumatic events. These memories maybe repressed or forgotten due to the impact the abusive incident has on the individual. These repressed memories may come back or surface only in therapy as part of addressing distressful emotions or feelings (Loftus & Davis, 2006). Research has also showed individuals' conscious effort in forgetting or avoiding the memories of trauma since they cause distress. Hence, these memories are labelled horrible and frightening and are pushed out of their minds (Edwards et al., 2007). Infantile amnesia, a condition characterized by the loss or absence of early life memories, could be a reason for the lack of disclosure and clarity of events. Polyvictimization which is caused due to multiple traumatic experiences in childhood is found to be another reason for lack of memory retrieval due to the intensity of distress caused by repeated trauma. Individuals with avoidant coping mechanisms due to attachment issues caused by early onset trauma are found to have greater loss of memory detail (Goodman et al., 2018).

Management of CSA

There are various treatment models that have been proposed to treat victims and survivors of CSA. The most widely used and studied method is the cognitive behavioural therapy (CBT). CBT used for trauma survivors is termed as trauma-focused cognitive behavioural therapy (TF-CBT) which is designed to address issues related to the traumatic incident. TF-CBT focuses on the trauma narrative that helps in addressing the fears and anxieties and to psycho-educate and equip the individuals with relaxation, healthy coping and self-regulation skills (Cohen & Mannarino, 2008). Another therapy model that is proposed to be very effective on trauma is Eye Movement Desensitization and Reprocessing (EMDR). Studies suggest that EMDR therapy has shown similar positive effects to that of CBT in adults with a few benefits on reducing behavioural issues (Jaberghaderi et al., 2004). Additionally, self-reports from groups that were treated with CBT and EMDR favoured EMDR due to rapid recovery as well as fewer number of sessions compared to CBT (Nijdam et al., 2012). However, the effectiveness of EMDR therapy on abuse trauma survivors is not clear due to the very few numbers of studies conducted on the success of EMDR.

Individual and group therapies are another form of evidence-based models that are used in treatment of trauma. Group therapy has shown more effect in improving self-concept, appropriate social skills and building trust while individual therapy has shown to reduce anxiety and depressive symptoms. Group therapy tends to be widely used and preferred due to the economic advantages as well as the benefits of belonging to a group (Knittle & Tuana, 1980; Kruczek & Vitanza, 1999).

Studies have proven play therapy and related treatment modalities to be effective for younger children. Since play therapy do not rely rigidly on verbal communication, children tend to enjoy and be able to work through their problems through play (Pifalo, 2006). Additionally, play therapy also aids in effective childhood abuse disclosure due to a difficulty in appropriately verbally reporting the incident (Paine & Hansen, 2002). Studies have also corroborated the efficiency of play therapy due to the reduction in externalized behaviours such as anger, aggression, conduct issues, antisocial as well as sexually inappropriate behaviours. Children who attended play therapy was also observed to have decreased internalizing concerns such as anxiety, self-blame, shame, guilt and nightmares (Greenspan et al., 2013).

A study conducted on combining psychotherapy and Hyperbaric Oxygen Treatment (HBOT) has shown to induce neuroplasticity and improves connectivity between the impacted areas of the brain, thus restoring the brain function. This mode of treatment which is carried out in three phases is proven to decrease levels of dissociation and elevate cognitive and emotional coping abilities. The three stages were designed in a way for a trauma survivor to recall and recollect the painful experiences and negative cognitions followed by reduction in distressing symptoms such as hypervigilance, anxiety, nightmares, and depression and were taken over by an emotional and physical relaxed state of being. In the third phase, newer physical and emotional energy and outlook instilled where participants tend to take on a future orientation shedding the past orientation. The findings of the study leads to a new understanding of treatment which focuses on a dual modality of treatment focusing the mind, brain and body and not merely reducing symptoms (Lev-Wiesel et al., 2018).

The aforementioned evidence-based trauma-focused interventions are widely used to treat survivors and victims of early abuse. Nonetheless, for individuals displaying severe distressing and persistent symptoms, alongside psychotherapy, medications in the form of antipsychotic drugs or mood stabilizers are provided to aid in ameliorating the symptoms as well as for a more optimistic treatment response to psychotherapy (McLaren et al., 2018). The American Academy of Child and Adolescent Psychiatry (AACAP) advises in the practice parameters the use of selective serotonin reuptake inhibitors (SSRIs) only after ineffective trials of evidence-based psychotherapies. AACAP also recommends pharmacotherapy with conjunction with psychotherapy in treatment of comorbid presentations (Cohen, 2010).

Treatment for adults who has disclosed and is experiencing the distress of early onset abuse includes factors that are specific and nonspecific to therapy approaches. Unconditional positive regard, attention, a trusted therapist-client relationship are some on the nonspecific factors that help mediate and regulate the therapy process (Jensen et al., 2005). The most common therapeutic approaches used to treat adults with sexual abuse trauma are cognitive behavioural therapy (CBT), cognitive processing therapy (CPT), supportive therapy, EMDR, exposure therapy and psychodynamic psychotherapy. These approaches help clients address the memories that are stuck and distressing and help change the trauma narrative (Wilen et al., 2017). Of the various types of treatment the above mentioned therapies have proven to be effective on many levels. There is no one best method of intervention that the literature suggests. There is some evidence in the effectiveness of each treatment type. More research is required on the treatment components that will help in advancing the treatment for early onset abuse victims and survivors (Tichelaar et al., 2020).

Conclusion

CSA still remains to be a major public health concern. Abuse of any kind has significant impact through the lifespan of an individual. It is shown to have debilitating effects on the physical, mental, emotional, sexual, personal and interpersonal aspects of an individual's life. Despite the precautionary measure taken by individuals, families and the social justice systems, sexual abuse is highly prevalent among children and youth. It is important to continue research on the topic of early life abuse and its long-term effects to better understand the severity and implications as well as to better the treatment outcomes and the modalities used by the healthcare professionals. The statistics and prevalence of childhood trauma throws light in to the importance of educating the public and especially adolescents and youth with ample information and normalization of disclosure and intervention to help work towards promoting better health outcomes. Improving disclosure facilitation and strengthening the disclosure resources has become the need of the hour due to the alarming rates at which traumatic incidences occur and the reason why victims and survivors remain silent. Awareness from a young age on the adverse effects of early onset trauma can help deal with the physical, emotional, psychological, cognitive, and socioeconomic factors in adulthood. Safer systems to support, disclose, and report an event as well as ameliorating the screening and intervention methods will help delineating the tremendous darkness associated with sexual abuse trauma. Educating individuals in families, society and other institutions on how to respond to and support disclosure of abuse will have far reaching effects in aiding better disclosure and awareness.

References

Afifi, T. O., Enns, M. W., Cox, B. J., de Graaf, R., ten Have, M., & Sareen, J. (2007). Child abuse and health-related quality of life in adulthood. *The Journal of Nervous and Mental Disease, 195*(10), 797–804.

Alaggia, R., Collin-Vézina, D., & Lateef, R. (2017). Facilitators and barriers to child sexual abuse (CSA) disclosures: A research update (2000–2016). *Trauma, Violence, & Abuse, 20*(2), 260–283.

American Psychological Association. (n.d.). *APA dictionary of psychology.* American Psychological Association. Retrieved March 19, 2022.

American Gastroenterological Association. (1997). American Gastroenterological Association medical position statement: Irritable bowel syndrome. *Gastroenterology, 112*, 2118–2137.

Anik, A. I., Towhid, M. I., Islam, S. S., Mallik, M. T., Azim, S., Rahman, M. G., & Haque, M. A. (2021). Deviance from the ethical standard of reporting child sexual abuse in daily newspapers of Bangladesh. *Humanities and Social Sciences Communications, 8*(1), 1–11.

Astbury, J. (2013). *Violating children's rights: The psychological impact of sexual abuse in childhood.* APS. Retrieved February 26, 2022.

Auerbach Walker, L. E., & Browne, A. (1985). Gender and victimization by intimates. *Journal of Personality, 53*(2), 179–195.

Bachmann, G. A., Bennet, J., & Moeller, T. p. (1988a). Consequences of childhood sexual abuse. *Journal of Nurse-Midwifery, 33*(5), 235–236.

Batchelder, A. W., Safren, S. A., Coleman, J. N., Boroughs, M. S., Thiim, A., Ironson, G. H., Shipherd, J. C., & O'Cleirigh, C. (2018). Indirect effects from childhood sexual abuse severity to PTSD: The role of avoidance coping. *Journal of Interpersonal Violence, 36*(9–10), NP5476–NP5495.

Beitchman, J. H., Zucker, K. J., Hood, J. E., DaCosta, G. A., Akman, D., & Cassavia, E. (1992). A review of the long-term effects of child sexual abuse. *Child Abuse & Neglect, 16*(1), 101–118.

Boden, J. M., Horwood, L. J., & Fergusson, D. M. (2007). Exposure to childhood sexual and physical abuse and subsequent educational achievement outcomes. *Child Abuse & Neglect, 31*(10), 1101–1114.

Boisset-Pioro, M. H., Esdaile, J. M., & Fitzcharles, M.-A. (1995). Sexual and physical abuse in women with fibromyalgia syndrome. *Arthritis and Rheumatism, 38*(2), 235–241.

Bonomi, A. E., Anderson, M. L., Rivara, F. P., Cannon, E. A., Fishman, P. A., Carrell, D., Reid, R. J., & Thompson, R. S. (2008). Health Care Utilization and costs associated with childhood abuse. *Journal of General Internal Medicine, 23*(3), 294–299.

Boynton-Jarrett, R., Wright, R. J., Putnam, F. W., Lividoti Hibert, E., Michels, K. B., Forman, M. R., & Rich-Edwards, J. (2013). Childhood abuse and age at menarche. *Journal of Adolescent Health, 52*(2), 241–247.

Bremner, J. D., Randall, P., Vermetten, E., Staib, L., Bronen, R. A., Mazure, C., Capelli, S., McCarthy, G., Innis, R. B., & Charney, D. S. (1997). Magnetic resonance imaging-based measurement of hippocampal volume in posttraumatic stress disorder related to childhood physical and sexual abuse—A preliminary report. *Biological Psychiatry, 41*(1), 23–32.

Breslau, N. (2002). Psychiatric morbidity in adult survivors of childhood trauma. *Seminars in Clinical Neuropsychiatry, 7*(2), 80–88.

Briere, J. (1996). Treating adults severely abused as children: The self-trauma model. In *Child abuse: New directions in prevention and treatment across the lifespan* (pp. 177–204).

Briere, J., Kaltman, S., & Green, B. L. (2008). Accumulated childhood trauma and symptom complexity. *Journal of Traumatic Stress, 21*(2), 223–226.

Brietzke, E., Sant'anna, M. K., Jackowski, A., Grassi-Oliveira, R., Bucker, J., Zugman, A., Mansur, R. B., & Bressan, R. A. (2012). Impact of childhood stress on psychopathology. *Revista Brasileira de Psiquiatria, 34*(4), 480–488.

Briggs, L., & Joyce, P. R. (1997). What determines post-traumatic stress disorder symptomatology for survivors of childhood sexual abuse? *Child Abuse & Neglect, 21*(6), 575–582.

Brown, R., & Kulik, J. (1977). Flashbulb memories. *Cognition, 5*(1), 73–99.

Brunello, N., Davidson, J. R. T., Deahl, M., Kessler, R. C., Mendlewicz, J., Racagni, G., Shalev, A. Y., & Zohar, J. (2001). Posttraumatic stress disorder: Diagnosis and epidemiology, comorbidity and social consequences, biology and treatment. *Neuropsychobiology, 43*(3), 150–162.

Campbell, R., Greeson, M. R., Fehler-Cabral, G., & Kennedy, A. C. (2015). Pathways to help. *Violence Against Women, 21*(7), 824–847.

Castro, Á., Ibáñez, J., Maté, B., Esteban, J., & Barrada, J. R. (2019). Childhood sexual abuse, sexual behavior, and revictimization in adolescence and youth: A mini review. *Frontiers in Psychology, 10*, 2018.

Choudhry, V., Dayal, R., Pillai, D., Kalokhe, A. S., Beier, K., & Patel, V. (2018). Child sexual abuse in India: A systematic review. *PLoS One, 13*(10), e0205086.

Christian, C. W., Lavelle, J. M., De Jong, A. R., Loiselle, J., Brenner, L., & Joffe, M. (2000). Forensic evidence findings in prepubertal victims of sexual assault. *Pediatrics, 106*(1), 100–104.

Cloitre, M., Garvert, D. W., Weiss, B., Carlson, E. B., & Bryant, R. A. (2014). Distinguishing PTSD, Complex PTSD, and borderline personality disorder: A latent class analysis. *European Journal of Psychotraumatology, 5*(1), 25097.

Cohen, J. A. (2010). Practice parameter for the assessment and treatment of children and adolescents with posttraumatic stress disorder. *Journal of the American Academy of Child & Adolescent Psychiatry, 49*(4), 414–430.

Cohen, J. A., & Mannarino, A. P. (2008). Trauma-focused cognitive behavioural therapy for children and parents. *Child and Adolescent Mental Health, 13*(4), 158–162.

Collings, S. J., Griffiths, S., & Kumalo, M. (2005). Patterns of disclosure in child sexual abuse. *South Africa Journal of Psychology, 35*(2), 270–285.

Collin-Vézina, D., De La Sablonnière-Griffin, M., Palmer, A. M., & Milne, L. (2015). A preliminary mapping of individual, relational, and social factors that impede disclosure of childhood sexual abuse. *Child Abuse & Neglect, 43*, 123–134.

Cook, A., Spinazzola, J., Ford, J., Lanktree, C., Blaustein, M., Cloitre, M., DeRosa, R., Hubbard, R., Kagan, R., Liautaud, J., Mallah, K., Olafson, E., & van der Kolk, B. (2005). Complex trauma in children and adolescents. *Psychiatric Annals, 35*(5), 390–398.

Daines, C. L., Hansen, D., Novilla, M. L., & Crandall, A. A. (2021). Effects of positive and negative childhood experiences on Adult Family Health. *BMC Public Health, 21*(1), 651.

Danese, A., Moffitt, T. E., Harrington, H., Milne, B. J., Polanczyk, G., Pariante, C. M., Poulton, R., & Caspi, A. (2009). Adverse childhood experiences and adult risk factors for age-related disease: depression, inflammation, and clustering of metabolic risk markers. *Archives of Pediatrics & Adolescent Medicine, 163*(12), 1135–1143. https://doi.org/10.1001/archpediatrics.2009.214

De Sousa, A. A., Shrivastava, A. K., Karia, S. B., & Sonavane, S. S. (2017). Child sexual abuse and the development of psychiatric disorders: A neurobiological trajectory of pathogenesis. *Industrial Psychiatry Journal, 26*(1), 4. https://doi.org/10.4103/ipj.ipj_38_15

DiLillo, D. (2001). Interpersonal functioning among women reporting a history of childhood sexual abuse: Empirical findings and methodological issues. *Clinical Psychology Review, 21*(4), 553–576.

Dong, M., Giles, W. H., Felitti, V. J., Dube, S. R., Williams, J. E., Chapman, D. P., & Anda, R. F. (2004). Insights into causal pathways for ischemic heart disease. *Circulation, 110*(13), 1761–1766.

Downing, N. R., Akinlotan, M., & Thornhill, C. W. (2021). The impact of childhood sexual abuse and adverse childhood experiences on adult health related quality of life. *Child Abuse & Neglect, 120*, 105181.

Dube, S., Andra, R., Whitefield, C., Brown, D., Felitti, V., Dong, M., & Giles, W. (2005). Long-term consequences of childhood sexual abuse by gender of victim. *American Journal of Preventive Medicine, 28*(5), 430–438.

Dube, S. R., Fairweather, D. L., Pearson, W. S., Felitti, V. J., Anda, R. F., & Croft, J. B. (2009). Cumulative childhood stress and autoimmune diseases in adults. *Psychosomatic Medicine, 71*(2), 243–250.

Easton, S. D. (2012). Disclosure of child sexual abuse among adult male survivors. *Clinical Social Work Journal, 41*(4), 344–355.

Easton, S. D., Saltzman, L. Y., & Willis, D. G. (2014). "Would you tell under circumstances like that?": Barriers to disclosure of child sexual abuse for men. *Psychology of Men & Masculinity, 15*(4), 460–469.

Edwards, V. J., Dube, S. R., Felitti, V. J., & Anda, R. F. (2007). It's OK to ask about past abuse. *American Psychologist, 62*(4), 327–328. https://doi.org/10.1037/0003-066x62.4.327

Elliott, D. M., Mok, D. S., & Briere, J. (2004). Adult sexual assault: Prevalence, symptomatology, and sex differences in the general population. *Journal of Traumatic Stress, 17*(3), 203–211.

Ensink, K., Borelli, J. L., Normandin, L., Target, M., & Fonagy, P. (2020). Childhood sexual abuse and attachment insecurity: Associations with child psychological difficulties. *American Journal of Orthopsychiatry, 90*(1), 115–124. https://doi.org/10.1037/ort0000407

Feiring, C., Rosenthal, S., & Taska, L. (2000). Stigmatization and the development of friendship and romantic relationships in adolescent victims of sexual abuse. *Child Maltreatment, 5*(4), 311–322.

Felitti, V. J., Anda, R. F., Nordenberg, D., Williamson, D. F., Spitz, A. M., Edwards, V., Koss, M. P., & Marks, J. S. (2019). Reprint of: Relationship of childhood abuse and household dysfunction to many of the leading causes of death in adults: The adverse childhood experiences (ACE) study. *American Journal of Preventive Medicine, 56*(6), 774–786.

Finkelhor, D., & Browne, A. (1985). The traumatic impact of child sexual abuse: A conceptualization. *American Journal of Orthopsychiatry, 55*(4), 530–541.

Fisher, C., Goldsmith, A., Hurcombe, R., & Soares, C. (2017). (rep.). *The impacts of child sexual abuse: A rapid evidence assessment.*

Fletcher, J., & Schurer, S. (2017). Origins of adulthood personality: The role of adverse childhood experiences. *The B.E. Journal of Economic Analysis & Policy, 17*(2).

Fontes, L. A., & Plummer, C. (2010). Cultural issues in disclosures of child sexual abuse. *Journal of Child Sexual Abuse, 19*(5), 491–518.

Frodl, T., Reinhold, E., Koutsouleris, N., Reiser, M., & Meisenzahl, E. M. (2010). Interaction of childhood stress with hippocampus and prefrontal cortex volume reduction in major depression. *Journal of Psychiatric Research, 44*(13), 799–807.

Fullwood, A., & Drossman, D. A. (1995). The relationship of psychiatric illness with gastrointestinal disease. *Annual Review of Medicine, 46*(1), 483–496.

Gelinas, D. J. (1983). The persisting negative effects of incest. *Psychiatry, 46*(4), 312–332.

Goodman, G. S., Quas, J. A., & Ogle, C. M. (2010). Child maltreatment and memory. *Annual Review of Psychology, 61*(1), 325–351.

Goodman, G. S., Gonzalves, L., & Wolpe, S. (2018). False memories and true memories of childhood trauma: Balancing the risks. *Clinical Psychological Science, 7*(1), 29–31. https://doi.org/10.1177/2167702618797106

Greenspan, F., Moretzsohn, A. G., & Silverstone, P. H. (2013). What treatments are available for childhood sexual abuse, and how do they compare? *International Journal of Advances in Psychology, 2*(4), 232.

Hadanny, A., & Efrati, S. (2016). Treatment of persistent post-concussion syndrome due to mild traumatic brain injury: Current status and future directions. *Expert Review of Neurotherapeutics, 16*(8), 875–887.

Hall, M., & Hall, J. (2011). *The long-term effects of childhood sexual abuse: Counseling implications*.

Halvorsen, J. E., Tvedt Solberg, E., & Hjelen Stige, S. (2020). "to say it out loud is to kill your own childhood." – an exploration of the first person perspective of barriers to disclosing child sexual abuse. *Children and Youth Services Review, 113*, 104999.

Harrop-Griffiths, J., Hickok, L., Russo, J., Holm, L., Walker, E., & Katon, W. (1988). Relationship of chronic pelvic pain to psychiatric diagnoses and childhood sexual abuse. *American Journal of Psychiatry, 145*(1), 75–80.

Hashemi, S. M., Yousefichaijan, P., Salehi, B., Almasi-Hashiani, A., Rafiei, M., Zahedi, S., Khedmati Morasae, E., & Maghsoudlou, F. (2020). Comparison of child abuse history in patients with and without functional abdominal pain: A case-control study. *BMC Psychiatry, 20*(1), 1–7.

Heim, C. M., Mayberg, H. S., Mletzko, T., Nemeroff, C. B., & Pruessner, J. C. (2013). Decreased cortical representation of genital somatosensory field after childhood sexual abuse. *American Journal of Psychiatry, 170*(6), 616–623.

Heiman, J. R., & Heard-Davison, A. R. (2004). Child sexual abuse and adult sexual relationships: Review and perspective. In *From child sexual abuse to adult sexual risk: Trauma, revictimization, and intervention* (pp. 13–47). American Psychological Association.

Hemmati, A., Newton-Howes, G., Falahi, S., Mostafavi, S., Colarusso, C. A., & Komasi, S. (2020). Personality pathology among adults with history of childhood sexual abuse: Study of the relevance of DSM-5 proposed traits and psychobiological features of temperament and character. *Indian Journal of Psychological Medicine, 43*(2), 135–143. https://doi.org/10.1177/0253717620928813

Hennessy, M. B., Deak, T., & Schiml-Webb, P. A. (2010). Early attachment-figure separation and increased risk for later depression: Potential mediation by Proinflammatory Processes. *Neuroscience & Biobehavioral Reviews, 34*(6), 782–790.

Henny, K. D., Kidder, D. P., Stall, R., & Wolitski, R. J. (2007). Physical and sexual abuse among homeless and unstably housed adults living with HIV: Prevalence and associated risks. *AIDS and Behavior, 11*(6), 842–853.

Henrichs, K. L., McCauley, H. L., Miller, E., Styne, D. M., Saito, N., & Breslau, J. (2014). Early menarche and childhood adversities in a nationally representative sample. *International Journal of Pediatric Endocrinology, 2014*(1), 14.

Herman, J. L. (1998). Recovery from psychological trauma. *Psychiatry and Clinical Neurosciences, 52*(S1).

Hershkowitz, I., Lanes, O., & Lamb, M. E. (2007). Exploring the disclosure of child sexual abuse with alleged victims and their parents. *Child Abuse & Neglect, 31*(2), 111–123.

Hovens, J. G., Giltay, E. J., Spinhoven, P., van Hemert, A. M., & Penninx, B. W. (2015). Impact of childhood life events and childhood trauma on the onset and recurrence of depressive and anxiety disorders. *The Journal of Clinical Psychiatry, 76*(07), 931–938.

Human breaking the silence - human rights watch. Human Rights Watch. (2013). Retrieved March 1, 2022.

IICSA. (2018, August 20). *3.2 the effects of child sexual abuse*. IICSA. Retrieved February 27, 2022.

Irish, L., Kobayashi, I., & Delahanty, D. L. (2009). Long-term physical health consequences of childhood sexual abuse: A meta-analytic review. *Journal of Pediatric Psychology, 35*(5), 450–461.

Jaberghaderi, N., Greenwald, R., Rubin, A., Zand, S. O., & Dolatabadi, S. (2004). A comparison of CBT and EMDR for sexually-abused Iranian girls. *Clinical Psychology & Psychotherapy, 11*(5), 358–368.

Jacobs-Kayam, A., & Lev-Wiesel, R. (2019). In limbo: Time perspective and memory deficit among female survivors of sexual abuse. *Frontiers in Psychology, 10*, 912.

Jensen, P. S., Weersing, R., Hoagwood, K. E., & Goldman, E. (2005). What is the evidence for evidence-based treatments? A hard look at our soft underbelly. *Mental Health Services Research, 7*(1), 53–74. https://doi.org/10.1007/s11020-005-1965-3

Kamiya, Y., Timonen, V., & Kenny, R. A. (2015). The impact of childhood sexual abuse on the mental and physical health, and healthcare utilization of older adults. *International Psychogeriatrics, 28*(3), 415–422.

Karr, T. M., Simonich, H., & Wonderlich, S. A. (2012). Psychological trauma and body image. In *Encyclopedia of body image and human appearance* (pp. 700–706). Academic Press.

Kaur, S., Kaur, S., & Rawat, B. (2021). Medico-Legal Evidence Collection in child sexual assault cases: A forensic significance. *Egyptian Journal of Forensic Sciences, 11*(1), 1–6.

Kendall-Tackett, K. (2009). Psychological trauma and physical health: A psychoneuroimmunology approach to etiology of negative health effects and possible interventions. *Psychological Trauma: Theory, Research, Practice, and Policy, 1*(1), 35–48.

Knittle, B. J., & Tuana, S. J. (1980). Group therapy as primary treatment for adolescent victims of intrafamilial sexual abuse. *Clinical Social Work Journal, 8*(4), 236–242.

Kruczek, T., & Vitanza, S. (1999). Treatment effects with an adolescent abuse survivor's group. *Child Abuse & Neglect, 23*(5), 477–485.

Larsson, S., Aas, M., Klungsøyr, O., Agartz, I., Mork, E., Steen, N. E., Barrett, E. A., Lagerberg, T. V., Røssberg, J. I., Melle, I., Andreassen, O. A., & Lorentzen, S. (2013). Patterns of childhood adverse events are associated with clinical characteristics of bipolar disorder. *BMC Psychiatry, 13*(1), 97.

Lemaigre, C., Taylor, E. P., & Gittoes, C. (2017). Barriers and facilitators to disclosing sexual abuse in childhood and adolescence: A systematic review. *Child Abuse & Neglect, 70*, 39–52.

Lepsy, N., Dering, M.-R., Fuge, J., Meltendorf, T., Hoeper, M. M., Heitland, I., Kamp, J. C., Park, D.-H., Richter, M. J., Gall, H., Ghofrani, H. A., Ellermeier, D., Kulla, H.-D., Olsson, K. M., & Kahl, K. G. (2022). Childhood maltreatment, mental well-being, and healthy lifestyle in patients with chronic thromboembolic pulmonary hypertension. *Frontiers in Psychiatry, 13*, 821468.

Leserman, J. (2005). Sexual abuse history: Prevalence, health effects, mediators, and psychological treatment. *Psychosomatic Medicine, 67*(6), 906–915.

Lev-Wiesel, R., Bechor, Y., Daphna-Tekoah, S., Hadanny, A., & Efrati, S. (2018). Brain and mind integration: Childhood sexual abuse survivors experiencing hyperbaric oxygen treatment and psychotherapy concurrently. *Frontiers in Psychology, 9*, 2535.

Li, N., Ahmed, S., & Zabin, L. S. (2012). Association between childhood sexual abuse and adverse psychological outcomes among youth in Taipei. *Journal of Adolescent Health, 50*(3 Suppl), S45–S51.

Lieberman, A. F., Van Horn, P., Grandison, C. M., & Pekarsky, J. H. (1997). Mental health assessment of infants, toddlers, and preschoolers in a service program and a treatment outcome research program. *Infant Mental Health Journal, 18*(2), 158–170.

Loftus, E. F., & Davis, D. (2006). Recovered memories. *Annual Review of Clinical Psychology, 2*(1), 469–498. https://doi.org/10.1146/annurev.clinpsy.2.022305.095315

London, K., Bruck, M., Ceci, S. J., & Shuman, D. W. (2005). Disclosure of Child Sexual Abuse: What does the research tell us about the ways that children tell? *Psychology, Public Policy, and Law, 11*(1), 194–226.

Maunder, R. G., & Hunter, J. J. (2001). Attachment and psychosomatic medicine: Developmental contributions to stress and disease. *Psychosomatic Medicine, 63*(4), 556–567.

McCarthy-Jones, S., & McCarthy-Jones, R. (2014). Body mass index and anxiety/depression as mediators of the effects of child sexual and physical abuse on physical health disorders in women. *Child Abuse & Neglect, 38*(12), 2007–2020.

McElroy, E., Shevlin, M., Elklit, A., Hyland, P., Murphy, S., & Murphy, J. (2016). Prevalence and predictors of axis I disorders in a large sample of treatment-seeking victims of sexual abuse and incest. *European Journal of Psychotraumatology, 7*(1), 30686.

McElvaney, R. (2013). Disclosure of Child Sexual Abuse: Delays, non-disclosure and partial disclosure. What the research tells us and implications for practice. *Child Abuse Review, 24*(3), 159–169. https://doi.org/10.1002/car.2280

McElvaney, R., & Culhane, M. (2015). A retrospective analysis of children's assessment reports: What helps children tell? *Child Abuse Review, 26*(2), 103–115.

McLaren, J. L., Barnett, E. R., Concepcion Zayas, M. T., Lichtenstein, J., Acquilano, S. C., Schwartz, L. M., Woloshin, S., & Drake, R. E. (2018). Psychotropic medications for highly vulnerable children. *Expert Opinion on Pharmacotherapy, 19*(6), 547–560.

McLean, C. P., Morris, S. H., Conklin, P., Jayawickreme, N., & Foa, E. B. (2014). Trauma characteristics and posttraumatic stress disorder among adolescent survivors of childhood sexual abuse. *Journal of Family Violence, 29*(5), 559–566.

McNeish, D., & Scott, S. (2018, June). *Key messages from research on intra-familial child sexual abuse.* www.csacentre.org.uk. Retrieved March 7, 2022.

McRobert, K. (2022). Childhood sexual abuse (CSA): Moving past the taboo and into the postcolonial. *Society Register, 6*(2), 17–34. https://doi.org/10.14746/sr.2022.6.2.02

Messman-Moore, T. L., & Long, P. J. (2003). The role of childhood sexual abuse sequelae in the sexual revictimization of women. *Clinical Psychology Review, 23*(4), 537–571.

Messman-Moore, T. L., Walsh, K. L., & DiLillo, D. (2010). Emotion dysregulation and risky sexual behavior in revictimization. *Child Abuse & Neglect, 34*(12), 967–976.

Montigny Gauthier, L., Vaillancourt-Morel, M. P., Rellini, A., Godbout, N., Charbonneau-Lefebvre, V., Desjardins, F., & Bergeron, S. (2018). The risk of telling: A dyadic perspective on romantic partners' responses to child sexual abuse disclosure and their associations with sexual and relationship satisfaction. *Journal of Marital and Family Therapy, 45*(3), 480–493.

Mullen, P. E., Martin, J. L., Anderson, J. C., Romans, S. E., & Herbison, G. P. (1994). The effect of child sexual abuse on social, interpersonal and sexual function in adult life. *British Journal of Psychiatry, 165*(1), 35–47.

Muntner, P. (2004). Trends in blood pressure among children and adolescents. *JAMA, 291*(17), 2107.

Najman, J. M., Dunne, M. P., Purdie, D. M., Boyle, F. M., & Coxeter, P. D. (2005). Sexual abuse in childhood and sexual dysfunction in adulthood: An Australian population-based study. *Archives of Sexual Behavior, 34*(5), 517–526.

Nelson, S., Baldwin, N., & Taylor, J. (2011). Mental health problems and medically unexplained physical symptoms in adult survivors of childhood sexual abuse: An integrative literature review. *Journal of Psychiatric and Mental Health Nursing, 19*(3), 211–220.

Newton, E. G., Jewett, L. R., & Thombs, B. D. (2009). Childhood psychosocial stressors and adult onset arthritis: A comment on Von Korff et al. *Pain, 144*(3), 340.

Niec, A. (2002). Forensic issues in the assessment of sexually assaulted adolescents. *Paediatrics & Child Health, 7*(3), 153–159.

Nijdam, M. J., Gersons, B. P., Reitsma, J. B., de Jongh, A., & Olff, M. (2012). Brief eclectic psychotherapy v. eye movement desensitisation and reprocessing therapy for post-traumatic stress disorder: Randomised controlled trial. *British Journal of Psychiatry, 200*(3), 224–231.

Paine, M. L., & Hansen, D. J. (2002). Factors influencing children to self-disclose sexual abuse. *Clinical Psychology Review, 22*(2), 271–295.

Paolucci, E. O. D. D. O. N. E., Genuis, M. L., & Violato, C. (2001). A meta-analysis of the published research on the effects of child sexual abuse. *The Journal of Psychology, 135*(1), 17–36.

Paras, M. L., Murad, M. H., Chen, L. P., Goranson, E. N., Sattler, A. L., Colbenson, K. M., Elamin, M. B., Seime, R. J., Prokop, L. J., & Zirakzadeh, A. (2009). Sexual abuse and lifetime diagnosis of somatic disorders. *JAMA, 302*(5), 550.

Paul, H. A. (2019). Treatment of disorders in childhood and adolescence. *Child & Family Behavior Therapy, 41*(4), 247–255.

Pifalo, T. (2006). Art therapy with sexually abused children and adolescents: Extended research study. *Art Therapy, 23*(4), 181–185.

Putnam, F. R. A. N. K. W. (2003). Ten-year research update review: Child sexual abuse. *Journal of the American Academy of Child & Adolescent Psychiatry, 42*(3), 269–278.

Quinney, R. (1972). Who is the victim? *Criminology, 10*(3), 314–323.

Raison, C. L., Capuron, L., & Miller, A. H. (2006). Cytokines sing the blues: Inflammation and the pathogenesis of depression. *Trends in Immunology, 27*(1), 24–31.

Rinne-Albers, M. A., van der Wee, N. J., Lamers-Winkelman, F., & Vermeiren, R. R. (2013). Neuroimaging in children, adolescents and young adults with psychological trauma. *European Child & Adolescent Psychiatry, 22*(12), 745–755.

Romans, S., Belaise, C., Martin, J., Morris, E., & Raffi, A. (2002). Childhood abuse and later medical disorders in women. *Psychotherapy and Psychosomatics, 71*(3), 141–150.

Ron, P. (2020). The relationship between internal and external resources, coping strategies, post-traumatic symptoms, and death-anxiety of round-the-clock paid Philippine immigrants and local workers taking care for the elderly during and after the Gaza War. *Psychology, 11*(04), 606–623.

Siervo, M., Ruggiero, D., Sorice, R., Nutile, T., Aversano, M., Iafusco, M., Vetrano, F., Wells, J. C., Stephan, B. C., & Ciullo, M. (2012). Body mass index is directly associated with biomarkers of angiogenesis and inflammation in children and adolescents. *Nutrition, 28*(3), 262–266.

Sigurdardottir, S., & Halldorsdottir, S. (2018). Screaming body and Silent Healthcare Providers: A case study with a childhood sexual abuse survivor. *International Journal of Environmental Research and Public Health, 15*(1), 94.

Sigurdardottir, S., Halldorsdottir, S., & Bender, S. S. (2012). Deep and almost unbearable suffering: Consequences of childhood sexual abuse for men's health and well-being. *Scandinavian Journal of Caring Sciences, 26*(4), 688–697.

Singh, M. M., Parsekar, S. S., & Nair, S. N. (2014). An epidemiological overview of child sexual abuse. *Journal of Family Medicine and Primary Care, 3*(4), 430.

Skinner, G. C. (2020). Disclosure of Child Sexual Abuse: A review of factors that impact proceedings in the courtroom. In *Reviewing crime psychology* (pp. 380–399). https://doi.org/10.432 4/9780429346927-21

Smedley, L. S. (2012). *CSA survivors: What heals and what hurts in a couple relationship* (UNLV Theses, Dissertations, Professional Papers, and Capstones). 1778.

Solberg, E. T., Halvorsen, J. E., & Stige, S. H. (2021). What do survivors of child sexual abuse believe will facilitate early disclosure of sexual abuse? *Frontiers in Psychiatry, 12,639341*

Stoltenborgh, M., van IJzendoorn, M. H., Euser, E. M., & Bakermans-Kranenburg, M. J. (2011). A global perspective on child sexual abuse: Meta-analysis of prevalence around the world. *Child Maltreatment, 16*(2), 79–101.

Stoltenborgh, M., Bakermans-Kranenburg, M. J., Alink, L. R., & van IJzendoorn, M. H. (2014). The prevalence of child maltreatment across the globe: Review of a series of meta-analyses. *Child Abuse Review, 24*(1), 37–50.

Su, W.-M., & Stone, L. (2020). Adult survivors of childhood trauma: Complex trauma, complex needs. *Australian Journal of General Practice, 49*(7), 423–430.

Summit, R. C. (1983). The child sexual abuse accomodation syndrome. *Child Abuse & Neglect, 7*(2), 177–193.

Taylor, M. L., Trotter, D. R., & Csuka, M. E. (1995). The prevalence of sexual abuse in women with fibromyalgia. *Arthritis and Rheumatism, 38*(2), 229–234.

Testa, M., VanZile-Tamsen, C., & Livingston, J. A. (2005). Childhood sexual abuse, relationship satisfaction, and sexual risk taking in a community sample of women. *Journal of Consulting and Clinical Psychology, 73*(6), 1116–1124.

The Ranch TN. (2021, December 7). *Child sexual abuse as a cause of PTSD (post-traumatic stress disorder)*. The Ranch TN. Retrieved February 25, 2022.

Tichelaar, H. K., Deković, M., & Endendijk, J. J. (2020). Exploring effectiveness of psychotherapy options for sexually abused children and adolescents: A systematic review of randomized controlled trials. *Children and Youth Services Review, 119*, 105519.

Tomoda, A., Navalta, C. P., Polcari, A., Sadato, N., & Teicher, M. H. (2009). Childhood sexual abuse is associated with reduced gray matter volume in visual cortex of young women. *Biological Psychiatry, 66*(7), 642–648.

Turkus, J. A. (1994). Trauma and recovery. by Judith Lewis Herman. Basic books: Glenview, IL, 1992, 276 pages. (hardbound $27.00, paperback $14.00). *Journal of Traumatic Stress, 7*(3), 497–498.

UNICEF. (2021). https://www.unicef.org/protection/sexual-violence-against-children

Walker, J. L., Carey, P. D., Mohr, N., Stein, D. J., & Seedat, S. (2004). Gender differences in the prevalence of childhood sexual abuse and in the development of pediatric PTSD. *Archives of Women's Mental Health, 7*(2), 111–121.

Waltke, H., LaPorte, G., Weiss, D., Schwarting, D., Nguyen, M., & Scott, F. (2017). *Sexual assault cases: Exploring the importance of non-DNA forensic evidence*. National Institute of Justice. Retrieved March 20, 2022.

Wegman, H. L., & Stetler, C. (2009). A meta-analytic review of the effects of childhood abuse on medical outcomes in adulthood. *Psychosomatic Medicine, 71*(8), 805–812.

Wilen, J. S., Littell, J. H., & Salanti, G. (2017). Psychosocial interventions for adults who were sexually abused as children. *Cochrane Database of Systematic Reviews*. https://doi.org/10.1002/14651858.cd010099.pub2

Willett, W. C. (1995). Weight, weight change, and coronary heart disease in women. *JAMA, 273*(6), 461.

Williamson, D. F., Thompson, T. J., Anda, R. F., Dietz, W. H., & Felitti, V. (2002). Body weight and obesity in adults and self-reported abuse in childhood. *International Journal of Obesity, 26*(8), 1075–1082.

Wolak, J., Finkelhor, D., Mitchell, K. J., & Ybarra, M. L. (2008). Online "predators" and their victims: Myths, realities, and implications for prevention and treatment. *American Psychologist, 63*(2), 111–128.

Wolf, M. R., & Nochajski, T. H. (2013). Child sexual abuse survivors with dissociative amnesia: What's the difference? *Journal of Child Sexual Abuse, 22*(4), 462–480.

Wosu, A. C., Gelaye, B., & Williams, M. A. (2015). Maternal history of childhood sexual abuse and preterm birth: An epidemiologic review. *BMC Pregnancy and Childbirth, 15*(1), 174.

Zielinski, D. S. (2009). Child maltreatment and adult socioeconomic well-being. *Child Abuse & Neglect, 33*(10), 666–678.

Zielinski, D. (2015, July 2). *Childhood maltreatment linked to adulthood economic problems*. National Institutes of Health. Retrieved March 20, 2022.

Chapter 5
Intimate Partner Violence and Victims

Rejani Thudalikunnil Gopalan

Introduction

Intimate partner violence (IPV), also known as domestic violence, spousal abuse, and relationship violence, among other names, is becoming a widely recognized social and public health problem (Burelomova et al., 2018). The definition of intimate partner violence varies among organizations and agencies. According to the World Health Organization (WHO), intimate partner violence is any behaviour within an intimate relationship that causes physical or sexual harm to those in the relationship (Heise et al., 1999). It highlights the intentional use of physical force or power, threatened or actual, against oneself, another person, or against a group or community, that either results in or has a high likelihood of resulting in injury, death, psychological harm, maldevelopment, or deprivation (WHO, 1996). The latest definition is that intimate partner violence refers to behaviour by an intimate partner or ex-partner that causes physical, sexual, or psychological harm, including physical aggression, sexual coercion, psychological abuse, and controlling behaviours (Krug, Dahlberg, Mercy, Zwi, Lozano, 2002). Centers for Disease Control (CDC, 2006) defined it as a single event or on-going occurrences of physical, sexual, or psychological harm or threats of harm between two people who are or have been in a romantic relationship. Working with victims may affect the understanding of intimate partner violence as noticed by Argyroudi and Flora (2021) that counsellors' work experience broadens the meaning of intimate partner violence which seems to affect simultaneously the counsellors' sense of (their) vulnerability to violence. In many cultures, the acceptance of IPV is difficult as it is considered normal that men can beat or injure women or partners. James-Hawkins et al. (2021) found that men in Vietnam often viewed IPV against women as normal and justified violence occurring when a husband was 'hot-tempered', drunk, or when the wife was

R. T. Gopalan (✉)
Mahatma Gandhi Medical College and Hospital, Jaipur, India

seen as at fault. It has been noticed that the rate of violence between intimate partners has increased tremendously during Covid-19 due to the stay-at-home policy (Tochie et al., 2020). Although the existence of IPV is reported across the world, according to Burelomova et al. (2018), there is no universally accepted definition of IPV, or a conceptual framework that would encompass the complexity of the phenomenon.

Types of Intimate Partner Violence

According to Krug et al. (2002), violence can be generally divided into three main categories according to the characteristics of those committing the violent act: self-directed, interpersonal, and collective which can be further divided into subcategories such as physical, sexual, psychological, deprivation, or neglect based on the nature of the violent acts. Self-directed can be subdivided into suicidal behaviour (suicidal thoughts, attempted suicides, and completed suicides) and self-abuse (e.g. self-mutilation); interpersonal violence is subdivided into family and intimate partner violence (violence mainly between members of the family, as well as intimate partners such as child abuse, elder abuse, and IPV) and community violence (violence between people who are unrelated, and may or may not know each other such as random acts of violence, rape, and sexual assault by strangers, and violence at institutional settings such as workplaces, schools, prisons, or nursing homes). Collective violence can be subdivided into three categories: social, political, and economic (as cited in Gulina et al., 2018).

Based on the severity of violence, the WHO (2010) divided the Interpersonal violence into three levels such as level I abuse which includes pushing, shoving, grabbing, and throwing objects to intimidation or damage to property, and pets; and Level II abuse (kicking biting, and slapping) and Level III abuse (use of a weapon, choking, or attempt to strangulate).

Prevalence

According to the WHO (2021), 1 in 3 (30%) of women worldwide has been subjected to either physical and/or sexual intimate partner violence or nonpartner sexual violence in their lifetime. In a study on global, regional, and country estimates, based on data from the WHO Global Database on Prevalence of Violence Against Women, Maheu-Giroux et al. (2022) included 366 studies conducted between 2000 and 2018 from 161 countries, and the sample was two million women aged 15 years or older comprising 90% of the global population of women and girls. On Bayesian multilevel model to jointly estimate lifetime and past-year intimate partner violence, they reported that globally, 27% of ever-partnered women aged 15–49 years are estimated to have experienced physical or sexual, or both, intimate partner violence in their lifetime. Recent studies of intimate partner violence (IPV) in high-resource countries suggest that men and women may perpetrate similar rates of violence against their partners and approximately 1.5% reported perpetrating violence and 35% reported victimization in Tanzania (Reese et al., 2021). The prevalence of IPV during pregnancy in China was found to be 7.7%, one of the highest reported in Asia (Wang et al., 2017).

Breiding et al. (2014) reported that 15.8% of women and 9.5% of men in the United States experienced other forms of sexual violence by an intimate partner during their lifetimes, 22.3% of women and 14.0% of men during their lifetimes experienced severe physical violence by an intimate partner. They concluded that among victims of contact sexual violence, physical violence, or stalking by an intimate partner, an estimated 71.1% of women and 58.2% of men first experienced these or other forms of intimate partner violence before the age 25 years. In the first exploratory study of the unique and diverse body of interpersonal violence research in the Chinese-language and scientific literature over a 37-year period covering 1982–2018 Zhang et al. (2021) reported that the total contribution of IPV research has increased significantly over time in China, with increasing growth in the past two decades especially. IPV against women in Arab countries represents a public health and human rights problem and Elghossain et al. (2019) studied the different types of IPV an against women in the 22 countries of the Arab League, between 2000 and 2016, and they found prevalence (ever) ranged from 6% to more than half (59%) (physical); from 3% to 40% (sexual); and from 5% to 91% (emotional/psychological). The rate of interpersonal violence among Saudi women is comparable to those of other countries (Alhalal et al., 2021). Ali et al. (2021) reported an overall prevalence of psychological violence as 31.3–83.6%, physical 10.0–98.5%, sexual violence as 2.5–77.0%, physical and sexual combined as 1.0–68.0%, and any other type as 6.9–90.0% among women in Pakistan. Lifetime IPV prevalence in Kenya was found to be 60.3% (Morris et al., 2022). In a systematic review, Kadir Shahar et al. (2020) reported IPV prevalence in Malaysia between the range of 4.94% and 35.9%. According to Bagwell-Gray et al. (2015), sexual violence is a part of IPV, but identification is difficult due to differences in terminology and measurements.

Married women are at high risk for IPV, and according to Yaya et al. (2021), IPV among married women of childbearing age can significantly enhance their risk of adverse health outcomes such as injury and disability, depression and anxiety, unwanted pregnancies, premature labour, complications with delivery, and perinatal and neonatal mortality, and they reported prevalence of experiencing any form of violence among ever-married women in Egypt as 29.4%. They found that women experienced physical, emotional, and sexual violence at 26.7%, 17.8%, and 4.6%, respectively. Another study reported a similar prevalence of IPV among ever-married women in reproductive age in Ethiopia (Chernet & Cherie, 2020). The rate of IPV among interracial marriages was also reported high in many studies. Brownridge et al. (2021) mentioned that research from the United States and Canada suggested that interracial relationships tend to have an elevated prevalence of intimate partner violence (IPV).

While studying IPV, many researchers tried to identify IPV among women during their pregnancy time and the rates are alarmingly high. In a review on IPV prevalence during pregnancy worldwide, Román-Gálvez et al. (2021) reported physical IPV as 1.6–78% and psychological IPV as 1.8–67.4%. Wang et al. (2017) reported that prevalence of IPV during pregnancy in China is considerable and one of the highest reported in Asia, and they found prevalence of IPV during pregnancy as 7.7%. The prevalence of IPV among pregnant women in Bengaluru, southern India, was found to be 3.7%, which was less compared to figures reported from other Indian study settings (Nath et al., 2021).

Intimate partner violence was noticed in special populations too. Hughes et al. (2011) mentioned that IPV occurs at elevated and disproportionate rates among women and men with disabilities, and the reported prevalence of any type of IPV among women with disabilities ranged from 26.0% to 90.0% for a lifetime and that for men ranged from 28.7% to 86.7% for lifetime. Wei et al. (2021) investigated the prevalence of IPV among men sex with men in China and reported 153 (35.5%) experienced any IPV experiences among 431 participants, and 119 (27.6%) reported themselves as being the perpetrator. Recent studies also found that women may perpetrate similar rates of violence against their partners and approximately 1.5% reported perpetrating violence (Reese et al., 2021).

Many studies reported an increase in IPV during COVID-19 pandemic and Peitzmeier et al. (2021) reported an increase in IPV in the majority of the sample (64.2%), IPV new to the relationship (34.1%), or of increased severity during COVID-19 (26.6%), representing 9.7% of the overall sample. Walsh et al. (2021) observed an increased prevalence of IPV perpetration (15.17%), 34.44% of which was new or more frequent and victimization prevalence was 14.95%, of which 46.88% was new or more frequent among gay, bisexual, and other men who have sex with men during COVID situation. In a study on IPV among adult Arab women before and during the COVID-19 lockdown, 490 adult Arab women aged 18 years have participated and half of the women reported that exposure to any type of IPV and exposure to psychological, physical, and sexual violence has significantly increased during the lockdown compared to before the lockdown (El-Nimr et al., 2021). It was also noticed that psychosocial factors like essential workers, pregnant, unable to afford rent, family income, unemployed/underemployed or had recent changes to their job, loss of job, had partners with recent changes to employment, those who had gotten tested or tested positive for COVID-19, and whether the husband lost his job during lockdown were associated with an increase in the IPV and lockdown affected the women's help-seeking behaviour (Peitzmeier et al., 2021; El-Nimr et al., 2021; Vives-Cases et al., 2021).

While considering the prevalence rate of IPV among different continents it can be confirmed that IPV exists and the rate is increasing. It is also possible that many women and men started reporting IPV without considering the stigma and stereotypes associate with IPV. The reports of IPV during pregnancy time was also high rate and IPV occurred in interracial and same-sex marriages, among person with disabilities which indicates the presence of IPV across the population. It is also interesting to notice that women perpetrate IPV although the rate is less.

Risk Factors for IPV

Intimate partner and sexual violence are the results of factors occurring at the individual, family, community and wider society levels that interact with each other to increase or reduce risk (protective) and some are associated with being a perpetrator of violence, experiencing violence or both (WHO, 2021). The same has been observed by many researchers that IPV results from a combination of factors including power differentials between partners and attitudes about the acceptability of using violence (Reese et al., 2021).

Individual Factors

Individual factors like women much younger than their partners, educational attainment, having children, partner's alcohol consumption, partner's decision-making, marital discord, and dissatisfaction; and difficulties in communicating between partners were found to be associated with IPV (Reese et al., 2021; WHO, 2021). Being housewives with children, controlling behaviour of partners and women who reported being afraid of their partner had a greater risk of IPV victimization (Occean et al., 2021). On personality factors related to IPV among teenage dating couples, Abilleira et al. (2019) found that aggression traits, antisocial characteristics, and mania were predicted the perpetration of IPV by girls but no particular traits were related to boys. Many factors from childhood also contribute to IPV, and Kouyoumdjian et al. (2013) reported risk factors for IPV from childhood and early adulthood as sexual abuse in childhood or adolescence, earlier age at first sex, lower levels of education, and forced first sex, and contemporary risk factors as younger age, married status with partner same or younger age, alcohol consumption before sex and acceptability of beating partner. Based on the ecological framework, Sabri et al. (2014) found from India that factors related to severe physical IPV and injuries included low or no education, low socioeconomic status, rural residence, the greater number of children, and separated or divorced marital status, husbands' problem drinking, jealousy, suspicion, control, and emotionally and sexually abusive behaviours.

Studies found a relationship between sexual orientation and IPV and in a study to explore the relationship between sexual orientation (heterosexual, homosexual, and bisexual), and demographic, cultural, and psychological factors and intimate partner violence among Hispanic men. Gonzalez-Guarda et al. (2013) reported that differences in education, income, and self-esteem were noted across participants identifying as heterosexual, homosexual, and bisexual, and bisexual Hispanic men had more chances for the perpetration of IPV compared to Homosexual Hispanic men.

There are common characteristics between perpetrators of IPV and homicide offenders. Abrunhosa et al. (2021) reported that IPV perpetrators were more prone to perpetrate violent behaviours against an intimate partner or ex-partner than intimate partner homicide (IPH) or intimate partner homicide (AIPH) offenders, the use of weapons and separation from the victim increases the probability of committing IPH or AIPH and being divorced, having no children, and committing other crimes than domestic violence were predictors of AIPH.

Jewkes et al. (2017) identified four groups of variables to be important in the experience of past-year sexual and/or physical IPV such as poverty, all childhood trauma, quarrelling and women's limited control in relationships, and partner factors (substance abuse, unemployment, and infidelity), and married women were also more at risk. According to Santambrogio et al. (2019), alcohol and substance use disorders and childhood abuse are the most risk factors related to IPV. Low educational attainment, IPV exposure in girlhood, and polygamy were significantly associated with the experience of IPV (Morris et al., 2022). Living in rural areas, being divorced, having primary and secondary education, being 25–39 years old, and being poor are found to be predictors of IPV against women in Ethiopia (Chernet & Cherie, 2020). The characteristics 'number of children' and 'unplanned pregnancy' were determined as risk factors for experiencing violence during pregnancy (Wang et al., 2017). Lower education background, lower socioeconomic status, history/ current substance abuse, exposure to prior abuse or violence, violence-condoning attitude; husbands or partners' controlling behaviour, substance abuse and involvement in fights and lack of social support were the reasons for IPV in Malaysia (Kadir Shahar et al., 2020). Nath et al. (2021) noted in the multivariate analysis that higher age (above 20 years) and the presence of depression were the risk factors for IPV in India. Women residing in urban areas, having only a primary-level education, being followers of Islam, and having husbands with no education reported having higher odds of experiencing any form of IPV in Egypt (Yaya et al., 2021). Victims possessed high morale, hopes, and positiveness (good virtues) that made them to tolerate others and interpersonal violence and made sacrifices with poor self-esteem and coping styles (Jadeja & Gopalan, 2016; Jagtap, Gopalan & Dahiya, 2017). Research findings from different countries showed that the risk factors for IPV related to particular sociocultural backgrounds though common factors are evident.

Some studies have found that particular occupations have the risk for IPV such as military personnel and being unemployed, experiencing abuse in childhood and having a partner who consumed alcohol increased partners' vulnerability to IPV (Igwe et al., 2021).

Gender

Some studies pointed out the importance of gender in IPV, and usually, it is considered that men have the authority to control female which is considered socially and culturally acceptable. According to WHO (2021), gender inequality and norms on the acceptability of violence against women are a root cause of violence against women. Kyler-Yano and Mankowski (2021) argued that integrated multiple dimensions of human diversity (e.g. culture, gender, and power) is important to understand IPV. They observed that Patriarchal gender role norms consistently predicted IPV perpetration by Asian American men that greater enculturation (Asian cultural identification) was associated with more patriarchal gender role norms and violence in the family of origin consistently predicted later IPV perpetration as an adult. Dako-Gyeke et al. (2019) explored gender norms held by men and women that might contribute to male perpetration of intimate partner violence in Ghana and reported that male perpetrated IPV is a common phenomenon in the studied community and woman's noncompliance with gender norms provided context for the male partner to enforce societal conformity through IPV. In addition to that, alcohol abuse exacerbates IPV. The influence of gender in IPV also noticed in immigrants by many studies. Immigrants arrive with limited support systems, wrestle with changing family dynamics, and may have to adapt to new gender roles and IPV often occurs in the private domain of the family and poses serious risks to women, children, families, and the broader society (Okeke-Ihejirika et al., 2020).

While considering the gender, men are more likely than women to report perpetrating IPV but recent findings suggesting that IPV may be bidirectional within relationships (Mulawa et al., 2018). According to Reese et al. (2021) studies of intimate partner violence (IPV) in high-resource countries suggested that men and women may perpetrate similar rates of violence against their partners. Violence among same sex relation also indicates the fact that it is not gender but power and other factors are responsible for IPV. Among male sex with male, self-esteem and age of first homosexual intercourse were identified as two significant factors contributing to IPV (Wei et al., 2021). As the society changed a lot from the traditional way of intimate relation between male and female to same sex relations and bisexual relations, the perception of relationship especially towards intimate relationship also changed drastically. The prior concept of male dominance and female submissiveness in heterosexual relation no longer applicable in same sex relations and the dynamics of such relations depends on many other dimensions and hence the vulnerabilities to IPV. The findings regarding perpetration of IPV by females in heterosexual relations also needs to be considered importantly and future studies need to focus on the risk factors among them.

Cultural Factors

Cultural factors are important in the causes of IPV which mainly explain the definition of masculinity and femininity in a society that set the boundaries and justification to the violence perpetrated to the opposite gender. In most culture, violence, especially IPV, is considered as normal not an offence. James-Hawkins et al. (2019) noticed that cultural definitions of masculinity in Vietnam and changes in women's participation in the labour force have contributed to status conflicts that normalize IPV as part of masculine superiority and violence is incorporated into the cultural definition of masculinity and illustrated how men use this definition to minimize their own and other men's perpetration. Sikweyiya et al. (2020) have observed similar pattern in Ghana. The social, cultural, and religious factors – stemming from patriarchy leads to construction of a traditional masculinity which included the notion that decision-making in the home is a man's prerogative, there should be rigid and distinct gender roles, men's perceptions of owning female partners and having the right to have sex with them whenever they desire, and the notion that wife beating is legitimate discipline and this form of masculinity that men used varying forms of violence against their female partners. Moreover, men use violence as a tactic for controlling women and emphasizing their authority and power over them. The cross-cultural constructions of IPV perpetration among men in treatment for substance use in England and Brazil also showed that substance use and IPV are culturally constructed and contextually defined (Radcliffe et al., 2017).

Social Factors

Sociodemographic vulnerabilities factors are important in predicting IPV, and sociodemographic risk markers (i.e. age, income, and education) in addition to couple functioning were found to be associated with IPV (Pu et al., 2021). Other factors included women's exposure to domestic violence in childhood, perpetration of IPV, and adherence to social norms that accept husbands' violence (Sabri et al., 2014). Attitudinal acceptance and justification of wife-beating and those who witnessed their father beating their mother reported high level of IPV perpetration (Reese et al., 2021). In a study to understand the extent to which the general public justifies intimate partner violence (IPV) to explain perpetration, victimization, and response to this behaviour, Waltermaurer (2012) reported that females tended to report a higher rate of IPV justification than males and younger respondents tended to report a higher rate IPV justification than their older counterparts. Peer behaviour also found to influence IPV and young people's perceptions that their peers perpetrate relationship violence have been shown to increase the incidence of self-reported perpetration (McKool et al., 2021). Many other factors like family of origin, alcohol and mental illness were found to influence IPV. Orozco-Vargas et al. (2021) reported that family-of-origin violence was significantly related to intimate partner violence via maladaptive emotion regulation strategies in the Mexican population. Exposure to parental IPV and past history of exposure to violence were linked with IPV (Reese et al., 2021; WHO, 2021). Among men, having ever consumed alcohol and experiencing childhood violence were associated with increased risk of most forms of IPV in Dar es Salaam, Tanzania (Mulawa et al., 2018). Victimization was found among women whose partners drank alcohol and had a polygynous relationship (Occean et al., 2021). Devries et al. (2014) examined the evidence of association between intimate partner physical or sexual violence (IPV) victimization and alcohol consumption in women and found a positive association. During the lockdown due to the COVID scenario in Uganda, Miller et al. (2022) reported increased alcohol consumption which exacerbated physical or verbal IPV and increased violence.

Mental illness was associated or mediated with the risk for IPV, and it was noted that greater ADHD symptoms severity, particularly inattention, indicated higher rates of psychological IPV perpetration and victimization, conduct disorder significantly predicted IPV perpetration both with and without injury, and while controlling for CD and hyperactivity/impulsivity, inattention independently predicted young adult IPV perpetration without injury. Mahoney and Iverson (2020) reported that alcohol use severity significantly moderated the association between PTSD symptoms and past-year physical IPV, especially with high levels of alcohol use, and no moderating effect was found.

The causes or risk factors for IPV have been a hot topic in the literature related to IPV and many postulated cultural factors, gender, power, mental health, personality factors, and use of alcohol and drugs as the major reasons for its occurrence but many studies are required to understand exact causes of IPV.

Theories of IPV

Many theories attempted to explain domestic violence, and these theories are on individualist, interactional, and sociocultural perspectives (Miller et al., 1999), and only major ones are described below.

Feminist Theory

According to McPhail, the feminist perspective has been one of the predominant theoretical models in the domestic violence field since the early 1970s, which is based on the assumption that the patriarchal system is the root cause of domestic violence and males possess more power and control over females in this system and considered male as the perpetrator and female as the victim (Dobash & Dobash, 1979; Walker, 1979). The main feature of feminist definitions is based on the use and abuse of power and dominance acquired from the patriarchal society and while applying to explain IPV, this single factor cause failed in many ways. While looking into the evolution of the feminist view, the understanding of IPV also changed accordingly. As mentioned by Kesselman et al. (2008), the first wave of feminism began in the mid-eighteenth century to abolish slavery, voting rights, and the right to inherit property and the second wave of feminism dates back to the mid-twentieth century for advocating for civil rights but failed to look at how race intersected with gender which made left out of the colour women that lead to the third-wave feminism to include marginalized people of both genders and different races, classes, and sexual orientations and it was termed as intersectionality coined by Crenshaw (1990). Moreover, studies on IPV experiences not only focused on women but men too which again put the question of a symmetric or asymmetric view on IPV. Overall, it can be said that feminism explained IPV from a single view to an intersectional view that relationship violence leads to an antioppression where as social justice perspective says patriarchy lies beside other oppressive factors which leads to IPV (Crenshaw, 1990; Kesselman et al., 2008; Taylor, 1998). According to George & Stith, most state Batterer Intervention Program standards based on second wave feminist perspective as the guiding framework that patriarchy is the overarching cause of IPV, that men are almost always the primary aggressors and that gender resocialization should be a key factor in treating all offenders which should be replaced with third-wave feminist move characterized by intersectional, socially just, feminist position. This movement should move beyond one-size-fits-all programme policies and interventions and make this change treatment providers or court officers will need to assess each offender to determine appropriate intervention(s).

Attachment Theory

The attachment theory by Bowlby (1988) has been used to explain intimate partner violence which is based on the influence of early childhood experiences on later attachments children can have four types of attachment such as secure, insecure-dismissing, insecure-preoccupied, and disorganized. Research on adult attachment became predominant during the 1980s, and adult attachment was perceived in two dimensions avoidance, and anxiety and the feelings of fear, uneasiness regarding intimacy, and difficulty accepting dependency on others are the predominant characteristics of the avoidance dimension while the anxious dimension characterized by reliability and availability of attachment figure. Based on these four prototypes were emerged such as the secure which shows low levels of avoidance and low levels of anxiety; preoccupied shows low levels of avoidance, but high levels of anxiety; dismissing shows a high level of avoidance and low levels of anxiety and the fearful style. people with an anxious attachment would tend to be ambivalent towards power and dominated people with an anxious attachment would tend to be ambivalent towards power and domination (Mikulincer & Shaver, 2007; Velotti et al., 2018; Shaver & Mikulincer, 2011). As noted by Finkel and Slotter (2007), individuals characterized by strong attachment anxiety deal with attachment threats by employing 'hyper activating strategies' which would lead individuals 'to feel chronically frustrated due to the unfulfilled need for demonstrations of love and commitment' and to engage in 'catastrophic appraisal of interpersonal conflicts, the perpetuation of the resulting negative affect, and conflict escalation'. The frequent frustration of attachment needs and negative effect characteristic of strongly anxiously attached individuals increases the likelihood that they will experience impulses towards IPV when facing threats to their attachment bonds. According to Hazan and Shaver (1987) in insecurely attached partners, one partner may perceive a threat when the other partner claims autonomy as if leaving he won't ever get back again, and he gains reassurance only by maintaining proximity and control over him and the other partner may perceive partner's need for closeness and intimacy as oppressing and threatening for its autonomy and this conflicting perspective can easily lead to a misunderstanding that often generates violence, perpetrated by one partner or both.

Many empirical pieces of evidence were there to support attachment theory in the explanation for interpersonal violence. Godbout et al. (2009) found that early exposure to parental violence in the family of origin is associated with adult IPV and dyadic adjustment, through attachment representations which stressed that exposure to violence during childhood to IPV and marital distress leads to abandonment anxiety and avoidance of intimacy. Studies have shown that exposure to domestic violence in childhood causes externalizing and internalizing problems and chances of becoming perpetrators of IPV in later life (Ryngala, 2003; Kincaid, 1982; Dutton, 1988). High levels of female attachment anxiety predicted high levels of male-perpetrated verbal and physical females and the female fear of abandonment and rejection may be a risk factor for becoming a victim of violence (Doumas et al., 2008). Doumas et al. (2008) noted that the 'mispairing' of an avoidant male partner with an anxious female partner was associated with both male and female violence.

On contrary, many studies could not find annelation between attachment theory with IPV. In their systematic review, Velotti et al. (2018) reported no significant associations between insecure attachment and IPV victimization or perpetration.

Cycle of Violence

The cycle of violence theory was proposed by Lenore Walker (1979) in the book *The Battered Woman*, and she proposed that three distinct stages are associated with recurring battering in cases of domestic violence such as the tension-building phase, the acute battering incident, and the honeymoon phase (tension-reduction theory) and violence follows a predictable pattern of these cycles and repeat itself and, the length of time required to complete it becomes shorter and the violence within it increases (Wilson, 2022). In the tension-building stage, there will be a gradual escalation of tension and fights and shouting are frequent but victims consider them isolated ones which can be controlled. In the violent episode phase, some trigger may lead to violent behaviour, mainly physical and then comes the reconciliation/honeymoon phase in which the abuser promises not to repeat it and shower lots of love and pampering on the victim and the victim may hope that it may not repeat but after some period the same cycle repeats. Though this theory is considered very important in the area of abuse and interpersonal violence, it is criticized for many reasons like lack of empirical approach and the difficulty in applying the cycle of violence universally (Dutton & Golant, 1997; Barnett, 2016).

Exchange Theory

Exchange theory is a behavioural approach to understanding social relationships in general. The assumptions and propositions of social exchange theory and control theory contributed to the exchange theory of family violence which states that individuals will use force and violence in their relationships with intimates and family members if they believe that the rewards of force and violence outweigh the costs of such behaviour because human interaction is guided by the pursuit of rewards and the avoidance of punishment and costs and a person who supplies reward services to another obliges the other to fulfil a reciprocal obligation; and thus, the second individual must furnish benefits to the first and if reciprocal exchange occurs, the interaction continues. However, if reciprocity is not received, the interaction will be broken off (Blau, 1964). Exchange theory can therefore be thought of as a perspective that emphasizes motivations for violence (Gelles, 1982). Willliams (1992) empirically supported this theory that those who were powerful and favouring the idea of hitting partners perceived the costs of arrest as low likely to assault their partners.

Identity Theory

The identity theory, formulated by Henri Tajfel and John Turner in 1979, argues that the meanings that people give themselves develop from the roles that they fulfil (Keenan, 2020). According to Mcleod (2008), this theory argues that people divide their world into an in-group and an out-group, and might discriminate against the out-group, thus enhancing their self-image. As mentioned by Stets and Burke (2005) in all interactions, the goal of individuals is to confirm their identities and when their identities are not confirmed, persons may control others in the situation to make them respond differently to confirm their identities. If the control does not work, aggression may be used as a last resort to obtain control and, in turn, confirmation of identity. Thus, identity theory can help explain domestic violence by showing how a lack of identity confirmation at the individual level is tied to the control process and aggression at the interactive level (http://criminal-justice.iresearchnet.com/).

Social Learning Theory

According to Bandura, learned behaviours are reinforced in childhood and can continue into adulthood through operant conditioning and act as a coping response to stress or as a method of conflict resolution. When applied to domestic violence, the theory states that violence is learned through role models provided by the family either directly or indirectly is reinforced in childhood, and continues in adulthood as a coping response to stress or as a method of conflict resolution which is always mentioned as the cycle of violence or intergenerational transmission theory, and it is a popular explanatory perspective in the marital violence literature (Ehrensaft et al., 2003: http://criminal-justice.iresearchnet.com/).

Victim-Blaming Theory

Victim blaming can happen in the context of domestic violence or IPV, and the term victim blaming is a devaluing act that occurs when the victim(s) of a crime or an accident is held responsible for the crimes that have been committed against them ('Victim Blame', 2007). Blaming the women who are treated with violence by their intimate partners is a form of second victimization that can undermine their mental health and hinder their recovery and psychosocial adjustment. In her study, Christine supported the existing findings that gender, lifetime trauma exposure, recent IPV victimization, and mental health symptoms for depression and PTSD are related to victim blame attributions and indirect IPV exposure increases the likelihood that a person will experience direct IPV victimization. According to Flood and Pease (2006), research should explore the reasons for victim-blaming attitudes by examining how these are influenced by factors at the individual, group and community levels and by macro-cultural determinants such as income inequality, legislative framework, gender role beliefs, patriarchal or 'honour' cultures, and gender inequality.

Though theories attempted to explain IPV, it was observed that a single theory doesn't fit all. As IPV is more influenced by culture, social perspectives, belief systems, gender inequality, stereotypes, attitudes, and behaviour, explaining it through a single or double lens will not capture all aspects. The underlying phenomena related to IPV are yet to be explored fully on different levels and thus more research is to be focused on multifactors on different dimensions.

Causes of IPV

The causes of IPV can be on different levels such as individual, relationship, community, and societal levels. On an individual level, many factors are associated with IPV such as young age, low education, alcohol and drug abuse, and history of childhood abuse. In a study, Abramsky et al. (2011) used data from ten countries included in the WHO Multi-country Study on Women's Health and Domestic Violence to identify factors that are consistently associated with abuse across sites and reported that alcohol abuse, cohabitation, young age, attitudes supportive of wife-beating, having outside sexual partners, experiencing childhood abuse, growing up with domestic violence, and being victim of IPV or perpetrating other forms of violence lead to the increased the risk of IPV. Orozco-Vargas et al. (2021) reported that family-of-origin violence was significantly related to intimate partner violence via maladaptive emotion regulation strategies in the Mexican population. Among men, having ever consumed alcohol and experiencing childhood violence were associated with increased risk of most forms of IPV in Dar es Salaam, Tanzania (Mulawa et al., 2018). Devries et al. (2014) examined the evidence of association between intimate partner physical or sexual violence (IPV) victimization and alcohol consumption in women and found a positive association. During the lockdown due to the COVID scenario in Uganda, Miller et al. (2022) reported increased alcohol consumption which exacerbated physical or verbal IPV and increased violence. Recent studies looked into the individual factors associated with the acceptability of IPV, and Atomssa, Medhanyie, and Fisseha (2021) reported 69% as acceptability and found women's education with secondary and above, partner's education secondary and above, women aged 35–49 years, fully empowered in household-level decision-making, literate and perceived existence of a law that prevents IPV were significantly associated with women's acceptance of IPV. Sandberg et al. (2021) reported that network characteristics affect IPV, and if the network is more acceptable towards IPV, more IPV can happen.

On the relationship level, factors like marital issues, dissatisfaction in prelateships, jealousy, economic hardships, and disparity among couples are related to IPV. In a systematic review and meta-analysis, Yakubovich et al. (2018) found the strongest evidence for modifiable risk factors for IPV against women were unplanned pregnancy and less educated parents. Jewkes (2002) mentioned that violence was used as a strategy to resolve the conflict among partners and reported relationships full of conflict, especially those in which conflicts occur about finances, jealousy, and women's gender role transgressions were more violent than peaceful relationships and were more vulnerable to IPV.

Various social and cultural factors are associated with IPV such as low socioeconomic strata, gender inequalities, and acceptable attitude towards violence and IPV. Priestley and Lee (2021) reported that being in a coresidential union, residing in an urban area, and having fair or poor health were significant demographic characteristics associated with IPV perpetration and witnessing violence between parents in childhood, being physically hit after age 15 years, and having a controlling nature were significant socialization and attitudinal predictors of perpetrating recent IPV. Cultural factors are important in the causes of IPV and James-Hawkins et al. (2019) noticed that cultural definitions of masculinity in Vietnam and changes in women's participation in the labour force have contributed to status conflicts that normalize IPV as part of masculine superiority and violence is incorporated into the cultural definition of masculinity and explained how the concept of masculinity used to normalize their own and other men's perpetration and similar pattern was observed in Ghana (Sikweyiya et al., 2020). The social, cultural, and religious factors stemming from patriarchy lead to construction of a traditional masculinity which included the notion that decision-making in the home is a man's authority with rigid gender roles, perception of owning female partners with right to have sex with them whenever desire occurs, and the notion that wife beating is legitimate discipline and this form of masculinity that men used varying forms of violence against their female partners. Moreover, men use violence as a tactic for controlling women and emphasizing their authority and power over them. The cross- cultural constructions of IPV perpetration among men in treatment for substance use in England and Brazil showed that substance use and IPV are culturally constructed and contextually defined (Radcliffe et al., 2017).

Kyler-Yano and Mankowski (2021) argued that integrated multiple dimensions of human diversity (e.g. culture, gender, and power) is important to understand IPV. They observed that Patriarchal gender role norms consistently predicted IPV perpetration by Asian American men that greater enculturation (Asian cultural iden- tification) was associated with more patriarchal gender role norms and violence in the family of origin consistently predicted later IPV perpetration as an adult. Immigrants arrive with limited support systems, wrestle with changing family dynamics, and may have to adapt to new gender roles and IPV often occurs in the private domain of the family and poses serious risks to women, children, families, and the broader society (Okeke-Ihejirika et al., 2020). Dako-Gyeke et al. (2019) explored gender norms held by men and women that might contribute to male per- petration of intimate partner violence in Ghana and reported that male perpetrated IPV is a common phenomenon in the studied community and woman's noncompli- ance with gender norms provided context for the male partner to enforce societal conformity through IPV. In addition to that, alcohol abuse exacerbates IPV.

In order to understand the causes of IPV, it is important to explore the vulnerable and risk factors for IPV at multilevels as well as the factors favouring the attitude of IPV on individual, relationship, social, and cultural levels. Recent studies have started focusing on what normalizes the IPV among community, and many more studies are required to make conclusions.

Consequences of IPV

The impact of IPV among the victims were found to be very detrimental and long term in terms of physical, emotional, psychological, economic, and social injuries. On physical level, increased health problems such as injury, chronic pain, fibromy- algia, gastrointestinal disorders like irritable bowel syndrome and gynaecological signs including sexually-transmitted diseases were found repeatedly associated with after effects of IPV and the impact was detrimental outcomes to mothers and infants if it happened during pregnancies (Campbell, 2002; Plazaola-Castaño & Pérez, 2004). Normann et al. (2020) reported in their study on breastfeeding out- comes (initiation, duration and exclusive breastfeeding) in women exposed to IPV in any form (physical, psychological, or sexual) and at any stage (1 year pre preg- nancy, during, or post pregnancy) that IPV exposure appears to associate negatively with some breastfeeding outcomes such as shortened breastfeeding duration, early termination of exclusive breastfeeding, and reduced breastfeeding initiation.

It is well established that intimate male partner violence (IPV) has a high impact on victims emotional, psychological, and mental health domains. The major impacts noticed were sadness, anger, self-blame, suicidal thoughts and attempts, depression, and posttraumatic stress disorder. Many studies repeatedly reported the association between IPV and depressive symptoms (Bacchus et al., 2018). On a systematic review and meta-analysis of longitudinal studies, Devries et al. (2013) noticed that in women, IPV was associated with incident depressive symptoms, and depressive symptoms with incident IPV and also IPV was associated with incident suicide attempts, and in men IPV was associated with incident depressive symptoms but not with suicide attempts. Blasco-Ros et al. (2010) reported on a follow-up study that while women exposed to physical/psychological IPV recovered their mental health status with a significant decrease in depressive, anxiety and PTSD symptoms. Soleimani et al. (2017) noticed their study that various forms of abuse are different from each other in terms of predicting a victim's mental health. Pico-Alfonso et al. (2006) observed that women exposed to physical/psychological and psychological IPV had a higher incidence and severity of depressive and anxiety symptoms, PTSD, and thoughts of suicide than control women and sexual violence was associated with a higher severity of depressive symptoms. The authors suggested that psychological IPV is as detrimental as physical IPV, with the exception of effects on suicidality, which emphasizes that psychological IPV should be considered a major type of violence by all professionals involved.

IPV is known to have resulted in occupational loss among victims or made them incapable of doing their work and thus faced economic crises which again worsened the situation or resulted in repeated abuse. The victims also faced insults or isolation or withdrawal from the society due to the stigma attached with IPV.

Though studies have focused mainly on females as victims, it is also necessary to look in to the impacts of IPV on males as victims. Many studies have pointed out that different types of assault had different impacts on males and females and future studies need to delineate these aspects.

Forensic Assessment and Investigations

There is no universal protocol for assessing and investigating domestic violence; hence, limitations appear in investigation, assessment, and report writing, and many studies have been indicating the same. Loots and Saayman (2019) noticed in a study that insufficient medicolegal documentation, wound description and evidence collection, by medical practitioners was identified across all wounding modalities and the medicolegal documentation in cases of IPV was suboptimal, with many important parameters not being routinely recorded, which is likely to impact negatively on criminal investigations and downstream legal proceedings. In a study on analysis of forensic documentation of domestic violence, Klopfstein et al. (2010) reported that domestic violence against female patients was documented in 0.4% over 6 years which was far below the proportions expected from the data and they opined that quality of the forensic documentation was poor and usually insufficient for criminal prosecution and mentioned about the requirement training for clinicians in the forensic aspects of medical records.

Police officers are typically the first responders when victims of intimate partner violence (IPV) report abuse, hence their attitudes towards IPV and victim blaming are crucial, and Kruahiran et al. (2022) reported significant effects of ambivalent sexism and victim's gender role on attitudes towards IPV and victim blaming by police officers and recommended sensitivity training programmes. In another study on police officers' views of IPV as well as whether policing philosophy is related to officers' attitudes towards IPV, it was found that officers expressed problematic views of IPV such as simplification of IPV, victim blaming, patriarchal attitudes towards women, and presumption of victim noncooperation and progressive views of IPV such as recognition of the complexity of IPV and awareness of barriers to leaving, and they considered IPV as serious problem and worthy of police intervention. Studies pointed out the fact that training programmes are required for those professionals involved in forensic investigations and procedures related to IPV.

Prevention

Many preventive strategies were used to tackle the problem of IPV including screening, education, teaching healthy relations and behaviours for children and adolescents, financial and occupational support for survivors, and family and social support. Many preventive techniques did not achieve the expected outcome fully which raised the question of implementing and modifying existing preventive methods. According to Sikweyiya et al. (2020), developers of interventions to prevent IPV need to recognize that there is a coherent configuration of aspirations, social norms and behaviours that are drawn on by some men to justify their use of IPV. Breiding et al. (2014) proposed that primary prevention of sexual violence, stalking, and intimate partner violence should begin early as these were experienced at a young age and strategies to be addressed known risk factors for perpetration and by changing social norms and behaviours by using bystander and other prevention strategies to deal with sexual violence and stalking victimization. They also suggested that primary prevention of intimate partner violence should focus on the promotion of healthy relationship behaviours and other protective factors, to help adolescents develop these positive behaviours before their first relationships. James-Hawkins et al. (2019) suggested that attempts to reduce IPV must address constructions of masculinity and the sociohistorical context of IPV by providing gender-sensitivity training and giving opportunity to assess how the concept of masculinity contributes their own families and communities.

Intervention

The treatment for IPV mainly focus on victims, perpetrator and couple together and many different paradigms are used to address stress, safety, social isolation and intimate relations, and emotional turmoil. The predominant treatments for victims are cognitive-behavioural therapy (CBT), interpersonal psychotherapy (IPT), eye movement desensitization reprocessing (EMDR), and emotional regulation and for perpetrators are feminist sociocultural and cognitive-behavioural therapy and couple treatment for both. According to Karakurt et al. (2022), the chronic physical and psychological effects of intimate partner violence (IPV) are complex, long-lasting, and chronic, and require treatments focusing on improving mental health issues, safety, and support, and various psychosocial intervention programmes are being implemented to improve survivor wellbeing. In their systematic review and meta-analysis, it was found that interventions could improve anxiety, depression, violence prevention, safety, health, self-esteem, social support, and stress management and also reported that empowerment plays a vital role, especially in the treatment of depression and posttraumatic stress disorder (PTSD). A systematic review on help-seeking and barriers to care in IPSV by Wright et al. (2021) reported that experiencing IPSV compared to experiencing nonsexual IPV (i.e. physical or psychological IPV) may increase help-seeking for medical, legal, and social services and barriers to seeking care in IPSV included social stigma, fear, and difficulty for individuals in identifying IPSV behaviours in their relationships as abuse. They also found that help-seeking can reduce the risk of future IPSV and decrease poor mental health outcomes. Orozco-Vargas et al. (2021) highlighted the importance of emotional regulation strategies in order to reduce IPV. Paphitis et al. (2022) suggested that a holistic view of the problem and individualized and trauma-informed support is required while using psychosocial interventions to improve the mental health of women survivors of IPV.

Social support was found to be a significant contributing factor to recovery, especially mental health and it was associated with increased resilience. Social support indicators including social connectedness, stronger network ties, and perceived supportive communities are key factors in fostering resilience among abused women, and it was reported that supportive community and availability of emergency fund helped women to be more resilient. Interventions should aim to promote stronger and more supportive social networks and increase women's utilization of formal support services (Blasco-Ros et al., 2010). According to Blasco-Ros et al. (2010), longitudinal studies are needed to improve knowledge of factors promoting or impeding health recovery to guide the formulation of policy at individual, social, and criminal justice levels. Burns et al. (2021) noticed that IPV-related training assists clinicians in making more accurate assessments of patients presenting with clinically significant relationship problems and recommended that IPV-related training programmes should be repeated, multicomponent, and include experiential training exercises, and guidelines for distinguishing normative relationship problems from clinically significant relationship problems and maltreatment.

Conclusion

Research pointed out the fact that intimate partner violence (IPV) is prevalent not only in heterosexual relationships but in the gay, lesbian, bisexual, and transgender communities; hence, the focus on victimization has undergone major changes. The traditional way of looking into the problems of IPV like male–female issues needs to be changed to different dimensions so as the dynamics. The causative factors, psychological vulnerabilities, relationship-specific factors, social and community factors like beliefs, stereotypies, gender-related assumptions in relationships, power, role, and responsibilities are required to be studied in different types of relationships as indicated by studies (e.g. Jadeja & Gopalan, 2016; Jagtap, Gopalan & Dahiya, 2017). As the different types of abuses in IPV result in various impacts, future studies need to focus on it to tailor suitable prevention and intervention methods in addition to the legal policies. The legal aid and policies for IPV mainly targeted help females in many countries, and this stance has to be changed when looking into the fact of the increased number of victimizations of males while females as perpetrators. As IPV is more closed to sociocultural factors, policies in the criminal justice system are to be amended in the view of scientific findings in the field.

References

Abilleira, M. P., Rodicio-García, M. L., Vázquez, T. C., Deus, M. P. R. D., & Cortizas, M. J. I. (2019). Personality characteristics of a sample of violent adolescents against their partners. Psicologia: Reflexão e Crítica, 32. https://doi.org/10.1186/s41155-019-0122-7.

Abramsky, T., Watts, C. H., Garcia-Moreno, C., Devries, K., Kiss, L., Ellsberg, M., et al. (2011). What factors are associated with recent intimate partner violence? Findings from the WHO multi-country study on women's health and domestic violence. BMC Public Health, 11(1), 1–17. https://doi.org/10.1186/1471-2458-11-109

Abrunhosa, C., de Castro Rodrigues, A., Cruz, A. R., Gonçalves, R. A., & Cunha, O. (2021). Crimes against women: From violence to homicide. Journal of Interpersonal Violence, 36(23–24), NP12973–NP12996. https://doi.org/10.1177/0886260520905547

Alhalal, E., Ta'an, W. A., & Alhalal, H. (2021). Intimate partner violence in Saudi Arabia: A systematic review. Trauma, Violence, & Abuse, 22(3), 512–526. https://doi.org/10.1177/1524838019867156

Ali, T. S., Karmaliani, R., Farhan, R., Hussain, S., & Jawad, F. (2021). Intimate partner violence against women: A comprehensive depiction of Pakistani literature. Eastern Mediterranean Health Journal, 27(2), 183–194. https://doi.org/10.26719/emhj.20.107

Argyroudi, A., & Flora, K. (2021 Jul). Meaning attribution to intimate partner violence by counselors who support women with intimate partner violence experiences in Greece. Journal of Interpersonal Violence, 36(13–14), 6578–6595. https://doi.org/10.1177/0886260518819877

Atomssa, E. M., Medhanyie, A. A., & Fisseha, G. (2021). Individual and community-level risk factors of women's acceptance of intimate partner violence in Ethiopia: multilevel analysis of 2011 Ethiopian Demographic Health Survey. BMC women's health, 21(1), 1–14.

Bacchus, L. J., Ranganathan, M., Watts, C., & Devries, K. (2018). Recent intimate partner violence against women and health: A systematic review and meta-analysis of cohort studies. BMJ Open, 8(7), e019995. https://doi.org/10.1136/bmjopen-2017-019995

Bagwell-Gray, M. E., Messing, J. T., & Baldwin-White, A. (2015). Intimate partner sexual violence: A review of terms, definitions, and prevalence. *Trauma, Violence, & Abuse, 16*(3), 316–335. https://doi.org/10.1177/1524838014557290

Barnett, P. (1993). *The Walker Cycle of Violence and Its Applicability to Wife Battering in the South African Context* (Doctoral Dissertation). University of the Witwatersrand, Faculty of Arts, School of Clinical Psychology.

Barnett, P. (2016). *The walker cycle of violence and its applicability to wife battering in the South African context. A dissertation submitted to the Faculty of Arts, University of the Witwatersrand, in partial fulfilment of the requirements for the Degree of Master of Arts in Clinical Psychology. Johannesburg 1993*

Blasco-Ros, C., Sánchez-Lorente, S., & Martinez, M. (2010). Recovery from depressive symptoms, state anxiety and post-traumatic stress disorder in women exposed to physical and psychological, but not to psychological intimate partner violence alone: A longitudinal study. *BMC Psychiatry, 10*(1), 1–12. https://doi.org/10.1186/1471-244X-10-98

Blau, P. M. (1964). *Exchange and power in social life*. Wiley.

Bowlby, J. (1988). Developmental psychiatry comes of age. *The American Journal of Psychiatry, 145*(1), 1–10. https://doi.org/10.1176/ajp.145.1.1

Breiding, M. J., Smith, S. G., Basile, K. C., Walters, M. L., Chen, J., & Merrick, M. T. (2014). Prevalence and characteristics of sexual violence, stalking, and intimate partner violence victimization–national intimate partner and sexual violence survey, United States, 2011. *Morbidity and Mortality Weekly Report. Surveillance Summaries (Washington, D.C.: 2002), 63(8), 1–18.*

Brownridge, D. A., Taillieu, T., Chan, K. L., & Piotrowski, C. (2021). Understanding the elevated prevalence of intimate partner violence in interracial relationships. *Journal of Interpersonal Violence, 36*(7–8), NP3844–NP3868. https://doi.org/10.1177/0886260518781803

Burelomova, A. S., Gulina, M. A., & Tikhomandritskaya, O. A. (2018). Intimate partner violence: An overview of the existing theories, conceptual frameworks, and definitions. *Psychology in Russia: State of the Art, 11*(3), 128–144. https://doi.org/10.11621/pir.2018.0309

Burns, S. C., Kogan, C. S., Heyman, R. E., Foran, H. M., Slep, A. M. S., Domínguez-Martínez, T., Grenier, J., Matsumoto, C., & Reed, G. M. (2021). Evaluating the relationship between intimate partner violence-related training and mental health professionals' assessment of relationship problems. *Journal of Interpersonal Violence.* https://doi.org/10.1177/08862605211005154

Campbell, J. C. (2002). Health consequences of intimate partner violence. *The Lancet, 359*(9314), 1331–1336. https://doi.org/10.1016/S0140-6736(02)08336-8

Centers for Disease Control and Prevention. (2006). *Understanding intimate partner violence fact sheet*. Retrieved from National Center for Disease Control and Prevention Website: http://www.cdc.gov/ViolencePrevention/pdf/IPV-FactSheet.pdf

Chernet, A. G., & Cherie, K. T. (2020). Prevalence of intimate partner violence against women and associated factors in Ethiopia. *BMC Women's Health, 20*(1), 1–7.

Crenshaw, K. (1990). Mapping the margins: Intersectionality, identity politics, and violence against women of color. *Stan. L. Rev., 43*, 1241. https://doi.org/10.3917/cdge.039.0051

Dako-Gyeke, P., Addo-Lartey, A. A., Ogum Alangea, D., Sikweyiya, Y., Chirwa, E. D., Coker-Appiah, D., et al. (2019). Small small quarrels bring about happiness or love in the relationships': Exploring community perceptions and gendered norms contributing to male perpetrated intimate partner violence in the Central Region of Ghana. *PLoS One, 14*(11), e0225296. https://doi.org/10.1371/journal.pone.0225296

Devries, K. M., Mak, J. Y., Bacchus, L. J., Child, J. C., Falder, G., Petzold, M., Astbury, J., & Watts, C. H. (2013). Intimate partner violence and incident depressive symptoms and suicide attempts: A systematic review of longitudinal studies. *PLoS Medicine, 10*(5), e1001439. https://doi.org/10.1371/journal.pmed.1001439

Devries, K. M., Child, J. C., Bacchus, L. J., Mak, J., Falder, G., Graham, K., Watts, C., & Heise, L. (2014). Intimate partner violence victimization and alcohol consumption in women: A systematic review and meta-analysis. *Addiction, 109*(3), 379–391. https://doi.org/10.1111/add.12393

Dobash, R. E., & Dobash, R. (1979). *Violence against wives: A case against the patriarchy* (pp. 179–206). Free Press.

Doumas, D. M., Pearson, C. L., Elgin, J. E., & McKinley, L. L. (2008). Adult attachment as a risk factor for intimate partner violence: The "mispairing" of partners' attachment styles. *Journal of Interpersonal Violence, 23*(5), 616–634. https://doi.org/10.1177/0886260507313526

Dutton, D. G. (1988). *The domestic assault o f women: Psychological and criminal justice perspectives.* Allyn & Bacon.

Dutton, D., & Golant, S. (1997). El golpeador; Un perfil psicológico. In El golpeador; Un perfil psicológico (pp. 234–234).

Ehrensaft, M. K., Cohen, P., Brown, J., Smailes, E., Chen, H., & Johnson, J. G. (2003). Intergenerational transmission of partner violence: A 20-year prospective study. *Journal of Consulting and Clinical Psychology, 71*(4), 741.

Elghossain, T., Bott, S., Akik, C., & Obermeyer, C. M. (2019). Prevalence of intimate partner violence against women in the Arab world: A systematic review. *BMC International Health and Human Rights, 19*(1), 1–16. https://doi.org/10.1186/s12914-019-0215-5

El-Nimr, N. A., Mamdouh, H. M., Ramadan, A., El Saeh, H. M., & Shata, Z. N. (2021). Intimate partner violence among Arab women before and during the COVID-19 lockdown. *Journal of the Egyptian Public Health Association, 96*(1), 1–8. https://doi.org/10.1186/s42506-021-00077-y

Finkel, E. J., & Slotter, E. B. (2007). An attachment theory perspective on the perpetuation of intimate partner violence. *DePaul Law Review, 56*, 895. Available at: https://via.library.depaul.edu/law-review/vol56/iss3/7

Flood, M., & Pease, B. (2006). *The factors influencing community attitudes in relation to violence against women: A critical review of the literature.* https://doi.org/10.1177/1524838009334131.

Gelles, R. J. (1982). An exchange/social control approach to understanding intrafamily violence. *The Behavior Therapist, 5*(1), 5–8.

Godbout, N., Dutton, D. G., Lussier, Y., & Sabourin, S. (2009). Early exposure to violence, domestic violence, attachment representations, and marital adjustment. *Personal Relationships, 16*(3), 365–384. https://doi.org/10.1111/j.1475-6811.2009.01228.x

Gonzalez-Guarda, R. M., De Santis, J. P., & Vasquez, E. P. (2013). Sexual orientation and demographic, cultural, and psychological factors associated with the perpetuation and victimization of intimate partner violence among Hispanic men. *Issues in Mental Health Nursing, 34*(2), 103–109. https://doi.org/10.3109/01612840.2012.728280

Gulina, M. A., Tikhomandritskaya, O. A., & Burelomova, A. S. (2018). Intimate partner violence: An overview of the existing theories, conceptual frameworks, and definitions. *Psychology in Russia, 11*(3), 128–144. https://doi.org/10.11621/pir.2018.0309

Hazan, C., & Shaver, P. (1987). Romantic love conceptualized as an attachment process. *Journal of Personality and Social Psychology, 52*(3), 511–524. https://doi.org/10.1037/0022-3514.52.3.511

Heise, L., Ellsberg, M., & Gottemoeller, M. (1999). Ending violence against women. *Population Reports, 27*(4), 1–1.

Hughes, R. B., Lund, E. M., Gabrielli, J., Powers, L. E., & Curry, M. A. (2011). Prevalence of interpersonal violence against community-living adults with disabilities: A literature review. *Rehabilitation Psychology, 56*(4), 302. https://doi.org/10.1037/a0025620

Igwe, C. P., Yusuf, O. B., & Fawole, O. I. (2021). Prevalence and correlates of intimate partner violence experience among partners of naval personnel in Lagos, Nigeria. *International Quarterly of Community Health Education, 42*(1), 63–72. https://doi.org/10.1177/0272684X20974223

Jadeja, M., & Gopalan, R. T. (2016). *Impact of intimate partner violence on victim's self-esteem, resilience, coping, problem solving and marital communication* (Unpublished M.Phil Dissertation).

Jagtap, M., Gopalan, R. T., & Dahiya, M. S. (2017). *The decision to stay in an abusive marital relationship: exploring coping strategies, resilience, attachment, forgiveness, empathy, commitment and spirituality among female victims.* Unpublished M.Phil Dissertation.

James-Hawkins, L., Salazar, K., Hennink, M. M., Ha, V. S., & Yount, K. M. (2019). Norms of masculinity and the cultural narrative of intimate partner violence among men in Vietnam. *Journal of Interpersonal Violence, 34*(21–22), 4421–4442. https://doi.org/10.1177/0886260516674941

James-Hawkins, L., Hennink, M., Bangcaya, M., & Yount, K. M. (2021). Vietnamese men's definitions of intimate partner violence and perceptions of women's recourse-seeking. *Journal of Interpersonal Violence, 36*(13–14), 5969–5990. https://doi.org/10.1177/0886260518817790

Jewkes, R. (2002). Intimate partner violence: Causes and prevention. *The Lancet, 359*(9315), 1423–1429. https://doi.org/10.1016/S0140-6736(02)08357-5

Jewkes, R., Fulu, E., Tabassam Naved, R., Chirwa, E., Dunkle, K., Haardörfer, R., et al. (2017). Women's and men's reports of past-year prevalence of intimate partner violence and rape and women's risk factors for intimate partner violence: A multicountry cross-sectional study in Asia and the Pacific. *PLoS Medicine, 14*(9), e1002381. https://doi.org/10.1371/journal.pmed.1002381

Kadir Shahar, H., Jafri, F., Mohd Zulkefli, N. A., & Ahmad, N. (2020). Prevalence of intimate partner violence in Malaysia and its associated factors: a systematic review. *BMC public health, 20(1), 1–9.*

Karakurt, G., Koç, E., Katta, P., Jones, N., & Bolen, S. D. (2022). Treatments for female victims of intimate partner violence: Systematic review and meta-analysis. *Frontiers in Psychology, 44.* https://doi.org/10.3389/fpsyg.2022.793021

Keenan, N. (2020). Theories of violence. *Philologia, 12*(1), 1–3. https://doi.org/10.21061/ph.222

Kesselman, A., McNair, L. D., & Schniedewind, N. (Eds.). (2008). *Women: Images and realities. A multicultural anthology* (4th ed.). McGraw-Hill.

Kincaid, P. J. (1982). The omitted reality: Husband-wife violence in Ontario and policy implication for education. *Dissertation Abstracts International, 42*(10A), 4301.

Klopfstein, U., Kamber, J., & Zimmermann, H. (2010). On the way to light the dark: A retrospective inquiry into the registered cases of domestic violence towards women over a six-year period with a semi-quantitative analysis of the corresponding forensic documentation. *Swiss Medical Weekly, 140*, w13047. https://doi.org/10.4414/smw.2010.13047

Kouyoumdjian, F. G., Calzavara, L. M., Bondy, S. J., O'Campo, P., Serwadda, D., Nalugoda, F., et al. (2013). Risk factors for intimate partner violence in women in the Rakai Community Cohort Study, Uganda, from 2000 to 2009. *BMC Public Health, 13*(1), 1–9. https://doi.org/1 0.1186/1471-2458-13-566

Kruahiran, P., Boonyasiriwat, W., & Maneesri, K. (2022). Thai Police Officers' attitudes toward intimate partner violence and victim blaming: The influence of sexism and female gender roles. *Journal of Interpersonal Violence, 37*(9–10), NP7426–NP7446. https://doi.org/10.1177/0886260520969405

Krug, E. G., Dahlberg, L. L., Mercy, J. A., Zwi, A. B., & Lozano, R. (2002). *World report on violence and health.* geneva, Switzerland: World Health Organization. Health Organization.

Krug, E. G., Mercy, J. A., Dahlberg, L. L., & Zwi, A. B. (2002). The world report on violence and health. *The Lancet, 360*(9339), 1083–1088. https://doi.org/10.1016/S0140-6736(02)11133-0

Kyler-Yano, J. Z., & Mankowski, E. S. (2021). A human diversity analysis of culture and gender in Asian American men's intimate partner violence perpetration. *Journal of Community Psychology, 49*(2), 653–671. https://doi.org/10.1002/jcop.22485

Loots, D. P., & Saayman, G. (2019). Medicolegal perspectives of interpersonal violence: A review of first-contact clinical notes. *South African Medical Journal, 109*(10), 792–800. https://doi.org/10.7196/SAMJ.2019.v109i10.13951

Maheu-Giroux, M., Stöckl, H., Meyer, S. R., & García-Moreno, C. (2022). Global, regional, and national prevalence estimates of physical or sexual, or both, intimate partner violence against women in 2018. *The Lancet, 399*(10327), 803–813. https://doi.org/10.1016/S0140-6736(21)02664-7

Mahoney, C. T., & Iverson, K. M. (2020). The roles of alcohol use severity and posttraumatic stress disorder symptoms as risk factors for women's intimate partner violence experiences. *Journal of Women's Health (2002), 29*(6), 827–836. https://doi.org/10.1089/jwh.2019.7944

McKool, M., Stephenson, R., Winskell, K., Teten Tharp, A., & Parrott, D. (2021). Peer influence on IPV by young adult males: Investigating the case for a social norms approach. *Journal of Interpersonal Violence, 36*(1–2), 83–102. https://doi.org/10.1177/0886260517725735

McLeod, S. (2008). *Social identity theory*. Retrieved from https://www.simplypsychology.org/social-identity-theory.html

Mikulincer, M., & Shaver, P. R. (2007). *Attachment in adulthood: Structure, dynamics, and change*. Guilford Press.

Miller, J. L., Dean, D. K., & Stacey, C. (1999). Family abuse and violence. In M. B. Sussman, S. K. Steinmetz, & G. W. Peterson (Eds.), *Handbook of marriage and the family* (pp. 705–741). Plenum Press.

Miller, A. P., Mugamba, S., Bulamba, R. M., Kyasanku, E., Nkale, J., Nalugoda, F., Nakigozi, G., Kigozi, G., Nalwoga, G. K., Kagaayi, J., Watya, S., & Wagman, J. A. (2022). Exploring the impact of COVID-19 on women's alcohol use, mental health, and experiences of intimate partner violence in Wakiso, Uganda. *PLoS One, 17*(2), e0263827. https://doi.org/10.1371/journal.pone.0263827

Morris, M., Okoth, V., Prigmore, H. L., Ressler, D. J., Mbeya, J., Rogers, A., Moon, T. D., & Audet, C. M. (2022). The prevalence of interpersonal violence (IPV) against women and its associated variables: An exploratory study in the Rongo Sub-County of Migori County, Kenya. *Journal of Interpersonal Violence, 37*(5–6), 2083–2101. https://doi.org/10.1177/0886260520935484

Mulawa, M., Kajula, L. J., Yamanis, T. J., Balvanz, P., Kilonzo, M. N., & Maman, S. (2018). Perpetration and victimization of intimate partner violence among young men and women in Dar es Salaam, Tanzania. *Journal of Interpersonal Violence, 33*(16), 2486–2511. https://doi.org/10.1177/0886260515625910

Nath, A., Venkatesh, S., Vindhya, J., Balan, S., & Metgud, C. S. (2021). Prevalence of intimate partner violence among pregnant women attending a public sector hospital in Bengaluru, southern India. *National Medical Journal of India, 34*(3). https://doi.org/10.25259/NMJI_309_19

Normann, A. K., Bakiewicz, A., Kjerulff Madsen, F., Khan, K. S., Rasch, V., & Linde, D. S. (2020). Intimate partner violence and breastfeeding: A systematic review. *BMJ Open, 10*(10), e034153. https://doi.org/10.1136/bmjopen-2019-034153

Occean, J. R., Thomas, N., Lim, A. C., Lovett, S. M., Michael-Asalu, A., & Salinas-Miranda, A. A. (2021). Prevalence and factors associated with intimate partner violence among women in Haiti: Understanding household, individual, partner, and relationship characteristics. *Journal of Interpersonal Violence, 36*(23–24), 11356–11384. https://doi.org/10.1177/0886260519898443

Okeke-Ihejirika, P., Yohani, S., Muster, J., Ndem, A., Chambers, T., & Pow, V. (2020). A scoping review on intimate partner violence in Canada's immigrant communities. *Trauma, Violence, & Abuse, 21*(4), 788–810. https://doi.org/10.1177/1524838018789156

Orozco-Vargas, A. E., Venebra-Muñoz, A., Aguilera-Reyes, U., & García-López, G. I. (2021). The mediating role of emotion regulation strategies in the relationship between family of origin violence and intimate partner violence. *Psicologia: Reflexão e Crítica, 34*. https://doi.org/10.1186/s41155-021-00187-8

Paphitis, S. A., Bentley, A., Asher, L., Osrin, D., & Oram, S. (2022). Improving the mental health of women intimate partner violence survivors: Findings from a realist review of psychosocial interventions. *PLoS One, 17*(3), e0264845. https://doi.org/10.1371/journal.pone.0264845

Peitzmeier, S. M., Fedina, L., Ashwell, L., Herrenkohl, T. I., & Tolman, R. (2021). Increases in intimate partner violence during CoViD-19: Prevalence and correlates. *Journal of Interpersonal Violence*, 08862605211052586. https://doi.org/10.1177/08862605211052586

Pico-Alfonso, M. A., Garcia-Linares, M. I., Celda-Navarro, N., Blasco-Ros, C., Echeburúa, E., & Martinez, M. (2006). The impact of physical, psychological, and sexual intimate male partner violence on women's mental health: Depressive symptoms, posttraumatic stress disorder, state anxiety, and suicide. *Journal of Women's Health, 15*(5), 599–611. https://doi.org/10.1089/jwh.2006.15.599

Plazaola-Castaño, J., & Pérez, I. R. (2004). Violencia contra la mujer en la pareja y consecuencias en la salud física y psíquica. *Medicina Clínica, 122*(12), 461–467. https://doi.org/10.1016/s0025-7753(04)74273-6

Priestley, S., & Lee, K. A. (2021). Understanding IPV perpetration among young Jamaican men: The role of socialization and attitudinal factors. *Journal of Interpersonal Violence, 36*(17–18), NP9053–NP9077. https://doi.org/10.1177/0886260519854553

Pu, D. F., Rodriguez, C. M., & Dimperio, M. D. (2021). Factors distinguishing reciprocal versus nonreciprocal intimate partner violence across time and reporter. *Journal of Interpersonal Violence,* 0886260521100147 5. https://doi.org/10.1177/08862605211001475

Radcliffe, P., d'Oliveira, A. F. P. L., Lea, S., dos Santos Figueiredo, W., & Gilchrist, G. (2017). Accounting for intimate partner violence perpetration. A cross-cultural comparison of English and Brazilian male substance users' explanations. *Drug and Alcohol Review, 36*(1), 64–71. https://doi.org/10.1111/dar.12450

Reese, B. M., Chen, M. S., Nekkanti, M., & Mulawa, M. I. (2021). Prevalence and risk factors of women's past-year physical IPV perpetration and victimization in Tanzania. *Journal of Interpersonal Violence, 36*(3–4), 1141–1167. https://doi.org/10.1177/0886260517738775

Román-Gálvez, R. M., Martín-Peláez, S., Martínez-Galiano, J. M., Khan, K. S., & Bueno-Cavanillas, A. (2021). Prevalence of intimate partner violence in pregnancy: An umbrella review. *International Journal of Environmental Research and Public Health, 18*(2), 707. https://doi.org/10.3390/ijerph18020707

Ryngala, D. J. (2003). *Role of attachment: The relationship between domestic violence and children's behavior problems* (Graduate Student Theses, Dissertations, & Professional Papers. 5299). https://scholarworks.umt.edu/etd/5299

Sabri, B., Renner, L. M., Stockman, J. K., Mittal, M., & Decker, M. R. (2014). Risk factors for severe intimate partner violence and violence-related injuries among women in India. *Women & Health, 54*(4), 281–300. https://doi.org/10.1080/03630242.2014.896445

Sandberg, J. F., Delaunay, V., Boujija, Y., Douillot, L., Bignami, S., Rytina, S., & Sokhna, C. (2021). Individual, community, and social network influences on beliefs concerning the acceptability of intimate partner violence in rural senegal. *Journal of Interpersonal Violence, 36*(11–12), NP5610–NP5642. https://doi.org/10.1177/0886260518805778

Santambrogio, J., Colmegna, F., Trotta, G., Cavalleri, P. R., & Clerici, M. (2019). Intimate partner violence (IPV) e fattori associati: una panoramica sulle evidenze epidemiologiche e qualitative in letteratura [Intimate partner violence (IPV) and associated factors: an overview of epidemiological and qualitative evidence in literature]. *Rivista di Psichiatria, 54*(3), 97–108. https://doi.org/10.1708/3181.31598

Shaver, P. R., & Mikulincer, M. E. (2011). *Human aggression and violence: Causes, manifestations, and consequences.* American Psychological Association.

Sikweyiya, Y., Addo-Lartey, A. A., Alangea, D. O., Dako-Gyeke, P., Chirwa, E. D., Coker-Appiah, D., Adanu, R., & Jewkes, R. (2020). Patriarchy and gender-inequitable attitudes as drivers of intimate partner violence against women in the central region of Ghana. *BMC Public Health, 20*(1), 682. https://doi.org/10.1186/s12889-020-08825-z

Soleimani, R., Ahmadi, R., & Yosefnezhad, A. (2017). Health consequences of intimate partner violence against married women: A population-based study in northern Iran. *Psychology, Health & Medicine, 22*(7), 845–850. https://doi.org/10.1080/13548506.2016.1263755

Stets, J. E., & Burke, P. J. (2005). Identity verification, control, and aggression in marriage. *Social Psychology Quarterly, 68*(2005a), 160–178.

Taylor, U. (1998). The historical evolution of black feminist theory and praxis. *Journal of Black Studies, 29*(2), 234. Retrieved 11/24/2012 from ProQuest database.

Tochie, J. N., Ofakem, I., Ayissi, G., Endomba, F. T., Fobellah, N. N., Wouatong, C., & Temgoua, M. N. (2020). Intimate partner violence during the confinement period of the COVID-19 pandemic: Exploring the French and Cameroonian public health policies. *The Pan African Medical Journal, 35*(Suppl 2), 54. https://doi.org/10.11604/pamj.supp.2020.35.2.23398

Velotti, P., Beomonte Zobel, S., Rogier, G., & Tambelli, R. (2018). Exploring relationships: A systematic review on intimate partner violence and attachment. *Frontiers in Psychology, 9*, 1166. https://doi.org/10.3389/fpsyg.2018.01166

Victim Blame. (2007). Retrieved March 3, 2008 from http://www.ibiblio.org/rcip//vb.html

Vives-Cases, C., Parra-Casado, D., Estévez, J. F., Torrubiano-Domínguez, J., & Sanz-Barbero, B. (2021). Intimate partner violence against women during the COVID-19 lockdown in Spain. *International Journal of Environmental Research and Public Health, 18*(9), 4698. https://doi.org/10.3390/ijerph18094698

Walker, L. (1979). *The battered woman*. Harper & Row.

Walsh, A. R., Sullivan, S., & Stephenson, R. (2021). Intimate partner violence experiences during COVID-19 among male couples. *Journal of Interpersonal Violence*, 8862605211005135. Advance online publication. https://doi.org/10.1177/08862605211005135.

Waltermaurer, E. (2012). Public justification of intimate partner violence: A review of the literature. *Trauma, Violence & Abuse, 13*(3), 167–175. https://doi.org/10.1177/1524838012447699

Wang, T., Liu, Y., Li, Z., Liu, K., Xu, Y., Shi, W., & Chen, L. (2017). Prevalence of intimate partner violence (IPV) during pregnancy in China: A systematic review and meta-analysis. *PLoS One, 12*(10), e0175108. https://doi.org/10.1371/journal.pone.0175108

Weingarten, C. A. (2016). Intimate partner violence and victim blaming. Wu, Y., Chen, J., Fang, H., & Wan, Y. (2020). Intimate partner violence: A bibliometric review of literature. *International journal of environmental research and public health, 17*(15), 5607.

Wei, D., Hou, F., Hao, C., Gu, J., Dev, R., Cao, W., Peng, L., Gilmour, S., Wang, K., & Li, J. (2021). Prevalence of intimate partner violence and associated factors among men who have sex with men in China. *Journal of Interpersonal Violence, 36*(21–22), NP11968–NP11993. https://doi.org/10.1177/0886260519889935

WHO. (1996). cited in Krug, Mercy, Dahlbers, & Zwi, 2002, p. 1084.

Willliams, K. (1992). Social sources of marital violence and deterrence: Testing and integrated theory of assaults between partners. *Journal of Marriage and the Family, 54*, 620–629.

Wilson, J. K. (2022). Cycle of violence. In F. P. Bernat & K. Frailing (Eds.), *The encyclopedia of women and crime*. https://doi.org/10.1002/9781118929803.ewac0083

World Health Organization. (2010). *World health statistics 2010*. World Health Organization.

World Health Organization. (2021). *Violence against women prevalence estimates, 2018: global, regional and national prevalence estimates for intimate partner violence against women and global and regional prevalence estimates for non-partner sexual violence against women.*

Wright, E. N., Anderson, J., Phillips, K., & Miyamoto, S. (2021). Help-seeking and barriers to care in intimate partner sexual violence: a systematic review. *Trauma, Violence & Abuse*, 1524838021998305. Advance online publication. https://doi.org/10.1177/1524838021998305.

Yakubovich, A. R., Stöckl, H., Murray, J., Melendez-Torres, G. J., Steinert, J. I., Glavin, C., & Humphreys, D. K. (2018). Risk and protective factors for intimate partner violence against women: Systematic review and meta-analyses of prospective-longitudinal studies. *American Journal of Public Health, 108*(7), e1–e11. https://doi.org/10.2105/AJPH.2018.304428

Yaya, S., Hudani, A., Buh, A., & Bishwajit, G. (2021). Prevalence and predictors of intimate partner violence among married women in Egypt. *Journal of Interpersonal Violence, 36*(21–22), 10686–10704. https://doi.org/10.1177/0886260519888196

Zhang, H., Zhao, R., Macy, R. J., Wretman, C. J., & Jiang, Y. (2021). A scoping review of 37 years of intimate partner violence research in China. *Trauma, Violence & Abuse, 22*(4), 752–765. https://doi.org/10.1177/1524838019881738

Chapter 6
Child Maltreatment and Forensic Interview Room in Turkey

Huseyin Batman and Çağatay Serkan Kaya

Introduction

Child maltreatment, which is one of the most common problems in the world, negatively affects millions of children around the world. It takes different forms: physical abuse, emotional abuse, sexual abuse, physical neglect, and emotional neglect (Chen et al., 2021). Child maltreatment not only adversely affects people's social functioning, mental health, and physical health in the short and long term, but also leads to a heavy economic burden (Chen et al., 2021). Child maltreatment includes serious negative early experiences with caregivers that may harm, potentially harm, or threaten the physical, social, and/or mental development of the child (Dias et al., 2014). Estimation of its prevalence is hindered by the absence of widely agreed thresholds at which actions or omissions towards children constitute maltreatment (Millsa et al., 2013). More than one in three of all US children are estimated to experience a child protective services (CPS) investigation before their 18th birthday. Over half of all official victimizations occur among children 5 years old or younger (U.S. Department of Health & Human Services, 2019), (Kim et al., 2017 as cited in Kovskil et al., 2021). Almost six cases of child maltreatment are report every minute in the United States (Daral et al., 2016). Beside that 1500 and 3000 children die from maltreatment each year in the United States (U.S. Department of Health and Human Services, 2020 as cited in Campbell et al., 2021).

Child maltreatment is a complex phenomenon, with four main types: (i) physical abuse, (ii) emotional abuse, (iii) sexual abuse, and (iv) neglect (Moore et al., 2015).

(i) *Physical Abuse*: Physical abuse is a widespread and global phenomenon that affects the lives of millions of children around the world and is in clear contradiction to the Convention on the Rights of the Child (Stoltenborgh, Kranenburg,

---

H. Batman (✉) · Ç. S. Kaya
Sandıklı School of Applied Sciences, Afyon Kocatepe University, Afyonkarahisar, Turkey

R. T. Gopalan (ed.), *Victimology*, https://doi.org/10.1007/978-3-031-12930-8_6

Ijzendoorn & Alink, 2013). Physical abuse is the risk of physical damage or injury to a child or young person under the age of 18 that will harm their health (Geçkil, 2017). The most common type of physical abuse may be tattooing, burns, incisive trauma, poisoning, asphyxia, suffocation, injury, or foetal death as a result of prenatal violence or shaken baby syndrome (Kara et al., 2004). In societies such as Turkey, which have accepted beating as a discipline method, cases of physical abuse are encountered more frequently (Polat, 2017).

(ii) *Emotional Abuse*: It is an attitude and behaviour that is humiliating and damaging the self-confidence of the child by an adult or an older person (Akyüz, 2013). Emotional abuse is more difficult to define, detect and prove legally, although they are seen quite frequently in daily life compared to other types of abuse (Şimşek & Cenkseven-Önder, 2011). Swearing at the child, humiliating, rejecting, hurting his pride, constantly ridiculing, excessive authority, not meeting his emotional needs, expecting responsibilities beyond his age, and not loving are the most common types of emotional abuse (Acehan et al., 2013). Emotional abuse or psychological abuse is a phenomenon that gathers all other forms of maltreatment under an umbrella. It can exist alone or in combination with physical and sexual abuse (Polat, 2017).

(iii) *Sexual abuse*: Child sexual abuse is defined by Munro (2022) as any form of sexual activity with a child by an adult, or by another child where there is no consent or consent is not possible; or by another child who has power over the child. According to Finkelhor et al. (2014), in 1999, the number of children who were victims of sexual abuse was 285,400, in addition to that 35,000 children were subjected to different types of sexual assaults. More than 55% of female children experienced sexual penetration, and most of the victims (89%) were females aged between 12 and 17 years. Globally, the majority of children face sexual abuse as every one in six boys, and one in every four girls faces sexual abuse during childhood (YWCA.org, 2017 as cited in Haykal et al., 2021). It is generally accepted that many cases go unreported. The National Center for Victims of Crime (NCVC, 2012) reported that children between the ages of 7–13 are particularly vulnerable for CSA (as cited in Zeglin et al., 2015). In Turkey, according to statistics of the Ministry of Justice 650 children are admitted to the Forensic Medicine Institute every month due to sexual abuse cases (İmdat & Asuma, 2016; İmdat & Asuma, 2018; Batman & Gökçearslan, 2022).

(iv) *Neglect*: It is the rejection and failure of child's basic needs and care by the parents or the caregiver. It is evaluated physically and emotionally. Negligence is more difficult to detect than abuse (Yağmur, 2008). The most basic point that separates neglect and abuse from each other is that abuse is an active phenomenon and neglect is a passive phenomenon (Sokullu Akıncı & Dursun, 2016).

Exposing the child to sexual abuse differs from other types of abuse (Bussey, 2009) because children are often the only eyewitness in sexual abuse cases (Brubacher et al., 2013). In addition to that, there is no physical evidence to reveal this abuse (Fanetti & Boles, 2004; Lamb et al., 2000). Child sexual abuse (CSA) is defined as the using child (18 years and under) for the purposes of sexual pleasure with or without physical contact by another individual whether known, unknown, older, or the same age (Olafson, 2011 as cited in Gray & Rarick, 2018). The issue of sexual abuse of children is a universal problem that continues from the past to the present. A review shows that the overall estimated global CSA prevalence was 12.7% in self-report studies between 1980 and 2008 (Stoltenborgh et al., 2011 as cited in Yu, 2020). Girls may have difficulty in expressing sexual abuse. The emphasis on girls' virginity and the embarrassment of losing it can create major barriers for girls to express this situation and make it hard for parents to seek professional support for their abused children (Fontes & Plummer, 2010). Işık and Uğurlu (2009) argued that the concept of honour stands out as a very important concept in Turkish society, that the concept of honour can be reason for individuals' life and can cause death for this cause, and that there are news about violence against women in the name of honour in the print media almost every day (Batman & Gökçearslan, 2022).

Not only men abuse children, women also may abuse children. Globally, a meta-analysis of 17 studies from 12 countries showed that (2.2%) of sexual offenses reported to authorities were committed by women (Cortoni et al., 2017 as cited in Kaylor et al., 2021). Children can be motivated to withhold information or deny that they were abused because they wish to protect familiar perpetrators, especially family members (Orbach & Shiloach, 2007). Also sometimes, family members do not report child sexual abuse cases within families, especially when the perpetrator is a breadwinner. The matter becomes complex when the perpetrator is the father, uncle, or brother, because family members then become divided as to whether to choose the perpetrator's side or the victim's side. This predicament creates dysfunction in the family and ultimately affects the family's social functioning (Masilo, 2018). Children refrain from reporting the incidents of sexual abuse if they feel they are going to lose or disrupt the family system (Zantsi, 2014 as cited in Masilo, 2018).

Apart from all of that in some west African countries such as Ghana and Togo, children are subjected to sexual abuse in the name of a religious ceremony called Trokosi. Virgin girls, as young as 10 years old, are sent to fetish shrines as slaves to atone for the sins and crimes committed by their relatives, who usually were already dead (Kasherwa & Twikirize, 2018). Children are sexually abused and impregnated by the custodial fetish priests in the shrines (Brooker, 1996; Gadzekpo, 1993; Laird, 2002 as cited in Sossou & Yogtiba, 2009).

The effect of sexual abuse on the child differs according to some factors. For example, duration, nature of sexual exploitation, relationship to the attacker, support system, and gender (Olafson, 2011 as cited in Gray & Rarick, 2018). Sexual abuse has some negative effect on the child. For example, low self-esteem, depression, anger and aggression, posttraumatic stress, dissociation, substance abuse, sexual difficulties, somatic preoccupation and disorder, self-injurious or self-destructive behaviour, self-harm and low self-esteem, unwanted pregnancy, anxiety, and exposure to sexually transmitted infections (Muridzo & Chikadzi, 2020). Studies on childhood abuse suggest that sexual abuse creates lasting effects on brain development that may lead to internalizing disorders (Hibbard et al., 2012; Teicher et al., 2006 as cited in Villalba et al., 2020). Child sexual abuse may result in unexplained fears, changes in eating habits, bed wetting, increased interest in sexual behaviours, itchy or inflamed genitalia, decreased social interest, or avoidance of physical touch (Hershkowitz, Lanes, & Lamb, 2007 as cited in Zeglin et al., 2015).

The characteristics of the families of children exposed to sexual abuse can be summarized as follows. A study (Black & DeBlassie, 1993) stated that studies have revealed that children who are victims of sexual abuse perceive their families as less capable of solving problems, setting appropriate role boundaries, and maintaining them. In addition, when the families of children who were victims of sexual abuse were examined, it was observed that they had a higher rate of general dysfunction and pathology. In a review of the research on the effects of childhood sexual abuse on adults (Bagley & Thurston, 1996) several interesting results were received. In particular, a family climate characterized by privacy, dialog and attachment problems, other types of abuse (e.g. emotional, physical), and feelings of shame and guilt on the part of the victim was found to be associated with greater psychological impairment among victims of crime. In addition, the family's reaction to the disclosure of sexual abuse was found to be critical (Romano & De Luca, 2001).

Though studies related to maltreatment has been reported in the past, mostly literature is available for sexual abuse and the current chapter will be focusing on sexual abuse and the victims. Different countries use their own legal protocols to interview the victims though common underlying principles are same and for more clarity, the authors use Turkey protocol as an example.

Forensic Interview

In particular, since the beginning of the 1980s, due to the increase in child abuse cases, the fact that the child finds more place in the judicial system and the child is both the victim and eyewitness of the incident (Goodman et al., 1998; Myers, 1992). Although children testify in a variety of types of cases, they most often testify about maltreatment, especially their own victimization (Bruck et al., 2006; Lamb et al., 2008; as cited in Malloy et al., 2012). Forensic interview is a broader term than interrogation, describing a fair, dualistic and open-minded communication to obtain accurate and reliable information conducted within framework of national law and the UN agreements on human, civil and political rights (Holmberg, 2014).

The effective interview with a witness requires a great deal of skill and ability on the part of the interviewer (Rogers & Lewis, 2007). Interviewing children is a complicated endeavour. The psychological research that was carried out recently has found that the quality of children's reports is dependent on the quality of the investigative interview (London, 2008). Sattar (2000) also asserts that interviewers can influence the quality of children's evidence.

Exposing the child to sexual abuse differs from other type of abuse (Bussey, 2009). Because children are often exposed to abuse is the only eyewitness (Brubacher et al., 2013). Since there is generally no other evidence, the implicit claim in forensic interviews with children is to get detailed and accurate answers from the child to analyse the applicability of criminal charges (Myklebust & Bjorklund, 2010 as cited in Phillips et al., 2012). For this reason, children should tell someone about their experiences or anyone who suspects that the child is abused should question this (Bussey, 2009). Sexually abused children may not be willing to participate in a prosecution and/or trial. We can state the reasons for this as follows:

(i) Fear of harm by the abuser.
(ii) Fear of rejection by the family.
(iii) Fear of disbelief.
(iv) Fear of others' reactions (e.g. carers being upset, professionals being insensitive).
(v) Fear of family break up, including their own removal from the family.
(vi) Fear of embarrassment (Westcott & Davies, 2014).

Repeated Interviewing of Children

Forensic interviewers have been counselled not to interview alleged victims of child sexual abuse repeatedly, not only because it may be distressing each time painful memories are revisited, but also because repeated interviewing is believed both to increase the amount of inaccurate information suggestively introduced by interviewers and to foster the incorporation of inaccurate information into children's memories (La Rooy et al., 2009).

Traditionally, repeated interviewers of children have been considered to be distressing because they generate painful memories, and also increase the likelihood of inaccurate information being suggestively obtained (Lamb, Hershkowitz, Orbach & Esplin, 2008a; La Rooy, Katz, Malloy & Lamb, 2010 as cited in Myklebust & Oxburgh, 2011). Experimental research has revealed that forensic interviews with the child more than once may lead to the message 'Your response in the previous interview is not correct' on the child. Especially young children (3–6 years old) when they are interviewed more than once they may attempt to change their responses (Holliday et al., 2012). Undertaking the second interview with the child a while after the first interview also causes problems. Ceci et al. (2000) argue that having a second interview with the child long after the event weakens the traces in the child's memory of the original event. Some authorities guess that, on average, a child may be questioned 12 times during an investigation (Whitcomb, 1992), and this figure may actually be an underestimate if one considers the most of the time parents, friends, or mental health professionals can question these children (Ceci et al., 2000).

A study conducted by the Ministry of Justice in Turkey revealed that children who were victims of sexual abuse had to testify an average of 17 times. In addition, it has been reported that having forensic interviews with the child more than once causes additional stress on children and families, increases the psychological effects on the child, and causes secondary emotional abuse because the additional interview leads to repetitive explanations.

Some measures are taken in order to prevent multiple judicial meetings with the child at the national and international level. For instance, in the United Kingdom, The Memorandum of Good Practice has warned that children should not be taken to forensic interviews more than once unless there is a valid reason in forensic cases (Home Office, 1992). The Criminal Procedure Code (5271: 236/2), which is still in force in Turkey says that; A child or victim whose psychology has been impaired by the effect of the crime may be heard once as a witness in the investigation or prosecution of this crime. Conditions that are necessary in terms of revealing the material truth are reserved. Therefore, this law revealed the necessity of taking the child to a forensic interview once unless there is a contrary situation (Batman & Gökçearslan, 2022).

Cognitive Interview (CI)

The cognitive interview (CI) was developed by Geiselman et al. (1984) to enhance the ability of eyewitnesses to recall information (Clarke, 2005). Initially, the cognitive interview was developed for use with adult interviewees. However, in recent years, the effectiveness of its use with children has been explored (Milne & Bull, 1999). The cognitive interview (CI) method was created by using psychological memory theories in order to get as much accurate information as possible from the willing interviewee. Based on the principle that memory is vulnerable and fallible, the CI uses a range of techniques that have been found to enhance memory and that support the communication of accurate recall of information about an incident (Shawyer et al., 2009). The first published paper on the use of the CI with children appeared in 1988. In this pilot study, Ed Geiselman (one of the originators of the technique) and Padilla found that children interviewed with a CI recalled 21% more correct information than did other children (Milne & Bull, 1999). The cognitive interview technique focuses on two main themes. These are respectively memory and communication (Fisher & Geiselman, 1992).

The original cognitive interview involved four instructions; these required the witness to i) reinstate mental context; ii) report everything; iii) recall events in different orders; and iv) change perspectives (Geiselman, Fisher, Firstenberg, Hutton, Sullivan, Avetissian & Prosk, 1984 as cited in Kebbell & Wagstaff, 1999). The cognitive interview techniques (Fisher & Geiselman, 1992) can be used to enhance the recall of witness, victims, and cooperative suspects. There is no reason why it could not also be used with witnesses with learning disability. Indeed, Milne and Bull (1996) provide evidence that the cognitive interview is effective for children with learning disability (Gudjonsson, 1999). Fisher et al. (2011) state that eyewitnesses and interviewers have cognitively difficult tasks. While eyewitnesses remember complex events and describe them to the interviewer in detail, the interviewers listen carefully and take notes, and on the other hand, they try to develop a crime theory by designing other questions that can be asked to the eyewitnesses. It is recommended to use the cognitive interviewing technique in the current judicial interviews currently used by the police in England and Wales (Dando, Wilcock & Milne, 2008; Dando et al., 2009).

Memory

Most academics working in the field of psychotherapy and psychology would agree that both in the short- and long-term periods human memory is malleable and can be fallible (Williams & Banyard, 1998). The brain, however, is immature at birth and requires more than a decade to mature fully. Understanding the intricate process of the brain's development may be helpful to those who work with children, for significant changes occur in a relatively short period of time (Perry & Wrightsman, 1991). It is also reported that memory can be influenced by the amount of stress or competing events during the time of memory storage and by other factors. Finally, it is well accepted that human beings do not have perfect recall for every event or thought they experience over periods of a few hours or days and certainly not over years (Williams & Banyard, 1998).

Regarding memory, researchers have proposed a three-stage process: encoding, storage, and retrieval (Melton, 1963). Encoding refers to the information transfer from our experiences into our memory (Atkinson & Shiffrin, 1971 as cited in La Rooy et al., 2011). Storage is the process of putting new information in memory. As people store information in memory, they usually modify it in some way; this process of encoding often helps them store the information more easily. Sometimes, encoding involves changing the form of the information (Ormrod, 2004). Retrieval is the process by which people find information they have previously stored so that they can use it again (Ormrod, 2004). Memory does not work like a video recorder that faithfully stores details completely, accurately and in chronological order so that they can be replayed at a later time (La Rooy et al., 2011). People remember in different ways and not in strict chronological sequence. Interviewers, therefore, should allow the interviewee to recall the event in their own order without the distraction of interruptions or any questions (Milne et al., 2007).

Developmental research highlights that younger child have poorer metamemory skills, that is they are less familiar with and less often use strategies that support retrieval (Wellman, 1978). They are less able to provide their own internal retrieval cues to access retained memories (Bauer, 1996). Through experience and age and the parallel development or other cognitive abilities children become more capable in their metamemory abilities and their abilities to create their own internal retrieval cues (Paterson, 2001). Memory retrieval issues occur due to insufficient cueing or incomplete memory search. The more elaborate a memory, the more easily the memory is cued: Adult memories contain information about time, place, person, actions, emotions, and the order of events (Reese & Fivush, 1993). Many of these components are missing from young children's memories (especially emotions, time, and event ordering), because the ability to perceive these components develops with age (Bourg et al., 1999).

According to psychological practitioners, people forget 50–80% of the details of what they have seen or heard within 24 hours of the event (Manley, 2009). This indicates how important it is that the child who is the victim of the abuse and the witness who saw the incident are taken to an interview immediately after the judicial incident (Batman & Gökçearslan, 2022). Finally, the longer the delay between the abuse experienced by children and the first meeting, the more likely it is that children will forget what they have experienced and be vulnerable to manipulation influences. Increased delay is especially a problem in sexual abuse cases, where children usually delay disclosure of the negative experience (Gitlin & Pezdek, 2009). Interviewers need to know how memory works in order to develop appropriate strategies to help the interviewee try to overcome memory loss without jeopardising the quality of information (Milne, 2009).

The Importance of Interviewer

Forensic interviewer is a professional staff who was trained on interview, who conducts interviews with children, and who considers the effects of trauma on children and takes measures to minimize the trauma who is a social worker or psychologist (Bağ & Alşen, 2016). The forensic interviewer must be equipped with some skills. For instance, the forensic interviewer should use a language that the child can understand, can interpret body language, ask simple questions, avoid asking more than one question at the same time, have basic information about the child's development, know interview techniques and child rights (Atılgan et al., 2014). Interviewers need to become competent in building rapport with children and using appropriate questions (Stewart et al., 2011). The person conducting the forensic interview is seen as a fact finder who collects details on legal compliance from an objective point of view, documenting the verbal statements of children where possible. The forensic interviewer is supportive but impartial towards the accuracy of the information presented, avoiding relationships that may unduly influence children's statements (Saywitz & Camparo, 2009).

Interviewers need to know about memory processes to be able to carry out an interview appropriately, as such knowledge will help interviewers to develop appropriate strategies to get as maximum information as possible from an interviewee (Milne & Bull, 2008). The forensic interviewer should be able to evaluate the social, psychological, medical, economic and legal factors affecting the child. All these should be done within the framework of ethical sensitivity (Atılgan et al., 2014).

Forensic Examination of the Child

In sexual assaults against individuals, preserving all kinds of medically evident materials and conducting the examination is a very important process in terms of both protecting the rights of the individual exposed to the attack and identifying the perpetrator of the act (Sözen & Aksoy, 2009; Yazar, 2018 as cited in Batman & Gökçearslan, 2022). The body examination consists of taking samples such as blood or similar biological substances, hair, saliva, and nails from the body of a person regarding a crime under investigation and performing medical examination inside the body when necessary is called body examination (Turhan, 2008). Also, sexual organ and anus examination are performed (Turhan, 2008). In Turkey, examination of victims for the purpose of evidence is carried out based on Article 76 of the Criminal Procedure Code (CMK) (Batman & Gökçearslan, 2022).

Before going to the examination, children who are victims of sexual abuse should be informed about the details of the examination in a way that they can understand, the procedures to be applied should be explained step by step, it should be said that he does not bore himself, that he is comfortable, that he is not afraid, that he is in a safe environment and that he will not suffer any harm due to the examination. Special attention should be paid to the confidentiality and privacy of the child, psychological relief and readiness for the examination should be ensured (Asrdizer, 2006).

In Turkey, the physical examination of the child who is a victim of sexual abuse is not carried out without the decision of the court or the prosecutor's office. Unless otherwise stated, the child's mother is present at the examination. It is argued that it would be useful to ask the adolescent child whether he wants his mother during physical examination. If the sexual abuse has occurred within the last 72 hours, if there is bleeding or acute damage, the examination should be done immediately. Repetition of physical examination should be avoided, and forensic examination of very young children should be performed under general anaesthesia. Considering that the victim child evaluates the physical examination as traumatic, the approach of the health personnel to the incident should be soft and reassuring (Aksoy et al., 1999). The examination should be carried out with an assistant health personnel in a comfortable, calm, enough light, ventilation, and heat environment where he/she can undress and take a shower when necessary.

The physician performing the examination should wear a gown to prevent contamination from outside. Important evidence can be obtained during the removal of one's clothes. For this purpose, it is recommended that the person undress on a wide sheet of paper. Torn, blood stain, semen stain, hair, button, stone, soil, etc. on clothes existence are investigated. The clothes of the person are packaged with the paper on which he was undressed, and his clothes during the event are duly taken, labelled, and sent to the laboratory. While performing these procedures, necessary precautions should be taken and gloves should be used to prevent contamination (Sözen & Aksoy, 2009). Forensic examinations of children who are victims of sexual abuse in Turkey are carried out in hospitals where child monitoring centres are located. It is possible for the child to be referred to services such as psychiatry in the hospital environment (Batman & Gökçearslan, 2022).

Interview Protocols

Memorandum of Good Practice

In the House of Commons in 1991, the home Office minister announced that his government department would be producing a code of practice for such video-recorded interviews to assist interviewers. The Home Office asked a psychologist

(Ray Bull) and a lawyer (Diane Birch) to produce a first working draft of the code by the summer of 1991 (Milne & Bull, 1999).

It has been stated that (Wellbourne, 2002) the Memorandum of Good Practice allowed children's evidence in chief to be given by way of video recording rather than 'live' in the courtroom. The Memorandum also provides a framework for the conduct of investigative interviews. The Memorandum gives interviewers guidance about various types of question and the order in which they should usually be presented (Milne & Bull, 1999). Furthermore, the Memorandum provides explicit guidance on conducting an interview with a child to enable the child to talk about his or her experience (Mortimer & Shepherd, 1999).

Achieving Best Evidence (ABE)

Many government services, law enforcement bodies, and NGO's have started to provide recommended guidelines. One of the leading organisations in this area is the British Home Office. Guidance was first issued in 1992 and then revised in 2002 and 2007. The renamed Memorandum of Good Practice (MOGP), and the retitled and revised Achieving Best Evidence (ABE) supplies particular guidelines for forensic interviews carried out by police and social workers that can be used in criminal and civil proceedings in the United Kingdom. The ABE Model is a four-stage, step-wise, cognitive interview model designed in order to be child friendly, evidentially sound and is formed to replace the child's examination-in-chief (the witness account for the prosecution) (Odeljan et al., 2017).

In the United Kingdom, in 2002, the government update of the 'Memorandum of Good Practice' retains the phased approach and it was largely written by psychologists. Thus, over the last 10 years, there have been several opportunities to re-evaluate the sense of the fundamental realization in the early 1990s that good interviewing of suspects and good interviewing of witnesses share many similarities (Bull & Milne, 2004). Selected officers now attend 'specialist' Achieving best Evidence (ABE) training to prepare them to interview vulnerable and intimidated witness (Shepherd & Milne, 2006).

The elements of the model include:

(i) Interviews should be conducted as soon as possible, if possible straight after receiving the accusations of abuse.
(ii) Interviews should be done in an informal environment with an interviewer that is trained for conducting investigative interview with children.
(iii) To enable the children to tell everything that has happened before the questioning phase starts.
(iv) To conduct interview in phases, starting with opened questions, specific questions should be used at the end of the interview.
(v) Duration of interview shouldn't be longer than 1 hour (Odeljan et al., 2017).

NICHD Protocol

One of the best studied guidelines for conducting forensic interviews with children is the NICHD Investigative Interview Protocol (Lamb, Hershkowitz, Orbach, & Esplin, 2008b). Close collaboration between researchers, interviewers, legal experts, and the police has been especially marked in this field, as exemplified by the achievements of the team who developed the National Institute of Child Health and Human Development (NICHD) Investigative Interview Protocol, a set of structured guidelines for interviewing children about experienced or witnessed events which has been validated extensively around the world. (Bull, 2010; Lamb et al., 2008; as cited in Malloy, La Rooy, Lamb & Katz, 2011). The NICHD protocol adapts forensic interviews to age-appropriate information requests and includes techniques that are effective in eliciting free-recall information from even young children (Lord & Cowan, 2011 as cited in Malloy et al., 2012). The NICHD Investigative Protocol seeks to orient both the interviewer and child towards open questioning and extended responding. Interviewers are taught to use the practice interview to encourage free narrative and extended answers to questions (Davies & Westcott, 2006).

This protocol, which covers all phases of the investigative interview (e.g. presubstantive phase including rapport building and narrative practice, substantive phase, disclosure phase, closure), was designed to translate professional recommendations into operational guidelines and guide interviewers to use prompts and techniques that maximize the amount of information elicited from free-recall memory (Lamb, Hershkowitz, Orbach, & Esplin, 2008b).

RATAC Protocol

The RATAC protocol was developed by Walters et al. The semi-structured RATAC protocol allows the development of spontaneity for each child and takes into account the child's age, cognitive, social, and emotional development (Anderson et al., 2010).

The RATAC protocol includes five elements:

- *Rapport.*
- *Anatomy Identification.*
- *Touch Inquiry.*
- *Abuse Scenario.*
- *Closure* (Toth, 2011).

The RATAC protocol encourages the use of media, including easel pads and drawing of 'face picture' and 'family circles' by the interviewer during the rapport stage. This is followed by asking children to give names for body parts using anatomically detailed drawings, and discussing touches as the primary method for introducing the topic of suspected sexual abuse situation with children under age 10. RATAC instructors encourage interviewers to consider the appropriateness of using anatomical dolls as demonstration aids following a child's verbal disclosure of sexual abuse (Toth, 2011).

Child Sexual Abuse in Turkish Penal Code

In Turkey, the crime of child sexual abuse is handled in the Turkish Penal Code (No:5237). According to the Turkish Penal Code, child sexual abuse is a sexual behaviour that occurs against the will of a child who is not yet 15 years old and does not know the legal meaning and consequences of abuse (Arslanturk, 2017). In The Turkish Penal Code (TCK), child sexual abuse is handled in two groups: children under the age of 15 and children over the age of 15 (Aydin, 2018). In Turkey, a person who sexually abuses a child is sentenced to imprisonment from 8 to 15 years according to Turkish Law (Turkish Penal Code). Cases related to child sexual abuse in Turkey are handled by the authorized criminal court (Aydin, 2018). Any person who had sexual intercourse with a child over the age of 15 without coercion, threat, or fraud is sentenced to imprisonment from 2 to 5 years upon filing of a complaint (Turkish Penal Code, 2016). As to sexual harassment crime, if a person is subject to sexual harassment by another person, the person performing such act is sentenced to a term of imprisonment from 3 months to 2 years or to a judicial fine; and in case of sexual harassment committed against child, the offender is sentenced to imprisonment from 6 months to 3 years upon complaint of the victim (Turkish Penal Code, 2016).

There is no definition for crime of child pornography in the Turkish Penal Code. This crime has been regulated by the tittle 'obscenity' (İmdat & Asuma, 2018). According to Turkish Penal Code, any person who (a) gives to a child obscene written or audio-visual material; or who reads or induces another to read such material to a child or makes a child watch or listen to such material, (b) makes public the content of such material in a place accessible or visible to a child, or who exhibits such material in a visible manner or who reads or talks about such material, or who induces another to read or talk about such material to a child... shall be sentenced to a penalty of imprisonment for a term of 6 months to 2 years and a judicial fine (Turkish Penal Code, 2016). Convention on the Rights of the Child article 34 encourages the countries that have signed to take actions to prevent pornographic exploitation of children (Polat, 2017 as cited in Batman & Gökçearslan, 2022).

How Safe to Take the Child to Courthouse

In Turkey, children who are victims of sexual abuse are called to the courthouse to conduct forensic interviews in Forensic Interview Rooms and sometimes to testify at the hearing. The extent to which the courtroom environment is safe for children is a controversial issue.

In the research conducted by Batman ve Gökçearslan, (2022) in three big court-houses in Istanbul, he met face to face with participating judges and professional staff and asked them whether the court environment poses a risk factor for the child. Professional staff especially stated that children who are victims of sexual abuse may face the risks of encountering the suspect and their relatives in the courthouse, being exposed to physical and verbal violence, withdrawing their complaints and being exposed to trauma again (Batman ve Gökçearslan, 2022).

Incest cases, in particular, can create a crisis that threatens family unity and all family members, and in cases where the intervention to the crisis is not good, the child may be blamed, excluded and exposed to violence (Zengin, 2014 as cited in Batman & Gökçearslan, 2022). In interviews with both judges and professional staff, it was stated that especially in incest cases, after the child's first statement, his family intervened, put pressure on the child, and some children changed their statements under the influence of this pressure and gave up on their complaints (Batman & Gökçearslan, 2022).

Tuğrul (2013) stated that the most common incest relationship in Turkey is between father and daughter, and it is common for the child to be exposed to abuse by more than one family member in the same home environment. In this respect, it is thought that there may be situations such as refusing to give information or deny-ing the event in order to protect the family member who abused them (Orbach & Shiloach, 2007) or for fear of revenge (Howitt, 2009) if they give correct informa-tion (Batman & Gökçearslan, 2022). Polat (2017) stated that especially in incest relationships, the perpetrator and her family can put the child under great pressure that the complaint is withdrawn.

In addition, some participating professionals have stated that the child's relatives are exposed to verbal violence, especially in incest cases, that the child may be attacked in some cases, and that he may be exposed to undeserved accusations (Batman & Gökçearslan, 2022). As it is known, cases of murder, extortion, terror-ism, etc. apart from sexual abuse cases, are seen in courthouses, and the density of cases may increase depending on the size of the courthouse.

It is thought that the fact that children who are victims of sexual abuse are in the corridors of courthouses, where cases related to all kinds of criminal cases are held, will cause them to face the risk of being caught in the middle of armed fights that may arise between opposing groups in different cases at any time (Batman & Gökçearslan, 2022). When all these issues are taken together, it strengthens the idea that children who are victims of sexual abuse may face multiple risks in the court environment.

Child Forensic Interview Centres in Turkey

In Turkey, there are three different centre structures for forensic interviewing with a child who is a victim of sexual abuse.

  (i) Child protection unit.
  (ii) Child monitoring centre (ÇİM).
  (iii) Child-friendly forensic interview room (Batman & Gökçearslan, 2022).

Child Protection Unit

Since the 1980s, the awareness of child abuse and neglect has increased in Turkey and the necessity of multidisciplinary work in this field has been realized, leading to the establishment of child protection unit (Bağ & Alşen, 2016). The first attempt to take statements of children exposed to sexual abuse in a place other than police stations and courthouses in Turkey was made possible with the establishment of Child Protection Units in some university hospitals in 1981, based on article 7 of the Higher Education Law (2547) (Cantürk, 2016). The first Child Protection Unit in Turkey was established in 1998 in Izmir province at Behçet Uz Children Hospital (Bağ & Alşen, 2016).

In Child Protection Unit, forensic medicine specialist, child mental health specialist, public health specialist, paediatrician, paediatric surgeon, social worker, psychologist, and nurse work together for children who are sexual abused (Cantürk, 2016). Child Protection Unit unlike the child monitoring centres works not only with children who are victims of sexual abuse, but also with children who have been exposed to other forms of abuse and violence (Humanistic Büro, 2014 as cited in Batman & Gökçearslan, 2022).

Child Monitoring Centres

Child monitoring centres (ÇİM) are new institutions where professionals working on child sexual abuse together under one roof. Thus, it shows the feature of multidisciplinary approach (Bağ & Alşen, 2016). Child monitoring centres (ÇİM) in Turkey was established based on the Child Monitoring Centre circular (No:28431) published on 04.10.2012 in order to prevent child abuse, to enable conscious and effective intervention, to minimize secondary traumatization of child victims. These centres ensure legal and medical procedures that were carried out at once by the professionals (Duyan & Bayır, 2016 as cited in Batman & Gökçearslan, 2022). Child monitoring centres are used in the investigation phase of child sexual abuse cases.

Forensic interview that was held in child monitoring centres is based on the principle that the child talks about this special event in a specially configured mirrored room to professional staff specially trained in this area, while the representative of each institution which will be stakeholder in the process monitors the interview and obtains their own data. Child monitoring centres minimize the obligation of the child re-express the traumatic event due to video and audio recordings (Bağ &

Alşen, 2016). Professionals such as social worker, psychologist, etc. who work in these centres were trained on child interview by some academics (Bayün & Dinçer, 2013). In child monitoring centres, only children who are victims of sexual abuse are evaluated (Bağ & Alşen, 2016). Child monitoring centres perform both forensic and medical examinations as well as social support and family counselling functions (Acehan et al., 2013 as cited in Aydemir & Yurtkulu, 2012).

Child monitoring centres were opened for the first time in Ankara for the purpose of pilot implementation, and then they were put into operation in different provinces (Kafadar, 2014). In Turkey, child monitoring centres work 7/24, and a forensic interviewer stays on duty every day (Bağ & Alşen, 2016). In child monitoring centres, interview rooms are big enough and especially suitable for meeting with children who are victims of sexual abuse. It is designed in a large hospital environment where medical examinations can also be performed. Children can be referred to the child psychiatry clinic if it is required in the hospital (Trabzon Bar Association Report, 2015 as cited in Batman & Gökçearslan, 2022).

Child-Friendly Forensic Interview Room

As the output of the 'Justice for Children Project' carried out in cooperation with the Ministry of Justice and UNICEF between 2012 and 2014, a Judicial Interview Room (AGO) has been established in courthouses in order to take the statements of the victims by experts. With this application, it is aimed to prevent secondary traumatization (Mağdur Hakları Daire Başkanlığı, 2017). Forensic interview room is a model to prevent secondary victimization of victims in the trial process and identify the need for protection by using appropriate interview methods. It is also a service model created for the purpose of routing (Aydin, 2017). In Turkey 90 forensic interview rooms were established in 70 different provinces and more than 500 judges, public prosecutors and professional staff were trained on child interview by some academics with the support of UNICEF (Mağdur Hakları Daire Başkanlığı, 2020).

Forensic interview rooms have been established primarily to take statements from victims, witnessed, delinquent children, victims of sexual crimes, domestic violence crimes and other vulnerable groups (Aydin, 2017). Within the scope of Child-Friendly Interview Rooms, there should be meeting, waiting and observation rooms. Also, the room should be in ideal temperature, and the size of the room should be at least 24 square meters with light, insulation, and ventilation. It should answer the needs of different age groups (Mağdur Hakları Daire Başkanlığı, 2018). During the forensic interview with sexually abused children, same-sex gender interviewer is assigned to them whenever possible. In addition to that, if the child's statement needs to be taken again, it is ensured that the interviewer who made the first interview with her is assigned (Aydin, 2017). It is important to emphasize that forensic interview rooms are used in the prosecution phase of child sexual abuse cases.

The Forensic Interview Rooms Regulation, which was prepared to determine the administrative functioning, workflows, and the service and working standards of the experts and other personnel who will work in the forensic meeting rooms, was signed on 24.02.2017 and entered into force (Mağdur Hakları Daire Başkanlığı, 2017). Forensic interview rooms operate under the juvenile prosecution offices within the judicial organization (Atılgan et al., 2014). There should be two cameras in the forensic interview room, one should be focused on the face of interviewee, and the second one should show the full screen of the room. Also microphone and headphone should be available. In the interview room, toy, painting pens, paper, etc. should be ready as an interview aid (Mağdur Hakları Daire Başkanlığı, 2018).

Conclusion

The phenomenon of child sexual abuse is one of the most emphasized and discussed issues in recent years. It is very important to protect and support the child against sexual abuse, which has devastating effects on children. In cases of sexual abuse, the importance of the child's statement increases when there is no material evidence. This situation increases the importance of having a forensic interview with the child in a suitable environment, right after the incident, by a trained forensic interviewer.

There have been attempts to take statements from children who are victims of sexual abuse since the 1980s in Turkey, and units such as Child Protection Centre, Child Monitoring Centre, and Child-Friendly Forensic Interview Room have been established in this regard. The judicial meeting rooms established in the courthouse with the joint efforts of the Ministry of Justice and UNICEF have eliminated the child's obligation to testify at the police station at the hearing and reduced the risk of coming face to face with the perpetrator. The importance of forensic interview rooms is increasing day by day in terms of protecting children who are victims of abuse and supporting them in the judicial process.

References

Acehan, S., Bilen, A., Ay, M. O., Gülen, M., Avcı, A., & İçme, F. (2013). Evaluation of child abuse and neglect. *Journal of Archival Sources, 22*(4), 591–614.
Aksoy, E., Cetin, G., Inanici, M. A., Polatu O., Sözen M. S., & Yavuz, F. (1999). *Child abuse and violation - forensic medicine lecture notes.*
Akyüz, E. (2013). *Children's law: Rights and protection of children.* Pegem.
Anderson, J., Ellefson, J., Lashley, J., Miller, L. A., Olinger, S., Russell, A., Stauffer, J., & Weigman, J. (2010). Cornerhouse forensic interview. *Journal of Practical and Clinical Law., 12,* 194–231.
Arslanturk, M. (2017). *Sexual offenses in Turkish penal code practice.* Distinguished Publishing.
Asrdizer, M. (2006). Physicians' approaches to child and female abuse cases applying to emergency services. *Turkiye Klinikleri Journal of Surgical Medical Sciences, 2*(50), 39–48.

Atılgan, U. E., Yağcıoğlu, S., & Çavdar, Y. (2014). *Forensic interview rooms with children: Their needs, examples of good practice and standards for forensic interviewing with children.* Ministry of Justice Publication.

Aydemir, D., & Yurtkulu, F. (2012). Fighting sexual abuse against children: Child fall up center. *Ankara Journal of Health Sciences, 1*(2), 151–165.

Aydin, M. (2017). *Basic legal knowledge for AGO app.* UNICEF.

Aydin, M. (2018). *Child sexual abuse.* Distinguished Publishing.

Bağ, Ö., & Alşen, S. (2016). A new model in the evaluation of child sexual abuse: Child Observation Centers. *İzmir Dr. Behçet Uz Children's Hospital. Journal, 6*(1), 9–14. https://doi.org/10.5222/buchd.2016.009

Bagley, C., & Thurston, W. (1996). *Understanding and preventing child sexual abuse.* Arena Social Work Publications.

Batman, H., Gökçearslan, E. (2022). Çocuğun *Cinsel İstismarında Adli Görüşme.* Seçkin yayıncılık.

Bauer, P. J. (1996). What do infants recall of their lives? Memory for specific events by one- to two-year-olds. *American Psychologist, 51*(1), 29–41. https://doi.org/10.1037/0003-066X.51.1.29.

Bayün, S., & Dinçer, C. N. (2013). Child observation center. *Journal of Legal Agenda, 2013*(2). Retrieved on 11.10.2021 http://www.ankarabarosu.org.tr/siteler/ankarabarosu/hgdmakale/2013-2/23.pdf

Black, C. A., & DeBlassie, R. R. (1993). Sexual abuse in male children and adolescents: Indicators, effects, and treatments. *Adolescence, 28*(109), 123–133.

Bourg, W., Broderick, R., Flagor, R., Kelly, M. D., Ervin, L. D., & Butler, J. (1999). *A child interviewer's guidebook.* Sage.

Brubacher, P. S., Malloy, C. L., Lamb, E. M., & Roberts, P. K. (2013). How do interviewers and children discuss individual occurences of alleged repeated abuse in forensic interviews. *Applied Cognitive Psychology, 27*, 443–450.

Bull, R., & Milne, B. (2004). Attempts to improve the police interviewing of suspects. In D. G. Lassiter (Ed.), *Interrogations, confessions and entrapment* (pp. 181–196) Kluwer Academic Plenium Pub.

Bussey, K. (2009). An international perspective on child witnesses. In B. L. Bottoms, C. J. Najdowski, & G. S. Goodman (Eds.), *Children as victims, witnesses and offenders, psychological science and law* (pp. 209–232). The Guildford Press.

Campbell, K. A., Wood, J. N., Lindberg, D. M., & Berger, R. P. (2021). A standardized definition of near-fatal child maltreatment: Results of a multidisciplinary Delphi process. *Child Abuse & Neglect, 112*, 1–7.

Cantürk, G. (2016). Ders notları. Ankara Üniversitesi Adli Tıp Enstitüsü.

Ceci, J. S., Bruck, M., & Battin, B. D. (2000). The suggestibility of children's testimony. In F. D. Bjorklund (Ed.), *False memory creation in children and adults* (pp. 169–202). Lawrence Erlbaum.

Chen, X., Zhang, S., Huang, G., Xu, Y., Li, Q., Shi, J., Li, W., Wang, W., Guo, L., & Lu, C. (2021). Associations between child maltreatment and depressive symptoms among Chinese college students: An analysis of sex differences. *Frontiers in Psychiatry*, 1–10. https://doi.org/10.3389/fpsyt.2021.656646.

Clarke, C. (2005). *A national evaluation of PEACE investigative interviewing* (Unpublished Ph.D thesis). Institute of Criminal Justice Studies. The University of Portsmouth.

Dando, C., Wilcock, R., & Milne, R. (2008). The cognitive interview: The efficacy of a modified mental reinstatement of context procedure for frontline police investigators. *Applied Cognitive Psychology, 23*, 138–147.

Dando, C., Wilcock, R., Milne, R., & Henry, L. (2009). A modified cognitive interview procedure for frontline police investigators. *Applied Cognitive Psychology, 23*, 698–716.

Daral, S., Khokhar, A., & Pradhan, S. (2016). Prevalence and determinants of child maltreatment among school-going adolescent girls in a semi-urban area of Delhi, India. *Journal of Tropical Pediatrics, 0*, 1–14. https://doi.org/10.1093/tropej/fmv106.

Davies, G., & Westcott, H. (2006). Investigative interviewing with children: Progress and pitfalls. In H. A. Armstrong, E. Shepherd, G. Gudjonsson, & D. Wolchover (Eds.), *Witness testimony, psychological, investigative and evidential perspectives* (pp. 153–170). Oxford University Press.

Dias, A., Sales, L., Hessen, D. J., & Kleber, R. J. (2014). Child maltreatment and psychological symptoms in a Portuguese adult community sample: The harmful effects of emotional abuse. *European Child & Adolescent Psychiatry.*, 1–12. https://doi.org/10.1007/s00787-014-0621-0.

Duyan, V., & Bayır, ÖÖ. (2016). Sosyal hizmete giriş: Öğrenciler ve uygulayıcılar için bir rehber. Sosyal çalışma yayınları.

Fanetti, M., & Boles, R. (2004). Forensic interviewing and assessment issues with children. In W. T. O'Donohue & E. R. Levensky (Eds.), *Handbook of forensic psychology: Resource for mental health and legal professionals* (pp. 245–265). Elsevier Science.

Fisher, R., & Geiselman, E. R. (1992). *Memory enhancing techniques for investigative interviewing.* Charles Thomas Publisher.

Fisher, P. R., Milne, R., & Bull, R. (2011). Interviewing cooperative witnesses. *Current Directions in Psychological Science, 20*(1), 16–19.

Finkelhor, D., Shattuck, A., Turner, H. A., & Hamby, S. L. (2014). The lifetime prevalence of child sexual abuse and sexual assault assessed in late adolescence. *Journal of Adolescent Health, 55*(3), 329–333. https://doi.org/10.1016/j.jadohealth.2013.12.026

Fontes, L. A., & Plummer, C. (2010). Cultural issues in disclosures of child Seual abuse. *Journal of Child Sexual Abuse., 19*(5), 491–518.

Geçkil, E. (2017). Çocuklarda Fiziksel İstismar ve Hemşirelik Yaklaşımı. *Gümüşhane Üniversitesi Sağlık Bilimleri Dergisi., 6*(1), 129–139.

Geiselman, R. E. et al. (1984). Enhancement of eyewitness memory: An empirical evaluation of the cognitive interview. *Journal of PoliceScience & Administration, 12*(1), 74–80.

Gitlin, B. I., & Pezdek, K. (2009). Children's memory in forensic contexts. In L. B. Bottoms, J. C. Najdowski, & S. G. Goodman (Eds.), *Children as victims, witnesses and offenders, psychological science and law* (pp. 57–80). The Guildford Press.

Goodman, G. S., Emery, R. E., & Haugaard, J. J. (1998). Developmental psychology and law: Divorce, child maltreatment, foster care and adoption. In W. Damon, I. E. Sigel, & K. A. Renninger (Eds.), *Handbook of child psychology: Child psychology in practice* (pp. 775–874). Wiley.

Gray, S., & Rarick, S. (2018). Exploring gender and racial/ethnic differences in the effects of child sexual abuse. *Journal of Child Sexual Abuse*, 1–19. https://doi.org/10.1080/10538712.2018.1484403.

Great Britain. Home Office. (1992). *Memorandum of good practice on video recorded interviews with child witnesses for criminal proceedings.* HMSO.

Gudjonsson, G. (1999). Testimony from persons with mental disorder. In H. A. Armstrong, E. Shepherd, & D. Wolchover (Eds.), *Analysing witness testimony* (pp. 62–75). Blackstone Press Ltd..

Haykal, A. H., Youssef, E., & Youssef, M. (2021). Child sexual abuse and the Internet-a systematic review. *Human Arenas*, 1–18. https://doi.org/10.1007/s42087-021-00228-9.

Holliday, E. R., Humphries, E. H., Brainerd, J. C., & Reyna, F. V. (2012). Interviewing vulnerable witnesses. In G. Davies & A. Beech (Eds.), *Forensic psychology: Crime, justice, law, interventions* (pp. 115–134). Wiley.

Holmberg, U. (2014). Interviewing suspect. In G. Davies & A. Beech (Eds.), *Forensic psychology: Crime justice law interventions* (pp. 135–150). Wiley.

Howitt, D. (2009). *Introduction to forensic & criminal psychology* (3rd ed.). Pearson Education Ltd.

İmdat & Asuma: Şiddeti Önleme ve Rehabilitasyon Derneği. Acıbadem Üniversitesi Suç ve Şiddetle Mücadele Uygulama ve AraştırmaMerkezi (2016). Child Abuse Report. https://www.imdat.org/kopyas%C4%B1-grooming

İmdat & Asuma: Şiddeti Önleme ve Rehabilitasyon Derneği. Acıbadem Üniversitesi Suç ve Şiddetle Mücadele Uygulama ve AraştırmaMerkezi (2018). Child Abuse Report 2. https://

cohum.giresun.edu.tr/Files/ckFiles/cohum-giresun-edu-tr/RAPOR-%C3%87OCUK-%C4%B0ST%C4%B0SMARI-tam_v2_cleancopy.pdf

Işık, R. Ş., Uğurlu, N. S. (2009). Namusa ve Namus Adına Kadına Uygulanan Şiddete İlişkin Tutumlar Ölçeklerinin Öğrenci ÖrneklemiyleGeliştirilmesi. *Türk Psikoloji Yazıları, 12* (24), 16–24.

Kafadar, H. (2014). Çocuk İzlem Merkezleri (ÇİM) ve Adli Tıp Yaklaşımı. *Journal of Clinical and Analytical Medicine., 5*(2), 279–281.

Kara, B., Biçer, Ü., & Gökalp, A. S. (2004). Çocuk İstismarı. *Çocuk Sağlığı ve Hastalıkları Dergisi., 2004*(47), 140–151.

Kasherwa, A. C., & Twikirize, J. M. (2018). Ritualistic child sexual abuse in post-conflict Eastern DRC: Factors associated with the phenomenon and implications for social work. *Child Abuse & Neglect, 81*, 74–81.

Kaylor, L. E., Winters, G. M., & Jeglic, E. L. (2021). Exploring sexual grooming in female perpetrated child sexual abuse. *Journal of ChildSexualAbuse.* 1–20. https://doi.org/10.1080/1053871 2.2021.1994505.

Kebbell, R. M., & Wagstaff, F. G. (1999). The effectiveness of the cognitive interview. In D. Canter & L. Alison (Eds.), *Interviewing and deception* (pp. 23–40). Ashgate-Darmauth Pub.

Kovskil, N. L., Hill, H. D., Mooney, S. J., Rivara, F. P., Morgan, E. R., & Rahbar, A. R. (2021). Association of state-level earned income tax credits with rates of reported child maltreatment, 2004–2017. *Child Maltreatment* , 1–9. https://doi.org/10.1177/1077559520987302.

La Rooy, D. J., Lamb, M. E., & Pipe, M. E. (2009). Repeated Interviewing: A criticial evaluation of the risks and potential benefits. *Researchgate*, 1–42. http://citeseerx.ist.psu.edu/viewdoc/downl oad?doi=10.1.1.565.3297&rep=rep1&type=pdf

La Rooy, J. D., Malloy, C. L., & Lamb, E. M. (2011). The development of memory in childhood. In E. M. Lamb, J. D. La Rooy, C. L. Malloy, & C. Katz (Eds.), *Children's testimony: A handbook of psychological research and forensic practice* (2nd ed., pp. 49–68). Wiley.

Lamb, M. E., Hershkowitz, I., Orbach, Y., & Esplin, P. W. (2008). Tell me what happened: Structured investigative interviews of child victims and witnesses. John Wiley & Sons.

Lamb, M. E., Hershkowitz, I., & Orbach, Y. (2008a). Interviewing children about abuse: An overview and introduction. In G. Davies & R. Bull (Eds.), *Tell me what happened* (pp. 1–17). Wiley.

Lamb, M. E., Hershkowitz, I., Orbach, Y., & Esplin, P. W. (2008b). The NICHD investigative interview protocol for young victims and witnesses. Tell me what happened. Structured investigative interviews of child victims and witnesses. John Wiley and Sons Ltd, Chichester, 83–101.

London, K. (2008). Investigative interviews of children: A review of psychological research and implications for police practices. In R. C. Bartol & M. A. Bartol (Eds.), *Current perspectives in forensic psychology and criminal behaviour* (2nd ed., pp. 39–48). Sage.

Mağdur Hakları Daire Başkanlığı. (2017). *Adli görüşme odaları*. http://www.magdur.adalet.gov.tr/ adli-gorusme-odalari-agotanitim-filmi-01681

Mağdur Hakları Daire Başkanlığı. (2018). *Adli görüşme odaları*. www.magdur.adalet.gov.tr/ ago-nedir-01587

Mağdur Hakları Daire Başkanlığı. (2020). *Adli görüşme odaları*. https://magdur.adalet.gov.tr/ Home/SayfaDetay/agonedir

Malloy, C. L., Wright, B. D., & Skagerberg, M. E. (2012). In Davies, G., & Beech, A. (Eds.), *Forensic psychology: Crime justice, law, interventions* (pp. 99–114). Wiley.

Malloy, C. L. Rooy, L. J. D. Lamb, E. M. Katz, C. (2011). Developmentally Sensitive Interviewing for Legal Purposes. In Lamb, E. M. Rooy, L.J. D. Malloy, C. L. Katz, C. (Eds.). Children's Testimony: A Handbook of Psychological Research and Forensic Practice (pp.1–14). Chichester: John Wiley & Sons Ltd.

Manley, A. (2009). *Elements of private investigation*. CRC Press.

Masilo, D. T. (2018). Prevention of child sexual abuse within the family system: Guidelines for an educational social group work program. *Journal of Child Sexual Abuse*, 1–13. https://doi.org/10.1080/10538712.2018.1430089.

Melton, A. W. (1963). Implications of short-term memory for a general theory of memory. *Journal of verbal Learning and verbal Behavior, 2*(1), 1–21.

Millsa, R., Scott, J., Alati, R., O'Callaghan, M., Najman, J. M., & Strathearn, L. (2013). Child maltreatment and adolescent mental health problems in a large birth cohort. *Child Abuse & Neglect, 37*, 292–302.

Milne, B. (2009). *Interviewing and testimony: masters level.* University Press.

Milne, R., & Bull, R. (1996). Interviewing children with mild learning disability with the cognitive interview. *Issues in Criminological & Legal Psychology, 26*, 44–51.

Milne, R., & Bull, R. (1999). *Investigative interviewing psychology and practice.* Wiley.

Milne, R., & Bull, R. (2008). Interviewing victims of crime, including children and people with intellectual disabilities. In R. K. Mark & M. D. Graham (Eds.), *Practical psychology for forensic investigations and prosecutions* (pp. 7–24). Wiley.

Milne, B., Shaw, G., & Bull, R. (2007). Investigative interviewing: The roles of research. In D. Carson, R. Milne, F. Pakes, K. Shalev, & A. Shawyer (Eds.), *Applying criminology to criminal justice* (pp. 65–80). Wiley.

Moore, S. E., Scott, J. G., Ferrari, A. J., Mills, R., Dunneh, M. P., Erskine, H. E., Devriesi, K. M., Degenhardte, L., Vose, T., Whiteford, H. A., McCarthyl, M., & Norman, R. E. (2015). Burden attributable to child maltreatment in Australia. *Child Abuse & Neglect., 48*, 208–220.

Mortimer, A., & Shepherd, E. (1999). The frailty of children's testimony. In H. A. Armstrong & D. Wolchover (Eds.), *Analysing witness testimony* (pp. 46–61). Blackstone Press Ltd..

Muridzo, N. G., & Chikadzi, V. (2020). Some impediments to child sexual abuse interventions and corresponding social work implications: Reflections on the Zimbabwean victim friendly system. *Journal of Human Rights and Social Work., 1*–10. https://doi.org/10.1007/s41134-020-00137-x.

Munro, K. (2022). Kalimunro Psychothrapist. *Incest & Child Abuse.* https://kalimunro.com/wp/articles-info/sexual-emotional-abuse/incest-and-child-sexual-abuse-definitions-perpetrators-victims-and-effects. Retrieved on 22.07.2022.

Myklebust, T., & Oxburgh, E. G. (2011). Reviewing the case (post interview). In E. M. Lamb, J. D. La Rooy, C. L. Malloy, & C. Katz (Eds.), *Children's testimony: A handbook of psychological research and forensic practice* (2nd ed., pp. 165–178). Wiley.

Myers, J. E. B. (1992). 'Steps towards forensically relevant research. In: Goodman, G., Taub, E., Jones, D., England, P., Port, L., Rudy, andPrado, L. *Testifying in Criminal Court: Emotional Effects on Child Sexual Assault Victims. Monographs of the Society for Research in Child Development., 57*(5), 143-152.

Odeljan, R., Butorac, K., & Bailey, A. (2017). Investigative interview with children. *Research Gate, 1*–11. https://www.researchgate.net/publication/313251118.

Orbach, Y., & Shiloach, H. (2007). Reluctant disclosures of child sexual abuse. In E. M. Pipe, E. M. Lamb, Y. Orbach, & C. A. Cederborg (Eds.), *Child sexual abuse: Disclosure, delay and denial* (pp. 115–134). Taylor & Francis Group.

Ormrod, J. E. (2004). *Human learning.* Pearson.

Paterson, B. (2001). *Improving children's eyewitness memory: Cognitive and social considerations* (Unpublished PhD dissertation). University of Portsmouth, Portsmouth.

Perry, W. N., & Wrightsman, S. I. (1991). *The child witness legal issues and dilemmas.* Sage Publication.

Phillips, E., Oxburgh, G., Gavin, A., & Myklebust, T. (2012). Investigative interviews with victims of child sexual abuse: The relationship between question type and investigation relevant information. *Journal of Police and Criminal Psychology., 27*(1), 45–54.

Polat, O. (2017). *Tüm boyutlarıyla çocuk istismarı.* Seçkin.

Reese, E., & Fivush, R. (1993). Parental styles of talking about the past. *Developmental Psychology, 29*(3), 596–606. https://doi.org/10.1037/0012-1649.29.3.596.

Rogers, C., & Lewis, R. (2007). *Introduction to police work.* Willan.

Romano, E., & De Luca, R. V. (2001). Male sexual abuse: A review of effects, abuse characteristics, and links with later psychological functioning. *Aggression and Violent Behaviour, 6*(1), 55–78.

Sattar, R. G. (2000). *The interviewing and preparation of child witness for legal purposes* (Unpublished PhD dissertation). University of Portsmouth.

Saywitz, J. K., & Camparo, B. L. (2009). Contemporary child forensic interviewing: Evolving consensus and innovation over 25 years. In L. B. Bottoms, J. C. Najdowski, & S. G. Goodman (Eds.), *Children as victims, witnesses and offenders, psychological science and law* (pp. 102–127). The Guildford Press.

Shawyer, A., Milne, B., & Bull, R. (2009). Investigative interviewing in the UK. In T. Williamson, B. Milne, & P. S. Savage (Eds.), *International developments in investigative interviewing* (pp. 24–38). Willan Pub.

Shepherd, E., & Milne, R. (2006). Have you told management about this? Bringing witness interviewing into the twenty-first century? In H. A. Armstrong, E. Shepherd, G. Gudjonsson, & D. Wolchover (Eds.), *Witness testimony: Psychological, investigative and evidential perspectives* (pp. 131–152). Oxford University Press.

Şimşek, S., & Cenkseven-Önder, F. (2011). Ergenlerde Davranış Problemlerinin, Anne-Babadan ve Öğretmenlerden Algılanan Duygusal İstismar Açısından İncelenmesi. *Elementary Education Online., 10*(3), 1124–1137.

Sokullu Akıncı, F., & Dursun, S. (2016). *Viktimoloji (Mağdurbilim)*. İnkılap Yayınevi.

Sossou, M. A., & Yogtiba, J. A. (2009). Abuse of children in *West* Africa: Implications for social work education and practice. *British Journal of Social Work., 39*, 1218–1234.

Sözen, Ş., & Aksoy, E. (2009). Cinsel Saldırılarda Hekim Sorumluluğu, Tıbbi ve Hukuki Yaklaşım. (2. Baskı). In S. Koç & M. Can (Eds.), *Birinci Basamakta Adli Tıp* (pp. 202–216). İstanbul Tabip Odası.

Stewart, H., Katz, C., & Rooy, L. J. (2011). Training forensic interviewers. In E. Lamb, M. Rooy, L. J. D. Malloy, C. L. Katz, & C. (Eds.), *Children's testimony: A handbook of psychological research and forensic practice* (pp. 199–216). Wiley.

Stoltenborgh, M., Bakermans-Kranenburg, M. J., Van Ijzendoorn, M. H., & Alink, L. R. (2013). Cultural–geographical differences in the occurrence of child physical abuse? A meta-analysis of global prevalence. *International Journal of Psychology, 48*(2), 81–94.

Toth, P. (2011). Comparing the Nichd and Ratac child forensic interview approaches - do the differences matter? *APSAC advisor.* https://umich.instructure.com/courses/90711/files/2366706/download?verifier=o0Qb0umZeetlMV5oCObHRLNWuzmx6xrOOEAsTAFU&wrap=1

Tuğrul, A. C. (2013). *Cinsel dokunulmazlığa karşı suçlar ve ensest ilişkiler*. Adalet.

Turhan, F. (2008). *Ceza Muhakemesinde Beden Muayenesi ve Tıp Hukuku*. V. Türk - Alman Tıp Hukuku Sempozyumu.

Turkish Penal Code (TCK). (2016). https://www.legislationline.org/download/id/6453/file/Turkey_CC_2004_am2016_en.pdf

U.S. Department of Health & Human Services, Administration for Children and Families, Administration on Children, Youth and Families, Children's Bureau. (2019). *Child maltreatment 2017*. Available from https://www.acf.hhs.gov/cb/research-data-technology/statistics-research/child-maltreatment

Villalba, K., Attonito, J., Gilles, M. J., Rosenberg, R., Sanchez, M., & Devieux, J. (2020). The effects of childhood sexual abuse: The role of anxiety and alcohol use among Haitian women living with HIV. *Journal of Child Sexual Abuse, 29*, 788–801.

Wellbourne, P. (2002). Videotaped evidence of children: Application and implications of the memeorandum of good practice. *British Journal of Social Work, 32*, 553–571.

Wellman, H. M. (1978). Knowledge of the interaction of memory variables: A developmental study of metamemory. *Developmental Psychology, 14*(1), 24–29. https://doi.org/10.1037/0012-1649.14.1.24.

Westcott, H. L., & Davies, G. (2014). Safeguarding witnesses. In G. Davies & A. Beech (Eds.), *Forensic psychology: Crime justice law interventions* (pp. 247–264). Wiley.

Whitcomb, D. (1992). When the victim is a child (2nd ed.). Washington, DC: US Department of Justice, Office of Justice Programs, National Institute of Justice.

Williams, L. M., & Banyard, V. (1998). *Trauma and memory*. Sage.

Yağmur, F. (2008). Çocuk İstismarı ve İhmali. *Sosyal Bilimler Araştırma Dergisi., 12*, 71–78.

Yazar, M. E. (2018). *2010–2016 yılları arasında pamukkale üniversitesine başvuran cinsel istismar ve cinsel saldırı olgularının adli tıp yönünden değerlendirilmesi* (Unpublished Expertise Dissertation in Forensic Medicine).

Yu, W. (2020). News portrayals of child sexual abuse in China: Changes from 2010 to 2019. *Journal of Child Sexual Abuse., 5*, 1–23.

Zeglin, R. J., DeRaedt, M. R., & Lanthier, R. P. (2015). Does having children moderate the effect of child sexual abuse on depression? *Journal of Child Sexual Abuse., 24*, 607–626.

Chapter 7
Cyberbullying

Michelle F. Wright

Introduction

Millions of youths use electronic technologies, such as mobile phones and the Internet, daily (Lenhart, 2015). These technologies allow youths many opportunities, such as the ability to communicate with just about anyone, quick access to information for leisure and homework purposes, and entertainment (e.g., watching videos). Despite the positives associated with electronic technology use, many youths are at risk for exposure to problematic online situations. Such situations might involve viewing unwanted electronic content through videos, images, and text, which contains glory or sexually graphic content. Problematic online situations also include experiencing identity theft and being targeted by sexual predators. Cyberbullying is another risk associated with youths' electronic technology use.

Defined as an extension of traditional bullying, cyberbullying involves being targeted by negative and unwanted behaviors via electronic technologies, including email, instant messaging, social networking websites, and text messages via mobile phones (Bauman et al., 2013b; Grigg, 2012). The anonymity of the cyber context allows cyberbullies greater flexibility to harm their victims without having to witness the reactions of the victims and/or experience any negative consequences as a result of their actions (Wright, 2014a). Cyberbullies' ability to remain anonymous is made possible by the ability to mask or hide their identity in cyberspace. Because youths can remain anonymous online, anonymity can trigger the online disinhibition effect. The online disinhibition effect is when youths do or say something to others that they typically would never do or say in the offline world (Suler, 2004; Wright, 2015). Another component of electronic technologies is the rapid transmission of communication. Because electronic technologies have such a feature, many cyberbullies can target their victims more quickly. For example, a rumor in the

M. F. Wright (✉)
DePaul University, Chicago, IL, USA

© The Author(s), under exclusive license to Springer Nature Switzerland AG 2022
R. T. Gopalan (ed.), *Victimology*, https://doi.org/10.1007/978-3-031-12930-8_7

offline world might take several hours to spread around school, while in the online world, this rumor could take a matter of minutes to spread to various classmates. Bullies can often target victims as often as they want as it is difficult to escape bullying in the online world as the behaviors can follow the person almost anywhere there is electronic technology access. Although it is possible to have many bystanders for traditional school bullying, cyberbullying has the potential to reach an audience of millions. These individuals can then perpetuate the cycle of cyberbullying by further sharing cyberbullying content (e.g., videos, pictures) with others.

The aim of this chapter is to review the topic of cyberbullying among youths, who might include children and adolescents from elementary school to high school. The literature reviewed includes studies from various disciplines, such as psychology, education, media studies, communication, social work, sociology, computer science, information technology, and gender studies. These studies might also include cross-sectional, longitudinal, qualitative, quantitative, and mixed-methods research designs. The chapter also draws on various studies across the world to conceptualize cyberbullying as a global health concern. The chapter includes seven sections, including:

(a) Background—It contains the definition of cyberbullying, the various characteristic behaviors, the various electronic technologies, the prevalence rates of cyberbullying, and the role of anonymity in perpetrating cyberbullying.
(b) Youths' characteristics and risk factors—It reviews the factors associated with youth's involvement in cyberbullying as perpetrators and/or victims.
(c) Negative psychosocial and academic outcomes—It explains research findings regarding the psychological, social, behavioral, and academic consequences associated with youths' cyberbullying involvement.
(d) Theoretical framework—It provides an overview of the social cognitive theory and the online disinhibition effect, and their application to cyberbullying.
(e) Solutions and recommendations—This section describes suggestions for prevention and intervention programs aimed at reducing cyberbullying involvement among youths, and public policy recommendations.
(f) Future research directions—It explains various recommendations for future research aimed at understanding youths' involvement in cyberbullying.
(g) Conclusion—It highlights closing remarks regarding the current nature of the literature on cyberbullying.

Background

Smith et al. (2013) defined cyberbullying as youths' use of electronic technologies to harass, embarrass, and intimidate others with hostile intent. The "hostile intent" portion of the definition is a requirement for a particular behavior or behaviors to qualify as cyberbullying. Cyberbullying can also include repetition and an imbalance of power between the perpetrator and the victim, similar to the traditional face-to-face bullying definition. In cyberbullying, the bully might target the victim multiple times by sharing a humiliating and embarrassing video or text message to one person or multiple people (Bauman et al., 2013b). It might also include only sending a message to someone once. Another opportunity for repetitiveness might be sending a video or a text message to one person and then that particular person shares the content again with another person or multiple people, who then again share the content with someone else. Repetitiveness of cyberbullying captures the potentially cyclic nature of this form of bullying.

The electronic technology component of the cyberbullying definition separates this form of bullying from traditional face-to-face bullying (Curelaru et al., 2009).

Examples of cyberbullying include sending unkind, mean, and/or nasty text messages, chat program messages, and emails, theft of identity information, pretending to be someone else, making anonymous phone calls, sharing secrets about the victim by posting or sending the secret to someone else, tricking someone to share a secret and then spreading the secret around, spreading nasty and/or untrue rumors using social networking websites, threatening to harm someone in the offline world, or uploading an embarrassing picture or video of a video who does not want to image shared (Bauman et al., 2013a, b). Many cyberbullying behaviors are similar to those perpetrate or experienced in the offline world, such as experiencing/perpetrating harassment, insults, verbal attacks, teasing, physical threats, social exclusion, gossip, humiliation.

Cyberbullying behaviors can occur through a variety of technologies, such as social networking websites, text messages via mobile phones, chat programs, online gaming, creation of a defamatory website against someone, and making fake social networking profiles using someone else's identity (Rideout et al., 2005). Another type of cyberbullying includes happy slapping, which involves a group of people who insult another person at random while filming the incident via a mobile phone and then posting the images or videos online for others to watch. Flaming is another type of cyberbullying behavior, and it involves posting a provocative or offensive message in a public forum with the desire of provoking a hostile response or triggering an argument with other members of the forum. The most frequently utilized technologies to harm others include gaming consoles, instant messaging tools, and social networking websites (Ybarra et al., 2007).

The prevalence rates of cyberbullying among youths have been frequently examined. In one study, 3767 middle school students (aged 11–14) were surveyed to examine their involvement in cyberbullying (Kowalski & Limber, 2007). Of this sample, 11% reported that they were cyberbullied at least once, 4% had bullied other youths, and 7% were involved as both perpetrator and victim. Higher prevalence rates were found by Patchin and Hinduja (2006). They found that 29% of the youths in their sample reported having experienced cyber victimization and 47% indicated that they were cyberbystanders. With an older sample of youths, grades 9th through 12th, Goebert et al. (2011) found that 56.1% of youths in their sample from the state of Hawaii reported that they were victims of cyberbullying. Taking into account the potential of cyberbullying experiences to extend from middle school to high school, Hinduja and Patchin (2012) surveyed youths in grades 6th through 12th. They found that 4.9% of their sample perpetrated cyberbullying in the past 30 days. Although differences in prevalence rates are the result of variations in sampling techniques and measurement techniques, it is important to understand these rates as they suggest that cyberbullying is a growing concern among children and adolescents. Cyberbullying is not just a problem localized to youths in the United States. Instead, it is a global problem with increasing evidence that cyberbullying occurs in Canada, Europe, Australia, Africa, Asia, and South America.

Cyberbullying in Canada

In comparison to cyberbullying prevalence rates in the United States, rates of youths' involvement in these behaviors are lower in Canada. In particular, Cappadocia et al. (2013) found that 2.1% of youths in their sample of 10th graders reported that they were perpetrators of cyberbullying, 1.9% reported being cyber-victims, and 0.6% explained that they were both cyberbullies and cybervictims. Slightly higher rates were found in another sample of Canadian adolescents in the 8th through 10th grades (Bonanno & Hymel, 2013). Bonnanno and Hymel found that 6% of their sample reported that they were cyberbullies, 5.8% reported that they were cybervictims only, and 5% indicated that they were both cyberbullies and cybervictims.

Cyberbullying in Europe

Using a sample of 22,544 Swedish youths, between the ages of 15 and 18, Laftman et al. (2013) found that 5% of their samples were cybervictims, 4% were cyberbullies, and 2% were both cybervicitms and cyberbullies. In a slightly younger sample of Swedish adolescents, seventh through ninth graders, Beckman et al. (2012) found that 1.9% of their samples were cybervictims, 2.9% were classified as cyberbullies, and 0.6% were cyberbullies and cybervictims. Cyberbullying has also been documented in Ireland in a sample of 876 12 through 17 year olds (Corcoran et al., 2012). Rates were 6% for cyber victimization among this group of Irish youths. Italian youths typically report higher levels of cyberbullying involvement when compared to youths in Northern and Western Europe. In one study, Brighi et al. (2012) found that 12.5% of the Italian youths in their sample of 2326, with an average age of 13.9 years, were classified as cybervictims. Similar rates have been found among German youths. In this research, Festl et al. (2013) found that 13% of their samples of 276, 13 through 19 year olds, were classified as cyberbullies and 11% were classified as cybervictims. Olenik-Shemesh et al. (2012) found that 16.5% of their participants ($N = 242$; 13–16 year olds) were cybervictims. The rate of Israeli adolescents identified as cybervictims or witnesses of cyberbullying was 32.4% of the sample ($N = 355$; 13–17 year olds; Lazuras et al., 2013).

Research has also been conducted with Turkish youths. In this research, Yilmaz (2011) found that 18% of the 756 7th graders in the study reported that they were victimized by cyberbullying and 6% reported that they were perpetrators of cyberbullying. Rates were much higher in Erdur-Baker's (2010) study. She found that 32% of the 276 youths, ages 14–18 years, in her study reported that they were cybervictims. Ayas and Horzum (2010) found that 19% of youths in the sample of 12–14 year olds had perpetrated cyberbullying. Slightly higher rates of cyberbullying perpetration were reported among Aricak et al.'s (2008) sample of 269 Turkish secondary school students. Of these students, 36% admitted that they had cyberbullied someone at least once.

Cyberbullying in Asia

Research on cyberbullying among Asian countries has been slower to develop than research in the United States, Canada, and Europe. In this research, Huang and Chou (2010) found that 63.4% of the 545 Taiwanese youths in their sample had witnessed cyberbullying, 34.9% were classified as cybervictims, and 20.4% were classified as cyberbullies. Jang et al. (2014) surveyed 3238 Korean adolescents, with findings revealing that 43% were classified as being involved in cyberbullying. Similar rates have been found among adolescents in China, with 34.8% in one sample ($N = 1438$) reporting that they were cyberbullies and 56.9% as cybervictims (Zhou et al., 2013). Focusing exclusively on Facebook cyberbullying, Kwan and Skoric (2013) reported that 59.4% of Singaporean adolescents in their study experienced cyber victimization through this social media website, while 56.9% perpetrated cyberbullying. In addition, Wong et al. (2014) found that 12.2% of adolescents in their sample ($N = 1912$) were cybervictims and 13.1% were classified as cyberbullying perpetrators.

Cross-Cultural Differences in Cyberbullying Involvement

Research on the cross-cultural differences in cyberbullying typically classified countries according to an independent self-construal or an interdependent self-construal. To have an independent self-construal view, the self is viewed as separate from the social context. On the other hand, someone with an interdependent self-construal view themselves within the context of their society. Typically, people from Western countries, like the United States, Canada, and the United Kingdom, reinforce and prime people to behave in ways aligned with an independent self-construal, while people from Eastern countries, like China, Korea, and Japan, are reinforced and primed for behavior consistently in regards to an independent self-construal. Differences in these self-construals affect people's social behaviors, particularly bullying and cyberbullying. Therefore, independent and interdependent self-construals have been used to explain these behaviors. In this research, youths from the United States typically reported higher rates of cyberbullying involvement, either as perpetrators or victims, when compared to Japanese youths (Barlett et al., 2013). Similar patterns have also been found among Austrian and Japanese youths (Strohmeier et al., 2013). In other research, Chinese youths reported less cyberbullying perpetration when compared to Canadian youths (Li, 2008) but more cyberbullying victimization than Canadian youths. Other research comparing East Asian youths from Canada with Canadian youths, Shapka and Law (2013) found that East Asian youths engaged in cyberbullying more for proactive reasons (i.e., to obtain a goal), while Canadian youths reported cyberbullying perpetration for reactive reasons (i.e., response to provocation). Wright et al. (2015) found that Indian youths reported higher levels of cyberbullying involvement than youths from China and Japan, with Indian boys reporting the highest rates of cyberbullying involvement.

Youths' Characteristics and Risk Factors for Cyberbullying

Despite differences in the estimates of cyberbullying rates, these studies provided evidence that cyberbullying is an experience that is reported among youths. With the recognition that cyberbullying is something to be concerned about among youths, researchers began to direct their attention to the characteristics and risk factors related to youths' involvement in cyberbullying.

Age was one of the first risk factors to receive attention. Findings from this research indicated that cyberbullying victimization peaked in early adolescences and that high school adolescents were more likely to perpetrated cyberbullying (Williams & Guerra, 2007). In addition, physical forms of cyberbullying, such as hacking, also peaked in middle school but generally declined in high school. On the other hand, Wade and Beran (2011) concluded that cyberbullying involvement was highest among 9th graders in their study when compared to middle school students.

Other research has focused on gender as a predictor of youths' cyberbullying involvement. Findings from this research indicated that boys were more often the perpetrators of cyberbullying when compared to girls (Boulton et al., 2012; Li, 2007; Ybarra et al., 2007). In contrast, other research (e.g., Dehue et al., 2008; Pornari & Wood, 2010) has revealed that girls were more often cyberbullies than boys. In some studies, girls reported that they were more often victimized by cyberbullying in comparison to boys (Hinduja & Patchin, 2007; Kowalski & Limber, 2007). Contrary to these findings, some research (e.g., Huang & Chou, 2010; Sjurso et al., 2016) has found that boys were more often cybervictims when compared to girls. Other studies (e.g., Stoll & Block, 2015; Wright & Li, 2013b) have revealed no gender differences in youths' involvement in cyberbullying.

Researchers have also directed their attention to considering youths' offline experience of perpetrators and victims of traditional school bullying as risk factors for youths' involvement in cyberbullying. These studies have considered the role of victim and perpetrator in both the face-to-face and cyber contexts. In these studies, positive associations are found between cyberbullying perpetration and traditional face-to-face bullying perpetration, cyber victimization and traditional face-to-face victimization and cyberbullying perpetration (Barlett & Gentile, 2012; Mitchell et al., 2007; Wright & Li, 2013a, b).

Another risk factor associated with youths' cyberbullying involvement is their use of electronic technology. The underlying conclusion in this research is that any exposure to electronic technology can increase youths' risk of cyberbullying. Higher use of the internet is associated positively with both the perpetration and victimization by cyber victimization (Ang, 2016; Aricak et al., 2008). Compared with non-victims, cybervictims spend more time using instant messaging tools, email, blogging sites, and online gaming (Smith et al., 2008). A possible explanation for the connection between electronic technology use and cyberbullying involvement is the likelihood that these youths disclose more personal information online, including geographical location (Ybarra et al., 2007). Disclosing this information puts them at risk for cyber victimization.

Internalizing problems, like depression and loneliness, as well as externalizing problems, like alcohol use, are also associated with youths' involvement in cyberbullying. To explain such relationships, researchers propose that victims' coping abilities are diminished or ineffective, which makes them vulnerable to cyberbullying (Cappadocia et al., 2013; Mitchell et al., 2007). Furthermore, Cappadocia et al. (2013) and Wright (2015) found that alcohol and drug use were each related positively to cyberbullying perpetration.

Researchers have also identified other variables that are linked to youths' cyberbullying involvement. Normative beliefs are the beliefs that a specific set of behavior, in this case cyberbullying, is an acceptable form of behavior. In this research, youths with higher normative beliefs concerning face-to-face bullying and cyberbullying were related positively to cyberbullying perpetration (e.g., Burton et al., 2013; Wright, 2014a). Therefore, cyberbullies believe that cyberbullying is an acceptable form of behavior to engage in. Provictim attitudes, defined as the belief that bullying is unacceptable and that defending victims is valuable, is another factor related to cyberbullying. Holding lower levels of provictim attitudes is associated positively with cyberbullying perpetration (Sevcikova et al., 2015). In addition, youths with lower levels of peer attachment, less self-control, and empathy, and greater moral disengagement were each related positively to cyberbullying perpetration (e.g., Wright, Kamble, Lei, Li, Aoyama, & Shruti, 2015).

Many of the studies on the characteristics and risk factors associated with cyberbullying involvement utilize cross-sectional research designs. Consequently, it is difficult to make understand the long-term associations of these characteristics and risk factors associated with cyberbullying involvement. Fanti et al. (2012) conducted a longitudinal study investigating youths' exposure to violent media and callous and unemotional traits in relation to cyberbullying involvement 1 year later. Findings revealed that media violence exposure related to greater cyber victimization. Perceived levels of stress from parents, peers, and academics also have a role in adolescents' perpetration of cyberbullying 1 year later (Wright, 2015).

In sum, there are a variety of characteristics and risk factors that make youths vulnerable to cyberbullying. Moving away from individual-related characteristics and risk factors, other researchers have examined the role of parents, schools, and teachers in youths' cyberbullying involvement.

Parents as Risk Factors

Parenting styles are linked to youths' involvement in cyberbullying. In particular, youths who are bully-victims often have parents who utilize indifferent-uninvolved parenting styles and inconsistent monitoring of their activities increases youths' involvement in cyberbullying (Totura et al., 2009). Neglectful parenting, or sometimes referred to as indifferent-uninvolved parenting, increased youths' involvement in cyberbullying in comparison to uninvolved youths (Dehue et al., 2012). Indifferent-uninvolved parents are often emotionally distance from their children, engage in little or no supervision, show little warmth and affection toward their children, place fewer demands on their children's behaviors, might and intentionally avoid their children. Cyber victimization was also increased among children who reported that their parents engaged in authoritarian parenting styles. Authoritarian parenting style is defined as parents who have high levels of demands and low levels of responsiveness. These parents have very high expectation but they display very low levels of warmth or nurturance.

Another aspect of parenting is the use of parental monitoring. The cyber context provides another opportunity for parents to monitor their children's online activity. In this research, Mason (2008) found that 50% of the children in his study reported that their parents monitored their online activities. One study explored the differences between what parents report in terms of how often they monitor their children's online activities and how often their children reported being monitored (McQuade et al., 2009). McQuade et al. found that 93% of parents in their study reported that they set limits on their children's online activities. However, only 37% of their children reported that their parents had given them rules regarding their online activities. These findings might indicate that parents overestimate the amount of monitoring they engage in or that the strategies they do implement are ineffective. Just like in the offline world, parents have an important role in protecting their children against online risks. Additional attention should be given to how parents navigate conversations with their children about online risks and opportunities.

Other research has focused on the role of parental monitoring and parental mediation in relation to reducing youths' risk of cyberbullying involvement. Wright et al. (2015) found that when youths reported more technology mediation by their parents they reported lower levels of cyber victimization and the associated negative adjustment difficulties. To explain these connections, Wright explains that parents who monitor their children's electronic technology use might have more opportunities to engage in discussions on the risks associated with cyberbullying involvement. Parents might also convey, during these discussions, that cyberbullying is unacceptable. Such a proposal is supported by the literature as Hinduja and Patchin (2013) and Wright (2013) found that youths who were concerned with being punished for negative online behaviors were much less likely to perpetrate cyberbullying. One study found little support that parental monitoring was helpful for preventing cyberbullying involvement. In this study, Aoyama et al. (2011) did not find that parental mediation and monitoring of their children's online activities were related to their children's cyberbullying perpetration and victimization. Aoyama et al. explained that many parents lack the technological skills to effectively monitor their children's online activities, which makes it difficult for them to know when and how to intervene in these activities. Another potential explanation might be that parents implement rules for electronic technology use that they do not follow-up on. Not following through with these rules can give the impression that parents are unconcerned with appropriate online behaviors, increasing the risk of engaging in cyberbullying. Failing to enforce rules might also indicate that parents do not often update strategies as their children become more independent electronic technology users. Research findings support this proposal as many parents report that they are not sure as to what type of online activities to discuss with their children (Rosen, 2007). When parents are not sure how to talk to their children about online activities, then it might lead many parents to not discuss appropriate online behaviors with their children.

There is also some research which investigates other family characteristics in relation to youths' cyberbullying involvement. Family income, parental education, and marital status of caregivers were unrelated to youths' involvement in cyberbullying (Ybarra & Mitchell, 2004). Other research indicates that parental unemployment increased youths' risk of cyberbullying perpetration and victimization (Arslan et al., 2012).

Schools as Risk Factors

Schools' role in monitoring and punishing youth's involvement in cyberbullying is a topic of great debate about school districts, parents, authorities, and researchers. This is because many of the cases involving cyberbullying are carried out off school groups, making it difficult for schools to be aware of such cases (deLara, 2012; Mason, 2008). However, many incidences of cyberbullying involve youths who attend the same school, making the schools' role in handling such incidences complex. Because cyberbullies and cybervictims might attend the same school, it is possible that knowledge of a cyberbullying incidence could spread throughout the school, leading to negative interactions between youths while on school grounds. These negative interactions could disrupt the learning process.

Regardless of the extent to which cyberbullying incidences can "spill over" onto school grounds, many administrators, teachers, and school districts have very different perceptions and awareness of cyberbullying. Some of these individuals might not even perceive cyberbullying as a significant event, warranting attention

(Kochenderfer-Ladd & Pelletier, 2008). It is problematic when administrators and teachers do not perceive cyberbullying as problematic because electronic technology and digital communication are embedded in the lives of the youths they teach. Furthermore, these administrators and teachers are often not likely to perceive any form of covert bullying behavior as serious and harmful as physical bullying (Sahin, 2010). They are often not likely to understand the consequences associated with relational bullying and cyberbullying. This could lead to the decision not to help youths who experience these behaviors or dealing with the situation by minimizing it. Teacher training might not properly inform teachers on how to deal with and recognize cyberbullying, making teachers' ability to intervene difficult. Cassidy et al. (2012a) found that many Canadian teachers were unfamiliar with newer technologies. Being unfamiliar with newer technologies made it difficult for these teachers to deal with cyberbullying as they were often unsure of how to respond to the incidence or of how to implement strategies to address the incident. Even when teachers were concerned with cyberbullying, their school district did not have policies and programs in place to deal with these behaviors (Cassidy et al., 2012b). This made it difficult for teachers to implement solutions and strategies.

Other research has revealed that teachers were often willing to participate in prevention programs aimed at reducing traditional face-to-face bullying but not cyberbullying prevention programs (Tangen & Campbell, 2010). This could be a product of few empirically and theoretical driven cyberbullying prevention programs or that administrators and teachers do not consider cyberbullying an important enough issue to warrant attention. Recognizing the importance of implementing policies and training programs on cyberbullying is important because youths' involvement in these behaviors has the potential to impact the learning environment (Shariff & Hoff, 2007).

Educators require training to increase their awareness of cyberbullying, with the hope of developing policies at the school level to reduce these behaviors. When teachers are more confident about their abilities and have a stronger commitment to their school, they are more likely to learn about cyberbullying, and have a greater awareness of these behaviors and knowledge to deal effectively with it (Eden et al., 2013). Such awareness and knowledge prevent children's and adolescents' cyberbullying perpetration and victimization. Furthermore, when teachers feel more confident, they intervene in cyberbullying incidences more often, which protects adolescents' from experiencing these behaviors (Elledge et al., 2013). Unfortunately, teachers' motivation for learning about cyberbullying decreases from elementary school to middle school, which is problematic as cyberbullying involvement usually increases in these years (Ybarra et al., 2007). Therefore, there is a need for educator training programs aimed at raising awareness of cyberbullying, particularly in the middle school years.

Youths' involvement in cyberbullying is less likely to perceive their school and teachers positively when compared to uninvolved youths (Bayar & Ucanok, 2012). Some youths might experience cyberbullying and fear that their classmates could be responsible. This decreases these youths' concentration on learning, thereby reducing their academic attainment and performance (Eden et al., 2013). Lower school commitment and perceptions of a negative school climate increase children's and adolescents' engagement in cyberbullying as they feel less connected to their school (Williams & Guerra, 2007). Youths' involvement in cyberbullying is linked to poor academic functioning (Wright, 2015).

Peer interactions are present in both the offline and online world. Through these interactions, youths learn about the social norms dictating acceptable and unacceptable behaviors within the peer group, and consequently they engage in more of the acceptable behaviors, even if they are negative. In this line of research, cyberbullying involvement is highest among classrooms in which these behaviors are elevated (Festl et al., 2013). Something about the classroom climate might be driving the levels of cyberbullying behaviors within a particular classroom. Furthermore, believing that one's friends engaged in cyberbullying also increases youths' risk of perpetrating cyberbullying (Hinduja & Patchin, 2013). Peer contagion might potentially explain these relationships. What this means is that one's friends "spread" negative online behaviors to others within their social network (Sijtsema et al., 2014).

Another peer-related variable associated with cyberbullying involvement is peer attachment. Peer attachment is defined as the closeness that youths feel with their same or similarly aged peers. Lower levels of peer attachment were associated positively with cyberbullying perpetration and victimization (Burton et al., 2013). When youths have poor peer attachment, they are likely to believe that their peers will not be there for them when they need it. This belief promotes negative interactions with peers. Cyberbullying involvement is higher when youths' experience peer rejection, whether perceived rejection or peer-reported rejection (Sevcikova et al., 2015; Wright & Li, 2013b). Wright and Li (2012) argue that peer rejection triggers negative emotional responses that lead to cyberbullying perpetration and victimization.

Cyberbullying perpetration might also be used to maintain and boost youths' social standing among their peer group, both online and offline. Wright (2014b) found that higher levels of perceived popularity, a reputational type of popularity in the peer group, were associated positively with cyberbullying perpetration 6 months later. With the prominent role of electronic technologies in youths' lives, Wright proposes that they might utilize these technologies as a tool for the promotion and maintenance of their social standing. The literature in this section suggests that it is important to consider the role of schools and peers in youths' cyberbullying involvement.

Negative Psychosocial and Academic Outcomes Associated with Youths' Involvement in Cyberbullying

Concerns with cyberbullying involvement among youths were triggered by the associated negative psychosocial and academic outcomes. Potential research for these linkages is that cyberbullying disrupts youths' emotional experiences, making them more vulnerable to negative outcomes, due to ineffective coping strategies.

Cybervictims are more likely than nonvictims to report lower levels of global happiness, general school happiness, school satisfaction, family satisfaction, and self-satisfaction (Toledano et al., 2015). In addition, cybervictims report more feelings of anger, sadness, and fear in comparison to noninvolved children and adolescents (Dehue et al., 2008; Machackova et al., 2013; Patchin & Hinduja, 2006).

Cyberbullying involvement also impacts youths' academic performance. In this literature, both cybervictims and cyberbullies are at an increased risk for difficulties at school, including academic problems, less motivation for school, poor academic performance, lower academic attainment, and more school absences (Yousef & Bellamy, 2015). Lower school functioning also relates to cyberbullying perpetration and cyber victimization (Wright, 2015). Cyberbullies and cybervictims experience the lower levels of school functioning when compared to cyberbullies, cybervictims, and uninvolved youths.

Internalizing and externalizing problems are both associated with youths' cyberbullying involvement (e.g., Mitchell et al., 2007; Patchin & Hinduja, 2006; Wright, 2014a; Ybarra et al., 2007). Cyberbullies and cybervictims both experience suicidal thoughts and attempt suicide more often than uninvolved youths (Bauman et al., 2013a). Similar results were found by Beckman et al. (2012). Beckman and colleagues also found that cyberbullying involvement increased youths' risk for experiencing mental health problems. Other research suggests that these youths are also at risk for psychiatric and psychosomatic problems (Sourander et al., 2010).

A limitation associated with the research on the psychosocial and behavioral consequences related to youths' cyberbullying involvement is that researchers do not account for youths' involvement in traditional face-to-face bullying. It is important to account for youths' involvement in traditional face-to-face bullying because this experience is associated with similar consequences as cyberbullying and due to the high correlation between the two (Williams & Guerra, 2007; Wright & Li, 2013b). One study accounted for traditional face-to-face bullying involvement and the findings suggested that cyberbullying perpetration and victimization might have worse psychological consequences when compared to the face-to-face bullying perpetration and victimization, after controlling for face-to-face bullying and victimization (Bonanno & Hymel, 2013).

Given the high correlation between cyberbullying and traditional face-to-face bullying involvement, some researchers have focused on the combined effects of these experiences on youths' psychosocial and behavioral outcomes. In this research, victims of both traditional face-to-face bullying and cyberbullying reported higher levels of internalizing symptoms when compared to youths who experienced only one type of victimization (Gradinger et al., 2009; Perren et al., 2010).

The research reviewed in this section suggests that a combination of various bullying experiences, whether online or offline, exacerbates youths' experience of depression, anxiety, and loneliness. These findings indicate the importance of considering youths' involvement in various bullying behaviors to better understand the best ways to intervene.

Theoretical Frameworks

In this section, two theories will be presented, along with their application to cyber-bullying involvement among youths. These theories include the social cognitive theory and the online disinhibition effect.

According to the social cognitive theory, parents and/or friends serve as impor-tant models of behaviors that are observed and replicated by youths (Hinduja & Patchin, 2008; Mouttapa et al., 2004). This theory has been extensively applied to youths' involvement in aggressive behaviors, including cyberbullying (Barlett & Gentile, 2012). According to Olweus (1993), children's aggressive behaviors are learned or modeled by someone who was stronger than the observer. The effects of the model on the observer depended on the observer's positive evaluation of the model. These perceptions have the potential to increase the likelihood of reducing children's inhibition for aggressive behaviors and increase aggressive acts, particu-larly when the model is rewarded for acting aggressively. In regard to cyberbullying, youths observe various incidences of successful cyberbullying acts (Barlett & Gentile, 2012). The more often they are exposed to these acts the greater the likeli-hood that they believe cyberbullying is acceptable, normative, and tolerable. The anonymity offered by the cyber context increases the chance that little or no imme-diate consequences occur after cyberbullying perpetration. When youths are posi-tively reinforced for cyberbullying behaviors, adolescents held greater positive attitudes toward these behaviors (Barlett & Gentile, 2012). These attitudes relate to future perpetration of cyberbullying behaviors (Wright & Li, 2013a, b).

The online disinhibition effect theory refers to the likelihood that the characteris-tics of the cyber context will increase the likelihood that youths engage in different ways online than they would offline (Suler, 2004). The cyber context allows people to loosen, reduce, or dismiss the typical social restrictions and inhibitions present in normal face-to-face interactions (Mason, 2008). The literature supports the premise that people behave differently in cyberspace than in the offline world. Research indicates that people are likely to be blunter when communicating with others via electronic technologies (McKenna & Bargh, 2000). In online communication, there are more misunderstanding, heightened hostility, and increase in aggressive behav-iors via electronic technologies when compared to face-to-face communication. It is also possible for communications through some electronic technologies might to not see emotional reactions. Not being able to see someone's emotional reactions in cyberspace prevents people from modulating their own behaviors because they are not able to witness the consequences of their actions, like they could in the offline world (Kowalski & Limber, 2007). Cyberbullying often occurs because cyberbullies cannot witness the cybervictims' reactions nor are their many opportunities to expe-rience social disapproval, punishment, or other consequences. Many cyberbullies recognize the ease of engaging in aggressive behaviors through electronic technolo-gies, which could potentially lead their behaviors to become more disinhibited over time, especially when they receive positive reinforcement for their behavior and are not able to recognize the consequences of their behaviors (Hinduja & Patchin, 2010;

Wright, 2015). Deindividuation, the process of not being accountable for one's actions, also occurs as a result of the online disinhibition effect (Joinson, 1998). Being able to remain anonymous through electronic technologies reduces youths' accountability for their online interactions. Coupling the reduction of accountability with the anonymity of the cyber context, might make it easier for youths to disengage from others, leading to increases in harmful online behaviors (Wright, 2015).

Solutions and Recommendations

Cyberbullying is a public health concern, warranting attention by all members of our communities, including educators, researchers, parents, and youths themselves. It is also important for education curriculum to include digital literacy skills training and citizenship in both the online and offline worlds (Cassidy et al., 2012b). Such curriculum should also focus on the positive uses of electronic technology, building empathy for negative online interactions, self-esteem, and social skills. To also improve school climate, administrators and teachers should learn students' names, praise good behavior, and stay technologically informed and up-to-date (Hinduja & Patchin, 2012).

Schools and parents should partner to help address cyberbullying. Parents should also increase their awareness and knowledge of electronic technologies (Cassidy et al., 2012a; Diamanduros & Downs, 2011). Increasing one's knowledge of electronic technologies can help parents understand the importance of technology in their children's lives and to recognize the risk and opportunities of their children's electronic technology use. Parents can also implement more effective monitoring strategies when they are more knowledge about electronic technologies and cyberbullying. Parents are encouraged to engage in open dialogue with children about appropriate electronic technology use.

Future Research Directions

There are some noticeable future directions for research on youths' involvement in cyberbullying. Anonymity is associated with youths' perpetration of cyberbullying involvement, but little attention has been given to this topic. Future research should focus on youths' perceptions of anonymous acts online and which factors might motivate them to engage in anonymous forms of cyberbullying. This research should also examine anonymous forms of cyberbullying versus nonanonymous forms of cyberbullying to better understand the motivators underlying these behaviors. This research should also investigate whether coping strategies and psychosocial adjustment difficulties vary as a function of whether cyberbullying was anonymous or nonanonymous. Additional investigations should be undertaken to understand the long-term impact of cyberbullying involvement among youths. Intervention and prevention programs could be developed which specific consideration to the specific age group identified as at the most risk for cyberbullying involvement.

Summary and Conclusion

The purpose of this literature review was to summarize research on cyberbullying involvement among youths by providing a description and definition, information about the characteristics and risk factors, the negative adjustment outcomes associated with the involvement in these behaviors, and theoretical frameworks. The studies reviewed in this chapter utilize cross-sectional, longitudinal, qualitative, quantitative, and mixed-methods research designs. Studies with various youths from across the world were also reviewed to shed more light on the cross-cultural research on youths' cyberbullying involvement. This cross-cultural research also provides support about youths' cyberbullying involvement being a global phenomenon.

The literature in this chapter provides a firm foundation for understanding youths' involvement in cyberbullying and the next directions for intervention, prevention, public policy, and research. The review suggests that much of the earlier research on cyberbullying focused on the prevalence rates of these behaviors. Current shifts in this research have changed the focus to understanding the causes and consequences of youths' involvement in cyberbullying. Although this research is still in its early stages in comparison to the literature on traditional face-to-face bullying, many of the published studies on cyberbullying focus on individual predictors of youths' involvement in these behaviors. More consideration is needed to understand the role of parents, schools, peers, and communities in youths' cyberbullying perpetration and victimization. Follow-up research on cyberbullying is important as this negative behavior impacts many aspects of our society, potentially undermining ethical and moral values. Consequently, it is imperative that we unite and do our part to reduce children's and adolescents' involvement in cyberbullying together.

References

Ang, R. P. (2016). Cyberbullying: Its prevention and intervention strategies. In D. Sibnath (Ed.), *Child safety, welfare and well-being: Issues and challenges* (pp. 25–38). Springer.

Aoyama, I., Utsumi, S., & Hasegawa, M. (2011). Cyberbullying in Japan: Cases, government reports, adolescent relational aggression and parental monitoring roles. In Q. Li, D. Cross, & P. K. Smith (Eds.), *Bullying in the global playground: Research from an international perspective*. Wiley-Blackwell.

Aricak, T., Siyahhan, S., Uzunhasanoglu, A., Saribeyoglu, S., Ciplak, S., Yilmaz, N., & Memmedov, C. (2008). Cyberbullying among Turkish adolescents. *CyberPsychology and Behavior, 11*, 253–261.

Arslan, S., Savaser, S., Hallett, V., & Balci, S. (2012). Cyberbullying among primary school students in Turkey: Self-reported prevalence and associations with home and school life. *CyberPsychology, Behavior, and Social Networking, 15*, 527–533.

Ayas, T., & Horzum, M. B. (2010). *Cyberbullg / victim scale development study*. Retrieved from: http://www.akademikbakis.org

Barlett, C. P., & Gentile, D. A. (2012). Long-term psychological predictors of cyber-bullying in late adolescence. *Psychology of Popular Media Culture, 2*, 123–135.

Barlett, C. P., Gentile, D. A., Anderson, C. A., Suzuki, K., Sakamoto, A., Yamaoka, A., & Katsura, R. (2013). Cross-cultural differences in cyberbullying behavior: A short-term longitudinal study. *Journal of Cross-Cultural Psychology, 45*, 300–313.

Bauman, S., Toomey, R. B., & Walker, J. L. (2013a). Associations among bullying, cyberbullying, and suicide in high school students. *Journal of Adolescence, 36*, 341–350.

Bauman, S., Underwood, M. K., & Card, N. A. (2013b). Definitions: Another perspective and a proposal for beginning with cyberaggression. In S. Bauman, D. Cross, & J. Walker (Eds.), *Principles of cyberbullying research: Definitions, measures, methodology* (pp. 26–40). Routledge.

Bayar, Y., & Ucanok, Z. (2012). School social climate and generalized peer perception in traditional and cyberbullying status. *Educational Sciences: Theory & Practice, 12*, 2352–2358.

Beckman, L., Hagquist, C., & Hellstrom, L. (2012). Does the association with psychosomatic health problems differ between cyberbullying and traditional bullying? *Emotional and Behavioural Difficulties, 17*, 421–434.

Bonanno, R. A., & Hymel, S. (2013). Cyber bullying and internalizing difficulties: Above and beyond the impact of traditional forms of bullying. *Journal of Youth and Adolescence, 42*, 685–697.

Boulton, M., Lloyd, J., Down, J., & Marx, H. (2012). Predicting undergraduates' self-reported engagement in traditional and cyberbullying from attitudes. *Cyberpsychology, Behavior and Social Networking, 15*(3), 141–147.

Brighi, A., Guarini, A., Melotti, G., Galli, S., & Genta, M. L. (2012). Predictors of victimisation across direct bullying, indirect bullying and cyberbullying. *Emotional and Behavioural Difficulties, 17*, 375–388.

Burton, K. A., Florell, D., & Wygant, D. B. (2013). The role of peer attachment and normative beliefs about aggression on traditional bullying and cyberbullying. *Psychology in the Schools, 50*, 103–114.

Cappadocia, M. C., Craig, W. M., & Pepler, D. (2013). Cyberbullying: Prevalence, stability and risk factors during adolescence. *Canadian Journal of School Psychology, 28*, 171–192.

Cassidy, W., Brown, K., & Jackson, M. (2012a). "Making kind cool": Parents' suggestions for preventing cyber bullying and fostering cyber kindness. *Journal of Educational Computing Research, 46*, 415–436.

Cassidy, W., Brown, K., & Jackson, M. (2012b). "Under the radar": Educators and cyberbullying in schools. *School Psychology International, 33*, 520–532.

Corcoran, L., Connolly, I., & O'Moore, M. (2012). Cyberbullying in Irish schools: An investigation of personality and self-concept. *The Irish Journal of Psychology, 33*, 153–165.

Curelaru, M., Iacob, I., & Abalasei, B. (2009). *School bullying: Definition, characteristics, and intervention strategies*. Lumean Publishing House.

Dehue, F., Bolman, C., & Vollink, T. (2008). Cyberbullying: Youngsters' experiences and parental perception. *Cyberpsychology and Behavior, 11*, 217–223.

Dehue, F., Bolman, C., Vollink, T., & Pouwelse, M. (2012). Cyberbullying and traditional bullying in relation to adolescents' perceptions of parenting. *Journal of Cybertherapy and Rehabilitation, 5*, 25–34.

deLara, E. W. (2012). Why adolescents don't disclose incidents of bullying and harassment. *Journal of School Violence, 11*(4), 288–305.

Diamanduros, T., & Downs, E. (2011). Creating a safe school environment: How to prevent cyberbullying at your school. *Library Media Connection, 30*(2), 36–38.

Eden, S., Heiman, T., & Olenik-Shemesh, D. (2013). Teachers' perceptions, beliefs and concerns about cyberbullying. *British Journal of Educational Technology, 44*, 1036–1052.

Elledge, L. C., Williford, A., Boulton, A. J., DePaolis, K. J., Little, T. D., & Salmivalli, C. (2013). Individual and contextual predictors of cyberbullying: The influence of children's provictim attitudes and teachers' ability to intervene. *Journal of Youth and Adolescence, 42*, 698–710.

Erdur-Baker, O. (2010). Cyberbullying and its correlation to traditional bullying, gender and frequent and risky usage of internet-mediated communication tools. *New Media & Society, 12*, 109–125.

Fanti, K. A., Demetriou, A. G., & Hawa, V. V. (2012). A longitudinal study of cyberbullying: Examining risk and protective factors. *European Journal of Developmental Psychology, 8*, 168–181.

Festl, R., Schwarkow, M., & Quandt, T. (2013). Peer influence, internet use and cyberbullying: A comparison of different context effects among German adolescents. *Journal of Children and Media, 7*, 446–462.

Goebert, D., Else, I., Matsu, C., Chung-Do, J., & Chang, J. Y. (2011). The impact of cyberbullying on substance uses and mental health in a multiethnic sample. *Maternal and Child Health Journal, 15*, 1282–1286.

Gradinger, P., Strohmeier, D., & Spiel, C. (2009). Traditional bullying and cyberbullying. *Journal of Psychology, 217*, 205–213.

Grigg, D. W. (2012). Definitional constructs of cyberbullying and cyber aggression from a triagnulatory overview: A preliminary study into elements. *Journal of Aggression, Conflict and Peace Research, 4*, 202–215.

Hinduja, S., & Patchin, J. W. (2007). Offline consequences of online victimization. *Journal of School Violence, 6*, 89–112.

Hinduja, S., & Patchin, J. W. (2008). Cyberbullying: An exploratory analysis of factors related to offending and victimization. *Deviant Behavior, 29*, 129–156.

Hinduja, S., & Patchin, J. W. (2010). Bullying, cyberbullying, and suicide. *Archives of Suicide Research, 14*, 206–221.

Hinduja, S., & Patchin, J. W. (2012). Cyberbullying: Neither and epidemic nor a rarity. *European Journal of Developmental Psychology, 9*, 539–543.

Hinduja, S., & Patchin, J. W. (2013). Social influences on cyberbullying behaviors among middle and high school students. *Journal of Youth and Adolescence, 42*, 711–722.

Huang, Y., & Chou, C. (2010). An analysis of multiple factors of cyberbullying among junior high school students in Taiwan. *Computers in Human Behavior, 26*, 1581–1590.

Jang, H., Song, J., & Kim, R. (2014). Does the offline bully-victimization influence cyberbullying behavior among youths? Application of general strain theory. *Computers in Human Behavior, 31*, 85–93.

Joinson, A. (1998). Causes and implications of behavior on the Internet. In J. Gackenbach (Ed.), *Psychology and the Internet: Intrapersonal, interpersonal, and transpersonal implications* (pp. 43–60). Academic Press.

Kochenderfer-Ladd, B., & Pelletier, M. (2008). Teachers' views and beliefs about bullying: Influences on classroom management strategies and students' coping with peer victimization. *Journal of School Psychology, 46*, 431–453.

Kowalski, R. M., & Limber, S. P. (2007). Electronic bullying among middle school students. *Journal of Adolescent Health, 41*, 22–30.

Kwan, G. C. E., & Skoric, M. M. (2013). Facebook bullying: An extension of battles in school. *Computers in Human Behavior, 29*(1), 16–25.

Laftman, S. B., Modin, B., & Ostberg, V. (2013). Cyberbullying and subjective health: A large-scale study of students in Stockholm, Sweden. *Children and Youth Services Review, 35*, 112–119.

Lazuras, L., Barkoukis, V., Ourda, D., & Tsorbatzoudis, H. (2013). A process model of cyberbullying in adolescence. *Computers in Human Behavior, 29*, 881–887.

Lenhart, A. (2015). *Teens, social media & technology overview 2015*. Retrieved from: http://www.pewinternet.org/2015/04/09/teens-social-media-technology-2015/

Li, Q. (2007). Bullying in the new playground: Research into cyberbullying and cybervictimization. *Australian Journal of Educational Technology, 23*, 435–454.

Li, Q. (2008). A cross-cultural comparison of adolescents' experience related to cyberbullying. *Educational Research, 50*, 223–234.

Machackova, H., Dedkova, L., Sevcikova, A., & Cerna, A. (2013). Bystanders' support of cyberbullied schoolmates. *Journal of Community & Applied Social Psychology, 23*(1), 25–36.

Mason, K. (2008). Cyberbullying: A preliminary assessment for school personnel. *Psychology in the Schools, 45*, 323–348.

McKenna, K. Y. A., & Bargh, J. A. (2000). Plan 9 from cyberspace: The implications of the internet for personality and social psychology. *Personality and Social Psychology Review, 4*, 57–75.

McQuade, C. S., Colt, P. J., & Meyer, B. N. (2009). *Cyber bullying: Protecting kids and adults from online bullies*. Praeger.

Mitchell, K. J., Ybarra, M., & Finkelhor, D. (2007). The relative importance of online victimization in understanding depression, delinquency, and substance use. *Child Maltreatment, 12*, 314–324.

Mouttapa, M., Valente, T., Gallagher, P., Rohrbach, L. A., & Unger, J. B. (2004). Social network predictor of bullying and victimization. *Adolescence, 39*, 315–335.

Olenik-Shemesh, D., Heiman, T., & Eden, S. (2012). Cyberbullying victimization in adolescence: Relationships with loneliness and depresisve mood. *Emotional and Behavioural Difficulties, 17(3–4), 361–374.*

Olweus, D. (1993). *Bullying at school. What we know and what we can do*. Blackwell Publishing.

Patchin, J. W., & Hinduja, S. (2006). Bullies move beyond the schoolyard: A preliminary look at cyberbullying. *Youth Violence and Juvenile Justice, 4*, 148–169.

Perren, S., Dooley, J., Shaw, T., & Cross, D. (2010). Bullying in school and cyberspace: Associations with depressive symptoms in Swiss and Australian adolescents. *Child and Adolescent Psychiatry and Mental Health, 4*, 1–10.

Pornari, C. D., & Wood, J. (2010). Peer and cyber aggression in secondary school students: The role of moral disengagement, hostile attribution bias, and outcome expectancies. *Aggressive Behavior, 36*, 81–94.

Rideout, V. J., Roberts, D. F., & Foehr, U. G. (2005). *Generation M: Media in the lives of 8-18-year-olds: Executive summary*. Henry J. Kaiser Family Foundation.

Rosen, L. D. (2007). *Me, Myspace, and I: Parenting the net generation*. Palgrave Macmillan.

Sahin, M. (2010). Teachers' perceptions of bullying in high schools: A Turkish study. *Social Behavior and Personality, 38*, 127–142.

Sevcikova, A., Machackova, H., Wright, M. F., Dedkova, L., & Cerna, A. (2015). Social support seeking in relation to parental attachment and peer relationships among victims of cyberbullying. *Australian Journal of Guidance and Counselling, 15*, 1–13. https://doi.org/10.1017/jgc.2015.1

Shapka, J. D., & Law, D. M. (2013). Does one size fit all? Ethnic differences in parenting behaviors and motivations for adolescent engagement in cyberbullying. *Journal of Youth and Adolescence, 42*, 723–738.

Shariff, S., & Hoff, D. L. (2007). Cyber bullying: Clarifying legal boundaries for school supervision in cyberspace. *International Journal of Cyber Criminology, 1*, 76–118.

Sijtsema, J. J., Ashwin, R. J., Simona, C. S., & Gina, G. (2014). Friendship selection and influence in bullying and defending. Effects of moral disengagement. *Developmental Psychology, 50*(8), 2093–2104.

Sjurso, I. R., Fandream, H., & Roland, E. (2016). Emotional problems in traditional and cyber victimization. *Journal of School Violence, 15*(1), 114–131.

Smith, P. K., Mahdavi, J., Carvalho, M., Fisher, S., Russell, S., & Tippett, N. (2008). Cyberbullying: Its nature and impact in secondary school pupils. *Journal of Child Psychology and Psychiatry, 49*, 376–385.

Smith, P. K., Del Barrio, C., & Tokunaga, R. S. (2013). Definitions of bullying and cyberbullying: How useful are the terms? In S. Bauman, D. Cross, & J. Walker (Eds.), *Principles of cyberbullying research: Definitions, measures, methodology* (pp. 26–40). Routledge.

Sourander, A., Brunstein, A., Ikonen, M., Lindroos, J., Luntamo, T., Koskelainen, M., Ristkari, T., & Helenius, H. (2010). Psychosocial risk factors associated with cyberbullying among adolescents: A population-based study. *Archives of General Psychiatry, 67*, 720–728.

Stoll, L. C., & Block, R. (2015). Intersectionality and cyberbullying: A study of cybervictimization in a Midwestern high school. *Computers in Human Behavior, 52*, 387–391.

Strohmeier, D., Aoyama, I., Gradinger, P., & Toda, Y. (2013). Cybervictimization and cyberaggression in Eastern and Western countries: Challenges of constructing a cross-cultural appropriate scale. In S. Bauman, D. Cross, & J. L. Walker (Eds.), *Principles of cyberbullying research: Definitions, measures, and methodology* (pp. 202–221). Routledge.

Suler, J. (2004). The online disinhibition effect. *CyberPsychology and Behavior, 7*, 321–326.

Tangen, D., & Campbell, M. (2010). Cyberbullying prevention: One primary school's approach. *Australian Journal of Guidance and Counselling, 20*, 225–234.

Toledano, S., Werch, B. L., & Wiens, B. A. (2015). Domain-specific self-concept in relation to traditional and cyber peer aggression. *Journal of School Violence, 14*(4), 405–423.

Totura, C. M. W., MacKinnon-Lewis, C., Gesten, E. L., Gadd, R., Divine, K. P., Dunham, S., & Kamboukos, D. (2009). Bullying and victimization among boys and girls in middle school: The influence of perceived family and school contexts. *The Journal of Early Adolescence, 29*, 571–609.

Wade, A., & Beran, T. (2011). Cyberbullying: The new era of bullying. *Canadian Journal of School Psychology, 26*, 44–61.

Williams, K. R., & Guerra, N. G. (2007). Prevalence and predictors of internet bullying. *Journal of Adolescent Health, 41, 14–21.* https://doi.org/10.1016/j.jadohealth.2007.08.018

Wong, D. S., Chan, H. C. O., & Cheng, C. H. (2014). Cyberbullying perpetration and victimization among adolescents in Hong Kong. *Children and Youth Services Review, 36*, 133–140.

Wright, M. F. (2013). The relationship between young adults' beliefs about anonymity and subsequent cyber aggression. *Cyberpsychology, Behavior, and Social Networking, 16*, 858–862.

Wright, M. F. (2015). Cyber victimization and perceived stress: Linkages to late adolescents' cyber aggression and psychological functioning. *Youth & Society, 47*(6), 789–810.

Wright, M. F. (2014a). Predictors of anonymous cyber aggression: The role of adolescents' beliefs about anonymity, aggression, and the permanency of digital content. *Cyberpsychology, Behavior, and Social Networking, 17*, 431–438.

Wright, M. F. (2014b). Longitudinal investigation of the associations between adolescents' popularity and cyber social behaviors. *Journal of School Violence, 13*, 291–314.

Wright, M. F. (2015). Adolescents' cyber aggression perpetration and cyber victimization: The longitudinal associations with school functioning. *Social Psychology of Education, 18*(4), 653–666.

Wright, M. F., & Li, Y. (2012). Kicking the digital dog: A longitudinal investigation of young adults' victimization and cyber-displaced aggression. *Cyberpsychology, Behavior, and Social Networking, 15*, 448–454.

Wright, M. F., & Li, Y. (2013a). Normative beliefs about aggression and cyber aggression among young adults: A longitudinal investigation. *Aggressive Behavior, 39*, 161–170.

Wright, M. F., & Li, Y. (2013b). The association between cyber victimization and subsequent cyber aggression: The moderating effect of peer rejection. *Journal of Youth and Adolescence, 42*, 662–674.

Wright, M. F., Kamble, S., Lei, K., Li, Z., Aoyama, I., & Shruti, S. (2015). Peer attachment and cyberbullying involvement among Chinese, Indian, and Japanese adolescents. *Societies, 5*, 339–353.

Ybarra, M. L., & Mitchell, K. J. (2004). Online aggressor/targets, aggressors, and targets: A comparison of associated youth characteristics. *Journal of Child Psychology and Psychiatry, 45,* 1308–1316.

Ybarra, M. L., Diener-West, M., & Leaf, P. (2007). Examining the overlap in internet harassment and school bullying: Implications for school intervention. *Journal of Adolescent Health, 1,* 42–50.

Yilmaz, H. (2011). Cyberbullying in Turkish middle schools: An exploratory study. *School Psychology International, 32*(6), 645–654.

Yousef, W. S. M., & Bellamy, A. (2015). The impact of cyberbullying on the self-esteem and academic functioning of Arab American middle and high school students. *Electronic Journal of Research in Educational Psychology, 23*(3), 463–482.

Zhou, Z., Tang, H., Tian, Y., Wei, H., Zhang, F., & Morrison, C. M. (2013). Cyberbullying and its risk factors among Chinese high school students. *School Psychology International, 34,* 630–647.

Key Terms & Definitions

Anonymity: The quality of being unknown or unacknowledged.

Anxiety: A mental health disorder which includes symptoms of worry, anxiety, and/or fear that are intense enough to disrupt one's daily activities.

Collectivism: A cultural value that stressed the importance of the group over individual goals and cohesion within social groups.

Cyberbullying: Children's and adolescents' usage of electronic technologies to hostilely and intentionally harass, embarrass, and intimidate others.

Empathy: The ability to understand or feel what another person is experiencing or feeling.

Externalizing difficulties: Includes children's and adolescents' failure to control their behaviors.

Individualism: The belief that each person is more important than the needs of the whole group or society.

Loneliness: An unpleasant emotional response to isolation or lack of companionship.

Normative belief: Beliefs about the acceptability and tolerability of a behavior.

Parental mediation and monitoring: The strategies that parents use to manage the relationship between their children and media.

Parenting style:The standard strategies that parents use in their child rearing.

Peer attachment: The internalization of the knowledge that their peers will be available and responsive.

Peer contagion: The transmission or transfer of deviant behavior from one adolescent to another.

Provictim attitudes: The belief that bullying is unacceptable and that defending victims is valuable.

Social exclusion: The process involving individuals or groups of people block or deny someone from the group.

Traditional face-to-face bullying: The use of strength or influence to intimidate or physically harm someone.

Additional Reading

Bauman, S. (2011). *Cyberbullying: What counselors need to know.* American Counseling Association.

Bauman, S., Cross, D., & Walker, J. (2013). *Principles of cyberbullying research: Definitions, measures, and methodology.* Routledge.

Hinduja, S., & Patchin, J. W. (2015). *Bullying beyond the schoolyard: Preventing and responding to cyberbullying.* Sage Publications.

Li, Q., Cross, D., & Smith, P. K. (2012). *Cyberbullying in the global playground*. Blackwell Publishing.

Menesini, E., & Spiel, C. (2012). *Cyberbullying: Development, consequences, risk and protective factors*. Psychology Press.

Tokunaga, R. S. (2010). Following you home from school: A critical review and synthesis of research on cyberbullying victimization. *Computers in Human Behavior, 26*, 277–287.

Wright, M. F. (2016). *A social-ecological approach to cyberbullying*. NOVA Publisher.

Chapter 8
Victims of War and Terrorism

Mahak Mathur, Gargi Chauhan Mehta, and Vikas Singh Rawat

War, in the popular sense, is a conflict between groups involving hostilities of considerable duration and magnitude. War is a species in the sort of violence; more specifically it is communal, unswerving, personal, intentional, planned, institutionalized, instrumental, sanctioned, and sometimes ritualized and structured, violence.

War is defined as:

> The violent rupture of the intricate and powerful fabric of the territorial taboos observed by social groups (E. Wilson, 1978).

> In another word war is defined as one or more governments to at least one other government, in which at least one of such governments no longer permits its relations with the others to be governed by the laws of peace (Sastry, 2016).

Wright (1942, 1965) has developed a typology of war as (a) Civil War which takes place within the boundaries of a sovereign nation; (b) the balance of Power War when members of a state system are at war among themselves; (c) the Defensive War to guard a civilization against the intrusions of an alien culture; and (d) the Imperial War where the population attempts to develop at the expense of another.

Consequences of War

War affects the lives adversely among different groups of people in many ways. The time, once the war gets over, is magnificently worse than the time throughout the war was squint. When there is war, everything is destroyed. War causes adverse losses ranging from physical property, infrastructure to the mental life, and social lives of the individuals. The people who are living below the poverty line and the

M. Mathur · G. C. Mehta (✉) · V. S. Rawat
Mahatma Gandhi Medical College and Hospital, Jaipur, India

169
R. T. Gopalan (ed.), *Victimology*, https://doi.org/10.1007/978-3-031-12930-8_8

low-income people will suffer more during and after the war. Wealthy people get accustomed to their normal life sooner. War negatively affects warriors and non-warriors alike, both physically and emotionally.

The emotional misery associated with war may occur not only due to direct exposure to life-threatening circumstances and violence but also through indirect stressors, such as injury to or death of family members or caretakers, economic hardships, geographic displacement, and continuous commotions of daily living (Jensen & Shaw, 1993). Death, injury, sexual violence, malnutrition, illness, and disability are some of the most threatening physical consequences of war, while post-traumatic stress disorder (PTSD), depression, and anxiety are some of the psychological or emotional effects.

Population Displacement

War causes citizens to leave their shelters in search of safety. In particular, refugees are at an elevated risk of contracting infectious diseases. The increased prevalence of infectious disease in refugee populations reveals itself during the conflict where the collapse of health systems leads to a spike in infectious diseases such as leishmaniasis, rabies, and tuberculosis in refugees. Civilians who lose their home during times of conflict are suspected to have numerous factors that contribute to putting them at a high risk of disease and illness. These factors include poverty, overcrowded living conditions, and increased likeliness of taking on work in cramped conditions. Displacement can double a person's risk of contracting an infectious disease, with recent studies in Organization for Economic Co-operation and Development (OECD) countries finding that the risk of infection for colonists is higher than the native population (Eiset & Wejse, 2017).

Access to clean water, food, and sanitation is unavoidably harmed by war. This raises the chance of spread of communicable diseases even more. It raises the risk of malnutrition and diseases associated with it. The increase in cholera and other waterborne infections can be exacerbated by a lack of clean water. Cholera can spread fast among those who live in crowded spaces. This is especially dangerous because cholera may kill a person very soon if left untreated. People who are forced to live in situations where diseases like cholera can thrive, such as those commonly associated with living in a conflict zone, have greater death rates than those who live in peaceful countries. People in war-affected areas are thrice as likely to defecate outside the toilet in open areas, due to lack of basic sanitation services and drinking water. The risk is particularly high among children under 5 years as they are more likely to die due to WASH-related illness than any other age group (Jeyakumar et al., 2021).

Limited Access to Healthcare Facilities

Hospitals and other facilities are frequently forced to change services in order to deal with the present crisis and may run out of resources. This reduces access to health care, especially in communities that are already underserved or under-resourced and have a shaky health infrastructure (Fernandes et al., 2019).

During war, healthcare workers are frequently targeted, patients with chronic conditions including asthma and diabetes are forced to wait for extended periods for care. It leads to mis diagnosed and undiagnosed conditions. During conflicts, routine immunization efforts are sometimes halted, leaving people vulnerable to epidemics and disease outbreaks that could have been avoided (Meiqari et al., 2018).

Women and Children

In a dangerous environment or during a conflict, children and women are more vulnerable to exploitation Armed conflicts' impact on children, particularly newborns and small children, must be evaluated alongside that of women. Women are the primary carers for children; thus, when they are harmed by war, so are the children. Many cultures have children's welfare shared by moms, elder sisters, aunts, and grandmothers. Physical and psychological growth of women are increasingly responsible for sustaining the social fabric of their communities while males depart to war. Women have an important role in establishing family and community continuity relationships during and after wars, which aids children's recovery from war-related trauma. One of the common ways that women are exclusively victimized by war is through sexual assault and rape. Women face an increased risk of rape during violent conflict. Rape and sexual violence are often used as tools of war with the intent of terrorizing the civilian population, shaming men to break military morale and promoting ethnic genocide. For example, during the last years of World War II, Soviet forces raped a substantial number of German women (Enloe, 2000a). The Pinochet administration in Chile employed rape of women as part of a formal state torture scheme to punish dissidents in the 1970s (Chinkin et al., 2020). Rape was used to commit ethnic genocide against Tutsi women by Hutu men as a formal attack on the Tutsi enemy. These war incidents result in physical and psychological injury to the women at the hands of the violent assaulters.

Role of women depends on many factors, including individual and country's global position and the type of war. A special report of the International Committee of The Red Cross (2013) concluded that women are not solely "victims" or "vulnerable" in need of protection and assistance. Women also take part in various military operations and provide essential support for the waging of war and maintenance of the military.

Women served in the military in large numbers around the world during the twentieth century. Beginning in 1942, the Soviet Union enlisted childless women as soldiers in World War II. Nurses and antiaircraft units were their primary roles (Enloe, 2000b). Around 800,000 women fought in the Soviet military during WWII, accounting for 8% of the total Soviet forces in their entirety (Goldstein, 2001). Women have also fought alongside males in guerrilla armies such as the Nicaraguan Sandinistas, Sri Lanka's Tamil Tigers, and others. Iraq is a country in which both men and women are required to serve in the military.

Women's physical and emotional health and survival are important. Women experience armed conflicts in a multitude of ways. In armed conflicts, international humanitarian law, human rights law, and refugee law provide protection tailored to the needs of women. Women now suffer in conflict not because of a lack of legislation, but because of a lack of enforcement and/or respect for existing rules (Krill, 1985).

Children's well-being during and after violent conflict. Nonetheless, children in war zones face a variety of challenges. Children are vulnerable to all forms of abuse and neglect, including sexual abuse, child trafficking, and kidnapping; both during and after war and conflict, children living in war zones and refugee camps are at risk of being neglected and abused as well as being used as human shields. Those who were seized by occupying armed forces, in particular, were subjected to sexual and physical abuse in prison. It is a significant issue that deserves to be addressed. Artillery fire has destroyed educational institutions in numerous nations, depriving millions of children and young people of their right to education (Snoubar & Hawal, 2015). The severe scarcity of schools and educational facilities, which has deprived many children of their right to education, has resulted in an upsurge in violence among students, leading to a slew of psychological and social issues. The rise in school violence can be linked to indirect violence such as violence on television or exposure to violence. Armed militias have attacked schools and educational infrastructure, which impacted the education of Youngsters and they started developing a propensity for hooliganism and aggressive behaviors (Snoubar & Duman, 2015).

Mental Health

Conflicts have a huge impact on mental health, in addition to their negative physical impacts. Long-term trauma exposure, death, disruption of normal social and work lives, and uncertainty about the future are all elements that contribute to significant mental and emotional stress. According to WHO data, mental illness is common among populations affected by conflict, with one in every five persons experiencing mental disease. Approximately 40% of young people have mental problems, 60–70% have post-traumatic stress disorder (PTSD), and 90% have other stress-related conditions (Chen et al., 2021).

In psychiatric history, wars have had an important part in a number of ways. After the world wars in the form of shell shock that supported the usefulness of psychological interventions during the first half of the twentieth century (Okello et al., 2007). Previous researches indicate that adverse situations cause more mortality and disability than any other major disease. War damages communities and families and often disrupts the development of the social and economic fabric of nations. Having an understanding of long-term effects of war on people's mental health and well-being is crucial for several reasons. On the one hand, the long-term recovery from wars is complicated as communities undergo reorganization and reconstruction of social and political life. On other hand, the struggle to provide adequate health and social support to those suffering from physical and mental health problems (Bracken et al., 1995).

Prevention Strategies for War

Terrorism dates back to the days of the Bible, while war has been around from the beginning of time. Combating war and terrorism is a challenging task due to their extensive histories. Sociologists and other social scientists, on the other hand, believe that there are a variety of avenues that may lead to a more peaceful world (Arquilla & Fogelson-Lubliner, 2011).

Arms control and diplomacy are two of the most popular methods used by political scientists and international relations experts to avert conflict. Different approaches to weapons control and diplomacy have varied degrees of success. As per literature, there has and will always be a place in the modern world for diplomacy and arms control, especially in the nuclear era when mankind is just minutes away from total catastrophe (Daase & Meier, 2012).

In addition to other considerations, the roots of war must be examined properly. As indicated by previous researches, political and military leaders' decision to go to war is a cultural phenomenon rather than a biological one. Moreover, deception is clearly a factor in the actions of many leaders who go to war for less noble causes. People and a free media in a democracy must always be prepared to question any reasons for war (Garcia, 2012). When the Vietnam War started, the Americans were far too tolerant of the 2003 decision to attack Iraq. Thus presumptions that a war is necessary should always be questioned in the media and by the general public, in order to avoid a war altogether.

Researches have provided various ways to avert war situations. Militarization and the amount of the military budget should be treated with the same level of preparedness (Solomon, 2006). Conflict may be avoided or stopped by social movements, as history shows, and the unbridled use of military force after a war has begun can also be prevented (Breyman, 2001; Staggenborg, 2010). War choices may be influenced by ideological differences and prejudice; therefore, measures to avert conflict must take these into consideration. Even though it seems utopian, the concept that governments and individuals should accept ideological differences and refrain from discriminating against people with differing religious or nonreligious views or ethnic origins is significant. International institutions like the United Nations may help prevent war and other violent conflict by promoting a greater level of understanding in this area. Additionally, initiatives aimed at promoting educational attainment have the potential to reduce the likelihood of violent conflict, since biasness reduces with education (Knight, 2011).

In addition to taking these different measures to avoid violence, a country's military budget must be reduced. Specialists in defense, who feel the budget is out of control, must call for reductions in nonessential military hardware and people, both at domestic and international level. Further, these measures will save the government a significant amount per year without putting the country at danger. The vast sum of money might then be utilized to fulfil the myriad internal requirements of the nation (Sustainable Defense Task Force, 2010).

Violent and armed conflicts are all impacted by a wide range of political, economic, and societal forces that are all interconnected. Conflict analysis may be used to provide a global perspective on the contributions of risk and protective variables. Nongovernmental organizations (NGOs) and other international organizations may use the interventions in an integrative and eclectic way to meet the demands of historical and political situations. More research is needed to better understand the interplay between political violence risk and protective variables, as well as the ways in which these factors vary by region and culture (de Jong, 2010).

Terrorism

The subject matter of terrorism is complex and sensitive. The complexities arise due to the fact that there are various aspects of human experiences and disciplines associated with it involving psychology, sociology, philosophy, military strategy, politics, history etc. Terrorism constitutes the illegitimate use of force to achieve a political objective when innocent people are targeted (Laqueur, 1999). US Department of Défense (2000) states it as the calculated use of violence or the threat of violence to inculcate fear; intended to coerce or to intimidate governments or communities with the motivation of obtaining certain goals which are religious, political, or ideological in nature.

Types of Terrorism

It is critical to underline the diverse nature of terrorism in order to categorize it into different typologies. Terrorism's nature varies depending on geographical, political, and cultural circumstances, among other things. Martin (2014) examined the following eight terrorist typologies.

Terrorism in the Twenty-First Century This type includes the modern terrorist environment that was seen towards the end of the twentieth century, emerging after the attacks on the USA on September 11 in 2001. Dissident terrorist organizations, organizational configurations, and transnational religious solidarity, which posed a threat of mass casualties, redefined the moral reasons for acts of violence.

State Terrorism This type of terrorism is perpetrated by governments in opposition to its perceived enemies. Externally, state terrorism can be directed against international adversaries, while internally it can be directed against the domestic adversaries.

Dissident Terrorism It is a type of terrorism that is known to be committed by nonstate societies and groups against governments, ethnonational, religious gatherings, and other potentially perceived oppositions.

Religious Terrorism This type of terrorism results from firm beliefs that almighty forces have permitted and commanded for the use of terrorist violence for the greater glory of God. Religious motivation to acts of violence is a rather common occurrence in the sphere of terrorism.

Ideological Terrorism This type is influenced by political systems of ideology (ideologies) that promote a group's or interest's self-perceived fundamental rights in defiance of another group's or interest's fundamental rights. The championed group utilizes their beliefs, theoretical and philosophical morals to justify violence and terrorism.

International Terrorism It is known as the terrorism that takes place globally. The targets are chosen owing to their relevance as representations of international importance, whether within the boundaries of own nation or outside over the state lines.

Criminal Dissident Terrorism Profits and politics drive this type of terrorism. Traditional organized criminals, for example, collect finances to fund their criminal activity and personal interests.

Gender-Selective Terrorism Men are exposed to systematic cruelty as a result of terrorism aiming to target males or women in a hostile population based on their gender because of their perceived inferiority. Males pose a threat as potential troops or sources of dissent. To obliterate an opposing group's cultural identity or intimidate them into surrender, women are subjected to systematic assault.

Causes of Terrorism

Different theorists have given different viewpoints into the understanding of terrorism as a single contributing factor is not sufficient precipitant that leads people to engage in acts of terror. Major consensus has been on the identification of three main perspectives to terrorism by the United Nations. These are mentioned below.

Psychological Perspective

This viewpoint considers a person's psychological processes to be the primary cause of terrorist attacks. Hatred or the thirst for power are said to be the driving forces behind such atrocities. For some terrorists, joining a terrorist organization provides social and psychological benefits such as adventure, companionship, and a stronger sense of self. They are also more likely to experience sentiments of rage, alienation, and disenfranchisement. Instead of pursuing any big ideological or strategic purpose, the terrorist may be more interested in gaining attention from others for his or her actions. For example, a terrorist by the name of Auguste Vaillant bombed the French Chamber of Deputies in 1893; his intentions stemmed from his aversion to the middle classes, and that he desired to tarnish their sense of economic and social status with his brutality.

Ideological Perspective

Ideology relates to the views, beliefs, principles, and values by which a group identifies its particular aims and agendas. Religion and political theories and programs are few ways that ideologies are expressed. It is a compelling message that inspires and motivates regular people to take action. Ideology is a dynamic and changing short system that is generated by ideologue's interpretation of events. It is inculcated by the dissemination of knowledge or propaganda in the form of lectures, speeches, pronouncements, publications, and other forms of communication. Several terrorist organizations have been determined to be ideologically motivated, including the Bader Meinhoff in Germany, Irish Republican Army (IRA), and the Liberation Tigers of Tamil Eelam (LTTE) in Sri Lanka.

Strategic Approach

This approach views terrorism as a logical adjunct to political collapse. Violence is viewed as the ultimate option by the individuals that have tried to seek solutions for their complaints through the government but failed to get their attention. Terrorism from this perspective is the product of a judicious analysis of a group's objectives and goals, as well as its assessment of the possibilities of victory. If victory through more conventional forms of resistance appears unlikely, terrorists may presume terrorism to be the better alternative (Education, n.d.)

Psychosocial Risk Factors Associated with Terrorism

Different studies have linked terrorism to a variety of root causes and risk factors. Terrorists' ideas typically involve considerable social reality distortions. One of the most common psychological grounds for terrorism is disruptive or psychopathological personalities (De la Corte, 2007). Some researchers have attempted to classify terrorists based on their proclivity for violence or inability to control aggressive urges. Terrorists, on the other hand, are not known for their impetuous aggressiveness. Individuals who become part of the same terrorist organization have varied intentions and personalities, according to biographical research. For example, paucity of empathy for their victims, opinionated or ideological attitude, or a utopian vision were all found to be the typical psychological traits among terrorists (De la Corte, 2007). Many studies in the 1970s and 1980s have explored the classic psychosocial attributes of terrorists. Hubbard (1971) in a research found five traits of skyjackers which are (1) violent behavior, often alcoholism in father; (2) extremely religious mother; (3) shy, timid and sexually demure and compliant; (4) overprotectiveness towards younger sisters and (5) social skills deficit. In another study, nine typical characteristics were found which are: (1) conflicts with authority, (2) poor awareness, (3) compliance to convention, (4) emotional distancing from the repercussions of unacceptable behavior, (5) uncertainties towards sexual duties, (6) magical thinking, (7) barbarism, (8) low levels of education, and (9) compliance of aggressive subculture norms and obsession towards weaponry. Additionally, some demographic, biographical, and psychological characteristics were found to be occurring with a high frequency: 25% of leftist had become orphans by the age of 14, 33% had significant conflicts with their parents, while out of all 33% had a previous account of juvenile criminal activities. Another factor that was recognized as a major factor in joining a terrorist organization was peer pressure along with a desire for higher social status. The amalgamation of young adult's individual selfhood with the group's selfhood and objectives were identified as a badge of membership (Ferracuti & Bruno, 1981).

Theories of Terrorism

There are two types of methods to explaining terrorist behavior: top down and bottom up. Top-down approaches attempt to identify the roots of terrorist activities in evolutionary, political, economic, and social contexts; on the other hand, bottom-up approaches attempt to explore the traits of individuals and organizations that opt for terrorism. These perspectives do not have isolated impacts. There is often found a fundamental overlap between theories. Several of these theories are discussed below (Wieviorka, 2004).

Psychoanalytic Views of Terrorism

The theory of psychoanalysis theory was born on the assumption that most of an individual's mental experiences are present in their unconscious mind and that each person passes through psychosexual stages of development in accordance to their primary sexual impulses. It propositions that most of the mental health issues have their source in unsettled intrapsychic frictions regarding those impulses (Gabbard, 2000). The psychoanalytical approach into understanding terrorist behavior can be loosely split into theory of narcissism, paranoia, and absolutist. These theories are discussed below.

Identity Theory

This theory suggests that young people with low self-esteem who have strong, if not desperate, needs to establish their identities tend to turn towards terrorism (Olsson, 1988). According to Böllinger (1981) conducted a study on eight members of a German terrorist group and found that overbearing parents hindered the children from establishing autonomy, resulting in identity conflicts that made violent conflict unavoidable. Those suffering from identity confusion may be plagued by feelings of solitude to the point of resorting to terrorist violence as a coping mechanism for the anguish of anomie (Ferracuti, 1982).

Narcissism Theory

Self-psychology was created by psychoanalyst Heniz Kohut (1972, 1978) as a deviation from Freud's orthodox ego psychology. This area of psychology has been used by John Crayton (1983), Eric Shaw (1986), Richard Pearlstein (1991), and many others to explore the process that leads young people to terrorism. Self-psychology highlights an infant's need for caring reactions in order to develop appropriately. Dearth of maternal empathy causes narcissistic harm, which causes growth to be halted in a couple of ways: recurrent immature grandiose fancies or errors to assimilate the parent's idealized image. These issues end up causing further problems in the formation of adult identity and morals. Additionally, political humiliation, such as subordination humiliation, could cause adult narcissistic damage, instigating the psychological attribute of infantile narcissism (Crayton, 1983). All of this could result into a pathological rise of self, the desertion of independence in favor of merging with the supreme powerful figure or a combination of both.

Paranoia Theory

Post (1998, 2004) proposed that the prominent attribute of terrorist psychology is mainly projection, which is an immature defense mechanism in which inner feelings which provoke anxiety gets assigned to an extraneous object/person. This usually occurs when a person who has grown up with a dysfunctional sense of self tends to idealize the good self and segregates it from the bad self. This defense mechanism is observed be the source of the "paranoid schizoid position," which Melanie Klein coined as an adult manifestation during the infantile phase of an individual's life (Robins & Post, 1997).

Absolutist/Apocalyptic Theory

Lifton (1999) suggested that many terrorist groups are in fact cults that use mass destruction with an aim to replace the corrupt world with a pure new social order. Apocalyptic organizations are known for their absolute moral extremity, idealization of a crusader symbol, weak reality testing, and imagining huge evil plots. Absolutist/totalist moral thinking leads to terrorist motives by attracting young adults with weak self-identities. Through this type of thinking, terrorists tend to defend themselves from the normal emotional responses to aggression through the method of denial, dissociation, or affect isolation.

Psychopathological Theory of Terrorism

The prevalent belief that terrorists must be mad or psychopathic is on one extreme of the spectrum (Hacker, 1976; Taylor, 1988). Current perspectives in psychiatry classify adult clinical and behavioral disorders using a multiaxial classification system. Axis I includes major mental disorders like schizophrenia, depressive disorders etc., while Axis II includes disorders of personality such as antisocial personality disorder (APD) (American Psychiatric Association, 2000). APD is a personality disorder which denotes pattern of remorseless contempt for the rights of other people. Very limited literature has been found incorporating a full psychiatric evaluation, pertaining to presence of Axis I disorders in terrorists. Ferracuti (1982) has found that while terrorist groups are in many instances led by people with mental health concerns, terrorists rarely meet the diagnostic criteria for mental disorders. Mostly, the studies linking terrorists to mental illness refer to the lack of remorse personality traits, psychopathy, or sociopathy (Taylor, 1988). Terrorists, just as psychopath lack mercy and are "outlaws" and "outcasts" that follow a deviated set of values that are away from societal norms (Cooper, 1977). Terrorism is sometimes also linked to innate personality traits, according to some psychological theories.

Developmental theories have stated that children with disordered and aggressive personalities are more drawn to joining terrorist organizations (Pettit, 1997). It is also linked to the desire for new experiences. Terrorist activities can be undeniably fascinating and may satisfy innate, possibly biologically predisposed desires of extreme emotional and physical incitement, risk, and ventilation (Hacker, 1983; Kellen, 1979; Levine, 1999).

Sociological Theories of Terrorism

Terrorism is one of the inalienable parts of the society, and the sociological understanding of terrorism will be able to valuably identify the underlying aspects to it. The sociological theories of terrorism are discussed below.

Rational Choice Theory

According to this theory, terrorist action is the result of a deliberate, rational, and calculated decision to use this particular method to achieve a sociopolitical goal. This theory is derived from economics, and explains how policy changes the rules of the "game" played between terrorists and governments might predictably alter behavior (Sandler, Tschirhart & Cauley, 1983; Lapan & Sandler, 1988; Crenshaw, 1992).

Social Learning Theory

Albert Bandura's (1973) theory propagates that violence is a result of repeated observation and modeling of a violent representation. This theory has its applications into understanding terrorist action as being a result of consequence of cognitive "reconstrual" of moral observations and leanings rather than innate aggression. For instance, adolescents living in the surroundings of political conflicts may be more exposed to terrorist activities and try to imitate and follow them. They may also end up learning public glorification of terrorists present in the culture (Crenshaw, 1992; Taylor & Quayle, 1994; Kelly & Rieber, 1995).

Frustration-Aggression Hypothesis

This theory states that those people who have political motivations reach an ending to the point of no return where their rising frustrations get transformed into violent action. Terrorist activities resulting from long-standing frustration also point towards suffered oppression and lack of response from government. This theory came into picture by observing the causes of violence observed in early twentieth-century Europe. It denotes terrorist action as the ultimate expression through anguish when in face of oppression (Dollard et al., 1939; Friedland, 1992).

Theory of Relative Deprivation

According to social theorists and political scientists, relative deprivation theory denotes that individual and groups who believe they are being deprived of life necessities like money, rights, political voice, or status end up to organize or join social movements dedicated to obtaining those things (Gurr, 1970). With respect to terrorism, a country's level of income inequality is intimately linked to its level of terrorists. As feelings of relative lack in terms of income inequality foster irritation, and frustration increases, it sows the seeds of terrorism (Gurr, 1970).

Oppression Theory

Researchers have implied political violence is often a consequence of oppression (Fanon, 1965; Whitaker, 1972; Schmid, 1983). Terrorist groups like ETA, PIRA, Hamas that are national separatist and ethnic sectarian have claimed much frequently the injustice they have faced by governments. Oppression occurs in the means of denial of people's identity, their dignity, security, and freedom which acts as a motivating factor for becoming a part of terrorist organization. As oppression can be tough to quantify, opinion differences in sociopolitical relationships occur, and the consequences of oppression can be experienced subjectively with differing intensities by people within a susceptible community (Crenshaw, 1986; Taylor & Quayle, 1994; Post, Sprinzak & Denny, 2003).

National Cultural Theory

Eubank and Weinberg (1994) have found occurrences of terrorism differs in "collectivist" vs "individualist" societies. This theory states that an individual's identity is primarily formed from the societal grounds. This leads the division of the world into in-groups and out-groups. There is correlation of personal welfare to the welfare of the group the member belongs to. In cultures that are individualistic in nature, identity emerges from personal aspirations. Additionally, Weinberg and Eubank have stated that the collectivist cultures are more vulnerable than individualist cultures to execute terrorist activities against out-groups, for example, foreigners. On the other hand, individualists are less hesitant to harm a fellow individual.

Humiliation-Revenge Theory

Another idea to understand what drives terrorists towards acts of violence is humiliation and the resulting internal need for vengeance (Juergensmeyer, 2000). Acts of revenge toward an oppressor's humiliation has been an ancient cultural custom. History is a proof that in Middle East countries the pattern of repeated oppression and humiliation was accompanied by aggressive action in the reverence of liberation. For example, Eyad el Sarraj, a Palestinian psychiatrist, has noted that humiliation is a significant motivator for teenage suicide bombers. Whether seen psychoanalytically as an unavoidable dynamic consequence of narcissistic injury or simply as a painful social stressor, humiliation appears conceivable as the source of a desire to revenge against governmental bodies perceived to be culpable.

Cognitive Theories of Terrorism

Cognitive style and quirks are also contributing factors to dysfunctional decisions. Lezak (1995) determined that cognitive functions such as attention, memory language, and executive processes, such as learning, planning, and following rules, judgment, reasoning, and carrying out appropriate risk-benefit calculations, are all characteristics of cognitive capability. Most of these functions take place in the brain's dorsolateral prefrontal cortex. Other cognitive functions such as ability of impulse control and performing socially acceptable behavior, on the other hand, relies on the ventromedial cortex (Gazzaniga, 2000; Mesulam, 2000). Cognitive biases, prejudices, distortions, and propensity to over- or underemphasize strategies in decision-making are all examples of cognitive style. Impairment and dysfunctions in these styles are contributing factors towards antisocial attitude and goals.

Group Process Theory

The majority of researches on terrorism explain it as a result of group psychological processes within distinctive subcultures that congeal in response to situations they deem unbearable (Taylor and Ryan, 1988; Friedland, 1992; Hoffman, 1998; Merari,

1998; Levine, 1999; Post, 2004; Sageman, 2004). Researchers have also proposed that even in the situations where the member of a terrorist group is not susceptible to mental health concerns, group dynamics like the likes of ideological indoctrination, repetitive instructions, and peer pressures have been known to affect the group's aggressive tendencies and behavior (Crenshaw, 1992; Clayton, Barlow, and Ballif-Spanvill, 1998).

Psychological Processes of Victims of Terrorism

The purpose of terrorism is to instill fear and precariousness among the community. The spread of this fear can be rapid and does not spread to those impacted primarily and secondarily; it has a direct impact on the families of victims and survivors. It also has impact on those individuals that come into contact with the televised footage of the event. The results of terrorist attacks are not just physical injury but also grave psychological injuries. An understanding of the psychological aftermaths of terrorism is essential to policy makers to create pre-crisis, crisis, and post-crisis intervention programs that will assist in reduction of the negative psychological impacts of terrorism.

Depending on the individual, the impact of psychological and physiological impact differs upon exposure to the traumatic event. Psychological response to traumatic event is based upon the interaction between several social, biological, and genetic vulnerabilities, past encounters, and future predictions (Ursano et al., 1992). Terrorism has several detrimental consequences on the spirit of community and a causes threat to sense of national security. Society's morale and unity as well as the ethnic, economic, racial, and religious gaps in our society all get negatively impacted (Human Rights Watch, 2002).

Identifying Vulnerable Populations at Risk

The vulnerable population involves a list of individuals who may have been remotely or closely impacted by the terrorist act. They are also the ones who were not present at the location of the event but witnessed it through media. Terrorist attacks also result in economic crashes and death of loved ones, which can be traumatic to the individuals. Goldfrank et al. (2003) in their research also found that the populations affected by terrorism vary in accordance to the nature of terrorism whether it is chemical, biological, radiological, nuclear bombing, or hijacking attack.

Pre-Attack Indications: Several factors like sex, age, previous experiences, and personality have all been linked to the ability to control negative effects of terrorism. In a study which was conducted after the 9/11 attacks, it was found that female gender was linked to more short-term outcomes (North et al., 2011; Schlenger et al., 2002; Silver et al., 2002). Further, Silver et al. (2002) also found that the past history of divorce and health problems has also contributed to greater mental health damages after terrorist attacks. Regarding age, Abenhaim et al. (1992) studied the influence of an individual's age on psychological responses to terrorism and found inconsequential relationship between the two especially in adults; few studies do mention of the psychological damages of terrorist acts on children and pubescents. Some studies also found that continual and immediate exposure to trauma leads to worse psychological problems in first responders and rescue workers (Duckworth, 1986; Jones, 2008), which is because of their frequent and direct exposure to traumatic happenings.

Indications during the attack: Research evidences have proved that terrorist acts are almost the same as traumatic events in terms of its effects on the psych of victims. In research by Silver et al. (2002) it was discovered that the extent of exposure to the 9/11 attacks was more foretelling of psychological distress than the extent of loss. Crucial event-related variables were identified as duration and type of attack. Studies have found that terrorist attacks might occur as a single massive attack, for example, the Oklahoma City Bombing, it can also be a multisite attack like the 9/11 attacks and also multisite continual or repeated event like the anthrax attacks of 2001 or a continuous or recurrent attack like the terrorist attacks in Northern Ireland (Ursano, 2002). The modus operandi of attack or the kind of attack may also control the consequence. For example, the attacks that are biological and radiological in nature may necessitate rapid exposure to the hazard and the development of health issues in victims, but bombing causes more immediate harm even though it occurs as mostly onetime event.

Post-Attack Indications: A variety of post-attack indicators may also help in identification of those people who are more likely to experience grave psychological consequences. Galea et al. (2002) in their research on the aftermath of 9/11, 2001 attacks discovered that episodes of panic at the time of or shortly after the terrorist attacks, as well as loss of assets, loved ones, jobs were some post-attack factors that foresaw post-traumatic stress disorder.

Secondary and Community Consequences of Terrorism

Terrorist attacks may have multifold consequences in the long term. Silver et al. (2002) have found in their research that terrorist activities were commonly observed as an act executed by certain racial, ethnic, or religious organizations. It is viewed as an intentional deed by an individual or a group which makes it different from other man-made disasters. The method of profiling of terrorist based on sociodemographics of race, ethnicity, and religion is still subject to controversies as it may cause further stigma and discrimination to the concerned racial, ethnic, or religious group. It also is matter of massive threat to community cohesion and psychological well-being of people. Consequentially, the outcomes of this type of profiling leads to more fear in people of their neighbors and strangers causing deterioration of unity of the community. Terrorist attacks, like other disasters, can, on the other hand, have surprisingly good implications for the community, according to the study. Because terrorism usually targets a specific group of people, the population's patriotism, unity, and pride often soars high in the aftermath.

Prevention Strategies for Terrorism

Since the increase in terrorist attacks, personal, business, and government efforts to combat terrorism have skyrocketed, with respect to the number of anti-terrorists programs. Government officials, legislators, scholars, and funding organizations must all work together to promote counterterrorism evaluation studies, including attempts to analyze these programs' results. Most evaluations of "ending terrorism" focus on this specific sort of terrorism because of transnational terrorism. Traditional approaches to countering transnational terrorism fall into two categories. Legal or military methods of apprehending and dismantling terrorist camps and infrastructure are among the initial options. Structural reform is the second alternative, which is founded on the understanding that terrorism has systemic origins. Terrorist specialists have a wide range of views on each tactic (White, 2012).

Law enforcement and military operations have been shown to diminish terrorist forces, yet terrorist organizations have survived despite these attempts. Terrorists may be encouraged to carry out further acts of terrorism and public support for their cause by these strategies. Structural reform is advocated by a number of terrorism specialists, believing that it may reduce terrorism by improving or removing the circumstances that drive individuals to commit terrorism. Terrorism's systemic foundations need to be considered even if there are no simple solutions. There will always be new terrorists to replace those who are captured or killed as long as these roots remain in place. So, it is important to understand why international terrorism exists in the first place. It is still critical that we address the root causes of terrorism in order to prevent it from happening in the first place. A law enforcement/military approach to combat terrorism may weaken terrorist organizations, but it also has the potential to inflict serious harm on civil freedoms (Kean & Hamilton, 2007).

Terrorism's underlying causes are seen as a subject with some conceptual obstacles. When the United Nations first considered terrorism in 1972, there were two main schools of thinking. For those who wished to get down to the roots of terrorism, there was the other side of the coin. Others, on the other hand, were more concerned with countering the expressions of terrorism. The second school of thought has grown in popularity during the previous three decades. Increasingly, people call for a contempt for the causes of terrorism, as if addressing them would somehow condemn the acts of terrorism and encourage their perpetrators to perpetrate even more atrocities in the future. One cannot overlook the circumstances that allow for the development of terrorism, whether they are called "breeding grounds" or the "fundamental causes."

On the other hand, concerns about terrorism's roots and aims must be tempered with sympathy for the victims and other groups harmed by the terrorist attacks. As part of a broader set of investigations and actions, the root cause investigation must be examined in conjunction with anything from prevention, early warning, and deterrent to prosecution or punishment, if those techniques fail. It is essential that all the many elements and parties engaged in a counterterrorism plan work together in unison. Although terrorism is illegal, it is commonly utilized to affect the political process, or the exchange of power between and among groups. Thus, law enforcement does not have the authority to intervene. In spite of governments' declared rules, there have been innumerable incidents of interactions with politically motivated murderers. Front organizations or representatives of political parties with political aims that are similar to those of the terrorists might be called violent political parties in their own right, if not directly with terrorists. When political parties utilize terrorism to share power rather than grab totalitarian control, there is generally considerable wiggle space for compromise. If a temporary or permanent political solution is established, amnesties have been issued. Terrorist victims typically have a hard time accepting such deals since some of their tormentors are being rewarded. Adopting proactive political actions rather than tolerating radicals and extremists who have already committed significant crimes motivated by politics is morally preferable. (Lum et al., 2006).

The strategies used to prevent violent crime and terrorism cannot be completely interchangeable. Though both contain the opportunity aspect, as well as the skills and equipment required to conduct a violent criminal are typically equivalent, however, the motives are significantly different: money in one instance and philosophy in the other. (The European Centre for Security studies, 2003). Terrorist funding is garnering a lot of attention in recent time. As for the terrorists, they risk being crushed by military force without arousing popular sympathy. As a result, they are unable to fund their terrorist actions. During 1976 and 1983, U.S. Government (2003) found that this was the situation in Argentina. Government-society relations are greatly affected by the decision between military maximum use of force (prone to being indiscriminate) and the police force philosophy (focused on restricted use of force). Putting the military in charge of battling terrorists sometimes leads in a 10-year or longer war on terror because of a failure to acknowledge the political and social roots of conflict.

Rule of law and essential human rights and international norms principles should guide the state, especially a liberal-democratic state, when faced with a national terrorist threat. Intelligence is the most significant tool in the fight against underground organizations that communicate in a language or coded language and are separated into cells. They need safe homes, cars, and money; identity and travel credentials; weapons and explosives; and the ability to communicate with each other and recruit new members. In large populations of innocent people, suspects can be weeded out using interrogation methods like matrix investigations. However, it creates privacy issues to examine the data of hundreds or thousands of individuals who are completely innocent in order to discover a few culprits. As long as proper due diligence is followed and an impartial review panel is in place, these concerns may be alleviated (Goodey, 2003).

An all-encompassing, multipronged strategy to countering terrorism includes specific police training to deal with terrorists. Maintaining proper and legal police conduct and adhering to the concept of minimal force, which confines fatal force to what is reasonable, justified, and proportional in a specific scenario to minimize additional damage, are the most significant concerns here (Bailey, 1995). A multi-pronged approach and a broad variety of reactions are required when armed terrorists randomly attack vulnerable citizens in the routine hours. It is important to remember that terrorism feeds on conflict, and also that the root causes of dispute must be dealt with (US Government, 2003).

No simple solution exists to the problem of terrorism. It is also worth noting that the amount of context of armed conflicts in the world is substantially more than previously thought when one considers not just interstate conflicts but also internal conflicts in which the government is not even a player (O'Neill, 2002). Conflict arises as a result of the divergent beliefs, pursuits, and goals of various social groupings. We can try to reduce the use of aggression in conflict situations by providing conflict parties with adequate dispute resolution procedures and tools. Fractional rather than winner-take-all governance in democracy is a powerful instrument for settling disagreements. A significant weapon in the fight against domestic terrorism is effective governance (rule of law) (Lund, 1996). Terrorism and major war crimes are not the norm in every internal political confrontation. It is possible that the solution to terrorism is the way to enhancing our capacity to prevent and control it (Alexander & Alexander, 2003).

It is important to remember that terrorism cannot be solved overnight. Because there are too many enabling circumstances at play, such as the absence or disagreement over the causes of terrorist acts and the underlying causes of terrorist attacks, political religiosities and media exploitation as well as a lack of political will for meaningful action against terrorism and the weak punishment of terrorists, to have much hope that this will be the case.

Psychological Rehabilitation of Victims of War and Terrorism

For decades, researchers in psychology and psychiatry have studied how traumatic experiences like war affect the mental health from both troops (Miller, 1920) and civilians (Baumgarten-Tramer, 1948). However, the fact that psychopathological effects of terrorist acts and therapies need have long been discussed in the psychological and psychiatric literature, this legacy is relatively new in the context of terrorism (Curran, 1988). However, none of these businesses had a formal testing program until the last 10–15 years. In reality, the most reliable knowledge on the mental health concerns that develop as a consequence of terrorist acts and how to treat them comes from examinations into a tiny number of instances. Despite this limitation, it should be noted that research into the causes and treatments of terrorism-induced mental illness has grown dramatically and meaningfully over the past century. Whereas at the turn of the century, much of our knowledge about these disorders and the people who suffer from them came from studies in the larger body of literature dedicated to traumatic events, today, the vast majority of our knowledge comes from the smaller but no less important body of literature dedicated to post-traumatic stress disorder (Difede et al., 2007).

According to meta-analytic (DiMaggio & Galea, 2006; DiMaggio et al., 2009) and narrative reviews (Bills et al., 2008; García-Vera & Sanz, 2008) a substantial proportion of terrorist attacks' victims (about 20–30%) would acquire post-traumatic stress disorder (PTSD) and other mental health issues. However, even if the percentage of secondary victims who get such diseases is reduced, the average frequency of those disorders is nonetheless higher than it was before to the terrorist activity. As a result, both direct and passive victims will need short, medium, and long-term mental health care. People who have been affected by the attack have a wide range of psychological needs, and it is important to address those, as well as the fact that these needs can shift over time and in different phases following the attack. It is also important to consider how eager people are to incorporate psycho-social therapies into a global response strategy (National Institute of Mental Health [NIMH], 2002).

As a result of war and terrorism, many people find themselves in a crisis scenario. People who have been affected by this tragedy feel powerless and hopeless. Interventions in times of crisis for those affected by war and terrorism, both directly and indirectly, become required. Counselors and psychologists may assist people with physical and mental health issues, get relief from their symptoms, go back to their prior levels of functioning, and learn new ways of coping that they can carry with them into the future. Interventions such as encouraging the sufferer in express-ing crisis-generated sentiments, aiding the victim in eradicating crisis-related nega-tive attitudes, pushing the victim to do more socializing, and manipulating the environment are all popular strategies in crisis intervention. Referring a victim to an organization that may help with financial concerns is one example of this (Foa et al., 2005).

In cognitive behavioral therapy for the treatment of overt and covert terrorist attack survivors, Duffy et al. (2007) found that treatment group participants demon-strated a substantial improvement at post intervention compared to those in the waiting comparison group. Post-traumatic stress disorder (PTSD) is the primary focus of research into the psychological well-being of terrorism survivors. Exposure therapies, trauma-focused cognitive-behavioral therapies (which include cognitive restructuring techniques and exposure techniques), anxiety control training (or stress-inoculation training), and eye movement desensitization and reprocessing (EMDR) are currently the treatments with the greatest empirical guarantees. Trauma-focused cognitive-behavioral treatment was shown to be effective in September 11, 2001, World Trade Center attack workers who had been diagnosed with PTSD or had substantial post-traumatic stress symptoms (Difede, Malta et al., 2007). The effectiveness and therapeutic relevance of trauma-focused cognitive-behavioral therapy for terrorist victims with post-traumatic stress disorder (PTSD) has not been extensively studied, although a few experimental and semigroup stud-ies have lately been published. This therapy combines stress management approaches with cognitive techniques and in some cases, in vivo and imaginal exposure. We can make use of this therapy over other treatments, including ones that have been shown to be beneficial, based on the results of these studies (Moreno et al., 2019). Future study should investigate if the same psychological therapies that have been shown to benefit survivors of other tragic incidents (including such combat veterans, survivors of physical rape and abuse, refugees, or victims of road accidents) might also aid terrorist victims.

Rehabilitation of a Terrorist

A terrorist detainee's fate hinges on the government's response. A detainee's ability to reintegrate may be hindered if the government places too much emphasis on security and surveillance, which elevates the stigma attached with this person in the community, in part. A former detainee's animosity of the state may be exacerbated if their freedom is severely restricted, making it harder that their beliefs and attitudes would change things for the better. Alternatively, the program's reputation will be seriously damaged if the inmate returns to terrorism due to a lack of adequate security. Psychologists must work closely with probation officials and police officers to handle and balance these responsibilities and dangers. The security posture should be determined by an individual's assessment of his or her psychological risk. Among terrorist prisoners, the most prevalent psychological hurdle is the fact that they have given up many of their prior identities in order to join a terrorist group. It is critical that they reawaken and remove all of their prior guises (e.g., parent, sibling, active community member, athlete, musician, and so on). It is important to emphasize that not every family is capable of providing a supportive environment for a detainee's transition from terrorist to non-terrorist identity (Australian Centre for Posttraumatic Mental Health, 2007).

Timing everything when it refers to interventions. When an offender is most open to change, the psychiatrist ought to be aware of this and adjust the treatment plan as appropriate. Terrorists must deal with a variety of psychological issues. It is clear that they have complaints, have identified a culprit, and also have rationalized aggression due to moral and instrumental grounds. However, it is most crucial that a prisoner is no longer tempted to use or advocate violence as an outlet for their frustrations, and this is the most doable of the three goals (Difede, Malta et al., 2007). Rather focusing on the individual's beliefs, psychologists should begin by focusing on the individual's behavior. Once rectified, psychologists should concentrate on modifying and questioning ideology when they believe that an offender is more vulnerable to this form of propaganda. The detainee's treatment options should be adapted to their specific requirements whenever feasible. A one-size-fits-all strategy will not work. It is essential to know why individuals join terrorist groups before deciding on the best place to concentrate rehabilitation efforts (Veldhuis, 2012).

Risk analysis and criminogenic needs should influence the kind of intervention to be used. For example, dealing with a former terrorist commander will need a different strategy than dealing with an ordinary soldier. A solution must be found for terrorist leaders/key characters in their new life to keep them from reverting to a life of violence, since their prominence in these groups typically satisfied their psychological needs. A person's need for "importance" lies at the heart of the matter. As part of the process of actual disengagement and desistance, correctional management and other stakeholders must allow for some degree of leniency in programming and allow for lapses in conduct. Often, detainees are reluctant to meet with psychiatrists and get therapy because they are afraid to accept that they need help or because they are ignorant of what therapists do or how they may help. Psychologists are employed by the state, which the inmate views as the cause of his issues and "the enemy," in rehabilitation programs for political dissidents. Psychologists who are seeking to build relationships of trust with inmates may find this to be a significant obstacle. Leadership and staff in jail are often skeptical of mental health professionals, finding it challenging for them to fully participate inside the system and be effective in their job. The term "terrorist" may frighten prison staff, administration, and other rehabilitative actors, making it much harder to connect with this prisoner population. The wording used to describe the programs may also impede progress. When it comes to "rehabilitation," some violent extremists are unwilling to take part because, in their minds, there is nothing wrong with them. Terrorists, unlike other violent criminals, tend to be intellectually fit and do not appear to suffer from evident psychopathologies, according to some research. To avoid diagnostic errors and poor treatment plans, further enquiry and a battery of tests should be conducted to uncover the sentimental issues at hand. In the case of detainees returning to culture, communities are usually wary of adopting supposedly changed terrorists, and their former networks are eager to tempt them back into the fold. The effectiveness of such types of rehabilitation services may be adversely affected by a lack of larger political support (Difede, Malta et al., 2007).

Conclusion

War and terrorism is a notorious counterpart of the modern world. The typologies, perspectives, risk factors, and theories of war and terrorism are crucial to understand the processes of it. These processes are viewed from the purview of sociology, politics, psychology, and other disciplines.

It is also the time for health professionals to view war and terrorism as a serious global public health problem. Moreover, they can provide and work on the strategies required to rehabilitate victims and terrorists detainees. Thus, a holistic approach encompassing different experts in the field becomes necessary. This would help in making others sensitive towards the suffering and make the world a more peaceful place.

References

Abenhaim, L., Dab, W., & Salmi, L. R. (1992). Study of civilian victims of terrorist attacks (France 1982–1987). *Journal of Clinical Epidemiology, 45*(2), 103–109.

Alexander, D. C., & Alexander, Y. (2003). *Terrorism and business: The impact of 11 September 2001* (p. 195). Transnational Publishers.

American Psychiatric Association. (2000). *Diagnostic and statistical manual of mental disorders* (4th ed. text rev ed.). American Psychiatric Association, Washington DC.

Arquilla, J., & Fogelson-Lubliner. (2011, March 13). The Pentagon's biggest boondoggles. *New York Times*, p. WK12.

Australian Centre for Posttraumatic Mental Health. (2007). *Australian guidelines for the treatment of adults with acute stress disorder and posttraumatic stress disorder*. ACPMH.

Bailey, W. G. (1995). *The encyclopedia of police science* (2nd. ed.). Garland Publishing.

Bandura, A. (1973). *Aggression: A social learning analysis*. prentice-hall.

Baumgarten-Tramer, F. (1948). Zur Psychologie der Ausgebombten [The psychology of the bombed-out]. *Gesundheit und Wohlfahrt, 28*, 158–163.

Bills, C. B., Levy, N. A., Sharma, V., Charney, D. S., Herbert, R., Moline, J., & Katz, C. L. (2008). Mental health of workers and volunteers responding to events of 9/11: Review of the literature. *The Mount Sinai Journal of Medicine, 75*, 115–127.

Böllinger, L. (1981). Die entwicklung zu terroristischem handeln als psychosozialer prozess: begegnungen mit beteiligten. Jäger H., Schmidtchen G., Süllwold L. (Hg.), *Lebenslaufanalysen* (pp. 175–231). Opladen.

Bracken, P. J., Giller, J. E., & Summerfield, D. (1995). Psychological responses to war and atrocity: The limitations of current concepts. *Social Science and Medicine, 40*(8), 1073–1082. https://doi.org/10.1016/0277-9536(94)00181-R

Breyman, S. (2001). *Why movements matter: The west German peace movement and US arms control policy*. State University of New York Press.

Chen, Y., Zhu, Z., Lei, F., Lei, S., & Chen, J. (2021). Prevalence and risk factors of post-traumatic stress disorder symptoms in students aged 8–18 in Wuhan, China 6 months after the control of COVID-19. *Frontiers in Psychology, 12*. https://doi.org/10.3389/FPSYG.2021.740575/FULL

Chinkin, C., Kaldor, M., & Yadav, P. (2020). Gender and new wars. *Stability, 9*(1). https://doi.org/10.5334/STA.733/

Clayton, C. J., Barlow, S. H., & Ballif-Spanvill, B. (1998). Principles of group violence with a focus on terrorism. In H. V. Hall & L. C. Whitaker (Eds.), *Collective violence* (pp. 277–311). Boca Raton, FL: CRC Press.

Cooper, H. H. A. (1977). What is a terrorist: A psychological perspective. *Legal Med. Q., 1*, 16.

Crayton, J. W. (1983). Terrorism and the psychology of the self. Perspectives on terrorism. *Wilmington, Delaware: Scholarly Resources, 33*(41), 1–70.

Crenshaw, M. (1992). Current research on terrorism: The academic perspective. *Studies in Conflict & Terrorism, 15*(1), 1–11.

Curran, P. S. (1988). Psychiatric aspects of terrorist violence: Northern Ireland 1969-1987. *British Journal of Psychiatry, 153*, 470–475.

Daase, C., & Meier, O. (Eds.). (2012). *Arms control in the 21st century: Between coercion and cooperation*. Routledge.

de Jong, J. T. (2010). A public-health view on the prevention of war and its consequences. In E. Martz (Ed.), *Trauma rehabilitation after war and conflict*. Springer. https://doi.org/10.1007/978-1-4419-5722-1_4

De la Corte, L. (2007). Explaining terrorism: A psychosocial approach. *Perspectives on Terrorism, 1*(2) 1–10.

Difede, J., Malta, L., Best, S., Henn-Haase, C., Metzler, T., Bryant, R., & Marmar, C. (2007). A randomized controlled clinical treatment trial for World Trade Center attack-related PTSD in disaster workers. *The Journal of Nervous and Mental Disease, 195*, 861–865.

DiMaggio, C., & Galea, S. (2006). The behavioral consequences of terrorism: A meta-analysis. *Academic Emergency Medicine, 13*, 559–566.

DiMaggio, C., Galea, S., & Li, G. (2009). Substance use and misuse in the aftermath of terrorism. A Bayesian meta-analysis. *Addiction, 104*, 894–904.

Dollard, J. (1939). *Frustration and aggression.*

Duckworth, D. H. (1986). Psychological problems arising from disaster work. *Stress Medicine, 2*(4), 315–323.

Duffy, M., Gillespie, K., & Clark, D. M. (2007). Post-traumatic stress disorder in the context of terrorism and other civil conflict in Northern Ireland: Randomized controlled trial. *BMJ, 334*, 1147–1150.

Education, Program. (n.d.). *TITLE Teaching guide on international terrorism: Definitions, causes, and responses.* INSTITUTION United States Inst. of Peace, Washington, DC.

Eiset, A. H., & Wejse, C. (2017). Review of infectious diseases in refugees and asylum seekers—Current status and going forward. *Public Health Reviews, 38*(1). https://doi.org/10.1186/S40985-017-0065-4

Enloe, C. H. (2000a). *Maneuvers: Intl. politics of militarizing women's lives.* 444. http://books.google.co.in/books?id=kTaa79pyr7EC

Enloe, C. H. (2000b). *Maneuvers: Intl. politics of militarizing women's lives.* University of California Press. https://www.ucpress.edu/book/9780520220713/maneuvers

Eubank, W. L., & Weinberg, L. (1994). Does democracy encourage terrorism? *Terrorism and Political Violence, 6*(4), 417–435.

European Center for Security Studies. (2003). The economic war on terrorism: Money laundering and terrorist financing, international conference sponsored by the Conference Center of the George C. Marshall European Center for Security Studies, co-sponsored by the US Department of the Treasury, the US Federal Bureau of Investigation and the US Department of Justice, Garmisch-Partenkirchen, Germany, 21–4 July. http://www.marshallcenter.org

Fanon, F. (1965). *The wretched of the earth.* New York, Pelican. Reprint of Les damnes de la terre (Paris, 1961).

Ferracuti, F. (1982). A sociopsychiatric interpretation of terrorism. *The Annals of the American Academy of Political and Social Science, 463*(1), 129–140.

Ferracuti, F., & Bruno, F. (1981). Psychiatric Aspects of Terrorism in Italy (From Mad, the Bad, and the Different, P 199–213, 1981, Israel L Barak-Glantz et al, ed.-See NCJ-84231).

Fernandes, R., Susarla, S., & Parmar, S. (2019). Vibration reduction for structures: Distributed schemes over directed graphs. *Lancet, 15*(2), 1613. https://doi.org/10.1177/19433875221096728

Friedland, N. (1992). Terrorist: Social and individual antecedents. In L. Howard (Ed.), *Terrorism: Roots, impact, responses.* New York: Praeger.

Foa, E., Cahill, S., Boscarino, J., et al. (2005). Social, psychological, and psychiatric interventions following terrorist attacks: Recommendations for practice and research. *Neuropsychopharmacology, 30*, 1806–1817. https://doi.org/10.1038/sj.npp.1300815

Garcia, D. (2012). *Disarmament diplomacy and human security: Regimes, norms, and moral progress in international relations.* Routledge.

García-Vera, M. P., & Sanz, J. (2008). A psychological umbrella for people affected by March 11 terrorist attacks: The role of self-help psychological guides and psychological intervention guidelines. In M. P. García-Vera, F. J. Labrador, & C. Larroy (Eds.), *Ayuda psicológica a las víctimas de atentadosycatástrofes [Psychological help for victims of terrorist attacks and disasters].* Editorial Complutense.

Galea, S., Ahern, J., Resnick, H., Kilpatrick, D., Bucuvalas, M., Gold, J., & Vlahov, D. (2002). Psychological sequelae of the September 11 terrorist attacks in new York City. *New England journal of medicisne, 346*(13), 982–987.

Gazzaniga, M. S. (Ed.). (2000). *The new cognitive neurosciences* (2nd ed.). Cambridge, MA: MIT Press.

Goldfrank, L. R., Panzer, A. M., & Butler, A. S. (Eds.). (2003). *Preparing for the psychological consequences of terrorism: A public health strategy*. National Academies Press.

Goodey, J. (2003). *Compensating victims of violent crime in the European Union*. National Roundtable on Victim Compensation. Gunaratna, R. Unpublished draft.

Gurr, T. R. (1970). *Why men rebel*. Princeton University Press.

Hacker, F. (1976). *Crusaders, criminals, crazies: Terror and terrorism in our time* (p. xi). New York: Norton.

Hoffman, B. (1998). *Inside terrorism*. New York: Columbia University Press.

Hubbard, D. G. (1971). *The skyjacker: His flights of fantasy*. Macmillan, New York.

Jensen, P. S., & Shaw, J. (1993). Children as victims of war: Current knowledge and future research needs. *Journal of the American Academy of Child and Adolescent Psychiatry, 32*(4), 697–708. https://doi.org/10.1097/00004583-199307000-00001

Jeyakumar, A., Godbharle, S. R., & Giri, B. R. (2021). Water, sanitation and hygiene (WaSH) practices and diarrhoea prevalence among children under five years in a tribal setting in Palghar, Maharashtra, India. *Journals.Sagepub.Com, 25*(2), 182–193. https://doi.org/10.1177/1367493520916028

Jones, J. (2008). *Blood that cries out from the earth: The psychology of religious terrorism*. Oxford University Press.

Juergensmeyer, M. (2000). *Terror in the mind of god*. Berkeley: University of California Press.

Kean, T. H., & Hamilton, L. H. (2007, September 9). Are we safer today? *The Washington Post*, p. B1.

Kellen, K. (1979). *Terrorists—What are they like? How some terrorists describe their world and actions*, Santa Monica, CA. RAND.

Kelly, R. J., & Rieber, R. W. (1995). Psycho-social impacts of terrorism and organized crime: The counterfinality of the practicoinert. *Journal of Social Distress and the Homeless, 4*(4), 265–286.

Knight, C. (2011). *Strategic adjustment to sustain the force: A survey of current proposals*. Project on Defense Alternatives.

Kohut, H. (1972). Thoughts on narcissism and narcissistic rage. In P. Omstein (Ed.), *The search for the self* (vol. 2 ed., pp. 685–724). New York: International Universities Press.

Kohut, H. (1978). *The search for the self*, New York: International Universities Press.

Lapan, H. E., & Sandler, T. (1988). To bargain or not to bargain: That is the question. *The American Economic Review, 78*(2), 16–21.

Laqueur, W. (1999). *The new terrorism: Fanaticism and the arms of mass destruction*. Oxford University Press.

Lezak, M. D. (1995). *Neuropsychological assessment* (3rd ed.). New York: Oxford University Press.

Lifton, R. J. (1999). *Destroying the world to save it: Aum Shinrikyo*. Apocalyptic Violence and the New Global Terrorism (Holt, New York, 2000).

Lum, C., Kennedy, L. W., & Sherley, A. (2006). Are counter-terrorism strategies effective? The results of the Campbell systematic review on counter-terrorism evaluation research. *Journal of Experimental Criminology, 2*, 489–516. https://doi.org/10.1007/s11292-006-9020-y

Lund, M. S. (1996). *Preventing violent conflicts: A strategy for preventive diplomacy*. US Institute of Peace Press.

Martin, G. (2014). Types of terrorism. In *Exchanging terrorism oxygen for media airwaves: The age of terroredia* (pp. 81–95). IGI Global.

Meiqari, L., Hoetjes, M., Baxter, L., & Lenglet, A. (2018). Impact of war on child health in northern Syria: The experience of Médecins Sans Frontières. *European Journal of Pediatrics, 177*(3), 371–380. https://doi.org/10.1007/S00431-017-3057-Y/FIGURES/5

Mesulam, M.-M. (2000). Behavioral neuroanatomy. In M.-M. Mesualm (Ed.), *Principles of behavioral and cognitive neurology* (2nd ed., pp. 1–120). Oxford, UK: Oxford University Press.

Merari, A. (1998). The readiness to kill and die: Suicidal terrorism in the Middle East. In W. Reich (Ed.), *Origins of terrorism: Psychologies, ideologies, theologies, states of mind* (pp. 192–207). Washington, DC: Woodrow Wilson Center Press.

Miller, H. C. (Ed.). (1920). *Functional nerve disease: An epitome of war experience for the practitioner*. Henry Frowde, Hodder & Stoughton.

Moreno, N., Sanz, J., García-Vera, M. P., Gesteira, C., Gutiérrez, S., Zapardiel, A., Cobos, B., & Marotta-Walters, S. (2019 Nov). Effectiveness of trauma-focused cognitive behavioral therapy for terrorism victims with very long-term emotional disorders. *Psicothema, 31*(4), 400–406. https://doi.org/10.7334/psicothema2018.165

National Institute of Mental Health. (2002). *Mental health and mass violence: Evidence based early psychological intervention for victims/survivors of mass violence a workshop to reach consensus on best practices*. NIH Publication No. 02-5138. U.S. Government Printing Office.

North, C. S., Pollio, D. E., Smith, R. P., King, R. V., Pandya, A., Suris, A. M., et al. (2011). Trauma exposure and posttraumatic stress disorder among employees of New York City companies affected by the September 11, 2001 attacks on the World Trade Center. *Disaster Medicine and Public Health Preparedness, 5*(S2), S205–S213.

O'Neill, W. G. (2002). Beyond slogans: How can the UN respond to terrorism? In *International peace academy responding to terrorism: What role for the United Nations?*, *Proceedings of a conference*, New York, 25–6 October, p. 7.

Okello, J., Onen, T. S., & Musisi, S. (2007). Psychiatric disorders among war-abducted and non-abducted adolescents in Gulu district, Uganda: A comparative study. *African Journal of Psychiatry (South Africa), 10*(4), 225–231. https://doi.org/10.4314/AJPSY.V10I4.30260

Pearlstein, R. M. (1991). *The mind of the political terrorist*. Scholarly Resources.

Plan, S. (2002). Human Rights Watch.

Post JM. (1998). *Terrorist psychologic: Terrorist behaviour as a product of psychological forces*. Origins of terrorism: Psychologies, ideologies, theologies, states of mind, W Reich. Johns Hopkins University Press, Baltimore, MD; 25–40.

Post, J. M. (2004). *Leaders and their followers in a dangerous world: The psychology of political behavior*. Ithaca, NY: Cornell University Press.

Post, J., Sprinzak, E., & Denny, L. (2003). The terrorists in their own words: Interviews with 35 incarcerated middle eastern terrorists** this research was conducted with the support of the Smith Richardson Foundation. *Terrorism and political Violence, 15*(1), 171–184.

Robins, R. S., & Post, J. M. (1997). *Political paranoia: The psychopolitics of hatred*. Yale University Press.

Sageman, M. (2004). *Understanding terror networks*. Philadelphia: University of Pennsylvania Press.

Sastry, K. R. R. (2016). International affairs: Legal controls of international conflict. By Julius Stone. (London, Stevens and Sons Ltd., 1954, pp. 851, $4–4 sh. net).: *doi: 10.1177/097492845601200212*, *12*(2), 182–183. https://doi.org/10.1177/097492845601200212.

Schlenger, W. E., Caddell, J. M., Ebert, L., Jordan, B. K., Rourke, K. M., Wilson, D., et al. (2002). Psychological reactions to terrorist attacks: findings from the National Study of Americans' reactions to September 11. *JAMA, 288*(5), 581–588.

Schmid, A. (1983). *Political terrorism: A research guide to the concepts, theories, databases and literature*. With a bibliography by the author and a world directory of "terrorist" organizations by A. J. Jongman. Amsterdam: North Holland.

Shaw, E. D. (1986). Political terrorists: Dangers of diagnosis and an alternative to the psychopathology model. *International Journal of Law and Psychiatry*.

Silver, R. C., Holman, E. A., McIntosh, D. N., Poulin, M., & Gil-Rivas, V. (2002). Nationwide longitudinal study of psychological responses to September 11. *Journal of the American Medical Association, 288*(10), 1235–1244.

Snoubar, Y., & Duman, N. (2015). Using social holistic approach in working with children who are in the war zone. *Mediterranean Journal of Social Sciences, 6*(2S5), 231–237. https://doi.org/10.5901/MJSS.2015.V6N2S5P231

Snoubar, Y., & Hawal, H. (2015). Young communities and the impact of wars and conflicts on the healthy growth of young people: Middle East as a model study. *European Journal of Interdisciplinary Studies, 1*(1), 129. https://doi.org/10.26417/EJIS.V1I1.P129-136

Solomon, N. (2006). *War made easy: How presidents and pundits keep spinning us to death* Hoboken. Wiley.

Staggenborg, S. (2010). *Social movements*. Oxford University Press.

Sustainable Defense Task Force. (2010). *Debt, deficits, & defense: A way forward.*

Taylor, M., & Ryan, H. (1988). Fanaticism, political suicide and terrorism. *Terrorism, 11*, 91–111.

Taylor, M., & Quayle, E. (1994). *Terrorist Lives*. Washington, Brassey's.

US Government. (2003, July). *Report of the Joint Inquiry into the Terrorist Attacks of 11 September 2001 to Congress, by the House Permanent Select Committee on Intelligence and the SenateSelect Committee on Intelligence*. Government Printing Office.

Ursano, R. J., Kao, T. C., & Fullerton, C. S. (1992). Posttraumatic stress disorder and meaning: Structuring human chaos.

Veldhuis, T. (2012). Designing rehabilitation and reintegration programmes for violent extremist offenders: A realist approach. *Terrorism and Counter-Terrorism Studies*. https://doi.org/10.19165/2012.1.02

Whitaker, B. (1972). *The fourth world: Victims of group oppression: Eight reports from the field work of thse minority rights group*. New York: Schocken.

White, J. R. (2012). *Terrorism and homeland security: An introduction* (7th ed.). Wadsworth.

Wieviorka, M. (2004). *The making of terrorism*. University of Chicago Press.

Wilson, E. (1978). *On human nature*. https://www.degruyter.com/document/doi/10.1515/9781400831296/pdf#page=354

Wright, Q. (1942). *A study of war* (2nd ed. 1965 ed.). Chicago Press.

Wright, Q. (1965). The escalation of international conflicts. *Journal of Conflict Resolution, 9*, 434–449.

Chapter 9
Trauma-Informed Psychological Supports When Natural Disasters Come

York Williams

Introduction

The World Health Organization reports that we are facing heavy toll with regard to natural disasters. Heath notes that subsequent to immediate deaths communicable diseases may threaten survivors' well-being. Rapidly escalating the death toll, inadequate and contaminated water and food that cause ill health, immune diseases, diarrhea, and more types of sicknesses have taken a toll on health organizations that treat places impacted by natural disasters. Heath also notes that even with well-developed emergency services in place, recent hurricanes in the USA such as Katrina demonstrate the immediate and ongoing needs of families and communities when disasters strike. Regardless of a community's size, location, and financial stability, some types of natural disaster pose a potential threat to the safety and well-being of its citizens (p. 289). This chapter's information is related to the domain of preventative and responsive services, as conceptualized in the National Association of School Psychologist model. This model offers specific examples of school psychologists' preventive and responsive services, including participation on school crisis teams, by offering "direct services in the context of crisis prevention, preparation, response and recovery".

Y. Williams (✉)
West Chester University, West Chester, PA, USA
e-mail: ywilliams@wcupa.edu

Natural Disasters

Depending on the location, some types of natural disasters are more likely to occur than others. Earthquakes, landslides, flash floods, tsunamis, avalanches, and fires are common examples of natural disasters that can strike at a moment's notice. In the USA, Gulf States are more prone to hurricanes which significantly impact families living in poverty. Tornados are common around the Appalachian Mountain ranges and Florida and Kansas, parts of North America with low terrains. Few individuals affected by disasters suffer serious long-term psychological harm such as Post-Traumatic Stress Disorder (PTSD), depression, and trauma. The vast majority of individuals are resilient and adapt to life after a natural disaster. These disasters do place families, communities, and students at risk. The personal impact of far-removed disasters appears to be negligible.

In general, natural disasters cause destruction and threaten livelihoods, economic activity, and cultures in every country across the globe. In addition to these economic losses, natural disasters lead to injury and loss of life, destruction of environmental quality, and psychological harm, as well as indirect losses. These major disruptions are huge shocks to human, social, economic, and environmental systems (Bakkensen et al., 2017). Natural disaster takes a significant toll on the health, well-being, and sense of efficacy in communities worldwide.

Best Practices in Crisis Intervention

A large body of research and natural disasters informs places like schools and public institutions. In order to keep children and vulnerable populations safe, schools and communities often implement research-based interventions and strategies to inform school psychologists in effectively planning and supporting students' needs in a natural disaster. Preventative practices are used to keep people and communities with vulnerable populations safe.

First, school and community crisis teams should prepare for the worst well in advance of a natural disaster happening. Next, schools and communities must prepare disaster services, which entails working within the prevention mitigation phase, where crisis teams must address potentially weak areas of response that might jeopardize the effectiveness of their school's disaster response efforts. Next, entities must prepare emergency kits. This may occur when local and school psychologists encourage teachers and community workers to prepare community and classroom emergency kits for distribution. Although these kits typically contain basic supplies and various items, the care workers should tailor these kits to their unique community and student population.

Next, community and interagency workers should train for emergency preparedness. This may entail community and school psychologists engaging in ongoing training opportunities for crisis intervention and prevention based on evidence and research-based strategies. Also, psychologists should remain up-to-date in CPR and first aid. Within the school setting, the roles of teachers and school staff should be refined and established in preparation for a disaster. This entails working with local and school psychologists to strengthen the role of teachers and school staff in crisis intervention that can support students in the event of a natural disaster (through trainings as crisis response team members).

Victims and Emotional Stages

Community and school psychologists must consider the impact of disaster on the child, their family, and community overall. Children will naturally worry and wish to become reunited with their family and loved ones. First, institutions and workers must attend to vulnerable children and their family members. This entails understanding the history of trauma within your school and general population and how an event will impact each child who suffers from the same. Additionally, institutions of care should consider age differences and how youth, seniors, children, and adults with disabilities may react to a crisis brought on by a natural disaster. The reactions of a child differs by age and history. Older children may understand the gravity of the event, whereas younger children and those with exceptional needs may not. Adults, seniors, and adults with special needs may become bewildered and overwhelmed, spurring the onset of medical reaction related to an ongoing health condition.

Psychologists and clinicians should also monitor children's behavioral and emotional needs. Typically, only the most extreme cases will require intermediate intervention needs. Physical injuries and the traumatic effects following an event should be considered for monitoring as well. Clinicians and psychologists should also monitor and assess internalizing and externalizing behaviors that can impede progress and stability in the event of a crisis. Monitoring for anxiety, depression, withdrawal as well as excitability, anger, opposition, and other more observable behaviors assists with managing the impact of the disaster or event on the students' or community member's social and emotional functioning. Clinicians must also monitor for symptoms of PTSD. Overall, PTSD is a trauma and stress-related disorder that may impact any individual at any age and typically emerge following a traumatic event, such as a natural disaster. Psychologists should watch for perseveration in children's play and how seniors react since oftentimes these issues are not easily articulated.

School and Community Interventions

Within the school setting, children need to be treated and cared for within the natural environment where the stressors of the event can be addressed. They need to be surrounded and cared for by adults and others who they trust when services are deemed necessary in the first place. Schools typically provide Tier I Interventions which are typically based on skills within a Cognitive Behavior Therapy (CBT)-based framework. For example, clinicians might utilize relaxation skills with minimal prompting to strengthen resilience and to return individuals back to a sense of normalcy. The same interventions can be utilized with adults and others within homes and community centers during and following the onset of a crisis.

Next, clinicians should consider Tier II and Tier III Interventions for students and adults still struggling with PTSD symptoms. These symptoms can persist beyond a month of the natural disaster and will require group or individual services based on CBT. Finally, care workers must assist children in developing a trauma narrative. Children should be encouraged to develop a story about their trauma and strategies to help them become aware of, observe, and manage their thoughts, feelings, and fears related to the event. Clinicians and caregivers during a disaster are encouraged to involve parents and caregivers in children's and vulnerable adults' interventions at all phases. Involving parents and or caregivers in the recovery process post disaster is important and can produce healing from the process. Given the diversity of residents, students, and community members from various backgrounds, clinicians and school psychologists must identify and treat students based on strategies that will meet their unique needs (Butler et al., 2017).

Heath notes that regardless of a community's location, size, or financial stability, some types of natural disaster pose a potential threat to the safety and well-being of children. Because most natural disasters occur with minimal or no warning, both prevention and intervention are critical components in school crisis plans. This chapter summarizes school psychologists' crisis prevention and intervention strategies to mitigate the impact of natural disasters and to strengthen social and emotional support for students. Prevention efforts must identify and address potentially vulnerable areas in crisis plans, including attending to the needs of students with disabilities, practicing the crisis plan, and coordinating efforts with emergency medical teams.

Helping schools return to their normal schedule as soon as possible supports student recovery and stabilizes the community. Additionally, research indicates the importance of social support in helping children recover following traumatic events. Sources of social support include parent involvement, peer group support, and a nurturing school and classroom environment. Another aspect for school psychologists to consider is strengthening the role of teachers and school staff in crisis intervention and increasing emotional support for students in their familiar classroom setting. Regarding counselling strategies to address anxiety and post-traumatic stress in children and adolescents, the bulk of research supports cognitive-behavioral therapy. Therapy based on cognitive-behavioral strategies helps students understand the connection between thoughts, feelings, and behaviors.

The Role of Counselors During Disaster

According to Uhernik (2008), counselors that understand the role of multidisciplinary work and Incident Control Systems (ICS) can join a multidisciplinary team in disaster response. Counselors can provide the team with unique skills and a behavioral health focus. Counselors who work in agency settings can assist in development or review of their agency internal emergency plans (Uhernik, 2008). Additionally, the behavioral expertise of the counsellor can assist in crafting messages for staff, public, and media. Uhernik notes that counsellors can collaborate with other emergency response groups as they engage in planning for different operational aspects during a disaster. Finally, counsellor expertise can be integral to emergency planning related to populations with special needs.

James and Gilliland (2017) also note that counsellors can be part of a School Crisis Response Team (SCRT) and also Crisis Intervention Team (CIT). Both can allow the counsellor to fulfil critical roles during a crisis. When a crisis is of such magnitude that local staff are overwhelmed or emotionally devastated because of personal involvement, then outside help should be summoned and the counsellor can assist with accessing this level of support. The counsellor may play an especially important role in a small or rural district where collaborative resources are scarce. James and Gilliland also suggest that counsellors bring a level of understanding to the needs of the CIT especially when resources are scarce and it is unclear with whom to collaborate. In situations when there is an immediate crisis, the counsellor is one who will be able to understand how the alliance network functions (James & Gilliland, 2017). Counsellors must also be mindful of the impact of the disaster on their sense of safety and well-being.

A traumatic event or situation creates psychological trauma when it overwhelms the individual's ability to cope, and leaves that person fearing death, annihilation, mutilation, or psychosis. According to the Administration for Children and Families (2021), Secondary Traumatic Stress or Vicarious Trauma can decrease staff functioning and create challenges in the working environment. Some of the documented negative organizational effects that can result from STS are increased absenteeism, impaired judgment, low productivity, poorer quality of work, higher staff turnover, and greater staff friction. Further evidence of secondary exposures can be inferred from student reactions to content, such as feelings of fear, helplessness, or horror (PTSD) subjective exposure.

Psychological First Aid and the Counselor's Role

Psychological First Aid (PFA) is described as a humane, supportive response to a fellow human being who is suffering and who may need support. The core of PFA involves the following themes: (a) providing practical care and support, which does not intrude; (b) assessing needs and concerns; (c) helping people to address basic needs (e.g., food and water, information); (d) listening to people, but not pressuring them to talk; (e) comforting people and helping them to feel calm; (f) helping people connect to information, services, and social supports; and (g) protecting people from further harm (Kantor & Beckert, 2011).

In general, PFA is aimed at helping people who have been very recently affected by a crisis event or natural disaster. One may provide PFA when you have contact with very distressed people. This is usually during or immediately after an event. Accordingly, PFA can be offered wherever it is safe enough for you to do so. This is often in community settings, such as at the scene of an accident, or places where distressed people are served, such as health centers, shelters or camps, schools, and distribution sites for food or other types of help (Kantor & Beckert, 2011). The three basic action principles of PFA are look, listen, and link. These action principles will help guide how you view and safely enter a crisis situation, approach affected people and understand their needs, and link them with practical support and information (Kantor & Beckert, 2011).

The five components/elements of PFA are: safety, calming, connectedness, self-efficacy, and hope. Additionally, training is critical in order to become an effective responder. There is a six-hour course that puts the participant in the role of provider in a post-disaster setting. The course is for individuals new to disaster response and want to learn the goals of PFA.

Victimization During and After Calamities

According to Vander Kolk (Van der Kolk, 2015), trauma affects not only those who are directly exposed to it, but also those around them. Vander Kolk suggests that trauma by definition is unbearable and intolerable. For example, he notes that most rape victims, combat soldiers, and children who have been molested become so upset when they think about what they experienced that they try to push it out of their minds while trying to act as though nothing happened so that they can attempt to move on (p. 2). According to Guarino and Bassuk (2010), trauma involves a threat to one's physical or emotional well-being related to an overwhelming experience that results in intense feelings of fear and lack of control and leaves people feeling helpless. These feelings change the way a person understands himself/herself, the world, and others.

Guarino and Bassuk maintain that trauma associated with the loss of home, safety, and a sense of security have a significant impact on how children and adults think, feel, behave, cope, and relate to others. Understanding trauma and its impact is essential to providing quality care to families who are experiencing homelessness. Becoming "trauma-informed" requires that service providers tailor their services to meet the unique needs of trauma survivors and avoid additional harm. The authors suggest that our bodies may also respond to trauma in a flight or fight pattern. The brain contains a natural alarm system designed to detect and evaluate potential threats and activate physical responses to keep the body safe. When the alarm system detects a threat (e.g., a loud noise, a violent situation, neglect), it readies the body to respond by releasing chemicals that lead to various physical responses such as sweating and increased heart rate and breathing (p. 15). The authors suggest that one of the keys towards unlocking a deeper understanding of trauma is through understanding triggers.

The term "trigger" refers to reminders of past traumatic experiences that people encounter in the present. Triggers may include sights, sounds, smells, feelings, or experiences that are associated with a previous traumatic experience (Van der Kolk, 2015; p. 15). When exposed to a trigger, the trauma survivor's brain remembers this as a danger signal based on past experiences and immediately prepares the body to respond. Prolonged exposure to trauma may also result in what the authors describe as complex trauma. The term "complex trauma" is used to describe prolonged, persistent traumatic stress that often originates within the caregiving system during critical developmental stages and leads to immediate and long-term difficulties in many areas of functioning (Van der Kolk, 2015; p. 16). It is important for helpers to understand the types of traumatic experiences the client has encountered so that they can provide better treatment and care.

Alexithymia

According to Zech, Luminet, Rime, and Wagner (Zech et al., 1999), patients are described as predominantly unimaginative and as often manifesting difficulties in verbal and symbolic expression of emotion. The authors note that at least three features characterize the alexithymic person: (i) a difficulty in recognizing, identifying, and describing emotions, and in distinguishing between emotional states and bodily sensations; (ii) an impaired symbolization, as evidenced by a paucity of fantasies and other imaginative activity; and (iii) a preference for focusing on external events rather than inner experiences. Alexithymia is more generally viewed as a cognitive style of language and of thoughts characterized by a deficit in the processing of emotional information, or as a deficit of affect regulation (Zech et al., 1999; p. 512). The authors further suggest that alexithymia has also been linked inextricably to the person's emotional regulation, such as emotional awareness, mood monitoring, mood labeling, and emotional intelligence. However, the authors note that the field of psychology must yield reliable instrumentation to further study and measure the presence of alexithymia with the correct psychometric properties in mind, some which may include five theoretically derived features: (i) difficulty describing feelings; (ii) difficulty distinguishing feelings and bodily sensations; (iii) lack of introspection; (iv) social conformity; and (v) paucity of fantasy. However, the authors contend that before further conclusions can be drawn about the type of alexithymia questionnaire to be recommended, different issues related to the BVAQ should be explored systematically.

According to Swart, Kortekaas, and Aleman (Swart et al., 2009), alexithymia or "no words for feelings" is a personality trait which is associated with difficulties in emotion recognition and regulation. It is unknown whether this deficit is due primarily to regulation, perception, or mentalizing of emotions. In order to further reconcile this issue, the authors studied participants in their research study who possessed a wide range of emotional tasks. Alexithymia has been reported to be a risk factor for a variety of medical and psychiatric disorders like substance use disorders, somatization, anxiety and depression, and even schizophrenia. Moreover, the authors report that alexithymia reduces life satisfaction. They maintain that unraveling the psychological mechanisms underlying alexithymia may have important clinical and societal implications (Swart et al., 2009).

In this research study (Swart et al., 2009), the authors hypothesized that alexithymics would underperform on all associated tasks. The two groups differed on the Emotion Regulation Questionnaire, Berkeley Expressivity Questionnaire, and Empathy Quotient. Specifically, the Emotion Regulation Quotient showed that alexithymic individuals used more suppressive and less reappraisal strategies. On the behavioral tasks, as expected, alexithymics performed worse on recognition of microexpressions and emotional mentalizing. Additionally, the authors report that groups did not differ on tasks of emotional semantics and prosody and associative emotional learning. The authors resolve those future studies are necessary to explore the specific emotion processing difficulties in alexithymia. For example, the use of brain imaging may help unravel brain mechanisms underlying emotional processing deficits in alexithymia can assist with at least understanding the physiological and chemical changes that take place during emotional experiences or the lack thereof (Swart et al., 2009).

Trauma-Informed Counseling Strategies

Vander Kolk suggests that we should revisit the way we diagnose alexithymia. He suggested in the video (2014) review that youth with this illness should be considered possessing an Alexithymia Disorder, which will provide the layers of progressiveness across emotional regulation or rather dysregulation. Further, Vanheule, Verhaeghe, and Desmet (Vanheule et al., 2011) maintain that alexithymic patients should focus on distressing situations, starting from which a three-step logic can be deployed. During therapy, mental representations on difficult situations in patients' lives need to be constructed by (1) putting into words the chain of events that makes up the distressing situation; (2) making the patient's appraisal of the difficult situation explicit; and addressing affective responses and discussing the patient's way of dealing with a difficult situation. The authors maintain that based on Freud's theory on actual neurosis and our reading of this theory via Lacan and contemporary attachment theory, alexithymia can be understood as a result of a representational failure in the relationship between subject and other. However, they argue that the failure of a traditional psychotherapeutic approach may lead to a repetition of the intersubjective mismatch that lies at the basis of the problem, without the therapist being aware of this.

Starting from Lacanian theory, the authors (Vanheule et al., 2011) note that therapy should largely focus on naming and verbally articulating specific problematic events in patients' lives. By means of language, experiences can be shared and situated in relation to culturally prevailing ideas and practices. From psychoanalytic attachment theory, the authors hold that that mirroring is a tool that is at the therapist's disposal in addressing the patient's distressing experience of arousal. First, as the authors demonstrate in their article using a case study approach, the therapists allow the patient to focus on letting her articulate specific tragic events that she qualified as difficult (Emma) that are typically interpersonal events or relationships. Second, as noted in the article with Emma, after constructing the chain of events, Emma was invited to indicate why exactly she thought she, or the others involved in the situation were acting correctly or not. Much of this time may be devoted to elaborating detailed appraisals of various situations which may give rise to multiple perspective seeking about the problem from various angles. Thirdly, efforts are made to adequately name experience of distress, and attention should be paid to how the client deals with it. For example, it was noted that Emma's spontaneous fleeing reactions were discussed post-session and alternative ways of reacting to troubling events were explored.

Upon additional therapeutic follow-up, the patient should be invited to discuss her own reactions to the painful situation she ran away from. The discussions can follow the three-step logic laid out here and explore the client's way of dealing with tension and distress in relation to the therapist's interventions. The authors resolve that these discussions will be difficult to the patient but are important in terms of enhancing her capacity to tolerate conflict. During the discussions with Emma, the authors noted that she often burst out in nervous laughter and showed nonverbal signs of disdain. The therapist in the study addressed these reactions and asked her what she was expressing. Using this therapeutic approach, Emma, like a typical client, may come to recognize her anger, helplessness, hopes, and sorrow, starting from which broader family-related problems may be further explored.

Resilience Post Disaster

Vargas (2021) suggests that clinicians and caretakers should implement a number of comprehensive preventions approaches that can address the multiplicity of risks and the cumulative trauma that many children and adults face. Some of these strategies may also emphasize the importance of promoting competence and building protection across multiple domains in order to achieve a positive outcome (Administration for Children and Families, 2021). According to the article entitled "Building Your Resilience" (APA, 2012), psychologists define resilience as the process of adapting well in the face of adversity, trauma, tragedy, threats, or significant sources of stress – such as family and relationship problems, serious health problems, or workplace and financial stressors. Moreover, the author maintains that resilience involves "bouncing back" from these difficult experiences. Much of the bounce-back is based on protective factors. For Paul, the love of his mother, was a source of continuing healing. Another protective factor Paul presented was the ability to find purpose (APA, 2012). Since mom was still recovering from her gunshot wounds, Paul needed to stay strong in order to support her in her continued transition to full parenthood and her role as caretaker of his siblings.

Post-Traumatic Stress Disorder (PTSD) and Natural Disaster

In Post-Traumatic Stress Disorder (PTSD), a number of changes in memory functioning have been identified that are comparable with other studies of patients who suffer with depression after a natural disaster or traumatic event. Some trends include a bias toward enhanced recall of trauma-related material and difficulties in retrieving autobiographical memories of specific incidents (Buckley et al., 2000). Additionally, more specific to PTSD is a cycle of traumatic events in the client that include emotion and memory. In some studies, high levels of emotion are associated with more vivid and long-lasting memories (Rubin & Kozin, 1984), while in others, they are associated with memories that are vague, lacking in detail, and error-prone. The DSM-V describes PTSD as characterized both by high-frequency, distressing, intrusive memories and by amnesia for the details of the event. Consistent with this are clinical studies and observations reporting that confusion and forgetting are as typical of trauma memories as is vivid, lasting recall. Mechanic et al. (1998) suggest that more systematic studies of patients' memories of personally experienced traumatic events confirm that recall tends to improve over the first few weeks (Mechanic et al., 1998), that their content may tend to be disorganized and contain gaps.

Relatedly, one other notable feature of memory in PTSD is when the client relives experiences or "flashbacks" to the trauma. When compared to normal autobiographical memory, these flashbacks are dominated by sensory detail such as vivid visual images and may include sounds and other sensations (Brewin & Saunders, 2001). However, these images and sensations are typically disjointed and fragmentary. As such, "reliving" of these memories is reflected in a distortion in the sense of time such that the traumatic events seem to be happening in the present rather than (as in the case of ordinary memories) belonging to the past. Additionally, as the client may relive episodes within these memories, they also do not seem to occur as a result of a deliberate search of memory but may be triggered involuntarily by separate events or specific reminders. Some reminders may come through the senses given the circumstances of the trauma, such as the sound of a police siren or the smell of smoke, or particular thoughts or images relating to the event (Ehlers & Clark, 2000).

Reynolds and Brewin (Reynolds & Brewin, 1998) interviewed matched groups of patients suffering from either PTSD or depression, as well as nonclinical controls, and asked them to describe the image or thought related to a stressful event that was most frequently coming to mind. The authors found that flashbacks, either on their own or in combination with other images and thoughts, were reported as the most frequent intrusive cognition by 43% of the PTSD patients, 9% of the depressed patients, and none of the nonpatients (Reynolds & Brewin, 1998). Overall, this finding adds further support to the claim that flashbacks are a distinctive feature of PTSD.

Forensic Aspects of Natural Disaster

One of the most difficult aspects of a Natural Disaster is managing the losses left behind, which often results in more grief and trauma for those caretakers and emergency personnel in charge of supporting the community (Morgan, 2004). To this end, worldwide, natural disasters claim thousands of lives each year. However, care of the deceased is often overlooked in disaster planning and the absence of guidance for first responders has recently been highlighted following several large disasters. More importantly for caretakers and personnel, the task becomes urgent for the identification and disposal of human remains. Additionally, forensic specialists are on hand to inspect the area and often a final determination about what has happened to the lost loved ones but may encounter issues such as an inability to access the affected area.

Additional concerns also extend to the identification of dead bodies, which is done by matching information from the deceased (physical features, clothes, etc.) This information often comes from information from individuals who are missing or presumed dead. At this point, the forensic investigators and caretakers must mobilize specific forensic resources which may take several days. During this time, bodies run the risk of decomposing which makes identifying bodies a priority. Forensic procedures (autopsies, fingerprinting, dental examinations, DNA) can be used after visual identification of bodies or photographs becomes impossible (Morgan, 2004). Overall, the process of analyzing, investigating, and composing the final reports around loss may expose the natural disaster personnel to a heightened level of vicarious trauma and secondary stress (Meadors et al., 2010).

Stages of TF-CBT		
1. Stabilization of Client ∘ Focus on Relationship with Client	2. Trauma Narrative & Processing – Remembrance & Mourning	3. Integration/Consolidation ∘ Conjoint sessions (parents) and/or support individuals ∘ Enhance Overall Safety in real live
∘ Establishing Safety (Perceived, Real threats)	∘ Processing of personal narrative/strengths/resiliency	∘ Mastery of Trauma Support Reminders
∘ Psychoeducation in CBT		
∘ Relaxation Techniques	∘ Desensitization to narrative and thoughts	
∘ Affect Modulation	∘ Mourn what did happen and what might have been	

Fig. 9.1 Stages of TF-CBT

Treatment for Victims

Trauma-Focused Cognitive Behavior Therapy (TF-CBT) is an evidence-based treatment that helps process traumatic memories, overcome problematic behaviors, and helps clients to develop effective coping skills while at the same time developing healthy interpersonal skills, especially following a natural disaster or major life event. This in turn may also help the client to reconnect with family and build upon their capacity for social supports (Cohen et al., 2012). Overall, TF-DBT (see Fig. 9.1) combines multiple approaches in stages and theories in order to meet the needs of the client. Through the use of cognitive and behavioral therapy, change can occur by harvesting traumatic memories that may cause the client to become stuck. Through desensitization, change behavior strategies can support growth through thoughts and perceptions. The goal is to change unhealthy behaviors and replace these with coping mechanisms. The background of TF-CBT is humanistic and where relationships matter. This approach also works well with family therapy (particularly for children and adolescents).

Figure 9.1 demonstrates the stages of TF-CBT that are especially important to address grief, loss, and mental illness-related needs following a natural disaster or traumatic event

The Stages of TF-CBT

The core of TF-CBT examines patterns of interactions in families through the use of Attachment Theory with a special focus on examining those relationships which makes it especially helpful for children. There is also a distinct aspect of TF-CBT that focuses on the development and neurobiology that also considers age-based understanding of individuals and also provides insight on development of the brain. Trauma-informed treatment is proposed in stages. Beginning in stage one, the clinician focuses on language that moves from "what is wrong with you" to "what happened to you." This approach reaffirms a sense of safety, trust, expression of feelings, and connectedness (Murray et al., 2013). There is also a focus on respect and unconditional positive regard for the client. The process of psychoeducation includes an understanding of trauma, implications of trauma, and treatment. Collaboration with client on treatment, skills learned, pace of sessions, choices, etc. are also introduced in phases of each of the three main stages of implementation. During self-care, there is a focus on regulation of emotions, self-soothing, and addressing dissociation. This is where the connection to traumatic memories as a psychological process may come in (Brewin et al., 2000).

Traumatic Memory and TF-CBT

Eye movement desensitization and reprocessing therapy (EMDR) is by now a well-established treatment for post-traumatic stress disorder (PTSD). There is good evidence for its efficacy and together with trauma-focused cognitive behavioral therapy (TF-CBT) it is considered to be the first-line treatment for PTSD (Bisson et al., 2013). As an adjunct with TF-CBT, the aspect of eye sensitization alone can be a powerful tool in assisting clients in managing traumatic memories, events, and experiences that otherwise keep them locked in a shadowy cold past. In recent years, short intensive CBT treatments for PTSD have been developed and found to be as effective as standard CBT applied on a weekly basis.

In addition to EMDR as an adjunct of TF-CBT in stage two of TF-CBT, traumatic memories can be processed through other interventions during therapy. Exposure to the trauma narrative as well as reminders of the trauma or emotions associated with the trauma are often used to help the client to both process what has happened to him or her and reduce avoidance and maladaptive associations with the trauma. Since the client may have difficulty regulating, this exposure is done in a controlled way, and planned collaboratively by the provider and patient so the patient chooses what they do. The goal is to return a sense of control, self-confidence, and predictability to the patient, and reduce escape and avoidance behaviors (Benight & Bandura, 2004). Additionally, psychoeducation about how trauma can affect the person is quite common as is instruction in various methods to facilitate relaxation. Managing stress and planning for potential crises can also be important components of CBT treatment. The provider, with the patient, has some latitude in selecting which elements of cognitive behavioral therapy are likely to be most effective with any particular individual.

Finally, the most important intervention to address the area of concern around memory in clients through the use of TF-CBT is during stage 2 in treatment using Trauma Narrative and Processing. This includes remembrance and mourning/grieving and retelling the story of the traumatic event while mourning the loss. Here, the clinician creates a narrative (art/bibliotherapy/psychodrama/sand tray) that allows a space where the client can rebuild the traumatic memory and begin to adapt it and process it in order to move on (Ehlers, 2013). Some steps in helping the client to recreate memories from his or her past begin with having them think of something from their past to practice a sense of trust in the process with you as a guide. This helps the client to begin to perceive any threat in order to end it, realize that they would survive and practice this in session a few times. This is where relaxation techniques and desensitization of the event come together in order to assist the client to normalize difficulties and unwanted thoughts while working to highlight strengths and to build resilience (Monson & Shnaider, 2014).

Challenges for Psychologists and Clinicians

Vanderkolk recommends understanding oneself in order to better manage and understand the triggers that ensue. Positive memories may minimize the impact of the trauma on the lives of individuals, such as playing an instrument, an intimate experience, and/or revisiting a favorite hobby (Van der Kolk, 2015). According to Vander Kolk (Van der Kolk, 2015), clinicians can hope to solve problems that children encounter when we can identify correctly what is going on with them and do more than developing new drugs to control them or trying to find the "gene" that is responsible for their "disease." Our goal is to assist them to lead productive lives and not medicate away their issues. As such, research is leading clinicians and scientists into new directions regarding understanding stressful experiences and the impact this has on gene expression. To this end, however, counselors also have to embody an ethic of self-care which can insulate oneself from compassion fatigue, vicarious or secondary traumatization, and counselor burnout (Meadors & Lamson, 2008).

Compassion Fatigue and Burnout

According to Burnett and Wahl (Burnett Jr & Wahl, 2015) Compassion Fatigue (CF), also sometimes known as burnout, can be broadly defined as a reduced capacity for empathy as manifested through emotional, behavioral, physical, spiritual, interpersonal, and cognitive reactions experienced by a disaster mental health service provider or any individual helping a traumatized person. Research has also shown the potential consequences of developing CF, which can include emotional exhaustion associated with depersonalization or lack of accomplishment.

Moreover, CF or burnout can be a result of being involved in situations that have been emotionally demanding for an extended period of time. A more multifaceted definition that encompasses three parallel dimensions: emotional exhaustion, depersonalization, and inefficacy. Studies have demonstrated a strong relationship between burnout and CF (Burnett Jr & Wahl, 2015). According to Wei et al. (2020), burnout is a psychological state resulting from a persistent negative reaction to work-related stress. The symptoms of burnout have been categorized into three dimensions: emotional exhaustion, feelings of cynicism, and a sense of inefficacy.

According to Gutierrez and Mullen (Gutierrez & Mullen, 2016), given the high intensity of counseling and the level of intimate and emotional processing that goes into counseling, counselors are often highly susceptible to counselor burnout. Gutierrez and Mullen argue that the profession of counseling requires counselors to confront any number of stressful scenarios that can lead to emotional exhaustion, empathy fatigue, and counselor burnout. Counselors are also required to empathize with patients which may cause exhaustion and mental fatigue over a period of time. As such, counselor burnout has been termed by the authors as a negative state characterized by physical, psychological, and emotional strain (Gutierrez & Mullen, 2016). To this end, the authors contend that emotional intelligence can play a positive role in buffering or minimizing the impact of counseling work with clients that may lead to burnout. In general, Emotional Intelligence (EI) consists of one's ability to identify, regulate, and use emotions effectively (Gutierrez & Mullen, 2016).

Secondary Traumatic Stress (STS) and Vicarious Trauma

Meadors, Lamson, Swanson, White, and Sira (Meadors et al., 2010) examined the impact of secondary traumatization and some of the personal and professional elements that affect how pediatric healthcare providers experience loss, stress, fear, anxiety, and depression all related to their duty of care with chronically ill patients and those impacted by a natural disaster or traumatic event. The authors note that traumatic events can have a profound and long-term impact on everyone who is directly and indirectly involved. They suggest that such occurrences are all too common and that most people in the USA will inevitably experience a trauma within their lifetime and some will experience multiple traumas directly (Meadors et al., 2010; p. 104). Healthcare providers, like clinicians, are one group of workers who are at a higher risk of experiencing secondary trauma, and as a result will experience multiple traumas as they extend care to patients facing irreversible medical conditions or who live in abusive environments. Vicarious traumatization can also occur when some of the personal and professional elements that affect how care workers experience loss, stress, fear, anxiety, and depression all related to their duty of care with chronically ill patients or extremely mentally ill patients. Meadors and Lamson (Meadors & Lamson, 2008) noted that unexpressed grief in mental and healthcare providers who tend to care for chronically or severely mentally ill patients, especially children, may lead to the development of core symptoms known as compassion fatigue.

A traumatic event or situation creates psychological trauma when it overwhelms the individual's ability to cope, and leaves that person fearing death, annihilation, mutilation, or psychosis. According to the Administration for Children and Families (Administration for Children and Families, 2021), Secondary Traumatic Stress or Vicarious Trauma can decrease staff functioning and create challenges in the working environment. Some of the documented negative organizational effects that can result from STS are increased absenteeism, impaired judgment, low productivity, poorer quality of work, higher staff turnover, and greater staff friction. Further evidence of secondary exposures can be inferred from student reactions to content – such as feelings of fear, helplessness, or horror (i.e., post-traumatic stress disorder [PTSD] subjective exposure).

Butler et al. (2017) maintain that as a consequence of secondary trauma exposures those with or without personal trauma histories are at risk for secondary traumatic stress (STS). STS describes the phenomenon wherein the sharing of traumatic experiences—particularly in circumstances where the listener is highly empathic or trying to be—stimulates trauma-related symptoms in the listener that can parallel those in the survivor. Additionally, these authors note that graduate training that incorporates trauma can involve secondary exposures not only in field but also in coursework, and contrary to students reported coursework to be at least as reactivating as fieldwork.

Post-Traumatic Events (PTE) has also impacted first responders such as firefighters (Kaurin et al., 2018). First responders, such as firefighters, are regularly exposed to traumatic stressors during their duties, including threats of violence, assaults, discovery of dead bodies or severely injured victims, and significant human suffering. Research also suggests between 80% and 90% of journalists have been exposed to a work-related traumatic event such as murder, mass casualties, war, and natural disasters. Most journalists exhibit resilience despite repeated exposure to such traumatic events. However, a significant minority are at risk for long-term psychological problems, including Post-Traumatic Stress Disorder (PTSD), depression, and substance abuse.

Secondary Stress and Burnout Interventions and Recommendations

One recommendation to address Secondary Traumatic Stress (STS), Vicarious Traumatization, and Burnout is the Bridge CAP model (Cognitive, Affective, Physical and Spiritual) (Cavicchioli & Maffei, 2020). This model allows a focus on accepting the reality where we are as client and helper, emotional pathways through the grief, loss, or crisis, and a transition to adjusting to self and the environment. The last phase includes a spiritual phase where we would then transcend the current issues in an attempt to make sense of what is happening in an existential sense. As such, since either you or the client might tend to become overwhelmed by framing the trauma, a strong intervention such as Bridge CAP will assist with keeping the parameters firm while we engage in crisis deconstruction.

Secondary traumatization can easily creep in if therapists and workers are not mindful of how they approach, and handle stressors related to work and their own internalization of the work. To this end, the author utilized a checklist approach as noted by Reidbord (2010) and ask critical questions about any feelings when they arise and examine them through a multifaceted lens with questions around: *where are these feelings coming from, what are the triggers, what did the client say or do to cause this feeling, and/or is the feeling uncharacteristic of a therapist?* In working with clients who might have experienced similar trauma as myself, this checklist approach might better enable me to stay within the therapist cascade and continue doing the work of a helper. As such, the checklist and reframing the dialogue will be essential as cautious steps in lessening the potential for countertransference into the future.

Finally, one strategy to support the clinician and client is Dialectical Thinking (open-mindedness) along with Positive Framing. To this end, remembering to let go of self-righteousness, moving beyond strict black and white thinking and finding a way to validate, not bury oneself into another person's point of view can take me— *the therapist*—a long way towards healing and insulate against vicarious traumatization and compassion fatigue. Additionally, it helps to consider positively framing every interaction rather than unhelpful thinking. For example, instead of grieving for what happened to a patient in crisis, we might focus on the good that resulted from her being able to share and discuss and find the silver lining in the current experience since there is so much grey.

Summary

It is important to consider other important issues related to the effects of different types of natural disasters and the timing of those disasters. Recovery and sustainability can be impacted by the type of population who experienced the event, such as a flooding, that might result in important economic and even human losses. Additionally, some communities given their location may be disproportionately impacted by the effects of an earthquakes such as those living in Spain and Chile where they may be more averse to the community or terrain and where the impact of the disaster may be less severe on their psychological functioning. Furthermore, it is important to bear in mind that resources for those impacted and the degree of evacuation procedures all have an impact on recovery towards a return to stability. The process of evacuation and its immediate aftermath is likely to encourage bonds among the evacuated individuals and might alter the impact of communal coping (Afifi et al., 2012). We also still have no clear idea of the time that elapses between a traumatic event and the onset of post-traumatic growth (Bitsch et al., 2011). Finally, it is important to consider other contextual aspects such as an adequate response from the authorities (Rhodes & Tran, 2012) and the social and organizational resources previously available to a community. No matter the variability of natural disaster, the return to normalcy should be monitored with fidelity inclusive of community and behavior health resources, clinical supports, and a culturally responsive approach by the crisis team members.

References

Administration for Children and Families. (2021). *Secondary traumatic stress.* https://www.acf. hhs.gov/trauma-toolkit/resilience

Afifi, W. A., Felix, E. D., & Afifi, T. D. (2012). The impact of uncertainty and communal coping on mental health following natural disasters. *Anxiety, Stress, & Coping: An International Journal, 25*, 329–347.

American Psychological Association (APA). (2012). Building you resilience. https://www.apa.org/ topics/resilience.

Bakkensen, L. A., Fox-Lent, C., Read, L. K., & Linkov, I. (2017). Validating resilience and vulnerability indices in the context of natural disasters. *Risk Analysis, 37*(5), 982–1004.

Benight, C. C., & Bandura, A. (2004). Social cognitive theory of posttraumatic recovery: The role of perceived self-efficacy. *Behaviour Research and Therapy, 42*(10), 1129–1148.

Bisson, J. I., Roberts, N. P., Andrew, M., Cooper, R., & Lewis, C. (2013). Psychological therapies for chronic post-traumatic stress disorder (PTSD) in adults. *Cochrane Database of Systematic Reviews,* (12).

Bitsch, L. J., Elklit, A., & Christiansen, D. M. (2011). *Basic problems with the measurement of posttraumatic growth.* Syddansk Universitet.

Brewin, C. R., & Saunders, J. (2001). The effect of dissociation at encoding on intrusive memories for a stressful film. *British Journal of Medical Psychology, 74*, 467–472.

Brewin, C. R., Andrews, B., & Valentine, J. D. (2000). Meta-analysis of risk factors for posttraumatic stress disorder in trauma-exposed adults. *Journal of Consulting and Clinical Psychology, 68*, 748–766.

Buckley, T. C., Blanchard, E. B., & Neill, W. T. (2000). Information processing and PTSD: A review of the empirical literature. *Clinical Psychology Review, 20*, 1041–1065.

Burnett Jr, H. J., & Wahl, K. (2015). *The compassion fatigue and resilience connection: A survey of resilience, compassion fatigue, burnout, and compassion satisfaction among trauma responders.*

Butler, L. D., Carello, J., & Maguin, E. (2017). Trauma, stress, and self-care in clinical training: Predictors of burnout, decline in health status, secondary traumatic stress symptoms, and compassion satisfaction. *Psychological Trauma: Theory, Research, Practice, and Policy, 9*(4), 416.

Cavicchioli, M., & Maffei, C. (2020). Rejection sensitivity in borderline personality disorder and the cognitive–affective personality system: A meta-analytic review. *Personality Disorders: Theory, Research, and Treatment, 11*(1), 1.

Cohen, J. A., Mannarino, A. P., Kliethermes, M., & Murray, L. A. (2012). Trauma-focused CBT for youth with complex trauma. *Child Abuse & Neglect, 36*(6), 528–541.

Ehlers, A. (2013). Trauma-focused cognitive behavior therapy for posttraumatic stress disorder and acute stress disorder. In G. Simos & S. G. Hofmann (Eds.), *CBT for anxiety disorders: A practitioner book* (pp. 161–190). Wiley.

Ehlers, A., & Clark, D. M. (2000). A cognitive model of posttraumatic stress disorder. *Behaviour Research and Therapy, 38*, 319–345.

Guarino, K., & Bassuk, E. (2010). Working with families experiencing homelessness: Understanding trauma and its impact. *Zero to Three, 30*(3), 11.

Gutierrez, D., & Mullen, P. R. (2016). Emotional intelligence and the counselor: Examining the relationship of trait emotional intelligence to counselor burnout. *Journal of Mental Health Counseling, 38*(3), 187–200.

James, R. K., & Gilliland, B. E. (2017). *Crisis intervention strategies.* Cengage Learning.

Kantor, E. M., & Beckert, D. R. (2011). Psychological first aid.

Kaurin, A., Schönfelder, S., & Wessa, M. (2018). Self-compassion buffers the link between self-criticism and depression in trauma-exposed firefighters. *Journal of Counseling Psychology, 65*(4), 453.

Meadors, P., & Lamson, A. (2008). Compassion fatigue and secondary traumatization: Provider self-care on intensive care units for children. *Journal of Pediatric Health Care, 22*(1), 24–34.

Meadors, P., Lamson, A., Swanson, M., White, M., & Sira, N. (2010). Secondary traumatization in pediatric healthcare providers: Compassion fatigue, burnout, and secondary traumatic stress. *OMEGA-Journal of Death and Dying, 60*(2), 103–128.

Mechanic, M. B., Resick, P. A., & Griffin, M. G. (1998). A comparison of normal forgetting, psychopathology, and information-processing models of reported amnesia for recent sexual trauma. *Journal of Consulting and Clinical Psychology, 66*(6), 948.

Monson, C. M., & Shnaider, P. (2014). *Treating PTSD with cognitive-behavioral therapies: Interventions that work.* American Psychological Association.

National Child Traumatic Stress Network. (2007, n.d.). *Trauma types.* from www.nctsn.org/what-is-child-trauma/trauma-types

Morgan, O. (2004). Infectious disease risks of dead bodies following natural disasters. *Revista Panamericana de Salud Pública, 15*(5), 307–312. http://publications.paho.org/english/dead_bodies.pdf

Murray, L. K., Dorsey, S., Skavenski, S., Kasoma, M., Imasiku, M., Bolton, P., et al. (2013). Identification, modification, and implementation of an evidence-based psychotherapy for children in a low-income country: The use of TF-CBT in Zambia. *International Journal of Mental Health Systems, 7*(1), 1–12.

Reidbord, S. (2010). Countertransference: An overview. *Sacramento Street Psychology.* https://www.psychologytoday.com/us/blog/sacramento-street-psychiatry/201003/overview-countertransference

Reynolds, M., & Brewin, C. R. (1998). Intrusive cognitions, coping strategies and emotional responses in depression, post-traumatic stress disorder, and a non-clinical population. *Behaviour Research and Therapy, 36*, 135–147.

Rhodes, A., & Tran, T. (2012). Predictors of posttraumatic stress and growth among black and white survivors of Hurricane Katrina: Does perceived quality of the governmental response matter? *Race and Social Problems, 4*, 144–157.

Rubin, D. C., & Kozin, M. (1984). Vivid memories. *Cognition, 16*(1), 81–95.

Swart, M., Kortekaas, R., & Aleman, A. (2009). Dealing with feelings: Characterization of trait alexithymia on emotion regulation strategies and cognitive-emotional processing. *PLoS One, 4*(6), e5751.

Uhernik, J. (2008). The counselor and the disaster response team: An emerging role. G. Walz, J. Bleuer, R. Yep, R.(Eds.), *Compelling counseling interventions: Celebrating vistas fifth anniversary*, 313–321.

Van der Kolk, B. A. (2015). *The body keeps the score: Brain, mind, and body in the healing of trauma.* Penguin Books.

Vanheule, S., Verhaeghe, P., & Desmet, M. (2011). In search of a framework for the treatment of alexithymia. *Psychology and Psychotherapy: Theory, Research and Practice, 84*(1), 84–97.

Vargas, C. (2021, May, 27). "One Bullet Can Do That to You': Losing a Generation to Gun Violence in Philadelphia." https://www.nbcphiladelphia.com/investigators/philadelphia-gun-violence-victims-shootings/2827615/

Wei, H., Kifner, H., Dawes, M. E., Wei, T. L., & Boyd, J. M. (2020). Self-care strategies to combat burnout among pediatric critical care nurses and physicians. *Critical Care Nurse, 40*(2), 44–53.

Zech, E., Luminet, O., Rimé, B., & Wagner, H. (1999). Alexithymia and its measurement: Confirmatory factor analyses of the 20-item Toronto Alexithymia Scale and the Bermond–Vorst Alexithymia Questionnaire. *European Journal of Personality, 13*(6), 511–532.

Chapter 10
Victimization at School and Workplace

Ashwini Deshpande Nagarhalli

Introduction

Victimization could be witnessed or experienced in any setting whether it is school or workplace. At the school level, among the peers, it is considered to be one of the most violent forms of expression (Zarate et al., 2017). Bullying as a concept is multidimensional. It includes synonyms like workplace harassment and behaviors that are oppressive (Bowling & Beehr, 2006). Imbalance of power and intention of harm over a period of time are the underlying ideas.

The bully may create opportunities to ensure that the victim does not succeed and might even suggest unrealistic timelines for tasks (Adams, 1997). There are other important indicators like workplace incivility which may lead to the experience of bullying (Estes & Wang 2008).

The concept of abusive supervision is linked to an imbalance of power between senior and subordinates. It is observed and reported in several forms like facial expressions, name-calling, tone, posture, intention to hurt, and disregard the contributions of the collaborators.

Due to the rise of cyberbullying, most indications suggest that the bullies have turned their attention to technology like the Internet and mobiles. Cyberbullies seem to believe that they can access their targets whenever and wherever they want (Smith et al., 2008). This seems to have become one of the powerful and direct means of exerting their power and control over others.

Cyberbullying, one more form of victimization takes variety of forms, includes activities like flaming, that is, transmission of angry messages, insulting or threatening messages. Then there is cyberstalking: using some kinds of threats of damage or intimidation, put-downs, spreading cruel rumors, masquerading or posing as

A. D. Nagarhalli (✉)
Little Pods, Mumbai, India

imposters, and sharing information to ruin a person's reputation. It may even include revealing classified or personal information about a person which was shared in confidence and finally exclusion by maliciously leaving a person out of a group, such as a chat rooms or even targeting a particular individual (Schenk & Fremouw, 2012).

Prevalence Rates

An inconsistency in the use of measurement methods, tools, and operational criteria also leads to variations in prevalence rates (Baguena, 2011). Elementary schools enlist bullying as one of the most common issue. An increased risk of becoming a bully or bully victim is linked to children who belong to socioeconomically disadvantaged families (Jansen et al., 2012).

Many researches are conducted on bullying and victimization in the Eastern high-income as well as Western countries. However, relatively lesser research is carried out in low- and middle-income countries (Zych et al., 2015).

Asian, North American, and African countries have high power distance and more of masculine values as compared to countries with low power distance and high feminine values. Hence, the former group of countries have a higher prevalence rate of victimization than the latter (Ciby & Raya, 2015).

About 52% of the prevalence rate of victimization was reported in Asia, predominantly Turkey and Pakistan. Whereas, the prevalence rate was lowest, that is, 1% in countries like Scandinavia. Cultural differences across the continents create a variation in prevalence rates (Einarsen, 2000; Ciby & Raya, 2015).

Causes

Most researchers have indicated and reviewed bullying as a multicausal phenomenon (Samnani & Singh, 2016).

However, studies suggest that both workers as well as antecedents leading up to the incidents of bullying need to be focused to grasp the origin of bullying (Samnani & Singh, 2016). Scholars have also identified some personal antecedents such as low self-esteem and poor social skills (Einarsen et al., 2011).

Often several causes are attributed to workplace bullying. Many studies focus on personality or individual factors being predominant in the face of bullying.

Bullying may even occur at top levels. Very often, it results in some kind of negative and destructive domino effect which leads bullying to cascade upwards or downwards resulting in the "kicking the dog" effects. Such an impact can be a threat not only to the employees but also the well-being of an organization (Williams, 2011).

Bullying can be viewed as a dynamic interaction between the bully and the victim, due to which the victim tends to feel powerless against the perpetrator (Menesini and Salmivalli 2017). This makes it really difficult for the victim to respond or cope with the problem (Hymel & Swearer, 2015).

One of the most common cause of bullying is personal envy: the person on the receiving end may be popular or may receive special attention from their colleagues. Such aspects can become intolerable for the bully. This could lead to some irrational assumptions as the bully sees the other person as a threat to his position. To cope with this aspect, often the victim is made to look incompetent professionally, and it could further lead to removal of the potential opposition (Adams, 1997).

According to researchers in this field, children who have any health condition were likely to be bullied more whereas children who had developmental or behavioral problems were involved in being victimized as well as being a bully (Van Cleave & Davis 2006).

However, among children, power can derive from a physical advantage (such as size and strength) or from a social advantage (such as a higher social status in a peer group or strength in numbers).

Consequences

As reported in the research by Finne et al. (2011), a common consequence of workplace bullying is psychological distress owing to the stressful as well as negative experiences. This may eventually lead to irritability, poor insight, and sometimes even impair one's decision-making skills (Arnsten et al., 2015; Giorgi et al., 2016).

Stressful experiences affect the biological parameters. Impairment in functions of the prefrontal cortex affecting emotions have been reported. Along with emotions, response inhibition, regulation of attention and insights could be affected (Arnsten et al., 2015).

Signs of being withdrawn and less communicative are observed in victims. They are often seen to be losing interest in their families. Some even act rudely or aggressively towards their loved ones. Along with changes in personality, they may develop drinking habits or become obsessed with the need to seek vengeance and ally with the ones who criticize the bully (Adams, 1997).

Once the self-esteem and self-confidence is affected as a result of bullying, such disturbances later affect the sleep pattern leading to anxiety and even depression. Suicidal thoughts may also lead to attempts (Adams & Lawrence, 2011).

Often individuals are threatened by a fear of loss of resources. They may experience heightened anxiety levels as there may be insecurities related to job or career. All these factors are known to affect the corporate image affecting satisfaction in life. Amongst several physiological indicators, sleep disturbance leads to depletion of resources and energy in an individual (Nauman et al., 2019).

Consequences of School Victimization

Documented researches on school victimization suggest consequences on both the victim and the bully. Several perspectives indicate negative outcomes like poor academic performance. Self-esteem issues, poor health, absenteeism, and other psychosomatic issues are reported in victims and perpetrators (Chen & Huang, 2015).

Children bullying others are manifested in the form of physical symptoms like aches and pain in stomach or head, psychosomatic symptoms like difficulty falling asleep or bed-wetting, depressive symptoms, symptoms of anxiety, substance use, dropping out of schools due to poor grades.

Extreme cases involve suicidal thoughts or suicide (Due et al., 2005; Williams et al., 1996). Such physical, psychosomatic, or psychological symptoms might be the first to present to a physician; these are often confirmed and further enquired into by conversation with school team, parents, and caregivers (Rigby, 2003; Nishina et al., 2005).

Children who have been victimized may express a dislike towards attending school (Rigby, 2003). Children who are high on physical aggression tend to drop out of schools easily. Some children may even develop serious psychosocial problems associated with attention, behavior, and emotional regulation. This may affect their school attendance (Nishina et al., 2005). Children who may have protective friends or older siblings may experience low risk of victimization. Children who are shy or nervous are easy targets.

In addition to these, children who are physically weak and disliked by others are more likely to be victimized against the ones with good friends and more popular (Hodges et al. 1997).

The impact of victimization is more evident in psychological symptoms than physical symptoms. Anxiety and depression are common (Due et al., 2005; Kaltiala et al., 1999). Similarly, victims who have been cyberbullied turn up with complaints of various forms of social and emotional difficulties. Some even express feeling unsafe at school; they tend to believe that no one supports them and even have multiple episodes of headaches (Sourander et al., 2010; Hinduja & Patchin, 2008).

Interventions

Though many researches support the idea of need for sensitive interventions, victimization at the workplace and school still demands evidence-based solutions for prevention of such incidents. The long-standing impact of bullying has forced all the countries to keep a check and introduce reforms for the same. The role of teachers is instrumental in identification of power struggles as well as introducing strategies to diffuse the same in classroom setups (Sorrentino et al., 2018). To avoid the power struggle between bullies and victims, intervention strategies are needed to neutralize such power dynamics and ensure that the children develop healthy relationships amongst themselves (Lamb et al., 2009).

Organizational setups that have high-power distance cultures should develop a culture of openly voicing out grievances (Morrison, 2014), to ensure victims are identified at the earliest. A culture of virtuousness, support, and positivity will be helpful in reducing the incidences of bullying (Malik & Naeem, 2016). Every growing organization needs to incorporate a code of conduct and policies that support respect and a culture of non-harassment. Also, supportive leadership can help tackle such issues in time. Supportive supervisors and leaders are instrumental in decreasing job-related stress in teams as well as mentoring-mentee relations (Sosik & Godshalk, 2000). Improved work outcomes can be expected. Additionally, policy makers and institutional reforms should be more proactive in this domain. Reports in the USA suggest that 38% to a drastic 90% of employees experienced workplace bullying at some point in their work life (Glendinning, 2001). Legislative measures seem to be missing here. Studies from countries like Norway and Finland report about 8–10% people having experienced bullying. Countries like Norway and Sweden in Europe have been quite successful in dealing with these issues. Norway has passed a Work Environment Act followed by Sweden with a similar one in 1997 (Vega & Comer, 2005).

Conclusion

Workplace bullying has become a sensational issue despite extensive research in the field. Many organizations and multinationals have been incorporating human resource practices which include training workshops, open discussions, and open channels of communication to create awareness, accept reporting, and encourage an inquiry into the matters related to victimization.

Despite these attempts, there is an increasing burden of victims who undergo emotional distress, setback to their confidence and self-esteem, and various physical ailments due to bullying behaviors in any form. By the time these issues are addressed by the higher authorities, victims feel burdened with such experiences and find it difficult to remain motivated and productive at work. Studies have also shown that peer leaders in school played a part in prevention of cyberbullying by creating bullying awareness in the school, developing leadership skills among students. Certain bullying intervention practices and team-building initiatives among the student community can be useful. This will encourage students to behave proactively. Brief psychotherapeutic models to help victims cope with the issues of anxiety and depression at the workplace as well as strengthening of self-management and emotional coping skills can be widely practiced in every occupational setup. There is a dearth of professionals who can be trained and sensitized to work with victims in any organizational setup, so that the higher authorities can address the issues smoothly. Future directions of this field could target interventions not only for victims but also the perpetrators so that incidence of this phenomenon gradually decreases. Physicians and other health professionals can be involved in directing parents toward resources, advocating on behalf of the children to school officials, community agencies. They can even help in encouraging parents to take an active role in monitoring their children and engaging them in positive school and community activities (Lamb et al., 2009).

References

Adams, A. (1997). Bullying at work. *Journal of Community & Applied Social Psychology, 7*, 177–180.

Adams, F. D., & Lawrence, G. J. (2011). Bullying victims: The effects last into college. *American Secondary Education, 40*, 4–13.

Arnsten, A. F., Raskind, M. A., Taylor, F. B., & Connor, D. F. (2015). The effects of stress exposure on prefrontal cortex: Translating basic research into successful treatments for post-traumatic stress disorder. *Neurobiological Stress, 1*, 89–99.

Baguena, M. (2011). Psychological harassment in the workplace: Methods of evaluation and prevalence. *The Open Criminology Journal, 4*, 102–108.

Bowling, N. A., & Beehr, T. A. (2006). Workplace harassment from the victim's perspective: A theoretical model and meta-analysis. *Journal of Applied Psychology, 91*, 998–1012.

Chen, Y. Y., & Huang, J. H. (2015). Precollege and in-college bullying experiences and health-related quality of life among college students. *Pediatrics, 135*(1), 18–25.

Ciby, M. A., & Raya, R. (2015). Workplace bullying: A review of the defining features, measurement methods and prevalence across continents. *IIM Kozhikode Society & Management Review, 4*, 38–47. https://doi.org/10.1177/2277975215587814

Due, P., Holstein, B. E., Lynch, J., Diderichsen, F., Gabhain, S. N., & Scheidt, P. (2005). Bullying and symptoms among school-aged children: International comparative cross-sectional study in 28 countries. *European Journal of Public Health, 15*(2), 128–132.

Einarsen, S. (2000). Harassment and bullying at work: A review of the scandinavian approach. *Aggression and Violent Behavior, 5*(4), 379–401.

Einarsen, S., Hoel, H., Zapf, D., & Cooper, C. L. (2011). The concept of bullying and harassment at work: The European tradition. In *Bullying and harassment in the workplace: Developments in theory, research, and practice*.

Estes, B., & Wang, J. (2008). Workplace incivility: Impacts on individual and organizational performance. *Human Resource Development Review, 7*(2), 218–240.

Finne, L. B., Knardahl, S., & Lau, B. (2011). Workplace bullying and mental distress — a prospective study of Norwegian employees. *Scandinavian Journal of Work, Environment & Health, 37*(4), 276–287.

Giorgi, G., Mancuso, S., & Perez, F. (2016). Bullying among nurses and its relationship with burnout and organizational climate. *International Journal of Nursing Practice, 22*(2), 160–168.

Glendinning, P. M. (2001). Workplace bullying: Curing the cancer of the American workplace. *Public Personnel Management, 30*(3), 269–286.

Hinduja, S., & Patchin, J. W. (2008). Cyberbullying: An exploratory analysis of factors related to offending and victimization. *Developmental Behaviour, 29*, 129–156.

Hodges, E., & Malone, M., & Perry, D. (1997). Individual risk and social risk as interacting determinants of victimization in the peer group. *Developmental psychology, 33*, 1032–1039. https://doi.org/10.1037/0012-1649.33.6.1032

Hymel, S., & Swearer, S. M. (2015). Four decades of research on school bullying: An introduction. *American Psychologist, 70*(4), 293–299.

Jansen, P. W., Verlinden, M., & Berkel, A. (2012). Prevalence of bullying and victimization among children in early elementary school: Do family and school neighborhood socioeconomic status matter? *BMC Public Health, 12*(494).

Kaltiala, R., Rimpelä, M., Marttunen, M., Rimpelä, A., & Rantanen, P. (1999). Bullying, depression, and suicidal ideation in Finnish adolescents: School survey. *British Medical Journal, 319*(7206), 348–351.

Lamb, J., Pepler, D. J., & Craig, W. (2009). Approach to bullying and victimization. *Canadian Family Physician (Médecin de Famille Canadien), 55*(4), 356–360.

Malik, S. Z., & Naeem, R. (2016). Organizational virtuousness, perceived organizational support and organizational citizenship behaviour: a mediation framework. *Journal of Behavioural Science, 26*, 113–129.

Menesini, E., & Salmivalli, C. (2017). Bullying in schools: The state of knowledge and effective interventions. *Psychology, Health & Medicine, 22*, 240–253. https://doi.org/10.1080/1354850 6.2017.1279740

Morrison, E. W. (2014). Employee voice and silence. *Annual Review of Organizational Psychology and Organizational Behavior, 1*, 173–197.

Nauman, S., Malik, S. Z., & Jalil, F. (2019). How workplace bullying jeopardises employees' life satisfaction: The roles of job anxiety and insomnia. *Frontiers in Psychology, 10*, 2292.

Nishina, A., Juvonen, J., & Witkow, M. R. (2005). Sticks and stones may break my bones, but names will make me feel sick: The psychosocial, somatic, and scholastic consequences of peer harassment. *Journal of Clinical Child Adolescent Psychology, 34*(1), 37–48.

Rigby, K. (2003). Consequences of bullying in schools. *Canadian Journal of Psychiatry, 48*(9), 583–590.

Samnani, A. K., & Singh, P. (2016). Workplace bullying: Considering the interaction between individual and work environment. *Journal of Business Ethics, 139*(3), 537–549.

Schenk, A. M., & Fremouw, W. J. (2012). Prevalence, psychological impact, and coping of cyberbully victims among college students. *Journal of School Violence, 11*, 21–37.

Smith, P. K., Mahdavi, J., Carvalho, M., Fisher, S., Russell, S., & Tippett, N. (2008). Cyberbullying: Its nature and impact on secondary school pupils. *Journal of Child Psychology and Psychiatry, 49*, 376–385.

Sorrentino, A., Baldry, A. C., & Farrington, D. P. (2018). The efficacy of the tabby improved prevention and intervention programs in reducing cyberbullying and cyber victimization among students. *International Journal of Environmental Research and Public Health, 15*, 2536. https://doi.org/10.3390/ijerph15112536, eid=2-s2.0- 85056669263; WOS:000451640500210.

Sosik, J. J., & Godshalk, M. (2000). The role of gender in mentoring: Implications for diversified and homogenous mentoring relationships. *Journal of Vocational Behavior, 57*, 102–122.

Sourander, A., Brunstein, K. A., Ikomen, M., Lindroos, J., Luntamo, T., & Koskelainen, M. (2010). Psychosocial risk factors associated with cyberbullying among adolescents. *Archives of General Psychiatry, 67*, 720–728.

Van Cleave, J., & Davis, M. M. (2006). Bullying and peer victimization among children with special health care needs. *Pediatrics, 118*(4).

Vega, G., & Comer, D. R. (2005). Sticks and stones may break your bones, but words can break your spirit: Bullying in the workplace. *Journal of Business Ethics, 58*, 101–109.

Williams, K. (2011). Bullying behaviors and attachment styles. *North American Journal of Psychology, 14*, 321–338.

Williams, K., Chambers, M., Logan, S., & Robinson, D. (1996). Association of common health symptoms with bullying in primary school children. *British Medical Journal, 313*(7048), 17–19.

Zarate, G., Biggs, B. K., Croarkin, P., Morath, B., Leffler, J., Cuellar-Barboza, A., & Tye, S. J. (2017). How well do we understand the long-term health implications of childhood bullying? *Harvard Review of Psychiatry, 25*(2), 89–95.

Zych, I., Ortega, R., & Del Rey, R. (2015). Scientific research on bullying and cyberbullying: Where have we been and where are we going. *Aggression and Violent Behavior, 24*, 188–198.

Chapter 11
Human Trafficking: Vulnerability, Impact, and Action

Sheeba Shamsudeen

Introduction

A global issue of unforeseen proportions, human trafficking has been increasingly referred to as 'modern-day slavery'. Human trafficking has been considered a lucrative criminal trade that has surpassed other organized crimes such as arms and drug smuggling (United Nations Office on Drugs and Crime, 2008a). An illegal trade of humans for commercial sexual exploitation and forced labour, human trafficking involves the movement of persons, including children, from one place to another using force, coercion, or deception in their economic and sexual manipulation (Naik, 2018).

Defining Human Trafficking

The United Nations Protocol to Prevent, Suppress and Punish Trafficking in Persons, Especially Women and Children, Supplementing the United Nations Convention against Transnational Organized Crime' (also called Palermo Protocol) provides a definition that includes three elements related to intent and consent (Einarsdóttir & Boiro, 2014, pp. 390–391): the act of trafficking (recruitment and transportation), the means of trafficking (force and deception), and the purpose of trafficking (exploitation). According to the Article 3 of the United Nations protocol, trafficking in persons is defined as:

> The recruitment, transportation, transfer, harbouring, or the receipt of persons, by means of the threat or use of force and other forms of coercion, abduction, fraud, deception, abuse of

S. Shamsudeen (✉)
Central Institute of Psychiatry, Ranchi, India

© The Author(s), under exclusive license to Springer Nature
Switzerland AG 2022
R. T. Gopalan (ed.), *Victimology*, https://doi.org/10.1007/978-3-031-12930-8_11

power or position of vulnerability or giving or receiving of payments or benefit to achieve consent of a person, having control over another, for the purpose of exploitation.

Exploitation here includes the exploitation of prostitution of others, or other forms of sexual exploitation, and also includes forced labour, slavery, servitude or forced removal of organs (United Nations, 2000).

Human trafficking can thus be conceptualized as, first, the transportation of any person; second, the use of force, fraud, or coercion; and third, exploitation (Sharma & Choudhary, 2016). Victims of trafficking could be of any age group, gender or nationality; yet, female victims are the primary targets. Globally, girls and women are trafficked mainly for sexual exploitation, while boys and men have been trafficked for forced labour (United Nations Office on Drugs and Crime, 2009).

Forms of Human Trafficking

Various forms of human trafficking exist, and the most commonly identified type is exploitation in the sex and entertainment industry. Victims have been tricked into having their organs removed, while children have been forced to serve as soldiers or for street begging (United Nations Office on Drugs and Crime, 2020a). Victims have also been trafficked to work in labour, work without pay, and under inhumane living conditions. Many individuals are also trafficked as domestic workers and for forced marriages (International Labour Organization, 2017).

Sexual Exploitation

Trafficking for sexual exploitation primarily impacts women and young girls forced and coerced into prostitution. Common patterns used to recruit victims into sex trafficking exist (Makisaka, 2009). The recruiters may be persons known to the victim or a neighbour, friend, romantic partner, family friend or acquaintance (Fisher, 2004). Some of them include a promise of better jobs, false marriage proposals, being sold by family members, and being kidnapped by traffickers.

Forced Labour

Victims trafficked for labour are exposed to exploitation and violence, including sexual, physical and psychological abuse. Victims are forced or deceived into providing their labour (United Nations Office on Drugs and Crime, 2021). Victims are usually women and adolescent girls who work and live with the perpetrators. However, they may also be men and young boys burdened with debt and use threats of deportation, detention and holding pay (United Nations Office on Drugs and Crime, 2009).

Forced Marriage

Marriage without consent is considered trafficking, mainly when women and girls are transported domestically and internationally. People use abuse and pressure to marry a victim against her will (United Nations Office on Drugs and Crime, 2020b), using deception for sexual exploitation and monetary gain.

Forced Removal of Organs

Organ trafficking involves exploiting people by selling their organs in a broader organ transplant scheme. The scarcity of organs creates desperation among those in need of a transplant who look for it illegally. Vulnerable, destitute victims are targeted and recruited through deception without complete information regarding the procedure or impact on health and recovery (MacInnis, 2013).

Methods of Coercing Victims of Trafficking

Human trafficking fuels the growing organized crime network (Office of the United Nations High Commissioner for Human Rights, 2014). Some traffickers use recruitment agencies as a cover to deceive potential migrants seeking work abroad and approach families in rural communities to convince them to send their children to work. Some standard methods used by traffickers include (Office on Trafficking in Persons, 2017) the following:

Force includes physical harm or restraint and sexual assault. Traffickers may use confinement during the early stages of victimization to break an individual's resistance.

Fraud includes false promises such as employment, wages, living conditions, marriage, or a better life. There are changes in the work conditions, and the compensation promised to victims in many cases.

Coercion includes threats to seriously harm an individual, use of manipulation, confiscation of documents, and inducing fear by threatening to share information or pictures with others.

Factors of Vulnerability for Human Trafficking

A 'vulnerable victim' is used to describe vulnerable individuals due to their age, physical or mental condition (United Nations Office on Drugs and Crime, 2021). In his book *Vulnerable Adults and the Law*, Herring (2016) defines a person as vulnerable if he/she (1) faces a risk of harm, (2) does not have resources to avoid the risk of harm from occurring, and (3) unable to adequately respond to the harm if the risk occurred. Various factors affect vulnerability to trafficking, and identifying these factors can help develop prevention programmes. These indicators help identify how individuals are vulnerable in particular contexts and provide a basis for interventions. To identify vulnerabilities to trafficking, a need for information regarding the environment within which trafficking occurs and awareness of vulnerable individuals and their communities exists (Ray, 2008).

Various studies have provided socio-economic and demographic profiles of victims of human trafficking. As most of the victims rescued from human trafficking are young, they may be easier to control by potential traffickers. However, a wide variation has been seen in victims' age, with some victims ranging from 15 to 45 years, while others are younger than 15 years (Gershuni, 2004). Women trafficked to the Middle East as housemaids are primarily below the age of 25 years (Paul & Hasnath, 2000), while research evidence from Albania shows that 74% of the victims rescued were in the age group of 18–24 years and 21% were between the ages of 25–30 years (Meese et al., 2002). In Romania, the age group most affected by trafficking was between 18 and 20 years (Save the Children, 2003). A survey from Tajikistan showed that victims were between the ages of 21 and 25 years (International Organization for Migration, 2001).

Around 80% of trafficked individuals are females (United States Department of State, 2003), while girls comprise 85% of victims exploited for commercial sex work and domestic servitude. A report on trafficked Indian child circus performers was 81% girls (Esther Benjamins Trust, 2003), while Italian cases showed 81% of the victims were females (Curtol et al., 2004).

The levels of education vary from primary education to college education. Trafficked circus performers in India revealed a high illiteracy rate of 61%, while 30% were educated until elementary school (Esther Benjamins Trust, 2003). Victims from Albania revealed that 65% had a high school education while 18% held a primary level education, with 4% holding college degrees (Meese et al., 2002). Victims trafficked as minors had a low education level as they had dropped out of school when they were trafficked (Save the Children, 2003).

These socio-economic and demographic profiles reveal that understanding vulnerability factors is not easy. Variations are seen in the economic circumstances of trafficked victims, with most reporting an average economic background compared to others (Surtees, 2005). Most trafficked individuals hail from troubled families; while some are orphans, others have been subjected to abuse and neglect. Many women reported troubled relationships with their husbands (Gershuni, 2004; Surtees, 2005; Save the Children, 2003). Many victims hail from ethnic minority groups; in India, children from the tribal and lower castes are more likely to be trafficked (UNICEF, 2001).

Victims of Trafficking as Vulnerable Subjects

In some marginalized urban areas, traffickers often have close relationships with victims and their families. The current discourse on the vulnerabilities to human trafficking involves various factors, including poverty, gender discrimination, individual personality factors, and, more significant community-based factors.

Children

Children are vulnerable differently from adults as it stems from the demands of adults and people in authority, including parents, teachers, and extended family members (Peek, 2008). Their inability to protect themselves physically and a lack of awareness of laws to protect them leave them in a position where they are unable to advocate for themselves. Even when rescued, they cannot articulate their experiences as adults can (United Nations Office on Drugs and Crime, 2008a).

Gender

Frequently excluded from economic and social systems like employment and higher education, women are vulnerable to human trafficking, specifically sex trafficking. Their secondary status in a family and society makes them vulnerable to rape, domestic violence and trafficking. Gender-based conditions of vulnerability apply to women and young girls who cannot protect themselves in the broader social and cultural conditions they live in (Woman's Commission for Refugee Women and Children, 2010). In patriarchal societies, marriage is considered universal, and a woman's marital status determines her status in family and society. At the same time, divorce, desertion, remarriage by the husband, or death of the husband leave her at a disadvantage (Ahmad, 2015). Traffickers may target divorcees and young married girls and introduce themselves to their parents as candidates for marriage or offer employment (Barry, 1995).

Poverty

Various conditions are associated with poor health, limited access to education, lack of food and resources, malnutrition, higher mortality rates, homelessness, social exclusion and discrimination. An increase in inflation decreases the incomes of those struck by poverty leading to migration and making migrants highly vulnerable to human trafficking (Asian Development Bank, 2004). The presence of debt also pushes individuals towards migration.

Social and Cultural Exclusion

Certain groups and classes benefit from privileges and have access to resources, while others suffer from discrimination in various domains such as education, employment, healthcare and other resources (Mosse, 2018). These groups are marginalized due to ethnicity, religion, and low social and minority status factors. As social exclusion prevents them from receiving economic benefits, their exclusion from mainstream activities puts them at risk for trafficking. Victims of commercial sexual exploitation are positioned as perpetrators and are excluded from services and opportunities they need, which dehumanizes them. It is also reinforced by other linked processes such as low income, poverty, unemployment, lack of adequate education, physical and mental health issues, housing problems, crime, lack of social support and other adverse life events (Shaw et al., 2017).

Limited Access to Education

Those with limited education have fewer income opportunities and thus do not know their rights regarding fair wages and working conditions. Education is an essential tool used by organizations as a preventive tool to reduce the vulnerability of people to human trafficking. It is also used to service trafficking survivors to improve their lives. Lack of access to education is an essential factor in the exposure to human trafficking in terms of domestic servitude, debt bondage, forced labour and other issues related to human trafficking (Spires, 2021).

Political Instability, War and Conflict

In armed conflict and political instability, traditional community life is disrupted and displaced, making individuals vulnerable to exploitation. It may include sexual assault, limited access to resources and abuse of power among women and girls, who are particularly vulnerable during such times of conflict (Woman's Commission for Refugee Women and Children, 2010).

Demand

Trafficking is driven by profits made by those who lie along the trafficking chain by exploiting men, women and children (International Labour Organization, 2017). Recruiters capitalize on the misery of individuals and victims'lack of familiarity with a new location or language. The fear of reprisal and mistrust of local authorities contributes to exploitation (International Labour Organization, 2005).

Family and Community-Based Factors

The role of an abusive and non-supportive family environment creates vulnerability to trafficking with variables such as infidelity, alcoholism, desertion by husbands, divorce, and death of husband or parents (Farley, 2003). Teenage pregnancy, gang participation, and substance abuse also combine with economic needs. Victims with childhood histories of being orphaned, abandoned or sexually abused make them vulnerable to traffickers who offer them false hopes of employment and a chance to escape oppressive family environments (Long, 2002).

Communities accept various forms of exploitation as tradition creating conditions of vulnerability. In many regions of West Africa, it is culturally acceptable for children to live with an extended family abroad for education or employment that is used to mask trafficking (Dottridge, 2002). The Devadasi system in India is another cultural system where specific communities dedicate their daughter to the service of the temple deity and are often sold into prostitution (Menon, 2019).

Personality Factors

The vulnerability for trafficking increases tenfold with migration; yet, only some people migrate, which disposes them to undertake risk and seek adventure, opportunities, and independence (Augustin, 2005). Young girls from smaller towns with more media exposure may be more vulnerable to trafficking (Feingold, 2005), where migration may lead to low self-esteem, family abuse, stalled education and a sense of life stagnation. Individuals without a heterosexual orientation are at risk of being trafficked due to the trauma caused by social exclusion and physical violence, leading to homelessness and vulnerability to being trafficked (Farley, 2003).

The causes of human trafficking may also be characterized as push and pull factors. Some factors exert pressure on victims and 'push' them towards migration and eventually under the control of traffickers. In contrast, other factors tend to 'pull' potential victims (United Nations Office on Drugs and Crime, 2009).

Push factors include war, genocide, violence, persecution, limited employment, educational opportunities and disasters (natural and artificial). These factors encourage migration and thus support a profitable market for human labour trade (Chuang, 2006). Other factors may include poverty, economic hardships, low status of women, low skill levels, sexual or physical abuse in the family of origin of victims, abuse by husband, death or desertion by husband, low-income family support and drug addiction in the family, among others.

Pull factors include safety and security, freedom from bad home life, availability of employment and labour market opportunities, improved quality of life, a promise of a more affluent lifestyle, and demand for cheap labour. Other factors may include opportunities to travel abroad and send home remittances, perception of acceptance in destination countries, temporary housing, food and gifts, false promises of love, and fake marriages (Kerr, 2014).

Theories on Human Trafficking

Theories concerning human trafficking and human rights violations help understand how and why injustice occurs. It also provides an understanding of the needs of those whose rights have been violated. Using these theories can predict how interventions and policies can be based on how they fit into the assumptions of theoretical foundations (Meshelemiah & Lynch, 2019). Some of the most common theories that apply to human trafficking include the following:

Bronfenbrenner's Ecological Model

Bronfenbrenner's ecological model considers that systems influencing an individual can be social or physical entities such as family, culture, workplace, and communities (Bronfenbrenner & Morris, 2007). The model views the relationship of an individual, their environment and behaviour, and understands the changes an individual's system undergoes when there is a change in a subsystem (Berg-Weger, 2019). Concerning human trafficking and human rights, Bronfenbrenner's ecological systems theory evaluates the risk factors for human trafficking, such as poverty, abuse, neglect, substance use, political instability, homelessness, and marginalized identities (Meshelemiah & Lynch, 2019).

Conflict Theory and Structural-Functional Theory

Conflict theory explores power structures and how power differentials affect social inequality. It operates on the principle that humans are interested in themselves and are competitive as they are forced into conflict over resources and the availability of wealth (Oberschall, 1978). From this perspective, social order only exists through coercion of the oppressed groups with the ruling of the more powerful classes. Every part of society serves to maintain the stability of the whole. However, when problems arise, it is due to a part of the social system that has become dysfunctional, which other parts of the system cannot compensate for adequately (Kingsbury & Scanzoni, 2009).

In human trafficking, conflict theory explains how social inequality and power disbalance occur while sexism, racism, and classism contribute to human rights violations. This has been seen in cases of child marriages, sex trafficking, organ trafficking, and other forms of victimization (Sellers, 1996). Thus, human rights violations can be examined from the perspective of the function of society.

Maslow's Hierarchy of Needs

Displayed as a pyramid to show needs to be met to reach optimal wellness, Maslow's physiological needs and safety needs make up the bottom two tiers. In comparison, love and belongingness needs and self-esteem needs make up the middle two tiers (Meshelemiah & Lynch, 2019). Self-actualization stands at the top of the pyramid, and in order to reach this, the basic needs need to be first met (Maslow, 1943). In the context of human trafficking, Maslow's hierarchy of needs understands why victims are drawn to and coerced by traffickers. These factors include homelessness, history of neglect and abuse, poverty, lack of housing, food, clothing, safety, and financial security that cover the basic needs in Maslow's hierarchy. Traffickers offer these things to victims, which draws them to traffickers; it is challenging to leave when intimate relationships and friendships that meet the psychological needs are offered and further bonds victims to them (Smith et al., 2009).

Labelling Theory

This is based on the theory that posits that the act of labelling and creating stigma serves to marginalize and force conformity as it alters one's view of self and its role in society. Marginalization causes secondary deviance and shifts self-concept and social expectations (Restivo & Lanier, 2015). Sex trafficking involves activities on the part of victims resulting in the criminalization of the victim rather than the trafficker. The victim then begins to fit into the label and view themselves as deviant criminal and continue their involvement in trafficking (Meshelemiah & Lynch, 2019).

Impact of Trafficking on Victims

The effects of trafficking have a significant impact on the well-being of victims, along with long-term physical, emotional and psychological consequences (United Nations Office on Drugs and Crime, 2008a). They experience abuse and poor health across the various stages of trafficking, during pre-movement, movement and post-movement, with forms of violence, deprivation, torture, forced use of substances, and abusive living conditions (United Nations Office on Drugs and Crime, 2008b). These can cause long-term psychological trauma and significant mental and physical health problems.

Physical Impact

Due to the abusive nature of trafficking, many victims may experience physical and sexual assault, with lasting physical and psychological effects (United Nations Office on Drugs and Crime, 2021). Children may experience stunted growth due to lack of nourishment, and some may also develop effects such as eye damage or lung disease (Zimmerman et al., 2003). All victims experience physical or sexual violence and are forced into performing sexual acts. Physical symptoms of women and girls trafficked for sex may include headaches; fatigue and weight loss; stomach, chest, back, pelvic and vaginal pain; and dental and eye, ear and skin problems. They also frequently experience vaginal discharge and reproductive infections, remaining untreated (Zimmerman et al., 2006).

HIV/AIDS

Women and children trafficked for sexual purposes are at a high risk of contracting and spreading HIV/AIDS and other sexually transmitted diseases. These can be attributed partly to the lack of bargaining power women hold concerning the use of condoms and other potentially dangerous sexual practices (Williams, 2006). The lack of education and information regarding HIV/AIDS and various misconceptions increases women and children's vulnerability to infections (United Nations Development Programme, 2003).

Mental Health Impact

Significant effects on the mental health of trafficked victims include trauma, anxiety, and fear (Rafferty, 2013). Victims'trauma symptoms include PTSD, depression, anxiety, sleep disorders, and dissociation. Victims experience sadness and hopelessness about the future, apart from suicidality, cognitive impairment, memory loss and withdrawal (Zimmerman et al., 2006). Problems with concentration and displays of anger are also common among victims. If they remain under the control of traffickers for prolonged durations, the effects of trauma may be severe and long-lasting. They may also continue after being rescued without proper treatment (Shkurkin, 2004).

Impact on Child Victims

Children are subjected to the same harmful effects as adults, but their age makes them vulnerable. Physical and sexual abuse, malnutrition, and stunted growth impact the development of trafficked children (Wood, 2020). With fewer negotiation skills and a lack of accurate information about diseases, these children are vulnerable to long-term physical and mental health consequences. The emotional well-being, self-esteem and ability to form healthy relationships of trafficked children are damaged (United Nations Office on Drugs and Crime, 2008a). They may have problems with attachment and show antisocial behaviours, aggression, developmental delays, language and cognitive difficulties, poor academic performance, and memory and verbal skills (Rafferty, 2013).

Substance Use

Women and children trafficked for sexual purposes are forced by their traffickers to use drugs to ensure their compliance, work longer hours, and perform reprehensible sexual acts. Victims may also turn to substance use to alleviate their pain resulting in addiction, organ damage, overdose, infections and even death (Zimmerman et al., 2003).

Behavioural Impact

The physical and psychological abuse causes an impact on the physical and emotional responses of trafficked victims. Victims find it difficult to make personal sense of the abuse experienced and may not be able to identify the form of help they need (Zimmerman et al., 2006). They may be reluctant to answer questions, show aggression and be hostile towards support persons. Rescued victims may be too traumatized and uncooperative as they refuse to obey contingent conditions such as zero tolerance of substance use and adherence to structured daily regimes (Meshelemiah & Lynch, 2019).

Stigma

The impact of the family and community is seen in the recovery of the trafficked persons. Victims choose to move away from their home areas and return to prostitution, while others may not reveal anything about the trafficking experience, which affects their recovery significantly (Limanowska, 2004). Victims face stigma due to sexual exploitation and social disapproval when they return home (Meshelemiah & Lynch, 2019). They face discrimination and rejection by their families and communities and may be blamed for their evil character.

Economic and Societal Impact

Human trafficking represents an irretrievable loss of human resources along with loss of remittances to developing countries. The cost of coercion and exploitation cannot be measured. However, the worst form of child labour is a loss of productive capacity of a generation of children who could otherwise gain from education and better health (Danailova-Trainor & Laczko, 2010). Trafficking also undermines extended family ties; for example, the forced absence of women may lead to neglect and breakdown of families (M'Cormack, 2011).

Gender Equity and Human Rights

The impact of trafficking falls disproportionately on girls and women as they constitute the primary victims trafficked. Being an ever-growing billion-dollar industry, the continued unequal power relations reinforce women's secondary status in society (Todres, 2010). Stripped of their human rights, trafficked individuals are deprived of their right to life, liberty and freedom from slavery, the right to be free from exploitation and abuse, and to develop in a protective environment. The right to adequate healthcare, freedom from discrimination, education, and employment are stripped from victims (M'Cormack, 2011).

Identifying Signs of Human Trafficking

Understanding the signs of trafficking is crucial to identification and assistance in healthcare settings (Dovydaitis, 2010). The presence of indicators does not prove or disprove the occurrence of trafficking, but its presence should lead to an investigation. Victims seek medical attention for consequences of assault and neglected health conditions, and emergency clinicians should be equipped to recognize them and intervene (Shandro et al., 2016).

Red Flags of Trafficking

Various red flags are seen when trafficked patients present in medical settings, including broken bones, traumatic brain injury, concussions, exhaustion, malnutrition, burns, vaginal tearing, HIV/AIDS, other sexually transmitted diseases, pelvic inflammatory diseases, and unplanned pregnancies, and miscarriages, among others. Among patients who have been trafficked for forced labour, red flags include body injuries, exhaustion, back pain, respiratory illness, hypothermia, dehydration, heat strokes, skin infections, and chemical burns (Orme & Ross-Sheriff, 2015).

Signs of a school-age child being trafficked include academic, behavioural, physical, emotional and social indicators. Some of these include: appearing malnourished, physical injuries, avoiding eye contact, looking dishevelled, appearing fearful, being aggressive, seeming to adhere to scripted responses in social interactions, lacking personal possessions, poor physical and dental health, and lack of identity documents, among others (Meshelmiah et al., 2018). Trafficked individuals also carry a high risk of developing PTSD and substance use disorders, apart from anxiety and panic disorders, depressive disorders, sleep disturbances, dissociative disorders, somatic symptoms and suicidal ideation and attempts (Greenbaum et al., 2018).

Profile of a Trafficker

Traffickers exploit innocent victims and lure them by manipulating and exploiting their vulnerabilities. Although law enforcements make efforts to identify individual traffickers, researchers have demonstrated that the profile of traffickers may vary significantly. Identifying the citizenship, gender, age, and education of traffickers can help to generate a broader understanding of traffickers (Clawson et al., 2006).

Although most offenders are citizens of their own country, some foreigners may also be traffickers. Many women have been convicted of trafficking in persons (Siegel & De Blank, 2010). Recruiters of trafficking are selected for their ability to establish quick trust with victims. Some may be victims themselves who may pursue trafficking as 'graduation' of their role due to the absence of other livelihood options (Kangaspunta, 2006). Recruiters are older victims as they can manipulate and coerce younger children (Toney-Butler & Mittel, 2017). Some may be married or be in domestic partnerships, while others are single; some have children, others do not. Family members of recruiters may be unaware of the traffickers' criminal activities, while some families collaboratively engage in trafficking operations. Many have professional occupations besides trafficking. While some have little to no education, others are highly educated (United Nations Global Initiative to Fight Human Trafficking, 2008). Not enough research has been undertaken into the profile of traffickers. What is known to date only reveals that the factors of traffickers differ in economic, social, cultural and educational backgrounds (Weitzer, 2014).

Preventing Human Trafficking

The response to human trafficking consists of anti-trafficking legislation and activities that work collaboratively with law enforcement agencies, local governments, and non-governmental organizations (Farrell, 2012). Their activities commonly consist of training, investigations, prosecutions, research, and victim services.

The broad areas of intervention in trafficking have been laid down in the UN protocol and are described as prevention, protection and assistance. The criminal justice system and social welfare policies are areas under which prevention is covered (United Nations Economic and Social Commission for Asia and the Pacific, 2002). While the criminal justice system includes national laws and international guidelines, social welfare focuses on rescue and rehabilitation measures.

Prevention efforts by local task forces assess the vulnerabilities of trafficking at an individual, familial and societal level, after which prevention strategies are implemented. These strategies under primary prevention include: (1) strengthening individual skills, (2) promoting community education, (3) educating healthcare providers, (4) fostering support networks, (5) changing organizational practices, and (6) influencing policy (Rafferty, 2013).

Successful primary prevention strategies shall employ approaches in various levels and settings. These include:

Violence and Crime Prevention strategies can be implemented by providing training in restorative justice, peace-making and intervention in neighbourhood problems. This can help create safe spaces and strengthen social support by implementing gang strategy to prevent and reduce gang violence using social interventions and monitoring youth (Gebo et al., 2015).

Housing and Urban Development strategies can address neighbourhood-level risk factors such as homelessness, supporting affordable housing, guaranteeing sufficient income and affordable healthcare, improving economic conditions for low-income populations, and early intervention to strengthen self-efficacy to overcome obstacles and maximize community resources (Burt et al., 2005).

Businesses can be encouraged to monitor and address labour trafficking in their supply chains, conduct investigations of forced labour, assist with workers' rights groups, educate workers to prevent forced labour on farms, provide legal support in case of exploitation, build awareness among individuals and businesses and create action against trafficking (Long et al., 2019).

Healthcare systems can be trained to identify potential victims who may seek care at any point during their exploitation. Healthcare professionals can be prepared to identify at-risk patients and refer them to necessary support services. Youth can be screened for substance use during paediatric check-ups using questionnaires to assess substance use disorders (Stoklosa et al., 2015).

Schools and Child Welfare strategies can target trafficking vulnerabilities involving educational challenges and substance use. Children's economic and social needs can be targeted by abuse, family disruption, and child welfare (Petersen et al., 2014). Youth programs teach youth to recognize and respond to signs of exploitation. School-based intervention can improve children's socio-emotional well-being and teach them coping skills to reduce the likelihood of substance use, reduce delinquent behaviours, and improve educational achievements. Safety planning with at-risk youth can ensure necessary knowledge in dangerous settings (Duger, 2015).

Principles of Prevention

The prevention of trafficking requires efforts to break its cycle and needs to be directed at preventing victims from being re-trafficked or becoming traffickers (Annex, 2000). The United Nations High Commissioner for Human Rights (United Nations Office on Drugs, Crime, & Global Programme Against Trafficking in Human Beings, 2008) recommends principles for guidance for anti-trafficking efforts. These include: (1) analysing factors that generate demand, (2) developing programmes to offer livelihood options, (3) improving children's access to education, (4) ensuring safe migration, (5) developing public awareness campaigns, (6) review policies related to migration, (7) increase opportunities to prosecute traffickers, and (8) use measures for reducing vulnerability.

Psychological Interventions for Trafficking-Related Trauma

Given the high degree of exposure to traumatic events among victims of human trafficking, significant psychological consequences include post-traumatic stress disorder, substance use, mood disorders, anxiety spectrum disorders, and dissociation. However, there is a paucity of research regarding treating the psychological sequelae of trafficking-related trauma (Hemmings et al., 2016).

The available treatment modules for victims of human trafficking have been borrowed from those for victims of sexual abuse and domestic violence. Treatment protocols aim to reduce the impact of trafficking while increasing the victims' psychological well-being and reducing the chance of re-victimization (Kangaspunta, 2006).

PTSD Treatment Among Victims of Human Trafficking

A study on trafficked women (Abas et al., 2013) revealed that risk factors for mental disorders include childhood sexual abuse, unmet needs and lack of social support, which are linked to PTSD, depression, anxiety, and self-harm in trafficked children and adolescents. As PTSD is a common reaction in trafficking victims, trauma-informed care aims to include victims'safety and recognize the impact of multiple traumatic events experienced throughout their lifespan. The pre-trafficking events are essential, increasing an individual's vulnerability to becoming a victim. Treatment providers should create flexible therapeutic interventions while assessing distress, symptoms and severity.

The most commonly used treatment modalities include Trauma-Focused Cognitive Behavioural Therapy (TF-CBT), Cognitive Processing Therapy (CPT), Prolonged Exposure Therapy (PET), and Eye Movement Desensitization Therapy (EMDR). These are rooted in trauma-informed care, but it is not yet clear which practices are most effective for responding to trafficking victims (Reid et al., 2018).

Cognitive Processing Therapy (CPT)

CPT is an evidence-based intervention that effectively treats PTSD and focuses on how a traumatic event is construed and coped with. Rooted in the emotional processing theory, CPT posits that repeated exposure to traumatic memories in a safe environment will lead to the habituation of fear. CPT uses cognitive restructuring techniques to change the maladaptive cognitions about self and the world that have developed due to the traumatic experience (Gilman et al., 2012).

Research has shown adequate evidence of CPT for treating trafficking-related PTSD, which causes complex psychological distress and manifests in interpersonal and behavioural difficulties (Edmond, 2018). A study by Castillo (2011) showed the efficacy of CPT for trauma and rape survivors to identify and challenge distorted thoughts from five themes: safety, trust, control, esteem, and intimacy. CPT has also been effective with physical abuse, survivors of childhood sexual abuse, military veterans and military personnel and refugees (Gold, 2017).

Prolonged Exposure Therapy (PE)

Prolonged exposure therapy aims to teach individuals to approach trauma-related memories, feelings, and situations gradually. These are stimuli that the individual has been avoiding since the traumatic event. PE aims to reduce excessive and unrealistic anxiety by confronting anxiety-provoking thoughts, activities, situations, and people who are not a threat to the individual (McLean & Foa, 2011).

Research has demonstrated that patients with trafficking-related PTSD have exhibited greater treatment adherence and reduced symptomology over time when they are given a choice between their preferred form of treatment (psychological vs pharmacological) as compared to those who are prescribed one or the other form (Zoellner et al., 2019). Other studies have also displayed the efficacy of PE in individuals affected by trauma (Salami et al., 2018; Schneier et al., 2012).

Trauma-Focused Cognitive Behaviour Therapy (TF-CBT)

The primary goal of TF-CBT is to reduce PTSD symptoms among children and adolescents (Cohen & Mannarino, 2015) and uses CBT principles in two contexts: (1) considering the role of the caregiver and (2) considering the developing nature of a child's coping and emotional regulation. PTSD symptoms associated with sexual abuse, such as depression, aggression, negative thoughts, shame and guilt, were designed to address in TF-CBT (de Arellano et al., 2014). It has now been adapted to other forms of abuse, domestic violence, loss, war and natural disasters.

TF-CBT has been conceptualized to address the emotional reactions of non-offending primary caregivers of the traumatized child, as they may also experience PTSD symptoms related to the abuse. TF-CBT involves psychoeducation, gradual exposure, behaviour modelling, body safety skills and coping strategies (de Arellano et al., 2014). TF-CBT also uses exposure and cognitive restructuring specific to traumatic experiences. In contrast, relaxation, affective modulation and cognitive coping skills develop these skills in the traumatized individual (Cohen & Mannarino, 2015). Literature has shown evidence of the use of TF-CBT for PTSD, especially for those with sexual abuse and PTSD. Many studies have demonstrated the efficacy of TF-CBT while working with survivors of human trafficking (Johnson, 2012; Burt, 2019).

Eye Movement Desensitization and Reprocessing (EMDR)

A treatment module that has proved efficacious in alleviating PTSD, EMDR developed by Shapiro (1989) targets PTSD resulting from disturbing past experiences and continues to cause distress due to inadequately processed memories. When memories are triggered, the disturbing elements stored are re-experienced. During

EMDR, an accelerated learning process is stimulated, incorporating eye movements and forms of rhythmic bilateral stimulation (e.g. using tones or taps). While clients focus briefly on the trauma memory and simultaneously experience bilateral stimulation, the emotions of the memory and its vividness are reduced (Shapiro, 1999).

Research evidence suggests that EMDR has demonstrated the ability to reduce PTSD, anxiety, and depression in individuals with ongoing traumatic stress such as sexual abuse, interpersonal violence, war veterans, prolonged violent conflicts, and internal displacement (Allon, 2015; Jarero et al., 2016).

Cognitive Analytic Therapy (CAT)

As a brief therapy, CAT has been applied to mental health problems with underlying trauma and neglect while also addressing neurotic problems, personality disorders, suicidality and deliberate self-harm (Ryle, 1995). CAT focuses on an individual's pattern of relating to themselves and others which are internalized from ongoing interpersonal interactions and are referred to as reciprocal roles. CAT utilizes the theoretical structure of the procedural sequence model, which can include cognitive, motivational, affective and behavioural elements and aims to alter a standard underlying faulty procedure which could be 'traps' (repetitive cycles of behaviour), 'dilemmas' (presentation of false choices) or 'snag' (negative aspects of a goal) (Denman, 2001).

CAT has shown effectiveness in studies exploring re-victimization and self-abuse (Clarke & Pearson, 2000). Other studies (Follette & Ruzek, 2007; Jones, 2020) have shown that CAT is a formidable tool in trauma treatment. Beyond symptom relief, it can help individuals dig deeper into distress, eventually leading to relief.

Narrative Exposure Therapy (NET)

NET is built on the theory of dual representations of traumatic memories (Elbert & Schauer, 2002). It contextualizes elements of the fear network, including sensory, affective, physiological and cognitive memories of traumatic experiences, to understand and process the memories during an individual's lifespan.

The efficacy of NET has been well established, with studies showing NET as a feasible treatment for PTSD for trafficking survivors (Brady et al., 2021; Robjant, 2021). NET therapists ask in detail regarding emotions, cognitions, sensory information, and physiological responses related to a traumatic event and then encourage the individual to relive these emotions and narrate the account without losing connection to the 'here and now' (Schauer et al., 2017). The therapist links their experiences to episodic facts, that is, time and place, facilitating reprocessing, meaning-making, and integration (Schauer et al., 2011).

Somatic Experiencing (SE)

A specific approach to somatic therapy, Somatic Experiencing (Levine, 2012) is based on the notion that traumatic experiences cause dysfunction in the nervous system, which stops one from processing the experience. With a naturalistic and neurobiological approach, this therapy aims to restore an individual's self with self-regulation, relaxation, aliveness and wholeness. SE aims to help one access their body's procedural memory of the traumatic event and then remap it to regain flow and aliveness. The body first approach of SE helps deal with trauma symptoms and create new bodily experiences. Thus, healing focuses on exploring the sensations underlying one's feelings and beliefs (Payne et al., 2015).

Research has shown that SE effectively reduces trauma symptoms and has been implicated as a long-term trauma treatment (Levine, 2010). It has also been effective as an early intervention for social service workers after natural disasters and ethnic minorities (Parker et al., 2008).

Alternative Treatment Approaches

In addition to the above-mentioned evidence-based approaches to treating trauma, various other therapeutic interventions are effective with trauma victims. Hypnotherapy serves as an adjunct to cognitive, exposure and psychodynamic therapies and is reinforced by the high hypnotic suggestibility of patients with post-traumatic conditions (Lynn & Cardeña, 2007). Trauma-focused psychodynamic psychotherapy for PTSD addresses the disruptions in narrative coherence and affective dysregulation, exploring the psychological meaning of symptoms and their relationship to traumatic events (Busch & Milrod, 2018). Other therapeutic modules such as art-based interventions, group psychotherapies, and brief eclectic therapies have also been effective in cases of complex traumas (Dorsey et al., 2017).

Forensic Medical Evaluation of Human Trafficking Victims

Human trafficking has been associated with physical and mental health risks such as psychological trauma, injuries from violence, sexually transmitted infections, HIV/AIDS, reproductive health outcomes, and substance misuse (Zimmerman et al., 2003). The physical examination and documentation need to be performed adequately and accurately to establish how an injury was caused. It is essential to apply forensic principles and skills used in forensic pathology to examine victims as it plays an essential part in legal proceedings (Alempijevic et al., 2007).

Various international standards of forensic medical examination for torture and sexual violence victims are available. The brief protocol 'Campaign to Rescue and Restore Victims of Human Trafficking' helps identify trafficking victims, including evidence of being controlled, inability to leave a job, bruises, signs of battering, fear of deportation, non-English speaking and a lack of passport or other documents (Dovydaitis, 2010).

Forensic medical evaluations for human trafficking victims should cover: (1) a head-to-toe examination, (2) record of injuries, (3) collection of forensic samples, (4) forensic diagnostic investigations, and (5) screening for diseases (Alempijevic et al., 2007). A methodological and detailed head-to-toe investigation may include laboratory tests, imaging and other diagnostics to document telltale markers of tools that may have inflicted injuries. Knowledge regarding the pattern of injuries and their anatomic location can assist physicians, and law enforcement agencies in determining the weapon used and determine if the injury is consistent with the history (Stark, 2011).

A medical examination can help reveal conditions such as malnutrition or deficiencies (Alempijevic et al., 2007). A forensic diagnosis is required in criminal investigations and consists of a clinical examination (including recordings of body measurements and an evaluation of signs of sexual maturity), x-ray and dental examination to record dentition status (Brkic et al., 2006). It is essential to collect appropriate forensic samples (swabs, hair, urine, or blood), including DNA analysis, fingerprints, fibres, and micro traces, indispensable in victim examinations.

Forensic Psychiatric Evaluation of Human Trafficking Victims

Mental health is an essential aspect of diagnostic assessment and documentation for trafficking victims due to the severity and frequency of trauma. Including psychological aspects and psychiatric diagnosis is considered obligatory in forensic evaluations (Wenzel et al., 2015). The psychological sequelae of trafficking-related trauma are relevant due to their long-lasting nature and can severely debilitate a victim's concentration, attention and memory functions. These aspects are essential for medical assessments that can preserve evidence of torture and identify the treatment needs of victims. While documenting diagnosis in comprehensive assessments, common co-morbidities and unspecific disorders, such as depression, somatoform and dissociative disorders, should also be considered (Kalt et al., 2013).

The European project 'Psychological Health Impact of Trafficking in Human Beings for Sexual Exploitation on Female Victims' analyses the psychological well-being of trafficking victims to account for their psychological conditions and prevent re-victimization. The psychiatric forensic evaluation of the mental health of victims in terms of psychopathology is necessary to diagnose the presence of mental disorders (Schultze-Lutter et al., 2018).

The *Manual on Effective Investigation and Documentation of Torture and Other Cruel, Inhuman or Degrading Treatment or Punishment* (the Istanbul Protocol) is a standard interdisciplinary protocol (Akar et al., 2014) that aims to help fight against violence by providing guidelines to ensure that a more effective assessment of the psychological sequelae occurs post trafficking.

A detailed assessment of trafficking survivors helps describe findings with or without offering a diagnosis in situations of ongoing differential diagnostic assessment based on the World Health Organisation's International Classification of Diseases (ICD) or a DSM diagnosis (Wenzel et al., 2015). While clinical interviews conducted by a licensed clinician are usually sufficient, questionnaires for trauma or standardized schedules, such as the Clinician-Administered PTSD Scale (CAPS), could also be used to screen and confirm the clinical diagnosis (Ozkalipci & Schlar, 1999).

Conclusion

Trafficking is a fundamental human rights violation that goes undetected, with its criminal enterprise estimated to affect millions of individuals and their families across the world. As a complex phenomenon, human trafficking is rooted in the socio-economic, political and cultural reality of the context in which it occurs. It is an economically lucrative industry that continues to enslave victims for sex, labour and service. Victims of human trafficking face many risks and psychological consequences as their vulnerabilities put them at a higher risk for it. Identifying these risk factors and utilizing this knowledge helps create preventive measures and tailor suitable treatment services (Schwarz et al., 2016). Professionals working in legislation, mental health practitioners, social workers and other service providers play a huge role in the war against human trafficking (Yakushko, 2009).

References

Abas, M., Ostrovschi, N. V., Prince, M., Gorceag, V. I., Trigub, C., & Oram, S. (2013). Risk factors for mental disorders in women survivors of human trafficking: A historical cohort study. *BMC Psychiatry, 13*(1), 1–11.

Ahmad, N. (2015). Trafficked persons or economic migrants? In *Trafficking and prostitution reconsidered: New perspectives on migration, sex work, and human rights* (p. 211). Routledge.

Akar, F. A., Arbel, R., Benninga, Z., Dia, M. A., & Steiner-Birmanns, B. (2014). The Istanbul protocol (manual on the effective investigation and documentation of torture and other cruel, inhuman or degrading treatment or punishment): Implementation and education in Israel. *Israeli Medical Association Journal, 16*(3).

Alempijevic, D., Jecmenica, D., Pavlekic, S., Savic, S., & Aleksandric, B. (2007). Forensic medical examination of victims of trafficking in human beings. *Torture, 17*(2), 117–121.

Allon, M. (2015). EMDR group therapy with women who were sexually assaulted in the Congo. *Journal of EMDR Practice and Research, 9*(1), 28–34.

Annex, I. I. (2000). *Protocol to prevent, suppress and punish trafficking in persons, especially women and children, supplementing the United Nations convention against transnational organized crime*. United Nations Office on Drugs and Crime, United Nations Convention against Transnational Organized Crime and the Protocols Thereto.

Asian Development Bank. (2004). *Combating trafficking of women and children in South Asia: Regional synthesis paper for Bangladesh, India, and Nepal*. Asian Development Bank.

Augustin, L. M. (2005). Migrants in the mistress's house: Other voices in the "trafficking" debate. *Social Politics: International Studies in Gender, State and Society, 12*(1), 96–117.

Barry, K. (1995). *The prostitution of sexuality*. New York University Press.

Berg-Weger, M. (2019). *Social work and social welfare: An invitation*. Routledge.

Brady, F., Chisholm, A., Walsh, E., Ottisova, L., Bevilacqua, L., Mason, C., et al. (2021). Narrative exposure therapy for survivors of human trafficking: Feasibility randomised controlled trial. *BJPsych Open, 7*(6).

Brkic, H., Milicevic, M., & Petrovecki, M. (2006). Age estimation methods using anthropological parameters on human teeth–(A0736). *Forensic Science International, 162*(1–3), 13–16.

Bronfenbrenner, U., & Morris, P. A. (2007). The bioecological model of human development. In *Handbook of child psychology* (Vol. 1). Wiley.

Burt, I. (2019). Modern-day slavery in the US: Human trafficking and counselor awareness. *International Journal for the Advancement of Counselling, 41*(2), 187–200.

Burt, M. R., Pearson, C., & McDonald, W. R. (2005). *Strategies for preventing homelessness: US Department of Housing and Urban Development Office of Policy Development and Research.*

Busch, F. N., & Milrod, B. L. (2018). Trauma-focused psychodynamic psychotherapy. *Psychiatric Clinics, 41*(2), 277–287.

Castillo, D. T. (2011). Cognitive and behavioral treatments for sexual violence. In T. Bryant Davis (Ed.), *Surviving sexual violence: A guide to recovery and empowerment* (pp. 91–107). Rowman & Littlefield.

Chuang, J. (2006). Beyond a snapshot: Preventing human trafficking in the global economy. *Global Legal Studies, 13*(1), 137–163.

Clarke, S., & Pearson, C. (2000). Personal constructs of male survivors of childhood sexual abuse receiving cognitive analytic therapy. *British Journal of Medical Psychology, 73*(2), 169–177.

Clawson, H., Dutch, N., & Cummings, M. (2006). *Law enforcement response to human trafficking and the implications for victims: Current practices and lessons learned.* US Department of Justice, National Institute of Justice.

Cohen, J. A., & Mannarino, A. P. (2015). Trauma-focused cognitive behavior therapy for traumatized children and families. *Child and Adolescent Psychiatric Clinics, 24*(3), 557–570.

Curtol, F., Decarli, S., Di Nicola, A., & Savona, E. U. (2004). Victims of human trafficking in Italy: A judicial perspective. *International Review of Victimology, 11*, 111–141.

Danailova-Trainor, G., & Laczko, F. (2010). Trafficking in persons and development: Towards greater policy coherence. *International Migration, 48*(4), 38–83.

de Arellano, M. A. R., Lyman, D. R., Jobe-Shields, L., George, P., Dougherty, R. H., Daniels, A. S., et al. (2014). Trauma-focused cognitive-behavioral therapy for children and adolescents: Assessing the evidence. *Psychiatric Services, 65*(5), 591–602.

Denman, C. (2001). Cognitive–analytic therapy. *Advances in Psychiatric Treatment, 7*(4), 243–252.

Dorsey, S., McLaughlin, K. A., Kerns, S. E., Harrison, J. P., Lambert, H. K., Briggs, E. C., et al. (2017). Evidence base update for psychosocial treatments for children and adolescents exposed to traumatic events. *Journal of Clinical Child & Adolescent Psychology, 46*(3), 303–330.

Dottridge, M. (2002). Trafficking in children in West and Central Africa. *Gender and Development, 10*(1), 38–42.

Dovydaitis, T. (2010). Human trafficking: The role of the health care provider. *Journal of Midwifery & Women's Health, 55*(5), 462–467.

Duger, A. (2015). Focusing on prevention: The social and economic rights of children vulnerable to sex trafficking. *Health and Human Rights Journal, 17*, 114.

Edmond, T. (2018). 5. Evidence-based trauma treatments for survivors of sex trafficking and commercial sexual exploitation. In *Social work practice with survivors of sex trafficking and commercial sexual exploitation* (pp. 70–96). Columbia University Press.

Einarsdóttir, J., & Boiro, H. (2014). The Palermo protocol: Trafficking takes it all. *Stjórnmál og stjórnsýsla, 10*(2), 387.

Elbert, T., & Schauer, M. (2002). Burnt into memory. *Nature, 412*, 883.

Esther Benjamins Trust. (2003). *A report on the use and abuse of children in circuses in India.*

Farley, M. (2003). *Prostitution, trafficking and traumatic stress*. Haworth Press.
Farrell, A. (2012). Improving law enforcement identification and response to human trafficking. In *Human trafficking: Exploring the international nature, concerns, and complexities* (pp. 181–206). CRC Press.
Feingold, D. A. (2005). Human trafficking. *Foreign Policy, 26–32.*
Fisher, B. (Ed.). (2004). *Violence against women and family violence: Developments in research, practice, and policy*. National Institute of Justice.
Follette, V. M., & Ruzek, J. I. (Eds.). (2007). *Cognitive behavioral therapies for trauma*. Guilford Press.
Gebo, E., Bond, B. J., & Campos, K. S. (2015). The OJJDP comprehensive gang strategy. In *The handbook of gangs* (pp. 392–405). Wiley.
Gershuni, R. (2004). Trafficking in persons for the purpose of prostitution. *Mediterranean Quarterly, 2004*, 133–146.
Gilman, R., Schumm, J. A., & Chard, K. M. (2012). Hope as a change mechanism in the treatment of posttraumatic stress disorder. *Psychological Trauma: Theory, Research, Practice, and Policy, 4*(3), 270.
Gold, S. N. (2017). *APA handbook of trauma psychology: Trauma practice* (Vol. 2, pp. xi–599). American Psychological Association.
Greenbaum, V. J., Dodd, M., & McCkracken, C. (2018). A short screening tool to identify victims of child sex trafficking in the healthcare setting. *Pediatric Emergency Care, 34*(1), 33–37.
Hemmings, S., Jakobowitz, S., Abas, M., Bick, D., Howard, L. M., Stanley, N., et al. (2016). Responding to the health needs of survivors of human trafficking: A systematic review. *BMC Health Services Research, 16*(1), 1–9.
Herring, J. (2016). *Vulnerable adults and the law*. Oxford University Press.
ILO (International Labour Organization). (2005). *A Global Alliance Against Forced Labour: Global Report Under the Follow-up to the ILO Declaration on Fundamental Principles and Rights at Work, 2005* (Vol. 93). International Labour Organization.
ILO (International Labour Organization). (2017). *Forced labour, modern slavery and human trafficking*.
International Organization for Migration. (2001). *Deceived migrants from Tajikistan*.
Jarero, I., Artigas, L., Uribe, S., & García, L. E. (2016). The EMDR integrative group treatment protocol for patients with cancer. *Journal of EMDR Practice and Research, 10*(3), 199–207.
Johnson, B. C. (2012). Aftercare for survivors of human trafficking. *Social Work & Christianity, 39*(4), 370.
Jones, L. (2020). Treatment approaches to trauma for those convicted of sexual crime: Interventions globally. In *Sexual crime and trauma* (pp. 1–31). Palgrave Macmillan.
Kalt, A., Hossain, M., Kiss, L., & Zimmerman, C. (2013). Asylum seekers, violence and health: A systematic review of research in high-income host countries. *American Journal of Public Health, 103*(3), e30–e42.
Kangaspunta, K. (2006). Trafficking in persons: Global patterns. In *International symposium on International Migration and Development* (Vol. 28, p. 30).
Kerr, P. R. (2014). Push and pull: The intersections of poverty, health disparities, and human trafficking. *Public Health & Social Justice, 3*(2), 1–5.
Kingsbury, N., & Scanzoni, J. (2009). Structural-functionalism. In *Sourcebook of family theories and methods* (pp. 195–221). Springer.
Levine, P. A. (2010). *In an unspoken voice: How the body releases trauma and restores goodness*. North Atlantic Books.
Levine, P. (2012). *Somatic experiencing*.
Limanowska, B. (2004). *Anti-trafficking action in South-Eastern Europe: Lack of effectiveness of law enforcement and migration approaches*. United Nations Division for the Advancement of Women (DAW), Sweden. UN Doc. CM/MMW/2003/EP, 6, 14.
Long, L. D. (2002). Trafficking in women and children as a security challenge in Southeast Europe. *Southeast European and Black Sea Studies, 2*, 53–68.

Long, E., Reid, J., McLeigh, J., Stoklosa, H., Felix, E., & Scott, T. (2019). *Preventing human trafficking using data-driven, community-based strategies.*

Lynn, S. J., & Cardeña, E. (2007). Hypnosis and the treatment of posttraumatic conditions: An evidence-based approach. *International Journal of Clinical and Experimental Hypnosis, 55*(2), 167–188.

M'Cormack, F. (2011). *Helpdesk research report: The impact of human trafficking on people and countries.* Governance and Social Development Resource Center.

MacInnis, N. (2013). Human trafficking: The complexities of a global definition. *Behavioural Sciences Undergraduate Journal, 1*(1), 39–51.

Makisaka, M. (2009). *Human trafficking: A brief overview.* World Bank.

Maslow, A. H. (1943). A theory of human motivation. *Psychological Review, 50*(4), 370.

McLean, C. P., & Foa, E. B. (2011). Prolonged exposure therapy for post-traumatic stress disorder: A review of evidence and dissemination. *Expert Review of Neurotherapeutics, 11*(8), 1151–1163.

Meese, et al. (2002). *Research report on third country national trafficking victims in Albania.* International Organization for Migration, ICMC.

Menon, N. (2019). Marxism, feminism and caste in contemporary India. In *Racism after apartheid: Challenges for Marxism and anti-racism* (pp. 137–156). WITS University Press.

Meshelemiah, J. C., & Lynch, R. E. (2019). *The cause and consequence of human trafficking: Human rights violations.*

Meshelmiah, J. C., Gilson, C., & Prasanga, A. P. A. (2018). Use of drug dependency to entrap and control victims of sex trafficking: A call for a US federal human rights response. *Dignity: A Journal on Sexual Exploitation and Violence, 3*(3).

Mosse, D. (2018). Caste and development: Contemporary perspectives on a structure of discrimination and advantage. *World Development, 110,* 422–436.

Naik, A. B. (2018). Impacts, causes and consequences of women trafficking in India from human rights perspective. *Social Sciences, 7*(2), 76–80.

Oberschall, A. (1978). Theories of social conflict. *Annual Review of Sociology, 4*(1), 291–315.

Office on Trafficking in Persons. (2017). *Fact sheet: Human trafficking.* Administration for Children and Families, U.S. Department of Health and Human Services. OTIP-FS-18-01.

OHCHR (Office of the United Nations High Commissioner for Human Rights). (2014). *Human rights and human trafficking.* New York and Geneva: GE.14-14023–June 2014–5,233.

Orme, J., & Ross-Sheriff, F. (2015). Sex trafficking: Policies, programs, and services. *Social Work, 60*(4), 287–294.

Ozkalipci, O., & Schlar, C. (1999). The Istanbul Protocol: International standards for the effective investigation and documentation of torture and ill treatment. *The Lancet, 354*(9184), 1117.

Parker, C., Doctor, R. M., & Selvam, R. (2008). Somatic therapy treatment effects with tsunami survivors. *Traumatology, 14*(3), 103–109.

Paul, B. K., & Hasnath, S. A. (2000). Trafficking in Bangladeshi women and girls. *The Geographical Review, 90,* 268.

Payne, P., Levine, P. A., & Crane-Godreau, M. A. (2015). Somatic experiencing: Using interoception and proprioception as core elements of trauma therapy. *Frontiers in Psychology, 6,* 93.

Peek, L. (2008). Children and disasters: Understanding vulnerability, developing capacities, and promoting resilience—An introduction. *Children Youth and Environments, 18*(1), 1–29.

Petersen, A. C., Joseph, J., Feit, M., & National Research Council. (2014). Consequences of child abuse and neglect. In *New directions in child abuse and neglect research.* National Academies Press (US).

Rafferty, Y. (2013). Child trafficking and commercial sexual exploitation: A review of promising prevention policies and programs. *American Journal of Orthopsychiatry, 83*(4), 559.

Ray, N. (2008). *Vulnerability to human trafficking: A qualitative study.* Washington University.

Reid, J. A., Strauss, J., & Haskell, R. A. (2018). 11. Clinical practice with commercially sexually exploited girls with intellectual disabilities. In *Social work practice with survivors of sex trafficking and commercial sexual exploitation* (pp. 218–238). Columbia University Press.

Restivo, E., & Lanier, M. M. (2015). Measuring the contextual effects and mitigating factors of labeling theory. *Justice Quarterly, 32*(1), 116–141.

Robjant, K. (2021). *Psychological sequalae of surviving modern slavery and its treatment using adapted narrative exposure therapy* (Doctoral dissertation).

Ryle, A. E. (1995). *Cognitive analytic therapy: Developments in theory and practice.* Wiley.

Salami, T., Gordon, M., Coverdale, J., & Nguyen, P. T. (2018). What therapies are favored in the treatment of the psychological sequelae of trauma in human trafficking victims? *Journal of Psychiatric Practice®, 24*(2), 87–96.

Save the Children. (2003). *Joint east west research project on trafficking in children for sexual purposes in Europe: Romania Country Report.*

Schauer, M., Neuner, F., & Elbert, T. (2011). *Narrative exposure therapy: A short term treatment for traumatic stress disorders* (2nd ed.). Hogrefe Publishing.

Schauer, M., Neuner, F., & Elbert, T. (2017). Narrative exposure therapy for children and adolescents (KIDNET). In *Evidence-based treatments for trauma related disorders in children and adolescents* (pp. 227–250). Springer.

Schneier, F. R., Neria, Y., Pavlicova, M., Hembree, E., Suh, E. J., Amsel, L., & Marshall, R. D. (2012). Combined prolonged exposure therapy and paroxetine for PTSD related to the World Trade Center attack: A randomized controlled trial. *American Journal of Psychiatry, 169*(1), 80–88.

Schultze-Lutter, F., Schmidt, S. J., & Theodoridou, A. (2018). Psychopathology—a precision tool in need of re-sharpening. *Frontiers in Psychiatry, 9*, 446.

Schwarz, C., Unruh, E., Cronin, K., Evans-Simpson, S., Britton, H., & Ramaswamy, M. (2016). Human trafficking identification and service provision in the medical and social service sectors. *Health and Human Rights, 18*(1), 181.

Sellers, J. (1996). Human behavior and the social environment: Shifting paradigms in essential knowledge for social work practice. *Journal of Baccalaureate Social Work, 2*(1), 155–156.

Shandro, J., Chisolm-Straker, M., Duber, H. C., Findlay, S. L., Munoz, J., Schmitz, G., et al. (2016). Human trafficking: A guide to identification and approach for the emergency physician. *Annals of Emergency Medicine, 68*(4), 501–508.

Shapiro, F. (1989). Eye movement desensitization: A new treatment for post-traumatic stress disorder. *Journal of Behavior Therapy and Experimental Psychiatry, 20*(3), 211–217.

Shapiro, F. (1999). Eye movement desensitization and reprocessing (EMDR) and the anxiety disorders: Clinical and research implications of an integrated psychotherapy treatment. *Journal of Anxiety Disorders, 13*(1–2), 35–67.

Sharma, S. S. S., & Choudhary, M. (2016). *Child trafficking in the Indo-Myanmar Region: A Case Study in Manipur* [Research].

Shaw, J. A., Lewis, J. E., Chitiva, H. A., & Pangilinan, A. R. (2017). Adolescent victims of commercial sexual exploitation versus sexually abused adolescents. *Journal of the American Academy of Psychiatry and the Law, 45*(3), 325–331.

Shkurkin, E. V. (2004). The consequences of the sexual abuse in human trafficking. In *Human trafficking conference* (Vol. 5).

Siegel, D., & De Blank, S. (2010). Women who traffic women: The role of women in human trafficking networks–Dutch cases. *Global Crime, 11*(4), 436–447.

Smith, L., Vardaman, S. H., & Snow, M. (2009). *The national report on domestic minor sex trafficking: America's prostituted children.* Shared Hope International.

Spires, B. (2021). Intersections between human trafficking and education: Toward new research agendas. *Journal of Contemporary Issues in Education, 16*(2).

Stark, M. M. (Ed.). (2011). *Clinical forensic medicine: A physician's guide* (Vol. 473). Humana Press.

Stoklosa, H., Grace, A., & Littenberg, N. (2015). Medical education on human trafficking. *AMA Journal of Ethics, 17*, 914–921.

Surtees, R. (2005). *Other forms of trafficking in minors: Articulating victim profiles and conceptualizing interventions.* NEXUS Institute to Combat Trafficking & International Organization for Migration.

Todres, J. (2010). Moving upstream: The merits of a public health law approach to human trafficking. *The North Carolina Law Review, 89,* 447.

Toney-Butler, T. J., & Mittel, O. (2017). *Human trafficking.*

UN GIFT (United Nations Global Initiative to Fight Human Trafficking). (2008). 016 Workshop: Profiling the traffickers. In *The Vienna Forum to fight human trafficking.* Austria Center Vienna, UN GIFT BP: 016.

UNDP (United Nations Development Programme). (2003). *From challenges to opportunities: Responses to trafficking and HIV/AIDS in South Asia.* United Nations Development Programme.

UNESCAP (United Nations Economic and Social Commission for Asia and the Pacific). (2002). *Recommended principles and guidelines on human rights and human trafficking.* Report of the United Nations High Commissioner for Human Rights to the Economic and Social Council. New York: UNESCAP.

UNICEF. (2001). *Children on the edge: Protecting children from sexual exploitation and trafficking in East Asia and the Pacific.*

United Nations. (2000). *Protocol to prevent, suppress and punish trafficking in persons, especially women and children, supplementing the United Nations convention against transnational organized crime.* United Nations Office on Drugs and Crime, United Nations Convention against Transnational Organized Crime and the Protocols Thereto.

United Nations Office on Drugs, Crime, & Global Programme Against Trafficking in Human Beings. (2008). *Toolkit to combat trafficking in persons.* United Nations Publications.

United States Department of State. (2003). *Trafficking in persons.* Washington, DC.

UNODC (United Nations Office on Drugs & Crime). (2008a). Global programme against trafficking in human beings. Toolkit to combat trafficking in persons. United Nations Publications.

UNODC (United Nations Office on Drugs and Crime). (2008b). *An introduction to human trafficking: Vulnerability, impact and action.* United Nations publication, V.07-88925-1500.

UNODC (United Nations Office on Drugs and Crime). (2009). *Global report on trafficking in persons.*

UNODC (United Nations Office on Drugs and Crime). (2020a). *Global report on trafficking in persons.* United Nations publication, Sales No. E.20.IV.3.

UNODC (United Nations Office on Drugs and Crime). (2020b). *Interlinkages between trafficking in persons and marriage.* Heuni, V19-02810.

UNODC (United Nations Office on Drugs and Crime). (2021). *Abuse of a position of vulnerability and other "means" within the definition of trafficking in persons.* New York: V.13-82591.

WCRWC (Woman's Commission for Refugee Women and Children). (2010). *Displaced women and girls at risk: Identifying risk factors and taking steps to prevent abuse.* University of New South Wales' Centre for Refugee Research.

Weitzer, R. (2014). New directions in research on human trafficking. *The Annals of the American Academy of Political and Social Science, 653*(1), 6–24.

Wenzel, T., Frewer, A., & Mirzaei, S. (2015). The DSM 5 and the Istanbul Protocol: Diagnosis of psychological sequels of torture. *Torture Journal, 25*(1), 11–11.

Williams, P. (2006). Sex work, the Palermo protocol and HIV/AIDS. *Global consultation on HIV/AIDS and sex work.*

Wood, L. C. (2020). Child modern slavery, trafficking and health: A practical review of factors contributing to children's vulnerability and the potential impacts of severe exploitation on health. *BMJ Paediatrics Open, 4*(1).

Yakushko, O. (2009). Human trafficking: A review for mental health professionals. *International Journal for the Advancement of Counselling, 31*(3), 158–167.

Zimmerman, C., Yun, K., Shvab, I., Watts, C., Trappolin, L., Treppete, M., et al. (2003). *The health risks and consequences of trafficking in women and adolescents: Findings from a European study*. London School of Hygiene & Tropical Medicine.

Zimmerman, C., Hossain, M., Yun, K., Roche, B., Morison, L., & Watts, C. (2006). *Stolen smiles: A summary report on the physical and psychological health consequences of women and adolescents trafficked in Europe*.

Zoellner, L. A., Roy-Byrne, P. P., Mavissakalian, M., & Feeny, N. C. (2019). Doubly randomized preference trial of prolonged exposure versus sertraline for treatment of PTSD. *American Journal of Psychiatry, 176*(4), 287–296.

Chapter 12
Crimes Against Persons

Afreen A. Hussain

Introduction

Crime and criminality encompasses a gamut of concepts and perspectives as seen in the diverse theories ranging from the characteristics of crime, the various ways in which they are manifested, the causative factors responsible for the crime such as environmental or economic, the role of personality characteristics and traits in an individual that might propel the person to commit a crime along with the psychosocial aspects of an individual's life that could determine or predict criminal behaviour (Khader, 2019; Barlow & Kauzlarich, 2010). The concept of crime in its varied elements has been explored by sociologists, psychologists, criminologists, anthropologists and professionals from the fields of criminal justice, thereby giving it a multidisciplinary approach and adding certain richness to it. Sarki (2019) defined crime from a social perspective as behaviour that is in contrast to the expected and acceptable norms of behaviours in a society which is invariably ensued by coercive measures. Lunden (1958) in his paper on Emile Durkheim elaborated on how Durkheim elucidated crime as a phenomenon that is not just normal but also necessary. Crime was a product of faulty social interactions in a society or 'social disorganization'. Opp's (2020) perspective on crime and criminality was that it involved an act of commission or non-commission of legally sanctioned behaviour. The Merriam-Webster online dictionary (n.d.) defines criminal acts as those which are punishable by a government for, they are prohibited and illegal and these also include offences against morality Criminal acts as defined in the Merriam-Webster dictionary (online) include those acts that are punishable by a government because they are prohibited and illegal and also against morality. Crime in this sense might thus be interpreted as a thought of wrongdoing or planning thereof as well as a

A. A. Hussain (✉)
Forensic Psychology Division of the Central Forensic Science Laboratory, Guwahati, India

realization of a misdemeanour that will incur penalty and punishment by an organization in authority, like a government because of the unlawful nature of the act.

Types of Crimes

The world of crime today is one that is highly developed and just as humankind has made progress in research and development in various fields, so has crime made progress in its evolution into novel forms and types (Buss, 2012). Since crime by its definition as stated above attracted sanctions and penalties, a classification was required considering the procedural practices of the courts. Most often, these would differ amongst different legal systems in the world. The categorization of the crimes along these lines also outlined the various ways in which crime can be manifested and further classified. In his chapter on the various types of crimes, Sarki (2019) elucidated how crimes can be distinguished based on the asperity of the criminal acts, the recipients or target population of the crimes, and the modes of committing the crimes by grouping them in three clusters: I, II, and III.

Cluster I: The categories of crimes in this cluster are defined as mala in se and mala prohibita.

Cluster II: This cluster comprised of crimes that are recipient-dependent, indicating that it takes into consideration the victims and the target of the crime along with the offender. Offences that are commonly included in this category are organized crime, financial crimes, corporate crimes, cybercrimes and victimless crimes and crimes that are considered traditional implying all those crimes that are other than the ones mentioned above.

Cluster III: The crimes listed in this cluster are specific to the Criminal Code Act, a criminal law applicable to northern Nigeria and they include felony, misdemeanor and simple crimes (Sarki, 2019).

Definitions and Categories of Crimes

- Mala in se and Mala prohibita: Mala in se identifies with crimes that are considered "evil in itself", and it therefore does not go by the diktats of governmental rules and regulations. Mala prohibita is Latin for wrongs prohibited and therefore implies any crime that is prohibited by the law of the land even though such crimes may not necessarily be wrongs on moral grounds as determined by the society (Columbia Law Review, 1930 & Black's Law Dictionary, 1990 in Gray, 1995).
- Organized crime: Two defining factors – "members" and "activities of a group" make up organized crime giving it the distinctive feature of "organization" described as "a group of people who cooperate to accomplish objectives or goals" (Mallory, 2012, p. 2). Corporate "crime"as described by Clinard, Yeager,

Brissette, Petrashek, and Harries (1979) included "violations" of which were included "administrative", "civil" and "criminal law" (p. 22). Sutherland (1940) is credited with the use of the term white-collar crime that he exemplified by tax frauds, embezzlement, forgery, bribery, manipulation in the stock exchange, miscalculation of funds and grants, among others. "Corporate crime is organizational crime..." (Kramer 1982, p. 79 as cited by Van Erp, 2018). Since the focus of this chapter is on crimes committed specifically against individuals, these concepts mentioned above shall not be delved into and the reader can follow up through the references if interested.

- Cybercrime: Cybercrime is the best example of technology being a double-edged sword. It can be simply defined as a type of crime that is committed in the virtual world through the use of a computer wherein the computer can work as both or either an instrument of 'attack' or a recipient of such an attack (Aghatise, 2006). While one face of cyberspace has benefitted the world in numerous ways, the other has been the cause of much loss and distress. Such illegal acts originate in the virtual world and eventually permeate into the physical world. The extent of this permeability was seen during the recent Covid-19 pandemic in 2020 where criminal acts like data theft, "online scams and phishing, disruptive malware, malicious domains, data harvesting malware, and misinformation" were found to be rampant in the cyberspace, the space that had become the global workplace of most individuals, organizations and corporations (Interpol., 2020, p. 5). Bada and Nurse (2019) discussed the psychological and social impact of cyberattacks and identified the following few unpleasant imprints that can potentially leave their mark on a victim of cybercrime:

  Emotional trauma
  Isolation and depression
  Anxiety
  Anger and grief
  Guilt
  Feeling of insecurity in the cyber world

- Victimless crimes: As the term indicates, such crimes are those that have a covert involvement of the victims which is why they are called victimless crimes. The difficulty with the word 'victimless' in studying victimless crimes comes from the perception that there can be no crime without the presence of both the perpetrator and the recipient (Fletcher, 2019). Siegel (2010) preferred replacing the term with public order crimes for these offences because they include offences such as substance abuse, begging, betting, prostitution, sale and consumption of prohibited substances and related offences. Such crimes do not have a direct impact on people but they are nonetheless punishable by law but in spite of that many such crimes go unpunished since there is little interest in reporting a crime that does not directly harm another (Jubaer, Hoque, Rahman, Moumi, & Deb, 2021).

- Conventional crimes: These are offences that are considered commonplace occurrences and therefore garner the attention of law enforcement agencies almost all the time. Crimes in this category encompass the wide range of offences from serious to minor transgressions. Crimes such as burglary, theft, larceny, assault, murder, robbery, rape, domestic violence and hate crimes are categorized as conventional crimes (Condirston, 2011 & Clinard & Yeager, 1978).

Crime keeps ever-evolving and the inevitability of the emergence of novel crimes must always be considered while reviewing its typology.

Crimes Against Persons

The focus of this chapter is on crimes committed against people. When one conceives of crimes against people, it is usually considered personal. A personal crime is one that directly affects an individual. Although crimes have been classified in a variety of ways, the core categories are almost constant. Hugh Lester (1924) in his report on the classification of crimes defined crimes against persons as "murder (including first degree and other), attempt, threat or conspiracy to murder, manslaughter, assault, kidnapping, and other" (p. 593). In the 1926 Report of the New York Joint Legislative Committee on the Coordination of the Civil and Criminal Practice Acts, crimes against persons included "abduction, assault, bigamy, manslaughter, murder, perjury, rape, and robbery". A subsequent subcommittee put forward the following as offences committed against people – murder, manslaughter, assault, and sex offences (as cited in Mac Donald, 1933, pp. 544–545). The following types of personal crimes affect an individual directly and are capable of causing immense physical, emotional or psychological hurt as will be seen later in the chapter.

Crimes against persons can thus be understood and summarized as under:

1. Homicide

    (a) Murder
    (b) Manslaughter

2. Assault (Home Office Counting Rules for Recorded Crime, 2021)

    (a) Serious assault (UNODC (2015) and aggravated assault (Federal Bureau of Investigation, 2004)
    (b) Minor assault

3. Criminal intimidation/threat
4. Harassment and stalking
5. Abduction
6. Sexual offences
7. Other types of crimes

1. Homicide
    Homicide is defined as the killing of one person by another and alludes to both the criminal and non-criminal aspects of the killing (Britannica, 2022) as

well as its legitimacy or lack thereof (Brookman, 2010). The principal difference between homicide and murder is that while homicide can be justified and can occur in many situations or circumstances, murder is a felony that cannot be legitimized. Homicide is considered lawful when it is pertains to death because of a duel, or killings during wars and is unlawful in the case of murder, manslaughter and infanticide as classified in England and Wales (Brookman, 2010). Murder is committed with an intention to hurt and is therefore treated as a criminal act (Law Reform Commission, 2008). An act that is considered homicidal may differ according to a country's legal frameworks, and as an example one can see how in the UK, homicide has two categories – murder and manslaughter (Lobingier, 1919).

(a) Murder is best understood by the definition given by Lord Chief Justice Edward Coke (Card, 1998 as cited by Brookman, 2010) in the early years of the seventeenth century as an act of illegal killing committed by "a person of sound memory, and of the age of discretion", within the jurisdiction of an region "any reasonable creature in rerum natura under the kings peace, with malice aforethought, either expressed by the party or implied by law", that results in the wounded or hurt party wounded, or hurt, etc., die of the wound or hurt, etc., within a year and a day after the same (p. 184). According to Hossain and Rahi (2018), the definition comprises of two parts – the external part called the actus rea which denotes the action part of anything wrong, and mens rea responsible for the thought or the mind behind the act thus implying that an unlawful act must be accompanied by an ill intention or motive.

(b) Manslaughter is defined as the act of causing death of another human being by being reckless or negligent (Fort Peck Tribes Comprehensive Code of Justice, 2019). Or simply, when a human being is killed without any ill intention it is termed as manslaughter (Mellor, 1982). Yet another perspective on manslaughter describes it as a form of "culpable homicide" which does not develop into murder and in the event that the cause is "negligence" it is termed as "manslaughter by negligence" (Criminal Offences Act, 1988). Mitchell and Mackay (2010) elaborated further and discussed voluntary and involuntary manslaughter, the components of which are the three offences – unlawful and dangerous act manslaughter, gross negligence manslaughter and reckless manslaughter. Voluntary manslaughter is murder as we know it and is an act committed out of a "loss of self-control (formerly provocation), diminished responsibility or suicide pact" (p. 1). Involuntary manslaughter is understood as the killing of another unintentionally. This might be a consequence of irresponsible behaviour and carelessness despite being lawfully correct in one's actions or acting in a way that is not deemed grave enough to be called a serious offence (Petherick & Petherick, 2019). Unlawful act manslaughter (or constructive manslaughter) as defined by Wheeler and Bloomer (2016) refers to death of a person due to the unlawful actions of another person. Citing the hearing of the DPP v. Newbury [1977] (A.C. 500) case, they emphasized that it is imperative that the actions must be legally wrong and dangerous with the likelihood of physically hurting another person. The likelihood or potential of causing harm is determined on the basis of the individual's capacity to predict the risks involved in the behaviour. Gross negligence manslaughter is interpreted as the lack of concern that a person's actions must have been to be determined guilty of unlawful behaviour while reckless manslaughter includes those individuals who were close to being sentenced for murder but could anticipate that that their actions have the potential for causing grievous hurt or even death (Mitchell & Mackay, 2010) even though they may have acted without any intent to cause such harm.

2. Assault (Home Office Counting Rules for Recorded Crime, 2021)

Perkins (1962) identified the concepts of assault and battery as interconnected. According to him, if any act of misconduct involves assault, then it invariably involves battery as well. He explained this with the example of two individuals. Let us assume that a certain individual A wants to hurt person B and because of which a stone is hurled at B by A. Now, if B just manages to avoid the stone and goes unharmed, then A would most likely be convicted for "criminal assault" as the act was an attempt to "commit a battery" (p. 71). Along with this, because A's actions put the fear of possible bodily harm into B, A would then be considered guilty of "trespass for assault" (p. 71) for this very reason. Rollison (1941) made a distinction between battery and assault and defined battery as a direct or indirect act of injury or attack on the physical body of a human being (the accuser in this case) carried out voluntarily and intentionally by the accused to hurt and cause harm. The emphasis of assault, on the other hand, is on anticipation. It involves the act of intentionally causing another human being to be in a fearful state in anticipation of an impending harm and injury that may be inflicted. The concept of assault was later simply understood as an "unlawful attack by one person upon another" (Federal Bureau of Investigation, 2004, p. 18). Views on the idea of assault are also country-specific and therefore thoughts on what are included or excluded in the definition differ (UNODC, 2015). Assault as an act involving coercion with the intention of either hurting or causing harm or threatening to do the same was given by the UNODC in 2015. This definition puts forward two categories of assault:

(a) Serious assault
(b) Minor assault

They surmised that any act involving the use of significant force by one to intentionally and recklessly hurt another to cause grievous bodily harm is understood to be a serious assault. Reckless behaviour here implies actions that are taken without considering the consequences of those actions. Aggravated assault almost fulfils the same criteria as that of a serious assault wherein the use of any dangerous weapons to cause fatal or grave injuries to the body is emphasized upon (Federal Bureau of Investigation, 2004). The weapons may be sharp instruments, firearms, poison, body parts like fists and feet that can be used as weapons and other weapons considered dangerous.

Minor assault is also intentional, reckless, and uses physical force to hurt another but it is of lesser intensity and results in minor or almost negligible physical injury. This can be understood as assault with intention to cause serious harm (UNODC, 2015).

3. Threat

The word threat is almost a commonplace term that is used loosely in routine conversation. The intensity of the damage that a threat can have can be gauged by its definitions even though it is true that not all threats are executed. Threat is an expression of intent to do harm or act out violently against someone or something. A threat was defined as that which can be "spoken, written, or symbolic" in nature where examples would include actions such as a gesture using one's hands as in a way that appears to be "shooting at another person" (O'Toole, 2008, p. 6). Threat is defined as any behaviour that threatens another individual particularly in the belief of the possibility of that threat being carried out (UNODC, 2015) and it has two categories:

(a) Serious threat which is a threat that is intended to cause serious or fatal harm
(b) Minor threat which is a threat that intends to cause only minor or negligible harm

A threat to kill another that is a category of violence without injury is legally defined as the act of threat made by a person to another without any legitimate explanation and intended to instil a fear into another of its fulfilment to kill that other or another (Home Office Counting Rules for Recorded Time, 2021). A threat and an attempt to harm is also one of the criteria for aggravated assault that could contribute to the vexatious situation (Federal Bureau of Investigation, 2006).

4. Harassment and Stalking

Harassment and stalking are acts that are both harmful and intend to cause harm to another person (UNODC, 2015). Heckels and Roberts (2010) outlined the concept of harassment as defined in the Protection of Harassment Act, UK 1997. He stated that harassment is behaviour that makes another person feel "alarm or distress" including acts that are capable of causing distress and those that have occurred at least twice (p. 367). Criminal harassment is in the simplest way understood as "harassing behaviour that includes stalking" (Department of Justice, Canada, 2003, p. 2). This behaviour must have no justifiable aim and meaning but must make one feel genuine fear for the security of one's person. However, such behaviour must be repetitive in nature, as an isolated case cannot be considered harassment unless there is a conspicuous threat to one's safety in the behaviour seen.

Meloy and Gothard (1995) as cited by Meloy (1999) defined stalking as behaviour that is persistent in its pursuance and harassment of an individual (s) and marked by obstinate, determined, malevolent thoughts and actions consequently threatening the other person's safety.

Stalking constitutes behaviour that is, in essence, an unwelcome and incessant pursual of a person consequently making the individual experience a sense of fear (Spitzer, n.d., p. 1). It is typically characterized by following an individual, threatening, watching, making phone calls, sending emails and messages, letters and gifts and other such tokens of affection, making contact and acquiring information on social media and other platforms through family, friends or colleagues (Heckels & Roberts 2010; Ministry of Justice, 2012). Laws related to stalking differ not just across countries but also jurisdictions (and therefore, the definitions get modified and the focus areas are altered accordingly). There are four components of stalking as propounded by Thomson and Dennison (2008) that can be interchanged as focus areas – (i). intent and motive of the stalker; ii. victim's feelings like fear and distress; iii. Repetition; and iv. persistence. Elaborating further, they described stalking to be typically conceived of as any behaviour towards another that intends to make the person uncomfortable and scared for his/her personal safety using tactics like repeatedly pursuing, watching, sometimes threatening, making unsolicited offers of affection through gifts, letters, and other modes of communication, approaching and involving other family members, friends, colleagues, and making threats to them as well all constitute stalking behaviour.

5. Abduction and Kidnapping

Abduction and kidnapping are crimes against persons but they do not always end up being violent. Abduction occurs when a person is wrongfully taken away by another through coercion, deception, or enticement and differs from kidnapping in that it does not involve any ransom (Uniform Crime Reporting, 2000). The acts of abduction and kidnapping are considered as acts that deprive or restrict an individual of the right to freedom of movement and liberty and include the following types of abductions:

(a) Abduction of a minor that involves the illegal taking away, restraining, and hiding of a minor from the "legal guardians" or "custodial parents" (p. 37)
(b) Parental abduction wherein a minor is abducted by a parent who does not have the legal sanction for custody of the minor
(c) Abduction by another family member that implies the abduction of a minor by a member of the family who is neither the parent nor the legal guardian
(d) Abduction by a legal guardian where a minor is abducted by a legal guardian who does not possess exclusive custodial rights, and is not a parent or some other family member
(e) Other abduction of a minor that involves all other categories of abduction other than the classifications made above (UNODC, 2015)

The different components of kidnapping are thus (The Law Commission, 2011):

(a) Taking or carrying away
(b) Force or fraud
(c) Without consent
(d) Lawful excuse

(e) Loss of liberty
(f) Sending abroad
(g) The fault element

6. Sexual Offences

Sexual violence as defined by the World Health Organization in their *World Report on Violence and Health* (Krug et al., 2002) included any actions that were sexual, or any efforts to acquire a "sexual act", or unsolicited remarks or advances that were sexual in nature, or attempts to traffic, or acts otherwise directed against an individual's sexuality or sexual orientation using force, by any person irrespective of their "relationship to the victim", and that which can happen in any environment whether in one's own residence or workplace (p. 149). The types of crimes that are listed under sexual offences are comprehensive and are also subject to a country's legal system that defines sexual offences. The categories of sexual offences have undergone constant evolution and what was once deemed prohibited may have legal sanction today (Green, 2015). This change is evidenced in the list below, and therefore, a compilation of the offences that comes under the purview of sexual offences (regardless of era) is cited here. These include:

(a) Rape
(b) Sexual assault
(c) Sexual offences against minors that include impairing morals of minors, child grooming, paedophilia, child trafficking, child pornography, and child marriage.
(d) Abduction
(e) Seduction
(f) Prostitution and human trafficking
(g) Adultery
(h) Castration in men and female genital mutilation and obligatory inspections for virginity
(i) Incest
(j) Exhibitionism
(k) Obscenity
(l) Voyeurism
(m) Abuse of position of trust
(n) Bestiality
(o) Necrophilia
(p) Sadomasochism
(q) Solicitation
(r) Pandering
(s) Sexual harassment and unwanted sexual advances
(t) Forced abortion, denial of the right to use contraception, and infanticide
(u) Violent acts against the sexual integrity of women
(v) Not registering as a sex offender

(w) Administering of a substance with intent to commit a sexual offence (Mac Donald, 1933, Green, 2015, Krug et al., 2002, A Guide to the Sexual Offences Act, 2010, Simons, 2015).

7. Other types of crimes against persons

    (i) Cause or abetting suicide
    (ii) Poisoning
    (iii) Custodial interference
    (iv) Neglect
    (v) Abuse of elders
    (vi) Criminal and negligent endangerment
    (vii) Hate crimes
    (viii) Crimes against the intellectually disabled
    (ix) Institutional violence

Crime Against Persons: Why Would Anyone Do It?

Criminality and criminal behaviour are best understood through the causes that are responsible for it. It is not enough to know the different types of crimes without having an understanding of what goes into making these crimes happen. It is therefore imperative to study crime and its causative factors to understand why a human being would want to hurt and harm another human being. As Lu (2016) aptly asked the question to determine the motivation that directs unlawful behaviour: "…is the lack of knowledge, or ignorance, the sole cause of evil-doings?" (p. 50).

1. *Homicide: Murder and Manslaughter*
    Morrall (2006) has provided a detailed description of the possible causes that might prompt an individual to want to kill another. He put forward the following topics to explain the commission of murder:

(a) Motives
(b) Mad-bad
(c) Individual
(d) Society
(e) Individual and society
(f) Devastation and fascination (pp. 36–37).

    He begins by first identifying the intentions that drive the acts of violence as the four 'Ls': "Lust; Love; Loathing; and Loot" (p. 36). Killing because of lust refers to murdering another out of passionate jealousy and also when one benefits sexually in exchange of the murder. One is guided to kill another out of love because of sympathy and care particularly when it involves a terminal illness. When an individual bears an intense hatred towards individuals or groups, or particular nationalities and cultures, it might cause that person to commit murder. Yet another motive is monetary advantage. If there is any gain to be got through endowment or other means of security, or being an assassin, or in a burglary then it might lead to the murder of the concerned person (s). The next probable cause for murder was the "Mad-bad" (p. 36) perspective. The contention was that the individuals with mental illness; those called 'mad' by a society and the ones who possess villainous characteristics are reason enough to commit murder. A contradiction to this approach presents itself in the fact that for the most part persons with mental illnesses do not commit murder; also, an individual perceived as a villain by some may be seen as a hero, thus, making it difficult to follow through with this assumption. The next factor to understand why people commit murder is related to individual features. Morrall (2006) referred to the biological make of human beings that make them prone to killing another. The physiology of males tends to make them more aggressive than women because of the presence of testosterone. He also noted the impact of glucose and alcohol content in the blood determining the proneness to murder. Citing David Buss (2012), the evolutionary psychologist, he stated that killing is a deep-seated component of human nature that fulfilled the demands required for survival, mostly reproduction and continuation of the species. It additionally portrayed man as a protector and provider, the subsequent traits that a woman would find attractive. Society and its relationship with the individual as a cause to commit murder were explored next. It was purported that a society that has a high exposure to violence and aggression would have a strong influence on its members; the consequence of which would be further perpetration of violent crimes like murder (Bloom, 2001, as cited in Morrall, 2006). The connection between an individual and the society the individual was considered "reflexive" (p. 37) in the sense that the social elements affected an individual psychosocially thereby worked as a catalyst to commit crimes like murder. Included here could be the role of sex workers in a society and the sex-related offences (Allen & Rotenberg, 2021; Balfour & Allen, 2014). It is true that crime fascinates and the glorification of crime through media and literature works as a double-edged sword. Violent crimes like murder leave behind deep-rooted psychological scars that may sometimes be responsible for further acts of crime. Although these elements strive to explain the incidence of murder, it is not without critique. Explaining the biology of man alone assumes that women are not murderers. The apparent evolutionary role of men being the provider-protector does not appear as a feasible notion to stomach in today's world.

2. *Assault*

   (a) Violence as a source of assaulting behaviour
   (b) Aggression as a source of assaulting behaviour

   Aggression maybe colloquially understood as behaviour which may be driven by a feeling of intense emotion that is seen in words or actions directed towards another which may cause the other hurt or harm, whether psychological or physical. Although violence and aggression tend to be used interchangeably and understood as similar, there is a thin line that separates the two. Berkowitz (1989) citing Dollard et al. (1939, p. 9) looked at aggression as any "sequence of behavior, the goal-response to which is the injury of the person toward whom it is directed" (p. 61). Felson (2009) while outlining violence stated that it is nothing but physical aggression when an individual uses brute force to hurt another. Another viewpoint given on human aggression suggests that it is behaviour "directed toward another individual that is carried out with the proximate (immediate) intent to cause harm" (Anderson & Bushman, 2002). They elaborated further and discussed the following major theories of aggression that are briefly mentioned below:

(a) Cognitive neoassociation theory

In its present form, this theory discusses the association between "feelings, ideas, and memories" connected as one structure in memory and subsequently creating "emotional networks". Consequently, when one section is set off, the other sections too get active because of the connection made between them. So, the assumption is that if unpleasant thoughts trigger the associated feelings and memories of negativity, then those thoughts should also trigger any experience that might be aggressive in nature (Berkowitz and Heimer, 1989 as cited by Berkowitz, 1989).

(b) Social learning theory

Social learning theories believe that all behaviour, not excluding criminal and deviant behaviour, is learned through observation and interaction with others – "People are not born with preformed repertoires of aggressive behaviour; they must learn them" (Bandura, 1978, p. 14). It thus surmises that the role of observation and social experiences is of paramount importance in moulding an individual's behaviour.

(c) Script theory

A script is formed when pieces of information are put together after which they work as a tool and guide for behaviour. The first step involves selecting a script. Anderson and Bushman (2002) cited the example of a child who having seen numerous times the use of a weapon (here, gun) to arbitrate any conflict is most likely to have a ready script that can be accessed any time a situation requires such behaviour. This recollection of the script is the second step.

(d) Excitation transfer theory

This theory propounded by Zillman (2008) illustrates behaviour through the concept of 'residue' and 'transfer'. It states that there are situations that elicit emotions and once that moment is gone the feelings and emotions that were triggered do not completely go away but stay as 'residue'. When another emotion-provoking circumstance arises, the residual emotions of the previous incident are added to the currently evoked emotions, thereby enhancing the emotional reaction which would have been less intense in nature had the earlier "residual excitation" not intensified it. This new enhanced response is significant of getting overexcited. Anderson and Bushman (2002) supposes that if anger was the activated emotion in the second of two emotion-arousing events, then it should follow that the individual will experience more anger in proportion to the situation and this would be because of the lingering feelings of anger of the first event that enhanced the current one.

(e) Social interaction theory

This theory understands acts of aggression to be an intentional deed committed as a means to achieve a goal or a target. According to Tedeschi and Felson (1994), as mentioned by Anderson and Bushman (2002), the concept can be best understood in the social context of behaviour. For example, an individual might employ aggression or arm-twisting tactics to acquire something he/she attaches value to or to avenge oneself or consolidate one's position in terms of authority and/or self-esteem. Simply put, the theory explains that aggressive conduct is "motivated by higher level (or ultimate) goals" (p. 32). Thus, such behaviour is guided by the end result that is to be achieved.

(f) General aggression model

The General Aggression Model (GAM) was created out of the amalgamation of the previously mentioned theories of aggression. The fundamental element of the GAM is the understanding of human aggression through the notion of "knowledge structures" (Allen, Anderson, & Bushman, 2018). The fundamental aspects of these knowledge structures consider the following: (i) they are generated from "experience" (Anderson & Bushman, 2002, p. 33), (ii) they have a bearing on "perception at multiple levels" (p. 33), ranging from the simplest to the most complex, (iii) they have the potential to become automatic in nature with frequent use, (iv) they are connected to "affective states, behavioral programs, and beliefs" (p. 33); and (v) act as a guide to direct an individual on how interpret and respond to the environment around them, whether it be the social or physical environment.

3. *Threat*

The act of threatening a person or a group of people is usually done with an aim and sometimes even an incentive is involved in the scheme of things. O'Toole (2008) provided a comprehensive list of reasons that may explain why threats are made and what purpose they may serve. A wide spectrum was given ranging from a need to warn, to intimidate, to cause injury, to bully, to frighten, to coerce someone into doing something, to protect oneself, to scare, to assert one's position in a situation, to reinforce control and power, to punishment, to seek vengeance, to challenge positions and people of authority and a need for attention. When threats are carried out, there are many emotions that operate on the individual (s) enacting that threat. Some common emotions include "love; hate; fear; rage; or desire for attention, revenge, excitement, or recognition" (p. 6). Despite the fact that the above factors may be at play, one cannot confirm with surety about what motivates an individual to carry out threats. When a threat is brought about, it is assumed that it is also a reflection of the state of mind of the individual and one must remember that an individual's frame of mind is not a permanent condition is subject to change and can be influenced by factors like alcohol and drugs (O'Toole, 2008).

4. *Harassment and Stalking*

An understanding of why an individual would harass and stalk another might be best explained by the two concepts listed below:

(a) Predatory-related violence and crime
(b) Dispute-related violence and crime (Felson, 2009)

How an individual perceives the hurt inflicted on another is dependent on whether the act is "predatory-related" or "dispute-related" crime (p. 7). Although these two notions sit well assaults and homicide, they can also be applied to what might lead to harassment and stalking. Dispute-related crimes have 'harming the other' as the focus of the act. If there is a contention between two individuals and if one of them might want to 'settle scores' with the other, this would be a method to adopt because in these crimes suffering of the victim is essential. In the predatory-related violence, the ultimate goal is not to cause harm to the victim but in the process they do not shy away from causing harm to the victim if it helps to serve their purpose. The role of mass media that portrays crime as something enticing and enthralling plays a significant role in promoting crimes like harassment and stalking though studies on this stance have mixed opinions. In a study on the effects of media on crime, the results indicated that even if media covers and depicts violent crimes, it does not necessarily promote or bring about an increase in crimes of violence, and the vice versa held true too, showing that an increase in crime rate does not reflect upon the increase in media coverage and if at all it does, it is insignificant (Rios, 2018).

5. *Abduction and Kidnapping*

In their paper on abduction of children, Miller et al. (2008) found that most of the time abductions are closely connected to divorce and subsequent custodial issues as family members appear to be the main perpetrators. They citing Finkelhor et al., (1991) identified the probable factors that might incite a family member (s) to carry out abduction and those were the decisions and insecurities around custodial rights that impacted the family life, alleged abuse on and by family members, and out of vengeance against previous partners.

Another factor that could explain why abductions happen might be poverty and unemployment. Poverty and unemployment have a cyclical relationship and the common understanding is that poverty follows unemployment and vice versa. Yaacoub (2017) citing Taylor (2000) explained the relationship between crime and poverty. Poverty reinforces crimes like robbery as it appears more feasible to steal and earn a living that way rather than be employed and sustain a job. At the same time, unemployment and homelessness may create frustration and dissension in society. Under such circumstances, abductions and kidnappings provide one with a relatively easy method to earn some money and therefore the temptation might be difficult to resist. It is not always that abductions or kidnappings end up with fatal consequences. Yet another contributing factor could be inadequate and compromised education. Poor judgment is usually a consequence of poor education and hence impaired decision-making skills. Such individuals tend to commit crimes either knowingly or unknowingly.

6. *Sexual Offences*

Sexual offences, in particular rape, assume certain characteristics of the offenders thereby predicting the motives behind the acts. Savino and Turvey (2004) uncovered some of these myths and by doing so also challenged some of the apparent causes that drive one to commit rape. One of the misconceptions around rape is its association with the fulfilment of sexual desires and also those uncontrollable sexual impulses drive one to rape. One more is the assumption that rapists are strangers. Yet, another challenged the myth that rapists are loners. One of the most significant causes of sexual offences constitutes the family and the familial climate around it. A family can be defined as a fundamental unit of kinship comprised of a group of individuals who are related to each other by blood, marriage, adoption or any other intimate bond (APA Dictionary of Psychology, n.d.). The definition clearly indicates the closeness and proximity of the members of a family and thereby the influence that these affiliations may have on the members. Family dysfunction that involves violence and crime has shown to have an adverse effect on individuals. The transition from the state of 'abused to abusing' is a common phenomenon seen amongst sex offenders (in particular, children) exposed to family dysfunctionality and violence. Krug et al. (2002) identified the factors that may put an individual at risk of and to commit sexual violence by categorizing them into two – one was concerned with the elements that are crucial in making women more vulnerable to sexual violence and the other looked at the factors that could lead men to rape. The factors that increased women's vulnerability to sexual violence included marriage and cohabitation, age, alcohol or drug consumption, previous sexual abuse or rape, multiple sexual partners, education and financial stability, participation in commercial sex, and poverty. The conditions that make men susceptible to rape have four components – individual, relationship, community, and societal under which are the determinants that increase the risk of committing rape.

7. *Other Offences*

Murder and ManslaRace and ethnicity have been found to contribute to criminal activities in those regions, particularly when it involves migration and immigration. This again is closely related to unemployment and poverty. Another aspect involves discrimination on the basis of race. Such discrimination that tends to create a racial superiority or inferiority complex can trigger feelings of aggression, hostility, depression and may sow seeds of discontent and disharmony. It has been reported that individuals experiencing racial discrimination are more likely to commit crime and that such discrimination can cause distress, have depressive effects, cause disengagement from social norms and can augment hostile views and behaviour (Burt, Simons & Gibbons, 2012).

Crimes Against Persons: Theories that Attempt to Explain Why a Human Hurts Another Human

1. *Biological Theories*

   Biological theories that explain why people commit crimes against other people look at the biological make of a human being and that includes the aspects of the physical body like facial structures, body shape, and so on. The proponent of this theory was Cesare Lombroso, who in the early years of the nineteenth century studied criminality from this point of view (Biological positivism). His contention was that an individual was "born" a criminal (The Scottish Centre for Crime and Justice Research (SCCJR), 2016, p. 2). This stance did not keep up with the newer theories that introduced elements making theories appear more plausible. Over time, biological theories expanded and began to probe into the "physiological, neurological and biochemical" determinants along with the genetic composition of human beings (Klimczuk, 2015). The biological theories of crime causation may potentially provide a reasonable explanation for crimes that people commit against other people. This is because an integral part of these theories addresses mental illness, primarily personality disorders. There are disorders that are genetically carried while some others are acquired. Crimes like assault and stalking another may be committed by individuals with mental illness for such individuals may have a diminished capacity to understand the consequences of their actions. This is important to note since biological theories also consider the concept of intelligence and levels of mental development as a causative factor of crime. Numerous studies conducted on families, twins and adoption have proved the influence of chromosomal abnormalities, the interplay of genes and the environment, brain injuries and foetal anomalies on the commission of crimes. In such a case, when an individual bearing such characteristics harms another individual, it might be assumed as accidental and with no intention to hurt. In their paper on abduction of children Miller et al. (2008) found that most of the time abductions are closely connected to divorce and subsequent custodial issues as family members appear to be the main perpetrators. Citing Finkelhor et al. (1991), they identified the probable factors that might incite a family member (s) to carry out abduction and those were the decisions and insecurities around custodial rights that impacted the family life, alleged abuse on and by family members, and out of vengeance against previous partners.

2. *Rational Choice Theory*

   This theory plays an important role in comprehending the reasons behind violence of humans on humans, especially crimes like homicide and assault. The rational choice theory is considered an offspring of the Right Realism of the 1980s USA and UK ((The Scottish Centre for Crime and Justice Research (SCCJR), 2016). Every individual is a rational being and is capable of making choices based the understanding of the possible consequences of those choices (Walsh and Ellis, 2007) and this is the crux of right realism. Rational choice theory, however, adds the element of actively 'choosing to commit a crime'; an idea posited by Cornish and Clarke that they called "choice structuring" and defined as "the constellation of opportunities, costs, and benefits attaching to particular kinds of crime" (Cornish & Clarke, 1987, p. 933, as cited by Walsh & Ellis, 2007). This theory appears to justify the offensive acts of individuals against others since those acts simply become a manifestation of the choices made by the individual after careful consideration of the outcomes of that choice. Thus, if an individual commits a homicide, it would be because he/she made a conscious choice to do it regardless of the reasons supporting or disagreeing with the choice.

3. *Left Realism/Relative Deprivation*

Left realism, like right realism, originated in the USA and the UK around the 1980s. Left realism, headed by Lea and Young and Elliot Currie in the mid-1980s believed that crime hugely affected the lives of the underprivileged. There are three notions that followers of this theory subscribe to:

(a) Relative deprivation
(b) Marginalization
(c) Subcultures (The Scottish Centre for Crime and Justice Research (SCCJR), 2016)

They described these concepts as vital to understanding the reason why certain classes or sections of people of a society are assumably inclined towards criminal activities or deviance. Relative deprivation speaks about the imbalance between the perception that one might have of a situation and its reality that creates a feeling of frustration and resentment (Džuverović, 2013). The role of poverty and unemployment may lead affected individuals to commit crimes like abduction and harassment. Criminal behaviour is mostly seen in the "lower" and "underclass" communities. Children from these sections of the society engage in criminal activities ('delinquent subculture') as a way to compensate for their failures and being discriminated upon. Adults may resort to crimes like sex trafficking, carry out paid assassinations, and abductions. Poverty might also drive one to kill one's own flesh and blood if one cannot afford to 'feed another mouth' (example of infanticide). Hate crimes may also be committed by individuals who feel discriminated against, and this discrimination could be based on race or ethnicity as well (Siegel, 2010).

4. *Social Learning Theories*

The social learning approach first emerged out of the studies done by Albert Bandura (1977–2021). He did not acknowledge the notions of learning as propounded by both classical and operant conditioning, and instead surmised that children learn the basics of behaviour and develop their perspectives mostly through observing and imitating the people around them, particularly the elders. Therefore, parents and other elders' behaviours and attitudes have a significant influence and impact on the youngsters who watch them and emulate their actions. Thus, Bandura's theory, later called Social Cognitive theory (Bandura,

1986 as cited by Moore, 2011), postulates that behaviour is a combination of three factors at play – observation, environment and behaviours (of others). According to this premise, behaviour that is "deviant, criminal or delinquent" in nature is a manifestation of these causative factors (Moore, 2011, p. 229). Social learning theories are seen to be at play mostly in the homes where violence is to be found. The above-mentioned factors of observation, environment and behaviours are predominantly seen with children or juvenile offenders or adults who have lived through a childhood having observed violence or criminal behaviour in the house. This theory can thus have a bearing on sexual offenders (who are adults) and juvenile offenders who may harass, bully or threaten others (Akers et al., 1979; Klimczuk, 2015).

Differential Association theory, built on the foundations of the learning theories, was introduced by Edwin Sutherland and its focus was primarily on the explanation of "individual criminality" and "aggregate crime rates" and to ascertain the circumstances that lead to the prevalence of crime or the absence thereof (Walsh & Ellis, 2007). Sutherland's theory is one of the first theories that viewed criminal conduct as an act that is learned from individuals who embody the very principles of criminal and deviant behaviour. When this theory is applied to individuals living in 'crime-infested' neighbourhoods with a lack of educational and occupational prospects, to assume that such individuals might have a tendency to commit crimes that affect other persons may be allowed. For example, gang members who undertake killings or abductions to 'earn a few bucks', or assault people if required, during 'mugging' seem to hint at the likelihood of such individuals hurting and harming others either as a means to an end or to achieve a goal. In fact, the theory states that not only is crime learned (how to commit a crime) but the justification behind it is also learned (why to commit a crime) from the others who influence that learning (Tibbetts, 2019). According to Jeffrey (1965), one of the concerns posed by Sutherland's theory is to identify what exactly constitutes the environmental factors that work as reinforcing reasons for criminal behaviour because other factors such as gratification (sex) and materialistic objects also appear to operate as causative factors of crime in a society. This would explain the existence of criminals who have had no association with criminals and vice versa and also why the theory's credibility was problematic since it could not precisely explain how criminal behaviour was learnt (Ward & Brown, 2015).

Social Learning theory (SLT) or as it is called now, the "social structure social learning theory" (Opp, 2020) was proposed by Robert Burgess and Ronald Akers (as cited in Ward & Brown, 2015). Initially known as the differential association reinforcement theory, it was an extension of Sutherland's theory of differential association the crux of which was that criminal and delinquent behaviour is learned by way of association with individuals who possess those very characteristics. Their theory put forward the perspective of the significance of the "learning content" as against the "learning process" in making the distinction between non-conforming and conforming behaviour (Ward & Brown, 2015, p. 410). A study of Akers theory brought to light the foundations on which the theory sits and its scope in providing answers to explain both non-compliant and compliant behaviour (Akers, Ronald L.: Social Learning Theory, n.d.). The focus of Akers' theory was the acknowledgment of the population of people who condone criminal and deviant behaviour as well as those who do not. This is because the two opposing types of people provide their respective views on their assertions, theories and/or perspectives. A significant outcome of the theory was the assertion that simply by virtue of affiliation with a 'criminal', it cannot be presumed that one will imbibe those very qualities of deviance because there are many other factors at play and those cannot be overlooked. In fact, deviant behaviour showed a tendency to increase when the "social and non-social reinforcement exceeded the social and non-social punishment of the behaviour" (p. 24). Akers' studies revealed that the theory had an advantage over the other social learning theories in its ability to "predict proclivity to use sexual aggression, actual use of physical sexual coercion, use of drugs and alcohol as a coercive strategy, and use of other nonphysical coercive strategies (p. 27)". Social learning theories thus, provide the much-needed clarity required to uncover unlawful behaviour.

5. *Personality Theories*

Moore (2011) who studied the different psychological theories associated with criminal behaviour surmised that theories of personality traits that explain criminal behaviour and delinquency do so by approaching the two as being a reflection of some "internal pathology". There were two distinct theories that were discussed. The first was Frued's psychodynamic theory that was able to explain delinquent behaviour as a result of instability between the id working on instincts, the ego operating on the reality principle, and the superego functioning around the moral compass of an individual and then, in an attempt to strike a balance between all three, adopts certain coping mechanisms called defence mechanisms (Siegel, Welsh, & Senna, 2006; Shoemaker, 2005) that can and sometimes do lead to problem behaviours. These malfunctioning behaviours could manifest itself as delinquency and other criminal behaviour. An individual hurting another individual might then simply be a reflection of one's inner hurt or distress.

Walsh and Ellis (2007) noted the following personality traits and characteristics responsible for criminal behaviour:

(a) Impulsiveness
(b) Negative emotionality
(c) Sensation-seeking
(d) Conscientiousness
(e) Empathy
(f) Altruism
(g) Moral reasoning (pp. 176–179)

Eysenck and Gudjonsson (1989) surmised that the concept of personality can be understood only when both its aspects are taken into consideration – ability and temperament for which they referred to ability in the context of general intelligence otherwise known as Spearman's g. For temperament, they put forward the components of Eysenck's personality structure (H. J. Eysenck, 1970; H. J. Eysenck, 1981; H. J. Eysenck & M. W. Eysenck, 1985 as cited in Eysenck and Gudjonsson, 1989) – psychoticism (P), neuroticism (N), introversion-extraversion (E). The theory posits that there is a positive and causative relationship between "criminality and antisocial conduct" high levels of psychoticism, high extraversion, and high neuroticism (p 55). Eysenck (1996) put forward the traits that were used to define psychoticism, extraversion, neuroticism in the following ways – "aggressive, cold, egocentric impersonal, impulsive, antisocial, unempathic, creative, and tough minded; sociable, lively, active, assertive, sensation-seeking, carefree, dominant, surgent, and venturesome; and anxious, depressed, guilt feelings, low self-esteem, tense, irrational, shy, moody, emotional" respectively (pp. 145–146).

Intelligence is considered as a determiner of criminal behaviour as suggested by Eysenck and Gudjonsson (1989). He believed that a high IQ (Intelligence Quotient) in individuals' words as an inhibitor to criminal or deviant conduct. This is because such people are better equipped to be successful in life in comparison to an individual with low IQ who may find it difficult to be in the same footing due to the deficiencies in education that work as a roadblock to achieving a successful life. It might be easier for the former to possess impressive academic credentials and get into respectably well-paying professions but the latter, because of the low IQ, may not get such opportunities and thereby look at other ways to live the same 'good life'. This is not to say that people with high IQs do not commit unlawful acts and in fact, when they do their chances of being caught are much less than those with low IQs. They surmised that even though intelligence plays a role in explaining criminal behaviour, it is not as significant as one would think it to be. It may thus be understood that any causal link between IQ and delinquent and adult criminal behaviour is in all likelihood "indirect" (Moore, 2011; Kendel et al., 1988).

The face of crime appears to be ever-evolving and that poses as both a challenge and an advantage for research and study to evolve accordingly in their approach to examine the theories and antecedents of criminal and deviant behaviour in individuals, juveniles as well as adults. This in turn creates a pool of individuals who become the unwilling recipients of such crimes. An inclusive commentary on these individuals who are called the 'victims of crime' is elaborated in the section below.

Victims of Crime: Who Are They?

The reasons to explain and comprehend why an individual or a group of individuals would want to hurt or harm another are certainly imperative to know but it is as essential and critical to recognize the other side of the story as well – the victim.

Exploring the varied facets that influence an individual to become a victim or make an individual vulnerable to becoming one is essential to protect this category of affected individuals as there is a compelling indication that certain people in comparison to other individuals seem to be more prone to becoming a victim of violence, crime, or accidents, including those that are natural calamities (Dillenburger, 2007). This section of the chapter takes an elaborate look into the victim perspective.

Victims of crime are individuals who may experience hurt – physical, emotional, financial, psychological or/and even a curtailment of the freedom and liberty that is fundamental to them. This might happen when a person or collectively a group persons commit crimes, and thereby 'break the law' by committing an act that is in gross violation of the law or by wilfully disregarding that which is instructed by the law (Declaration of Basic Principles of Justice for Victims of Crime and Abuse of Power, 1985). The different aspects that are studied in crime victims are their individual characteristics, their behaviour, their environment and demographics, the association between the victim and the perpetrator, the victim's part, if any, in the crime, along with customs, norms, rules including value systems of a society that the victim and perpetrator belong to, the effects of the crime on the victim, and profiling (Sergianni, 2012; Dillenburger, 2007).

Risk Factors for Victimization: What Makes an Individual Vulnerable to Being a Victim of Crime

One of the key areas of victimology is to examine the factors that make an individual or a group of individuals susceptible to becoming a victim of a crime or a violent attack. Ibrahimi, Marinescu, Ibrahimi, and Luciani (2018) categorised certain elements that may work as both risk and protective factors for the victims of crime:

- Individual protection factors
- Family protection factors
- Extra family protection factors
- Flexibility factors (para. 22–25)

The above-mentioned classification includes individual elements like "temperament, ability to reflect, cognitive attitudes" (para. 22), and family components like the ability of family members to express emotions like warmth and compassion, the interpersonal relationships amongst them, and their influence on a victim. They (Ibrahimi et al., 2018) also added an additional protective element provided by the family that included members who are not related by blood but form the social support system. Flexibility factors take into consideration the role of a victim's tenacity and coping to deal with the stressful experiences and bearing in mind the role of the physical, psychosocial, environmental elements in the victim's life.

Apart from the categories mentioned there is another multi-factors list which influence the risk of victimization (CDC, 2008a; Crandall, et al., 2004; Heise ND Garcia-Moreno, 2002; Tjaden & Thoennes, 2000 as cited in Domestic Violence/ Intimate Partner Violence: Applying Best Practice Guidelines, n.d.). They are listed below as:

1. "Individual Factors:

   - Prior history of DV/IPV (domestic violence/intimate partner violence).
   - Gender.
   - Young age.
   - Heavy alcohol and drug use.
   - High-risk sexual behaviour.
   - Childhood experiences of witnessing or being the recipient of violence.
   - Being less educated.
   - Unemployment.
   - In the case of men, differences in ethnicity in partners appear as a factor.
   - For women, level of education plays a role particularly if it is higher than that of their partner.
   - For women, being American Indian/Alaska Native or African American.
   - With regard to women, the presence of a partner displaying verbally abusive behaviour, jealousy and possessiveness seem to increase the risk.

2. Relationship Factors

   - Partners who have differences in their financial, educational or professional standings
   - An imbalance of power and control in the relationship with one partner dominating

3. Community Factors

   - Poverty and associated factors (e.g. overcrowding).
   - When there is a reduced degree of social capital in terms of an absence or dearth of institutions or relationships or principles of social behaviour that are responsible for establishing healthy social interactions (both qualitatively and quantitatively) within a community, it can work as a potential risk factor.
   - Domestic Violence and/or Intimate Partner Violence do not always have strong community sanctions. and this is sometimes seen in the unwillingness of the police to intervene and take action.

4. Societal Factors

   - Patriarchal gender norms (e.g. women should stay at home, not enter work-force, should be submissive) (p. 20)

Interventions for Victims and Perpetrators of Personal Crime

"Victim Assistance, Support or Services" was a term given by Dussich (2006) referring to practices in response to victimizations with the sole purpose of alleviating victim suffering and facilitating recovery. These activities included here were extending information to all the concerned individuals, conducting assessments, designing individual interventions, along with case and system advocacies, public policies and programmes and overseeing their growth.

Interventions for Victims of Crime

Interventions for victims of crime go beyond the traditional subdivision between criminal and general victimology. There is another field of thought and of the victim profiling movement established that deals with the prevention, care, mitigation and minimization of the victimization effects on the victim from a physical, psychological, and social point of view (Ibrahimi et al., 2018). They were referring to what Van Dijk (1997) termed as "assistance-oriented victimology"(p. 5) wherein he was primarily concerned with the clinical approach to the victims. He believed that the effects of victimization can be assessed in the results of post-traumatic stress disorder as victimology has to deal with the diagnosis, prevention and treatment of its effects.

Clinical victimology has its greatest model in Gérard Lopez. His object of study focussed on the following aspects (Lopez-Bornstein, 1995, as cited in Ibrahimi et al., 2018):

(a) The medical-psychosocial consequences of the victimization process
(b) The treatment of complications
(c) The assessment done medically and pedagogically of the degree of damage inflicted for purposes of compensation in the court

They identified the physical and psychological injuries and the corresponding complications that may derive from it for each type of victim (of crime or catastrophes or accidents). In addition to the consequences and complications of a physical and psycho-traumatic nature, there are economic consequences and relations with the criminal justice system coupled with several social consequences, which may or may not be related to the post-traumatic stress disorder, such as difficulties in family relationships, degradation of intimate relationships of couples, professional work, and so on (Lopez-Bornstein, 1995, as cited in Ibrahimi et al., 2018).

To summarize, it would be acceptable to state that what a victim of a crime requires is the fulfilment of the basic human need for safety and security – physical, emotional, and psychosocial. One of the ways to achieve this for victims is to be able to express themselves without the fear of judgment and consequent secondary victimization that might sometimes be seen during the investigative and legal process, overwhelming media coverage, to cite a few examples (Canadian Resource Centre for Victims of Crime, 2005).

Interventions for Perpetrators of Crime

The National Research Council in their book, *Service Provider Perspectives on Family Violence Interventions* (1995) explains that the treatment, control, and punishment of offenders who engage in child abuse, intimate violence, or elder abuse have been affected by the legal and social services function in American society causing discrepancies and disruptions in setting standards. It is seen that while certain forms of assault as a crime are categorized within criminal law where victims may claim protection from law enforcement agencies, in other areas laws that address criminals are far and few between or are undecided.

The line of competent treatment and management of such offenses may require therapeutic or educational interventions. The focus in such cases would be on altering or modifying the parent or caretaker's perceptions or expectations of the child's behaviour. An attempt to distinguish between a behaviour that is abusive and originating from "ignorance or inappropriate perceptions" and those that are defined by ambitions to "harm a child" might be a daunting task both for the people who work with such victims and other public officials (National Research Council, 1995, p. 65).

Offenders' treatment programs have evolved over the years and have seen its presence in a wide range of environs like mental health services and law enforcement settings for assaulters and sexual offenders. This is also witnessed in social service agencies that tend to physically abusive or neglectful parents. The interventions for offenders employ a wide range of conceptual models, including cognitive, psychoeducational, therapeutic, use of medications, lie detectors, deterrence, and other systems, that work as control or monitoring mechanisms to help determine and identify and rehabilitate offenders (National Research Council, 1995).

Associated Methods of Investigation Used in the Forensic Investigations of Personal Crime

Victimology is an essential component in the crime scene analysis and related to the Criminal Profiling process. Criminal profiling can be understood as a tool to aid an investigation that makes use of the available information regarding an offence and crime scene and finally puts together a "psychosomatic representation" of the mastermind recognized behind the crime (Douglas & Olshaker, 1995 cited in Abumere, 2012, p. 1). The task of a criminal profiler and crime scene analyst would thus be to offer their expertise in the forensic examination and investigation of crimes and integrate the acquired information in the study of victims. This can be done through assistance in the analysis of modus operandi or MO, case linkage, or motivational analysis or simply to provide their impression of the victim's risk factors and/or their vulnerabilities to different types of harm or loss. An essential requirement while incorporating victimology during investigative purposes is victim history. Neglecting or undermining the importance of victim history, in part or whole, results in lacunae in the investigative and factual records that will make victim-related interpretation incomplete, if not inaccurate (Turvey, 2014).

Criminal profiling is typically used with the help of victimology and crime scene analysis with serious crimes like serial crimes, murders or rape were identity of criminals. The effectiveness of a criminal profile may be questioned in its accuracy or assistance to enforcement agencies as sometimes it might inadequately mislead the police, in ways that might give a criminal more time to escape detection, and as a consequence, the death of an innocent person may be witnessed. However, this does not imply that profiles should be ignored or should never be used by police again, but that profiling should be approached with caution (Abumere, 2012).

Yet another method that is used as an investigative tool is psychological autopsy. In the field of forensic science and forensic psychology, it helps the criminal justice system in examining deaths that are uncertain and in victimology while working with the assumption that everybody's "psychic life" leaves behind certain imprints, through "documents, the place where he/she lived, the subject's interaction to others" (Perez Delgado, Parra, Munoz Valero, & Perdomo Espinoza, 2015, para. 16). It is believed that initial contributions to such examinations were made by Shneidman and Farberow at the Los Angeles Suicide Prevention Centre during the 1950s wherein they defined psychological autopsy as a "retrospective reconstruction" of the life of an individual where the core emphasis is on "lethality", a term that explains those features of the individual that decode the intentions of that person's related to his/her own demise. It also offers cues with regard to the type of death and the degree (if any) of his/her contribution in his/her own death, and the explanation regarding the time of death (Shneidman and Farberow, 1961, p. 51 as cited in Canter, 2000). Psychological autopsy is a technique that entails reviewing the psychological aspects of a victim's life. It a procedure that aids in the investigation of the nature of a death, in particular the psychological aspects and what is known as "equivocal deaths" – understood as situations that do not directly ascertain the cause or intention of death, like accidents, suicide, or an unknown/ undetermined cause and involves a reconstruction of the deceased's life (Knoll, 2008; Shneidman, 1981). This technique that uses interviews and examination documents to recreate the behaviour, personality, lifestyle, habits and history of the victim prior to death can also effectively decipher the victim's psychological intent and motives. Psychological autopsy as an investigative tool is not without its limitations and does face challenges with regard to its validity and reliability. Notwithstanding, numerous courts in the USA have considered the expertise of psychologists and other professionals working with mental health in making their judgments and decisions.

Conclusion

Victims of crime can be considered as comprising one of the most fragile sections of a society and therefore working with them and for them requires expertise and the use of constructive investigative tools. The perception towards victims and the notion of victimology cannot be based simply on the portrayal done by media or public attitude. It is imperative to understand where a victim of crime comes from, what a victim undergoes, what they do, how to deal with their experiences, and where does a victim of crime wish to go from there. All of this needs to be done with utmost caution and sensitivity and the best possible approach is multidisciplinary as it involves teamwork that works holistically for the victim and the perpetrators of crime as one cannot exclude them from the study of these victims.

References

Abumere, F. I. (2012). *Effectiveness of criminal profiling*. uPublish.Info. https://www.academia.edu/2333675/Effectiveness_of_Criminal_Profiling

Access Continuing Education Inc. (n.d.). *Domestic Violence/Intimate Partner Violence: Applying Best Practice Guidelines*. https://www.accesscontinuingeducation.com/ACE4000-09/coursebook.pdf

Aghatise, J. (2006). *Cybercrime definition*. Cyber Crime.

Akers, R. L. (n.d.). *Social learning theory*. http://faculty.washington.edu/matsueda/courses/401D/Readings/Akers.pdf

Akers, R. L., Krohn, M. D., Lanza-Kaduce, L. & Radosevich, M. (1979). Social learning and deviant behaviour: A specific test of a general theory. *American Sociological Review, 44(4), 636–655*.

Allen, J. J., Anderson, C. A., & Bushman, B. J. (2018). The general aggression model. *Current Opinion in Psychology, 19*, 75–80. https://doi.org/10.1016/j.copsyc.2017.03.034

Allen, M., & Rotenberg, C. (2021). Crimes related to the sex trade: Before and after legislative changes in Canada. *Juristat, 41*(1), 1–29.

Anderson, C. A., & Bushman, B. J. (2002). Human aggression. *Annual Review of Psychology, 53*, 27–51.

Bada, M., & Nurse, J. R. C. (2019). The social and psychological impact of cyber-attacks. In V. Benson & J. Mcalaney (Eds.), *Emerging cyber threats and cognitive vulnerabilities*. Academic Press Inc.

Balfour, R., & Allen, J. (2014). *A review of the literature on sex workers and social exclusion*. University College London. Institute of Health Equity. Retrieved from https://assets.publishing.service.gov.uk/government/uploads/system/uploads/attachment_data/file/303927/A_Review_of_the_Literature_on_sex_workers_and_social_exclusion.pdf

Bandura, A. (1978). Social learning theory of aggression. *Journal of Communication, 28*(3), 12–29. https://doi.org/10.1111/j.1460-2466.1978.tb01621.x

Barlow, H. D. & Kauzlarich, D. (2010). *Explaining Crime. A Primer in Criminological Theory. Rowman & Littlefield Publishers, Inc.*

Berkowitz, L. (1989). Frustration-aggression hypothesis: Examination and reformulation. *Psychological Bulletin, 106*(1), 59–73.

Britannica, T. Editors of Encyclopaedia (2022, May 26). Homicide. *Encyclopedia Britannica*. https://www.britannica.com/topic/homicide

Brookman, F. (2010). Homicide. In F. Brookman, M. Maguire, T. Bennett, & H. Pierpoint (Eds.), *The handbook of crime*. Willan.

Burt, C. H., Simons, R. L. & Gibbons, F. X. (2012). Racial discrimination, ethnic-racial socialization, and crime: A micro-sociological model of risk and resilience. *American Sociological Review, 77(4), 648–677*. https://doi.org/10.1177/0003122412448648

Buss, D. M. (2012). The evolutionary psychology of crime. *Journal of Theoretical and Philosophical Criminology, 1*(1), 90–98.

Canadian Resource Centre for Victims of Crime. (2005). *The impact of victimization*. Retrieved from https://www.crcvc.ca/docs/victimization.pdf

Canter, D. V. (2000). Psychological autopsies. In *Encyclopedia of forensic sciences*. Elsevier.

Columbia Law Review. (1930). The distinction between "Mala Prohibita" and "Mala in se" in criminal law. *Criminal Law Review Association, 30*(1), 74–86.

Condirston, E. (2011). *Traditional crime vs. corporate crime: A comparative risk discourse analysis* [Master's thesis, The University of Ottawa]. Retrieved from https://ruor.uottawa.ca/bitstream/10393/20315/1/Condirston_Erin_2011_thesis.pdf

Clinard, M. B., Yeager, P. C., Brissette, J., Petrashek, D., & Harries, E. (1979). *Illegal corporate behavior*. The Law Enforcement Assistance Administration.

Clinard, M. B., & Yeager, P. C. (1978). Corporate crime. Issues in research. *Criminology, 16*(2), 255–272.

Department of Justice, Canada. (2003) *Stalking is a crime called criminal harassment*. https://www.justice.gc.ca/eng/rp-pr/cj-jp/fv-vf/stalk-harc/pdf/har_e-har_a.pdf

Dillenburger, K. (2007). A behaviour analytic perspective on victimology. *International Journal of Behavioral Consultation and Therapy, 3*(3), 433–448.

Dussich, J. P. J. (2006). Victimology – Past, present and future. *131st International Senior Seminar Visiting Experts' Papers*, pp. 116–129.

Džuverović, N. (2013). Does more (or less) lead to violence? Application of the relative deprivation hypothesis on economic equality – Induced conflicts. *CIRR, XIX*(68), 115–132.

Eysenck, H. J. (1996). Personality and crime: Where do we stand. Psychology, *Crime & Law, 2, 143–152*.

Eysenck, H. J. & Gudjonsson, G. H. (1989). *The causes and cures of criminality*. New York: Plenum Press.

FBI Releases its 2006 Crime Statistics. (n.d.). FBI. Retrieved September 20, 2022, from https://archives.fbi.gov/archives/news/pressrel/press-releases/fbi-releases-its-2006-crime-statistics

Federal Bureau of Investigation. (2004). *Uniform Crime Reporting Handbook. U.S Department of Justice*. https://ucr.fbi.gov/additional-ucr-publications/ucr_handbook.pdf.

Felson, R. (2009). Violence, crime, and violent crime. *International Journal of Conflict and Violence, 3(1), 1–16*.

Finkelhor, D., Hotaling, G., & Sedlak, A. (1991). Children abducted by family members: A national household survey of incidence and episode characteristics. *Journal of Marriage and the Family, 53*(3), 805–817. https://psycnet.apa.org/doi/10.2307/352753

Fort Peck Tribal Court. (2019). *Fort peck tribes comprehensive code of justice* (p. 4).

Fletcher, R. (2019). Victimless crime. *Criminology*. https://doi.org/10.1093/OBO/9780195396607-0272

General Assembly resolution 40/34. (1985, November 29). *Declaration of basic principles of justice for victims of crime and abuse of power*. Retrieved from https://www.un.org/en/genocideprevention/documents/atrocity-crimes/Doc.29_declaration%20victims%20crime%20and%20abuse%20of%20power.pdf

Gray, R. L. (1995). Eliminating the (absurd) distinction between malum in se and malum prohibitum crimes. *Washington University Law Review, 73*(3), 1369–1398.

Green, S. P. (2015). What are sexual offences. In C. Flanders & Z. Hoskins (Eds.), *The new philosophy of criminal law* (pp. 61–80). Rowman and Littlefield.

Heckels, V., & Roberts, K. (2010). Stalking and harassment. In Brookman et al. (Eds.), *Handbook of crime*. Palgrave Macmillan.

Home Office Counting Rules for Recorded Crime. (2021). *Violence against the person*. Home Office. United Nations Office on Drugs and Crime.

Hossain, M. B., & Rahi, S. T. (2018). Murder: A critical analysis of the common law definition. *Beijing Law Review, 9*, 460–480. https://doi.org/10.4236/blr.2018.93028

Ibrahimi, S., Marinescu, V. E., Ibrahimi, E., & Luciani, E. (2018, November). Forensic victimology: A step forward the psychosocial profile of victimology. In *International Conference on Social Sciences and Humanities (p. 1)*.

International Labour Organization. (1988). Criminal Offences Act. *Tonga*. Retrieved from https://www.ilo.org/dyn/natlex/docs/ELECTRONIC/73337/95725/F665862081/TON73337.pdf

Interpol. (2020). *Cybercrime: Covid-19 impact*. Interpol General Secretariat.

Jeffrey, C. R. (1965). Criminal behaviour and learning theory. *Journal of Criminal Law and Criminology, 56*(3), 294–300.

Jubaer, S. M. O. F., Hoque, L., Rahman, F., Moumi, A., & Deb, B. (2021). Victimless crime and victimology under different national legal system: A global approach. *European Scholar Journal, 2*(5), 6–16.

Kendel, E., Mednick, S., Kirkegaard-Sorensen, L., Hutchings, B., Rosenberg, R., & Schulsinger, F. (1988). IQ as a potential factor for subjects at high risk for antisocial behaviour. *Journal of Counselling and Clinical Psychology, 56*, 224–226.

Khader, M. (2019). *Crime and behaviour. An introduction to criminal and forensic psychology*. Nanyang Technological University, Singapore Home Team Behavioural Sciences Center, Singapore.

Klimczuk, A. (2015). Causes of crime. In F. F. Wherry (Ed.), *The Sage encyclopedia of economics and society* (pp. 308–311). Sage Publications. https://doi.org/10.4135/9781452206905.n128

Knoll, J. L. (2008). The psychological autopsy, part I: Applications and methods. *Journal of Psychiatric Practice, 14(6), 393–397*.

Krug, E. G., Dahlberg, L. L., Mercy, J. A., Zwi, A. B., & Lozano, R. (2002). *World report on violence and health*. World Health Organization, Geneva. http://apps.who.int/iris/bitstream/handle/10665/42495/9241545615_eng.pdf

Law Reform Commission. (2008, January). *Homicide: Murder and involuntary manslaughter*.

Lester, H. (1924). Report upon classification of crimes. *Journal of Criminal Law and Criminology, 14*(4), 593–604.

Lobingier, S. C. (1919). Homicide concept. *Journal of Criminal Law and Criminology, 9*(3), 373–377.

Lu, Y. (2016). Socrates, crime, and punishment. *Rerum Causae, 8*(2), 50–57.

Lunden, W. A. (1958). Pioneers in criminology XVI – Emile Durkheim (1858–1917). *Journal of Criminal Law and Criminology, 49*(1).

Mac Donald, J. W. (1933). Classification of crimes. *Cornell Law Review, 4*(7), 524–563.

Mallory, S. L. (2012). An introduction to organized crime. In *Understanding organized crime*. Jones and Bartlett Learning.

Mellor, L. (1982). In J. Swart & L. Mellor (Eds.), *Homicide. A forensic psychology casebook*. CRC Press.

Meloy, J. R. (1999). Stalking: An old behaviour, a new crime. *Psychiatric Clinics of North America, 22*(1), 85–99. https://psycnet.apa.org/doi/10.1016/S0193-953X(05)70061-7

Merriam-Webster. (n.d.). Crime. In *Merriam-Webster.com dictionary. Retrieved March 30, 2022, from* https://www.merriam-webster.com/dictionary/crime

Miller, J. M., Kurlycheck, M., Hansen, J. A., & Wilson, K. (2008). Examining child abduction by offender type patterns. *Justice Quarterly, 25*(3), 523–543.

Ministry of Justice. (2012). *Help starts here. Information on stalking (Criminal harassment)*. British Columbia.

Mitchell, B., & Mackay, R. D. (2010). Investigating involuntary manslaughter: An empirical study of 127 cases. *Oxford Journal of Legal Studies, 1–27*. https://doi.org/10.1093/ojls/gqq034

Moore, M. (2011). Psychological theories of crime and delinquency. *Journal of Human Behavior in the Social Environment, 21*(3), 226–239. https://doi.org/10.1080/10911359.2011.564552

Morrall, P. (2006). Murder and society: Why commit murder? *Criminal Justice Matters, 66*(1), 36–37. https://doi.org/10.1080/09627250608553401

National Research Council. (1995). Treatment of offenders. In *Service provider perspectives on family violence interventions*. The National Academies Press. https://doi.org/10.17226/9053

Opp, K.-D. (2020). The concept of crime, the definition of "theory", and the characteristics of a good theory. *Analytical Criminology*, 6–20. https://doi.org/10.4324/9780429026980-2

O'Toole, M. E., National Center for the Analysis of Violent Crime (US), & Critical Incident Response Group. (2008). *The school shooter: A threat assessment perspective*. Critical Incident Response Group (CIRG), National Center for the Analysis of Violent Crime (NCAVC), FBI Academy.

Perez Delgado, W., Parra, I. L., Munoz Valero, C., & Perdomo Espinoza, A. (2015). Biopsychosocial autopsy: Post mortem investigation tool in forensic expert studies in ago's technical unit for the assistance to women, children and adolescents. *Attorrney's General's Office Magazine*, 103–130.

Petherick, W., & Petherick, N. (2019). Homicide: An introduction. In *Homicide* (pp. 1–18). Academic Press. https://doi.org/10.1016/B978-0-12-812529-8.00001-X

Perkins, R. M. (1962). An analysis of assault and attempts to assault. *Minnesota Law Review, 47, 71–91.*

Rios, V. (2018). *Media effects on crime and crime style*. https://scholar.harvard.edu/files/vrios/files/rios_mediaeffectscrime-style.pdf

Rollison, W. D. (1941). Torts: Assault, battery. *Notre Dame Law Review, 17*(1), 1–21.

Sarki, Z. M. (2019). Types of crime: The three clusters. In S. A. Abdullahi (Ed.), *Readings in criminology*. (forthcoming).

Savino, J., & Turvey, B. (2004). Defining rape and sexual assault. In *Rape investigation handbook*. Academic Press.

Shneidman, E. S. (1981). The psychological autopsy. *Suicide and Life-threatening Behavior, 11*(4), 325–340.

Sergianni, V. (2012). *Victims of crime*. A European Association of Psychology and Law.

Siegel, L. J. (2010). *Criminology, criminology: Theories, patterns, and typologies* (10th ed.). Wadsworth Cengage Learning.

Siegel, L. J., Welsh, B. C., & Senna, J. J. (2006). *Juvenile delinquency: Theory, practice and law*. Thomson/Wadsworth.

Simons, A. (2015). *Adult sex offender typologies* (pp. 1–8). Office of Justice Programs.

Shoemaker, D. J. (2005). *Theories of delinquency: An examination of explanations of delinquent behavior*. Oxford University Press.

Spitzer, E. (n.d.). *Stalking. Realities and responses*. State of New York. Office of the Attorney General.

Sutherland, E. H. (1940). White-collar criminality. *American Psychological Review, 5*(1), 1–12.

Tibbetts, S. G. (2019). *Criminological theory: The essentials. Sage Publications*.

The Law Commission. (2011). *Simplification of criminal law: Kidnapping* (Consultation Paper No. 200). https://s3-eu-west-2.amazonaws.com/lawcom-prod-storage-11jsxou24uy7q/uploads/2015/04/cp200_kidnapping_consultation.pdf

The Scottish Centre for Crime and Justice Research (SCCJR). (2016). *Theories and causes of crime*. [online] Glasgow: University of Glasgow, pp. 1–8. Retrieved from http://www.sccjr.ac.uk/wp-content/uploads/2016/02/SCCJR-Causes-of-Crime.pdf

Thomson, C. M., & Dennison, S. M. (2008). Defining relational stalking in research: Understanding sample composition in relation to repetition and duration of harassment. *Psychiatry, Psychology and Law, 15*(3), 482–499. https://doi.org/10.1080/13218710802389432

Turvey, B. E. (2014). Victimology. In *Forensic victimology*. Academic Press. https://doi.org/10.1016/C2012-0-06694-X

United Nations Children's Fund. (2010). *A guide to the Sexual Offences Act 2010*. https://www.unicef.org/lac/media/4701/file/PDF%20Sexual%20Offences%20Act.pdf

United Nations Office on Drugs and Crime (UNODC). (2015). *International Classification of Crime for Statistical Purposes (ICCS). Version1.0. United Nations Publication.*

Van Dijk, J. J. (1997, August). *Introducing victimology.* The Ninth International Symposium of the World Society of Victimology, Free University of Amsterdam, pp. 1–12.

Van Erp, J. (2018). The organization of corporate crime: Introduction to special issue of administrative sciences. *Administrative Sciences, 8(36). 1–12.*

Walsh, A. & Ellis, L. (2007). *Criminology: An interdisciplinary approach. Sage Publications.*

Ward, J. T., & Brown, C. N. (2015). Social learning theory and crime. *International Encyclopedia of the Social & Behavioural Sciences, 22*, 409–414.

Wheeler, R., & Bloomer, J. (2016). Death investigation systems: Murder, manslaughter, homicide, and attempts – Definitions. *Encyclopedia of Forensic and Legal Medicine*, 32–34. https://doi.org/10.1016/B978-0-12-800034-2.00126-9

Yaacoub, S. (2017). Poverty, inequality and the social causes of crime: A study between United States and Europe. *International Journal of Science and Research, 6(10), 629–634.* https://doi.org/10.21275/ART20176722

Zillman, D. (2008). Excitation transfer theory. In W. Donscbach (Ed.), *The international encyclopedia of communication* (pp. 1–6). https://doi.org/10.1002/9781405186407.wbiece049

Chapter 13
Psychological Factors in Property Crimes: Theories, Traits, and Treatment

Dorothy Bhandari Deka

A crime is an offense that evidences community disapproval and punishment mostly by the way of a fine or imprisonment (Julian, 2012). Any crime against a person, such as murder and rape, is considered extremely atrocious but crimes against property can cause huge loss, suffering, and even personal injury or death. Crimes against property include theft, crimes associated with theft, and crimes that damage property. This chapter includes the types and theories behind property crimes along with how crime is related to mental health such as the type and trait of personality who commits the crimes, the psychological impact on victims, and what are the possible support and intervention available for helping the victims to cope up with the situation. It is known, for example, that people with high economic standards are more exposed to property crime than is the general population (Tseloni et al., 2002).

In the book, *Essentials of Criminal Law* (pp. 207–209), the main property crimes are as follows:

- Larceny: The act of stealing can be carried out in more than one way. When the defendant steals by a physical taking, the theft is generally a larceny theft, such as a pickpocket takes the wallet from your purse and walks away. The crime seems comparatively rare in North America, Australia and New Zealand whereas in countries of Eastern Europe it is unusually high and also in Latin America, Asia, and Africa (Van Dijk et al., 1992).
- Embezzlement: Embezzlement refers to a form of white-collar crime in which a person or entity misappropriates the assets entrusted to them. For example, a bank official steals money from your account. Rates are significantly higher in South Africa and the lowest rates are found in Switzerland and Italy (Larsson, 2006)

D. B. Deka (✉)
Sarvodaya Healthcare, Guwahati, India

- False pretenses: A behavior intended to deceive others, such as you sell a car to a friend who lies and falsely promises that he or she will pay you in the morning.
- Receiving stolen property: The offense of acquiring goods with the knowledge that they have been stolen, extorted, embezzled, or unlawfully taken in any manner, such as buying a car knowing that it is stolen. Research has revealed that a larger proportion of those who are poor are more exposed to property crimes than others (Larsson, 2006)
- Forgery and uttering. Forgery is the changing or making of a document with the intent to defraud someone and uttering is passing that document to someone with the intent to defraud. For example, a friend takes one of your checks, makes it payable to himself or herself, signs your name, and cashes the check at your bank.
- Robbery: The crime of stealing from a place or a person, especially using violence or threats, such as you are told to hand over your wallet by an assailant who points a loaded gun at you. Research reveals that the highest rates of robbery were observed in Latin America; the risk for individual citizens here to be victimized by robbery is three times higher than the global average (Van Dijk 2007)
- Extortion: Extortion is typically nonviolent, but the elements of extortion are very similar to robbery, which is considered a forcible theft offense. You are told to pay to a gang leader who states that otherwise you will suffer retaliatory attacks in the coming months.

An individual's house is a safe and secure shelter where we are free to express our personalities and interests without fear of uninvited intrusions. There are four crimes that threaten the security of an individual's home. It can be involved cheating, destruction, and taking of property like stealing money (Julian, 2012).

- Burglary: An individual breaks into your home with the intent to commit a felony. Attempts of burglary are highest in Africa and Latin America. In many developing countries, completed burglaries are more common (van Kesteren & Alvazzi del Frat, 2002).
- Trespass: Members of a street gang gather in your front yard to sell narcotics.
- Arson: An angry neighbor sets your house on fire.
- Malicious mischief: A neighbor angry over your parking in his or her space defaces your home (Zar Rokh, 2007).

In the book Child and Ormerod (2017), it was mentioned that English philosopher John Locke viewed the protection of private property as the most important duty of government and as the bedrock of democracy. According to Locke, people originally existed in a "state of nature" in which they were subject to the survival of the fittest. Later, the individuals came together and agreed to create and maintain loyalty to a government that in return promised to protect individuals and their private property. The seventeenth-century English philosopher John Locke's opinion was taken in the Fifth Amendment to the U.S. Constitution which prohibits the taking of property without due process of law. Therefore, even today, individuals recognize that the ownership of private property is a right that provides us with a source of personal enjoyment, profit, and motivation and also serves as a way of self-worth. The development of various offenses was necessary to protect and punish the illegal taking of private property. Currently, roughly 30 states have simplified the law by combining the various property crimes into a single theft statute.

Crimes against property include burglary, motor vehicle theft, theft, arson, vandalism, and shoplifting that involves the taking of property or money and usually does not include a threat of force. Here the object is to obtain money, property, or some other benefits (Grabosky, 1997) *Theories of opportunity of property crime* focus on how offenders, rather than going out and actively looking for opportunities to commit a crime, simply come across them as they go about their daily activities; that is why more property crimes occur on busy streets or near heavy-traffic areas than in quiet, seldom-used ones. According to *routine activity theory*, most offenders do not go out of their way to look for crimes to commit; instead, they discover criminal opportunities while engaging in their routine activities and choose to take advantage of them. As per routine activity theory, in any crime that occurs, at least these three objects must be present at the same time and place: a suitable target, a motivated offender, and a lack of guardianship. According to *rational choice theory* potential, offenders weigh the costs and benefits of a given crime. When they come across an opportunity for crime, they informally assess the situation to see whether or not it is worth taking (Klaus, 2006).

Causes and Risk Factors of Criminal Behavior

The scientific approach towards studying criminal behavior is known as criminology. One of the oldest scientific approaches in criminal behavior theories highlights physical and biological abnormality as the prominent mark of the criminal. Ernest Jones, in the year 1954, delineated seven major principles of Freud's approach within the psychoanalytic perspective criminal and delinquent behaviors are attributed to disturbances or malfunctions in the ego or superego.

- *Biological Cause and Risk Factors that Can Lead to Criminal Acts*

  Modern biological theories observe the entire range of biological characteristics, counting those that are environmentally induced. The theories argue that certain biological conditions enhance the likelihood in an individual, will engage in maladaptive behavior patterns such as violent or antisocial behavior and behavioral patterns that include actions that are legally defined as crime or criminal acts. Contemporary theories increasingly focus on the interaction between biological characteristics and the social environment rather than only focusing in the sole effects of biological factors. Activity in the behavioral approach system, on the other hand, causes an individual to instigate or increase movement toward a goal. Due to prenatal experiences or genetic factors, some children are born with a hyper-persistent behavior approach system or an underactive behavioral inhibition system (Fowles, 2001). The basolateral amygdale and orbitofrontal cortex, on the other hand, expand dendrites as a result of chronic stress, causing increased aggressiveness (Hunter & McEwen, 2013). Neurobiological deficits may result in self-regulatory problems which again increase the risk of antisocial behavior (Calkins & Keane, 2009). Chronic stress diminishes the dendrites of neurons in the hippocampus and medial prefrontal cortex that causes reduced synaptic input, decreases abilities for self-regulation (Lupien et al., 2009). A number of studies have tried to determine the role of heredity in criminality. One of the earlier studies was by German physiologist Johannes Lange (1929). He found that in a group of 13 pairs of adult male identical twins, when one twin had a record of imprisonment, the other similarly had been imprisoned in almost 77% of the cases but in a comparable group of 17 pairs of fraternal twins, when one twin had been imprisoned, the other had a prison record by only 12% of the cases. Even in other studies, similar findings were observed about criminal behavior among identical twins and fraternal twins. Neurotransmitters (biological factors), chemicals that allow for the transmission of electrical impulses within the brain, are the basis for the brain's processing of information which might underline all types of behavior along with antisocial behavior. A study by Moul et al. (2013) on the relationship between neurotransmitter levels and antisocial behavior stated that antisocial people have significantly lower levels of serotonin than normal population. Although in most of the studies norepinephrine and dopamine did not show differences as such, in few of the studies that used a direct measure of neurotransmitter functioning, an effect of norepinephrine on antisocial behavior was also found (Beaver & Wright, 2005). The serotonin system, the dopamine system, and the noradrenaline system make up the three major monoamine systems in the brain. Serotonin is positively associated with inhibition, dopamine with approach, and noradrenaline with arousal (Zuckerman, 2007). The behavioral inhibition system is an aversive motivational system (Carver & White, 1994) that inhibits behavior that may lead to negative outcomes (Gray, 1987).

Low Birth Weight

Low birth weight below 2500 grams is assumed to cause damage to the central nervous system, therefore a reasonable proxy for increased risk for neuropsychological disorders (Brennan et al., 1984). There is abundant evidence that the relationship between low birth rate and antisocial behavior can be tied to early central nervous system dysfunction or development, neurological abnormalities, and neurodevelopmental problems and deficits (Tibbetts & Piquero, 1999). Therefore, it can be said that various biological aspects including the modern approaches, along with twin studies, neurotransmitters-related studies, and aspects related to birth like low birth weight can lead to antisocial behavior.

- *Physical Appearance and Crime*
  In 1775, John Caspar claims about the suspected relation between facial features and human conduct, whereas Lombroso in the year 1931 had proclaimed that criminals, compared with the general population show differences of head height, head width, and degree of receding forehead and differences in head circumference, head symmetry. Based on Seldon's theory, the association between mesomorph and delinquency was also found in a study by the Gluecks (1991), who compared 500 persistent delinquents with 500 proven nondelinquents. The two groups were matched in terms of age, general intelligence, ethnic-racial derivation, and residence in underprivileged areas. It was found that mesomorphs were more highly categorized by traits particularly suitable to the commission of acts of aggression such as physical strength, insensitivity, energy along with a relative freedom from such inhibitions to antisocial adventures such as feelings of inadequacy, emotional instability. It was revealed that mesomorphs who became delinquent were categorized by a number of personality traits not normally found in mesomorphs and sociocultural factors such as careless household routine, and lack of family group recreations associated with delinquency in mesomorphs. Therefore, it can be concluded that delinquents and possibly criminals differ from nondelinquent and noncriminals in being physically more mesomorphic, energetic, and aggressive in temperament along with showing the higher need for achievement and power motivationally (Fox, 1961).

- *Psychoanalytical Causes of Crime*
  The term psychoanalysis was coined by Sigmund Freud in the year 1896. Several studies based on the theory provide the basic orientation for psychoanalytic explanations of criminal behavior. As per the psychoanalytic perspective, criminal and delinquent behaviors are ascribed to conflicts or malfunctions in the ego or superego, that is, either in the reality principle pattern or moral principle pattern, excessive guilt from an overdeveloped superego is one source of criminal behavior (Denno, 2005). A psychoanalytically oriented psychologist, August Aichhorn (1925) found that many children in his organization had underdeveloped superego, therefore the delinquency and criminality behavior were primarily expressions of an unregulated id that works on pleasure principle. He attributed this particular behavior to the fact that the parents of these children were either absent or unloving, as the children failed to form the loving attachments necessary for the appropriate development of their superegos. Marital conflict among parents further heightens the risk of low inter- and intra-parental consistency in parenting practices, both of which generate an unpredictable environment for children that can alter the development of structure of superego.

- *Social Causes and Risk Factors of Criminal Behavior*
  Differential association theory proposed in the year 1939, showed that crime was mostly due to social disorganization that resulted from the social processes of mobility, conflict, and competition. In 1947, Sutherland modified his theory by adding other materials that took shape. According to the theory, criminal behav-

ior is learned through the interaction with other persons in the process of communication. The principal part of the learning of criminal behavior occurs within close personal groups. The criminal behavior learning process includes various procedures of committing the crime, both complicated and simple, along with the specific direction of motives, drives, rationalizations, and attitudes. The process of learning criminal behavior by association with criminal and anti-criminal patterns involves all of the mechanisms that are involved in any other learning. A differential association may vary in frequency, duration, priority, and intensity (Benson, Buehler, & Gerard, 2008). The spillover hypothesis suggests that parents whose relationship is characterized by a high level of conflict are more liable to engage in dysfunctional parenting practices, and disharmony in one relationship spills into other relationships within the family. Approximately 20% of the population variation in antisocial behavior is due to the environment shared by family members, preventing environmental influences occupied in interactions between genetic and environmental factors. Most of the behavior is due to interactions between genes and environmental factors thus, it is clearly understood that 20% of population variation in antisocial behavior is due to direct environmental effects (Moffitt, 2005). Exposure to violence, in terms of abuse or witnessing domestic violence, is stressful experience that strongly impacts children's well-being (Krug et al., 2002).

- *Stress Reactivity as a Mediator*
Van Goozen et al. (2008) proposes a theoretical module in which stress hyporeactivity mediates the influences of early adversity and genetic factors on persistent and severe antisocial behavior. Van Goozen et al. (2008) discuss two theories why lower stress sensitivity might describe antisocial individuals. One of the theories says that antisocial individuals are less responsive to the negative consequences of behavior; therefore they are less receptive to learning from punishment (Raine, 1996) whereas the second theory talks about sensation-seeking. Antisocial personalities tend to participate more in high-risk behaviors, suggesting that they have higher stress thresholds (Zuckerman, 1979). Also, in support of the latter theory, the personality trait of sensation-seeking has shown to be vital in the prediction of antisocial behavior among antisocial individuals recorded higher than the general population (Herrero & Colom, 2008). Higher scores for neuroticism characteristics are defined as a chronic tendency to experience negative emotional states such as depression, anxiety, and anger and has been found among high sensation-seeking inmates compared to the general population (Rebollo et al., 2002; Ellis et al., 2009).

According to the standard economics of crime model (Becker, 1968; Chiu & Madden, 1998), criminals are individuals who commit a crime according to the maximization of their expected utility. According to the model, inequality leads to more crime because it increases the incentives to commit property crimes. Crime rates depend on the potential gain from crime and the associated opportunity cost. According to Chiu and Madden (1998), if income inequality rises, then the level of crime also rises up by two sources. The alternative to crime is less attractive for criminals and the potential proceeds from crime are greater. Apart from various theories, there is another rising issue in the present scenario: Internet and technological advances have increased than earlier times as they play an important role in a wide range of criminal activities. Just the Internet can be used to enhance the daily lives of individuals and the functioning of services, it has given rise to cybercrime. Cybercrime is a global phenomenon and is as borderless as the Internet itself. The attack surface continues to grow as society becomes increasingly digitized, with more citizens, businesses, public. The Internet is of course fundamentally a source of information and an environment where communities of like-minded individuals can meet. The list of information that could be used to assist criminals is essentially endless, but key examples include access to detailed map data, including satellite and street views for reconnaissance, shipping routes, and schedules, tutorials, guides, and recipes for drugs or explosives, and tips on operational security (Agrafiotis et al., 2018).

Human Nature, Mental Health, and Crime

Homo sapiens tend to have a dark side that likes crime and violence; usually everyone denies it, but the contrary is true. It applies to anyone regardless of our age, region, caste, social status, education, or religion. It can amuse and at the same time can frighten us. Crime somehow intrigues people as it can attract or repel but it happens. It can cause anger when the near or dear ones in our society are affected (Rao, 2007).

According to Bartol (2007), there are three major domains of underlying assumptions about human nature:

- *Conformity perspective*: The strain theory of Merton (2020) argues that 'humans are fundamentally good people and conforming beings who are strongly influenced by values and attitudes of the society in which they live'. It assumes that humans, as creatures of conformity, want to do the 'right' thing'. Education, social network, friends, and family influence can help access well-advertised goals but not to all. Therefore, if there is a 'perceived discrepancy' between materialist values and goals cherished and the availability of legitimate means that is when any kind of crime and delinquency occurs.
- *Nonconformist perspective*: It assumes that human beings are basically undisciplined creatures; if given a chance he/she would disobey society's settlement and would commit crimes extensively. The social control theory by Travis (1960) states that crime and delinquency can occur when a person is tied to the normative standards that are weak or nonexistent. Therefore, it is assumed that human nature is fundamentally 'bad' or 'antisocial'.
- Another perspective assumes that human beings are basically 'neutral' by birth; a child develops most of the perspectives, beliefs, and tendencies from his/her

social environment, and various methods of learning can be used to learn different things. As per Sutherland's differential association theory (1947), criminal acts are learned through social interaction with various people. Different individuals learn about criminal acts as a result of communication or learnings they get from other people who were also thought to be criminals; it is not because of emotional disturbance, mental illness, or innate qualities of 'goodness' or 'badness'. The conventional wisdom that 'bad company promotes bad behavior' appropriately reviews the concept of the third perspective.

Crime and Personality

A crime that is perceived as a social mirror constitutes one of the biggest social ills and poses a great challenge to eradicate. The available literature evidenced psychological traits such as personality traits as important as environmental factors in explaining criminal and antisocial behavior in an individual (Larsson, 2006) defined as any act that violates the criminal law while crime indicates the specific action of criminal behavior such as rape and murder. There are four psychological traits that are considered important aspects of criminal behavior: personality traits, low self-control, aggressive behavior, and cognitive distortion (Robinson, 2004).

Personality and Personality Traits

According to the Diagnostic and Statistical Manual of Mental Disorders of the American Psychiatric Association (APA, 2013), personality traits are defined as the enduring patterns of perceiving, relating to, and thinking about the environment and oneself that are exhibited in a wide range of social and personal contexts.

Big Five and Criminal Behavior

The "Big Five" components of trait personality, agreeableness, and conscientiousness have been found to be predictive of adult criminal behavior. Earlier John et al. (1994) found that delinquents aged 12–13 years old who had engaged in burglary, drug dealing, and strong-arming behavior scored lower on Agreeableness, Conscientiousness, and Openness and obtained higher scores on Extraversion than nondelinquents. Studies by Heaven (1996) found that neuroticism in addition to agreeableness and conscientiousness to be predictive of delinquent behavior along with Neuroticism to be positively, and Conscientiousness and Agreeableness to be negatively related to self-reported vandalism. The antisocial undercontrollers were characterized by extremely low scores on Agreeableness and Conscientiousness, and moderate scores on Extraversion, Openness, and neuroticism compared to non-delinquent adolescents. Also, as per gender comparisons, it is reported that physical aggression in men and women is found to be associated with low agreeableness, low conscientiousness, and high neuroticism (Caprara et al., 1996; Van Aken et al., 1998).

Studies in partner violence by Heaven (1996) provided some evidence of a correlation between low agreeableness with partner violence for men and women. Partner violence perpetration for women is highly associated with personality-type neuroticism (Ibid). A Malaysian study among offenders by Mohammad Rahim et al. (2014) noted significant associations between certain Alternative Five-Factor Model personality traits with specific types of aggression.

Psychoticism, Extraversion, and Neuroticism Factors and Criminal Behavior

Psychoticism, extraversion, and neuroticism are the three essential personality factors in Eysenck (1991). This model is one of the theories that explicitly relate personality traits to criminal behavior. It was found that delinquents scored high in Eynseck's PEN dimensions. Higher neuroticism scores reflect emotional instability and impulsive and antisocial behavior, and psychoticism is defined by a lack of empathy, cruelty, hostility, psychopathy, aggressiveness, and socialization deficit. Some of the literature reviews on criminology indicate high scores on psychoticism and neuroticism to be associated with juvenile delinquency (Romero et al., 2001). Several other studies found juvenile delinquency to be positively related to psychoticism and extraversion instead of psychoticism and neuroticism. High scores on psychoticism and neuroticism are even found in adult offender-related data (Blackburn, 1993; Aleixo & Norris, 2000). Furthermore, characteristics of psychoticism such as aggressive, hostile, low empathy, and impulse are the common characteristics shared by criminals and delinquents. However, Blackburn (1993) convincingly stated that high psychoticism scores reflected more serious and persistent offenders. People with high scores on impulsive sensation-seeking are more likely to engage in criminal acts since they are used to risky and socially unacceptable activities. The involvement in criminal behavior stems from searching for high arousal and sensation-seeking. Studies have found positive associations between sensation-seeking, a wide range of impulsive and criminal acts such as smoking, alcohol and illicit drug abuse, and risky sexual behavior. Impulsive sensation-seeking is also related to a wide range of troubles like childhood conduct issues, aggressive behavior, and nonpsychopathic murder (Fossati et al., 2007; Buker, 2011).

Influence of Self-Control

Self-control is considered as an important concept in influencing the likelihood of an individual's violent act. Literature reviews related to psychological, sociological and criminology reveals that poor self-control is perceived to be the primary cause of criminal and delinquent behavior (Buker, 2011). Other studies have associated low self-control to more prone to substance use and reckless behavior during adolescence or young adult period, also been associated with self-reported juvenile delinquency and bullying by juveniles (Nofziger, 2001; Vazsonyi et al., 2001). Empirical assessment on the General Theory of Crime (GTC) supports the claim that low self-control is significantly related to crime and impulsive behaviors (Pratt & Cullen, 2000). Therefore, the role of self-control as an important predictor of crime and criminal acts, which is evidenced by Vazsonyi et al. (2001), proposed a theoretical argument that stresses the importance of self-control as the primary cause of crime.

Aggression: Core Emotion in Crime

Aggression is described as an overt behavior carried out intentionally to harm another person who is motivated to avoid the harm. Aggression is often evaluated in relation to behavioral and conduct-related issues (Bushman & Huesmann, 2010). In psychosocial terms, aggression can be defined as a psychological phenomenon that describes a broad category of behavior that intends to harm another by means of physical or verbal attacks (Comer & Gould, 2001). From the neurobiological perspective, aggression has been linked with high levels of testosterone and low levels of certain neurotransmitters such as serotonin (Dabbs et al., 2001). Aggression has also been linked to genetics and social learning. Other predisposing factors for aggression include genetic factors, obstetric complications, the rearing environment, biological factors, and psychiatric disorders such as substance abuse, psychosis, depression, and personality disorders (Citrome & Volavka, 2003; Landsford, 2012). Another study by Warren et al. (2002) recognized a significant relationship between aggression and antisocial behavior that might lead to an individual's participation in violent behavior that also includes murder. According to Feshbach (1964), there are two types of aggression known as instrumental aggression and expressive aggression. The types are distinguished by their goals or the rewards that they offer the perpetrator. The instrumental type of aggression comes from the desire for objects or the status possessed by another person, such as jewelry, money, or territory. It is conceived as a premeditated means of obtaining some goal other than harming the victim and being proactive rather than reactive. The expressive aggression is a reflection of hostile reactions and has historically been conceived as being impulsive, thoughtless (e.g., unplanned), driven by anger, having the ultimate motive of harming the target, and occurring as a reaction to some perceived provocation. It is determined that most murders, rapes, and other violent crimes directed at harming the victims are precipitated by hostile aggression and anger (Geen, 2001).

One of the models that have been used in criminological studies is the Four Structure Aggression Model by Buss and Perry (1992). Aggression is characterized as the outcome of the links between emotions (anger), thoughts (hostility), and aggressive behavior. Buss and Perry's model describes four dispositional sub-traits of aggression. The types of aggression are physical aggression, verbal aggression, and cognitive and emotional components of aggression. There are strong pieces of literature and theoretical foundation for all the four types of aggression as a global conceptualization of aggression and criminal acts. Physical and verbal aggression reflects the motor component of aggression, usually conceived as premeditated means of obtaining some goals and harming the victim. It is also known as instrumental aggression. The facet of physical aggression consists of kicking, beating, and hurting. Examples of verbal aggression include shouting, threatening, and insulting others. In the cognitive component. Hostility reflects the cognitive component of aggression which involves negative feelings such as feelings of ill will, opposition, and injustice directed towards others. Hostility is a cognitive reaction of a perceived threat or insult that differentiates it from the motor component of aggression. The emotional component is another type that reflects anger. The emotional component of aggression is due to the perceived provocation which motivates to harm the target. It is usually conceived as impulsive and thoughtless driven by anger (Trninic et al., 2008).

Ferguson et al. (2008) evidenced that personality factors are more critical than environmental factors in developing aggressive traits in an individual. However, it was argued that there is no single factor credible enough to determine the root of aggression. The current consensus is that aggression is multidetermined. Earlier research had highlighted aggression as the basic ingredient of violent crime. Along with that, it has also indicated that aggression leads to violence and claimed violence as aggression has the goal of extreme harm, including death (Sarchiaopone et al., 2009). Aggressive behavior seems to be the outcome of the frustration due to hindrances in goal attainment. Another study on aggression emphasized aggression as the basic ingredient of violent crime. Since then, many theories have been created to understand how it contributes to violent behavior. Anderson and Bushman (2002) claimed that violence although described as aggression but in some of the instances is not considered to be violent. There are a variety of mechanisms linking aggression and violent acts.

Influence of Cognitive Distortion

The importance of cognitive distortion has been recently examined within the field of criminology and social psychology while determining the possible factors for criminal acts. A cognitive distortion is defined as inaccurate or biased ways of attending to or conferring meaning upon experiences (Andrews & Bonta, 2010). Literature attempts to explain the commencement, development, and persistence of antisocial behavior and violent acts. Also, social cognitive theories have proved cognitive distortion as a result of antisocial behavior or some deficiency in interpreting social events (Nas et al., 2008). Based on theories, cognitive distortions attempt to explain that people tend to block moral judgments in order to justify avoiding responsibility for their own behavioral or attitudinal problems. A self-serving cognitive distortion is often labeled as an antisocial attitude that insulates the individual from blame or negative self-concept. Earlier studies have recognized the role of cognitive distortion as the catalyst for a wide range of aggressive and antisocial behavior. Various researches have also provided some evidence of the criminal population, such as cognitive distortions and their contribution to problematic emotional and behavioral responses which eventually lead to criminal and deviant behavior. Over the past decades, cognitive distortion is often linked to externalizing behavioral issues (Liau et al., 1998; Andrews & Bonta, 2010). Studies suggest that murderers who used multiple killing methods display higher levels of cognitive distortions compared to those who killed their victim using a single method. Also, cognitive distortion among sexual offenders and juvenile delinquents is strongly associated with child sexual abuse. And it is elevated among the offender population such as adolescents who have committed sexual offenses. Evidence also indicates that cognitive distortions have been observed among youths who exhibit delinquency. Studies also revealed that juvenile delinquents showed higher levels of cognitive distortions than nondelinquents. (McCrady et al., 2008; Ward, 2000). Cognitive distortion among sexual offenders emerged from underlying causal theories than stemming from unrelated or independent beliefs. Beech et al. (2005) determined five cognitive distortions after interviewing 28 sexual murderers in the United Kingdom. Those were: dangerous world, male sex drive is uncontrollable, entitlement, women as sexual objects, and women as unknowable and prepared to kill to avoid detection.

Individuals committing financial crime are generally someone good in financial decision-making, and it is mostly affected by several psychological factors, such as intelligence, an individual's personality traits, and his/her ability to make rational decisions (Patterson & Daigler, 2014). Dearden (2019) describes the manner in which heuristics and biases, which have an adverse effect on rational decision-making, could promote criminal economic activity. One type of disorder includes pathological liars (Nee et al., 2019), who succeed to a certain extent in covering their negative attributes, exhibit control over their impulses, and convey an impression of being normal and successful. Narcissism typifies individuals with a mania for succeeding sometimes into antisocial behavior (Bromberg, 1965). Recent studies have focused on associations between the characteristics of the so-called dark triad psychopathy, narcissism and Machiavellianism (Babiak et al., 2010; Trompeter et al., 2013) and white-collar crime. High level of narcissism is found among white-collar offenders. The type of psychopathy found to be associated with white-collar offences is manifested in impulsiveness, outbreaks of violence, risk-taking and antisocial learnings with no acceptance of responsibility and no setting of long-term goals (Alalehto & Azarian, 2018). It is observed that particularly dominant psychopathy in occurrences where white-collar offenders become red collar criminals (Perri, 2016).

Mental Health of Victims

In a study by Harvey et al. (2014) victims describe three factors that are linked to financial crime vulnerabilities; one factor is the *financial resources* available to them, such as any recent changes in their situation, and the extent and quality of their financial social networks. The other factor is *family circumstances,* such as immediate pressure to increase their income due to family responsibilities or a strong desire to provide for family members' long-term security. The third one is the *psychological aspect,* such as the personality traits that enabled the fraud qualities like being trusting or compared with those that were protective, also individuals experiencing psychological stress at the time of contact can increase their vulnerability to the fraud. The needs and experiences of victims of crime have become increasingly recognized as an important aspect of criminal justice and public policy. It is a necessity to examine closely the nature and relationship between becoming a victim of crime and a person's succeeding mental health conditions and issues. There are several ways through which a victim of crime can be affected. Firstly, it is the financial loss experienced as a direct consequence of property being stolen and indirect financial costs such as loss of income through time spent in court, medical expenses, etc. Victims of violent crime may experience a physical injury of variable severity that may have short-term or long-term effects. Along with it, the effects of victimization may include feelings of fear, anxiety, sadness, helplessness, guilt, and social withdrawal (Shapland & Hall, 2007).

Slade et al. (2009) found that there are associations between being a victim of violence and poor mental health; some of the several plausible explanations for the relationship are:

- Exposure to violence causes a decline in mental health
- People with poor mental health are more likely to experience violence
- There are common risk factors for both mental health problems and becoming a victim of violence

Also, studies have revealed that determining whether crime victimization causally affects mental health is somewhat complicated at times due to the contribution of the individuals' socioeconomic background such as family background and psychosocial and behavioral factors related to mental health. Demographic characteristics associated with the prevalence of mental disorders include age, employment status, country of birth, education, and partnership status. Some of the literature reviews have identified a range of sociodemographic factors and health behaviors shown to be associated with poor mental health, such as childhood abuse or trauma (Willits et al., 2013; Scott et al., 2010), stressful life events, social connectedness, financial strain, general health and health behaviors, such as physical activity smoking and problematic alcohol use have also been associated with mental health status. Inability to control these important risk factors when examining the relationship between crime victimization and mental health leads to erroneous conclusions, such as there is an independent effect of victimization on mental health or might be led to overestimate the size of any such effect.

The Psychological Impact of Victimization

According to National Organization for Victim Assistance (2001), it is almost impossible to predict how an individual will respond to crime. Psychological injuries created by crime are often the most difficult to cope with and have long-lasting effects. As crime is usually experienced as more serious than an accident or misfortune, it is difficult to come to terms with the fact that loss and injury have been caused by the deliberate act of another human being.

According to Illingworth (2007), common reactions to crime were split into four stages:

- The initial reaction usually is shock, fear, anger, helplessness, disbelief, or guilt; some of the reactions might reoccur at a later stage as well, for example when attending a trial or going to the hospital for medical treatment. A period of disorganization might occur and might even manifest itself in psychological effects such as distressing thoughts about the event, depression, nightmares, fear of loss, guilt, and lack of confidence and self-esteem.
- Secondly, behavioral responses might occur, such as increased alcohol or substance abuse, the disintegration of social relationships, staying away from people and situations, or social withdrawal.
- The third phase is reconstruction and acceptance where the victims often try to come to terms with the crime by longing for everything to be as it was before and to turn the clock back.
- Finally, in the fourth phase of normalization/adjustment, the recovery of the victims begins, accepting the reality of what happened. He/she may try to reinterpret their own experience and try to give an explanation for what has happened or to decide that the situation has led to personal growth.

The boundaries between these different stages are not very clear-cut as outlined here and victims may not progress effortlessly through all the stages. Victims at one extreme may shrug off very serious crimes with no noticeable effects sometimes and on the other extreme victims might get stuck in a particular stage and have difficulty moving on (Warren et al., 2002).

According to Robinson et al. (2021), emotional and psychological symptoms the victims usually experience are as follows:

- Shock, denial, or disbelief: At the very initial phase, individuals may find it difficult to believe that they have become a victim of crime. They might even pretend that it did not happen to them at all (denial) that may last for a few moments or maybe for months and even years. Victims might experience a 'childlike' state or maybe when a crime occurred, they were in a dreamlike state; after the initial shock, they may experience other emotions.

- Confusion and difficulty concentrating: A state of confusion might occur, such as being unsure of what actually happened, as it was quick and also very chaotic. They might even become confused thinking about why it happened to them or maybe when questioned they find it difficult to answer.
- Anger, irritability, mood swings: Being angry is the second stage of the grief cycle, where the victim may be angry at God, question why it happened with them only. Anger can also be expressed by the family members, friends, the justice system, and even sometimes themselves.
- Anxiety and fear: This is one of the common emotions experienced by the victims after experiencing a crime that involved a threat to one's safety or life. It can lead to panic attacks if ever reminded of the crime and is unresolved. Fear can last for quite some time that can be unhealthy and, in such cases, an individual should seek mental health support.
- Guilt, shame, and self-blame: Blaming self is very common. Victims feel that things happened because of their mistake or carelessness. Also, guilt is common; they feel guilty for not being to do more to prevent what happened. In crimes involving sexual acts, offenders often degrade the victim by making them do humiliating things. Because of this some victims even feel self-hatred because they believe that they can no longer be loved by those who are close to them.
- Frustration: Victims are usually frustrated by the feelings of helplessness that surface when the crime takes place. Also, individuals may continue to feel frustrated if they are unable to access the support and information that is necessary for their healing.
- Withdrawing from others: Usually after experiencing crime, victims tend to isolate themselves, avoid people around or experience interpersonal issues.
- Feeling sad or hopeless: The feeling of intense sadness is often the most powerful long-term reaction to any crime. It is common for victims to become depressed and anxious after a crime occurs.

Along with psychological and emotional symptoms, some physical and behavioral issues are also observed symptoms such as insomnia or nightmares, fatigue, being startled easily, difficulty concentrating, increased heartbeat, agitation, aches and pains, muscle tension, issues related to appetite, and daily functioning (Warren, 2012).

Forensic Procedures After Property Crime and Its Legal Aspects

Forensic laboratories have grown almost fourfold since the early 1970s; there is pressure on the police and courts to increase their reliance on more objective forms of evidence. Earlier studies in the 1960s and 1970s specified physical evidence was available at most crime scenes, but minute scientific evidence was collected, and that had a nominal impact on case outcome (Briody, 2004). The *level of contact of the offender with the victim* and the crime scene environment is what produces the physical evidence in the first place. Physical evidence is acquired from the target and evidence left behind on whomever or whatever the offender had come in contact. The *condition of crime scenes* is an important factor, with indoor scenes and those committed in clean and orderly environments, allowing investigators to distinguish the newly created evidence from the background environment but crimes committed in commercial establishments and public areas (sidewalks and roadways) pose special problems for preserving evidence and protecting its contamination. The *time elapsed* from the crime commission and its report to the police, and the delay in police response to the scene, have long been considered factors not only in apprehending criminals but also in the preservation of scene evidence (Peterson et al., 2010).

According to the Federal Bureau of Investigation CODIS Program (2009), the steps usually taken for forensic investigation are:

- *Preliminary report:* The initial report is critical in the success that physical evidence is preserved and collected; most of the time fragile and transient nature of physical evidence allows it to be easily contaminated or destroyed through careless handling.
- *Follow-up investigation*: All the crimes do not receive follow-up investigations such as burglaries that mostly involve only a telephone call to police and the taking of a report over the telephone.
- *Crime scene search:* This takes place where different agencies have various policies with respect to calling a crime scene specialist to the crime scene.
- *Submission of evidence to the laboratory:* Physical evidence is taken to the police department property storage area or to the crime laboratory directly.
- *Examination of evidence and report of findings:* The following steps are followed in the process:

  (a) Establishing element of the crime
  (b) Identification of a suspect
  (c) Testing statements and alibis
  (d) Reconstruction

Based on all the evidence and forensic reports, legal actions are taken and punishments are decided.

The Prevention Methods and Interventions for Victims at the Individual Level and Society at Large

All crimes are serious and should be treated as crucial. It is important to remember that even minor crimes can be overwhelming in a person's life. Any type of crime can affect everyone in a different manner. Generally, crime victims are most directly affected by crime along with family members, relatives, neighbors or friends, and others who care about the victim. These people, along with the victim, do require help, information, and support.

According to National Organization for Victim Assistance (2001), victimization is stressful, and knowing what to expect in the outcome of crime can help relieve anxiety. In the aftermath of the crime, victims usually need a variety of support, services, and understanding.

- Victims need to feel safe first as crime often leaves them feeling helpless, vulnerable, and frightened. Various emotional issues may arise like fear, shock, denial, etc. Emotional distress might be expressed in some strange ways, such as laughter. Sometimes victims feel rage at the sudden, unpredictable, and uncontrollable threat to their safety or lives.
- Victims should be able to express their emotions well and vent out their stories of trauma as a victim of a crime. Along with that their story and expression need to be accepted and should be judged as that can help them recover early.
- Once able to express and vent out emotion, victims may need to know what comes next. Various preventive measures can be used to make them feel better and strong and accept the reality.
- Victims should also be prepared for legal procedures related to crime. They are usually concerned about their role in the investigation of the crime and in the legal proceedings or the role of the media.

Victimization often causes trauma and depending upon the level of trauma that a person has already experienced in their lifetime, crime can be devastating. To support an individual who has been the victim of violent crime, psychotherapy should be emphasized in both concrete ways and practical helping strategies; also some subtle, reconstructive and integrative modalities can be used. Psychotherapy provides preventive and treatment methods for crime victims and survivors to recover from the traumatizing effects of human malice (Miller, 1998).

According to Herman (2003) and Williamson et al. (2008), various strategies can be used for victims in order to help them cope with the experience they went through. The whole intervention and preventive measure can be divided into two parts:

A. *Core psychotherapies that are important for victims to overcome trauma*

1. Psychological first aid (PFA): Psychological first aid is a systematic set of helping actions aimed at reducing initial post-trauma distress and supporting short- and long-term adaptive functioning. It reduces symptoms such as anxiety through nonjudgmental listening, encouragement, and assurance of the practitioner. Psychological first aid is designed as an initial component of a comprehensive disaster/trauma response, and it is created around eight core actions:

   - Contact and engagement
   - Safety and comfort
   - Stabilization

- Information gathering
- Practical assistance
- Connection with social supports
- Information on coping support
- Linkage with collaborative services (Bisson & Andrew, 2007)

Psychological first aid is concept-driven and its administration requires assessment and clinical judgment by the professional, given the complexity of presentations, variability of context, needs, and logistical constraints. Psychological first aid is proposed for use by disaster mental health responders, counselors, and others who may provide immediate support for survivors at a crime scene. There are two major advantages of psychological first aid: it is highly movable and designed for delivery anywhere recent victims can be found such as shelters, schools, hospitals, homes, staging areas, feeding locations, family assistance centers, and other community settings. The principles of psychological first aid can also be applied immediately after a traumatic event in non-disaster field settings, including hospital trauma centers, rape crisis centers, and war zones (Rothbaum & Davis, 2003).

2. Psychological debriefing interventions: Debriefing is typically offered in a single session within hours or days after the event to everyone exposed to the event. The aim is to make victims aware and educate them about how to normally react to trauma so as to encourage them to share their experiences and emotional responses to the event and help them cope with the situation (Hembree & Rothbaum, 2007). One of the most common forms of psychological debriefing is Critical Incident Stress Debriefing.

   - Critical Incident Stress Debriefing (CISD) is a secondary prevention intervention originally established for the use with individuals indirectly exposed to traumatic events because of their occupation, such as police officers, firefighters, or emergency medical personnel. Critical incident stress debriefing is usually managed in a single 120–180 min session by a team composed of individuals familiar with the organization, such as police officers and mental health professionals (Hetrick et al., 2010). Along with normalizing the responses of individuals to stress and reassuring them, the professional also trains them in coping skills and offers additional resources for those who may need them. Cochrane review (2002) measured the effectiveness of brief, single-session psychological debriefing for the prevention and management of psychological distress after trauma among the victims. It is a very flexible and loosely structured approach.

3. Crisis intervention: A short-term management technique designed to reduce possible permanent damage to a victim affected by a crisis, it focuses on four goals for symptom reduction that are chosen by the victim. The approach helps the victim in developing a short-term framework so that they can be

aware of the experience and accordingly work on it (Cusack et al., 2016). One of the crisis intervention programs is the critical incident stress management program.

- Critical Incident Stress Management (CISM): It is a program with multi-component that aims to reduce the severity related to the impairment associated with the traumatic stress of the victims (Schnurr, 2017). Critical incident stress management includes methods such as pre-incident training for people with high-risk occupations, one-on-one individual crisis support, demobilizing, and defusing. Critical incident stress management also has a family support component whereby family members of the emergency personnel are debriefed (Hembree & Rothbaum, 2007; Schnurr, 2017).

4. Cognitive therapy is a relatively short-term form of psychotherapy based on the concept that the way we think and our thought process functions about things affects how we feel emotionally. Cognitive therapy basically challenges dysfunctional thoughts that are usually irrational or illogical related to victimization (Monson et al., 2012).

- Cognitive restructuring is one of the intensive approaches that is used in cognitive therapy programs. It is based on the theory that how we perceive the event and based on that our thought and moods get affected. It aims to facilitate relearning thoughts and beliefs generated from a traumatic event and increase awareness of dysfunctional trauma-related thoughts and correct or replace those thoughts with more adaptive and/or rational cognitions. Cognitive restructuring generally takes place over 8–12 sessions of 60–90 min (Sloan et al., 2018).
- Cognitive processing therapy: Cognitive restructuring focuses on addressing maladaptive beliefs about the traumatic event and the implications of the trauma on one's life. Cognitive processing therapy components include psychoeducation, written accounts about the impact of the traumatic event on one's life, and cognitive restructuring. In this technique, people evaluate their thoughts and feelings and learn to challenge irrational thoughts and distorted beliefs about safety, trust, power, control, and intimacy. In some cases, the victims are allowed to write a detailed account of the trauma and narrate it in the presence of the therapist. Cognitive processing therapy can be administered in both individual and group settings but studies suggest that individual therapy may be more effective (Resick et al., 2002).

5. Cognitive-behavioral therapy: It is a form of psychological treatment that has been demonstrated to be effective for a range of problems including depression, anxiety disorders, alcohol, and drug use problems, marital problems, eating disorders, and severe mental illness. The therapy deals with both the cognitive and behavioral aspects related to the issue (Cahill et al., 2009). As we know, in cognitive therapy, the psychotherapist helps the victim or the

patient to identify and correct distorted, irrational, and maladaptive beliefs, whereas in behavioral therapy it is important to practice the goals that are made in order to overcome the issues it facilitates – symptom reduction and improved day-to-day functioning. Using Cognitive approaches along with behavioral techniques can help overcome trauma or traumatic symptoms. Cognitive-behavioral therapy uses principles of learning and conditioning to deal with and manage disorders and their symptoms; it includes components from both behavioral and cognitive therapy and a combined method to deal with the trauma (Foa et al., 2009).

- In trauma-focused cognitive behavioral therapy, components such as exposure, cognitive restructuring, and various coping skills have been used in various eclectic approaches. Common forms of trauma-focused cognitive behavioral therapy sessions are usually brief and involve weekly sessions lasting 60–90 min (Cahill et al., 2009). Additional practices and training such as relaxation exercises, coping skills training, stress management, or assertiveness training are often included as part of cognitive-behavioral therapy either as a group or individual-based therapy program (Shapiro, 2003).

Coping skills therapy may include training such as stress inoculation therapy, assertiveness training, biofeedback and relaxation training (imagery, progressive muscular relaxation), role-playing to manage anxiety, depression, or any other trauma-related symptoms. This therapy is designed to enhance coping skills for present situations. Coping skills training programs usually require at least eight 60–90-min sessions whereas more comprehensive interventions such as stress inoculation therapy require 10–14 sessions of similar time sets (Sloan et al., 2018).

6. Eye movement desensitization and reprocessing (EMDR): This technique associates imaginal exposure with the concurrent induction of saccadic eye movements that are believed to provide assistance to reprogram brain function so that the emotional impact of trauma can be resolved. Eye movement desensitization and reprocessing is a form of psychotherapy that has components of cognitive-behavioral therapy and exposure therapy but also incorporates saccadic eye movements during exposure (Fao et al., 2019). In the eye movement desensitization and reprocessing process, the victim is instructed to imagine a traumatic event that is part of their recurrent thought and memory and then gradually engages in negative cognition. Here the technique involves the patient imagining a scene from the trauma, focusing on the accompanying cognition and arousal, and then followed by articulating an incompatible positive cognition (such as personal worth) while the therapist moves two fingers across the patient's visual field and instructs the patient to track the fingers and asks the client to consider memory while focusing on the rapid movement of the therapist fingers. After an eye move-

ment round of 10–12 times (back and forth), the victim or the patient is asked to rate the strength of the negative memory along with the victim's or the patient's belief in the positive cognition. The order is repeated until anxiety decreases, at which point the patient is instructed to generate a more adaptive thought. Earlier eye movement desensitization and reprocessing procedure were short and it consisted of 1–3 sessions but with further modifications, the current procedure consist of 8–12 weekly sessions of 90 min each (Sloan et al., 2018).

7. Exposure-based therapy: It involves confrontation with terrifying or anxious stimuli and is a continuous process until anxiety is reduced. Exposure therapy is a psychological intervention technique that was developed to help people challenge their unreasonable fears and thoughts; usually irrational thoughts are challenged in actual situations to reduce anxiety and fears related to victimization. The exposure technique is based on mental imagery from memory or introduced in scenes presented by the therapist (imaginal exposure) (Rothbaum et al., 2001). In some cases, experience is from the actual scene or similar events in life, which is known as in vivo exposure and the idea is to extinguish the habituated emotional response to traumatic stimuli; such training basically helps the victim or the patient to realize that nothing bad is going to happen that gradually reduces or eliminates escaping from feared situations and the effect related with it. Re-experiencing the trauma memories through exposure let the victim tolerate the trauma to be emotionally processed so that the memories become less distressing. Through exposure, the individual learns to cope with situations that they may have been avoiding due to erroneous beliefs (Foa & Rauch, 2004). The procedure is usually conducted for 8–12 weekly or biweekly sessions lasting 60–90 min (Sloan et al., 2018).

   Exposure therapies usually vary in numbers and types of components; the number and frequency of exposure sessions are based on the victim's or patient's need. The homework assignments and methods of exposure usually differs from case to case. The therapy sessions are generally proceeded based on the requirement of the patient; therefore, the therapist and the patient usually decide on how to address the individual's emotional response to the exposure maladaptive thoughts (Resick et al., 2002).

   According to Foa and Rauch (2004), there two most practiced forms of exposure therapies; those are:

   • Prolonged exposure therapy: Prolonged exposure therapy usually involves 12–14 sessions that includes breathing retraining or practice along with psychoeducation about common issues and reactions about the trauma situation. Various studies have showed that effectiveness for prolonged exposure had been established among victims experiencing single or multiple types of traumas along with comorbidities such as substance use disorder, personality disorder, and psychosis (Hamblen et al., 2019).

Exposure types vary and depend on what the patient is avoiding, patient willingness, and accessibility of reminders of the trauma (Foa & Rauch, 2004).

- Written exposure therapy: In this particular method of therapy, victims or patients are asked to write about their traumatic situation in response to specific prompts. After the written activity, both the therapist and patient discuss the written matter and during the process of discussion the patient is motivated to pay attention to his or her thoughts and emotions that the situation evokes (Sloan & Marx, 2019).

There are various methods and techniques used in exposure therapy:

- Imaginal exposure: This method is a typical way wherein the patient is asked to imagine and explore the traumatic event, re-experienced through verbal description, writing, or other means, in the presence of the therapist, and usually the patients are made relaxed during the session so that rationally the evaluation and analysis regarding the situation can be done in order to cope with the situation.
- In vivo exposure: The technique is known as in vivo exposure, as the patients during the session try to challenge their fear in a real-life setting, a generally safe situation but they typically avoid it because it reminds them of the challenges, and they emotionally get vulnerable and cognitive functioning is challenged (Markowitz et al., 2015).
- Virtual reality exposure: It is a method for providing exposure therapy through virtual reality that is usually well designed to recreate situations that may aid imagined exposure, such as disastrous disasters or severe motor vehicle accidents. The therapy technique uses a typical head-mounted computer display to present victims with sensory material that includes visual, auditory, tactile, and other sensory material that stimulates distressing memories and emotional responses (Difede & Hoffman, 2002).

B. *Supportive Psychotherapies that are important for victims to overcome trauma*
Although the therapies discussed under this umbrella is used as a supportive method for patients. And sometimes when trauma-focused therapies are not available as it has to be conducted by experts or the patient is ready for or wants it, the following interventions help in managing their issues.

- Coping skills training: Training on coping skills is often part of a more inclusive therapy program; here the techniques that are included are role-playing, assertiveness training, stress management training, relaxation training, biofeedback, and psychoeducation about psychological needs like sleep hygiene, nutrition, and self-care (Collins, 2004).
- Mindfulness-based stress reduction: This approach teaches victims to attend to the present moment in a nonjudgmental, accepting manner and

may represent an alternative to trauma-focused treatments (Boyd et al., 2018).

- Acceptance and commitment therapy: The therapy involves training acceptance along with working on behavioral modification toward value-driven goals. Studies have revealed that there are various symptomatic changes that has taken place with the application of this therapy (Varra, 2009; Hayes et al., 2006).
- Present-centered therapy: It was originally developed as a strong comparator treatment that captured many of the effective components of "good psychotherapy"; it demonstrated effects beyond common psychotherapeutic benefits. It is a time-limited treatment for trauma victims that focuses on growing adaptive responses to existing life stressors and complications that are directly or indirectly related to trauma or stressful incident-related symptoms (Schnurr et al., 2001).
- Interpersonal therapy: Interpersonal therapy appears to be effective with limited usefulness for trauma victims. It might be a satisfactory alternative for patients who are reluctant to take up exposure-based therapy methods. Interpersonal psychotherapy focuses on disorder-specific indications in the framework of present issues, especially social or interpersonal-related (Markowitz et al., 2015).
- Psychodynamic psychotherapy: Treatment with the therapy with victims focuses on improving ego strength, self-concept, and dimensions for interpersonal relatedness (Collins, 2004).

A variety of psychotherapies are also used with the victims as per their needs and requirements. Eclectic and integrative therapists draw concepts and techniques from a variety of diverse kinds of therapy that includes dynamic, cognitive, and behavioral approaches. Along with all the above-mentioned therapies, other therapies are also given to the victims and their family members for better coping and future prevention. Community-based therapies are also provided for traumatic people and communities (Palmer & Woolfe, 1999).

Conclusion

Any type of crime can be harmful and shocking for the victim and the person who commits the crime also can have various reasons behind it. Understanding every perspective is difficult; yet, we have tried to find out the various theories behind the offender and criminal behavior along with its psychological impact on the victim which cannot be neglected. It is important to provide support and help for better development and managing the situation as well as the individual. Various theories and therapy strategies can help develop new perspectives towards various criminal acts and accordingly better strategies can be developed to make this world a better place to live in.

References

Agrafiotis, I., Nurse, J. R., Goldsmith, M., Creese, S., & Upton, D. (2018). A taxonomy of cyber-harms: Defining the impacts of cyber-attacks and understanding how they propagate. *Journal of Cybersecurity, 4*(1), tyy006.

Aichhorn, A. (1925). *Neglected youth; Psychoanalysis in Nursing Education: 10 Introductory Lectures* (11th ed., 2005). Berne: Huber.

Alalehto, T., & Azarian, R. (2018). When white collar criminals turn to fatal violence: The impact of narcissism and psychopathy. *Journal of Investigative Psychology and Offender Profiling, 15*(2), 215–226.

Aleixo, P. A., & Norris, C. E. (2000). Personality and moral reasoning in young offenders. *Personality and Individual Differences, 28*, 609–623.

Anderson, C. A., & Bushman, B. J. (2002). Human aggression. *Annual Review of Psychology, 53*, 27–51.

Andrews, D. A., & Bonta, J. (2010). *The psychology of criminal conduct* (5th ed.). Matthew Bender.

American Psychiatric Association (APA). (2013). *Diagnostic and Statistical Manual of Mental Disorders (DSM-V)* (5th ed.). American Psychiatric Publishing.

Babiak, P., Neumann, C. S., & Hare, R. D. (2010). Corporate psychopathy: Talking the walk. *Behavioral Sciences & the Law, 28*(2), 174–193.

Bartol, C. R. (2007). *Criminal behaviour: A psychosocial approach* (5th ed., p. 07458). Prentice Hall, Upper Saddle River.

Beaver, K. M., & Wright, J. P. (2005). Evaluating the effects of birth complications on low self-control in a sample of twins. *International Journal of Offender Therapy and Comparative Criminology, 49*, 450–471.

Becker, G. S. (1968). Crime and punishment: An economic approach. *Journal of Political Economy, 76*, 169–217.

Benson, M. J., Buehler, C., & Gerard, J. M. (2008). Interparental hostility and early adolescent problem behavior: Spillover via maternal acceptance, harshness, inconsistency, and intrusiveness. *The Journal of Early Adolescence, 28*(3), 428–454.

Beech, A., Fisher, D., & Ward, T. (2005). Sexual murderer' implicit theories. *Journal of Interpersonal Violence, 20*, 1366–1389.

Bisson, J., & Andrew, M. (2007). *Psychological treatment of post-traumatic stress disorder (PTSD)*. Cochrane Database System Revision.

Blackburn, R. (1993). *The psychology of criminal conduct: Theory, research and practice*. Wiley.

Brennan, P. A., Mednick, S. A., & Raine, A. (1984). Biosocial interactions and violence: A focus on perinatal factors. In A. Raine, P. A. Brennan, D. P. Farrington, & S. A. Mednick (Eds.), *Biosocial bases of violence* (pp. 163–174). Plenum Press.

Briody, M. (2004). The effects of DNA evidence on homicide cases in court. *Australian & New Zealand Journal of Criminology, 37*(2), 231–252.

Bromberg, W. (1965). *Crime and the mind*. Macmillan.

Buker, H. (2011). Formation of self-control: Gottfredson and Hirschi's general theory of crime and beyond. *Aggression and Violent Behavior, 16*, 265–276.

Bushman, B. J., & Huesmann, L. R. (2010). Aggression. In S. T. Fiske, D. T. Gilbert, & G. Lindzey (Eds.), *Handbook of social psychology* (5th ed., pp. 833–863).

Buss, A. H., & Perry, M. P. (1992). The aggression questionnaire. *Journal of Personality and Social Psychology, 63*, 452–459.

Boyd, J., Richardson, L., Anderson, S., Kerr, T., Small, W., & McNeil, R. (2018). Transitions in income generation among marginalized people who use drugs: A qualitative study on recycling and vulnerability to violence. *International Journal of Drug Policy, 59*, 36–43.

Cahill, S., Rothbaum, B., Resick, P., & Follette, V. (2009). Cognitive-behavioral therapy for adults. In *Effective treatments for PTSD: Practice guidelines from the International Society for Traumatic Stress Studies* (2nd ed.). Guilford Press.

Calkins, S. D., & Keane, S. P. (2009). Developmental origins of early antisocial behaviour. *Development and Psychopathology, 21*, 1095–1109.

Caprara, G. V., Barbaranelli, C., & Zimbardo, P. G. (1996). Understanding the complexity of human aggression: Affective, cognitive, and social dimensions of individual differences in propensity toward aggression. *European Journal of Personality, 10*, 133–155.

Carver, C. S., & White, T. L. (1994). Behavioral inhibition, behavioral activation, and affective responses to impending reward and punishment: The BIS/BAS scales. *Journal of Personality and Social Psychology, 67*, 319–333

Child, J., & Ormerod, D. (2017). *Smith, Hogan, and Ormerod's Essentials of Criminal Law*. Oxford University Press.

Chiu, W. H., & Madden, P. (1998). Burglary and income inequality. *Journal of Public Economics, 69*, 123–141.

Citrome, L., & Volavka, J. (2003). Treatment of violent behavior. In A. Tasman, J. Kay, & J. Lieberman (Eds.), *Psychiatry* (2nd ed.). Wiley.

Collins, P. H. (2004). *Black sexual politics: African Americans, gender, and the new racism*. Routledge.

Comer, R., & Gould, E. (2001). *Psychology around us* (p. 82). Wiley.

Cusack, K., Jonas, D. E., & Forneris, C. A. (2016). Psychological treatments for adults with post-traumatic stress disorder: A systematic review and meta-analysis. *Clinical Psychology Review, 43*, 128–141.

Dabbs, J. M., Riad, J. K., & Chance, S. E. (2001). Testosterone and ruthless homicide. *Personality and Individual Difference, 31*, 599–603.

Dearden, T. E. (2019). How modern psychology can help us understand white-collar criminals. *Journal of Financial Crime, 26*, 61–73.

Denno, D. W. (2005). Criminal law in a post-Freudian world. *University of Illinois Law Review, 2*, 601–174.

Difede, J., & Hoffman, H. G. (2002). Virtual reality exposure therapy for World Trade Center post-traumatic stress disorder: A case report. *Cyberpsychology & Behavior, 5*(6), 529–535.

Dijk, V. (2007). *The world of crime: Breaking the silence on problems of security, justice, and development across the world* (pp. 15–44). SAGE Publications, Inc.

Dijk, V., et al. (1992). Circadian and sleep/wake dependent aspects of subjective alertness and cognitive performance. *Journal of Sleep Research, 1*(2), 112–117.

Ellis, L., Beaver, K. M., & Wright, J. (2009). *Handbook of crime correlates*. Academic Press.

Eysenck, H. J. (1991). Dimensions of personality: 16, 5 or 3? Criteria for a taxonomic paradigm. *Personality and Individual Differences, 12*(8), 773–790.

Eysenck, H. J., & Thomas. (1967). *The biological basis of personality*. Thomas.

Fao, M., Shipro, F., & Solomon, R. (2019). The role of eye movement desensitization and reprocessing (EMDR) therapy in medicine: Addressing the psychological and physical symptoms stemming from adverse life experiences. *The Permanente Journal., 1*, 71–77.

FBI (Federal Bureau of Investigation). (2009). *CODIS Program*. Retrieved from http://www.fbi.gov/hq/lab/html/codis1.htm

Feshbach, S. (1964). The function of aggression and the regulation of aggressive drive. *Psychological Review, 71*, 257–272. Wiley & Sons.

Ferguson, C. J., Cruz, A. M., Martinez, D., Rueda, S. M., Ferguson, D. E., & Negy, C. (2008). Personality, parental, and media influences on aggressive personality and violent crime in young adults. *Journal of Aggression, Maltreatment, and Trauma, 17*(4), 395–414.

Foa, E. B., & Rauch, S. A. (2004). Cognitive changes during prolonged exposure versus prolonged exposure plus cognitive restructuring in female assault survivors with posttraumatic stress disorder. *Journal of Clinical Psychology, 72*(5), 879–884.

Foa, E. B., Keane, T. M., Friedman, M. J., & Cohen, J. (2009). *Effective treatments for PTSD: Practice guidelines from the International Society for Traumatic Stress Studies* (2nd ed.). Guilford Press.

Fossati, A., Barratt, E. S., Borroni, S., Villa, D., Grazioli, F., & Maffe, C. (2007). Impulsivity, aggressiveness, and DSM-IV personality disorders. *Psychiatry Research, 149*, 157–167.

Fowles, D. C. (2001). Biological variables in psychopathology: A psychobiological perspective. In P. B. Sutker & H. E. Adams (Eds.), *Comprehensive handbook of psychopathology* (pp. 85–104). Kluwer Academic/Plenum Press.

Fox, V. (1961). *Community-based corrections*. Prentice-Hall.

Geen, R. G. (2001). *Human aggression* (2nd ed.). Taylor & Francis.

Gluecks, L. (1991). *Predicting delinquency and crime*. Harvard University Press.

Grabosky, P. (1997). *Strategic approaches to property crime control* (PDF). Second National Outlook Symposium: Violent Crime, Property Crime and Public Policy, Canberra, Australia.

Gray, J. A. (1987). *The psychology of fear and stress*. Cambridge University Press.

Hamblen, J. L., Norman, S. B., & Sonis, J. H. (2019). A guide to guidelines for the treatment of posttraumatic stress disorder in adults. *Journal of Psychotherapy (Chicago), 56*(3), 359–373.

Harvey, S., Kerr, J., Keeble, J., & Nicholls, C. M. (2014). *Understanding victims of financial crime Understanding victims of financial crime: A qualitative study with people affected by investment fraud*. NatCen Social Research. Financial Conduct Authority.

Hayes, S., Luoma, J., Bond, F., Masuda, A., & Lillis, J. (2006). Acceptance and commitment therapy: Model, process and outcomes. *Behaviour Research and Therapy, 44*, 1–25. https://doi.org/10.1016/j.brat.2005.06.006

Heaven, P. (1996). Personality and self-reported delinquency: Analysis of the "Big Five" personality dimensions. *Personality and Individual Differences, 20*, 47–54.

Hembree, E. A., & Rothbaum, B. O. (2007). *Prolonged exposure therapy for PTSD: Emotional processing of traumatic experiences: Therapist guide*. Oxford University Press.

Herman, J. L. (2003). The mental health of crime victims: Impact of legal intervention. *Journal of Traumatic Stress, 16*(2), 159–166.

Herrero, Ó., & Colom, R. (2008). Distinguishing impulsive, unsocialized sensation seeking: A comparison between criminal offenders and the general population. *Journal of Individual Differences, 29*(4), 199.

Hetrick, S. E., Purcell, R., Garner, B., & Parslow, R. (2010). Combined pharmacotherapy and psychological therapies for post-traumatic stress disorder (PTSD). *Cochrane Database System Review*, (7), CD007316.

Hunter, R. G., & McEwen, B. S. (2013). Stress and anxiety across the lifespan: Structural plasticity and epigenetic regulation. *Epigenomics, 5*(2), 177–194.

Illingworth, H. (2007). *Canadian Resource Centre for Victims of Crime*.

John, O. P., Caspi, A., Robins, R. W., Moffitt, T. E., & Stouthamer-Loeber, M. (1994). The little five: Exploring the nomological network of the five factor model of personality in adolescent boys. *Child Development, 65*, 160–178.

Julian, A. (2012). *"Crimes against property", Introduction to criminal law, creative commons*, pp. 484–543. Retrieved from: http://creativecommons.org/licenses/by-nc-sa/3.0/

Klaus, P. (2006). *National crime victimization survey: Crime and the nation's households, 2004*. Bureau of Justice Statistics.

Krug, E. G., Mercy, J. A., Dahlberg, L. L., & Zwi, A. B. (2002). The world report on violence and health. *Lancet, 360*, 1083–1088.

Landsford, J. E. (2012). Boys' and girls' relational and physical aggression in nine countries. *Aggressive Behavior, 38*(4), 298–308.

Lange, J. (1929). The importance of twin pathology for psychiatry. *Allgemeine Zeitschrift für Psychiatrie und Psychisch- Gerichtliche, 90*, 122–142.

Larsson, D. (2006). Exposure to property crime as a consequence of poverty. *Journal of Scandinavian Studies in Criminology and Crime Prevention, 7*, 45–60.

Liau, A. K., Barriga, A. Q., & Gibbs, J. C. (1998). Relations between self-serving cognitive distortions and overt vs. covert antisocial behavior in adolescents. *Aggressive Behavior, 24*, 335–346.

Lupien, S. J., McEwen, B. S., Gunnar, M. R., & Heim, C. (2009). Effects of stress throughout the lifespan on the brain, behaviour and cognition. *Nature Reviews Neuroscience, 10*, 434–445.

Markowitz, J. C., Petkova, E., Neria, Y., Meter, P. E., Zhao, Y., Hembree, E., Lovell, K., Biyanova, T., & Marshall, R. D. (2015). Is exposure necessary? A randomized clinical trial of Interpersonal psychotherapy for PTSD. *American Journal of Psychiatry, 172*, 430–440.

McCrady, F., Kaufman, K., Vasey, M. W., Barriga, A. Q., Devlin, R. S., & Gibbs, J. C. (2008). It's all about me: A brief report of incarcerated adolescent sex offenders' generic and sex-specific cognitive distortions. *Sexual Abuse: A Journal of Research and Treatment, 20*, 261–271.

Merton, R. K. (2020). Opportunity structure: The emergence, diffusion, and differentiation of a sociological concept, 1930s–1950s. *In The legacy of anomie theory* (pp. 3–78). Routledge.

Miller, L. (1998). Psychotherapy of crime victims: Treating the aftermath of interpersonal violence. *Psychotherapy: Theory, Research, Practice, Training, 35*(3), 336–345. https://doi.org/10.1037/h0087801

Moffitt, T. E. (2005). Genetic and environmental influences on antisocial behaviors: evidence from behavioral–genetic research. *Advances in Genetics, 55*, 41–104.

Mohammad Rahim, K., Nadiah, M. S., Azizah, O., Khaidzir, I., & Geshina, M. S. (2014). Associations between personality traits and aggression among Malay adult male inmates in Malaysia. *ASEAN Journal of Psychiatry, 2*, 176–185.

Monson, C. M., Macdonald, A., & Fredman, S. J. (2012). Effect of cognitive-behavioral couple therapy for PTSD: A randomized controlled trial. *Journal of the American Medical Association, 308*(7), 700–709.

Moul, C., Dobson-Stone, C., Brennan, J., Hawes, D., & Dadds, M. (2013). An exploration of the serotonin system in antisocial boys with high levels of callous-unemotional traits. *PLoS One, 8*(2), e56619.

Nas, C. N., Brugman, D., & Koops, W. (2008). Measuring self-serving cognitive distortions with the how I think questionnaire. *European Journal of Psychological Assessment*, 181–189.

National Organization for Victim Assistance (NOVA). (2001). *National Organization for Victim Assistance (NOVA)*. National Sexual Violence Resource Center. Retrieved September 21, 2022, from https://www.nsvrc.org/organizations/81

Nee, C., Button, M., Shepherd, D., Blackbourn, D., & Leal, S. (2019). The psychology of the corrupt: Some preliminary findings. *Journal of Financial Crime, 26*(2), 488–495.

Nofziger, S. (2001). *Bullies, fights, and guns: Testing self-control theory with juveniles*. LFB Scholarly.

Palmer, S., & Woolfe, R. (1999). *Integrative and eclectic counseling and psychotherapy*. SAGE Publications.

Patterson, F. M., & Daigler, R. T. (2014). The abnormal psychology of investment performance. *Review of Financial Economics, 23*, 55–63.

Perri, F. S. (2016). Red collar crime. *International Journal of Psychological Studies, 8*, 61–84.

Peterson, J., Skeem, J. L., Hart, E., Vidal, S., & Keith, F. (2010). Analyzing offence patterns as a function of mental illness to test the criminalization hypothesis. *Psychiatric Services, 61*(12), 1217–1222.

Pratt, T. C., & Cullen, F. T. (2000). The empirical status of Gottfredoson and Hirschi's general theory of crime: A meta-analysis. *Criminology, 38*, 931–964.

Raine, A. (1996). Autonomic nervous system activity and violence. In D. M. Stoff & R. B. Cairns (Eds.), *Aggression and violence: Genetic, neurobiological and biological perspectives* (pp. 145–168). Erlbaum.

Rao, S. (2007). Psychiatrist and the science of criminology: Sociological, psychological and psychiatric analysis of the dark side. *Indian Journal of Psychiatry, 49*(1), 3–5.

Rebollo, I., Herrero, O., & Colom, R. (2002). Personality in imprisoned and non-imprisoned people: Evidence from the EPQ-R. *Psicothema, 4*, 540–543.

Resick, P. A., Nishith, P., & Weaver, T. L. (2002). A comparison of cognitive-processing therapy with prolonged exposure and a waiting condition for the treatment of chronic posttraumatic stress disorder in female rape victims. *Journal of Clinical Psychology*.

Robinson, M. (2004). *Why crime? An integrated systems theory of antisocial behaviour.* Pearson Prentice Hall.

Robinson, G., Brewster, B., Silverman, B. W., & Walsh, D. (2021). Covid-19 and child criminal exploitation in the UK: Implications of the pandemic for county lines. *Trends in Organized Crime*, 1–24.

Romero, E., Luengo, M., & Sobral, J. A. (2001). Personality and antisocial behaviour: Study of temperamental dimensions. *Personality and Individual Differences, 31*, 329–348.

Rothbaum, B. O., & Davis, M. (2003). Applying learning principles to the treatment of post-trauma reactions. *Annals of the New York Academy of Sciences, 1008*(1), 112–121.

Rothbaum, B. O., Hodges, L. F., & Ready, D. (2001). Virtual reality exposure therapy for Vietnam veterans with posttraumatic stress disorder. *Journal of Clinical Psychiatry, 62*(8), 617–622.

Sarchiaopone, M., Carli, V., Cuomo, C., Marchetti, M., & Roy, A. (2009). Association between childhood trauma and aggression in male prisoners. *Psychiatry Research, 165*, 187–192.

Schnurr, P. P., Friedman, M. J., Lavori, P. W., & Hsieh, F. Y. (2001). Design of department of veterans affairs cooperative study no. 420: Group treatment of posttraumatic stress disorder. *Controlled Clinical Trials, 22*(1), 74–88.

Schnurr, P. (2017). Focusing on trauma-focused psychotherapy for posttraumatic stress disorder. *Journal of Clinical Psychology, 14*, 56–60.

Scott, A. J., Lloyd, R., & Gavin, J. (2010). The influence of prior relationship on perceptions of stalking in the United Kingdom and Australia. *Criminal Justice and Behavior, 37*(11), 1185–1194.

Shapiro, D. (2003). Individual rights, drug policy, and the worst-case Scenario. *Criminal Justice Ethics, 22*(1), 41–45.

Shapland, M., & Hall, A. (2007). Self-reported delinquency in boys aged 11 to 14. *British Journal of Criminology, 18*, 255–266.

Slade, T., Johnson, A., Oakley, M., & Andrews, G. (2009). 2007 national survey of mental health and wellbeing: Methods and key findings. *Journal of Psychiatry, 43*, 594–605.

Sloan, D. M., & Marx, B. P. (2019). *Written exposure therapy for PTSD: A brief treatment approach for mental health professionals.* American Psychological Press.

Sloan, D. M., Marx, B. P., Lee, D. J., & Resick, P. A. (2018). A brief exposure-based treatment vs cognitive processing therapy for posttraumatic stress disorder: A randomized noninferiority clinical trial. *JAMA Psychiatry, 75*(3), 233–239.

Tibbetts, S. G., & Piquero, A. R. (1999). The influence of gender, low birth weight, and disadvantaged environment in predicting early onset of offending: A test of Moffitt's interactional hypothesis. *Criminology, 37*, 843–877.

Travis, H. (1960). *Key ideas in criminology and criminal justice* (pp. 163–196). Sage Publications.

Trninic, V., Barancic, M., & Nazor, M. (2008). The five-factor model of personality and aggressiveness in prisoners and athletes. *Kinesiology, 40*, 170–181.

Trompeter, G. M., Carpenter, T., Desai, N., & Riley, R. A. (2013). A synthesis of fraud related research. *Journal of Practice and Theory, 32*, 287–321.

Tseloni, G., Jason, R., Goldsmith, M., Creese, S., & Upton, D. (2002). Burglary victimization in England and Wales, the United States and the Netherlands. A cross-national comparative test of routine activities and lifestyle theories. *The British Journal of Criminology, 1*(33), 37–44.

Van Aken, M. A., van Lieshout, C. F., & Scholte, R. H. (1998). The social relationships and adjustment of the various personality types and subtypes. *Society for Research on Adolescence, 1*, 420–449.

Van Goozen, S. H. M., Fairchild, G., & Harold, G. T. (2008). The role of neurobiological deficits in childhood antisocial behavior. *Current Directions in Psychological Science, 17*, 224–228.

van Kesteren, J. N., & Alvazzi del Frate, A. (2002). The ICVS in the developing world. *International Journal of Comparative Criminology, 2*(1), 57–76.

Varra. (2009). Acceptance and commitment therapy: Model, process and outcomes. *Journal of Behaviour Research and Therapy, 1*(43), 1–25.

Vazsonyi, A. T., Pickering, L. E., Junger, M., & Hessing, D. (2001). An empirical test of a general theory of crime: A formation comparative study of self-control and the prediction of deviance. *Journal of Research in Crime and Delinquency, 38*, 91–131.

Ward, T. (2000). Sexual offenders' cognitive distortions as implicit theories. *Aggression and Violent Behavior, 5*, 491–507.

Warren. (2012). Pharmacotherapy for post-traumatic stress disorder in combat veterans. *Journal of Managed Care and Hospital Formulary Management, 37*(1), 32–38.

Warren, J. I., Hurt, S., Loper, A. B., Bale, R., & Friend., R, & Chauhan, P. (2002). Psychiatric symptoms, history of victimization, and violent behavior among incarcerated female felons: An American perspective. *International Journal of Law and Psychiatry, 25*, 129–149.

Williamson, E., Dutch, N. W., & Clawson, H. J. (2008). *Evidence-based mental health treatment for victims of human trafficking*. Office of the Assistant Secretary for Planning and Evaluation, U.S. Department of Health and Human Service.

Willits, D., Broidy, L., & Denman, K. (2013). Schools, neighborhood risk factors, and crime. *Crime & Delinquency, 59*(2), 292–315.

Zar Rokh, E. (2007). Crimes Against Property & Ownership. Available at SSRN: https://ssrn.com/abstract=963613. https://doi.org/10.2139/ssrn.963613.

Zuckerman, M. (1979). *Sensation seeking: Beyond the optimal level of arousal*. Lawrence Erlbaum.

Zuckerman, M. (2007). *Sensation seeking and risky behavior*. American Psychological Association.

Chapter 14
Elder Abuse and Victims with Disabilities

Vaitsa Giannouli

Elder Abuse

The expected increase of older population in the USA (Vincent, 2010) and also worldwide (Bergman et al., 2013) is related to numerous challenges and dilemmas regarding medical issues, psychological, economic, social, philosophical, political as well as legal issues (Giannouli, 2017, 2019, 2020; Heisler, 2019). Healthy aging is related to a number of changes (Coll, 2019), and although there are cases of disease-free older adults, there is a high frequency of reported major morbidities including dementia, cancer, cerebrovascular accident(s), heart failure, and myocardial infarctions (Newson et al., 2010) that may affect older individuals in many ways in their everyday life. Longevity reported in older adults is also linked to physical, mental and financial dependency, something that increases the chances of abuse against older adults (Alon, 2021; Giannouli, 2022a; Govil & Gupta, 2016; Jamshidi et al., 1992). Elder abuse or abuse of seniors is a common, but not thoroughly investigated phenomenon around the world with devastating effects on the victims (individual consequences) (Abolfathi Momtaz et al., 2013) as well as with broader societal costs (Pillemer et al., 2016), that exists internationally not only in older institutionalized older patients or minority older adults (Dong, 2015) but also in community-dwelling elderly people aged 65 years and older, who suffer from abuse or are at risk of being abused (Gorbien & Eisenstein, 2005). This differentiation in research is based on the discrimination of two groups: (a) community and (b) institutional living older adult populations (Acierno et al., 2010). World Health Organization (WHO), defines 'elder abuse' as a "single or repeated act, or lack of appropriate action, occurring within any relationship where there is an expectation of trust, which causes harm or distress to an older person" (WHO, 2002). Although a dramatic discrepancy has been found between the prevalence rates of elder abuse

V. Giannouli (✉)
Aristotle University of Thessaloniki, Thessaloniki, Greece

R. T. Gopalan (ed.), *Victimology*, https://doi.org/10.1007/978-3-031-12930-8_14

and the number of elder abuse cases actually reported (Roberto, 2016), the prevalence of elder abuse in (private and public) institutions is still high (Yon et al., 2019), and although there is a lack of prevalence studies in community-dwelling older adults in low-income and middle-income countries, elder abuse seems to affect one in six older adults worldwide (Yon et al., 2017). Especially during COVID-19 crisis, an 83.6% increase in elder abuse was found, compared to prevalence estimates prior to the pandemic (Chang & Levy, 2021), while factors such as physical distancing was associated with reduced risk of elder abuse, but financial strain was associated with an increased risk of abuse (Chang & Levy, 2021).

Therefore, for this mixed population of healthy elders as well as older patients with diverse intermittent health problems or chronic conditions, there is a growing attention of policymakers, healthcare systems, social welfare agencies, and the general public (Giannouli, 2018; Giannouli et al., 2019a, b; Pillemer et al., 2016). Although many theories and models exist to interpret elder abuse (Nerenberg, 2008), some focusing on intra-individual explanations, on stress, on dependency on isolation and transgenerational violence (Payne, 2005), one major problem for research as well as for society is the lack of consensus in the definitions of elder abuse (Giannouli, 2018; Pillemer et al., 2016). For example, a widely accepted definition coming from the U.S. National Academy of Sciences, defines elder as "(1) intentional actions that cause harm or create a serious risk of harm (whether or not harm is intended) to a vulnerable elder by a caregiver or other person who stands in a trust relationship, or (2) failure by a caregiver to satisfy the elder's basic needs or to protect the elder from harm" (Wallace & Bonnie, 2003). The National Center on Elder Abuse (2005) distinguishes between seven different types of elder abuse, that may occur with varying frequency and severity, and in different settings (in the older adults' own home, in organizational/institutional and/or community settings) (Baker et al., 2016). The forms that elder abuse can take are namely (1) physical abuse, (2) sexual abuse/assault, (3) psychological/emotional abuse, (4) financial/material exploitation, (5) neglect, (6) abandonment, and (7) self-neglect (Hardin & Khan-Hudson, 2005). These types of abuse can be perpetrated in isolation or can co-occur, something that is known as 'poly-victimization' (Hamby et al., 2016).

Physical Abuse

Physical abuse refers to the use of physical force that may result in bodily injury, physical pain, and/or impairment (National Center on Elder Abuse, 2005). Physical abuse also refers to cases of body actions related to 'annoyance to the body causing the pain or serious or less serious injury, physical compulsion or drug-induced restraint' (Paul & Parkins PA, 2017). This involves at least one act of violence, such as hitting, burning, pushing, grabbing, stabbing, cutting, beating, striking, slapping, physical restraint, or intentional overmedication negatively affecting the older adult (Friedman et al., 2015; Mouton et al., 2005; World Health Organization, 2002).

Unfortunately, many incidents of elder abuse (e.g. psychological) are not identified by professionals in healthcare (Reis & Nahmiash, 1998), but only the more severe cases of physical abuse may be identified due to the visible signs that it leaves (Abolfathi Momtaz et al., 2013; Gordon & Brill, 2001). Physical abuse seems to be the most consistently measured mistreatment type (Pillemer et al., 2016), with the use of information based on the Conflict Tactic Scale (CTS) and a relevant modified version of this scale, as developed by Pillemer and Finkelhor (1988). There are contradicting evidence regarding the possible factors predicting physical abuse as depression-depressive symptoms, which are associated specifically with physical abuse in China (Wu et al., 2012), U.K. (O'Keeffe et al., 2007) and Canada (Podnieks, 1993). In addition to that, gender may be another factor, as female older adults who also face poor physical health get more frequently exposed to abuse (that they feel ashamed to report) more than males cross-culturally (Ayalon & Huyck, 2001; Briones et al., 2002; Cadmus & Owoaje, 2012; Ghodoosi et al., 2014; Jeon et al., 2019; Lai et al., 2014). This reported gender issue may be due to the fact that women tend to face higher abuse or mistreatment or elder abuse in the form of intimate partner violence and domestic violence prior to old age (Aitken & Griffin, 1996; Penhale, 2003). Another intergenerational family issue is the finding of physical and emotional sibling violence through the life course and its relationship to elder physical abuse (Perkins et al., 2018). Finally, anatomically it is of interest to report that two-thirds of injuries are to the upper extremity and maxillofacial region (Murphy et al., 2013).

The identification and intervention of elder abuse involves many obstacles that can be described in three levels: clinical, organizational, and policy (Mohd Mydin & Othman, 2020). At the clinical level, primary care physicians recognize that they lack the confidence and knowledge of elder abuse and neglect intervention (Mohd Mydin & Othman, 2020; Rosen et al., 2018a, b). Interventions regarding physical abuse have been shown to be effective, when education and anger management intervention programs for individuals, who physically abuse or neglect their elderly dependents, are employed (Campbell Reay & Browne, 2002).

Sexual Abuse/Assault

Sexual abuse/assault involves non-consensual sexual contact(s) of any kind (such as sexual activities ranging from unwanted sexual touching to rape) with an elderly person (National Center on Elder Abuse, 2005). Sexual abuse is the least frequently reported form of elder mistreatment (Shields et al., 2004) not only in healthy older adults, but mainly in vulnerable (physically and cognitively) older adults living in long-term care facilities (Ramsey-Klawsnik et al., 2007).This may be due to the fact that sexual abuse in Western countries, such as the USA, is much more a taboo issue than reporting psychological or physical abuse (Anme et al., 2005). It is true that there are sexual behavioural changes, such as inappropriate/improper sexual behaviours, hypersexuality and disinhibition found in Alzheimer's disease patients

(Bardell et al., 2011; Bartelet et al., 2014; Black et al., 2005; Canevelli et al., 2011, 2017; Cipriani et al., 2016; De Medeiros et al., 2008; Gomes-Pinto, 2014; Rosen et al., 2010; Thom et al., 2017; Vloeberghs et al., 2007; Wallace & Safer, 2009; Ward & Manchip, 2013), a symptomatology that opens a discussion regarding informed consent.

More specifically, it has been supported that gender (women), origin (Aboriginal Canadians), and family status (elders who are divorced), as well as geographical (living in urban areas) and economic status (low income) are risk factors not only of physical abuse but mainly of sexual abuse (Brozowski & Hall, 2010). In the case of sexual abuse of older victims, the myth-stereotype of young attractive female attacked by a stranger is not confirmed (Bows & Westmarland, 2017). In addition to that, there is a reported variability in findings regarding male and female alleged and/or confirmed sexual perpetrators as well as both male and female elderly sexual abuse victims (Ramsey-Klawsnik et al., 2008). This variability renders difficult the prediction of sexual abuse cases, especially when the perpetrator characteristics, the victim vulnerabilities, the type of abuse act(s), and the location(s) of assault(s) are all simultaneously taken into consideration (Ramsey-Klawsnik et al., 2008).

Elders with a diagnosis of a major neurocognitive disorder (dementia), when compared to those without a diagnosis, are found to be abused more often by individuals known to them (such as a family member, a caregiver or another nursing home resident in cases that these older patients are institutionalized) than by a total stranger (Alon, 2021; Burgess & Phillips, 2006). More specifically, there are three patterns of abuse within the family: (a) long-term domestic violence, (b) recent onset of sexual abuse within a long-term marriage, and (c) sexual victimization within a new marriage (Ramsey-Klawsnik, 2003). Additionally, incestuous elder abuse is mainly committed by adult children, other relatives, and quasi-relatives (Ramsey-Klawsnik, 2003). Here, we should mention that there are reports from India and Africa where widows are being forced into marriage, something that is linked to this type of elder abuse (Kumari, 2014; McFerson, 2013).

Recent studies have found that elderly sexual assaults are more frequently committed by strangers (Chopin & Beauregard, 2021). For vulnerable (physically and mentally) older adults living in nursing homes, it has been supported that the victims tend to be predominately white males with cognitive and physical deficits that limit their ability for self-care, and the most typical sexual abuse alleged and substantiated is fondling (Teaster et al., 2007). Sexual crimes against the elderly have been found to be more violent and resulting in more severe injuries, than those in younger individuals, and they occur more often in the victim's residence (for the elders that are not institutionalized) (Chopin & Beauregard, 2020). The motivation behind elderly sexual abuse can be categorized in four clusters: sex, anger, opportunities, and experimentation (Chopin & Beauregard, 2021), but also power-control issues have been documented especially for male perpetrators (Cartwright & Moore, 1989). It is of interest that these elders show distress rather than verbal disclosures, they are easily confused and verbally manipulated (mainly due to their cognitive disabilities), and are frequently also beaten (Burgess & Phillips, 2006). Although, all reported suspected cases of elder sexual abuse need a complete physical examination accompanied by a sexual assault evidence kit, we should not disregard verbal, behavioral and/or physical changes of elders, which can be used to support an allegation of sexual assault (Burgess & Phillips, 2006). These difficulties in verbal communication are also a point to keep in mind, especially when working with non-verbal elders (that is those diagnosed as severe stage of dementia) (Ramsey-Klawsnik, 1993). Also, marginalized elders are at risk of increased vulnerability to elder abuse related to oppression experienced as a consequence of ageism, sexism, ableism/ disability, racism, heterosexism/homophobia, classism, and various intersecting types of oppression (Walsh et al., 2010). Prevention strategies could include apart from the routine check of the elders also relevant criminal background checks on staff caring for elders in nursing homes or performing services in the homes of elders (Burgess et al., 2005).

Psychological/Emotional Abuse

Psychological/emotional abuse is the infliction of mental anguish, pain, or distress through verbal or non-verbal acts (Hall et al., 2016; National Center on Elder Abuse, 2005). In addition to this definition, insensitivity and disrespect (e.g. treating older adults like infants or isolating older adults from their family, friends, or regular activities) are considered to be forms of emotional/psychological abuse (Conrad et al., 2010a, b). Psychological/emotional abuse in a recent study in Poland is more often experienced by older women, older adults living in urban areas as well as older individuals with a reported low socioeconomic status and those suffering from a chronic disease (Filipska et al., 2020). Prevalence estimates for abuse reported by older residents in institutional settings were found to be highest for psychological abuse, followed by physical, financial, neglect, and sexual abuse (Acierno et al., 2010; Yon et al., 2019), and especially for (physically or mentally) dependent older adults a high percentage has been found to report emotional/psychological abuse (Cooper et al., 2008). It is of interest that emotional/psychological abuse is the most prevalent type of abuse among older adults suffering from dementia/major neurocognitive disorders (Downes et al., 2013). A point to consider is that the estimated prevalence might differ depending on researchers' definition of emotional/psychological abuse and the relevant measures that were used in the assessment (Conrad et al., 2010a). One such widely used measure in use is the Older Adult Psychological Abuse Measure (OAPAM) (Conrad et al., 2010a, 2011).

Regarding the risk factors, so far an emphasis is given on the characteristics of the abusers, for example substance abuse by abusers is associated with a higher probability of elder emotional/psychological abuse (Hwalek, 1996). Additionally, mental health problems and abuser dependency on the older adult are also common abuser characteristics (Johannesen & LoGiudice, 2013) as well as financial dependency (Jackson & Hafemeister, 2011a). One prominent factor is the caregiver stress as expressed in the victim–abuser interaction, which has been found to be the most predictive of emotional/psychological abuse (Pillemer & Finkelhor, 1988). More specifically, a review supports that abusers experiencing caregiver burden and/or stress, or who had psychiatric illness, or psychological problems, were more likely to be perpetrators of psychological abuse (Johannesen & LoGiudice, 2013). A poor premorbid or current relationship between the caregiver and the older adult (for the cases of elder patients) characterized by conflict and aggression is also a risk factor particular to the occurrence of emotional/psychological abuse (Downes et al., 2013).

Another reported risk factor is the lack of social support or social isolation as experienced by the older adults. Lower global cognition (measured by lower Mini-Mental Status Examination scores) is associated with emotional/psychological abuse (Dong et al., 2011), as well as depression and anxiety which are also correlated with emotional/psychological abuse (Beach et al., 2010; Begle et al., 2011; Fisher & Regan, 2006). Alcohol use is cross-culturally associated with increased risk of emotional/psychological abuse (Tredal et al., 2013), and in the USA, it was found that the need for assistance with activities of daily living (ADLs) is also correlated with emotional abuse (Acierno et al., 2010). Thus, older adults with a diagnosis of psychiatric illness(es), psychological problems, poor physical heath or fragility are more likely to become victims of emotional/psychological abuse (Johannesen & LoGiudice, 2013). These factors could be targeted in early identification and prevention programs (Burnett, Achenbaum, & Murphy, 2014a).

Financial Abuse/Material Exploitation

Financial abuse/material exploitation is defined as the illegal or improper use of an elder's funds, property, and/or assets (National Center on Elder Abuse, 2005) in terms of thefts of money and materials, scams, overcharging for services, coercion, forged checks, mismanagement of finances, unauthorized ATM charges, influence or pressure to resign money or to transfer real property as a 'gift to others', estate changes, and abuse of trust (Conrad et al., 2010b; Setterlund et al., 2007; Wood et al., 2014). Financial elder abuse is usually linked to a trusted individual, differentiating it from cases of fraud and/or scams, which are usually perpetrated by strangers (Burnes et al., 2017). Among the above-mentioned types of abuse, financial exploitation becomes increasingly important in the modern era not only in healthy older adults, but also in patients suffering with different types of diseases (Giannouli, 2018, 2022a). Exploitation by primary contacts is contrasted to fraud by secondary contacts, such as home repair frauds, insurance frauds, medical frauds, confidence games, telemarketing frauds, and phony contests frauds (Payne, 2005). Financial abuse/material exploitation is difficult to detect and prosecute, mainly because of the many problems that existin defining elder financial abuse (Gibson & Qualls, 2012). Given that social isolation and loneliness is common in old age (even in healthy older adults), and thus impaired social interactions may alienate the individuals from exterior sources of support (e.g. friends, family) (Tragantzopoulou & Giannouli, 2021), and the 'financial reality' (current prices of goods, new forms of financial scams, etc.), this may render them possible victims of financial abuse

(Giannouli, 2022a; Lichtenberg, 2017). Financial abuse may have clearer or singular motives from the side of the perpetrator (e.g. financial gain) than physical or psychological abuse, where motives may be multiple and complex (Fraga Dominguez et al., 2021).

So far, financial abuse is defined as the illegal or improper use of a person's finances or property by another individual, with an emphasis given on the abusive event and the associated risk factors, but 'routine activities theory' directs attention more to developing prevention strategies that focus on everyday activities and hence seeks to reduce the opportunities for illegal activity (Setterlund et al., 2007). As a consequence, a new emphasis is given to the intersection of financial exploitation and decision-making capacity (Lichtenberg, 2016a, b, c). Financial incapacity risk factors that may be involved in financial exploitation are numerous. For example, a diagnosis of a major or minor neurocognitive disorder (e.g. Alzheimer's disease, vascular dementia, frontotemporal dementia, Parkinson's disease, and even mild cognitive impairment) plays a vital factor (Giannouli & Tsolaki, 2014, 2016; Giannouli et al., 2018). In addition to that, the volume of specific brain areas (e.g. left angular gyrus and amygdala volumes) have been found to influence financial capacity (Giannouli & Tsolaki, 2019a), while impaired cognitive skills, such as perseveration in arithmetic skills, are found to be impaired in older adults (Giannouli, 2013), and more specifically these impaired skills in the Mini-Mental State Examination (MMSE) item that examines subtraction of serial sevens can predict financial incapacity (Giannouli & Tsolaki, 2022a). The diagnosis of comorbid depression also affects cognitive skills, including financial capacity skills, not only in the above-mentioned neurocognitive disorders (Giannouli & Tsolaki, 2019b, 2021a, b, c), but also in healthy older individuals (Giannouli & Tsolaki, 2019b, 2021a, b, c). These findings are also supported longitudinally, as the cognitive capacity for financial issues is declining both in Alzheimer's Disease as well as Mild Cognitive Impairment (MCI), thus increasing the chances of financial abuse as dependency increases and help-seeking behaviours may decrease (Giannouli et al., 2022; Martin et al., 2008; Triebel et al., 2009). Another point to be mentioned is the role of vascular burden, and its detrimental impact on financial capacity (Giannouli & Tsolaki, 2022b). Finally, the role of impaired self-awareness and insight in Alzheimer's Disease as well as MCI has been correlated with deficits in financial capacity, a finding that also supports that impaired self-awareness of cognitive efficiency may also be a risk factor for financial abuse in the abovementioned patient groups (Giannouli & Tsolaki, 2022c). These situations wherein both members of a dyad may manifest excessive dependency of one form or another are called synergistic dependencies and play a role in the prediction of financial abuse (Borenstein, 2019).

A new interesting finding supports that apathy instead of depression plays a key role in predicting financial capacity in Parkinson's disease with dementia and frontotemporal dementia (Giannouli & Tsolaki, 2021d). One more interesting finding supports that genetic information, such as Apoe ε4 allele, cannot be used in the prediction of financial capacity performance in Mild Alzheimer Disease (Giannouli & Tsolaki, 2021e). A clear influence of education (formal education in years) as well as financial (il)literacy may be a fundamental influence on financial (in)capacity and financial abuse (Giannouli & Tsolaki, 2021g).

It has been reported that older women with high socioeconomic status, as well as Latina older women do not identify financial abuse as a type of elder abuse, whereas working-class white women do (Roberto, 2016). Of course, one problem that arises is the fact that overestimation or underestimation of financial capacity and incapacity can play the role of a confusing factor and as a result high levels of financial abuse and exploitation may arise (Giannouli & Tsolaki, 2021f). Sentimentality and nostalgia may also be negative factors influencing not only cognitive functions related to financial (in)capacity, but also behaviours linked to financial exploitation (Stoyanova et al., 2017).

Although there is a plethora of relevant tools regarding the assessment of financial capacity/incapacity in old age (Ghesquiere et al., 2019), mainly coming from the USA, such as Lichtenberg Financial Decision Screening Scale (LFDSS) (Lichtenberg, 2016a, b, c) and the Financial Capacity Instrument (FCI) (Marson, 2013; Marson et al., 2000, 2005, 2009), there is also the dimension regarding financial exploitation, measuring by a self-report instrument, the Older Adult Financial Exploitation Measure (OAFME) (Conrad et al., 2010b). So far the cross-cultural differences and the different legal systems and the diversity of the theoretical models on which these instruments are based render predictions of financial exploitation difficult to reach (Jackson & Hafemeister, 2011b).

The experiences of victims of financial exploitation in general are characterized as linked to negative affect and loss of financial control (Giannouli et al., 2019a, b). In many cases, the influence of interventions based on spirituality may assist the individuals' resilience and fostering of self-esteem (Giannouli & Giannoulis, 2020; Giannoulis & Giannouli, 2020a, b). Additionally, cognitive impairment predicts perceptions regarding self-stigma of seeking help in older adults, and as a result this perception of stigma may hinder reports of financial abuse and therefore should be aimed at when interventions are discussed (Giannouli, 2022b).

Although information sharing between healthcare experts and older adults/families/caregivers has been claimed to be of importance, especially in the case of elder abuse (Giannouli & Tsolaki, 2015), it is not enough when prevention, intervention and rehabilitation methods are concerned (Giannouli et al., 2017). One more reason for this complex issue is that there are not only cases of pure financial exploitation, but also of hybrid financial exploitation, in which psychological abuse, physical abuse, or neglect is found along with financial exploitation at the same time (Jackson & Hafemesiter, 2012).

In addition to that, the introduction of medical technologies renders necessary the implementation of e-health applications not only in the assessment of cognitive and emotional factors that may influence financial (in)capacity and therefore the possibilities of financial exploitation (Greene, 2022), but also in intervention programs, such as online educational programs focusing on strengthening relevant financial skills in older individuals as well as their families and caregivers (Giannouli & Hyphantis, 2017). Although Internet (applications) may assist communication, diminish isolation, provide the place where information is provided and financial education is achieved, at the same time it may be a new medium where abuse takes place (Greene, 2022). Points on which interventions should focus on are the financial knowledge and skills and financial decision-making, with special care for the contextual factors (financial situational awareness, psychological vulnerability, undue influence, and past financial exploitation), intellectual factors (expression of choice, rationale, understanding, and appreciation), consistency with values, and integrity of financial decisional ability (Adams & Lichtenberg, 2014; Lichtenberg et al., 2015).

There is a great emphasis on the role of banks and bank employees as the first to be able to detect financial abuse (Pratt, 2003), and this reflects the need of prevention and intervention programs to enhance banks' responses, through additional and focused education and training, in an attempt to promote integrated inter-sectorial collaboration (Phelan et al., 2021). In this line, there are multidisciplinary teams, such as Financial Abuse Specialist Team (FAST) who follow a rapid-response system providing immediate intervention in cases of financial abuse against elders, which provides the community with both a deterrent to prevent future incidence of financial abuse and the ability to move quickly to prevent losses by creating a seamless system of collaboration (Malks et al., 2003).

Neglect

Neglect is related to (intentional/willful) refusal or (unintentional/non-willful) failure, to fulfil any part of a person's obligations or duties to an elderly person, that is the physical and/or emotional needs of the older adult (National Center on Elder Abuse, 2005). Neglect may also include "the failure of a person who has fiduciary responsibilities to provide care for an elder (e.g. pay for necessary home care services), or failure on the part of an in-home service provider to provide necessary care" (National Center on Elder Abuse, 2013). Neglect can take two forms: passive or active, depending on the intent of the caregiver (Kruger & Moon, 1999). Passive neglect may be due to the caregiver's ignorance, lack of skills, or the caregiver's own failing health (Ahmad & Lachs, 2002).

Reviews showing prevalence rates or measurement of elder abuse conclude that neglect in older adults is not so far measured sufficiently (Cooper et al., 2008; Dong, 2015; Gallione et al., 2017; McCarthy et al., 2017; Sooryanarayana et al., 2013). Neglected older adults are often subject to lower quality of life, poorer self-rated health, and higher levels of depression; thus there is an urgent need to detect and prevent neglect at the earliest stages (Hall et al., 2016). Neglect may play a determining role in the deaths of older adults (especially those with intellectual as well as physical disabilities), thus making it necessary for healthcare workers to be more alert to the clinical signs of neglect (Ventura et al., 2018). Urban older women in USA face more often passive neglect than rural women (Dimah & Dimah, 2003). In a recent study of thematic analysis in Ghana, four categories emerged regarding neglect: "(1) Since the death of my husband: neglect as a function of a natural cause;

(2) I did not plan well by then: neglect attributed to the self; (3) They do to all of us: neglect resulting from the failure of government institutions; and, (4) Our family do not even come to see us: neglect attributed to the breakdown of the extended family system" (Awuviry-Newton et al., 2020). Again as in the previously mentioned types of elder abuse, operational definitions of neglect differ significantly between research studies, and at the same time demographic, socioeconomic, and cultural differences influence in differential ways the perceptions of neglect in different countries, thus making all these factors possible causes of discrepancies in reported prevalence rates of neglect in various countries (Dong, 2015; Stodolska et al., 2020).

Elderly living in social homes usually have the characteristics to be defined as neglected elderly and are at a high risk of depression due to lack of social support (Kartinah & Sumarni, 2021). This is a point for interventions, such as psychotherapy, and more specifically logotherapy for neglect (Elsherbiny & Al Maamari, 2018; Kartinah & Sumarni, 2021).

Abandonment

Abandonment refers to the desertion of an elderly person by a person who has physical custody of the elder or by a person who has assumed responsibility for providing care to the elder (National Center on Elder Abuse, 2005). Abandonment is neglect by family members concerning some of their family members (Martínez et al., 2020). The majority of states in the USA do not recognize elder abandonment as a form of elder abuse in their statutes (Rzeszut, 2017). Older adults are abandoned in retirement homes and at hospitals, usually documented as a sudden change in their living arrangement (Villarreal et al., 2017).

For example, this phenomenon is frequently reported in India (Chokkanathan & Lee, 2005), where police is considered to be a valuable community resource for identifying and returning lost and abandoned elders or by informing relevant institutions (Kardile & Peisah, 2017). In addition to that, there are reports regarding widows coming from some traditional societies, who are at greater risk of having their property seized and being abandoned by their families, something that is not considered in their societies as problematic (Pillemer et al., 2016). In Western countries, abandonment can also be seen as lack of attention and care not only on the part of the family members, but also on the part of society in general (Martínez et al., 2020). Although elderly care by family members is an important traditional culture of the people in countries such as Greece, Bulgaria, Romania (Giannouli et al., 2019a, b), and Nigeria (Dimkpa, 2015), a reported decline in elderly care in Nigeria has been attributed to the erosion of the traditional culture by foreign cultures, modernization and urbanization as well as economic and social problems (Dimkpa, 2015). Although little is known about how the elderly experience abandonment, there is a study showing that they progress from resisting, occupying, pondering, and embracing phases toward successful coping (de Guzman et al., 2012), while data from older women show that they experience a range of negative emotions such as feeling of "abandonment", "feeling of rejection", "feeling of loneliness", " concerns about decrepitude and overload" and "concerns of dying alone" (Alikarami et al., 2021). This data may fill in the gap of "elders' missing voices" and assist healthcare providers with knowledge of appropriate interventions in the provision of holistic care.

Self-neglect

Self-neglect involves behaviors of an elderly person that threaten the elder's health or safety (National Center on Elder Abuse, 2005), and it involves profound inattention to health and hygiene by the individual herself (Pavlou & Lachs, 2008). Four subtypes of self-neglect have been found: physical and medical neglect, environmental neglect, global neglect, and financial neglect (Burnett et al., 2014a, b). Although there is a debate whether self-neglect is actually a geriatric syndrome, there is strong evidence to support this, based on its multifactorial aetiology, its clear association with increased mortality as well as with higher rates of hospitalization (Dong et al., 2012), and the fact that two other geriatric syndromes (cognitive impairment and depression) are risk factors for self-neglect (Pavlou & Lachs, 2006).

Clinical evaluation is recommended to focus on medical history, cognitive function, social networks, psychiatric screening and environment as comorbidity, dementia, depression, alcoholism, anxiety disorders, schizophrenia, obsessive-compulsive disorder, personality disorders, social isolation, low education, poverty, adverse life events, pride in independence, sensory and physical impairments have been proposed as possible risk factors (Pavlou & Lachs, 2008). Most of the times, the individual's capacity is under question, and interventions are case-based (Pavlou & Lachs, 2008). Of course, there is another interpretation to the above-mentioned, as self-neglect as well as neglect may be attributable to frail older adults' and their families' lack of resources to pay for essential goods and services and the inadequate public policy coverage (inadequate existing healthcare and other formal support programs) for the older adults (Choi et al., 2009). Older adults who are vulnerable to self-neglect may demonstrate an intact capacity to make decisions, but their capacity to identify and extract themselves from harmful situations, circumstances, and/or relationships may be diminished (Naik et al., 2008). Eight instruments have been proposed for the measurement of self-neglect (Qian et al., 2021), such as the Self-neglect Severity Scale (SSS) (Kelly et al., 2008), the Chicago Self-Neglect Scale, and the Texas Self-Neglect Scale (Dong & Simon, 2013). A plethora of ethical dilemmas arise in the medical treatment of older adults with self-neglect, as is the case of rehabilitation nurses, who are obligated to uphold the autonomy of older adults and strengthen their independence, but when poor health behaviors put older adults or others at risk for negative consequences, the basic principles of autonomy, beneficence, nonmaleficence, and capacity raise complicating questions (Mauk, 2011).

Despite the paucity of empirical evidence of specific intervention strategies, a multidisciplinary team approach is strongly suggested (Dong, 2017). Possible interventions should aim at the risk factors, such as depressive symptoms and/or cognitive impairment, found in elderly individuals living in the community (Abrams et al., 2002). More specifically, as shown by a recent review, some specific characteristics such as sociodemographic (male, older age, low economic status, ethnicity, lower educational level, marital status, and lower number of children), health-related characteristics (existence of cognitive impairment, lower level of physical function, nutritional status, higher number of medical comorbidities, and pain), psychological characteristics (with most prominent a diagnosis of depression), and social context characteristics (living alone, lower social networks and social engagement, lower neighbourhood cohesion, and neighbourhood disorder) may all be points to take into consideration in detection and prevention of self-neglect (Yu et al., 2021).

Older Victims with Disabilities

An individual with a disability is defined by the Americans with Disabilities Act (ADA) as a person who has a physical or mental impairment that substantially limits one or more major life activities, a person who has a history or record of such an impairment, or a person who is perceived by others as having such an impairment. As stated above, healthy elders usually do not fall in the above definition (with the exception of cases of formally undiagnosed disorders), but older adults with a diagnosis of age-related neurocognitive disorder or other physical disorders (medical diagnoses related to the cognitive disorder or not), are frequently referred as victims or as individuals very vulnerable to crimes (Giannouli, 2022a).

In addition to that, there is a special population of older adults, that is, those who form a growing number of older adults with intellectual disabilities, for example in the case of Down syndrome, who have intellectual disabilities diagnosed early in their life with additional comorbid condition(s), due to the documented increase in life expectancy (Bittles et al., 2007) and premature aging (Tolksdorf & Wiedemann, 1981). Although vulnerable individuals are considered to be even more vulnerable as they age (Fulmer et al., 1992), the disability requirement is also a hypothesis behind normal aging, as well as in the case of elders with dual diagnosis, this is easier to understand when undue influence is examined in this special population. Of course, in the case of older adults with disabilities, there is no extensive research on their experiences, although the way elders interpret their own abuse experience and the pattern of abuse can influence the patterns of help-seeking behaviors (Yan, 2015), while findings support that the more dependent upon the perpetrators the victims are (e.g. due to physical disabilities), lower help-seeking is expected (Burnes et al., 2019).

Age-related mental disorders in people with already diagnosed intellectual disabilities (Sinai et al., 2012) may multiply and aggravate the severity of cases of elder abuse, as victimization of older adults with lifelong disabilities is more frequent (Ansello & O'Neill, 2010). For example, in the case of sexual abuse between partners, failing health and the progression of a disease (e.g. dementia) can impair the already diminished capacity to communicate whether or not sexual contact is desired (Brandl et al., 2006). In addition to that, for mentally impaired and/or physically handicapped older adults, abuse is similar to that found in child abuse and it is of interest that physically it often includes characteristic burn patterns on the body in contrast to older adults without such disabilities (Bowden et al., 1988).

Elder abuse of individuals with intellectual disabilities is underreported and there is also a lack of standardized research, or in the scarce existing research there is no common definition of elder abuse for elders with disabilities (Giannouli, 2022a). Given that victims seek help mostly from medical and health services (Lowenstein et al., 2009) as they usually tend to be isolated and their interactions mainly with physicians are many times the only opportunity for abuse detection (Lachs & Pillemer, 2015), health-related policies and programs as a first step in prevention should begin to identify elder abuse and neglect in a more organized and systematic way that must be cross-culturally validated (Oveisi et al., 2014). Possible points for consideration are the alternative communication strategies required when interviewing this special population as well as the special skills needed for case assessment (Baladerian, 1997) in order to overcome physical, environmental and social barriers, as well as to achieve a change in attitude towards the needs of older people with disabilities (Marhulumba & Nel, 2021).

Forensic Assessment and Procedures: Legal Concerns and Beyond

Differences in elder abuse definitions in different countries hinder the application of a unique assessment protocol and relevant procedures in forensic assessment in different cultures and countries worldwide (Daly & Jogerst, 2001). There is an approach in abuse identification, supporting that the discrepancy between what is normal and expected and what is abnormal or unexpected at a specific setting should be our compass in abuse detection (Gilhooly et al., 2013). Nevertheless, when determining legally sufficient consent, mental health experts as well as legal experts keep in mind autonomy and self-determination (Giannouli, 2020) taking the forms of: (1) knowledge of the relevant information and/or facts relevant to the decision to be made (e.g. risks and benefits), (2) the mental capacity to realize and rationally process the risks and benefits of engaging in an activity in a way that is consistent with the individual's general prior values, and (3) voluntariness, which is a stated choice combined with the absence of coercion or unfair persuasion or inducements and the presence of a realistic choice between engaging or refraining from the activity (American Psychological Association, 2005, 2006).

For the forensic assessment regarding elders, there is published literature that supports the simultaneous use of (neuro)psychological tests, questionnaires, and other instruments, as well as medical procedures, and other assessment techniques provided by multidisciplinary teams consisting of a diverse array of professionals (Falk & Hoffman, 2014; Navarro et al., 2010). At these specialized forensic centres, medical experts coming from different specialties, geriatricians, psychologists, social workers, legal experts, public guardian deputies, ombudsmen, mental health services, victim advocates, and domestic violence experts work together in an efficient and effective way (Falk et al., 2010; Wiglesworth et al., 2006). The 'forensic center approach' can facilitate cooperation and group problem-solving among key professionals, and provide complete/detailed assessments that can assist authorities in determining if a case of abuse has occurred, and thus possible referrals can be made in a timely manner to the Office of the Public Guardian (PG) for investigation and possible conservatorship or guardianship (Gassoumis et al., 2015; Morris, 2010). In this way, the medical, legal and social providers jointly engage in case review, consultation, and provision of supportive professional services (Yonashiro-Cho et al., 2019), and increased rates of prosecution can be achieved (DeLiema et al., 2016; Navarro et al., 2013). For example, regarding the evaluation of legal competencies, there is a plethora of competencies to be examined, such as competence to stand trial, criminal responsibility, competence to care for self and property, competence to consent to treatment, as well as other competencies (Grisso, 2006).

Unfortunately, so far, no common forensic assessment protocols and procedures are followed while dealing with crimes among elderly population and more specifically for elders with disabilities. In different European countries (Diaz et al., 2016), as well as in different US states, even within the same states but at different forensic centres, a variety of procedures are followed (Giannouli & Tsolaki, 2015). Although the individualized/personalized approach is the dominant paradigm (Horley, 2004), there are some general principles regarding the process which include: (1) multidisciplinary data collection, (2) key decisions for consideration, and (3) strategic actions utilized by an interprofessional team focused on elder justice (Navarro et al., 2016).

It is of interest, that although the same theoretical principles are adopted, the forensic center team members make home visits with Adult Protective Services (APS) or other similar protective services (provided by the states or other governmental agencies or any private organizations), and other healthcare and legal professionals for the purposes of conducting psychological or medical evaluations, lessening the burden of multiple interviews for the alleged abuse victims, and gathering evidence for possible prosecution (Schneider et al., 2010).

In the case of the above-mentioned types of elder abuse, it is of utmost importance to investigate the neuropsychological correlates of behaviour (Wood et al., 2014), and thus geriatric neuropsychology and classic neuropsychological assessment protocols form the basis of forensic conclusions, when legal concerns arise (Jamora et al., 2008).

How Do We Deal with Crimes Among Elderly Population?

The rights of older adults to lead a life of dignity and independence should be recognized and respected, regardless of the sociocultural context (Giannouli, 2020). Based on the above, there are eight trends in practice that all future interventions should take into account when prevention and recognition of adult abuse is discussed, namely: (1) the increasing number of frail elders living at home, (2), the shift from protection to empowerment of older adults, (3) the heightened understanding of victims, (4) the burgeoning prevention networks, (5) the Adult Protective Services (APS) Network that is imitated by many countries (other than the USA), (6) the criminalization of elder abuse, (7) the focus on forensics, and (8) the introduction of international multi-agency initiatives (Nerenberg, 2008). Interventions regarding elder abuse involve medical, social, therapeutic and educational services as well as legal interventions (Payne, 2005), applied both at an individual level (empowerment of elders to prevent victimization) and at caregivers/providers of healthcare services to be aware of the characteristics and effectively document suspected mistreatment and prevent elders mistreatment (Payne, 2005). One more point to consider is the fact that the guidance given to professionals working in different contexts has gaps and inconsistencies (Gilbert et al., 2013), and therefore needs to be improved by relevant interventions focusing on providing to professionals with relevant state-of-the-art knowledge and skills (Du Mont et al., 2016; Rosen et al., 2018a, b).

Generally, interventions must incorporate the needs of the victims as well as the perpetrators, the type of abuse involved, the variations in perpetrator culpability, and the continuum of complexity among these cases (Jackson, 2016). Although there is a proclivity towards individualized interventions and family-centred interventions (Ryan & Roman, 2019), multi-agency work that respects all involved professional and scientific fields (Giannouli, 2021; Giannouli & Syrmos, 2021) requires much more to be clarified both in research, as well as clinical and legal practice (Brandl et al., 2006). Finally, social inclusion of elderly with or without disabilities is another trend in the literature in the direction of protecting them (Podnieks, 2006), and this may be supported by societal demands (e.g. through the media) for educating and preparing those caring older adults to report elder abuse (Starr, 2010), but also by passing relevant legislation that will prevent, identify, and treat abuse cases in an evidence-based way shared by different institutions, professionals, and countries (Leedahl & Ferraro, 2007).

From Alpha to Omega: What Is Still Missing in Elder Abuse?

Although there is a growing interest in the causes and antecedents of elder abuse, and more specifically in older adults with disabilities, still there is no broad consensus among healthcare experts-practitioners, researchers (in humanities and social sciences), and legal experts and legal systems regarding not only the ways to spot this phenomenon (and thus driving us to fail to detect abuse), but also the ways to prevent violence (Giannouli, 2022a; Dong & Wang, 2016). In numerous countries, there are legislative strategies in prevention including mandatory reporting laws, penalty enhancement statutes, criminal background checks for those living and working near the older adults, and the Elder Justice Act, which is the first comprehensive legislation to address the abuse, neglect, and exploitation of older adults (Payne, 2005). It is true that we have reached an agreement regarding the recognition of the above-mentioned types of abuse, but still cross-cultural differences in the attitudes and the representations that the public laypeople as well as 'experts' hold on various health issues (Giannouli & Stoyanova, 2014, 2018), and specifically regarding this multifaceted topic, render it difficult to deal with it effectively (Giannouli, 2022a). It must be noted here that attitudes towards elders, their healthcare and mental capacity as well as the links with the different forms of abuse and possible prevention and interventions vary across cultures (Giannouli, 2014; Giannouli et al., 2019a, b), mainly due to differences on the views on independence and protection (Giannouli et al., 2019a, b), thus rendering research difficult. At this point, we should not forget the relative gatekeeping powers not only of welfare professionals, but also of family members and carers, and the fact that demands have increased, especially upon older people with higher needs and who may lack economic and cultural capital (Carey, 2021).

Therefore, interventions should be based on the existing knowledge of risk factors (for both victim and perpetrator), without ignoring the personal factors that may affect each older adult individually. There are interventions for elder victims that focus on different dimensions, such as on maximizing independence, on resolving crises, on ensuring the victim's safety, on fostering empowerment and support, and on preserving and recovering assets (Nerenberg, 2008), while at the same time interventions for the perpetrators include counselling, domestic violence programs, and programs for educating caregivers (Nerenberg, 2008). Thus, a number of general interventions have been proposed and are in use, such as caregiver interventions, money management programs, helplines, emergency shelter, and multidisciplinary teams (Pillemer et al., 2016). All these approaches are based on the idea of the least restrictive alternatives (Nerenberg, 2008).

Future research should focus on the characteristics and predictive factors of elder abuse through the lenses of cross-cultural differences and in multicultural societies, but an emphasis should also be given on interventions and the education on perceived abuse among healthcare and legal professionals, which could be a starting point for a change (Giannouli, 2022a). Therefore, there is not only a dire need to develop more cross-culturally appropriate measures-tools-instruments, but it is also necessary that professionals follow developments in the field by adopting evidence-based approaches to elder abuse (Pillemer et al., 2016), by following holistic approaches, within a continuum of coordinating and collaborating service options, and with available long-term services for older adults (Nerenberg, 2008). Some unanswered questions that remain to be answered focus on how we (professionals and laypeople) can raise the awareness on the problem of elder abuse, what prevention programs have countries across the world implemented nationally, and to which extent have various countries been developing national action plans to coordinate action against elder abuse (Yon et al., 2020).

References

Abolfathi Momtaz, Y., Hamid, T. A., & Ibrahim, R. (2013). Theories and measures of elder abuse. *Psychogeriatrics, 13*(3), 182–188.

Abrams, R. C., Lachs, M., McAvay, G., Keohane, D. J., & Bruce, M. L. (2002). Predictors of self-neglect in community-dwelling elders. *American Journal of Psychiatry, 159*(10), 1724–1730.

Acierno, R., Hernandez, M. A., Amstadter, A. B., Resnick, H. S., Steve, K., Muzzy, W., & Kilpatrick, D. G. (2010). Prevalence and correlates of emotional, physical, sexual, and financial abuse and potential neglect in the United States: The National Elder Mistreatment Study. *American Journal of Public Health, 100*(2), 292–297.

Adams, S. D., & Lichtenberg, P. A. (2014). How to protect and help clients with diminished capacity. *Journal of Financial Planning, 27*(4), 22–25.

Ahmad, M., & Lachs, M. S. (2002). Elder abuse and neglect: What physicians can and should do. *Cleveland Clinic Journal of Medicine, 69*(10), 801–808.

Aitken, L., & Griffin, G. (1996). *Gender issues in elder abuse*. Sage.

Alikarami, K., Maleki, A., Abdollahyan, H., & Rezaei, M. (2021). Phenomenology of the lived experiences of lonely aged women from abandonment and rejection. *Social Welfare Quarterly, 21*(80), 231–260.

Alon, S. (2021). Cognitive impairment and dementia: A risk factor for elder abuse and neglect. In M. Kapur Shankardass (Ed.), *Dementia care* (pp. 269–282). Springer.

American Psychological Association, (2005). Assessment of older adults with diminished capacity. A handbook for lawyers.. American Bar Association Commission on Law and Aging-American Psychological Association.

American Psychological Association, (2006). Assessment of older adults with diminished capacity. A handbook for psychologists.. American Bar Association Commission on Law and Aging–American Psychological Association.

Anme, T., McCall, M., & Tatara, T. (2005). An exploratory study of abuse among frail elders using services in a small village in Japan. *Journal of Elder Abuse & Neglect, 17*(2), 1–20.

Ansello, E. F., & O'Neill, P. (2010). Abuse, neglect, and exploitation: Considerations in aging with lifelong disabilities. *Journal of Elder Abuse & Neglect, 22*(1–2), 105–130.

Awuviry-Newton, K., Nkansah, J. O., & Ofori-Dua, K. (2020). Attributions of elder neglect: A phenomenological study of older people in Ghana. *Health & Social Care in the Community, 28*(6), 2172–2178.

Ayalon, L., & Huyck, M. H. (2001). Latino caregivers with Alzheimer's disease. *Clinical Gerontologist, 24*(3/4), 93–106.

Baker, P. R., Francis, D. P., Hairi, N. N., Othman, S., & Choo, W. Y. (2016). Interventions for preventing abuse in the elderly. *Cochrane Database of Systematic Reviews, 16*(8), CD010321.

Baladerian, N. J. (1997). Recognizing abuse and neglect in people with severe cognitive and/or communication impairments. *Journal of Elder Abuse & Neglect, 9*(2), 93–104.

Bardell, A., Lau, T., & Fedoroff, J. P. (2011). Inappropriate sexual behavior in a geriatric population. *International Psychogeriatrics, 23*(7), 1182–1188.

Bartelet, M., Waterink, W., & van Hooren, S. (2014). Extreme sexual behavior in dementia as a specific manifestation of disinhibition. *Journal of Alzheimer's Disease, 42*(s3), S119–S124.

Beach, S. R., Schulz, R., Castle, N. G., & Rosen, J. (2010). Financial exploitation and psychological mistreatment among older adults: Differences between African Americans and non-African Americans in a population-based survey. *The Gerontologist, 50*, 744–757.

Begle, A. M., Strachan, M., Cisler, J. M., Amstadter, A. B., Hernandez, M., & Acierno, R. (2011). Elder mistreatment and emotional symptoms among older adults in a largely rural population: The South Carolina elder mistreatment study. *Journal of Interpersonal Violence, 26,* 2321–2332.

Bergman, H., Karunananthan, S., Robledo, L. M., Brodsky, J., Chan, P., Cheung, M., & Bovet, P. (2013). Understanding and meeting the needs of the older population: A global challenge. *Canadian Geriatrics Journal, 16*(2), 61.

Bittles, A. H., Bower, C., Hussain, R., & Glasson, E. J. (2007). The four ages of Down syndrome. *European Journal of Public Health, 17*(2), 221–225.

Black, B., Muralee, S., & Tampi, R. R. (2005). Inappropriate sexual behaviors in dementia. *Journal of Geriatric Psychiatry and Neurology, 18*(3), 155–162.

Borenstein, R. F. (2019). Synergetic dependency in partner and elder abuse. *American Psychologist, 74,* 713.

Bowden, M. L., Grant, S. T., Vogel, B., & Prasad, J. K. (1988). The elderly, disabled and handicapped adult burned through abuse and neglect. *Burns, 14*(6), 447–450.

Bows, H., & Westmarland, N. (2017). Rape of older people in the United Kingdom: Challenging the 'real-rape' stereotype. *British Journal of Criminology, 57*(1), 1–17.

Brandl, B., Dyer, C. B., Heisler, C. J., Otto, J. M., Stiegel, L. A., & Thomas, R. W. (2006). *Elder abuse detection and intervention: A collaborative approach.* Springer Publishing Company.

Briones, D. F., Ramirez, A. L., Guerrero, M., & Ledger, E. (2002). Determining cultural and psychosocial factors in Alzheimer disease among Hispanic populations. *Alzheimer Disease and Associated Disorders, 16*(Supplement 2), S86–S88.

Brozowski, K., & Hall, D. R. (2010). Aging and risk: Physical and sexual abuse of elders in Canada. *Journal of Interpersonal Violence, 25*(7), 1183–1199.

Burgess, A. W., & Phillips, S. L. (2006). Sexual abuse, trauma and dementia in the elderly: A retrospective study of 284 cases. *Victims and Offenders, 1*(2), 193–204.

Burgess, A. W., Hanrahan, N. P., & Baker, T. (2005). Forensic markers in elder female sexual abuse cases. *Clinics in Geriatric Medicine, 21*(2), 399–412.

Burnes, D., Henderson, C. R., Sheppard, C., Zhao, R., Pillemer, K., & Lachs, M. S. (2017). Prevalence of financial fraud and scams among older adults in the United States: A systematic review and meta-analysis. *American Journal of Public Health, 107*(8), e13–e21.

Burnes, D., Acierno, R., & Hernandez-Tejada, M. (2019). Help-seeking among victims of elder abuse: Findings from the National Elder Mistreatment Study. *The Journals of Gerontology: Series B, 74*(5), 891–896.

Burnett, J., Achenbaum, W. A., & Murphy, K. P. (2014a). Prevention and early identification of elder abuse. *Clinics in Geriatric Medicine, 30*(4), 743–759.

Burnett, J., Dyer, C. B., Halphen, J. M., Achenbaum, W. A., Green, C. E., Booker, J. G., & Diamond, P. M. (2014b). Four subtypes of self-neglect in older adults: Results of a latent class analysis. *Journal of the American Geriatrics Society, 62*(6), 1127–1132.

Cadmus, E. O., & Owoaje, E. T. (2012). Prevalence and correlates of elder abuse among older women in rural and urban communities in South Western Nigeria. *Health Care for Women International, 33*(10), 973–984.

Campbell Reay, A. M., & Browne, K. D. (2002). The effectiveness of psychological interventions with individuals who physically abuse or neglect their elderly dependents. *Journal of Interpersonal Violence, 17*(4), 416–431.

Canevelli, M., Troili, F., Talarico, G., Tosto, G., Letteri, F., Lenzi, G. L., & Bruno, G. (2011). Inappropriate sexual behaviors in dementia: A review of literature. *Cognitive Sciences, 6*(2), 183–203.

Canevelli, M., Lucchini, F., Garofalo, C., Talarico, G., Trebbastoni, A., D'Antonio, F., et al. (2017). Inappropriate sexual behaviors among community-dwelling patients with dementia. *The American Journal of Geriatric Psychiatry, 25*(4), 365–371.

Carey, M. (2021). Welfare conditionality, ethics and social care for older people in the UK: From civic rights to abandonment? *The British Journal of Social Work,* bcab233.

Cartwright, P. S., & Moore, R. A. (1989). The elderly victim of rape. *Southern Medical Journal, 82*(8), 988–989.

Chang, E. S., & Levy, B. R. (2021). High prevalence of elder abuse during the COVID-19 pandemic: Risk and resilience factors. *The American Journal of Geriatric Psychiatry, 29*(11), 1152–1159.

Choi, N. G., Kim, J., & Asseff, J. (2009). Self-neglect and neglect of vulnerable older adults: Reexamination of etiology. *Journal of Gerontological Social Work, 52*(2), 171–187.

Chokkanathan, S., & Lee, A. E. (2005). Elder mistreatment in urban India: A community based study. *Journal of Elder Abuse & Neglect, 17*(2), 45–61.

Chopin, J., & Beauregard, E. (2020). Elderly sexual abuse: An examination of the criminal event. *Sexual Abuse, 32*(6), 706–726.

Chopin, J., & Beauregard, E. (2021). Sexual abuse of elderly victims investigated by the police: From motives to crime characteristics. *Journal of Interpersonal Violence, 36*(13–14), 6722–6744.

Coll, O. (Ed.). (2019). *Healthy aging: A complete guide to clinical management*. Springer.

Conrad, K. J., Iris, M., Ridings, J. W., Langley, K., & Anetzberger, G. J. (2010a). Self-report measure of psychological abuse of older adults. *The Gerontologist, 51*, 354–366.

Conrad, K. J., Iris, M., Ridings, J. W., Langley, K., & Wilber, K. H. (2010b). Self-report measure of financial exploitation of older adults. *The Gerontologist, 50*(6), 758–773.

Conrad, K. J., Iris, M., Ridings, J. W., Rosen, A., Fairman, K. P., & Anetzberger, G. J. (2011). Conceptual model and map of psychological abuse of older adults. *Journal of Elder Abuse & Neglect, 23*, 147–168.

Cooper, C., Selwood, A., & Livingston, G. (2008). The prevalence of elder abuse and neglect: A systematic review. *Age and Ageing, 37*, 151–160.

Cipriani, G., Lucetti, C., Danti, S., Carlesi, C., & Nuti, A. (2016). Violent and criminal manifestations in dementia patients. *Geriatrics & Gerontology International, 16*(5), 541–549.

Daly, J. M., & Jogerst, G. (2001). Statute definitions of elder abuse. *Journal of Elder Abuse & Neglect, 13*(4), 39–57.

de Guzman, A. B., Lacorte, J. C., Lacsamana, A. K. G., Lagac, M. L. M., Laguador, J. M., Lapid, J. J. R., & Lee, L. M. C. (2012). Who says there is no life after abandonment? A grounded theory on the coping of abandoned Filipino elderly in nursing homes. *Educational Gerontology, 38*(12), 890–901.

De Medeiros, K., Rosenberg, P. B., Baker, A. S., & Onyike, C. U. (2008). Improper sexual behaviors in elders with dementia living in residential care. *Dementia and Geriatric Cognitive Disorders, 26*(4), 370–377.

DeLiema, M., Navarro, A. E., Moss, M., & Wilber, K. H. (2016). Prosecutors' perspectives on elder justice using an Elder Abuse Forensic Center. *American Journal of Criminal Justice, 41*(4), 780–795.

Diaz, A., Balackova, N., Gronqvist, R., Rohra, H., Rochford-Brennan, H., Orheim, A., ... & Pearson, J. (2016). Dementia in Europe yearbook 2016: Decision making and legal capacity in dementia.. Alzheimer Europe.

Dimah, K. P., & Dimah, A. (2003). Elder abuse and neglect among rural and urban women. *Journal of Elder Abuse & Neglect, 15*(1), 75–93.

Dimkpa, D. (2015). Perspectives on elder bias and abandonment in Nigeria: Implications for gerontological counselling. *International Journal of Education and Research, 3*(4), 221–232.

Dong, X. Q. (2015). Elder abuse: Systematic review and implications for practice. *Journal of the American Geriatrics Society, 63*(6), 1214–1238.

Dong, X. (2017). Elder self-neglect: Research and practice. *Clinical Interventions in Aging, 12*, 949.

Dong, X., & Simon, M. (2013). Elder self-neglect: Implications for health care professionals. *Canadian Geriatrics Journal, 3*(1), 25–28.

Dong, X., & Wang, B. (2016). 2015 Rosalie Wolf Memorial Award Lecture: Past, present, and future of elder abuse. *Journal of Elder Abuse & Neglect, 28*(4–5), 345–365.

Dong, X., Simon, M., Rajan, K., & Evans, D. A. (2011). Association of cognitive function and risk for elder abuse in a community-dwelling population. *Dementia and Geriatric Cognitive Disorders, 32*, 209–215.

Dong, X., Simon, M. A., & Evans, D. (2012). Elder self-neglect and hospitalization: Findings from the Chicago Health and Aging Project. *Journal of the American Geriatrics Society, 60*(2), 202–209.

Downes, C., Fealy, G., Phelan, A., Donnelly, N., & Lafferty, A. (2013). *Abuse of older people with dementia: A review.* NCPOP, University College Dublin.

Du Mont, J., Kosa, D., Macdonald, S., Elliot, S., & Yaffe, M. (2016). Development of skills-based competencies for forensic nurse examiners providing elder abuse care. *BMJ Open, 6*(2), e009690.

Elsherbiny, M. M. K., & Al Maamari, R. H. (2018). The effectiveness of logotherapy in mitigating the social isolation of neglected institutionalised older people. *British Journal of Social Work, 48*(4), 1090–1108.

Falk, E., & Hoffman, N. (2014). The role of capacity assessments in elder abuse investigations and guardianships. *Clinics in Geriatric Medicine, 30*(4), 851–868.

Falk, E., Landsverk, E., Mosqueda, L., Olsen, B. J., Schneider, D. C., Bernatz, S., & Wood, S. (2010). Geriatricians and psychologists: Essential ingredients in the evaluation of elder abuse and neglect. *Journal of Elder Abuse & Neglect, 22*(3–4), 281–290.

Filipska, K., Biercewicz, M., Wiśniewski, A., Kędziora-Kornatowska, K., & Ślusarz, R. (2020). Prevalence and associated factors of elder psychological abuse-A cross-sectional screening study, based on a hospitalized community from Poland. *Archives of Gerontology and Geriatrics, 90*, 104152.

Fisher, B. S., & Regan, S. L. (2006). The extent and frequency of abuse in the lives of older women and their relationship with health outcomes. *The Gerontologist, 46*, 200–209.

Fraga Dominguez, S., Ozguler, B., Storey, J. E., & Rogers, M. (2021). Elder abuse vulnerability and risk factors: Is financial abuse different from other subtypes? *Journal of Applied Gerontology*, 07334648211036402.

Friedman, B., Santos, E. J., Liebel, D. V., Russ, A. J., & Conwell, Y. (2015). Longitudinal prevalence and correlates of elder mistreatment among older adults receiving home visiting nursing. *Journal of Elder Abuse and Neglect, 27*(1), 34–64.

Fulmer, T., McMahon, D. J., Baer-Hines, M., & Forget, B. (1992). Abuse, neglect, abandonment, violence, and exploitation: An analysis of all elderly patients seen in one emergency department during a six-month period. *Journal of Emergency Nursing, 18*(6), 505–510.

Gallione, C., Dal Molin, A., Cristina, F. V. B., Ferns, H., Mattioli, M., & Suardi, B. (2017). Screening tools for identification of elder abuse: A systematic review. *Journal of Clinical Nursing, 26*, 2154–2176.

Gassoumis, Z. D., Navarro, A. E., & Wilber, K. H. (2015). Protecting victims of elder financial exploitation: The role of an elder abuse forensic center in referring victims for conservatorship. *Aging & Mental Health, 19*(9), 790–798.

Ghesquiere, A. R., McAfee, C., & Burnett, J. (2019). Measures of financial capacity: A review. *The Gerontologist, 59*(2), e109–e129.

Ghodoosi, A., Fallah Yakhdani, E., & Abedi, H. A. (2014). Studying the instances of elder abuse and their relationship with age and sex in the hospitalized elderly. *Iranian Journal of Forensic Medicine, 20*(1), 367–376.

Giannouli, V. (2013). Number perseveration in healthy subjects: Does prolonged stimulus exposure influence performance on a serial addition task? *Advances in Cognitive Psychology, 9*(1), 15–19.

Giannouli, V. (2014). What do Greeks believe about elders and mental capacity. *AGORA International Journal of Juridical Sciences, 8*(3), 1–5.

Giannouli, V. (2017). Alzheimer's disease: Psychosocial dimensions of a modern plague. *Encephalos, 54*, 33–38.

Giannouli, V. (2018). Elder abuse and consent capacity: Our collective nemesis? In R. T. Gopalan (Ed.), *Social, psychological, and forensic perspectives on sexual abuse* (pp. 207–221). IGI Global.

Giannouli, V. (2019). Judging Antigone in old age: (Neuro)psychology in the twenty-first century. *Problems of Psychology in the 21st Century, 3*(2), 72–74.

Giannouli, V. (2020). Et in Arcadia ego. *Philosophy Now, 138,* 32–33.

Giannouli, V. (2021). Exploring hubris in physicians: Are there emotional correlates? *Psychiatria Danubina, 33*(1), 57–59.

Giannouli, V. (2022a). Reflecting on crime and legal issues in people with intellectual disabilities: Theory, perspectives, and future approaches. In M. Khosrow-Pour (Ed.), *Research anthology on physical and intellectual disabilities in an inclusive society* (pp. 1539–1567). IGI Global.

Giannouli, V. (2022b). Does cognition predict perceptions regarding self-stigma of seeking help in older adults? *Revista Colombiana de Psiquiatría,* in press.

Giannouli, V., & Giannoulis, K. (2020). Gazing at Medusa: Alzheimer's Dementia through the lenses of spirituality and religion. *Health Psychology Research, 8*(1), 47–52.

Giannouli, V., & Hyphantis, T. (2017). In the labyrinth of e-Health: Exploring attitudes towards e-Health in Greece. *Journal of Psychology and Clinical Psychiatry, 8*(2), 474–476.

Giannouli, V., & Stoyanova, S. (2014). Does depressive symptomatology influence teenage patients and their mothers' experience of doctor-patient relationship in two Balkan countries? *Psychological Thought, 7*(1), 19–27.

Giannouli, V., & Stoyanova, S. (2018). Exploring emotional aspects of infertility in women from two countries. *Psychiatrike = Psychiatriki, 29*(1), 34–41.

Giannouli, V., & Syrmos, N. (2021). The flight of Icarus: A preliminary study of the emotional correlates of hubris in gerontological nurses during the SARS-CoV-2 pandemic. *Psychiatria Danubina, 33*(Suppl 10), 109–113.

Giannouli, V., & Tsolaki, M. (2014). Legal capacity of the elderly in Greece. *Hellenic Journal of Nuclear Medicine, 17,* 2–6.

Giannouli, V., & Tsolaki, M. (2015). A neglected drama for elders: Discrepancy between self-perception and objective performance regarding financial capacity in patients with cognitive deficits. *Psychological Thought, 8*(2), 142–147.

Giannouli, V., & Tsolaki, M. (2016). Questions about dementia with Lewy bodies, personal beliefs and real performance for financial capacity tasks. *European Psychiatry, 33*(S1), S469–S470.

Giannouli, V., & Tsolaki, M. (2019a). Are left angular gyrus and amygdala volumes important for financial capacity in mild cognitive impairment? *Hellenic Journal of Nuclear Medicine, 22,* 160–164.

Giannouli, V., & Tsolaki, M. (2019b). Depression and financial capacity assessment in Parkinson's disease with dementia: Overlooking an important factor? *Psychiatriki, 30*(1), 66–70.

Giannouli, V., & Tsolaki, M. (2021a). Mild Alzheimer Disease, financial capacity and the role of depression: Eyes wide shut? *Alzheimer's Disease and Associated Disorders, 35*(4), 360–362.

Giannouli, V., & Tsolaki, M. (2021b). Vascular dementia, depression and financial capacity assessment. *Alzheimer's Disease and Associated Disorders, 35*(1), 84–87.

Giannouli, V., & Tsolaki, M. (2021c). Unraveling Ariadne's thread into the labyrinth of aMCI: Depression and financial capacity. *Alzheimer's Disease and Associated Disorders, 35*(4), 363–365.

Giannouli, V., & Tsolaki, M. (2021d). Is depression or apathy playing a key role in predicting financial capacity in Parkinson's disease with dementia and frontotemporal dementia? *Brain Sciences, 11,* 785.

Giannouli, V., & Tsolaki, M. (2021e). Apoe ε4 allele and financial capacity performance in Mild Alzheimer Disease: A pilot study. *Journal of Alzheimer's Disease Reports, 5*(1), 93–97.

Giannouli, V., & Tsolaki, M. (2021f). Frontotemporal dementia and financial capacity: Facing the Cerberus of overestimation or underestimation? *Australasian Psychiatry, 30*(1), 41–43.

Giannouli, V., & Tsolaki, M. (2021g). Financial capacity and illiteracy: Does education matter in aMCI? *Journal of Alzheimer's Disease Reports, 5*(1), 715–719.

Giannouli, V., & Tsolaki, M. (2022a). Financial incapacity of patients with Mild Alzheimer's Disease: What neurologists need to know about where the impairment lies. *Neurology International, 14*(1), 90–98.

Giannouli, V., & Tsolaki, M. (2022b). Liberating older adults from the bonds of vascular risk factors: What is their impact on financial capacity in aMCI? *Psychiatry and Clinical Neurosciences*, in press.

Giannouli, V., & Tsolaki, M. (2022c). Self-awareness of cognitive efficiency, cognitive status, insight, and financial capacity in patients with Mild AD, aMCI, and healthy controls: An intriguing liaison with clinical implications? *Neurology International, 14*, 628–637.

Giannouli, V., Mistraletti, G., & Umbrello, M. (2017). ICU experience for patients' relatives: Is information all that matters? *Intensive Care Medicine, 43*(5), 722.

Giannouli, V., Stamovlasis, D., & Tsolaki, M. (2018). Exploring the role of cognitive factors in a new instrument for elders' financial capacity assessment. *Journal of Alzheimer's Disease, 62*(4), 1579–1594.

Giannouli, V., Ivanova, D., Stoyanova, S., & Drugas, M. (2019a). When is a person with dementia in need of palliative care? Opinions of healthcare professionals and university students from three South East European countries. *Psychiatria Danubina, 31*(4), 465–472.

Giannouli, V., Tegos, T., Zilakaki, M., & Tsolaki, M. (2019b). Elders and mental capacity: Using a qualitative approach to examine views on independence and protection across the Balkans. *Hellenic Journal of Nuclear Medicine, 22*(2), 122–139.

Giannouli, V., Stamovlasis, D., & Tsolaki, M. (2022). Longitudinal study of depression on amnestic Mild Cognitive Impairment and financial capacity. *Clinical Gerontologist*, 1–7.

Giannoulis, K., & Giannouli, V. (2020a). Subjective quality of life, religiousness, and spiritual experience in Greek Orthodox Christians: Data from healthy aging and patients with cardiovascular disease. In *GeNeDis 2018* (pp. 85–91). Springer.

Giannoulis, K., & Giannouli, V. (2020b). Religious beliefs, self-esteem, anxiety, and depression among Greek orthodox elders. *Romanian Journal Anthropological Researches and Studies, 10*, 84–90.

Gibson, S., & Qualls, S. H. (2012). A family systems perspective of elder financial abuse. *Generations, 36*(3), 26–29.

Gilbert, A., Stanley, D., Penhale, B., & Gilhooly, M. (2013). Elder financial abuse in England: A policy analysis perspective related to social care and banking. *The Journal of Adult Protection, 15*(3), 153–163.

Gilhooly, M. L., Cairns, D., Davies, M., Harries, P., Gilhooly, K. J., & Notley, E. (2013). Framing the detection of financial elder abuse as bystander intervention: Decision cues, pathways to detection and barriers to action. *The Journal of Adult Protection, 15*(2), 54–68.

Gomes-Pinto, A. (2014). A case of inappropriate sexual behaviour in mixed dementia. *Progress in Neurology and Psychiatry, 18*(4), 21–22.

Gorbien, M. J., & Eisenstein, A. R. (2005). Elder abuse and neglect: An overview. *Clinics in Geriatric Medicine, 21*(2), 279–292.

Gordon, R. M., & Brill, D. (2001). The abuse and neglect of the elderly. In D. N. Weisstub, D. C. Thomasma, S. Gauthier, & G. F. Tomossy (Eds.), *Aging: Caring for our elders* (pp. 203–218). Springer.

Govil, P., & Gupta, S. (2016). Domestic violence against elderly people: A case study of India. *Advances in Aging Research, 5*(5), 110–121.

Greene, A. J. (2022). Elder financial abuse and electronic financial instruments: Present and future considerations for financial capacity assessments. *The American Journal of Geriatric Psychiatry, 30*(1), 90–106.

Grisso, T. (2006). *Evaluating competencies: Forensic assessments and instruments* (Vol. 16). Springer.

Hall, J. E., Karch, D. L., & Crosby, A. E. (2016). *Elder abuse surveillance: Uniform definitions and recommended core data elements for use in elder abuse surveillance.* Centers for Disease Control and Prevention, National Center for Injury Prevention and Control, Division of Violence Prevention.

Hamby, S., Smith, A., Mitchell, K., & Turner, H. (2016). Poly-victimization and resilience port-folios: Trends in violence research that can enhance the understanding and prevention of elder abuse. *Journal of Elder Abuse & Neglect, 28*(4–5), 217–234.

Hardin, E., & Khan-Hudson, A. (2005). Elder abuse – "society's dilemma". *Journal of the National Medical Association, 97*, 91–94.

Heisler, C. J. (2019). Ethical dilemmas, vulnerable elders, and elder abuse. *Innovation in Aging, 3*(Suppl 1), S238.

Horley, J. (2004). *Personal construct perspectives on forensic psychology.* Routledge.

Hwalek, M. (1996). The association of elder abuse and substance abuse in the Illinois Elder Abuse System. *The Gerontologist, 36*, 694–700.

Jackson, S. L. (2016). All elder abuse perpetrators are not alike: The heterogeneity of elder abuse perpetrators and implications for intervention. *International Journal of Offender Therapy and Comparative Criminology, 60*(3), 265–285.

Jackson, S. L., & Hafemeister, T. L. (2011a). Risk factors associated with elder abuse: The impor-tance of differentiating by type of elder maltreatment. *Violence and Victims, 26*, 738–757.

Jackson, S. L., & Hafemeister, T. L. (2011b). *Financial abuse of elderly people vs. other forms of elder abuse: Assessing their dynamics, risk factors, and society's response.* Final report pre-sented to the National Institute of Justice.

Jackson, S. L., & Hafemeister, T. L. (2012). Pure financial exploitation vs. hybrid financial exploi-tation co-occurring with physical abuse and/or neglect of elderly persons. *Psychology of Violence, 2*(3), 285–296.

Jamora, C. W., Ruff, R. M., & Connor, B. B. (2008). Geriatric neuropsychology: Implications for front line clinicians. *NeuroRehabilitation, 23*(5), 381–394.

Jamshidi, R., Oppenheimer, A. J., Lee, D. S., Lepar, F. H., & Espenshade, T. J. (1992). Aging in America: Limits to life span and elderly care options. *Population Research and Policy Review, 11*(2), 169–190.

Jeon, G. S., Cho, S. I., Choi, K., & Jang, K. S. (2019). Gender differences in the prevalence and correlates of elder abuse in a community-dwelling older population in Korea. *International Journal of Environmental Research and Public Health, 16*(1), 1–13.

Johannesen, M., & LoGiudice, D. (2013). Elder abuse: A systematic review of risk factors in community-dwelling elders. *Age and Ageing, 42*, 292–298.

Kardile, M. S., & Peisah, C. (2017). Elder abuse by abandonment in India: A novel community awareness and intervention strategy. *International Psychogeriatrics, 29*(6), 1035–1036.

Kartinah, K., & Sumarni, S. (2021). The effect of for group empowerment for reducing depression in elderly. *Open Access Macedonian Journal of Medical Sciences, 9*(5), 90–94.

Kelly, P. A., Dyer, C. B., Pavlik, V., Doody, R., & Jogerst, G. (2008). Exploring self-neglect in older adults: Preliminary findings of the Self-Neglect Severity Scale and next steps. *Journal of the American Geriatrics Society, 56*, S253–S260.

Kruger, M. R. M., & Moon, C. C. H. (1999). Can you spot the signs of elder mistreatment? *Postgraduate Medicine, 106*(2), 169–183.

Kumari, S. (2014). Social position and deprivation among elderly widows: A study of rural Jharkhand. *Indian Journal of Gerontology, 28*, 112–125.

Lachs, M. S., & Pillemer, K. A. (2015). Elder abuse. *New England Journal of Medicine, 373*(20), 1947–1956.

Lai, W. L., Daoust, G. D., & Li, L. (2014). Understanding elder abuse and neglect in aging Chinese immigrants in Canada. *The Journal of Adult Protection, 16*(5), 322–334.

Leedahl, S. N., & Ferraro, F. R. (2007). Why is elder abuse overlooked? Media and ageism. *Psychology and Education-Orangeburg, 44*(1), 1–9.

Lichtenberg, P. A. (2016a). The intersection of financial exploitation and financial capacity. *The American Psychologist, 71*(4), 312.

Lichtenberg, P. A. (2016b). Financial exploitation, financial capacity, and Alzheimer's disease. *American Psychologist, 71*(4), 312.

Lichtenberg, P. A. (2016c). New approaches to preventing financial exploitation: A focus on the banks. *Public Policy & Aging Report, 26*(1), 15–17.

Lichtenberg, P. A. (2017). New approaches to determining financial capacity and risk for exploitation. *Journal of Mental Health Care, 1,* 1–3.

Lichtenberg, P. A., Stoltman, J., Ficker, L. J., Iris, M., & Mast, B. (2015). A person-centered approach to financial capacity assessment: Preliminary development of a new rating scale. *Clinical Gerontologist, 38*(1), 49–67.

Lowenstein, A., Eisikovits, Z., Band-Winterstein, T., & Enosh, G. (2009). Is elder abuse and neglect a social phenomenon? Data from the first national prevalence survey in Israel. *Journal of Elder Abuse & Neglect, 21*(3), 253–277.

Malks, B., Schmidt, C. M., & Austin, M. J. (2003). Elder abuse prevention: A case study of the Santa Clara County financial abuse specialist team (FAST) program. *Journal of Gerontological Social Work, 39*(3), 23–40.

Marhulumba, T., & Nel, V. (2021). The neglect of people with disabilities in integrated development planning in Ngangelizwe Township, Mthatha. In H. H. Magidimisha-Chipungu & L. Chipungu (Eds.), *Urban inclusivity in Southern Africa* (pp. 327–345). Springer.

Marson, D. C. (2013). Clinical and ethical aspects of financial capacity in dementia: A commentary. *The American Journal of Geriatric Psychiatry, 21*(4), 382–390.

Marson, D. C., Sawrie, S. M., Snyder, S., McInturff, B., Stalvey, T., Boothe, A., et al. (2000). Assessing financial capacity in patients with Alzheimer disease: A conceptual model and prototype instrument. *Archives of Neurology, 57*(6), 877–884.

Marson, D., Hebert, T., & Solomon, A. (2005). Civil competencies in older adults with dementia: Medical decision-making capacity, financial capacity, and testamentary capacity. In G. Larrabee (Ed.), *Forensic neuropsychology: A scientific approach* (2nd ed.). Oxford University Press.

Marson, D. C., Martin, R. C., Wadley, V., Griffith, H. R., Snyder, S., Goode, P. S., et al. (2009). Clinical interview assessment of financial capacity in older adults with mild cognitive impairment and Alzheimer's disease. *Journal of the American Geriatrics Society, 57*(5), 806–814.

Martin, R., Griffith, H. R., Belue, K., Harrell, L., Zamrini, E., Anderson, B., et al. (2008). Declining financial capacity in patients with mild Alzheimer disease: A one-year longitudinal study. *The American Journal of Geriatric Psychiatry, 16*(3), 209–219.

Martínez, W. S. N. F., González, M. D. J. J., Pérez, N. E. M., & Guerrero-Castañeda, R. F. (2020). Meaning of well-being of older institutionalized persons in abandonment situation. *Revista Brasileira de Enfermagem, 73,* e20200123.

Mauk, K. L. (2011). Ethical perspectives on self-neglect among older adults. *Rehabilitation Nursing, 36*(2), 60–65.

McCarthy, L., Campbell, S., & Penhale, B. (2017). Elder abuse screening tools: Systematic review. *The Journal of Adult Protection, 19,* 368–379.

McFerson, H. M. (2013). Poverty among women in Sub-Saharan Africa: A review of selected issues. *The Journal of International Women's Studies, 11,* 50–72.

Mohd Mydin, F. H., & Othman, S. (2020). Elder abuse and neglect intervention in the clinical setting: Perceptions and barriers faced by primary care physicians in Malaysia. *Journal of Interpersonal Violence, 35*(23–24), 6041–6066.

Morris, J. R. (2010). The Bet Tzedek legal services model: How a legal services model addresses elder abuse and neglect. *Journal of Elder Abuse & Neglect, 22*(3–4), 275–280.

Mouton, C. P., Larme, A. C., Alford, C. L., Talamantes, M. A., McCorkle, R. J., & Burge, S. K. (2005). Multiethnic perspectives on elder mistreatment. *Journal of Elder Abuse and Neglect, 17*(2), 21–44.

Murphy, K., Waa, S., Jaffer, H., Sauter, A., & Chan, A. (2013). A literature review of findings in physical elder abuse. *Canadian Association of Radiologists Journal, 64*(1), 10–14.

Naik, A. D., Lai, J. M., Kunik, M. E., & Dyer, C. B. (2008). Assessing capacity in suspected cases of self-neglect. *Geriatrics, 63*(2), 24.

National Center on Elder Abuse. (2005). *Elder abuse prevalence and incidence.* National Center on Elder Abuse.

National Center on Elder Abuse. (2013). *An introduction to elder abuse for professionals: Neglect*. NCEA.

Navarro, A. E., Wilber, K. H., Yonashiro, J., & Homeier, D. C. (2010). Do we really need another meeting? Lessons from the Los Angeles county elder abuse forensic center. *The Gerontologist, 50*(5), 702–711.

Navarro, A. E., Gassoumis, Z. D., & Wilber, K. H. (2013). Holding abusers accountable: An elder abuse forensic center increases criminal prosecution of financial exploitation. *The Gerontologist, 53*(2), 303–312.

Navarro, A. E., Wysong, J., DeLiema, M., Schwartz, E. L., Nichol, M. B., & Wilber, K. H. (2016). Inside the black box: The case review process of an elder abuse forensic center. *The Gerontologist, 56*(4), 772–781.

Nerenberg, L. (2008). *Elder abuse prevention: Emerging trends and promising strategies*. Springer.

Newson, R. S., Witteman, J., Franco, O. H., Stricker, B. H., Breteler, M., Hofman, A., & Tiemeier, H. (2010). Predicting survival and morbidity-free survival to very old age. *Age, 32*(4), 521–534.

O'Keeffe, M., Hills, A., Doyle, M., McCreadie, C., Scholes, S., Constantine, R., et al. (2007). *UK study of abuse and neglect of older people: Prevalence survey report*. Department of Health.

Oveisi, S., Karimi, R., & Mahram, M. (2014). Note from Iran: Self-reported elder abuse in Qazvin, 2012. *Journal of Elder Abuse & Neglect, 26*(3), 337–340.

Paul & Perkins PA. (2017). *Physical abuse. Nursing home abuse guide*. Available at: http://nursinghomeabuseguide.com/elder-abuse/physical-abuse/. Accessed 5 Jan 2022.

Pavlou, M. P., & Lachs, M. S. (2006). Could self-neglect in older adults be a geriatric syndrome? *Journal of the American Geriatrics Society, 54*(5), 831–842.

Pavlou, M. P., & Lachs, M. S. (2008). Self-neglect in older adults: A primer for clinicians. *Journal of General Internal Medicine, 23*(11), 1841–1846.

Payne, B. K. (2005). *Crime and elder abuse: An integrated perspective*. Charles C Thomas Publisher.

Penhale, B. (2003). Older women, domestic violence, and elder abuse: A review of commonalities, differences, and shared approaches. *Journal of Elder Abuse & Neglect, 15*(3–4), 163–183.

Perkins, N. H., Spira, M., & Key, J. E. (2018). Intergenerational transmission of physical and emotional sibling violence: A potential connection to elder abuse. *Families in Society, 99*(3), 256–268.

Phelan, A., O'Donnell, D., & McCarthy, S. (2021). Financial abuse of older people by third parties in banking institutions: A qualitative exploration. *Ageing & Society*, 1–22.

Pillemer, K., & Finkelhor, D. (1988). The prevalence of elder abuse: A random sample survey. *The Gerontologist, 28*(1), 51–57.

Pillemer, K., Burnes, D., Riffin, C., & Lachs, M. S. (2016). Elder abuse: Global situation, risk factors, and prevention strategies. *The Gerontologist, 56*(Suppl_2), S194–S205.

Podnieks, E. (1993). National survey on abuse of the elderly in Canada. *Journal of Elder Abuse & Neglect, 4*, 4–58.

Podnieks, E. (2006). Social inclusion: An interplay of the determinants of health—New insights into elder abuse. *Journal of Gerontological Social Work, 46*(3–4), 57–79.

Pratt, C. (2003). Banks' effectiveness at reporting financial abuse of elders: An assessment and recommendations for improvements in California. *California Law Review, 40*, 195.

Qian, M., Shi, Y., Lv, J., & Yu, M. (2021). Instruments to assess self-neglect among older adults: A systematic review of measurement properties. *International Journal of Nursing Studies, 123*, 104070.

Ramsey-Klawsnik, H. (1993). Interviewing elders for suspected sexual abuse: Guidelines and techniques. *Journal of Elder Abuse & Neglect, 5*(1), 5–18.

Ramsey-Klawsnik, H. (2003). Elder sexual abuse within the family. *Journal of Elder Abuse & Neglect, 15*(1), 43–58.

Ramsey-Klawsnik, H., Teaster, P. B., Mendiondo, M. S., Abner, E. L., Cecil, K. A., & Tooms, M. R. (2007). Sexual abuse of vulnerable adults in care facilities: Clinical findings and a research initiative. *Journal of the American Psychiatric Nurses Association, 12*(6), 332–339.

Ramsey-Klawsnik, H., Teaster, P. B., Mendiondo, M. S., Marcum, J. L., & Abner, E. L. (2008). Sexual predators who target elders: Findings from the first national study of sexual abuse in care facilities. *Journal of Elder Abuse & Neglect, 20*(4), 353–376.

Reis, M., & Nahmiash, D. (1998). Validation of the indicators of abuse (IOA) screen. *Gerontologist, 38*(4), 471–480.

Roberto, K. A. (2016). The complexities of elder abuse. *American Psychologist, 71*(4), 302.

Rosen, T., Lachs, M. S., & Pillemer, K. (2010). Sexual aggression between residents in nursing homes: Literature synthesis of an underrecognized problem. *Journal of the American Geriatrics Society, 58*(10), 1970–1979.

Rosen, T., Stern, M. E., Elman, A., & Mulcare, M. R. (2018a). Identifying and initiating intervention for elder abuse and neglect in the emergency department. *Clinics in Geriatric Medicine, 34*(3), 435–451.

Rosen, T., Stern, M. E., Mulcare, M. R., Elman, A., McCarthy, T. J., LoFaso, V. M., et al. (2018b). Emergency department provider perspectives on elder abuse and development of a novel ED-based multidisciplinary intervention team. *Emergency Medicine Journal, 35*(10), 600–607.

Ryan, J., & Roman, N. V. (2019). Family-centred interventions for elder abuse: A narrative review. *Journal of Cross-Cultural Gerontology, 34*(3), 325–336.

Rzeszut, S. M. (2017). The need for a stronger definition: Recognizing abandonment as a form of elder abuse across the United States. *Family Court Review, 55*(3), 444–457.

Schneider, D. C., Mosqueda, L., Falk, E., & Huba, G. J. (2010). Elder abuse forensic centers. *Journal of Elder Abuse & Neglect, 22*(3–4), 255–274.

Setterlund, D., Tilse, C., Wilson, J., McCawley, A. L., & Rosenman, L. (2007). Understanding financial elder abuse in families: The potential of routine activities theory. *Ageing & Society, 27*(4), 599–614.

Shields, L. B., Hunsaker, D. M., & Hunsaker, J. C. (2004). Abuse and neglect: A ten-year review of mortality and morbidity in our elders in a large metropolitan area. *Journal of Forensic Sciences, 49*(1), 122–127.

Sinai, A., Bohnen, I., & Strydom, A. (2012). Older adults with intellectual disability. *Current Opinion in Psychiatry, 25*(5), 359–364.

Sooryanarayana, R., Choo, W. Y., & Hairi, N. N. (2013). A review on the prevalence and measurement of elder abuse in the community. *Trauma, Violence & Abuse, 14*, 316–325.

Starr, L. A. (2010). Preparing those caring for older adults to report elder abuse. *The Journal of Continuing Education in Nursing, 41*(5), 231–235.

Stodolska, A., Parnicka, A., Tobiasz-Adamczyk, B., & Grodzicki, T. (2020). Exploring elder neglect: New theoretical perspectives and diagnostic challenges. *The Gerontologist, 60*(6), e438–e448.

Stoyanova, S. Y., Giannouli, V., & Gergov, T. K. (2017). Sentimentality and nostalgia in elderly people in Bulgaria and Greece–Cross-validity of the questionnaire SNEP and cross-cultural comparison. *Europe's Journal of Psychology, 13*(1), 109–128.

Teaster, P. B., Ramsey-Klawsnik, H., Mendiondo, M. S., Abner, E., Cecil, K., & Tooms, M. (2007). From behind the shadows: A profile of the sexual abuse of older men residing in nursing homes. *Journal of Elder Abuse & Neglect, 19*(1–2), 29–45.

Thom, R. P., Grudzinskas, A. J., & Saleh, F. M. (2017). Sexual behavior among persons with cognitive impairments. *Current Psychiatry Reports, 5*(19), 1–7.

Tolksdorf, M., & Wiedemann, H. R. (1981). Clinical aspects of Down's syndrome from infancy to adult life. *Trisomy, 21*, 3–31.

Tragantzopoulou, P., & Giannouli, V. (2021). Social isolation and loneliness in old age: Exploring their role in mental and physical health. *Psychiatriki, 32*(1), 59–66.

Tredal, I., Soares, J. J. F., Sundin, Ö., Viitasara, E., Melchiorre, M. G., Torres-Gonzales, F., et al. (2013). Alcohol use among abused and non-abused older persons aged 60–84 years: An European study. *Drugs: Education, Prevention, and Policy, 20*, 96–109.

Triebel, K. L., Martin, R., Griffith, H. R., Marceaux, J., Okonkwo, O. C., Harrell, L., et al. (2009). Declining financial capacity in mild cognitive impairment: A 1-year longitudinal study. *Neurology, 73*(12), 928–934.

Ventura, F., Caputo, F., & Molinelli, A. (2018). Medico-legal aspects of deaths related to neglect and abandonment in the elderly. *Aging Clinical and Experimental Research, 30*(11), 1399–1402.

Villarreal, J. F., Cárdenas, V. H., & Miranda, J. M. (2017). Functional assessment of older adults related to family abandonment. *Enferm Investiga [Internet], 2*(1), 14–17.

Vincent, G. K. (2010). *The next four decades: The older population in the United States: 2010 to 2050 (No. 1138).* US Department of Commerce, Economics and Statistics Administration, US Census Bureau.

Vloeberghs, E., Van Dam, D., Franck, F., Staufenbiel, M., & De Deyn, P. P. (2007). Mood and male sexual behaviour in the APP23 model of Alzheimer's disease. *Behavioural Brain Research, 180*(2), 146–151.

Wallace, R. B., & Bonnie, R. J. (Eds.). (2003). *Elder mistreatment: Abuse, neglect, and exploitation in an aging America.* National Academies Press.

Wallace, M., & Safer, M. (2009). Hypersexuality among cognitively impaired older adults. *Geriatric Nursing, 30*(4), 230–237.

Walsh, C. A., Olson, J. L., Ploeg, J., Lohfeld, L., & MacMillan, H. L. (2010). Elder abuse and oppression: Voices of marginalized elders. *Journal of Elder Abuse & Neglect, 23*(1), 17–42.

Ward, R. F., & Manchip, S. (2013). 'Inappropriate'sexual behaviours in dementia. *Reviews in Clinical Gerontology, 23*(1), 75–87.

Wiglesworth, A., Mosqueda, L., Burnight, K., Younglove, T., & Jeske, D. (2006). Findings from an elder abuse forensic center. *The Gerontologist, 46*(2), 277–283.

Wood, S., Rakela, B., Liu, P. J., Navarro, A. E., Bernatz, S., Wilber, K. H., et al. (2014). Neuropsychological profiles of victims of financial elder exploitation at the Los Angeles County elder abuse forensic Center. *Journal of Elder Abuse & Neglect, 26*(4), 414–423.

World Health Organization. (2002). *The Toronto declaration on the global prevention of elder abuse.* WHO.

Wu, L., Chen, H., Hu, Y., Xiang, H., Yu, X., Zhang, T., et al. (2012). Prevalence and associated factors of elder mistreatment in a rural community in People's Republic of China: A cross-sectional study. *PLoS One, 7*, e33857.

Yan, E. (2015). Elder abuse and help-seeking behavior in elderly Chinese. *Journal of Interpersonal Violence, 30*(15), 2683–2708.

Yon, Y., Mikton, C. R., Gassoumis, Z. D., & Wilber, K. H. (2017). Elder abuse prevalence in community settings: A systematic review and meta-analysis. *The Lancet Global Health, 5*(2), e147–e156.

Yon, Y., Ramiro-Gonzalez, M., Mikton, C. R., Huber, M., & Sethi, D. (2019). The prevalence of elder abuse in institutional settings: A systematic review and meta-analysis. *European Journal of Public Health, 29*(1), 58–67.

Yon, Y., Lam, J., Passmore, J., Huber, M., & Sethi, D. (2020). The public health approach to elder abuse prevention in Europe: Progress and challenges. In A. Phelan (Ed.), *Advances in elder abuse research* (pp. 223–237). Springer.

Yonashiro-Cho, J., Rowan, J. M., Gassoumis, Z. D., Gironda, M. W., & Wilber, K. H. (2019). Toward a better understanding of the elder abuse forensic center model: Comparing and contrasting four programs in California. *Journal of Elder Abuse & Neglect, 31*(4–5), 402–423.

Yu, M., Gu, L., Shi, Y., & Wang, W. (2021). A systematic review of self-neglect and its risk factors among community-dwelling older adults. *Aging & Mental Health, 25*(12), 2179–2190.

Chapter 15
Secondary Victimization of Sexually Assaulted Women

Milica Boskovic and Gordana Misev

Introduction

Victimization is the act and process of making someone a victim. Victim, as a term, can be viewed in a narrower and broader sense. In a narrower sense, it is a person whose right or good has been violated by committing a crime or by violating international human rights norms. In a broader sense, besides individuals, other entities are also included, such as organizations and social groups, whose rights or goods have been violated in the same way. UN *Declaration* of *Basic Principles of Justice for Victims of Crime and Abuse of Power* (Resolution No. 40/34,1985) categorizes victims as:

1. Victims of criminal acts
2. Victims of power misuse and
3. Indirect victims (family members, people that helped victims, etc.)

Phenomenology of victimization and victims, more scientific interests have got at beginning of XX Century, basicly inside criminology as science. Edwin Sutherland (1924), Hans von Henting (1979), and Benjamin Mendelsohn (1976) have taken important steps toward victimology in their works. In the late 1970s, academic researchers gave wider attention to questions about victimization consequences, secondary victimization, and vistims' protection at court proceedings.

Throughout history, there were different theoretical approaches trying to explain the root of crime, and also the role of victims at crime. The syntagm "role of victim"

M. Boskovic (✉)
Faculty of Diplomacy and Security, Belgrade, Serbia
e-mail: milica.boskovic@fdb.edu.rs

G. Misev
Center for Multidisciplinary Research and Communication, Belgrade, Serbia
e-mail: gordana.misev@zvezdara.org.rs

describes the main approaches in early works that tried to implicate that victims probably challenged possible perpetrators. Von Henting and Mendelsohn focused their attention on explaining the interaction between criminal and victim, and implied that victims are not totally innocent in this "relationship." The idea that victim is a sort of challenger was presented by Marvin Wolfgang (1957 and 1958) and Menachem Amir (1967). Their works were some kind of mainstream for those who tried to blame the victim for what happened to her, especially in cases of rape. Garofalo (1914) was one of the first to note that a victim may provoke another into attack (Meier & Miethe, 1993). Von Henting highlighted personal attributes that make someone more vulnerable to crime, but also implied guilty of such victims. Most efforts to put part of the blame on victim could be found in the works of Wolfgang, and later Amir. Many studies at those time focused on explaining victims' precipitation in crime. These terms were used for crimes such as assault, rape, and murder – victims were sort of blamed for trying to resist against violence or even provoking criminal behavior. Researching Wolfgang and Amir made, supported previously descibed statements and opinions of society, Amir presented that almost 40% of rape victims were prostitutes or had "bad reputation" (Amir, 1967). The most dangerous thing at those times was that tradition and social constellation of women's role were supported by scientific views on gender and its rights. Strong social beliefs and theoretical support did not give women too much space to protect their rights, especially as victims, and to get a fair trial and understanding. Many other similar studies have been conducted, including those that explain a participant's likelihood to victim blame paralleled with some other personal factors, such as their religious beliefs (Writes), their views and values about marriage (Whatley, 2005), whether they have ever been victimized (Mason and Riger), men's sexuality and the sexuality of the victim (Wakelin & Long, 2003), and their likelihood of adhering to rape myths (Conaway, 2017:52).

Today, statements previously descibed surely are unacceptable, but decades has to past until different and new theories substituted those represented by Mendelsohn, Wolfgang, and others. Surely, their works did not have wider academic and political support (Meier & Miethe, 1993:459). This concept was focused on improper distribution of victimizing factors, interpersonal violent crimes, and how victim contributes to own victimization (Nikolić-Ristanović & Konstantinović-Vilić, 2018:436). Support to these statements, victims who suffered multiple and repeated victimization, pointing that their personal performances have influence on becoming victims. Lawrence Cohen and Marcus Felson (1979) represented Routine Activity Theory. Main postulate of this theory was that people will be motivated to satisfy their violent and criminal needs if knew they will avoid the punishment. This is the so-called predatory crime. Miethe and Meier (1990) worked inside Structural-Choice Theory, consistent with Theory of routine activities. Routine activity and lifestyle patterns "help" creating a criminal opportunity, providing knowledge and experience to the predator, of when and how the potential victim is more exposed to attack. Routine activities may predispose some persons and their property to greater risks, but the selection of a particular crime victim within a socio-spatial context was determined by the expected utility of one target over another (Miethe & Meier, 1990, p. 245).

Predator also estimate victims' weaknesses, strength, eventual personal safety measures or their non-existence, and these are important things for abuser when tracking someones' lifestyle and routine patterns. Lifestyle-exposure approach presented by Hindelang et al. (1978) primarily focuses on differences between social groups and sub-groups, their lifestyles, surrounding, socio-economic status. The basic premise of his theory was that differences in the places, social cohesion, culture, and status make some groups and living hoods more exposed to crime. Previous posture we can define as correct, having in mind existence of dangerous places, gangs, dangerous jobs; but, objective circumstances of geographical or architectural characteristics, risking jobs or existence of street violent groups cannot put blame on victims, that they that influenced their own victimization, as well as either theories should not do that.

Theoretical analysis of the causes and forms victimizations also created typology of victims. Mendelsohn (1956), defines six types of victims: The typology consists of six categories: (1) completely innocent victims, (2) victims with minor guilt, (3) voluntary victims, (4) victims more guilty than the offender, (5) victims who alone are guilty, and (6) the imaginary victims (Sengstock, 1976:2). Innocent victim is someone who did not contribute to the victimization and is in the wrong place at the wrong time, Victims with minor guilt are those who do not actively participate in their victimization but contribute to it in some minor degree. Voluntary victims, or guilty victims, guilty offenders are those where victim and offender may have engaged in a criminal activity together. Victims more guilty than offenders are those who have been primary attackers, but the offender won the fight. Imaginary victims are those who lied about their victimization. Guilty victims are those who instigated a conflict but are killed in self-defense. Looking at this typology, we could say that, for Mendelsohn, only one type is completely innocent, while all other types have minor or bigger impact on own victimization. Ellenberger (1970) uses the term "latent victim" for people who have predispositions to become victims – these predispositions come from their profession, biological or medical characteristics or state, gender, or age. Fattah (1978 and 1991) defined several types of victims – those who did not provoke own victimization, latent victims and provocateurs, and victims with active role in a criminal act.

Having in mind all previously mentioned, and knowing that victims did not always throughout history had same important status at trials, it is not surprising why, besides primary victimization, people often suffer impacts of secondary victimization.

Women Victimization

Women victimization, especcially by sexual assaults Violence against women and rape as most brutal form have been subjects of many theoretical and practical researching and articles. Still, most researches focus on some form of violence and victimization or some groups of women. Not many articles cover the problems of violence and rape as well as the phenomena of different secondary victimization. Holstrom and Burgess (1975) studied problems that occurred after sexual assault by interviews with victims, which provided three diagnostic categories of sexual trauma. Even the studies made during the mid-1970s provide valuable clinical explanations that can be used today for understanding trauma and explore further victimization. Novakovic (2007) also examined the types of rape victimization. Postmus and Severson (2006) in their research provided the history of sexual and physical victimization, reported by incarcerated and non-incarcerated women and aimed to define different consequences after these traumas. Those researchers defined and explained health, mental health suicidality and other consequences.

Many authors examined domestic violence, its effects, and possible secondary victimization. Ferraro and Johnson (1983) wrote about wife battering in the USA. Their research provided data on domestic violence, ways of support, and the problem of non-rationalization of a woman that she is the victim and does not deserve violence. Aing (2016) at the study researched experiences of 22 domestic violence survivors at Australia. Ekram (2012) researched on the treatment of victims of domestic violence and their possible secondary victimization, and based on the results from that study and women's experiences, provided the understanding of why women fear to report abuse to officials. Direct statements and expression of feelings provided by victims helped understand the complexity and the potential negative approach of officials toward victims.

When secondary victimization is the main subject of study, most of them refer to victimization at the justice system, medical system, or at society; but, as we said, not many of them explore the many possible forms and sources of secondary victimization. Campbell and Raja (1999) indicate that there is a lot of literature indicating that many victims feel revictimized by the medical system. Campbell (2006) examined what victims felt when they asked for help after the attack, through researching if rape survivors who had the assistance of rape victim advocates had better and more positive experiences with the legal and medical systems compared to those who did not work with advocates. Rivera et al. (2012) examined victims of domestic violence and their possible secondary victimization in the court. As they underline, their study was designed to gain an in-depth understanding of abused mothers' court mediation experiences and how those experiences impact future court help-seeking when the fathers of their children have been abusive to them. Victim perspectives on advocacy support in the criminal justice process were research themes for Brooks and Burman (2016) also researched about victims' perspectives about advocacy support in the criminal justice process. Avery (2020) examined the role rape myth acceptance (RMA) and society play on victims, and how it is important to utilize RMA by all bodies of criminal justice system. Here, we could underline studies about victimization and sexual assaults focused on very special groups, such as women with physical disabilities, provided by Olsvik (2009), or among undergraduate students, examined by Hernández-Romero, Rincón, and Castro-Alzate (2018).

Violence, trauma, and secondary victimization have very serious negative impact on all victims, but here specially referring women, as they are one of vulnerable groups; although every form of attack on person itself is specific, it is useful to collect and describe possible sources of secondary victimization victimization and re-traumatization at on one comprehensive way, as this phenomenon becomes even wider, because of impact mass media and social networks has on people and their behavior today.

Consequences of Victimization

Primary victimization is the process of causing direct harm or damage to the person and, by that, developing trauma. Besides physical injuries or illness, the act of victimization also causes emotional, psychological, and social consequences. Most influent reactions on trauma are anxiety and depression, and at longer time – PTSD. Victims could deny that a criminal act happened to them, avoid to accept that fact, which is the most dangerous way of thinking – because it delays the process of confrontation and healing. Emotional reactions can be fear, confusion, anger, hopelessness, but from position of healing and empowering – sense of guilty and shame are one of most serious consequences and feelings that delay and slow down therapeutic process. From a psychological perspective, stress and trauma may cause confusion, concentration and sleep disorder, and hallucinations. All these consequences may lead to social exclusion, imbalance of living and working activities, and state of introversion. Further, without adequate psychological and social care, and personal sense of hope, victim can get into posttraumatic stress disorder (PTSD), which complicates the already present negative emotions, powerless state, and antisocial behavior. Victims with PTSD can lose interest in working activities, in regular family ties, and become abusers of drug and alcohol and even have suicidal thoughts.

Some authors describe social injuries as consequences of victimization and explain them as inadequate or even malicious and abusive treatment of victim by society, groups, institutions, or even family members. This is actually one of the forms of secondary victimization. Secondary victimization is an act of primary victimization tightening, through the negative reaction of the society or even the wrong reaction of institutions (Nikolić Ristanović, 2003:3). Secondary victimization can happen in family, work, or even at every step of police investigation or trial. Even improper medical treatment or media news can increase trauma and humiliate the victim. When children are victims, school can be place of secondary victimization.

Some societies have intention to humiliate the victims, to decrease her/his trauma and what they suffer, and even blame them for their own victimization. Those attitudes are mostly the effect of tradition, culture, and the historical perspective of human rights. Ignorance or partiality can cause secondary victimization at institutions; as Nils Cristie (1985) asserts, victims are unprofessional outsiders at criminal processes, who probably see the court building for the first time. Mawby and Walklate (1994) said that when victims report crime to police, usually they do not know anything about further trial. Secondary victimization through the process of criminal justice system may occur because of difficulties in balancing the rights of the victim against the right of the accused. For example, (1) Secondary victimization as the result of procedure. (2) Secondary victimization as outcome of justice from criminal justice process. (3) Secondary victimization by the denying effect of the society. (4) Secondary victimization by the unfair treatment of victims by the other institution (Baisla, 2010).

Lack of understanding and protection during trials, as well as misunderstanding and absence of support from familiar people, make victims suffer the psychological trauma again and even deeper. What the victim needs is social understanding, emotional support, physical protection, and information about her/his rights. Absence of some of these factors is mainly the cause for the victim not deciding to report the crime. Unreported crimes cause the so-called dark number of victimizations – much higher numbers of unreported crimes than those that are reported, many victims stayed uncovered and maybe without adequate help, and criminals go unpunished.

Trauma After Rape

The strongest traumas for women are probably violence and sexual assault and rape. Rape is forced, violent sexual penetration against the victim's will, and without the victim's consent (Holstrom & Burges, 1975:1288). These kind of assaults and the act of rape cause deep psychological and emotional trauma, as well as serious injuries. Based on interviews with rape victims, Holstrom and Burges developed three diagnostic categories of sexual trauma: rape trauma syndrome, accessory-to-sex reaction, and sex-stress situation. This categorization is helpful in understanding what this type of victimization causes to women, what short- and long-term consequences could be, and why comprehensive help and support is needed. Holstrom and Burges (1975) provided and explained these three possible states:

- Rape trauma syndrome is acute phase and include gastrointestinal irritability, muscular tension, sleep-pattern disturbance, as well as disorganization of lifestyle. Long-term effects include nightmares, emotional disturbance, changing living place, and social surrounding.
- Accessory-to-sex-reaction puts victim in a subordinate position, because of their stage of personality, cognitive development, and/or age (children and adolescents). Offender has a dominative figure and power over victim, as elder person and authority. By using manipulation and gifts (material goods, money, candy), the offender tries to make relationship with the victim and explain that sexual activity is desirable and appropriate. When the victim is an accessory to sexual activity, trauma often shows itself through a gradual social and psychological withdrawal from usual activities;
- Sex-stress situation is an anxiety reaction that results from the circumstances surrounding sexual activity to which both parties initially consented. The person for whom the sexual situation produces the most anxiety usually brings the matter to the attention of a professional, such as a police officer or one of the hospital staff members (Holstrom & Burges, 1975:1289).

Rape as an act of forced sexual relation, followed by violence, is the most brutal form of sexual abuse. Act of rape includes use of physical force, threats, torture and violent sexual act, which is unwilling by victim, and it is one of most brutal forms of violence and abuse. At a symbolical level, this annuls the victim's subjectivity (Ignjatović & Simeunović-Patić, 2015:100). Consequences are various and serious, some of them could be long-term. This is a very specific form of violence and criminal act – the offender needs to humiliate the victim to dominate over her and hurt. These sexual acts are degradation of human being; after the act, victims feel frightened, ashamed, and helpless. Most scholarly discussions on women's higher levels of fear focuses on the horror of rape that may arise from another face-to-face victimization (Ferraro, 1995:669).

Besides anxiety, fear, and depression, rape victims can get many emotional impacts and feelings. From aspect of psychological help, as well as for decision to report crime, some of most problematic behaviors are shock and denial. Victim find difficulty in accepting what happened and that she has become a victim. After shock and partial or total acceptance of the fact, some of them could feel anger. This anger and rage that victims feel are is irrational as they are not guilty for what happened to them, as well as surrounding is not guilty, but victimized persons sometimes get angry on justice system, police, social workers, and even family members, as the mode of theor own inner defence mechanism. For fear as emotional condition, we can say is rational, as women become victim of brutal act, even worse if offender is someone they know and trust. But fear can get anxiety to get deeper and worse, for the victim may get panic attacks and become introverted and unsocialized. As long as these emotional states occupy the victim, her treatment and recovery are harder and slow, as she could start feeling helplessness. This is why adequate social and legal approach to question of women, gender role and sexual behavior are important, as secondary victimization, made by officials or by social surrounding or media, can push victim into more serious emotional disturbance and aggravate her psychological and physical recovery.

Physical injuries that result from crime may be classified as minor (scratches), moderate (bruises, broken bones, and similar), and severe (stabbing by different sharp objects, gunshot wounds). It may not be possible to see all physical injuries such as internal organ injuries or brain injuries, or those internal injuries caused by sexual assault (Canadian Resource Centre for Victims of Crime, 2005:3). Knowing this, even from amateur and human level, it is clear why sensitive, compassionate, and measured approach of medical staff is important.

It is not unusual that women do not report they were raped, if it is known females gone through tradition of gender enueual relationships established at societies and that even sometimes legal system formalize that dominant/submissive relationships between men and women, through formalization of these ratios., at judical decisions. Male dominated through social and religion construction of family and life roles – he is dominated at home, job, politics; Even today, at modern times, there are countries where women do not have right to vote or even go to school and drive a car. Sexual violence has historically been utilized as "a pervasive, systemic method of creating and sustaining male dominance over women," as such rape myths seek to further justify (Avery, 2020:34).

Males were those who wrote definitions and laws, and by that, rape had dark side of legal history at past. Woman's sexual propriety has long been a significant measure of her worth in our society (Pruitt, 2003:967). In the early 1900s, from the aspect of rape, law recognized two types of women: chaste and unchaste. Chaste women were respected at society and protected by law, men were punished for raping chaste women. On the other hand, unchaste women were degraded and their rapes were usually not punished. Rape at marriage was not recognized, and husbands were excluded from legal responsibility. Changes and legal reform, started after 1960s, and three reasons were dominated for society, as well as law authorities start to look at women and act of rape differently. Number of reported acts of rape dramatically increased and law system was confronted with facts that rape is violent and criminal act, no matter how society and tradition estimate or underestimate women. Political activism was the third factor – they encouraged legal reform and putting victim at a central place, she/he deserves. Feminist movements of 1980s made a strong impact on improving a woman's place in the society and even science. Prominent attempts to counter violence against women therefore focus on changing people's views on whether it is acceptable to engage in such violence (Wagman et al., 2015) Feminist authors explain gender-based dimension of victimization as a product of imbalance of power and fight against sexism in the judicial system (Barberet, 2010).

Canadian criminologists point out on several prejudices that formed cultural construction, which effect was low compassion and underestimation of this brutal criminal act (Ignjatović & Simeunović-Patić, 2015). Those delusions are that "raping is not possible," "woman wants to be raped," they provoke by their style and behavior, "rape is sexual act," because man have natural needs, and sometimes cannot control them, "No means Yes" and "Once said Yes, always mean Yes." These attitudes were deeply rooted into patriarchal societies and main politics, and it is not rare that some groups still believe that a woman "gets what she deserves." On researching the causes of family violence, Dragisic-Labas (2019) used the term "power" as the power of those who are "beyond," and say that it is a consequence of cultural and social constructions, which is copied and misused in marriages. In traditional societies, men have forced power and used it even for sexual victimization of women. Necić also points out that women's role in societies were historically defined, based on imbalance of power between men and women (Necić, 2019:38). Baeza et al. (2022), talked about social capital as factor of "accepting" or disapproval of women rape. The definition of social capital refers to resources available to victimized person through social networks and belonging to groups through social norms, trust, and reciprocity that facilitate help and cooperation for mutual benefit (Putnam & Feldstein, 2009). Regarding cases of sexual violence, social capital would not be a protective factor in those communities where this type of violence is justified or ignored (Baeza et al., 2022:3). Depending on political order at state, economic freedom, collective spirit, and social ties - previously described social capital can be protective factor for respect of human rights and equality orcan be another ballast for women at traditionally gender-based societies.

Secondary Victimization After Rape

Although the collective state of mind has changed, gender-based roles are mainly outdated, and women are equal at social life, work, and judicial system, still many women avoid to say and report that they are victims of family or other kind of violence and/or rape. The response of community members and public institutions to the crimes of rape and sexual assault has been, historically, disappointing. Victims have felt forced into silence, ashamed to speak out about their experiences (Hunter, 2019:8).

Even today, some women that report violence and/or rape, are stigmatized, misunderstood, deprived of support and empowerment, and go through psychologically painful trials. Before a woman can report a rape to the police, two preconditions are necessary; First, she must identify herself as a victim of a crime. Second, she must be confident that others—parents, friends, and especially the police—will perceive her as a victim (Williams, 1984:461). Faced by inadequate social and media reaction, absence of support from close persons, misunderstanding of authorities, and inefficient trials, victimized women experience secondary victimization, which extends their trauma and complicates recovery. Secondary victimization stems from how a victim is perceived by family members and close social surrounding, police investigators, medical personnel, prosecutors, jurors, and even media. Rather than receiving necessary assistance from police officers, healthcare professionals, and mental health professionals, victims of sexual assault face judgment, blame, and shame (Hunter, 2019:13). Secondary victimization is not rare, and has serious consequences on victims, as well as on whole society, their empathy, cultural changes and empowerment of human rights. In a study by Campbell, findings showed that the more a victim encounters these secondary victimization behaviors, the more symptoms of posttraumatic stress they develop (Campbell, 2008). Victim can feel secondary victimization through language and used terms, which can be inappropriate and even degrading (by offender, police officer, social worker, lawyer), through absence of emotional and psychological support, adequate medical help, or exclusion from social groups or work, and strenuous trials. As Baisla mentions in her article, secondary victimization through the process of criminal justice system may occur because of difficulties in balancing the rights of the victim against the right of the accused (Baisla, 2010). For example: (1) Secondary victimization, which is the outcome of procedure, (2) Secondary victimization, which is the outcome of justice from criminal justice process, (3) Secondary victimization from the denying effect of the society, and (4) Secondary victimization by the unfair treatment of victims by the other institution (Baisla, 2010:62).

Canadian Resource Centre for Victims of Crime (2005) gives a few examples of secondary victimization:

- The refusal to recognize their experience as criminal victimization.
- Intrusive or inappropriate conduct by police or other criminal justice personnel.
- The whole process of criminal investigation and trial (decisions about whether or not to prosecute the case, the trial itself, the sentencing of the offender, and punishment).
- The victim perceives difficulties in balancing their rights with those of the accused or the offender.
- Criminal justice processes and procedures do not take the perspective of the victim into account.
- Relatives may have restricted access to the body of a loved one due to hospital policies and procedures.
- The hurried schedule of the emergency room may affect a sexual assault victim's privacy or sense of dignity.
- School personnel may discount child disclosure of abuse.
- Doctors may not acknowledge signs of spouse abuse.
- Spiritual leaders may try to guide victims into paths of healing and forgiveness before they are ready or against their wishes.
- Intrusive or inappropriate investigation and filming, photographing, and reporting bythe media (p.7).

One of most important international documents about preventing secondary victimization is Recommendation No. R (85) 11 on the position of the victim in the framework of criminal law and procedure, from 1985. This Recommendation No. R 85 (11) is one of based documents, for creating and involving into practice many other legal recommendations and conclusions. This document and the UN Declaration of Basic Principles of Justice for Victims of Crime and Abuse of Power, adopted by General Assembly resolution 40/34, have the following similar demands:

1. Informing about trial and procedure;
2. Allowing victim to speak and say their opinion;
3. Help and support to victim during trial;
4. Providing maximum safety for victim;
5. Avoiding unnecessarily long trial.

Committee Recommendation indicates that direct secondary victimization is insensitive police treatment, repeated questioning, and insufficient protection from inappropriate publicity, as well as from revenge. Indirect secondary victimization occurs when information flow between victim and judicial system is insufficient and when victim has difficulty to compensate damage by state or offender.

The criminal justice system is often characterized as causing secondary victimization among crime victims (Orth, 2002:314). Many research studies showed that secondary victimization during trials is not rare. A study by Campbell and associates showed that 52% of rape victims found legal system as harmful (Campbell, Wasco, Ahrens, Sefl, & Barnes, 2001). Besides the effects of the psychological difficulties caused by the primary victimization, secondary victimization by criminal proceedings could negatively influence other psychological variables such as the victim's self-esteem, faith in the future, trust in the legal system, and faith in a just world (Orth, 2002:314). These consequences are not surprising, as the legal system should be a place of safety and justice, and when victims do not feel that protection and respect, trauma continues and insecurity grows.

Campbell and Raja provided researching at which participants were employes at Illinois licensed mental health, and were mental health professionals (i.e., clinical/ counseling psychologists, clinical social workers, social workers and professional counselors). The majority of mental health professionals surveyed (84%) agreed that contact with social service providers re-traumatizes rape victims. Campbell and Raja (1999) provided these facts from their research:

(a) Eighty-one percent of study participants believed that the legal system's treatment of rape victims is psychologically detrimental,
(b) Eighty-nine percent of study participants agreed that the medical, post-rape exam was traumatizing for rape survivors,
(c) Fifty-eight percent of study participants implicated mental health professionals in contributing to secondary victimization of rape survivors through harmful practices (Campbell & Raja, 1999)

Every step of crime/rape investigation and proceeding should provide trust and care. Experiences of rape survivors with the medical system can also be questionable. When rape victims seek post-assault emergency medical care, most receive a medical exam and forensic evidence collection kit, less than one-half receive information on the risk of pregnancy (40–49%), and between 20% and 43% are able to obtain emergency contraception to prevent pregnancy (Campbell, 2006:2).

It is not unusual for a victim to be unsatisfied with verdict and punishment. If the offender is in prison, the victim perceives that she/he is definitely safe, trauma is at least compensated, and other potential victims are safe. Victims may react with moral dissatisfaction if the perpetrator receives better or more costly rehabilitation than they themselves. Victims frequently have a critical attitude toward the perpetrator's rehabilitation, primarily because it improves the outcome of the perpetrator and therefore worsens the relative outcome for the victim (Orth, 2002:315). Knowing the legal history and the position of female victims during the early 1900s, fear and doubts are expected. This mistrust, however, has not been limited to legal requirement and officers of the court; Case histories indicate the great reluctance of juries to convict an apparently normal male for rape except under aggravated circumstances (Giacopassi & Wilkinson, 1985:369).

Very special form of secondary victimization during trialsis happening at cases about human trafficking. Victims of human trafficking mostly are targeted by traffickers based on vulnerabilities they already have; they past multiple physical and sexual torture during their "slavery," with very serious and mostly long-term psychological, health and social consequences. Being witness at trails for traffickers is very stressful and sometimes dangerous for these victims – this places the victim in a dual role, namely, on the one hand as witness and informant for law enforcement and on the other hand as beneficiary of protection measures in place for trafficking victims (Goodey, 2004). Article 12(4) of the Directive 2011/36 states that victims of trafficking should receive specific treatment aimed at preventing secondary victimization by avoiding unnecessary repetition of interviews, visual contact with defendant, giving evidence in open court and unnecessary questioning concerning the victim's private life (Rijken & Khadraoui, 2020:69).

We could say that special treatment deserves women raped at war and similar arm conflicts. Their trauma is multiplied by fact that their state and society are at war, that every kind of existence, even hers and the life of her loved ones, is seriously disturbed and in danger. As Jones et al. (2014) point out, sexual violence in conflict is far from a discrete trauma; it often has lifelong and even intergenerational impacts. Rape and other forms of sexual violence during armed conflict are now acknowledged as weapons of war, designed not only to inflict bodily harm on primarily – but not exclusively – female victims, but also to terrify and humiliate them, their families and their communities (UN Women, 2013; Domingo et al., 2013; UNICEF, 1996, at Jones et al., 2014:1). As armed conflicts are almost unavoidable reality, we are witness that many women become victims of rape, during war, but unfortunately sometimes at states they migrate. As Wood (2018) says when rape by an armed organization occurs frequently, it is often said to be a strategy of war. Having in mind that behind most of the armed conflicts are politics, different ideologies, and religion, it is easy for these women to experience re-traumatization and secondary victimization, depending on treatment at court, if offenders are even identified and processed. Also, media reporting and their objectivity is often interrogative. Survivors – women and girls, as well as men and boys (who are even less likely to report the violence because of hostility around homosexual acts) – can face stigma that forces them out of their families, isolates them from their communities and leaves them to deal with their physical and psychological trauma alone (Jones et al., 2014:3).

It is not a rare phenomenon that women, victims of violence or rape, are secondary victimized by media. This kind of indecent and sometimes ironically reporting about women victims of sexuall assault, are also induced by traditional gender-based roles and inequality, as well as by needof media to have sensational headlines. As Jugovic, Jugovic, and Bogetic said, the media's approach to women victimized by violence is colored by "three S" – sex, scandal, and spectacle (Jugović et al., 2016). In a research on media presentation in Serbia, specially monitored on World's Day of violence against women (25.11.2017.), Necic argued that 67% of reports had negative context, 3% with positive context, while at other times, in 26 cases women were presented as victims, in 9 cases media gave more publicity to the offender, and 10 reports were neutral (Necić, 2019).

News media play an important role in public perception of events. If talking about gender roles and sexuality – advertising, movies, and even some artworks, did not help creating adequate sociopolitical view of women personality, identity and right on having choice. Film and advertising often reinforce rape myths that trivialize sexual assault as a pleasurable, even romantic, experience (McCaul et al., 1990). In pornography, women are usually presented as sexually aggressive, and even "desired" for being raped. It is not unusual to hear that many young actresses or models say that they were forced to sex, in line to get (better) role and piece of glory. Even today, the most famous Hollywood actresses are much less paid than their male colleagues; same thing we can say for men and women in sports, even business. If all these inequalities and sometimes derogation of women are widely presented by media, what would stop one unarticulated and violent person to harass or rape a woman? In their qualitative analysis of newsmagazine coverage of ten high-profile sexual assaults that occurred between 1980 and 1996, Ardovini-Brooker and Caringella-Macdonald (2002) found that reports covering acquaintance rape cases were more likely to blame the victim than those covering stranger rape cases (Gravelin, 2016).

Another problem is a lack of respect for the individual's dignity, as well as their privacy. In some cases, newspapers print personal details which are not relevant to the crime, but make for interesting copy (Mulley, 2001:30). Anastasio and Costa (2004) provided several researching on women and victims' treatment by media. At one of their researching (Anastasio & Costa, 2004), they examined whether victims of violent crime (excluding sex crimes) are treated differently according to their gender. Data showed that accounts of violent crime personalize male victims more than female victims: more personal information was included about male victims, and males were significantly more likely to be referred to by name rather than by a noun ("the victim") or pronoun; Also, empathy for the victim was increased across victim gender by both inclusion of personal information and referring to the victim by name. Victim blame was also increased by the inclusion of personal information. Implications of how the news media may subtly reduce empathy and engender blame for female victims are discussed (Anastasio & Costa, 2004). Historically using descriptors such as "pretty" and "flirtatious" to characterize survivors; help keeping alive "rape as normal and pleasurable" myth and undermines its origin as a violent crime which is committed in search of power and control, not sexual pleasure (Thacker, 2017:92).

Ardovini-Brooker and Caringella-Macdonald (2002) qualitatively analyzed newsmagazine coverage for 10 sexual assaults that happened during the 1980s and mid-1990s. Data showed that reports covering acquaintance rape cases were more likely to blame the victim than those covering stranger rape cases. Media wish to know and show victim's name, lifestyle, place of living, friends, habits, rather than to talk and write about attacker, his psychological and social profile. Women are often held responsible for solving their own problems, and rape is no exception – especially since women are often accused of "provoking" the abuse somehow (Thacker, 2017:89).

If we want to be clear about some media and their "hunger" for publicity, we should say that they seek for so-called high-profile crime and rape cases. When this happens, media outlets and journalists can be relentless in their attempts to get the story (Canadian Resource Centre for Victims of Crime, 2010). Cases become high-profile when the victim is an attractive, white, middle-class female (Canadian Resource Centre for Victims of Crime, 2010), when the nature of crime is bizarre, and including even children or old people. Vulnerable groups are more "attractive" for covering, while prostitutes or some of minorities usually are not an "interested topic" or even are blamed for what happened to them.

Primary and Secondary Victimization at Social Networks

It is unquestionabe that the Internet and applications created during decades brought connection between people, helped share their culture, thoughts, experiences, and art. Especially, social networks have become a place of virtual meeting of people around the world, living at different traditions, political orders, and social surroundings. Sharing ideas, successes, and promoting cultural differences is a fortune for the global society. During Covid-19 crisis, web applications showed as almost irreplaceable tools for learning, working, and spending free time. Mass media are a central component of daily life (Bovill & Livingstone, 2001). The use of social networking sites has increased significantly in the last decade, especially among young people. Social media sites such as Facebook, Instagram, and Twitter have become an integral part of people lives. It is indicated that there are 2.23 billion monthly active Facebook users with an annual increase of 11% around the world (Çimke & Cerit, 2021). Many useful things got its stronger promotion with help of World Wide Web, such as freedom movements and exposing global corruption. Since the mid-nineteenth century, the feminist movement in Western countries, United States at first, have significantly increased in strength. With the help of social media, a fourth wave of feminism began in the United States and other Western countries during 2012 (Zhang et al., 2022). But although knowing this, we must underline that mass media and social networks are the main provider of information, but also generator of delusions and fraud. News media play an important role in public perception of events (McCombs & Reynolds, 2002). Internet applications and social networks, as many other achievements, have their dangerous and manipulative side. Criminals, bullies and fraudsters find their hidden comfortable place at the net, for victimizing people. Talking about social networks and secondary victimization, we specially speak about women, as most frequent victims of web "dark side." Even though social networking websites have opened a wide window for socializing, they have also opened the floodgates for various crimes against women in the cyber space (Halder, 2009:5). Social networks are a debatable place for meeting and dating people, knowing that it is very easy to create profile and be whoever someone wants to be. Giving trust to someone behind an online profile, women can become victims of violence, rape, and, most dangerously, human trafficking. Not only that, people can be victims of different ridicules and bullying, even without knowing that. The fact that the Internet and Wi-Fi connections are present in all areas of life trhough applications and cell phones, for socially disordered people provides opportunity to make pictures or videos of different people at different situations (without their knowledge), and share it online, with putting inappropriate comments. Cyber violence is also presented at intimate partner relationships. Even though cyber intimate partner violence usually occurs in an ongoing relationship, it can also occur after the relationship has ended. Several studies have shown that the moment when a woman tries to leave a relationship is a critical time where she is most likely to experience traditional violence from her partner (Felmlee & Faris, 2016). What is most terrifying and for wider psychological, anthropological, and even philosophical consideration is the fact that people seek for sensation, drama, do the action of recording violence, but without the need to come and help the victim. By this, a whole new sphere of deviation is established – cyber aggression. Cyber aggression refers to electronic or online behavior intended to harm another person psychologically or damage his or her reputation (Felmlee & Faris, 2016:244). Unfortunately, online news comments and social networks, besides being a supportive tool, have become a place of victimization and secondary victimization. Women are exposed to primary as well as to secondary victimization through social networks. Behind virtual profiles there could be rapists, human traffickers, and drug dealers. Famous persons, influencers, and bloggers are faced with many disturbing, humiliating, and even threatening comments and messages by unknown virtual profiles. Behind these profiles, mostly are frustrated, asocial, and unfulfilled persons, but their thoughts can push someone to harm some of "targeted" people. On the other hand, victimized women, especially those who were deceived, raped, and trafficked, are faced with malicious online comments, referring mostly that they deserved that by way they were dressed, way they lived (specially explained by Theory of routine activities and at works of Von Henting and Amir), popularity they tried to achieve, and similar. As Higson-Bliss (2017) said, anyone can become a victim of abuse online, but it is apparent that certain behaviors are gender specific. For instance, women are more likely to have comments aimed at them threatening rape and other forms of sexual violence. This is particularly the case for women in the public eye (Higson-Bliss, 2017). But what is important is, these kinds of comments come from women, as much as from men. By these virtual attacks and comments, these women are being secondary victimized. Virtuality often makes possible for victim and attacker to change places at "guilty chair" at eyes of cyber jury. It is especially dangerous when someone from that virtual jury is capable, not only to make secondary, but even primary victimization of some woman. Media news on trial reports, and supportive social networks are strength for victimized women, but on other hand that is also cyber sphere at which exist many virtual profiles which use that area and own anonimity for manipulation, degradation, spitting out frustrations and even supporting violence. Explosion of web applications and social networks leave law practitioners a few steps behind, discussing on how to regulate freedom of speech and right on privacy and humanity. IT sphere is the one trying to protect people, blocking politically or in any other way incorrect messages.

Most articles provide researching on secondary victimization at juridical processes. Not having adequate and sensible approach and justice at trials does not give strength for other victims to speak about their trauma and ask for help and punishment for those who are guilty. But what is not researched enough is secondary victimization of assaulted women at social networks. Online media and networks provide people to write and talk about their opinion even when it is politically or in other way incorrect and unhuman, hiding behind false names and profiles. It is not rare that, at social media posts and after reportets' news about women victimization, especially if she is famous one, people write posts with comments about attack, saying that these victims deserved beacuse of way they live, way they dress or similar atributes, that someone finds "too atractive". Social networks provide a huge space for frustrated or violent people to express their aggressive and deviant opinions and even intentions. Future research should pay more attention on secondary victimization by media, online news, and social networks, especially on readers' comments. Results of these researching would be helpful for media and IT experts to prevent harmful and inappropriate comments, not just at cases when they are opposite to constitutional or criminal law.

Conclusion

Victim blaming can have different psychological, social, religious, and even normative roots. Sometimes it is easier to support a "stronger" person to not go against violence, but to protect people/women in need. Passivation, even jealousy ("she is pretty," "good dressed"), or unconscious fear and denial of fact that it might happen to them even put some women in a position to blame the victim for being assaulted and raped. Non-existence of psychological mechanisms for coping with man-world challenges and their own degradation at family, society, or job place make some women non-solidary with victims. The worst that can happen from these attitude and beliefs is for women to blame themselves for being attacked. This attitude, unfortunately, perfectly describes the Theory of Just World – people believe that world is a safe place, but they only get what they deserve. Described beilefs are passiveand even religiously interwoven attitude, similar to "It is God's will," which lead to behavior unmotivated for empowerment, for fighting and believing that thing can be different and that it depends on us, and our will and acting. Those who blame themselves also help increasing those factors in their socialization and victimization that contributed to their feelings of responsibility. These factors included miseducation about rape, adherence to rape myths, and blame addressed to them by their support people (Conaway, 2017:53). Victims are sometimes wrongfully portrayed as passive individuals who seek out and submit to the violence they endure (The Canadian Resource Centre for Victims of Crime, 2009).

Other, and more dangerous side of phenomenon of victim – blaming is seeing offender as someone who simplycannot control his natural sexual needs/forces. What differentiates human beings from animals is conscience and possibility to distinguish right from wrong. So, hiding behind needs that cannot be controlled is conceited and perfidious. Serious mental illness combined with physiological disorders can lead to lack of needs' control, but even then, women cannot be blamed for any forced violent and sexual attack. Women have the fear of rape, but the mistake is when they learn that the attack is their fault, and when from a young age, they learn that they have to control and modify their behavior, in order to avoid societies' misunderstanding and even blaming for victimization. Violence and sexual attack start point have at the attacker's own feeling of supremacy, gender-based social power, and the will to show and "confirm" that attitudes, even by degradation and sexual disrespect of women and their personal will and integrity. The shift of the blame onto the victim is largely a result of people's preconceived notions about rape. People are less likely to believe a victim and less likely to hold her assailant accountable when she reports being assaulted in a manner that is not consistent with stereotypes (Michele & Brown, 2012:76). By all previously mentioned and described attitudes and actions, so called rape myth is created and even being dominated phrase at some point at history. Rape myths are believed to vary across cultures and societies, but constantly follow a trend by which the victim is blamed. Promoting gender-based stereotypes, religious and traditional beliefs, and even presenting rape as women' fault or imagination can have serious impacts on how police, medical or social service, judge, or even their own family will look on them and react. Unfortunately, we are witnessing that in some countries (mostly pure areas of Asia and Africa), women are not just abused and subordinated, but even are "goods" that can be sold, mostly to human traffickers. This fact shows how many cultural, time, and space gaps we need to solve to bring equality and human rights to all parts of the world.

Every person has some level of resiliency – ability to face with sudden and traumatic events. Some person has stronger resilience mechanisms and some of them weaker. Many psychological, physical, and socio-economic factors create strength of personal resiliency. No matter how personal mechanisms are developed, the first helping approach to victim needs to be very measured and focused. First therapeutic help (emergency help) has three steps: (1) In the first step, the therapist or supporting person needs to have an empathic approach and help victim to free herself from the negative emotions she currently feels; (2) In the second step, the victim needs to speak about the traumatic event, her thoughts, and feelings; (3) In the third step, the therapist should decide which further therapeutic approach and support is the best for victim to restore her mental strength and mechanisms of resilience. What victim needs at moments of shock and trauma is expert help, social support, and a feeling of understanding, sympathy, and belief in justice. Any kind of rude, inappropriate approach, by officials, medical staff, or the surrounding, pushes the victim into deeper anxiety, helplessness, and feeling that she is guilty.

Canadian Resource Centre for Victims of Crime (2005) provide what victims need after facing crime:

- Victims need to feel safe as crime often leaves them feeling helpless, vulnerable, and frightened.
- In addition to fear, victims often have feelings of self-blame, anger, shame, sadness,or denial. Emotional distress may surface in seemingly peculiar ways, such as laughter.
- Sometimes victims feel rage at the unpredictable and/or uncontrollable threat to their safety. This rage can even be directed to the people who try tohelp them.
- Victims should be able to express their emotions. Victims often need to share their emotions and tell their stories after the trauma of the crime. They may also need tohave their feelings accepted by their surroundings and have their story heard by a nonjudgmental listener.
- Victims may need to know "what comes next." Following victimization, victims often have concerns about their role in the investigation of the crime and the legal

proceedings. They may also be concerned about issues such as media attention and reporting about their victimization and personal details. Victims can also be concerned about payment for health care or property damage. Victimization is stressful, and knowingwhat to expect in the aftermath of crime can help relieve anxiety (p.8)

Rape is an act of brutal violence, which not only physically hurts a person but also humiliates her dignity and disrespects her free will. The last thing victims need is to be excluded from society, to be stigmatized, and secondary victimized by lack of trust, support, and absence of justice.

Secondary victimization not only pushes victims into deeper psychological trauma effects but also by some way encourages possible offenders to "materialize" their sense of supremacy, strength, and look, by showing force and sexual necessity over women.

References

Amir, M. (1967). Victim-precipitated forcible rape. *Journal of Criminal Law, Criminology, and Police Science, 58*, 99.493–99.502.

Anastasio, P. A., & Costa, D. M. (2004). Twice hurt: How newspaper coverage may reduce empathy and engender blame for female victims of crime. *Sex Roles: A Journal of Research, 51*(9–10), 535–542.

Anderson, K. L. (2002). Perpetrator or victim? Relationships between intimate partner violence and well-being. *Journal of Marriage and Family, 64*(4), 851–863.

Ardovini-Brooker, J., & Caringella-Macdonald, S. (2002). Media attributions of blame and sympathy in ten rape cases. *The Justice Professional, 15*(1), 3–18.

Avery, E. (2020). The 'effective decriminalisation' of acquaintance rape: Rape myth acceptance, secondary victimisation and anti-rape campaigns. *Plymouth Law Review, 3* 59.

Baeza, P. I., et al. (2022). Social, economic and human capital: Risk or protective factors in sexual violence? *International Journal of Environmental Research and Public Health, 19*. https://doi.org/10.3390/ijerph19020777

Baisla, D. K. (2010). Secondary victimization under the criminal justice system. *Issues in Legal and Political Philosophy* (November 15, 2010). Available at SSRN: http://ssrn.com/abstract=1742165 or https://doi.org/10.2139/ssrn.1742165 (visited on 01.12.2021.)

Barberet, R. (2010). Feminist victimology. In B. S. Fisher & S. P. Lab (Eds.), *Encyclopedia of victimology and crime prevention* (Vol. 1). Sage Publication, Inc.

Bošković, M., et al. (2017). Exploring the link between commiting acts of cruelty to animals and violence against people. In T. G. Rejani (Ed.), *Handbook of social, psychological, and forensic perspectives on sexual abuse*. IGI Global Publishing.

Bovill, M., & Livingstone, S. (2001). *Bedroom culture and the privatization of media use.*

Brooks, O., & Burman, M. (2016). Reporting rape: Victim perspectives on advocacy support in the criminal justice process. *Criminology and Criminal Justice*. http://eprints.gla.ac.uk/122862/

Bugarski, T. D. (2018). Borba protiv nasilja u porodici u praksi nadležnih organa u Novom Sadu. *Zbornik radova Pravnog fakulteta u Novom Sadu, I*, 95–121.

Burgess, A. W., & Holmstrom, L. L. (1975). Coping behavior of the rape victim. *American Journal of Psychiatry, 133*(4), 413–418.

Campbell, R. (2008). The psychological impact of rape victims. *The American Psychologist, 63*(8), 702–717.

Campbell, R., & Raja, S. (1999). Secondary victimization of rape victims: Insights from mental health professionals who treat survivors of violence. *Violence and Victims, 14*(3), 261–275.

Campbell, R., Sefl, T., Barnes, H. E., Ahrens, C. E., Wasco, S. M., & Zaragoza-Diesfeld, Y. (1999). Community services for rape survivors: Enhancing psychological well-being or increasing trauma? *Journal of Consulting and Clinical Psychology, 67*, 847–858.

Campbell, R., Wasco, S. M., Ahrens, C. E., Sefl, T., & Barnes, H. E. (2001). Preventing the "Second rape" rape survivors' experiences with community service providers. *Journal of interpersonal violence, 16*(12), 1239–1259.

Campbell, R. (2006). Rape survivors' experiences with the legal and medical systems: Do rape victim advocates make a difference?. *Violence against women, 12*(1), 30–45.

Canadian Resource Centre for Victims of Crime. (2005). p. 1–11.

Christie, N. (1985). Crime control as drama. *JL & Soc'y, 13*, 1.

Çimke, S., & Cerit, E. (2021). Social media addiction, cyberbullying and cyber victimization of university students. *Archives of Psychiatric Nursing, 35*(5), 499–503.

Cohen, L. E. (1981). Modeling crime trends: A criminal opportunity perspective. *Journal of Research in Crime and Delinquency, 18*, 138–164.

Cohen, L. E., & Cantor, D. (1980). The determinants of larceny: An empirical and theoretical study. *Journal of Research in Crime and Delinquency, 17*, 140–159.

Conaway, E. (2017). *VictimBlaming.* https://www.csustan.edu/sites/default/files/honors/documents/journals/entries/Conaway.pdf

Dragišić-Labaš, S. M. (2019). Suicidno ponašanje korisnika psihijatrijskih usluga - teorije i istraživanja. *Sociološki pregled, 53*(4), 1521–1552.

Ellenberger, H. F. (1970). The discovery of the unconscious: The history and evolution of dynamic psychiatry (Vol. 1, pp. 280–281). New York: Basic books.

Ekram, A. (2012). Do victims of domestic violence suffer from secondary victimization? An exploration into the causes, processes and treatments. Bachelor Thesis. p. 1–50.

Emerson, E., et al. (2022). The association between disability and risk of exposure to peer cyber victimization is moderated by gender: Cross-sectional survey. *Disability and Health Journal, 15*(1), 101170. https://doi.org/10.1016/j.dhjo.2021.101170. Epub 2021 Jul 7. PMID: 34253505.

Farrell, G. (1995). Preventing repeat victimization. *Crime and Justice, 19*, 469–534.

Fattah, E. A. (1978). Moving the right: a return to punishment. *Crime and Justice, 6*(2), 79–92.

Fattah, E. A. (1991). From crime policy to victim policy. the need for a fundamental policy change. *Int'l Annals Criminology, 29*, 43.

Felmlee, D., & Faris, R. (2016). Toxic ties: Networks of friendship, dating, and cyber victimization. *Social Psychology Quarterly, 79*(3), 243–262.

Felson, M., & Cohen, L. (1980). Human ecology and crime: A routine activity approach. *Human Ecology, 8*, 389–406.

Ferraro, K. F. (1995). Women's fear of victimization: Shadow of sexual assault? *Social Forces, 75*(2), 667–690.

Ferraro, K. F., & Johnson, J. M. (1983). How women experience battering: The process of victimization. *Social Problems, 30*(3), 325–339.

Garofalo, R. (1914). *Criminology.* Little, Brown.

Giacopassi, D. J., & Wilkinson, K. R. (1985). Rape and the devalued victim. *Law and Human Behavior, 9*(4), 367–383.

Goodey, J. (2004). Sex trafficking in women from Central and East European countries: Promoting a 'victim-centred' and 'woman-centred' approach to criminal justice intervention. *Feminist review, 76*(1), 26–45.

Gravelin, C. R. (2016). *Assessing the impact of media on blaming the victim of acquaintance rape* (Dissertation). e Faculty of the University of Kansas.

Greathouse, S. M., et al. (2013). Female Sexual Assault Perpetrators. In *A review of the literature on sexual assault perpetrator characteristics and behaviors.* RAND Corporation.

Halder, D. (2009). Cyber socializing and victimization of women. *TEMIDA,* 5–26.

Hernández-Romero, H., Rincón, P., & Castro-Alzate, E. S. (2018). Prevalence of victimization and perpetration of sexual aggression in undergraduate students: a systematic review 2008-2018. *Revista Ciencias de la Salud, 17*(1), 85–107.

Higson-Bliss, L. (2017). The law, social media and the victimisation of women. In *Socio-Legal Studies Association Annual Conference*, Newcastle.

Hindelang, M. S., Gottfredson, M., & Garofalo, J. (1978). *Victims of personal crime*. Ballinger.

Hunter, K. M. (2019). Secondary victimization of young adult female sexual assault victims. *UCF Thesis and Dissertations*, pp. 1–148.

Ignjatović, Đ., & Simeunović-Patić, B. (2015). *Viktimologija*. Univerzitet u Beogradu-Pravni fakultet.

Jones, N., et al. (2014). *The fallout of rape as a weapon of war: The life-long and intergenerational impacts of sexual violence in conflict* (pp. 1–7). Overseas Development Institute.

Jugović, A., Jugović, J., & Bogetić, D. (2016). Socio-kulturni kontekst i karakteristike nasilja nad ženama u Srbiji. *Godišnjak Fakulteta političkih nauka, X*(15), 105–123.

Knežević, B. S., et al. (2018). Odnos lekara prema nasilju u porodici. *Opšta medicina., 24*(3–4), 63–72.

Kornhauser, R. (1978). *Social sources of delinquency*. University of Chicago Press.

Meier, R.F., Miethe, T.D. (1993). Understanding theories of criminal victimization. *Crime and Justice*, Vol. 17, 459–499

Mendelsohn, R (1976). Victimology and contemporary society's trends. *Victimology, an international journal*, 1, pp. 8–28

McCaul, K. D., Veltum, L. G., Boyechko, V., & Crawford, J. J. (1990). Understanding attributions of victim blame for rape: Sex, violence, and foreseeability. *Journal of Applied Social Psychology, 20*(1), 1–26.

McCombs, M., & Reynolds, A. (2002). News influence on our pictures of the world. In *Media effects* (pp. 11–28). Routledge.

Media Guide for Victims. (2010). Published by: Canadian Resource Centre for Victims of Crime. www.crcvc.ca

Meier, R. F., & Miethe, T. D. (1993). Understanding theories of criminal victimization. *Crime and Justice, 17*, 459–499.

Mendelsohn, R. (1976). Victimology and contemporary society's trends. *Victimology, an International Journal, 1*, 8–28.

Michele, S. A., & Brown, J. (2012). Rape and victim-blaming: A critical examination of the tendency to blame victims and exonerate perpetrators in cases of rape. *Prized Writing*, 75–88.

Miethe, T. D. (1985). The myth or reality of victim involvement in crime: A review and comment on victim-precipitation research. *Sociological Focus, 18*, 209–220.

Miethe, T. D. (1991). Citizen-based crime control activity and victimization risks: Examination of displacement and free-rider effects. *Criminology, 29*, 419–439.

Miethe, T. D., Hughes, M., & McDowall, D. (1991). Social change and crime rates: An evaluation of alternative theoretical approaches. *Social Forces, 70*, 165–185.

Milić, A. (2010). Porodične vrednosne orijentacije – vrednosni raskol. In A. Milić i sarad (Ed.), *Vreme porodica, Sociološka studija o porodičnoj transformaciji u savremenoj Srbiji*. Čigoja štampa.

Milutinovic, I., & Pavlovic, J. (2019). Diskurs o nasilju prema ženama u srpskim onlajn medijima: dominantne komunikacijske strategije. *CM: Communication and Media XIV, 45*, 5–36.

Mulley, K. (2001). Victimized by the media. *CJM, 43*, 30–31.

Nečić, N. (2019). Reprezentacija nasilja prema ženama u srpskoj štampi. *CM: Communication and Media, XIV*(45), 37–60.

Nikolić Ristanović, V. (2003). Podrška žrtvama I sprečavanje sekundarne viktimizacije: savremena zakonska rešenja I praksa. *TEMIDA, 03*, 3–11.

Nikolić-Ristanović, V. (ur.) (2002). Porodično nasilje u Srbiji. Beograd: Viktimološko društvo Srbije, Prometej.

Nikolić-Ristanović, V. (2003). Krivično delo nasilje u porodici u društvenom kontekstu i pravnom sistemu Srbije i Crne Gore. *Temida, 6*(2), 5–10.

Nikolić-Ristanović, V. (2019). *Od žrtve do pobednika: Viktimologija kao teorija, praksa i aktivizam*. Prometej.

Nikolić-Ristanović, V., & Konstantinović-Vilić, S. (2018). *Kriminologija*. Prometej.

Novakovic, M., et al. (2017). Importance of Mental Disorders in Victimization.

Olsvik, V. M. (2009). *Multiple and repeat victimization of women with physical disabilities*. Paper presented at the 11th European Conference on Traumatic Stress (ECOTS), Oslo.

Orth, U. (2002). Secondary victimization of crime victims by criminal proceedings. *Social Justice Research, 15*(4).

Postmus, J. L., & Severson, M. (2006). *Violence and victimization: Exploring women's histories of survival*. Final Report to the National Institute of Justice, USA, p. 1–332.

Pruitt, J., & Grudin, J. (2003, June). Personas: practice and theory. In Proceedings of the 2003 conference on Designing for user experiences (pp. 1–15).

Putnam, R. D., & Feldstein, L. (2009). *Better together: Restoring the American community*. Simon & Schuster.

Republički zavod za statistiku. (2018). *Bilten 643: Punoletni učinioci krivičnih dela u Republici Srbiji, 2017. – prijave, optuženja i osude*. Dostupno na: http://publikacije.stat.gov.rs/G2018/Pdf/G20185643.pdf stranici pristupljeno 16.8.202020

Rijken, C., & Khadraoui, L. (2020). Secondary victimization of trafficking victims and law enforcement interventions. In *Psychological health impact of THB for sexual exploitation on female victims* (pp. 57–74).

Rivera, E., Sullivan, C., & Zeoli, A. (2012). Secondary victimization of abused mothers by family court mediators. *Feminist Criminology, 7*(3), 234–252.

Sengstock, M. C. (1976). The Culpable Victim in Mendelsohn's Typology.

Sutherland, E. H. (1924). *Principles of criminology*. University of Chicago Press.

Thacker, L. K. (2017). Rape culture, victim blaming, and the role of media in the criminal justice system. *Kentucky Journal of Undergraduate Scholarship, 1*(1), 8.

Von Hentig, H. (1979). *The criminal & his victim: Studies in the sociobiology of crime*. Knopf Doubleday Publishing Group.

Wagman, J. A., Gray, R. H., Campbell, J. C., Thoma, M., Ndyanabo, A., Ssekasanvu, J., et al. (2015). Effectiveness of an integrated intimate partner violence and HIV prevention intervention in Rakai, Uganda: Analysis of an intervention in an existing cluster randomised cohort. *The Lancet Global Health, 3*(1), e23–e33.

Wakelin, A., & Long, K. M. (2003). Effects of victim gender and sexuality on attributions of blame to rape victims. *Sex Roles, 49*(9), 477–487.

Walklate, S., & Mawby, R. I. (1994). Critical Victimology: International Perspectives. *Critical Victimology*, 1–224.

Whatley, M. A. (2005). The effect of participant sex, victim dress, and traditional attitudes on causal judgments for marital rape victims. *Journal of Family Violence, 20*(3), 191–200.

Williams, L. S. (1984). The classic rape: When do victims report? *Social Problems, 31*(4), 459–467.

Wolfgang, M. (1957). Victim-precipitated criminal homicide. *Journal of Criminal Law, Criminology, and Police Science, 48*, 1–11.

Wolfgang, M. (1958). *Patterns of criminal homicide*. University of Pennsylvania Press.

Wood, E. J. (2018). Rape as a practice of war: Toward a typology of political violence. *Politics and Society*, 1–25.

Zhang, J., Sun, C., & Hu, Y. (2022). Representing victims and victimizers: An analysis of #MeToo movement related reports. *Women's Studies International Forum, 90*, 1–7.

Zweig, J. M., et al. (1999). A longitudinal examination of the consequences of sexual victimization for rural young adult women. *The Journal of Sex Research, 36*(4), 396–409.

Chapter 16
Revictimization: Towards a New Theoretical Concept

Rejani Thudalikunnil Gopalan

Introduction

The concept of revictimization has been defined in many different ways, but the common theme that arises is the repetition of the victimization of the same person, which can be physical, sexual, emotional, or any form of abuse. It is defined in terms of legal, psychological, and social perspectives. According to UNODC Model Law and Related Commentary on Justice in Matters involving Child Victims and Witnesses of Crime (UNICEF, 2009, 5), revictimization is a situation in which the same person has been the victim of more than one offence over a specific period. As per the Care and Protection of Children Act (2000), it means a situation in which a person suffers more than one criminal incident over some time. In the empirical literature, it is defined as an increased likelihood of adult victimization of women following the victimization as a child, which exacerbates issues associated with the initial abuse in childhood (Classen et al., 2005; Messman & Long, 1996; Ports et al., 2016; Sutton et al., 2021). Previous studies have been mainly focused on child sexual abuse, its repetition, and the abuses in the adulthood (adult sexual victimization), which made the definitions mostly related to sexual abuse, such as revictimization defined as incidents of sexual abuse a woman experiences in childhood and at least one other sexual assault experience in her adult years. A great deal of confusion in the literature stems from researchers using the terms recidivism, revictimization, and multiple victimizations interchangeably and the failure to define and give parameters to the phenomenon of revictimization accounts for some of this confusion (Conturo et al., 1999).

R. T. Gopalan (✉)
Mahatma Gandhi Medical College and Hospital, Jaipur, India

R. T. Gopalan (ed.), *Victimology*, https://doi.org/10.1007/978-3-031-12930-8_16

Prevalence of Revictimization

Most research on sexual revictimization is conducted among college students, hence the prevalence studies on revictimization mainly dominate sexual abuse, though studies have been reported on physical abuse and other forms of abuse. In one of the first reports on revictimization, Kaplan & Miller, (1978) reported 24% of revictimization (recidivist victims) among the rape victims. According to Walsh et al. (2020), 20–25% of women and 7–8% of men will experience sexual assault during college, ranging from unwanted sexual contact through completed penetration and found repeated victimization (64%) for students who experienced sexual assault at college. In a meta-analysis, Walker et al. (2019) mentioned that the mean prevalence of sexual revictimization across studies was 47.9% suggesting that almost half of the child sexual abuse survivors are sexually victimized in the future. Similar trends were noticed in the previous studies too (Neumann et al., 1996; Wyatt et al., 1992). Many methodological issues have been found in the prevalence studies of revictimization such as variations in definition, measurements, and sample, but still overall studies indicate the high occurrence of revictimization.

Revictimization Theories

The concept of revictimization can be viewed from the victim perspective and the offender perspective, and what is known about victims and offenders is based on an incomplete picture of the true extent of victimization (Gopalan & Aravind, 2018); longitudinal studies are required to understand the exact process of victimization and therapeutic effectiveness (Steffi et al., 2017). Many attempts to explain why revictimization happens with different theoretical orientations and each one has its own merits and limitations. The following section mentions a few relevant theories.

Re-enactment Theory

Victims of trauma relive their trauma, to some extent compulsively and Freud called this repetitive behaviour repetition compulsion he argued that re-enacting their past trauma was to gain mastery through later studies did not prove this. Many observed that individuals re-create and repetitively relive the trauma in their present lives, which is called re-enactment, and when this happens, survivors take the role of victim or perpetrator (Van der Kolk, 1989; Levy et al., 1998; McFarlane & van der Kolk, 1996). The phenomenon of re-enactment was explained in terms of biological urgency and considered as spontaneous repetitions that have never been verbalized or even remembered; some conceived it as a result of psychological vulnerabilities such as ego deficits and poor coping strategies, while others argued it as mastery to remember, assimilate, integrate, and heal from the traumatic experience (the Chu, 1991, 1992; Miller, 1984; Kluft, 1990; Janet, 1919).

According to van der Kolk (1989), trauma can be repeated on behavioural, emotional, physiological, and neuroendocrinological levels. He explained the re-enactment of trauma at all these levels and argued that traumatized individuals' direct anger against the self or others leads to repetitive re-enactment of real events from the past. To cope with traumatization, they form attachment bonds mostly with perpetrators to deal with the inadequate resources which further cause confusion of pain and love and the hyperarousal states created by trauma affect memory to be state-dependent or dissociated, which interferes with good judgment, and also activate neurochemical changes which make them respond to contemporary stimuli as a return of the trauma and causes a return to earlier behaviour patterns. As noted by van der Kolk (1989) high arousal causes people to engage in familiar behaviour, regardless of the rewards, and when novel stimuli are perceived to be anxiety-provoking, they return to familiar patterns, even if they cause pain, and he argued that victimized people may try to neutralize their hyperarousal by a variety of addictive behaviours such as compulsive re-exposure to the victimization of self and others.

Levy et al. (1998) divided re-enactments into four general categories. In the first category, he argued that re-enactment is an attempt to master which can be an adaptive solution or leads to revictimization and difficulties. In the second category, re-enactments are caused by rigidified defences and in the third, re-enactments are caused by affective dysregulation and cognitive reactions. In the fourth category, re-enactments are caused by ego deficits, where trauma survivors' psychological vulnerabilities can lead to re-enactments and revictimization.

Studies have tried to explain the revictimization of sexual abuse by using re-enactment theory and found it to be useful. According to Lahav et al. (2019) identification with the aggressor or perpetrator may serve as a multifaceted phenomenon in the context of sexual revictimization, especially in childhood sexual abuse, and it existed above and beyond the effects of chronicity of the abuse and PTSD symptoms. Studies also supported that victim of childhood sexual abuse re-enacted the activities as perpetrators later in life. Burgess, Hazelwood, Rokous & Hartman (2006) reported that serial rapists had childhood sexual abuse history, mainly forced sex perpetrated by family members and they re-enacted the abuse as a preadolescent with their earliest victims being known to them and the onset of rape fantasies in mid-adolescence crystalizes the earlier sexually initiated behaviours into juvenile behaviours of spying, fetish burglaries, molestations, and rapes and its repetition targeted on strangers. Though many studies supported re-enactment theory, some studies did not favour it as indicated by Irwin (1999), who studied the relationship between the severity of childhood trauma and proneness to victimization in adulthood and found both violent and non-violent revictimization, but opined that the classical repetition compulsion theory of revictimization is less able to accommodate these findings.

Underdeveloped Detection of Danger as Reason for Revictimization

Another theory to explain revictimization is risk recognition and response, which postulates that childhood abuse leads to impaired risk recognition (inability to detect danger in a social situation) and thus prone to revictimization (Soler-Baillo et al., 2005; Chu et al., 2014). It is also argued that the inability to detect risk may be associated with trauma symptoms experienced by the survivor and also the response to the identified risk is important and many times response may be nil or get delayed among survivors (Naugle, 2000; Volkert et al., 2013). Bockers et al. (2014) have reported that lack of increased risk recognition ability in combination with higher attachment anxiety, lower self-efficacy, and higher state dissociation may increase the risk of revictimization. Though many studies support this theory, a few did not (Logan-Greene et al., 2010; Chu et al., 2014). One major criticism of this study is that most studies related to risk detection have been conducted among college students who are already known to be at high risk for victimization and revictimization.

Ecological System Theory

An ecological framework for considering factors influencing revictimization was proposed by Grauerholz (2000) who emphasized the importance of understanding factors in the microsystem, exosystem (like unsafe neighbourhoods, poverty), macrosystem, and exosystem factors (extreme lack of resources like homelessness). This theory has received lots of empirical support. Many used Bronfenbrenner's (1979, 1986, 1995) ecological theory of human development to study sexual abuse and revictimization (e.g. Kubiak et al., 2018). In one study, individual-level factors (e.g., sociodemographics, biological/genetic factors), assault characteristics (e.g., victim–offender relationship, injury, alcohol use), microsystem factors (e.g., support from family and friends), meso/ exosystem factors (e.g., support from legal and medical teams), macrosystem factors (e.g., acceptance of socialmyths), and chronosystem factors (e.g., sexual revictimization and history of other victimizations) affect adult sexual assault survivors' mental health outcomes (e.g., post-traumatic stress disorder, depression, suicidality, and substance use) were the multilevel factors to study victimization (Campbell et al., 2009). Many recent studies follow ecological system theories to explain revictimization, though it is not yet a fully explained phenomena. To understand the mechanisms underlying the relationship between CSA and sexual revictimization in adulthood, Messman-Moore and Long (2003) suggested an ecological framework that can consider factors outside of the victim, including childhood factors such as family environment, contextual factors including the behaviour of the perpetrator, and societal and cultural factors that impact revictimization. Pittenger et al. (2018) reported an ecological explanation for sexual revictimization among childhood or adolescence that factors such as younger children, girls, ethnoracial minority youth, and those with an identified mental health problem at individual level, presence of a non-caregiving adult in the home, being in mental health treatment, and domestic violence in the family factors at interpersonal level predicted revictimization but could not predict any factors at community level and when combined all factors, only individual-level factors significantly predicted the risk for revictimization.

Wöller (2005) reported that the term repetition compulsion has little explanatory value without additional theoretical assumptions, and within the psychodynamic framework, an ego-psychological view conceives trauma repetition as an attempt to master traumatic experience, and as per object relations perspective, revictimization is explained by the influence of traumatic introjects. Negative cognitions of being worthless, bad, and guilty can endorse the conviction that abuse is justified and reduce the capacity of self-care and negative learning experiences from traumatic helplessness and powerlessness account for low self-efficacy expectations and prevent the establishment of self-boundaries. Trauma repetition can also be understood as an enactment in relation to affect regulation. Research in the field of attachment theory identified attachment styles predisposing to revictimization, and research dealing with post-traumatic stress disorder emphasizes the importance of traumatic effects recurring in daily life, and inappropriate coping with effects and dissociation may lead to traumatization. According to Castro et al. (2019), the traumagenic dynamics model and the information-motivation-behavioural skills model are helpful to understand partially the relation between the tendency of risky sexual behaviours among those had childhood sexual abuse episode and further episodes of sexual victimization during adolescence and early youth. Senn et al. (2012) studied whether constructs suggested by the traumagenic dynamics (TD) model (a theory of the effects of CSA) or constructs suggested by the information-motivation-behavioural skills (IMB) model (a theory of the antecedents of sexual risk behaviour) better mediated the relation between CSA and sexual risk behaviour in adulthood among 481 women participants. They found that the TD constructs mediated the relation between CSA and the number of sexual partners, whereas the IMB constructs mediated the relation between CSA and unprotected sex.

Revictimization in Sexual Violence and Intimate Partner Violence

Studies showed that revictimization exists and it happens in sexual assault and intimate partner violence. Though these are two distinctive forms of violence, some underlying features may be there as common core reasons for revictimization. Though it was noted that prevalence of sexual abuse and revictimization varies according to the type of concept and definitions, legal criteria, method of data collection, and source of data (Gopalan, 2018), studies have shown that revictimization happens. This section of the chapter will explore the factors associated with the revictimization of sexual abuse and intimate partner violence (IPV) to delineate the common factors in both violations.

Revictimization in Sexual Violence

The risk factors or vulnerabilities for revictimization of sexual abuse have been studied in many types of research, mainly among college students, and the focus was on victims and perpetrators. The major factors of vulnerabilities or risk on the part of the victim as well as the perpetrator (though not much) were documented but the main factors were studied personal characteristics of the victim and perpetrators and the recent studies have started focusing on multifactor or ecological viewpoints. The most studied factors were childhood sexual abuse, adolescent sexual abuse, childhood physical abuse, individual characteristics, and socio-cultural factors from the victim domain, which are listed below.

Childhood Sexual Abuse and Revictimization

Childhood sexual abuse (CSA) was consistently predicted revictimization in later life as found in many studies. In one study, Senn and Carey (2010) reported that sexual abuse, physical abuse, psychological abuse, and neglect are associated with adult sexual risk behaviour, but only CSA was uniquely associated with adult sexual risk behaviour. On childhood victimization and risk of revictimization in young adulthood, Desir and Karatekin (2021) noticed that a number of childhood victimization experiences significantly predicted the number of adulthood victimization experiences, and nearly every type of childhood victimization significantly increased the risk of experiencing each type of adulthood victimization. Lacelle et al. (2012) also reported that child sexual abuse survivors were more likely to report having experienced other forms of childhood victimization and multiple forms of victimization were at greater risk of experiencing more adverse outcomes, including risky sexual behaviours, sexual problems, and negative sexual self-concept. Reese-Weber and Smith (2011) found that CSA was significantly related to sexual victimization during the first semester of college with attachment anxiety playing an important role. Orcutt, Cooper, & Garcia (2005) reported that a history of CSA was associated with a twofold increase in the likelihood of experiencing ASA (Adult sexual abuse) and psychological distress (i.e., depression, anxiety), and the use of sex to reduce negative affect partially mediated the relation between CSA and prospective adult sexual assault. According to Conturo et al., (1999) women who had multiple experiences of rape in childhood had the highest percentage of revictimization as adults and incestuous childhood sexual abuse was closely associated with revictimization noticed that revictimization begins in childhood, and that sexual abuse by family members creates a particular vulnerability to revictimization in both childhood and later adulthood. Sexual victimization, specifically, child sexual abuse (CSA), has been associated with compulsive sexual behaviour (CSB) (Slavin et al., 2020). Senn et al. (2006) found that CSA was associated with greater sexual risk behaviour, including more sexual partners, unprotected sex, and sex trading and alcohol use for men and drug use for women mediated the relation between CSA and the number of sexual partners, intimate partner violence mediated the relation between CSA and the number of episodes of unprotected sex for women. Ménard and MacIntosh (2021) reported in a review the connections between CSA and later adult sexual risk behaviours (e.g., unprotected intercourse, sexually transmitted infection diagnosis) and mentioned that sexual risk behaviours occurred under the influence of alcohol/substances and reports of concurrent sexual partners/infidelity.

The effects of force and type of sexual abuse on sexual behaviour outcomes have been less well-studied. In one study Senn et al. (2007) used 1177 Patients attending an STD clinic as a sample to find the impact of penetration and force and reported that those who reported sexual abuse involving penetration and/or force reported more adult sexual risk behaviour, including the number of lifetime partners and several previous STD diagnoses, and more severe sexual abuse is associated with riskier adult sexual behaviour. Das and Otis (2016) have studied distinctive linkages of mild and severe childhood sexual contact with lifetime sexual and psychological outcomes among women and men aged 60–99 years by using data from the 2010 to 2011 wave of the National Social Life, Health, and Aging Project—a nationally representative probability sample of older U.S. adults. The study reported that among women, sequelae of childhood contact seemed consistently negative for the mild rather than severe variant, potentially channelling women into revictimization and finally to elevated sexuality and poor mental health in late life, and for men, it was noticed lifelong eroticizing but not psychological effects of this early experience-with the co-presence of revictimization potentially enhancing rather than lowering their mental health.

Age and gender affect the sexual abuse impacts and from the data of a longitudinal study of a birth cohort born in Dunedin, New Zealand in 1972/1973, Van Roode et al. (2009) reported that gender and age were critical when considering the effect of CSA and the profound early impact of CSA demonstrated for women appears to lessen with age (increased rates were observed for several sexual partners, unhappy pregnancies, abortion, and sexually transmitted infections) but abused men appear to carry increased risks into adulthood in terms of more number of partners and acquisition of herpes simplex virus type 2. Most of the studies have been conducted among females and not much is known about the impact of sexual abuse among males in the long term. In a retrospective cohort study from 1995 to 1997 among 17,337 adult HMO members in San Diego, California, Dube et al. (2005) have examined the impact of CSA on both gender and men reported female perpetration of CSA nearly 40% of the time, and women reported female perpetration of CSA 6% of the time. CSA significantly increased the risk of the outcomes, and the magnitude of the increase was similar for men and women who had an increased risk of marrying an alcoholic and problems with their marriage. Many studies have noted that convicted offenders, especially males, have a history of child sexual abuse. In a study on 101 incarcerated males who were convicted of and imprisoned for CSA in the United Kingdom (UK), 40 of them reported to have had sexual abuse in childhood (Roberts, 2020).

Research consistently predicted the relationship between childhood sexual abuse and adverse mental health outcomes. To develop a model for predicting adult/adolescent sexual revictimization and post-assault functioning, Arata (2000) developed a path model which indicated that mediators of relationship between revictimization and child sexual abuse were found to be self-blame, post-traumatic symptoms, and consensual sexual activity. Women with revictimization and multiple adult assaults reported more difficulties compared to women with only one form of adult abuse or no victimization. They also reported higher levels of distress and were more likely to experience anxiety and PTSD-related symptoms as compared to women with only adult abuse (Messman-Moore et al., 2000). Hannan et al. (2017) examined whether symptoms of post-traumatic stress disorder (PTSD), adolescent sexual assault (ASA), and drinking motivations (e.g., drinking to regulate emotional experiences) mediate the relationship between a history of childhood sexual abuse (CSA) and subsequent alcohol-related problems among college women at a Midwestern university. Using a serial mediation model, they reported the relationship between CSA and subsequent alcohol-related problems via two separate paths. In one path, CSA was associated with PTSD, which in turn predicted drinking to regulate emotional experiences, which then was related to alcohol-related problems in adulthood. In the second path, association of CSA and ASA predicted drinking to regulate emotional experiences, which may lead to alcohol-related problems in adulthood. Classen et al. (2005) reviewed 90 empirical studies on sexual revictimization and found that the occurrence of childhood sexual abuse and its severity, higher distress, and certain psychiatric disorders predicted revictimization and noted that revictimized individuals showed difficulty in interpersonal relationships, coping, self-representations, and affect regulation and exhibited greater self-blame and shame. The study also reported multiple traumas, especially childhood physical abuse and recency of sexual victimization were also associated with higher risk. Hay et al. (2021) reported distress, mental health and substance use problems, distrust, and interpersonal difficulties as the consequences of CSA among college students (Hay et al., 2021). In a systematic review on the role of sexual revictimization in the emergence of mental disorders in adulthood, Cividanes, Feijo-Mello & Mello (2018) noted that PTSD symptoms were most prevalent in the CSA with adult sexual assault groups which proves the role of the revictimization hypothesis that sexual revictimization predicts mental disorders in adulthood.

Studies also reported a link between CAS and psychological vulnerabilities to revictimization. Papalia, Mann & Ogloff (2021) found that CSA victims are vulnerable to a range of revictimization experiences later in life, and victim sex, age at index abuse, and several psychiatric diagnostic categories were independently associated with revictimization risk and different patterns of vulnerability emerging depending on the nature of revictimization. Lau & Kristensen (2010) found an increased psychological vulnerability among women with adult sexual abuse such as psychological distress and the factors like fear, scared, shyness and mistrust. Research has suggested that psychological processes initiated by sexual victimization, especially in childhood and adolescence, result in behaviours that can increase victims' exposure to potential offenders and make them more vulnerable to the tactics of the offenders they encounter (Robert et al., 2006).

Many other factors were also found to be associated with revictimization such as a lack of increased risk recognition ability in combination with higher attachment anxiety, lower self-efficacy, and higher state dissociation (Bockers et al., 2014), sexual self-esteem, sexual concerns, and high-risk sexual behaviours (Van Bruggen, Runtz & Kadlec, 2006), mirror dissociative beliefs (Lahav, Ginzburg, & Spiegel, 2020), borderline personality organization (Izdebska & Beisert, 2021), and lower self-efficacy to refuse sex (Swahn et al., 2022).

Adolescence Sexual Victimization and Revictimization

Like childhood sexual abuse, abuse in adolescence also increases the revictimization of sexual abuse in later life. Humphrey and White (2000) noted that victimization occurred before the age of 14 years almost doubled the risk for later adolescent victimization and highest for those who had been first assaulted in early adolescence, severe adolescent experiences associated with greater risk of collegiate revictimization, adolescent victims of rape or attempted rape were more likely to be as seriously assaulted during their first year of college and they concluded that childhood victimization increased the risk of adolescent victimization, which in turn significantly affected the likelihood of revictimization among college women. Exposure to childhood sexual abuse (CSA) was associated with increased rates of sexual risk-taking behaviours and sexual revictimization during adolescence. A birth cohort of 520 New Zealand born young women who were studied at regular intervals from birth to the age of 18 reported that exposure to CSA was associated with increased sexual vulnerability in adolescence (Fergusson et al., 1997). By using structural equation modelling to study direct and indirect social and behavioural risk factors for adult sexual revictimization among 147 predominantly sexually abused adult African American women, Fargo (2009) reported that the relationship between the child and adolescent sexual victimization is indirect, mediated by adolescent risk-taking behaviour, and the relationship between the adolescent and adult sexual victimization is also indirect, mediated by risky sexual behaviour. Also, the residual effects of early childhood family environment and childhood physical abuse indirectly predict sexual revictimization.

Childhood Physical Abuse and Sexual Revictimization

The relationship between childhood physical abuse and sexual victimization in adolescence or adulthood has been studied much, though limited research on this aspect indicated a positive link. The effect of child physical abuse on child sexual abuse and future revictimization has been studied by many researchers and found conflicting results though the majority of studies favour future revictimization (Schaaf & McCanne, 1998; Merrill et al., 1999). Rivera-Rivera et al. (2006) noted that physical violence during childhood occurred "almost always" and was associated with physical and sexual violence during her adult life, and frequent violence during childhood was associated with more occurrence of violence during adulthood. Also, a positive association was found between physical and sexual abuse before 15 years of age, and experiencing rape during adulthood was also associated with sexual abuse before 15 years of age. Senn and Carey (2010) state that sexual abuse, physical abuse, psychological abuse, and neglect are associated with adult sexual risk behaviour. Many studies have reported adverse effects of physical violence in later life such as a higher number of arrests, history of a personal offence, family problems, and suicidality in men and anxiety or depressive disorder in women and lifetime depression and HIV acquisition in adulthood (Clark et al., 2020; Chaplin et al., 2021; De Venter et al., 2013; Shamu et al., 2019). Studies on the relationship between childhood physical abuse and sexual victimization in adolescence or adulthood have been limited but indicated a positive link (Schaaf & McCanne, 1998; Merrill et al., 1999). The separate effect of physical abuse and future victimization of sexual abuse was not fully explored mostly in studies though some studies pointed out that physical abuse risk future sexual victimization.

Relation Between Sexual and Physical Abuses and Revictimization

It was noted from many studies that there is a relationship between sexual victimization and future physical victimization or vice versa. Noll (2005) suggested that there is evidence of a persistent cycle of violence perpetrated against women that begins in childhood in the form of sexual abuse, re-emerges later in adolescence and early adulthood in the form of physical assault or sexual revictimization, and ultimately places the next generation at considerable risk for victimization. In a 15-year prospective, the longitudinal study examines adolescent and young-adult female self-reports of traumatic sexual and physical experiences occurring after substantiated childhood sexual abuse-revictimizations, Barnes et al. (2009) that abused females were almost twice as likely to have experienced sexual revictimization and physical revictimization perpetrated by older, non-peers and characterized by physical injury. Noll et al. (2003) reported from a longitudinal, prospective study participated by females that those who had childhood sexual abuse reported twice as many subsequent rapes or sexual assaults, 1.6 times as many physical affronts including domestic violence, almost four times as many incidences of self-inflicted harm, and more than 20% more subsequent, significant lifetime traumas. It was also noted that physical revictimization was positively correlated with PTSD symptoms, pathological dissociation, and sexually permissive attitudes, and self-harm was positively correlated with both peritraumatic and pathological dissociation. Though many studies have addressed the relation between childhood/adolescence sexual abuse and adulthood physical assault, and the relation between childhood/adolescence physical abuse and adulthood sexual victimization and its impacts, the studies indicated the confirmation of this relationship.

Intimate Partner Violence and Revictimization

Intimate partner violence is another form of violence and it occurs repeatedly. Researchers attempted to understand why it occurs repeatedly and why the partner continues the relationship. The concept of the abuse cycle proposed by Lenore Walker (1979) is very relevant to answering these questions. According to her, domestic violence goes through different stages: the first one is the tension building stage where the wife feels like giving extra care to the partner's needs and frustration, in the second stage, the acute battering incident in which the partner physically abuses the wife, in the third stage, the remorseful stage, the partner feels guilt about the incident and expresses apology and promises not to repeat and shows loving behaviour, and there will be a calming period for some time till anything triggers to repeat the cycle. LaMotte et al. (2019) have studied the positive and negative reactions and conciliatory behaviours after IPV by the perpetrator and found that the vast majority of participants (89.8%) reported negative reaction(s) after IPV like feeling ashamed; 32.7% reported positive reaction(s) like feeling justified, and 67.5% reported conciliatory behaviour (s) like buying flowers for the partner. It was also noted that positive reactions were associated with positive outcome expectancies of IPV, more frequent abuse perpetration, and antisocial features; negative reactions were associated with greater motivation to change, more frequent abuse perpetration, and borderline features, and were inversely linked to psychopathic traits; and conciliatory behaviours were associated with motivation to change, borderline characteristics, and lower levels of psychopathic traits. Tharp et al. (2013) reported among perpetrators of IPV that hostility is a predictor of physical IPV perpetration, and impulsiveness is a predictor of sexual and psychological IPV perpetration. Norlander and Eckhardt (2005) mentioned that elevated anger and hostility are distinguishing characteristics of IPV perpetrators.

Neal and Edwards (2017) reviewed empirical evidence regarding male and female perpetrators' endorsed attributions for their IPV perpetration, as well victims'attributions for their partners' IPV perpetration. It was observed that IPV perpetrator similar to attributions of physical and psychological IPV perpetrators which consisted of control, anger, retaliation, self-defence, to get attention, and an inability to express oneself verbally. Victims'attributions for physical IPV perpetration consisted of anger, control, jealousy, and the influence of drugs/alcohol, which are similar to perpetrators' self-reported attributions for engaging in IPV perpetration and attribution of victims related to psychological IPV were included perpetrator's personality, relationship dissolution, alcohol, and their partners' jealousy. Victims'attributions for their partners' sexual IPV perpetration, however, differed from perpetrators' attributions, consisting of the victim's belief that the perpetrator thought they wanted it, being under the influence of alcohol/drugs, and doing it out of love. Flynn and Graham (2010) suggested a need for more standardization of measurement and larger representative samples to identify more systematically reasons that are perceived by victims and perpetrators to be most the important contributors to IPV, and more research on perceived reasons for IPV also needs to address gender differences as well as differences related to self-partner attributions.

Recent studies reported that both genders are perpetrating IPV, and currently researches focus on the bidirectional nature of the phenomenon, which underlines that both women and men can equally be victims and perpetrators of IPV. In one study Kahya (2021) noted that emotional maltreatment, physical abuse and neglect, and sexual abuse were associated with the victimization of and perpetration by women, rejection sensitivity mediated the association between these factors and being a victim of IPV while hostility was a mediator between these factors and perpetration of IPV. Moreover, childhood emotional maltreatment (CEM) was the only trauma type which predicted victimization by rejection sensitivity and perpetration by hostility above and beyond the effects of co-occurring trauma types.

Researches confirm that revictimization in IPV happens due to many factors such as personality factors of victim and perpetrator, attribution and justification of violence by both parties though differently, social conformity, and normalization of violence. More studies are required for bidirectional perpetration and victimization and IPV among same-sex and bisexual relationships.

Common Factors for Sexual Abuse and Intimate Partner Violence

It is argued that intimate partner violence and sexual abuses differ in terms of their occurrences and the underlying process, and it was noted that sexually abused children became perpetrators of sex-related crimes and the same is predicted for childhood victims of physical abuse. Felson & Lane (2009) reported that male offenders who were sexually abused as a child are more likely to commit sexual offences, particularly sexual offences against children, than nonsexual offences, and offenders who were physically abused are more likely to engage in violent offences than non-violent offences. In addition to that, they reported that sexual offenders, and to a lesser extent violent offenders, are likely to specialize in those offences. Jespersen et al. (2009) observed a higher prevalence of sexual abuse history among adult sex offenders than among non-sex offenders and a significantly lower prevalence of sexual abuse history among sex offenders against adults compared to sex offenders against children, but the opposite was found for physical abuse. Moreover, there are differences in the process of execution of the crime as indicated by Felson and Massoglia (2012) that robbery offenders planned their crime ahead of time than homicide and physical assault offenders, and sexual assault offenders are no more likely to report planning than homicide offenders and domestic violence was less likely to be planned than violent offences involving strangers.

Research proved that there is a link between sexual abuse in childhood and intimate partner violence in later life. Herrero et al. (2018) analysed the data from 23,863 heterosexual women from the 28 countries of the European Union and reported that childhood abuse experiences negatively affect the development of healthy interpersonal relationships in adulthood, and thus, some female victims of child abuse are more likely to select potentially abusive intimate male partners. They noticed that when sexually abused children become adults, they tend to select partners who are either traditional or generally violent and there was a persistent influence of social structural conditions throughout this process. Jadeja & Gopalan (2016) also noted that women who have witnessed violence between parents in childhood are more likely to experience violence when they grow up as adults.

According to the violence model, IPV and other forms of violence have common etiologies and the risk factors are the same for IPV and other types of violence that men and women who attack their partners are equally likely to have a predisposition towards violence as men and women who attack other people. In other words, they are typical violent offenders whose characteristics and experiences are similar to those of other violent offenders in terms of prior records of violence, engaging in substance abuse, being intoxicated during the incident, having been abused as a child, and/or have been abused as an adult by a non-partner. The evidence suggests that men and women who attack their partners are typical violent offenders and also found evidence of retaliation and mutual violence by partners. Offenders who assaulted their partners were more likely to have been abused by their partners and more likely to have been physically abused as children (Felson & Lane, 2009). In support of this view, many studies suggested that sexual abuse, physical abuse, and domestic violence are linked to each other as reported that the risk for sexual revictimization was consistently found to be associated with the presence of domestic violence and physical abuse in the family (Hornor & Fischer, 2016), the association between vulnerability for revictimization and domestic violence in the family (Pittenger et al., 2018), and childhood exposure to violence predicts physical and sexual abuse (Hayes & van Baak, 2017). The common patterns can be observed in IPV among same-sex, heterosexual, and bisexual relations, as gender is no more a very important factor in IPV, but the power struggle and other dynamics between the couple are the causes of IPV. All these are pointing out that there are common factors among different forms of violence.

Towards a New Theoretical Concept

From the background of ecological and violence perspectives, and clinical and research experiences with different forms of violence and crimes, the author introduces a conceptual framework for revictimization. From previous studies it can be noted that multiple factors are involved in the revictimization of violence, such as individual, interpersonal, and socio-cultural levels, and common aetiologies are also noticed for violence.

Sex is a multi-factor concept as it involves personal, interpersonal, and socio-cultural beliefs and a person's sexual activities are influenced by all the factors. While trying to explain a perpetrator or victim's behaviour, all these factors are to be considered. Previous studies have focused on any single factor such as individual characteristics and social factors, but a comprehensive approach is more appropriate for a thorough understanding of the process. Even in the case of IPV, the same viewpoint is applicable and it is very important to note that both in sexual victimization and IPV, the common factor is that it involves human interaction or it occurs in human context. How the perpetrator sees the victim and his/her vulnerabilities and revictimizes the crime is important, the same as how the victim evaluates the situation, the thought process, and socio-cultural contexts. Why the spouse does not leave the partner even though IPV is frequent and why the sexual revictimization happens even when there are opportunities to escape from that situation or vulnerabilities to future victimization can be answered by using ecological and violence perspectives. In the first incidence of abuse (sexual or physical), a violation happens in individual, interpersonal, and socio-cultural belief systems based on the severity of abuse. At an individual level, personality factors, coping abilities, emotional regulations, and cognitive factors play an important role in how the victim perceives the whole scenario. On an interpersonal level, the victim goes through the violation of trust and bond and the shattering of this fuels the two extremes of emotions or numbness. If the victimization is done by a stranger, mostly the fear factor and the inability to handle that fear may be the reason for revictimization. The same fear factor may play role in IPV though the spouse is not a stranger. The vulnerabilities at individual and interpersonal levels lead to revictimization by trying to conform to the socio-cultural belief system. If the social beliefs favour the IPV, the victim tries to justify the abuse by making her/him believe that it is ok to be slapped by a partner, she must sacrifice and make the marriage workable, and everything will become alright. It is noticed that emotionally dependent, seeking love and validation, high moral and religious values, and high virtues play a significant role in revictimization (Jadeja & Gopalan, 2016; Jagtap, Gopalan & Dahiya, 2017). It is important to understand that some factors or a factor is holding back the victim, which allows the revictimization, and if those factor/factors get fulfilled by the abuser, chances are there for more victimization, which can be emotional factors, economic, and social or cultural beliefs system. Acceptance of abuse as part of life, helplessness, poor economic condition, no shelter, and sociocultural pressure to conform to the norms accelerate the revictimization. Not those victims are not at fault they have high morale, hopes and positiveness (good virtues) that make to tolerate others, and sacrifice behaviour as noted in study Jagtap, Gopalan & Dahiya, 2017. It is important to look from a multifactor perspective including social, cultural, spiritual/religious value systems, emotional, economical, physical needs, cognitive, psychological/personality factors, and coping abilities while considering the causes of revictimization. One factor and a combination of a few make the victim continue the relationship or predict more chances of revictimization in sexual and intimate partner violence. Victims feel helpless or fear of losing something on an individual, interpersonal, or socio-cultural level or a combination of these which makes them feel uncomfortable (which can be termed as deficits) that allow the revictimization. When those deficits (e.g., poor self-esteem and coping as noticed in the study by Jadeja & Gopalan, 2016) are getting a boost, they can break that cycle. For example, when the victim has deficits in decision-making and getting support or a boost for that deficit allows the victim to break the cycle. The same happens in deficits in terms of shelter, emotional support, reduction of fear, etc. In sum, it can be stated that revictimization happens when the victim is having some deficits in terms of personal, interpersonal, and socio-cultural levels, and the victim can break the cycle of revictimization when a boost is given to the deficits, mostly at different levels by an external source or by self, which I call as multifactorial deficits and boost theory. As it is a thread of conceptual formulation of theory, empirical studies are required to validate it.

References

Arata, C. M. (2000). From child victim to adult victim: A model for predicting sexual revictimization. *Child Maltreatment, 5*(1), 28–38. https://doi.org/10.1177/1077559500005001004

Barnes, J. E., Noll, J. G., Putnam, F. W., & Trickett, P. K. (2009). Sexual and physical revictimization among victims of severe childhood sexual abuse. *Child Abuse & Neglect, 33*(7), 412–420. https://doi.org/10.1016/j.chiabu.2008.09.013

Bockers, E., Roepke, S., Michael, L., Renneberg, B., & Knaevelsrud, C. (2014). Risk recognition, attachment anxiety, self-efficacy, and state dissociation predict revictimization. *PLoS One, 9*(9), e108206. https://doi.org/10.1371/journal.pone.0108206

Bronfenbrenner, U. (1979). Contexts of child rearing: Problems and prospects. *American psychologist, 34(10), 844.*

Bronfenbrenner, U. (1986). Recent advances in research on the ecology of human development. In R. Silbereisen, K. Eyferth & G. Rudinger (Eds.), *Development as action in context* (pp. 287–309). Berlin: Spronger-Verlag.

Bronfenbrenner, U. (1995). Developmental ecology through space and time: A future perspective. In P. Moen, G. H. Elder Jr., and K. Lüscher (Ed.), *Examining lives in context: Perspectives on the ecology of human development* (pp. 619–647). Washington, DC: American Psychological Association.

Burgess, A.,Hazelwood, R.,Rokous, F., Hartman, C., & Burgess, A. (2006). Serial Rapists and Their Victims: Reenactment and Repetition. *Annals of the New York Academy of Sciences, 528,* 277–295. https://doi.org/10.1111/j.1749-6632.1988.tb50871.x

Campbell, R., Dworkin, E., & Cabral, G. (2009). An ecological model of the impact of sexual assault on women's mental health. *Trauma, Violence, & Abuse, 10*(3), 225–246. https://doi.org/10.1177/1524838009334456

Castro, Á., Ibáñez, J., Maté, B., Esteban, J., & Barrada, J. R. (2019). Childhood sexual abuse, sexual behavior, and revictimization in adolescence and youth: A mini review. *Frontiers in Psychology, 10,* 2018. https://doi.org/10.3389/fpsyg.2019.02018

Chaplin, A. B., Jones, P. B., & Khandaker, G. M. (2021). Sexual and physical abuse and depressive symptoms in the UK Biobank. *BMC Psychiatry, 21*(1), 1–10. https://doi.org/10.1186/s12888-021-03207-0

Chu, J. A. (1991). The repetition compulsion revisited: Reliving dissociated trauma. *Psychotherapy: Theory, Research, Practice, Training, 28*(2), 327. https://doi.org/10.1037/0033-3204.28.2.327

Chu, J. A. (1992). The revictimization of adult women with histories of childhood abuse. *The Journal of Psychotherapy Practice and Research, 1*(3), 259.

Chu, A. T., DePrince, A. P., & Mauss, I. B. (2014). Exploring revictimization risk in a community sample of sexual assault survivors. *Journal of Trauma & Dissociation, 15(3), 319–331.*

Cividanes, G., Feijo-Mello, A., & Mello, M. (2018). Revictimization as a high-risk factor for development of posttraumatic stress disorder: a systematic review of the literature. *Brazilian Journal of Psychiatry, 41, 1–8.* https://doi.org/10.1590/1516-4446-2017-0013

Clark, C. B., Reiland, S. A., Armstrong, J. D., Ewy, R., & Cropsey, K. L. (2020). Characteristics associated with a history of physical and sexual abuse in a community corrections sample. *Substance Use & Misuse, 55*(3), 512–518. https://doi.org/10.1080/10826084.2019.1686023

Classen, C. C., Palesh, O. G., & Aggarwal, R. (2005). Sexual revictimization: A review of the empirical literature. *Trauma, Violence, & Abuse, 6*(2), 103–129. https://doi.org/10.1177/1524838005275087

Conturo, T. E., Lori, N. F., Cull, T. S., Akbudak, E., Snyder, A. Z., Shimony, J. S., ... & Raichle, M. E. (1999). Tracking neuronal fiber pathways in the living human brain. *Proceedings of the National Academy of Sciences, 96(18), 10422–10427.*

Das, A., & Otis, N. (2016). Sexual contact in childhood, revictimization, and lifetime sexual and psychological outcomes. *Archives of Sexual Behavior, 45*(5), 1117–1131. https://doi.org/10.1007/s10508-015-0620-3

De Venter, M., Demyttenaere, K., & Bruffaerts, R. (2013). The relationship between traumatic childhood events, anxiety, depression, and substance abuse in adulthood; a systematic literature review. *Journal of Psychiatry, 55*(4), 259–268.

Desir, M. P., & Karatekin, C. (2021). Characteristics of disclosing childhood victimization and risk of revictimization in young adulthood. *Journal of Interpersonal Violence, 36*(21–22), NP12225–NP12251. https://doi.org/10.1177/0886260519889932

Dube, S. R., Anda, R. F., Whitfield, C. L., Brown, D. W., Felitti, V. J., Dong, M., & Giles, W. H. (2005). Long-term consequences of childhood sexual abuse by gender of victim. *American Journal of Preventive Medicine, 28*(5), 430–438. https://doi.org/10.1016/j.amepre.2005.01.015

Fargo, J. D. (2009). Pathways to adult sexual revictimization: Direct and indirect behavioral risk factors across the lifespan. *Journal of Interpersonal Violence, 24*(11), 1771–1791. https://doi.org/10.1177/0886260508325489

Felson, R. B., & Lane, K. J. (2009). Social learning, sexual and physical abuse, and adult crime. *Aggressive Behavior: Official Journal of the International Society for Research on Aggression, 35*(6), 489–501. https://doi.org/10.1002/ab.20322

Felson, R. B., & Massoglia, M. (2012). When is violence planned? *Journal of Interpersonal Violence, 27*(4), 753–774. https://doi.org/10.1177/0886260511423238

Fergusson, D. M., Horwood, L. J., & Lynskey, M. T. (1997). Childhood sexual abuse, adolescent sexual behaviors and sexual revictimization. *Child Abuse & Neglect, 21*(8), 789–803. https://doi.org/10.1016/s0145-2134(97)00039-2

Flynn, A., & Graham, K. (2010). "Why did it happen?" A review and conceptual framework for research on perpetrators' and victims' explanations for intimate partner violence. *Aggression and Violent Behavior, 15*(3), 239–251. https://doi.org/10.1016/j.avb.2010.01.002

Gopalan, R. T. (2018). Influence of concept, definitions, assessments methods, and source of data on prevalence of sexual abuse. In *Social psychological, and forensic perspectives on sexual abuse IGI Global.* https://doi.org/10.4018/978-1-5225-3958-2-Ch001

Gopalan, R. T., & Aravind, A. (2018). An update on theories and treatment of sexual offenders. In *Social psychological, and forensic perspectives on sexual abuse (pp. 284–298). IGI Global.* https://doi.org/10.4018/978-1-5225-3958-2-Ch019

Grauerholz, L. (2000). An ecological approach to understanding sexual revictimization: Linking personal, interpersonal, and sociocultural factors and processes. *Child Maltreatment, 5*(1), 5–17.

Hannan, S. M., Orcutt, H. K., Miron, L. R., & Thompson, K. L. (2017). Childhood sexual abuse and later alcohol-related problems: Investigating the roles of revictimization, PTSD, and drinking motivations among college women. *Journal of Interpersonal Violence, 32*(14), 2118–2138. https://doi.org/10.1177/0886260515591276

Hay, C., Grobbelaar, M., & Guggisberg, M. (2021). Mothers' Post-separation Experiences of Male Partner Abuse: An Exploratory Study. *Journal of Family Issues, 0192513X211057541.*

Hayes, B. E., & van Baak, C. (2017). Risk factors of physical and sexual abuse for women in Mali: Findings from a nationally representative sample. *Violence Against Women, 23*(11), 1361–1381. https://doi.org/10.1177/1077801216658979

Herrero, J., Torres, A., & Rodríguez, F. J. (2018). Child abuse, risk in male partner selection, and intimate partner violence victimization of women of the European Union. *Prevention Science, 19(8), 1102–1112.* https://doi.org/10.1007/s11121-018-0911-8

Hornor, G., & Fischer, B. A. (2016). Child sexual abuse revictimization: Child demographics, familial psychosocial factors, and sexual abuse case characteristics. *Journal of Forensic Nursing, 12*(4), 151–159. https://doi.org/10.1097/JFN.0000000000000124

Humphrey, J. A., & White, J. W. (2000). Women's vulnerability to sexual assault from adolescence to young adulthood. *Journal of Adolescent Health, 27*(6), 419–424. https://doi.org/10.1016/s1054-139x(00)00168-3

Irwin, H. J. (1999). Violent and nonviolent revictimization of women abused in childhood. *Journal of Interpersonal Violence, 14*(10), 1095–1110. https://doi.org/10.1177/088626099014010006

Izdebska, A., & Beisert, M. (2021). The level of personality organization and revictimization in lives of child sexual abuse survivors. *Journal of Interpersonal Violence, 36*(5–6), 2199–2226. https://doi.org/10.1177/0886260518759061

Jadeja, M., & Gopalan, R. T. (2016). *Impact of intimate partner violence on victim's self-esteem, resilience, coping, problem solving and marital communication.* Unpublished M.Phil Dissertation.

Jagtap, M., Gopalan, R. T., & Dahiya, M. S. (2017). *The decision to stay in an abusive marital relationship: exploring coping strategies, resilience, attachment, forgiveness, empathy, commitment and spirituality among female victims.* Unpublished M.Phil Dissertation

Janet, P. (1919). *Les médications psychologiques: études historiques, psychologiques et cliniques sur les méthodes de la psychothérapie (Vol. 3). Librairie Félix Alcan.*

Jespersen, A. F., Lalumière, M. L., & Seto, M. C. (2009). Sexual abuse history among adult sex offenders and non-sex offenders: A meta-analysis. *Child Abuse & Neglect, 33(3), 179–192.* https://doi.org/10.1016/j.chiabu.2008.07.004

Kahya, Y. (2021). Intimate partner violence victimization and perpetration in a Turkish female sample: Rejection sensitivity and hostility. *Journal of Interpersonal Violence, 36(7–8), NP4389–NP4412.* https://doi.org/10.1177/0886260518786499

Kaplan, M. F., & Miller, L. E. (1978). Effects of jurors' identification with the victim depend on likelihood of victimization. *Law and Human Behavior, 2*(4), 353–361.

Kluft, R. P. (1990). Dissociation and subsequent vulnerability: A preliminary study. *Dissociation: Progress in the Dissociative Disorders, 3*(3), 167–173.

Kubiak, S. P., Brenner, H., Bybee, D., Campbell, R., & Fedock, G. (2018). Reporting sexual victimization during incarceration: Using ecological theory as a framework to inform and guide future research. *Trauma, Violence, & Abuse, 19(1), 94–106.* https://doi.org/10.1177/1524838016637078

Lacelle, C., Hébert, M., Lavoie, F., Vitaro, F., & Tremblay, R. E. (2012). Child sexual abuse and women's sexual health: The contribution of CSA severity and exposure to multiple forms of childhood victimization. *Journal of Child Sexual Abuse, 21*(5), 571–592. https://doi.org/10.1080/10538712.2012.688932

Lahav, Y., Ginzburg, K., & Spiegel, D. (2020). Post-traumatic growth, dissociation, and sexual revictimization in female childhood sexual abuse survivors. *Child Maltreatment, 25*(1), 96–105.

Lahav, Y., Talmon, A., Ginzburg, K., & Spiegel, D. (2019). Reenacting past abuse–identification with the aggressor and sexual revictimization. *Journal of Trauma & Dissociation, 20*(4), 378–391. https://doi.org/10.1080/15299732.2019.1572046

LaMotte, A. D., Remington, N. A., Rezac, C., & Murphy, C. M. (2019). Examining positive and negative reactions and conciliatory behaviors after partner violence perpetration. *Journal of Interpersonal Violence, 34(3), 599–620.* https://doi.org/10.1177/0886260516644596

Lau, M., & Kristensen, E. (2010). Sexual revictimization in a clinical sample of women reporting childhood sexual abuse. *Nordic Journal of Psychiatry, 64*(1), 4–10.

Levy, S. R., Stroessner, S. J., & Dweck, C. S. (1998). Stereotype formation and endorsement: The role of implicit theories. *Journal of Personality and Social Psychology, 74*(6), 1421. https://doi.org/10.1037/0022-3514.74.6.1421

Logan-Greene, P. L., Nurius, P. S., Herting, J. R., Walsh, E., & Thompson, E. A. (2010). Violent victimization and perpetration: joint and distinctive implications for adolescent development. *Victims & Offenders, 5(4), 329–353.*

McFarlane, A. C., & van der Kolk, B. A. (1996). Trauma and its challenge to society. In B. A. van der Kolk, A. C. McFarlane, & L. Weisaeth (Eds.), *Traumatic stress: The effects of overwhelming experience on mind, body, and society* (pp. 24–46). The Guilford Press.

Ménard, A. D., & MacIntosh, H. B. (2021). Childhood sexual abuse and adult sexual risk behavior: A review and critique. *Journal of Child Sexual Abuse, 30(3), 298–331.* https://doi.org/10.1080/10538712.2020.1869878

Merrill, L. L., Newell, C. E., Thomsen, C. J., Gold, S. R., Milner, J. S., Koss, M. P., & Rosswork, S. G. (1999). Childhood abuse and sexual revictimization in a female Navy recruit sample. *Journal of Traumatic Stress: Official Publication of The International Society for Traumatic Stress Studies, 12*(2), 211–225.

Messman, T. L., & Long, P. J. (1996). Child sexual abuse and its relationship to revictimization in adult women: A review. *Clinical Psychology Review, 16(5), 397–420.* https://doi.org/10.1016/0272-7358(96)00019-0

Messman-Moore, T. L., & Long, P. J. (2003). The role of childhood sexual abuse sequelae in the sexual revictimization of women: An empirical review and theoretical reformulation. *Clinical Psychology Review, 23*(4), 537–571. https://doi.org/10.1016/s0272-7358(02)00203-9

Messman-Moore, T. L., Long, P. J., & Siegfried, N. J. (2000). The revictimization of child sexual abuse survivors: An examination of the adjustment of college women with child sexual abuse, adult sexual assault, and adult physical abuse. *Child Maltreatment, 5(1), 18–27.* https://doi.org/10.1177/1077559500005001003

Miller, J. G. (1984). Culture and the development of everyday social explanation. *Journal of Personality and Social Psychology, 46*(5), 961. https://doi.org/10.1037/0022-3514.46.5.961

Naugle, A. E. (2000). Identifying behavioral risk factors for repeated victimization using videotaped stimulus materials. (Doctoral dissertation, University of Nevada, Reno). *Dissertation Abstracts International, 61*, 1091.

Neal, A. M., & Edwards, K. M. (2017). Perpetrators' and victims' attributions for IPV: A critical review of the literature. *Trauma, Violence, & Abuse, 18*(3), 239–267. https://doi.org/10.1177/1524838015603551

Neumann, D. A., Houskamp, B. M., Pollock, V. E., & Briere, J. (1996). The long-term sequelae of childhood sexual abuse in women: A meta-analytic review. *Child Maltreatment, 1*(1), 6–16. Van der Kolk 1989.. https://doi.org/10.1177/1077559596001001002

Noll, J. G. (2005). Does childhood sexual abuse set in motion a cycle of violence against women? What we know and what we need to learn. *Journal of Interpersonal Violence, 20(4), 455–462.* https://doi.org/10.1177/0886260504267756

Noll, J. G., Horowitz, L. A., Bonanno, G. A., Trickett, P. K., & Putnam, F. W. (2003). Revictimization and self-harm in females who experienced childhood sexual abuse: Results from a prospective study. *Journal of Interpersonal Violence, 18*(12), 1452–1471. https://doi.org/10.1177/0886260503258035

Norlander, B., & Eckhardt, C. (2005). Anger, hostility, and male perpetrators of intimate partner violence: A meta-analytic review. *Clinical Psychology Review, 25*(2), 119–152. https://doi.org/10.1016/j.cpr.2004.10.001

Orcutt, H. K., Cooper, M. L., & Garcia, M. (2005). Use of sexual intercourse to reduce negative affect as a prospective mediator of sexual revictimization. *Journal of Traumatic Stress: Official Publication of the International Society for Traumatic Stress Studies, 18*(6), 729–739.

Papalia, N., Mann, E., & Ogloff, J. R. (2021). Child sexual abuse and risk of revictimization: Impact of child demographics, sexual abuse characteristics, and psychiatric disorders. *Child maltreatment, 26*(1), 74–86.

Pittenger, S. L., Pogue, J. K., & Hansen, D. J. (2018). Predicting sexual revictimization in childhood and adolescence: A longitudinal examination using ecological systems theory. *Child Maltreatment, 23*(2), 137–146. https://doi.org/10.1177/1077559517733813

Ports, K. A., Ford, D. C., & Merrick, M. T. (2016). Adverse childhood experiences and sexual victimization in adulthood. *Child Abuse & Neglect, 51, 313–322.* https://doi.org/10.1016/j.chiabu.2015.08.017

Reese-Weber, M., & Smith, D. M. (2011). Outcomes of child sexual abuse as predictors of later sexual victimization. *Journal of Interpersonal Violence, 26*(9), 1884–1905. https://doi.org/10.1177/0886260510372935

Rivera-Rivera, L., Allen, B., Chávez-Ayala, R., & Avila-Burgos, L. (2006). Physical and sexual abuse during childhood and revictimization during adulthood in Mexican women. *Salud publica de Mexico, 48*(S2), 268–278. https://doi.org/10.1590/s0036-36342006000800007

Robert, D., Pamela, G., Timothy, R., & Chris, O. (2006). *Reducing sexual revictimization: A field test with an urban sample.* https://nij.ojp.gov/library/publications/reducing-sexual-revictimization-field-test-urban-sample

Roberts, S. (2020). Untold stories: Male child sexual abusers' accounts of telling and not telling about sexual abuse experienced in childhood. *Journal of Child Sexual Abuse, 29*(8), 965–983. https://doi.org/10.1080/10538712.2020.1841351

Schaaf, K. K., & McCanne, T. R. (1998). Relationship of childhood sexual, physical, and combined sexual and physical abuse to adult victimization and posttraumatic stress disorder. *Child Abuse & Neglect, 22*(11), 1119–1133.

Senn, T. E., & Carey, M. P. (2010). Child maltreatment and women's adult sexual risk behavior: Childhood sexual abuse as a unique risk factor. *Child Maltreatment, 15*(4), 324–335. https://doi.org/10.1177/1077559510381112

Senn, T. E., Carey, M. P., Vanable, P. A., Coury-Doniger, P., & Urban, M. A. (2006). Childhood sexual abuse and sexual risk behavior among men and women attending a sexually transmitted disease clinic. *Journal of Consulting and Clinical Psychology, 74*(4), 720. https://doi.org/10.1037/0022-006X.74.4.720

Senn, T. E., Carey, M. P., Vanable, P. A., Coury-Doniger, P., & Urban, M. (2007). Characteristics of sexual abuse in childhood and adolescence influence sexual risk behavior in adulthood. *Archives of Sexual Behavior, 36*(5), 637–645. https://doi.org/10.1007/s10508-006-9109-4

Senn, T. E., Carey, M. P., & Coury-Doniger, P. (2012). Mediators of the relation between childhood sexual abuse and women's sexual risk behavior: A comparison of two theoretical frameworks. *Archives of Sexual Behavior, 41*(6), 1363–1377. https://doi.org/10.1007/s10508-011-9897-z

Shamu, S., Shamu, P., Zarowsky, C., Temmerman, M., Shefer, T., & Abrahams, N. (2019). Does a history of sexual and physical childhood abuse contribute to HIV infection risk in adulthood? A study among post-natal women in Harare, Zimbabwe. *PLoS One, 14*(1), e0198866. https://doi.org/10.1371/journal.pone.0198866

Slavin, M. N., Scoglio, A. A., Blycker, G. R., Potenza, M. N., & Kraus, S. W. (2020). Child sexual abuse and compulsive sexual behavior: A systematic literature review. *Current Addiction Reports, 7*(1), 76–88. https://doi.org/10.1007/s40429-020-00298-9

Soler-Baillo, J. M., Marx, B. P., & Sloan, D. M. (2005). The psychophysiological correlates of risk recognition among victims and non-victims of sexual assault. *Behaviour Research and Therapy, 43*(2), 169–181.

Steffi, B., Mnik, B., & Gopalan, R. T. (2017). Management of sexual offenders. *International Research Journal of Human Resources and Social Sciences, 4*(2), 29–41.

Sutton, T. E., Edwards, K. M., Siller, L., & Shorey, R. C. (2021). An exploration of factors that mediate the relationship between adverse childhood experiences and sexual assault victimization among LGBTQ+ college students. *Child Maltreatment, 10775595211041970.* https://doi.org/10.1177/10775595211041970

Swahn, M. H., Culbreth, R. E., Gilmore, A. K., Parrott, D. J., Daigle, L. E., Kasirye, R., & Bukuluki, P. (2022). Sexual victimization, self-efficacy to refuse sex while drinking, and regretting alcohol-involved sex among underserved youth in Kampala, Uganda. *International*

Journal of Environmental Research and Public Health, 19(4), 1915. https://doi.org/10.3390/ijerph19041915

Tharp, A. T., Schumacher, J. A., Samper, R. E., McLeish, A. C., & Coffey, S. F. (2013). Relative importance of emotional dysregulation, hostility, and impulsiveness in predicting intimate partner violence perpetrated by men in alcohol treatment. *Psychology of Women Quarterly, 37*(1), 51–60. https://doi.org/10.1177/0361684312461138

UNICEF. (2009). Justice in Matters involving Child Victims and Witnesses of Crime: Model Law and Related Commentary. https://www.unodc.org/documents/justice-and-prison-reform/Justice_in_matters...pdf

Van der Kolk, B. A. (1989). The compulsion to repeat the trauma: Re-enactment, revictimization, and masochism. *Psychiatric Clinics of North America, 12*(2), 389–411. https://doi.org/10.1016/S0193-953X(18)30439-8

Van Bruggen, L. K., Runtz, M. G., & Kadlec, H. (2006). Sexual revictimization: the role of sexual self-esteem and dysfunctional sexual behaviours. *Child Maltreatment, 11*(2), 131–145. https://doi.org/10.1177/1077559505285780

Van Roode, T., Dickson, N., Herbison, P., & Paul, C. (2009). Child sexual abuse and persistence of risky sexual behaviors and negative sexual outcomes over adulthood: Findings from a birth cohort. *Child Abuse & Neglect, 33*(3), 161–172. https://doi.org/10.1016/j.chiabu.2008.09.006

Volkert, J., Schulz, H., Härter, M., Wlodarczyk, O., & Andreas, S. (2013). The prevalence of mental disorders in older people in Western countries–a meta-analysis. *Ageing Research Reviews, 12*(1), 339–353.

Walker, L. E. (1979). *Battered women: A psychosociological study of domestic violence.*

Walker, H. E., Freud, J. S., Ellis, R. A., Fraine, S. M., & Wilson, L. C. (2019). The prevalence of sexual revictimization: A meta-analytic review. *Trauma, Violence, & Abuse, 20(1), 67–80.* https://doi.org/10.1177/1524838017692364

Walsh, K., Choo, T. H., Wall, M., Hirsch, J. S., Ford, J., Santelli, J. S., et al. (2020). Repeat sexual victimization during college: Prevalence and psychosocial correlates. *Psychology of Violence, 10*(6), 676. American Cancer Society. (2019). Breast cancer facts & figures 2019–2020. *American Cancer Society*, 1–44. https://doi.org/10.1037/vio0000339

Wöller, W. (2005). Traumawiederholung und Reviktimisierungnachkörperlicher und sexuellerTraumatisierung. *Fortschritte der Neurologie·Psychiatrie, 73*(02), 83–90. https://doi.org/10.1055/s-2004-830055

Wyatt, G. E., Guthrie, D., & Notgrass, C. M. (1992). Differential effects of women's child sexual abuse and subsequent sexual revictimization. *Journal of Consulting and Clinical Psychology, 60*(2), 167.

Chapter 17
Early Childhood Violence Exposure and Subsequent Antisocial Behavior: Canadian Indigenous Young Offenders Case Study

Claude R. Shema

Introduction

Antisocial behavior among juvenile delinquents' population has long been a great concern for caregivers, teachers, parents, and communities and nations at large (Goodman & Scott, 2012). Despite acknowledgement and awareness of juvenile delinquents' antisocial behavior and associated criminal implications, the underlying factors leading to juvenile delinquency differ from one individual to another and from one culture to the next (Puri & Treasaden, 2009). However, despite plethora of factors, a common denominator significantly associated with juvenile delinquency across culture has been found to be early childhood exposure to violence and trauma (Leschied & Wormith, 1997; Shema, 2019).

Moreover, despite the findings suggesting strong correlation between psychiatric disorders (or mental disorders in general) and juvenile criminal behavior, empirical studies at larger scale are needed, to examine more correlation of mental disorders and juvenile delinquency. Furthermore, available statistics in North America, Canadian Indian youths are by far overrepresented in young offender facilities in Canada (Allard et al., 2010), in comparison to white Caucasians or other minority youth groups. Additional to overrepresentation of the Indian youths among young offenders' population, some studies also have found more prevalence of mental disorders among young offenders of Indigenous youths than in any other category of young offenders' ethnic groups (Corrado et al., 2015).

C. R. Shema (✉)
Lancaster University, Lancaster, UK

Characteristics of Psychiatric Disorders

Multiple studies also suggest that a juvenile delinquent involved with justice system respectively suffers multiple mental disorders (Shema, 2019 pp.49–92), such as:

- Depression,
- Over-anxiety,
- Substance abuse disorders,
- Psychosis, schizophrenia,
- Personality disorders traits
- Attention deficit and hyperactive disorders,
- Cognitive disabilities,
- FASD (fetal alcohol syndrome disorder)
- Conduct disorder.

And there are more disorders that need urgent consideration in legal process and appropriate mental health interventions (Lecshied, 2011). Moreover, juvenile delinquency phenomenon has become a nerve-wrecking problem, and more so complex, due to the nature of conduct behaviors that stem from multi-factorial aspects associated with it (Cassey et al., 2010).

Background

Antisocial behavior leading to criminal involvement among children and adolescents continues to challenge families and communities on different levels, from psychological anxieties to socioeconomic burdens. Although treatments such as cognitive behavioral therapy-based strategies help at certain degree, preventive measures are relatively plugged with inefficacy, due to the scarcity of studies pertaining to antisocial and related criminal behavior among youth and the causal factors.

Factors Associated with Juvenile Delinquency

Hypothetically, juvenile delinquency behavior can be better understood through a biopsychosocial model approach, which includes:

1. Biological factors
2. Psychological factors
3. Social/environment factors

Moreover, these three factors also can play key roles in juvenile delinquents' behavior, as moderating factors leading to transformational journey for change, or for worse in the following roles:

I. Predisposing factor
II. Precipitating factors
III. Perpetuating factors

It is important also to understand that juvenile delinquency behavior can be significantly fueled by predisposing factors. For example, among Canadian young offenders, study has found that Aboriginal youth with preexisting conditions such as FASD were highly prone to be involved in crimes and subsequent involvement with the legal system due to the pattern of offending behavior (Popova et al., 2011). Other examples related to predisposing factors associated with juvenile delinquency have been suggested in multiple studies, including brain structure, traumatic brain injury impact, and neural system (Yoder et al., 2016; Frick, 2016).

For example, some severe cases of chronic and callous juvenile criminal behavior have been linked to brain structure as predisposing factors, especially in the interaction between monoamine oxidase type A (MAOA), catechol-*o*-methyltransferase (COMT), and serotonin transporter (5HTT). Multiple studies (Huizinga et al., 2006; Kim-Cohen et al., 2006; Fergusson et al., 1996; Ouellet-Morin et al., 2016) concluded that predisposing factors are highly influenced by the environment and subsequently lead to criminal behavior in adolescence. Another element to consider is the potential personality change due to traumatic brain injury (TBI) among children and adolescents with history of exposure to physical violence (Frick, 2016). Unfortunately, due to a number of reasons, these TBI cases are overlooked, which complicates efforts aimed at treating juvenile delinquents' antisocial behavior and related violence and criminal behavior.

Moreover, through developmental neuropsychophysiological process and gradual trajectory of learning, it is understood that early childhood exposure to violence and trauma experience often lead to psychological disorders (Ozer et al., 2010). These adverse events, including, but not limited to, child neglect, child physical/sexual/psychological abuse, and abandonment events, are highly associated with pediatric disruptive behavior, and subsequently juvenile delinquency and related antisocial behavior at later age, especially in adolescence (Thapar & Stergiakouli, 2008). However, positive parenting skills and positive natural social support have been proven to be a protective and transformative factor among others, due to their role in positive reversal of maladaptive behavior, and pro-social skills acquisition (p.280).

In terms of social factors, family dynamic and family structure/interaction, high-rate crime neighborhood (environment), and negative peer pressure have been found to be highly associated with maladaptive and antisocial behaviors among children and adolescents (Boccio & Beaver, 2019).

Juvenile Delinquency

Violent Behavior

The broader definition of juvenile delinquency is based on a youth or juvenile individual under the age of 18 involved in crimes and subsequently with justice system, or young persons in conflict with the law, or simply the juvenile law-breakers (Mulder et al., 2019). The evidence suggests serious concerns related to juvenile delinquency and violent crimes worldwide, on both individual and group-related offences level (p.824). Since the early 1980s, several studies in juvenile delinquency behavior have merged, trying to understand this phenomenon, which sometimes can be exacerbated or confound with normal developmental stage of youth, especially pruning period in which changes in behavior and mood occur, such as anti-social behavior, aggression, disobedience, and violence. Hence a great number of them become involved with law enforcement and justice system, at a rate of about 120,000 any given day in North America for instance (Odjers et al., 2005).

Furthermore, studies in juvenile delinquency behavior also suggest that the severe delinquency behavior usually occurs in the same period of developmental age, adolescence, marked by rebellion behavior against rules or authorities. Moreover, in quest to find the causal factors associated with juvenile delinquency, it has been suggested that some mental health issues might be the key in juvenile delinquency and antisocial-related behavior (Kendall et al., 1992; Glenn et al., 1994), whilst social and environment factors are believed also to be risk and key factors alongside medical, biological, or organic factors (Murray et al., 2010). Thus, there is no standalone factor associated with juvenile delinquency, but a multitude of factors embodied in the entire functioning systems of youth delinquents, such as biological predisposing factors, psychological and social-environment, including but not limited to socioeconomic status (SES) associated with high violence-rated neighborhood (Fontaine et al., 2019). For example, an international study examining comparison of young offending behavior in different select countries in the world (Egli et al., 2010) has found mental disorders to be the most predominant risk factors. However, some other relevant factors, such as SES, psychological factors, history of endless violence in neighborhood, alongside deviant peers, have been found be consistently associated with the development of juvenile delinquency and violence, or other criminal behaviors (pp.155–159).

Canadian Aboriginal Young Offenders' Perspective

Canadian history of notorious "Indian Residential School (IRS.)" system has left long-lasting psychosocial impacts among survivors and their generations, in what is known as "trans-generational trauma" (Bombay et al., 2014). There is strong evidence for IRS's far-reaching impacts on survivors and their descendants. Among others, chronic posttraumatic stress disorder (PTSD) and anxiety, all leading to other psychiatric comorbidities, such as high rate of suicide attempts, self-injury behavior disorders, substance abuse and chronic alcoholism as negative coping strategies (Tait, 2003). Moreover, the unhealed mental disorders caused by IRS system led to significant disintegration of the families, significantly diminished parenting skills, and uprooted positive practice of indigenous culture and traditions (Kirmayer, 2019).

Based on literature, the impacts of IRS also contributed to the pattern of moderate to severe domestic violence behavior in Aboriginal families, which subsequently continued to the downward spiral of trauma-violence-trauma cycle, from parents to children and grandchildren in that order for generations (p.23). Therefore, based on theory of trauma, and childhood adverse events-related behavior, it is fair stating that IRS and its trans-generational trauma trajectory, contributed significantly to subsequent Aboriginal young offending behavior, and related violence and other antisocial behavior.

Criminogenic Hypothetical Analysis

(a) *Mental Disorders and Substance Use*

Despite findings of potential correlation between juvenile delinquents and mental disorders in general, substance abuse or substance possession and drug trafficking or known street as dealing, has been found to be highly associated with criminal charges or criminal involvement among Aboriginal young offenders in Canada, which may explain the overlapping numbers of Aboriginal young offenders in Canadian criminal justice system, as previously study has suggested (Semenza et al., 2019).

(b) *Identity Seeking and Abnormal Conformity*

From statistic standpoint, it has been reported that Aboriginals' (Indians, Indigenous, First Nations, Metis, Inuit people) numbers in Canadian criminal justice system are higher than other ethnic groups' ratios, both in youth and adults (Cesaroni et al., 2019). The impact of this duo overrepresentation also plays an important role in perpetuation of offending behavior among Aboriginal youth, especially through cultural identity formation, and conformity (Miller & Collette, 2019). Therefore, household with close family member or members involved with criminal justice system is highly prone to juvenile offending behavior for young ones. This can also be understood through neuropsychodevelopmental perspective and learning process as well. The reason being the strong evidence suggesting that children learn primarily from their close (in proximity) guardians, caregivers, parents, or peers, especially through observations, adaptation, and repetitive imitation practice process (Yılmaz et al., 2019).

(c) *Violence-Trauma-Violence Vicious Cycle*

The third component of hypothetical analysis related to Aboriginal young offenders' behavior can be better understood through the phenomenology of violence-trauma-violence cycle (McGee et al., 2017). In this regard, evidence suggests that some of the victims of trauma due to violence subsequently become perpetrators of violence as well. In some instances, evidence also demonstrated that some children and youth victims of multiple childhood episodes of trauma due to violence are more likely to become violent perpetrators, if no preventive measures such as psychosocial strategies had been taken (Turner et al., 2016).

Therefore, exposure to violence or antecedent victimhood of violence are highly associated with perpetuation of violence as well, which can also be explained through desensitization and abnormal adaptation to violence, leading to normalization of trauma and violence, as a way of life or lifestyle.

The notion of victim–victimizer cycle has been also observed in some cases of sexual related violence, where children victims of sexual abuse become sexual abusers at later age, especially in adolescence (Glasser et al., 2001). This finding validates sexual violence among Aboriginal young offenders in Canada, and majority of offenders are believed to be victims of sexual assault at early childhood and adolescence as well, whereas vast majority of the abusers have been also found to have antecedent history of trans-generational sexual abuse victimhood (Maxwell, 2014).

Intergenerational Trauma in Aboriginal Young Generation

The Genesis of Emotional Dysregulation

Coercive residential schools' programs introduced and enforced in Canada between 1860 and 1980s aimed at educating and modernizing or civilizing native (Aboriginals and Inuit) children had done so, but the practice also has generated unspeakable family dysfunctionality and cascade of trauma among Canadian aboriginal families (Kaspar, 2014). The practice component, among others, is that children were coercively sent away from their parents for educational or "civilizational" purpose, a prolonged school term that would last at least 10 months or longer per year, which had substantially generated anxiety disorders, cultural and social detachment feelings among the Aboriginal children, or stress, depression, anxiety, powerlessness, helplessness. and other related psychological impacts among their parents as well (LaFrance & Collins, 2003).

Moreover, studies also suggest enormous trauma among the aboriginal children who attended residential school, due to direct abuse, including starvation, physical abuse, or corporal punishment (58.1%), emotional and cultural abuse (37.9%), sexual abuse by residential school staff and teachers (22.6%), and prolonged forced separation from their biological parents, relatives, and families (Braveheart-Jordan & De Bruyn, 1995). Technically, three generations of family were affected, the aboriginal family structure was uprooted, and majority of aboriginal parents thereafter exhibited lack of proper child rearing, inadequate parenting skills, associated with one or more mental health issues, especially those affected by the cascade of trauma generated from residential school era (LaFrance & Collins, 2003; McCormick & Wong, 2006), therefore generated trans-generational transmission of serious mental health among Aboriginal population (Kirmayer et al., 2019). It was not publicly known until the mid-1990s, when the historical revelation of trauma related to colonial era was exposed, suggesting correlates between historical oppression, and psychological trauma exhibited through unusual behaviors and serious health concerns among Indigenous peoples of North America (Kirmayer & Valaskakis, 2009).

In one of a handful studies conducted in this regard thus far, Sochting et al. (2007) systematically analyzed case files of former Indian residential schools (IRS) students survivors ($n = 127$) in British Columbia province to unfold their mental health issues embodied with the IRS era. The most relevant findings were strong evidence of complex posttraumatic stress disorders associated with IRS practice and abuse, including children removal from parents for a long period of time, physical-emotional-cultural-and psychological abuse (p.321).

Furthermore, the study has found that approximately 93 individuals out of 127 (73.2%) were diagnosed with numerous of mental disorders such as PTSD (64.2%) and associated somatic complaints, substance abuse (26.3%), major depression (21.1%), dysthymia (20.0%), anxiety disorders (12.6%), antisocial personality disorder (3.2%), obsessive compulsive personality disorder (7.4%), schizoid personality disorder (6.3%), and avoidant personality disorder (3.2%), and subjects have been found to be highly delinquent (64.5%), involved in revictimizing circle, and became more violent from petit crimes to serious offending behaviors such as murder (p.324). Therefore, the hypothesis suggests a strong correlation between poverty, and possible intergenerational inheritability of trauma context, as one of the major attributable factors to the Aboriginal/Métis juvenile delinquency-related emotional dysregulation behavior, and juvenile organized criminal behavior, such as gang affiliation, as one of perpetuating factors associated with Aboriginal youth delinquency (Bracken et al., 1994).

IRS and Intergenerational Violence Among Indigenous Youth

Based on available literature, it is inarguable that the IRS's practice and related policy (1800s–1990s) have caused severe and nearly irreparable negative psychological impacts among Canadian Indigenous people. From the psychodevelopmental perspective of learning, adult behaviors such as domestic violence due to mental health issues have inarguably been perpetuated onto younger generations, leading to the cascade of trauma and violence vicious cycle, also known as trans-generational trauma and related behavior. In this regard, to be able to grasp the impact of IRS on Aboriginal youth of second, third, and fourth generation or beyond, it is important to compare characteristic of Indigenous social structure and interaction between children and their parents (Barker et al., 2019).

But most importantly, the deeper damage was done in terms of Indigenous culture in teachings and child rearing values, and healthy natural attachment embodied with Indigenous culture, practice, beliefs, and environment context (Fig. 17.1). These damages or negative impacts also have led to circle of violence and criminal

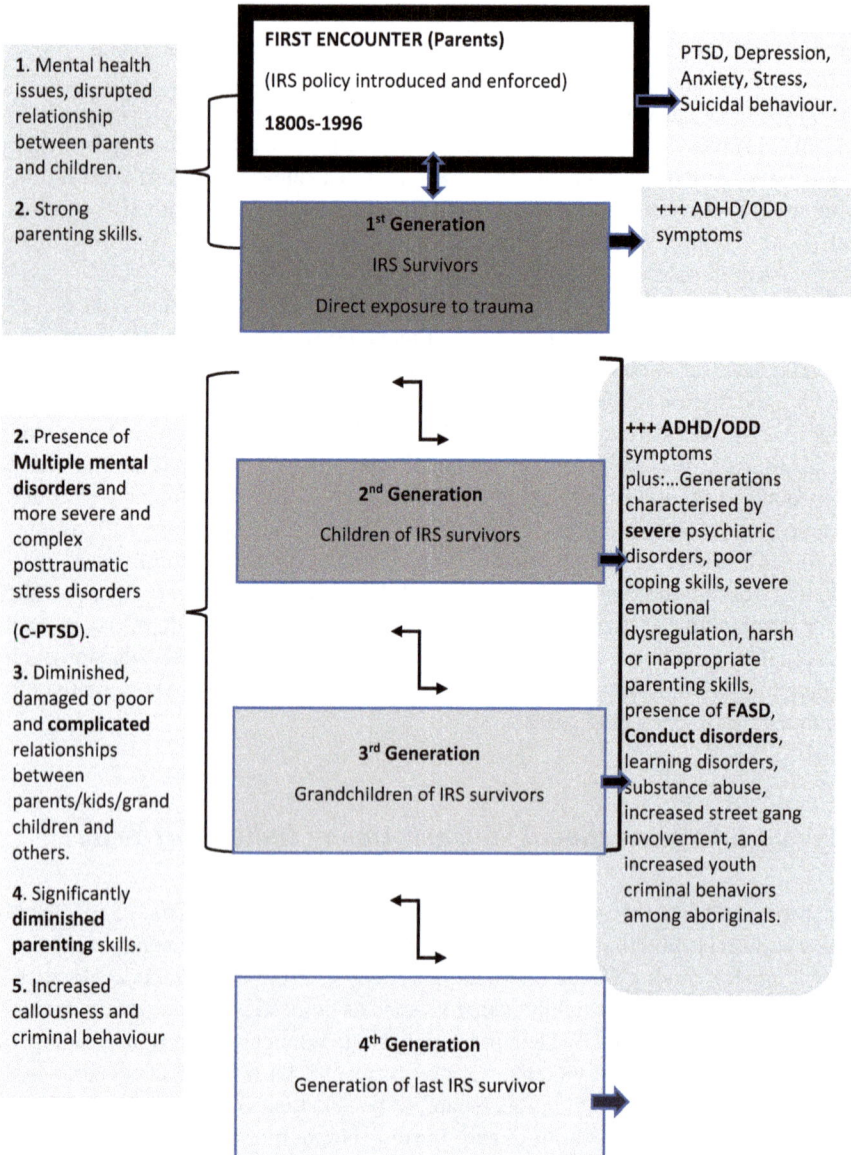

Fig. 17.1 Hypothetical narrative and clinical model of intergenerational trauma (Indigenous Peoples of Canada). Legend: +++(Increase)

related behavior among Aboriginal children and youth (Hinkson & Fullenwieder, 2019), not to mention that these youth are more likely to be diagnosed with concurring psychiatric and personality disorders, including conduct disorder (Shema, 2018).

Psychopathological Analysis of Conduct Disorder and Violence

Origin of Canadian Indigenous Youth's Violence

As finding from research across the culture suggests (Ulzen & Hamilton, 1998; Ulzen & Hamilton, 2003; Colins et al., 2011; Ali & Awadelkarim, 2016; Choi et al., 2017), juvenile delinquents suffer from psychiatric comorbidities (and or personality) disorders symptoms such as oppositional defiant disorder and conduct disorder. However, the disorder highly associated with violence in these psychiatric comorbidities is conduct disorder, which has also been predominantly found among Canadian Aboriginal young offenders (Shema, 2018 pp.123–203). Although Conduct Disorder (CD) and related clinical or behavioral features seem to be a new field of interest in contemporary clinical psychology, clinical features of CD can be also explained and succinctly discerned through early developmental psychological history (Woody & Viney, 2017). For example, early theorists such as Darwin, Rousseau, Locke, Haeckel, Preyer, Freud, and others had included child's psychology, cognition, conduct and behavior, or children's mental health in their work (Woody & Viney, 2017, p.208).In this regard, it is worth noting that early philosophers and theorists in psychology stated that childhood psychological or mental disorders-related behavior can be attributed to nature and nurture (pp.209–210), which is consistent with contemporary or current knowledge in studies related to CD as mentioned earlier.

Moreover, pediatric psychopathology of Indigenous youth-related violence can also be better understood through nature vs. nurture theory as well. The reason being in this regard, is that strong evidence suggests that Indigenous social structure has been disabled, through a systemic political (power) coercive acculturation, and subsequent psychological and social negative impacts, which perpetuated a vicious domestic violence (Hamilton, 2019).

Moreover, as most of the children learn through observing how adults around them behave, talk, and react, these children become violent youth, who learned the use of violence as the only survival strategy in a perceived harsh life in a violent environment. In Canadian context, the family domestic violence among aboriginals on reserves is higher than the rest of population (Halseth & Greenwood, 2019). Therefore, Aboriginal domestic violence is believed to be one of the contributing factors of violence and related conduct disorder and street-related life. Thus, family, or vicious domestic violence, high rate of violence in neighborhood, conduct disorder, and related maladaptive behaviors among Canadian Aboriginal youth are the most significant contributing factors associated with the circle of violence in this population.

Family Dynamic, Parenting Style, and CD

Parenting style, especially poor parenting, or harsh parenting has been associated with development of inappropriate behavior, and CD has high correlates of negative or harsh parenting as factor (Comer, 2010). In this case, it is understood that harsh or poor parenting style leads to maladaptive behavior in children, who would subsequently employ violence and callousness as tool to get what they want, or simply as way of life, because of their parents' or caregivers' behavior (Max et al., 2005). Although some isolated cases of CD have been reported in children and adolescents from functional and positive upbringing as well, studies across the board have demonstrated that family dysfunctionality is a constant catalyst of likelihood in developing CD in children and adolescents (Max, 2014). Moreover, psychopathological hypotheses related to this phenomenon suggest that through developmental trajectory of children embedded with adverse experiences, and negative social interaction with parents or caregivers, contribute to child's maladaptive behavior, due to learning process interfered with inadequate or inappropriate learning process (Puri & Treasaden, 2009).

Thus, the absence of parents, dysfunctional family structure, or domestic violence often lead to violent brain in children, which is usually corrected at an early age. Otherwise, it can potentially escalate into anti-social personality disorder, known as sociopaths, psychopaths, and antisocial personality disorder in adulthood (Frick, 2016). Therefore, positive parenting style, functional family, and natural support system are the beacon and strong pillar to prevent CD. Conversely, the absence of family structure and poor parenting or lack of adequate natural social support are the major factors that often lead to CD and related callous and unemotional traits. Despite strong evidence suggesting that cognitive behavior therapy and multisystemic therapy address all underlying factors associated with CD, prognosis suggests that at least a half of CD sufferers usually carry over the disorder into adulthood, and become lifelong or chronic offenders due to antisocial personality disorder and related antisocial and criminal behavior (Puri & Treasaden, 2009).

Hypothetical Psychopathology Pathways

As mentioned earlier, based on the finding of the research pertaining to criminal behavior and psychiatric disorders in children and adolescents, CD has become the main focus, due to its engraved clinical features imprinted in criminal motives or intentions of antisocial behavior found in kids with criminal minds. From transcultural psychiatry perspectives, it is evident that sociopolitical system and power played a very significant role in interfering and interrupting normal and natural cultural norms of First Nations in Canada. More so, normal child psychodevelopmental trajectory was interfered with and indescribably impeded (McQuaid et al., 2017), resulting in subsequent trans-generational adverse psychological, socioeconomical, and potentially genetic changes as outcomes (Bombay et al., 2014).

Moreover, from a wealthy contemporary history of Canadian literature, it is understood that First Nations (Aboriginals) children, at a very early age, were forcefully and brutally separated from their biological mothers, fathers, brothers, and were forced to stay and live with strangers. Subsequently, these Indigenous children were sexually, emotionally, physically, mentally, psychologically, culturally abused, and some were tortured to death by their capturers and masters (Grant, 2008; Partridge, 2010). Therefore, based on the facts parents who survived from residential school had been deprived the normal trajectory of developmental growth, it is evident that their neuropsychophysiological developmental trajectory has been impacted negatively by severe trauma they endured during residential schools (Gone, 2013).

Moreover, parents' narratives were corroborated by empirical research-based report by Dr. Peter H. Bryce (1853–1932), who stated that Indigenous kids in residential schools experienced extreme trauma and cruelty, such as electric shock, unconventional and unsafe medical experiments, sexual molestation, starvation, unexplained disappearance, poisoning, and freezing to death (Bryce, 1922). Hence, majority of Indian residential school survivors (only about 52% survived, 42% died) and subsequent generations became entangled with slew of medical, psychological, and social vulnerability leading to substance abuse, transiency, and potential developmental of conduct disorder and concurring psychiatric disorders in their young age, as manifestation of trauma and childhood severe adversities they endured (Ross et al., 2015).

But mostly alarming, these survivors of residential schools in Canada have lost ability to be parents and deprived the right to teach their kids (Jaine, 1995). In return, they transmitted those symptoms and negative behavior and medical/health issues to their children, grandchildren and great grandchildren, and potentially generations to come, depending on how healing process goes (Kaspar, 2015). Although, some people with little to no knowledge of trans-generational trauma often deny that trauma can be transmitted or inherited. However, epigenetic studies suggest otherwise, strongly suggesting robust evidence that Canadian Indigenous trauma and other related psychological issues may have been transmitted epigenetically through generation to generation (Aguiar & Halseth, 2015).

Conduct Disorder in Youth and Violent Behavior

Conduct disorder (CD) is regarded as one of the most prevalent mental disorders in childhood and adolescence and the most anti-social behavior factor associated with juvenile delinquency (Frick, 2016). In terms of description, CD is characterized as a pattern of antisocial and rule breaking behaviors, in which the basic rights of others and normal social standards are violated (Puri & Treasaden, 2009). Most of recent research with focus on childhood anti-social behavior, attention has been given to CD, as currently the most prevalent mental disorder among juvenile offenders in correctional facilities around the world (Ulzen & Hamilton, 1998; Ulzen &

Hamilton, 2003; Colins et al., 2011; Ali & Awadelkarim, 2016; Ouellet-Morin et al., 2016; Choi et al., 2017). Moreover, CD sufferers are highly prone to psychiatric comorbidities as well, which makes this disorder more complex than it sounds. For example, literature suggests a high rate of presence of other mental disorders coexisting with CD, such as substance abuse, oppositional defiance disorder, and more (Bevc et al., 2003).

The impacts of CD on sufferers range from cognitive and learning impairment, impaired social connections and relationships, low self-esteem, vulnerability to social predators such as street gang groups (Vitaro et al., 2014), with high rate of early death due to suicide or homicide among sufferers, due to high risk-taking behavior. Among Canadian young offenders, CD prevalence has been found to be higher than average of the rest of the young offenders' group (Shema, 2018). This overrepresentation also can also explain the high rate of violence among aboriginal youth, both in and out detention centres.

Therefore, the fact that young offenders exhibit CD related symptoms or suffer from CD as the most prevalent psychiatric disorder among them, it is imperative to understanding the link between CD and criminal behavior in children and adolescents. Moreover, CD itself is characterized by criminal intent-related behavior. Thus, it is clear that CD is the most psychiatric disorder, and the most relevant factor associated with juvenile delinquency behavior, such as violence, which deserves more focus and strong emphasis. Furthermore, CD complexity is also linked to psychiatric comorbidity aspects, such as co-occurrence of other disruptive, emotional, and mental health issues including Attention Deficit and Hyperactive Disorder (ADHD), substance abuse, learning disabilities, depression, oppositional defiance disorder, and burdens embodied with it (Goodman & Scott, 2012). It has also been documented that CD sufferers are often misunderstood, due to the nature of this disorder, such as anti-social behavior, which often can be mistakenly perceived as a maladaptive behavior in social context, rather than a psychological or psychiatric disorder. Even more so, CD sufferers exhibit inability to follow the social norms, to be able to fit in the community and families, due to their criminal behaviors, which causes intrapersonal struggles and burdens to sufferers and society (Erskine et al., 2014).

Etiology

The etiology of CD remains an enigmatic subject to clinicians, thus not fully understood. Some studies have found some evidence of potential genetic factors, leading to the development of CD and its anti-social behaviors (Kendler et al., 2013). Other findings of potential predisposing factors of CD, such as aggressive behavior, as one of its clinical features, is the monoamine oxidase A (MAOA) genotype (Byrd & Manuck, 2014). The MAOA genotype hypothesis involves childhood adversity, such as trauma and maltreatment, and subsequent development of antisocial behaviors known as "gene–environment interaction." However, the findings suggest more studies, due to the insufficient evidence of the study outcome (p.11). Nevertheless, CD can be analyzed from developmental perspective, and environmental factors contexts or neurogenetic, and brain structure (Buckholtz & Meyer-Lindenberg, 2008). Moreover, family structure and parent–children interaction, including parenting styles such as harsh, inconsistent, and inadequate parenting, have been proven to be the most leading underlying factors associated with CD (Greeson et al., 2014). Therefore, historically, Canadian young offenders of Aboriginal ethnic groups are embedded with all the genetic, environmental, and socioeconomic risk factors leading to CD and related disruptive and anti-social behavior, including violence.

Brain Structure and CD

Furthermore, the results the results of functional magnetic resonance imaging (fMRI) applications suggested a strong link between CD, brain structure abnormalities, and neurological issues, irrespective of the brain's abnormalities causes (Yoder et al., 2016). Like any other disorders, CD can be characterized by severity or levels: mild, moderate, and severe. The severe type of CD, mostly associated with callousness and unemotional traits, has been linked to severe abnormalities in the brain, involving reduced corpus callosum in the brain anatomy, and the development of CD, irrespective of early childhood adverse events or psychiatric comorbidity (Lindner et al., 2016).

Besides potential organic deficits such as brain structure, CD has been often confounded with disruptive behaviors due personality change, in pediatric posttraumatic brain injury (Max et al., 2005; Max, 2014). For example, in a neurological study, Lindner et al. (2016, p.11) has also found strong association between reduced corpus callosum in the brain anatomy, and the development of CD, irrespective of early childhood adverse events or psychiatric comorbidity. Like any other behavior-related disorder, CD also has been significantly linked to the environmental factors, as stated in clinical study findings (Max et al., 2005; Max, 2014; Frick, 2016).

In this regard, it is understood that some genetic–environment interaction, biochemical on brain structure level, and psychophysiological aspects are strongly related to CD in children and adolescents, which means that a biopsychosocial model approach should be taken into consideration when dealing with CD children and adolescents (Scott, 2007). Another factor related to CD and violence among juvenile delinquents is commonly known as undiagnosed personality change disorder due to the brain injuries. As matter of fact, results from advanced studies examining CD and brain structure correlates (Lindner et al., 2015; Michalska et al., 2016; Noordermeer et al., 2016; Yoder et al., 2016; Rogers et al., 2017) suggested abnormalities and deficit in gray matter, insula, anterior cingulate cortex, and neuroanatomical disconnect. These findings also underscore the lack of empathy, callousness, violence, and impulsivity associated with CD sufferers as well, especially among young offenders (Moore et al., 2014).

Conclusion and Recommendations

The Indian residential schools (IRS) policy and practice have caused severe historical trans-generational trauma among Canadian Indigenous people. Despite paucity in scientific research-related studies, the overrepresentation of all negative psychosocial spheres among Canadian Aboriginal young offenders in criminal justice system, mental disorders, and endless domestic violence inarguably stem from the outcomes of IRS. Therefore, from forensic psychoanalysis and psychosocial perspectives, it is fair to conclude that some criminal behaviors among the Aboriginal youths, are highly related to their mental disorders such as conduct disorder (CD) and its psychiatric comorbidities. Moreover, the IRS also uprooted the cultural strengths of Aboriginals, resulting in a vicious cycle of domestic violence of all kinds, as a catapult of children and adolescents' subsequent violence.

Therefore, from cascade of trauma to domestic violence, children of Canadian Aboriginal parents with unhealed trans-generational trauma and less natural or ecological supporting system are likely to be exposed to early childhood domestic violence exposure. Thus, through developmental growth and learning, these children are prone to adopt violence and become violent in adolescence (and adulthood), as negative coping skills, due to the lack of positive coping skills. On the other hand, the use of violence becomes a survival strategy in a violent environment in which these children live, which unfortunately leads to involvement with law enforcement and criminal justice system in most cases. Hence, they become young offenders, with violent behavior and other related anti-social behavior.

References

Aguiar, W., & Halseth, R. (2015). *Aboriginal peoples and historic trauma: The processes of intergenerational transmission.* National Collaborating Centre for Aboriginal Health = Centre de collaboration nationale de la santé autochtone.

Ali, A. S. A., & Awadelkarim, M. A. (2016). The nature and prevalence of psychiatric disorders in a Sudanese juvenile correctional facility. *Sudanese Journal of Paediatrics, 16*(2), 28.

Allard, T., Stewart, A., Chrzanowski, A., Ogilvie, J., Birks, D., & Little, S. (2010). Police diversion of young offenders and Indigenous over-representation. *Trends and Issues in Crime and Criminal Justice, 390*, 1.

Barker, B., Sedgemore, K., Tourangeau, M., Lagimodiere, L., Milloy, J., Dong, H., et al. (2019). Intergenerational trauma: The relationship between residential schools and the child welfare system among young people who use drugs in Vancouver, Canada. *Journal of Adolescent Health., 65*(2), 248–254.

Bevc, I., Duchesne, T., Rosenthal, J., Rossman, L., Theodor, F., & Sowa, E. (2003). *Young offenders' diagnoses as predictors of subsequent adult criminal behavior.* Accessed from: https://files.eric.ed.gov/fulltext/ED481072.pdf. 17 March 2018.

Boccio, C. M., & Beaver, K. M. (2019). The influence of family structure on delinquent behavior. *Youth Violence and Juvenile Justice, 17*(1), 88–106.

Bombay, A., Matheson, K., & Anisman, H. (2014). The intergenerational effects of Indian Residential Schools: Implications for the concept of historical trauma. *Transcultural Psychiatry, 51*(3), 320–338.

Braveheart-Jordan, M., & De Bruyn, L. (1995). *So, she may walk in balance: Integrating the impact of historical trauma in the treatment of Native American Indian women.*

Bryce, H. P. (1922). The story of a national crime: Being an appeal for justice to the Indians of Canada; the wards of the nation, our allies in the revolutionary war, our brothers-in-arms in the great war. *U of Alberta Libraries, 1922.* Retrieved from: http://peel.library.ualberta.ca/bibliography/4734/1.html on October 7, 2019.

Buckholtz, J. W., & Meyer-Lindenberg, A. (2008). MAOA and the neurogenetic architecture of human aggression. *Trends in Neurosciences, 31*(3), 120–129.

Byrd, A. L., & Manuck, S. B. (2014). MAOA, childhood maltreatment, and antisocial behavior: Meta-analysis of a gene-environment interaction. *Biological Psychiatry, 75*(1), 9–17.

Cesaroni, C., Grol, C., & Fredericks, K. (2019). Overrepresentation of Indigenous youth in Canada's Criminal Justice System: Perspectives of Indigenous young people. *Australian & New Zealand Journal of Criminology, 52*(1), 111–128.

Choi, B. S., Kim, J. I., Kim, B. N., & Kim, B. (2017). Comorbidities and correlates of conduct disorder among male juvenile detainees in South Korea. *Child and Adolescent Psychiatry and Mental Health, 11*(1), 44.

Colins, O., Vermeiren, R., Vahl, P., Markus, M., Brockaert, E., & Doreleijers, T. (2011). Psychiatric disorder in detained male adolescents as risk factor for serious recidivism. *La Revue Canadienne de Psychiatrie, 56*(1), 44–50.

Comer, R. J. (2010). *Abnormal psychology.* Macmillan.

Corrado, R. R., Lussier, P., & Leschied, A. D. (2015). *Serious and violent young offenders and youth criminal justice: A Canadian perspective.* Simon Fraser University Publications.

Egli, A. N., Vettenburg, N., Savoie, J., Lucia, S., Gavray, C., & Zeman, K. (2010). Belgium, Canada and Switzerland: Are there differences in the contributions of selected variables on self-reported property-related and violent delinquency? *European Journal on Criminal Policy Research, 16*(3), 145–166.

Erskine, H. E., Ferrari, A. J., Polanczyk, G. V., Moffitt, T. E., Murray, C. J., Vos, T., et al. (2014). The global burden of conduct disorder and attention-deficit/hyperactivity disorder in 2010. *Journal of Child Psychology and Psychiatry, 55*(4), 328–336.

Fergusson, D. M., Horwood, L. J., & Lynskey, M. T. (1996). Childhood sexual abuse and psychiatric disorder in young adulthood: II. Psychiatric outcomes of childhood sexual abuse. *Journal of the American Academy of Child & Adolescent Psychiatry, 35*(10), 1365–1374.

Fontaine, N. M., Brendgen, M., Vitaro, F., Boivin, M., Tremblay, R. E., & Côté, S. M. (2019). Longitudinal associations between delinquency, depression and anxiety symptoms in adolescence: Testing the moderating effect of sex and family socioeconomic status. *Journal of Criminal Justice, 62,* 58–65.

Frick, P. J. (2016). *Conduct disorder: Recent research and implications for serving children and adolescents in the juvenile justice system.* Retrieved from sites01.lsu.edu September 19, 2019.

Glasser, M., Kolvin, I., Campbell, D., Glasser, A., Leitch, I., & Farrelly, S. (2001). Cycle of child sexual abuse: Links between being a victim and becoming a perpetrator. *The British Journal of Psychiatry, 179*(6), 482–494.

Glenn, A., Pease, K., & Kendall, K. (1994). Health and offence histories of young offenders in Saskatoon, Canada. *Journal of Criminal Behaviour and Mental Health, 4*(3), 163–180.

Gone, J. P. (2013). Redressing First Nations historical trauma: Theorizing mechanisms for indigenous culture as mental health treatment. *Transcultural Psychiatry, 50*(5), 683–706.

Goodman, R., & Scott, S. (2012). *Child and adolescent psychiatry.* Wiley.

Grant, H. (2008). American Indians: Working with American Indians and historical trauma. *Illness, Crisis, and Loss, 16,* 125–136.

Greeson, M. R., Kennedy, A. C., Bybee, D. I., Beeble, M., Adams, A. E., & Sullivan, C. (2014). Beyond deficits: Intimate partner violence, maternal parenting, and child behavior over time. *American Journal of Community Psychology, 54*(1–2), 46–58.

Halseth, R., & Greenwood, M. (2019). *Indigenous early childhood development in Canada: Current state of knowledge and future directions.* National Collaborating Centre for Aboriginal Health.

Hamilton, J. W. (2019). Reforming residential tenancy law for victims of domestic violence. *The Annual Review of Interdisciplinary Justice Research, 8*(2019), 245.

Hinkson, M., & Fullenwieder, L. (2019). Imaging crisis in Indigenous Australia and Canada: Towards an analysis of neoliberal primitivism. *Visual Studies*, 1–18.

Huizinga, D., Haberstick, B. C., Smolen, A., Menard, S., Young, S. E., Corley, R. P., Stallings, M. C., Grotpeter, J., & Hewitt, J. K. (2006). Childhood maltreatment, subsequent antisocial behavior, and the role of monoamine oxidase A genotype. *Biological Psychiatry, 60*(7), 677–683.

Jaine, L. (1995). *Residential schools: The stolen years* (p. 1995). University Extension Press, Extension Division, University of Saskatchewan.

Kaspar, V. (2015). The lifetime effect of residential school attendance on indigenous health status. *American Journal of Public Health, 104*(11), 2184–2190.

Kendall, K., Glenn, A., & Pease, K. (1992). Health histories of juvenile offenders and a matched control group in Saskatchewan, Canada. *Criminal Behaviour and Mental Health, 2*, 269–286.

Kendler, K. S., Aggen, S. H., & Patrick, C. J. (2013). Familial influences on conduct disorder reflect two genetic factors and one shared environmental factor. *Journal of the American Medical Association Psychiatry, 70*, 78–86.

Kim-Cohen, J., Caspi, A., Taylor, A., Williams, B., Newcombe, R., Craig, I. W., & Moffitt, T. E. (2006). MAOA, maltreatment, and gene–environment interaction predicting children's mental health: New evidence and a meta-analysis. *Molecular Psychiatry, 11*(10), 903.

Kirmayer, L. J. (2019). Toward an ecosocial psychiatry. *World Social Psychiatry, 1*(1), 30.

Lafrance, J., & Collins, D. (2003). *Residential schools and Aboriginal parenting: Voice of parents*.

Leschied, A. D. W., & Wormith, J. S. (1997). Assessment of young offenders and treatment of correctional clients. In D. R. Evans (Ed.), *The law, standards of practice, and ethics in the practice of pschology* (pp. 233–255J), Edmond Publishing.

Lindner, P., Savic, I., Sitnikov, R., & Budhiraja, M. (2015). Conduct disorder in females is associated with reduced corpus callosum structural integrity independent of comorbid disorders and exposer to maltreatment. *Translational Psychiatry, 6*, e714. https://doi.org/10.1038/tp.2015.216

Max, J. E. (2014). Neuropsychiatry of pediatric traumatic brain injury. *Psychiatry Clinical North America, 37*, 125–140.

Max, J. E., Levin, H. S., Landis, J., Schachar, R., Saudners, A., Ewing-Cobbs, L., et al. (2005). Predictors of personality change due to traumatic brain injury in children and adolescents in the first six months after injury. *Journal of the American Academy of Child and Adolescent Psychiatry., 44*(5), 434–442.

Maxwell, K. (2014). Historicizing historical trauma theory: Troubling the trans-generational transmission paradigm. *Transcultural Psychiatry, 51*(3), 407–435.

McCormick, R., & Wong, P. T. (2006). Adjustment and coping in Aboriginal people. In *Handbook of multicultural perspectives on stress and coping* (pp. 515–531). Springer.

McGee, Z. T., Logan, K., Samuel, J., & Nunn, T. (2017). A multivariate analysis of gun violence among urban youth: The impact of direct victimization, indirect victimization, and victimization among peers. *Cogent Social Sciences, 3*(1), 1328772.

McQuaid, R. J., Bombay, A., McInnis, O. A., Humeny, C., Matheson, K., & Anisman, H. (2017). Suicide ideation and attempts among First Nations Peoples living on-reserve in Canada: The intergenerational and cumulative effects of Indian Residential Schools. *The Canadian Journal of Psychiatry, 62*(6), 422–430.

Michalska, K. J., Zeffiro, T. A., & Decety, J. (2016). Brain response to viewing others being harmed in children with conduct disorder symptoms. *Journal of Child Psychology and Psychiatry, 57*(4), 510–519.

Miller, R. L., & Collette, T. (2019). Multicultural identity development: Theory and research. In *Cross-cultural psychology: Contemporary themes and perspectives* (pp. 614–631), Wiley Online Library. https://doi.org/10.1002/9781119519348.ch30

Moore, E., Indig, D., & Haysom, L. (2014). Traumatic brain injury, mental health, substance use, and offending among incarcerated young people. *The Journal of Head Trauma Rehabilitation, 29*(3), 239–247.

Mulder, E., Brand, E., Bullens, R., & van Marle, H. (2019). Toward a classification of juvenile offenders: Subgroups of serious juvenile offenders and severity of recidivism. *International Journal of Offender Therapy and Comparative Criminology, 63*(6), 819–836.

Noordermeer, S. D., Luman, M., & Oosterlaan, J. (2016). A systematic review and meta-analysis of neuroimaging in oppositional defiant disorder (ODD) and conduct disorder (CD) taking attention-deficit hyperactivity disorder (ADHD) into account. *Neuropsychology Review, 26*(1), 44–72.

Odjers, C. L., Burnette, M. L., Chauhan, P., Mortetti, M. M., & Repucci, N. C. (2005). Misdiagnosing the problem: Mental health profiles of incarcerated juveniles. *Canadian Child and Adolescent Psychiatry Reviews, 14*(1), 26–29.

Ouellet-Morin, I., Côté, S. M., Vitaro, F., Hébert, M., Carbonneau, R., Lacourse, É., Turecki, G., & Tremblay, R. E. (2016). Effects of the MAOA gene and levels of exposure to violence on antisocial outcomes. *British Journal of Psychiatry, 208*(1), 42–48. https://doi.org/10.1192/bjp.bp.114.162081

Ozer, K., Gillani, S., Williams, A., & Hak, D. J. (2010). Psychiatric risk factors in pediatric hand fractures. *Journal of Pediatric Orthopaedics, 30*(4), 324–327.

Partridge, C. (2010). *Residential schools: The intergenerational impacts on Aboriginal peoples.*

Popova, S., Lange, S., Bekmuradov, D., Mihic, A., & Rehm, J. (2011). Fetal alcohol spectrum disorder prevalence estimates in correctional systems: A systematic literature review. *Canadian Journal of Public Health, 102*(5), 336–340.

Puri, B., & Treasaden, I. (2009). *Psychiatry: An evidence-based text.* CRC Press.

Rogers, J., Gonzalez, K., Baker, R., Clanton, R., Pauli, R., Smaragdi, A., et al. (2017). 433. Investigation of white matter microstructure differences in male and female youths with conduct disorder in the FemNAT-CD study. *Biological Psychiatry, 81*(10), S177.

Ross, A., Dion, J., Cantinotti, M., Collin-Vézina, D., & Paquette, L. (2015). Impact of residential schooling and of child abuse on substance use problem in Indigenous Peoples. *Addictive Behaviors, 51*, 184–192.

Scott, S. (2007). Conduct disorders in children. *BMJ: British Medical Journal, 334*(7595), 646. https://doi.org/10.1136/bmj.39161.370498.BE

Semenza, D. C., Meldrum, R. C., Jackson, D. B., Vaughn, M. G., & Piquero, A. R. (2019). School start times, delinquency, and substance use: A criminological perspective. *Crime & Delinquency.* https://doi.org/10.1177/0011128719845147

Shema, R. C. (2018). *Kids with criminal minds. Psychiatric disorders or criminal intentions?* LAP, Publishing.

Sochting, I., Corrado, R., Cohen, I. M., Ley, R. G., & Brasfield, C. (2007). Traumatic pasts in Canadian Aboriginal people: Further support for a complex trauma conceptualization? *British Columbia Medical Journal, 49*(6), 320.

Tait, C. L. (2003). *Fetal alcohol syndrome among Aboriginal people in Canada: Review and analysis of the intergenerational links to residential schools.* Aboriginal Healing Foundation.

Thapar, A., & Stergiakouli, E. (2008). Genetic influences on the development of childhood psychiatric disorders. *Psychiatry, 7*(7), 277–281.

Turner, H. A., Shattuck, A., Finkelhor, D., & Hamby, S. (2016). Polyvictimization and youth violence exposure across contexts. *Journal of Adolescent Health, 58*(2), 208–214.

Ulzen, T. P. M., & Hamilton, H. (1998). The nature and characteristics of psychiatric comorbidity in incarcerated adolescents. *Canadian Journal of Psychiatry, 43*, 57–63.

Ulzen, T. P. M., & Hamilton, H. (2003). Post traumatic stress disorder in incarcerated adolescents. *Canadian Child and Adolescent Psychiatry Review, 12*(4), 113–116.

Vitaro, F., Brendgen, M., & Lacourse, E. (2014). *Peers and delinquency: A genetically-informed, developmentally sensitive perspective.* Springer International.

Woody, W. D., & Viney, W. (2017). *A history of psychology: The emergence of science and applications.* NY Taylor & Francis.

Yılmaz, M., Yılmaz, U., & Demir Yılmaz, E. N. (2019). *The relation between social learning and visual culture.*

Yoder, K. J., Lahey, B. B., & Decety, J. (2016). Callous traits in children with and without conduct problems predict reduced connectivity when viewing harm to others. *Scientific Reports, 6*, 20216. https://doi.org/10.1038/srep20216

Chapter 18
Understanding Adolescent Behavior and Victimization of Special Populations Through Bronfenbrenner's Bioecological Theory

York Williams

Introduction

Adolescents tend to engage in more risk-taking behavior than any other age group due to physical and cognitive development, the adolescent period in which their behavior occurs, and the impact that major normative and idiosyncratic transitions have on their lives at the time (McMahan, 2009; Steinberg, 2010; Tudge et al., 2009). According to Konrad et al. (2013) adolescence is the phase of life between late childhood and adulthood. Typically, adolescents seek diversion, new experiences, and strong emotions, sometimes putting their health at serious risk. In Germany, for example, 62% of all deaths among persons aged 15–20 are due to traumatic injuries. Neuroscientific explanations have been proposed for typical adolescent behavior; with these explanations in mind, one can derive appropriate ways of dealing with adolescents. To this end, educators, researchers, and child clinicians must develop an understanding of risk-taking behavior in youth in order to address high-risk, oppositional, and other behaviors that may be related to the chemistry in the brain and brain-based developmental stages that are now considered a natural part of adolescence and not simply student will or volition (Konrad et al., 2013; McMahan, 2009).

There is a strong correlation between the development of students who are considered exceptional or who have special needs and Bronfenbrenner's bioecological framework (McMahan, 2009; Rosa & Tudge, 2013; Tudge et al., 2016). Using Bronfenbrenner's ecological theory as a guide, researchers have been able to develop a more nuanced understanding of the social and cultural risk factors that may cause child maltreatment and social adjustment issues, that may also lead to victimology for students who are considered members of special populations

Y. Williams (✉)
West Chester University, West Chester, PA, USA
e-mail: ywilliams@wcupa.edu

R. T. Gopalan (ed.), *Victimology*, https://doi.org/10.1007/978-3-031-12930-8_18

(Marshal et al., 2003; Redmond & Rice, 1998). This chapter attempts to elucidate the factors that impact psychosocial development for adolescents. The author explores social-cultural risk factors using Bronfenbrenner's bioecological theory of development. Finally, a lens is developed through which to understand adolescents who may have disabilities or disorders as special populations that may cause them to be viewed as both victims and perpetrators of socially deviant behavior. For this chapter, the author defines "special populations" by age (minors younger than 18 years of age), historically underrepresented ethnic or racial groups, and adolescents who live in rural or high-needs areas (Guterman et al., 2019).

Developmental Victimology

According to Finkelhor (2007), children are among the most highly victimized segments of the population. They suffer from high rates of the same crimes and violence adults do, and then they suffer from much victimization specific to childhood such as child abuse and neglect. Second, victimization has enormous consequences for children, derailing normal and healthy development trajectories. Additionally, children are also subject to a number of social cultural and home variables that influence behavior (McMahan, 2009; Rosa & Tudge, 2013; Tudge et al., 2016). Adding in the extra element of disability (See Fig. 18.1) has the potential to make these youth more so vulnerable to reacting to some of these influences that may cause them to be both victims and or perpetrators of others at a higher rate than their

Fig. 18.1 Represents examples of variables impacting adolescent decision-making

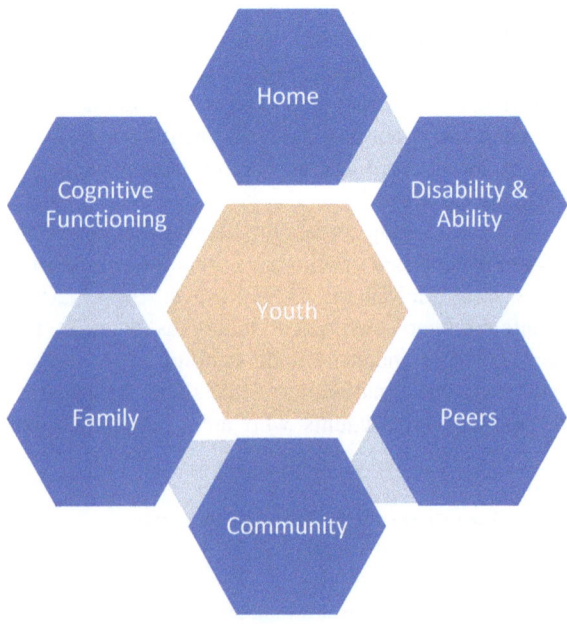

nondisabled peers. This is not meant to suggest that children with disabilities are perpetrators at a higher rate than those children or adolescents without disabilities at all. More so, children with disabilities, such as emotional and or cognitive impairments may present as a class of protected youth under the Individual Disabilities Education Act (IDEA, 2004) that data has shown may be a higher risk at responding in ways that may cause harm to themselves and or others as a result of their disability (Marshal et al., 2003; Redmond & Rice, 1998).

Finkelhor notes that victimization has enormous consequences for children, derailing normal and healthy development trajectories. It can affect personality formation, have major mental health consequences, impact academic performance, and also is strongly implicated in the development of delinquent and antisocial behavior (Finkelhor, 2007; Margolin & Gordis, 2000). For conceptual purposes, Finkelhor has proposed a definition of victimization around child development that is defined as including three categories: (1) conventional crimes in which children are victims (rape, robbery, assault), which the author calls "crimes"; (2) acts that violate child welfare statutes, including some of the most serious and dangerous acts committed against children, such as abuse and neglect, but also some less frequently discussed topics such as the exploitation of child labor, which the author calls "child maltreatment"; and (3) acts that would clearly be crimes if committed by adults against adults, but by convention, are not generally of concern in the criminal justice system when they occur among or against children. Clinicians must be aware of the factors that impact the categorization of child victimization and maltreatment, as the population of adolescent youth with developmental disabilities, cognitive impairments, and social and emotional disabilities and disorders are amongst the most vulnerable population to be both victims and perpetrators (Marshal et al., 2003; Redmond & Rice, 1998). As such, Bronfenbrenner proposes that there are social and bioecological influences that impact the overall development of children across their lifespan, thus culminating into the last stage of adolescence where the greatest outcomes are readily seen (Konrad et al., 2013; McMahan, 2009).

Bronfenbrenner and the Bioecological Theory

The primary objective of this final phase of Bronfenbrenner's Bioecological theory was to show how individual characteristics, in conjunction with aspects of the context, both spatial and temporal, influence what Bronfenbrenner now called "proximal processes" (Rosa & Tudge, 2013). In this final version of his theory, named both the bioecological theory and the bioecological model of human development, Bronfenbrenner gave pride of place to proximal processes and included the Process-Person-Context Time ("PPCT") model of how to conduct bioecological research. Here, this model assists us to understand phases of development for youth with extreme deviant behaviors. The bioecological model is seen as "an evolving theoretical system for the scientific study of human development over time" This system presupposes that the four elements of which it is formed (process, person, context, time) simultaneously influence human beings' developmental outcomes; their effects are not merely additive (Tudge et al., 2016). Bronfenbrenner also emphasized the role played by the person in his or her own development by means of a mechanism termed proximal processes. Proximal processes are the center of bio-ecological theory and are viewed as the driving forces of human development. Here, the individual interacts with his or her environment making meaning and exploring variables across the context which makes that person's development even more so unique.

Bronfenbrenner identified three types of person characteristics that he maintained are likely to influence a person's development (Tudge et al., 2009). The first type is force, which is most likely to impact a person's development (initiate and engage proximal processes). The next type is resource (engagement), which considers how the individual uses and engages with the variables within her environment. The last type is demand (encourage and invite reactions from the social environment), which entails the way the individual negotiates relationships with others within the immediate environment. Overall, human development takes places through processes which becomes progressively more complex with reciprocal interaction between a human being and the people, objects and symbols in their immediate external environment (See Fig. 18.2). Accordingly, this interaction must occur on a fairly regular basis over extended periods of time which culminate into what Bronfenbrenner terms "proximal processes."

Context is broken down into four spheres: micro, meso, exo, and macro. The microsystem entails the environment, such as home, school, or peer group. There is also a great deal of time that entails a number of activities and interactions. The mesosystem entails interrelations among more than one microsystem. Some examples include the interaction with school, neighborhood, and family. The exosystem entails the individual not actually interacting in the situation as such but is more so indirectly influenced in her development (Rosa & Tudge, 2013). Finally, the macrosystem entails any group where members share values and belief systems (culture, resources, lifestyles). The macrosystem influences and is influenced by all other systems (McMahan, 2009).

Finally, time was considered the chronosystem – but broadened to account for what happens over the course of both ontogenic and historical time periods – here a child's life (Tudge et al., 2009). Historical events impact the development of the child over her lifetime. Bronfenbrenner believed that change evolved within a phenomenological perspective. This change has meaning based on the individual's understanding of the experiences and her interactions within all of the other systems at work within the PPCT model. For Bronfenbrenner, there were three subsystems of time that each played a crucial role in the development of the individual: micro-time (what is occurring during the course of some specific activity or interaction); meso-time (the extent to which activities and interactions occur with consistency in the environment); and macrotime (earlier term is chronosystem) developmental processes can vary depending on certain historical events that are occurring as individuals are at certain ages (Tudge et al., 2009).

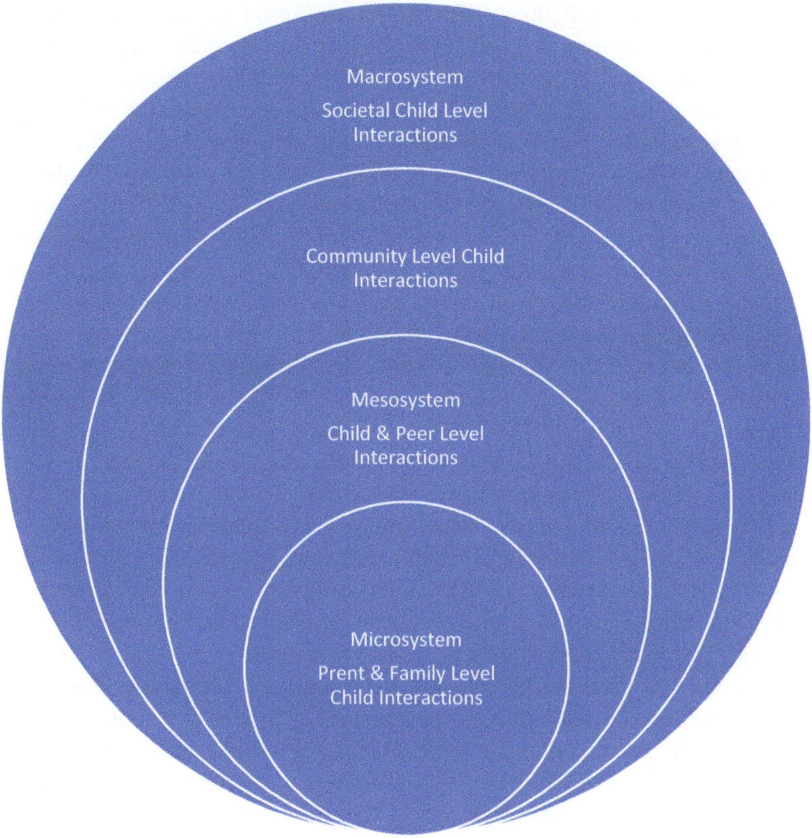

Fig. 18.2 Demonstrates child interactions across Bronfenbrenner's systems

Adolescents and Child Development

According to McMahan, on the most basic level, adolescents go through the various stages of ecological systems that entail fundamental changes in their biological, cognitive, self-esteem and more in which each set of these changes is initiated and or acted on by the others (p. 4). For example, a physical change in puberty for an 11-year-old girl may posit feelings of awkwardness and irritability, especially if these changes occur during the early adolescence period. The young lady may tend to become anxious about appearing so physically more mature than her friends, along with hormonal changes and natural physical and brain-based transitions that accompany prepubescent stages of adolescence (2009). She may also threaten to leave school or run away from home. These changes may also cause temper out-bursts towards peers, in addition to a sudden feeling of independence, autonomy and opposition since these rapid physical and brain-based developmental changes may make the child feel like she is old enough to be respected only as a result of her early onset physical development. This may in fact result in risk-taking behaviors, trouble in school, and may be impacted by outside of school factors which may be idiosyncratic in nature, such as her parent's divorcing. When the student is interviewed and the concern about the family transition arises, in addition to feelings of awkwardness and anxiety around these sudden and early prepubescent changes; the theories and hypothesis might appear to be confirmable, valid and reliable about the developmental risks and challenges the adolescent may encounter. Hence, adolescents tend to engage in more risk -taking behavior than any other age group due to physical and cognitive development, the adolescent period in which their behavior occurs, and the impact that major normative and idiosyncratic transitions have on their lives at the time (Finkelhor, 2007; Margolin & Gordis, 2000). However, when analyzing the behaviors of adolescents with exceptional needs, one must consider alternative theories to explain behavior.

According to Steinberg (2010) heightened vulnerability to risk-taking in middle adolescence may be due to the combination of relatively higher inclinations to seek rewards and still maturing capacities for self-control. The study employed five data collection sites: Denver; Irvine (California), Los Angeles, Philadelphia, and Washington, D.C. The sample included 935 individuals between the ages of 10 and 30 years, recruited to yield an age distribution designed both to facilitate the examination of age differences within the adolescent decade and to compare adolescents of different ages with young adults (p. 218). Participants completed a 2-h assessment that consisted of a series of computerized tasks, a set of computer-administered self-report measures, a demographic questionnaire, and several computerized tests of general intellectual function. The central measures utilized in this study included a questionnaire, the assessment of IQ, self-report measures of impulsivity and reward-seeking, a computerized version of the Tower of London task (used as a behavioral measure of impulsivity), and a computerized adaptation of the Iowa Gambling Task (IGT; used as a behavioral measure of reward-seeking). The process entailed examining whether the two behavioral tasks did, as proposed, differentially index reward-seeking and impulsivity; regression analyses were conducted in which the two self-report measures were considered as simultaneous predictors of the two behavioral tasks' principal outcome measures (p. 219).

Steinberg noted that participants reported their age, gender, ethnicity, and household education. Individuals under 18 reported their parents' education, whereas participants 18 and older reported their own educational attainment. The sample included 935 individuals between the ages of 10 and 30 years, recruited to yield an age distribution designed both to facilitate the examination of age differences within the adolescent decade and to compare adolescents of different ages with young adults (p. 218). The sample was reportedly evenly split between males (49%) and females (51%) and was reportedly ethnically diverse, with 30% African-American, 15% Asian, 21% Latino (a), 24% White, and 10% other. Participants were predominantly working and middle class (p. 218). Generalizability may have been achieved based on the sample size in addition to the diverse sample based on demographics, age, race, SES, and lifestyle. It was reported that in the regression predicting average time to first move on the Tower of London from self-reported impulsivity and reward-seeking, self-reported impulsivity was a significant predictor, but self-reported sensation seeking was not. In contrast, in the comparable regression analysis predicting draws from the advantageous decks in the final block of the IGT (when participants presumably had begun to figure out which decks were advantageous), self-reported impulsivity is not a significant predictor, but self-reported reward-seeking was (See quantitative results (p. 219). Additionally, the authors noted that in order to test the hypothesis that reward-seeking increases in early adolescence and then declines, but that impulsivity shows a gradual decline with age, continuing through late adolescence and into young adulthood, age differences in these self-reports were examined via sets of two hierarchical multiple regression analyses. Age, IQ, and SES were entered on the first step, and the quadratic term for age entered on the second step (pp. 219–220).

In summary, related research findings support the theory that adolescents tend to engage in more risk-taking behavior than any other age group due to physical and cognitive development, the adolescent period in which their behavior occurs, and the impact that major normative and idiosyncratic transitions have on their lives at the time. The author's sample included a number of adolescents from middle years to young adults who reported risk-taking behaviors in the Tower of London task using a behavior measure on impulsivity in which the focus was on differentially index reward-seeking and impulsivity related behaviors. Overall, child maltreatment and social maladjustment research usually focus on the impact of the home, physical changes and idiosyncratic transitions that impacted the overall development of the child at each stage (Casey et al., 2008).

Steinberg (2010) and Casey et al.'s (2008) work does not drill down to the level of the ecosystem impacting choices made by the adolescents in their study, but their work does confirm the body of research on adolescent brain and physical development, which points to extensive and dramatic remodeling of reward circuitry early in adolescence and more so a lengthier period of more gradual maturation of brain systems implicated in self-regulation (p. 222). This finding confirmed that physical changes (biological and brain based) in addition to sensory/reward-seeking behaviors within the environment (ecosystem) may impact overall development, and well into adulthood (Steinberg, 2010). Steinberg maintained that vulnerability toward heightened risk-taking during middle adolescence is likely to be normative, which poses a challenge to those interested in the health and well-being of this age group (p. 222).

Parental Influences as Social Cultural Factor on Adolescent Development and Behavior

According to McMahan (2009), families form complex social systems where each family member affects the whole built upon individual relationships. The family would fit into Bronfenbrenner's micro system. Also, each family member affects others and relationships within the household, in both positive and negative feedback loops. Within the family dynamic are also some significant changes that create imbalance or disequilibrium in phase transitions where even minor events can have major consequences for the family unit. McMahan also suggests that expectations about authority and control tend to change over time and teens expect more say earlier on in development, but at the same time many parents may lack skills adolescents need to proceed with developmental boundaries in place. Figure 18.3 represents the primary styles of parenting that can overall impact how and in what ways adolescents respond to their family and related stressors within their microsystem.

Moreover, developmental issues also are salient for parents; conflict with adolescents among parents who are facing midlife issues contributes to psychological symptoms and life dissatisfaction, particularly for mothers (Smetana et al., 2006). Additionally, structural changes in the family, like divorce and remarriage, have been found to lead to a temporary disruption of adolescent–parent relationships, including increased conflict, particularly in the first two years following a divorce and with the new stepparent. Also, the authors cite a recent meta-analysis, which shows that socioeconomic disadvantage is strongly and consistently related to harsh, unresponsive parenting (Grant et al., 2003). Relatedly, the authors maintain that closeness and intimacy and objectively observed assessments of warmth and cohesion in adolescent–parent relationships decline during adolescents.

Adolescents raised in authoritative homes have been shown to be more academically competent than adolescents reared in homes where parents are consistent but not authoritative in their parenting (Smetana et al., 2006). However, accordingly, high levels of psychological parental control have been associated with both

Fig. 18.3 Represents the dimension of parenting styles on adolescent development

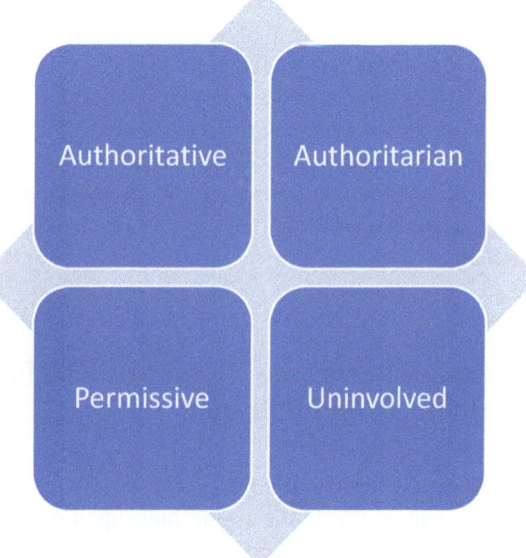

internalizing and externalizing problems. But, the authors maintain that recent findings also suggest the need for greater attention to how parents acquire knowledge of adolescents' activities and act on that knowledge (Smetana et al., 2006). Relatedly, while parental involvement in decision-making is advantageous in early and middle adolescence, adolescents' increased decision-making autonomy between middle and late adolescence leads to better adjustment in late adolescence (Smetana et al., 2006). Overall, parental conflict, agreement, and disagreement have been found to diverge with age.

According to Davids et al. (2017) the familial home environment, where parenting takes place, plays an important role in the health behaviors that children and adolescents engage in and has implications on health and well-being in later life. The authors maintain that lifestyle-related behaviors predispose children and adolescents to the global burden of noncommunicable and other lifestyle-related diseases. Health behavior has been defined as the behaviors and actions that individuals engage in that concerns their physical health, nutritional and dietary practices, physical activity as well as addictive behaviors, and parents play a central role in this endeavor. The authors engaged in a systematic review attempting to establish the relationship between child and adolescent health behavior and parenting approaches. The authors created a meta-analysis of the literature that focused on healthy lifestyle and parenting. An instrument was used to assess the methodological quality of the studies that met the inclusion criteria. After the methodological quality was appraised for each of the studies, only those studies that met the criteria for the categories of satisfactory to good were reviewed.

The authors (Davids et al., 2017) utilized a narrative synthesis approach: a three-staged synthesis approach entailed: (1) developing a preliminary synthesis of findings of included studies, (2) exploring the relationships which exist in the data, and (3) an assessment of the robustness of the synthesis. Of the 33 studies that were initially retrieved, 10 studies met the criteria for methodological appraisal. Health behaviors have been defined as the behaviors that individuals engage in that form part of one's daily routines; these include diet, physical activity, sedentary behaviors, and sleep. The parenting approaches identified within the various studies were categorized into being either positive or negative parenting approaches based on the definition of the approaches used within the studies examined. Overall, (2017) noted that the developmental phase of adolescence often is associated with engaging in behaviors that could either promote positive health or hinder it. The behaviors that are established during this developmental phase have been associated with outcomes in later life. However, central to the establishment of health-related behaviors has been the influential role of the parent–child relationship. Health-related behaviors were found to be influenced by any number of factors which could be behavioral, psychosocial, or sociocultural (p. 603). The authors maintain that the findings presented, in the review, might aid recommendations for program development and implementation particularly in addressing some of the lifestyle-related diseases that pose a threat to children and adolescents (Davids et al., 2017).

Brain-Based Activity and Deviant Behavior

Research indicates that the prefrontal cortex, a part of the brain deeply involved in assessing risks and making complex judgments, is still developing during the adolescent years (Yurgelun-Todd, 2002). As consistent with Inside the Teenage Brain (Yurgelun-Todd, 2002), children's brains are still developing, so if they commit a serious crime at a tender and young age then they must have an opportunity to be reformed. As such, the possibility of a life sentence without the possibility of parole for juvenile offenders has been considered by the Supreme Court as harsh and unusually cruel since as most states just recently reversed these life sentences for youth. In any case, the minimum threshold of criminal action has to consider all the aforementioned in light of sentencing guidelines in cases where youth are vulnerable, and age is a factor. As a society we have to consider the crime and punishment, with an understanding of the complexities of the developing brain in youth in adolescence (McMahan, 2009). The minimum threshold of criminal action that might warrant such a sentence should be determined by practitioners in the field and take into consideration the offenders' ability to be reformed.

According to Broderick and Blewitt (2015) the *Invincibility Fable* occurs when an adolescent thinks that he or she has no consequences for his or her actions. As such, there is no penalty for misbehavior or reckless behavior, and what happens simply happens to others and it may or may not be the victim's fault. For example, an 11-year-old charged with the murder of his father's girlfriend and her unborn child may not have been aware of the consequences of his actions when he allegedly pulled the gun, but first we have to determine if he was even emotionally and cognitively able to reach this level of egocentric thought, since he was only 11 years of age, and by all accounts, still developing both cognitively and emotionally (Broderick & Blewitt, 2015; Crimeinsider; Yurgelun-Todd, 2002). In the *Teenage Brain Issue* (Watanabe, 2017), the author and colleagues maintained that the teenage brain is undergoing an important and dramatic transition that leaves it vulnerable to a number of environmental influences that can push it into a negative trajectory. Watanabe (2017) contends that the blood-brain barrier, which protects the brain from toxins, is still maturing until the age of 20 or more. Also, take care if the largely beneficial neurohormone melatonin is being considered for therapy for adolescents, because it may interfere with the pubertal changes in the brain. The core of this research review confirms the presence of a number of social-cultural factors related to teenage brain development and at-risk behavior in youth and these youth are more at-risk if they have a learning disability and or come from a high-needs and or economically disadvantaged home or community. Race is also a critical factor in understanding social-cultural factors that influence at-risk behaviors and impact how we understand victimology.

The primary objective of this final phase of Bronfenbrenner's bioecological theory was to show how individual characteristics, in conjunction with aspects of the context, both spatial and temporal, influence what Bronfenbrenner now called "proximal processes" (Rosa & Tudge, 2013). In this final version of his theory, named both the bioecological theory and the bioecological model of human development, Bronfenbrenner gave pride of place to proximal processes and included the Process-Person-Context Time ("PPCT"). To this end, researchers, advocates, teachers, parents, and clinicians must develop a nuanced understanding of the impact of the PPCT model on adolescent development during the last middle and final stages of adolescence. For example, a teenager experiencing difficulty building peer relationships and trusting adults as a result of home trauma and dysfunction in addition to possibly a learning disability should have interventions and conceptual supports put into place by a school Multi-Tiered System of Support (MTSS) team (behavior, IEP, intervention, and guidance). These and other revelations have the potential to enhance one's overall understanding and improve knowledge that can be applied to individual student cases dealing with child maltreatment, trauma, depression, and delinquent behavior (Marshal et al., 2003; Redmond & Rice, 1998).

Bronfenbrenner and Social Cultural Factors

Mental health disorders often have an onset in adolescence (Kessler et al., 2005). The heightened vulnerability to psychiatric conditions during adolescence has been proposed to relate to genetically preprogrammed neural development at the same time as new stresses and challenges emerge in the environment, including social stress, during adolescence may be longer lasting and qualitatively different from stress exposure at other periods of life. Additionally, exposure to social isolation during adolescence increases the likelihood of depressive-like behaviors as well as alterations in the structure of the prefrontal cortex (Leussis & Andersen, 2008). Social emotions—such as guilt, embarrassment, shame, and pride—require representing another's mental state, whereas basic emotions such as fear and disgust do not. Because adolescence is a period of increased sensitivity to peer evaluation, there may be changes in how social emotions are processed. One fMRI study investigated changes in neural recruitment during a social emotional task between adolescence (11–18 years) and adulthood (23–32 years) (Burnett et al., 2009). The authors found that social context modulates risk attitudes adopted by adolescents. In another student, relative to adults, adolescents showed greater risk-adverse behavior after receiving expert advice, and this effect is modulated by increased engagement of the dorsolateral PFC by adolescents during valuation in the presence of advice (Engelmann et al., 2012).

The above makes adolescents a subset of special populations when it comes to understanding behavior that may result in harm to self or others and therefore culminating into victimization. Additionally, adolescents with identified learning needs and or disabilities are another tier of this adolescent group thus making them an at-risk population of adolescents. De Ruiter et al. (2008) argue that in general, apart from rapid physical and biological changes, adolescence is a period of growing autonomy, and changing social relations with peers and parents. During the transition from adolescence into young adulthood, youths leave the relatively safe and familiar educational system, are likely to enter a more demanding work environment, and might start (thinking about) living away from their parents. However, youths with mild to moderate and borderline intellectual disability are at risk for persistent psychopathology to a similar degree. Different informants showed to have a different evaluation of the level and the amount of change of problem behavior and should be considered complementary in the diagnostic process.

De Ruiter et al. (2008) maintain that it is expected that children with intellectual disability, especially those who are more intellectually challenged, will encounter more stress as they are faced with more personal limitations in adaptive functioning during these major transition periods, which might increase their vulnerability to developing emotional and behavioral problems. However, in general this field is understudied. For several reasons, the development of psychopathology is expected to differ between youth with mild to borderline intellectual disability (MiID) versus MoID. The authors note that some emotional and behavioral problems that require more advanced (cognitive) development (e.g. depressive symptoms, delinquent behavior) might only emerge at a later chronological age or not at all in children with MoID. Similarly, young children without intellectual disability are less likely to be diagnosed with depression and more likely to show high levels of inattention, while an increase of depressive symptoms is known to occur in adolescents without intellectual disability. It is also suggested that children with MoID have more difficulties in expressing their feelings of discomfort and anxiety, and instead express these feelings through aggression.

Redmond and Rice (1998) argue that one interpretive account of child behavioral influences linked to disability can be seen in the Social Adaptation Model (SAM). The SAM considers the behavioral differences between children with SLI and their normally developing peers to be the result of an interaction between the children's primary language limitations, social context, and the biases people associate with limited verbal proficiency. The second account, referred to here as the Social Deviance Model (SDM), considers differences between children with SLI and non-affected children to be manifestations of differences in underlying socioemotional traits. These two models lead to clear and contrasting assumptions, predictions, and clinical implications. Children may be more at-risk to socially maladaptive influences on behavior and or seek out social groups or peers that can influence them in a myriad of ways because of their limited expressive and receptive abilities.

Marshal et al. (2003) suggest that deviant peer group affiliation has an impact on behavior and is associated as a risk factor for substance use in adolescents with childhood attention-deficit/hyperactivity disorder (ADHD). Results showed that deviant peer affiliation mediated the relationship between ADHD and substance use, suggesting that children with ADHD are more likely than children without ADHD to become involved with deviant peers and, as a result, more likely to use substances. Moreover, the relationship between deviant peer affiliation and substance use was stronger for adolescents with ADHD, suggesting that once they are immersed in a deviant peer group, adolescents with ADHD are more vulnerable to the negative social influences of that group. Additionally, the authors cite to research that shows that adolescents with childhood hyperactivity more often reported cigarette, alcohol, and marijuana use than did control participants (Barkley et al., 1990). Taken together with victimization studies, adolescents as members of this special population calls for further research.

Maercker and Horn (2013) maintain that lifespan developmental psychologists widely agree on the transactional or contextual models of psychological functioning. Individual factors interact with contextual factors over time and constitute risk and/or protective factors for the development of a disorder or psychological health. However, interpersonal and socio-ecological aspects are known to be highly relevant risk and protective factors in the aftermath of a trauma. Meanwhile, contextual approaches and changes in developmental and interpersonal processes over time provide promising and heuristically inspiring avenues for further research in the area of trauma and posttraumatic stress disorders (2013). In his seminal work, Belsky (1980) concludes that more specifically, by drawing attention to the nested relationships that exist between causative agents, this framework should stimulate investigators to move beyond the mere identification of individual variables that are correlated with child abuse and neglect to the study of relationships between variables. Although the strategy of identifying individual correlates has proven fruitful in the past, and in fact has generated the data base on which the present report rests, it is clear that the predictive value of such research is exceedingly limited.

The microsystem is the immediate environment in which the child lives. Microsystems include any immediate relationships or organizations the child interacts with, such as, the family, peer group, or school setting. The mesosystem describes interrelationships between different microsystems. For example, parental involvement in children's schooling can have a positive influence on children's academic competence through children's valuing of academics. The exosystem level has indirect effect on an individual's developmental outcome and is the setting in which the individual does not actively participate. Examples of the exosystem include the parents' workplace. Events happening at the workplace can affect children through how parents interact with their children. Bronfenbrenner's final level is the macrosystem. It involves the society, and includes cultural values and describes the economic conditions under which families live along with material resources, and opportunity structures. The interrelations among these nested environments allow for examination of how patterns of interactions within these systems influence each other and affect individuals' developmental outcomes (Ashiabi & O'Neal, 2015).

One variable that can influence child behavior is parenting experiences in the microsystem, which may have one of the greatest influences on how youth respond to stressors within the other areas of Bronfenbrenner's system (See Fig. 18.4). Ashabi and O'Neal suggest (Ashiabi & O'Neal, 2015) that parents, a microsystem for their children, are also impacted by socioeconomic circumstances. Parents from lower SES backgrounds often experience higher levels of parenting stress, psychological distress, and depression. Another variable that can influence adolescent behavior is neighborhood. Ashabi and O'Neal (Ashiabi & O'Neal, 2015) maintain that neighborhoods, a microsystem construct, are also linked with children's developmental outcomes. The associations between neighborhoods and children's behavioral and emotional problems are less consistent than those reported for cognitive

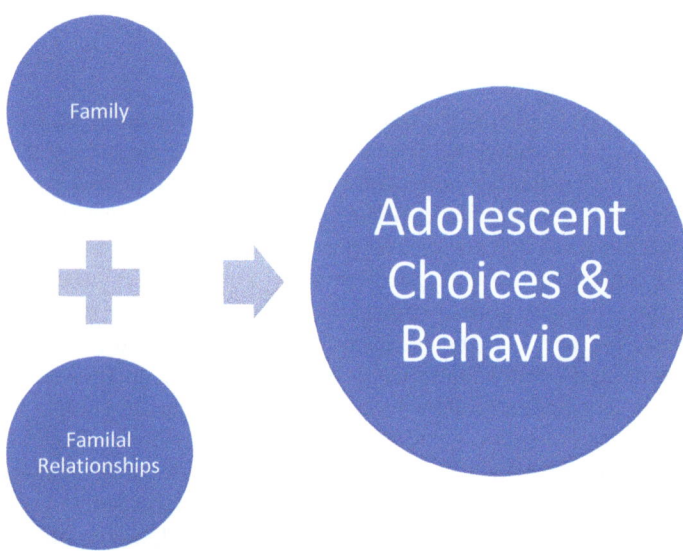

Fig. 18.4 Demonstrates the impact on familial relationships on adolescent choices and behaviors that result

and school outcomes. The authors found that neighborhood social capital indicators were also mostly positively correlated with parent–child interactions and positive social behaviors, and negatively with parenting and family stress and negative social behaviors.

Conclusion

In summary, adolescents engage in more risk-taking behavior than any other age group due to physical and cognitive development, the adolescent period in which their behavior occurs, and the impact that major normative and idiosyncratic transitions have on their lives at the time (REF). According to Konrad et al. (2013) adolescence is the phase of life between late childhood and adulthood. Clinicians and educators have to develop an understanding of risk-taking behavior in youth that can also assist teachers and parents to do the same, as some of these high-risk and oppositional and other behaviors may be related to chemistry in the brain and brain-based developmental stages that are now considered a natural part of adolescence and not simply student will or volition (Konrad et al., 2013; McMahan, 2009). The added presence of disability, social emotional disorders, and social maladjustment during adolescence makes this group a special population that is more at-risk of victimization, as both a victim and perpetrator of harmful behaviors, to self and others.

The correlation has been established between the development of students who are considered exceptional or who have special needs and Bronfenbrenner's bioecological framework (McMahan, 2009; Rosa & Tudge, 2013; Tudge et al., 2016). Using Bronfenbrenner's ecological theory as a guide, researchers have been able to develop a more nuanced understanding of the social and cultural risk factors that may cause child maltreatment and social adjustment issues, that may also lead to victimology for students in special education (Marshal et al., 2003; Redmond & Rice, 1998). Finkelhor noted that victimization has enormous consequences for children, derailing normal and healthy development trajectories. It can affect personality formation, have major mental health consequences, impact on academic performance, and also is strongly implicated in the development of delinquent and antisocial behavior (Finkelhor, 2007; Margolin & Gordis, 2000). As such, Bronfenbrenner's bioecological theory demonstrates the importance of understanding the social and bioecological influences that impact the overall development of children across their lifespan, thus culminating into the last stage of adolescence where the greatest outcomes are readily seen (McMahan, 2009; Rosa & Tudge, 2013; Tudge et al., 2016).

References

Ashiabi, G. S., & O'Neal, K. K. (2015). Child social development in context: An examination of some propositions in Bronfenbrenner's bioecological theory. *SAGE Open, 5*(2). https://doi.org/10.1177/2158244015590840

Barkley, R. A., Fischer, M., Edelbrock, C. S., & Smallish, L. (1990). The adolescent outcome of hyperactive children diagnosed by research criteria: I. An 8-year prospective follow-up study. *Journal of the American Academy of Child & Adolescent Psychiatry, 29*(4), 546–557.

Belsky, J. (1980). Child maltreatment: An ecological integration. *American Psychologist, 35*(4), 320.

Broderick, P. C., & Blewitt, P. (2015). *The life span: Human development for helping Professionals.* Merrill/Prentice Hall.

Burnett, S., Bird, G., Moll, J., Frith, C., & Blakemore, S. J. (2009). Development during adolescence of the neural processing of social emotion. *Journal of Cognitive Neuroscience, 21*(9), 1736–1750.

Casey, B. J., Getz, S., & Galvan, A. (2008). The adolescent brain. *Developmental Review, 28,* 62–77.

Davids, E. L., Roman, N. V., & Leach, L. (2017). The link between parenting approaches and health behavior: A systematic review. *Journal of Human Behavior in the Social Environment, 27*(6), 589–608.

De Ruiter, K. P., Dekker, M. C., Douma, J. C., Verhulst, F. C., & Koot, H. M. (2008). Development of parent-and teacher-reported emotional and behavioural problems in young people with intellectual disabilities: Does level of intellectual disability matter? *Journal of Applied Research in Intellectual Disabilities, 21*(1), 70–80.

Engelmann, J. B., Moore, S., Monica Capra, C., & Berns, G. S. (2012). Differential neurobiological effects of expert advice on risky choice in adolescents and adults. *Social Cognitive and Affective Neuroscience, 7*(5), 557–567.

Finkelhor, D. (2007). Developmental victimology. *Victims of Crime, 3,* 9–34.

Grant, K. E., Compas, B. E., Stuhlmacher, A. F., Thurm, A. E., McMahon, S. D., & Halpert, J. A. (2003). Stressors and child and adolescent psychopathology: Moving from markers to mechanisms of risk. *Psychological Bulletin, 129*(3), 447.

Guterman, H. G., Ponomareva, E., Shapira, Y., & Davidovitch, N. (2019). The role of institutional climate and tolerance in integration of special populations. *Education and Society, 37*(1), 79–96.

Individuals with Disabilities Education Act, 20 U.S.C. § 1400. (2004).

Kessler, R. C., Berglund, P., Demler, O., Jin, R., Merikangas, K. R., & Walters, E. E. (2005). Lifetime prevalence and age-of-onset distributions of DSM-IV disorders in the National Comorbidity Survey Replication. *Archives of General Psychiatry, 62*(6), 593–602.

Konrad, K., Firk, C., & Uhlhaas, P. J. (2013). Brain development during adolescence: Neuroscientific insights into this developmental period. *Deutsches Ärzteblatt International, 110*(25), 425.

Leussis, M. P., & Andersen, S. L. (2008). Is adolescence a sensitive period for depression? Behavioral and neuroanatomical findings from a social stress model. *Synapse, 62*(1), 22–30.

Maercker, A., & Horn, A. B. (2013). A socio-interpersonal perspective on PTSD: The case for environments and interpersonal processes. *Clinical Psychology & Psychotherapy, 20*(6), 465–481.

Margolin, G., & Gordis, E. B. (2000). The effects of family and community violence on children. *Annual Review of Psychology, 51*(1), 445–479.

Marshal, M. P., Molina, B. S., & Pelham, W. E., Jr. (2003). Childhood ADHD and adolescent substance use: An examination of deviant peer group affiliation as a risk factor. *Psychology of Addictive Behaviors, 17*(4), 293.

McMahan, I. (2009). *Adolescence*. Pearson Education.

Redmond, S. M., & Rice, M. L. (1998). The socioemotional behaviors of children with SLI: Social adaptation or social deviance? *Journal of Speech, Language, and Hearing Research, 41*(3), 688–700.

Rosa, E. M., & Tudge, J. (2013). Urie Bronfenbrenner's theory of human development: Its evolution from ecology to bioecology. *Journal of Family Theory & Review, 5*(4), 243–258.

Smetana, J. G., Campione-Barr, N., & Metzger, A. (2006). Adolescent development in interpersonal and societal contexts. *Annual Review of Psychology, 57*, 255–284.

Steinberg, L. (2010). A dual systems model of adolescent risk-taking. *Developmental Psychobiology, 52*(3), 216–224.

Tudge, J. R., Mokrova, I., Hatfield, B. E., & Karnik, R. B. (2009). Uses and misuses of Bronfenbrenner's bioecological theory of human development. *Journal of Family Theory and Review, 1*(4), 198–210.

Tudge, J. R. H., Payir, A., Merçon-Vargas, E., Cao, H., Liang, Y., Li, J., & O'Brien, L. (2016). Still misused after all these years? A reevaluation of the uses of Bronfenbrenner's bioecological theory of human development. *Journal of Family Theory & Review, 8*(4), 427–445.

Watanabe, M. (2017). The teenage brain issue. *Birth Defects Research, 109*(20), 1611–1612.

Yurgelun-Todd, D. (2002). Inside the teenage brain. *Frontline*.

Chapter 19
Working with Victims: Psychological Assessment of Victims

Mauro Siri

Introduction

The etymology of the word victim is obscure in the Latin language. Primarily refers to "Living being, animal or man, consecrated and immolated to divinity". Taking the steps from a purely historiographical perspective, the role of the victim appears to be designated and linked to a purpose: sacrifice. The field of victimology is a scientific study of victims and the victimization process (Muratore & Tagliacozzo, 2008) and the concept of sacrifice, purged of the spiritual meaning that every culture and religion approach. Sacrifice means "to make sacred" and involves the intentional act of accepting a bond or violence for a higher moral purpose. All this provides a significant degree of free choice. Victims from a victimological perspective cannot always choose; they are often victims of physical or psychological violence, natural disasters, wars or other traumatic events (Van Dijk, 1999). Clinical victimology has had its most significant contributions to theoretical and didactic accommodation within the French school of which the most outstanding exponent is Gérard Lopez. This chapter mainly focuses on three aspects: the consequences of the victimization process, complications of treatment and the medical-psychological evaluation of the damage caused by victimization. Karmen (2012) mentioned "differential risk" to identify in a more schematic and organized way, those characteristics that can be considered risk factors. It can therefore be summarized, perhaps in a reductive way, that there is a sort of potential distance between the victim and the risk, and this can produce consequences, which must be addressed with appropriate tools.

M. Siri (✉)
University of Genoa, Genoa, Italy

Trauma

The very fact of being exposed to forms of violence can create negative physical, psychological, behavioural and social outcomes. Behind every form of violence, there is a common element or trauma (Van Dijk, 1999). First, the aspect linked to the psychological changes deriving from the chain of endocrine events induced by stress will be explored.

According to the stress-vulnerability model (Selye, 1936), stressful experiences, which are faced in the course of life, interact dynamically with the individual biological vulnerability to various mental pathologies, inducing a series of psychological and biological changes that can lead to the expression of disorders (Myin-Germeys & van Os, 2007). Stressors also promote changes in emotional and cognitive states: concentration and learning are aimed solely at stressful factors, leaving out any other stimuli. Long exposure to stressful factors, with the consequent hyperproduction of glucocorticoids, would damage brain structures such as the hippocampus. Studies conducted on animals have shown that glucocorticoids can induce dendritic regression, inhibit neurogenesis in the dentate gyrus and contribute to neuronal death (Sapolsky, 2003). In patients with a first psychotic episode, an association was found between an increase in cortisol levels and a decrease in left hippocampal volume (Mondelli et al., 2010). Furthermore, an inverse relationship has been highlighted between cortisol levels and those of BDNF (Brain-Derived Neurotrophic Factor) found in the prefrontal cortex of animals and post-mortem studies carried out on a sample of schizophrenic subjects (Issa et al., 2010). The persistent hyperproduction of cortisol, therefore, has implications on cognitive functions such as memory, where the hippocampus plays a fundamental role; in fact, memory deficits have been found in patients with a volume reduction of the hippocampus (O'Brien et al., 2004). The organism's autonomous response to stress, described by Walter Cannon as the "fight or flight" syndrome consists of a massive release of catecholamines (Cannon, 1939, 1940). The "fight or flight" response originates within the brain stem, is immediate but short-lived and acts through the stimulation of the sympathetic and parasympathetic efferent pathways that lead to rapid alterations of physiological states, thanks to the innervation of the organs target (Ulrich-Lai & Herman, 2009). The neuroendocrine response, described by Selye, is, on the other hand, mediated by the activation of the hypothalamus-pituitary-adrenal axis. As a whole, the stress system coordinates the adaptive response of the individual to various environmental stimuli, external or internal to the organism, and its activation involves systemic and behavioural changes that improve homeostatic capacity, increasing the chances of survival. However, conditions of chronic stress, psychosocial load, and real or imagined events can facilitate the imbalance of the nervous, immune, cardiovascular and metabolism systems in general, making the body more susceptible to the development and/or progression of diseases. Current knowledge deriving from pharmacology and genomics studies confirms this morpho-functional integration, and above all the unity between mental phenomena and the so-called somatic processes in continuous interaction with the environmental and social context. As later observed by Mason (1971), the individual's adaptive reaction to the environment is triggered by an emotional reaction that can determine different physiological responses to the stimulus itself.

Furthermore, man does not passively undergo an external stimulus, but, through a cognitive evaluation, gives it meaning; physiological responses therefore arise, differentiated for each individual, in response to exposure to the same stressor (Lazarus, 1993; Fredrickson & Joiner, 2002). There are considerable differences in sensitivity to the effects of stress, and this variability can be affected by development. It is known that the stress suffered in the early life period can have long-term consequences, increasing vulnerability to subsequent stresses. In turn, insufficient adrenal hormone secretion increases anxiety and the response to fear (Edwards, 1990), while in brain ageing an increase in susceptibility to stress is still observed (McEwen, 2002). Among other things, the action of antidepressant drugs is expressed by normalizing the function of the HPA axis with reduction of adrenal hyperplasia, restoration of hormonal suppression after administration of dexamethasone and specific actions on CRH receptors. The inhibition of the synaptic reuptake of monoamines initiates a cascade of events whose final result involves various metabolic changes, with an increase in the capacity and function of corticosteroid receptors (Jedema & Grace, 2003). Repeated stimuli or non-targeted activation of the allostatic system can cause the organism to wear out. For example, recurrent depression represents a pattern of physical and mental allostatic load, and in several studies, it has been associated with an increased incidence of cardiovascular disorders, increased platelet reactivity, increased insulin resistance with abdominal fat deposition, decreased bone mineral density and atrophy of the hippocampus, amygdala and prefrontal cortex; the latter phenomenon has also been reported in post-traumatic stress disorder (Bremner et al., 1997). It is plausible that, through this mediator of peripheral origin, conditions of fasting or abundance of food, but also thinness or overweight, can modify the regulation of the HPA axis. Corticosteroid hormones have both direct and insulin-mediated effects on adipose tissue and ultimately promote visceral adiposity with insulin resistance, dyslipidemia and hypertension (metabolic syndrome) and effects on the bone which cause low turnover osteoporosis. Another example of allostatic loading, directly related to prolonged exposure to high levels of circulating glucocorticoids, includes the regulation of the immune response, which, possibly mediated by the endogenous opioidergic system, can be stimulated or inhibited in an intensity-related manner by acute stressful stimuli, or chronic (Yin et al., 2000). Chronic stress, due to adrenal dysregulation, can negatively affect cognitive performance. The hippocampus has diurnal function is perhaps seasonal is maintained by adrenal steroids, through alpha and beta-noradrenergic innervation and 5-HT1A-serotoninergic, it is a key structure in spatial and episodic learning, in memory, as well as in situations of expectation and reward. In this regard, the role of corticosteroids in the phenomenon of jet lag has been demonstrated (McEwen, 1992a) and that the dietary intake of tryptophan, the precursor of 5-HT, increases serotoninergic activity and improves cognitive functions, especially in the subjects most vulnerable to stress (Markus, 2002). During repeated stress, as in Cushing's syndrome (Bordeau, 2009), circulating hormones interfere with the structural plasticity of the hippocampus causing remodelling of dendrites in the CA3 region and suppressing neurogenesis at the level of granules in the dentate gyrus, while in death neuronal pyramidal cells caused by severe and prolonged seizures, ischemia and psychosocial stress, NMDA3 receptors are also involved. On the other hand, the ability to recover after the stress reaction is entrusted to the correction of hypercortisolism itself (Bordeau, 2009) or to agents, such as estrogens and perhaps androgens, which counteract the negative effects of the allostatic load, regulating the formation of synapses through the stimulation of nerve growth factors (McEwen, 1992b). These phenomena can condition the responses to fear or anxiety and justify their maintenance even in situations not connected to reality, for example, the experience of stress with separation from the mother, in the neonatal period, leads to a reduction in the levels of neuropeptide Y (NPY) in the hippocampus and striatum and the increase in hypothalamic NPY and CRH (Husum et al., 2002).

Trauma, Stress and Diagnosistic Framework

At the diagnostic level, the trauma is classified by the 5th version of the DSM in the category of Trauma- and Stressor-Related Disorders (APA, 2013). Disorders characterized by pathological reactions to stress have been included in this chapter. All these disorders are characterized by having experienced trauma with the appearance of clinically significant emotional and behavioural symptoms. In the diagnostic category found reactive attachment disorder, uninhibited social engagement disorder, acute stress disorder, post-traumatic stress disorder and adaptation disorders. Disorders related to trauma and stress are triggered by exposure to stress or traumatic events, although the symptomatic manifestations can be very different from disorder to disorder. The symptoms related to severe psychological stress resulting from exposure to a traumatic event can be quite different from person to person. In some cases, the psychological trauma can manifest itself through emotions of fear and anxiety, often linked to the stressful context. In other cases, instead of anxiety, it is possible to observe other symptoms such as anhedonia or dysphoria, feelings of anger and aggression, or even dissociative symptoms. Post-traumatic stress disorder can manifest itself in different ways but the main feature is the development of a series of anxious-depressive symptoms following a traumatic event. In some patients, symptoms related to fear, avoidance and anxiety prevail, in others, a drop in mood and anhedonia are observed, still, others may show dissociative symptoms, although a combination of these symptoms is often observed in patients suffering from PTSD. We can distinguish the symptoms of post-traumatic stress disorder into certain categories: intrusive symptoms, avoidance strategies, mood and thinking changes and increased psychomotor activation. Generally, in PTSD patients, we can observe symptoms of these different categories often mixed. The intrusive symptoms mainly concern images relating to the traumatic event. These images are precisely defined as intrusive as the subject feels that he is not in control of them and that he is powerless, they present themselves to the conscience of the subject disturbingly and involuntarily. They can be present during the day or even at night, in the form of dreams or nightmares. Symptoms of psychological distress may also occur in the presence of a stimulus that recalls the traumatic episode (such as an image or a sound). Avoidance in PTSD, another symptom of post-traumatic stress disorder, is the use of experiential avoidance strategies to avoid coming into contact with any stimulus that remembers the trauma. Subjects tend to avoid places, situations or people who remember the traumatic event. This method of avoidance can lead to a significant reduction in the vital area of the subject as he can generally begin to avoid places that are particularly important to him (for example, places that remind him of the traumatic event) progressively reducing his quality of life. Changing the way of thinking the PTSD In the face of a traumatic event, symptoms of a cognitive and emotional nature may also arise. Specifically, patients with PTSD may not remember the traumatic event (post-traumatic amnesia), or develop negative ideas about themselves, others and the world. Finally, patients suffering from post-traumatic stress disorder may present symptoms of a drop in mood, feel emotionally distant from everyone or even no longer be able to experience positive emotions. Patients with PTSD may also exhibit symptoms of impaired and excessive psychomotor activation (Aupperle et al., 2019). These subjects can show themselves particularly angry and irritable, up to having violent and destructive behaviours. Patients may also show excessive anxiety, sleep problems and impaired attention and memory. All these symptoms can be particularly disturbing and significantly worsen the quality of life of the subjects. This is why it is important to deal with the traumatic event within a psychotherapeutic setting. Trauma and PTSD. However, it should be remembered that not all traumatic life events lead to the development of post-traumatic stress disorder. It is common for traumatic events to naturally cause a form of psychological distress, but in many cases (about 70–80% of cases) these symptoms tend to resolve spontaneously (Di Blasio, 2016) over time. However, when these symptoms do not resolve, they present themselves in a very intense way for a prolonged period (the DSM-5 defines 1 month as the minimum period to be able to diagnose PTSD). Furthermore, in recent years, the concept of "microtrauma" or "cumulative psychic injury" (Crastnopol, 2015) is upcoming in clinical psychology and psychiatry. So not only a serious or catastrophic event can cause PTSD, but also the presence of multiple small stressful or adverse events (for example mobbing) can lead to developing the same symptoms as a single larger and more relevant PTSD. For this reason, it is important to deal promptly with situations of psychological distress, through appropriate psychotherapeutic strategies, to favour quick processing of the trauma.

Victim Assessment

We are frequently led to consider violence as a momentary and partial loss of control on the part of the aggressor, a sort of condition of decontrol. In reality, the statistical data from the literature give a different image. There is an emotional climate in which one person tries to control another through a variety of actions or behaviours. Some authors (Gargiullo & Damiani, 2016) divide the acts of violence based on a precise taxonomy: there is psychological neglect that is expressed in an attitude of indifference, continuous forgetfulness, promises not maintained and emotional coldness. We then move on to physical neglect, minimizing or completely ignoring the other's physical health problems and not worrying sufficiently about family safety. We are faced with emotional and psychological abuse when a subject tends to humiliate, blame, control actions and decisions, illicitly withhold personal information, belittle, criticize, isolate and limit the autonomy of another. Sexual harassment consists of a series of jokes and teasing of a sexual nature even in the presence of strangers, vulgar jokes, obscene acts, insistent requests, blackmailing sexual ports and requests of a perverse nature. We arrive at real emotional and psychological violence in the presence of vandalism, physical threats, defamatory accusations, mistreatment of pets, threats of abandonment, persecutory behaviour, ridicule of values and religious faith and induction into behaviour contrary to common morality. It falls into this type of violence hypercuria (excessive care of a minor compared to his real physical and educational needs), Munchausen Syndrome (production and simulation of physical symptoms and or psychics to attract the attention of others to themselves through continuous research clinics and unnecessary hospitalization. Subject a person to periodic specialist visits for induced symptoms or invented by the applicant family member), Ganser Syndrome (frequent in prisoners awaiting trial, but found in hysteroid subjects that simulate a pathological psychiatric logic to force the other, for example, not to ask for separation one) and Gaslighting (mental manipulation, cruel and planned, agitated with the intent to undermine all certainty and security of her in the intended victim); economic violence (e.g., financial revenue control, impeding decisions on purchases of goods and services, forcing people to leave work, hindering the looking for a job outside the home, borrowing debt to meet their expenses); and physical violence (e.g., slapping, stapling, biting, choking, hitting them with objects you, pull by the hair, punch and/or kick, burn with cigarettes and/or with red-hot objects, injure with objects or with the use of weapons).

The severity of the injuries can range from bruises, grazes, broken bones and teeth to permanent injuries (in- validity) until death; sexual violence (e.g., sexual assault, rape, incest, coercion of perverse sexual tensions, incitement to prostitution, sexual exploitation through prostitution and/or the production of pornographic material); stalking (a form of psychological aggression, and often also physical, by a persecutor who breaks in a repetitive, unwanted and destructive way in the victim's private life with serious physical and psychological consequences); mobbing: parental or environmental incompatibility (intrusive and persistent forms of control, for example by in-laws, in the life of the spouses); conjugal (delegitimation of one spouse by the other through recurrent offences and humiliation relations both in private and in the presence of relatives, friends and strangers. This kind of mobbing behaviour can go so far as to discredit the victim in the eyes of her children to "isolate" her from the family context and make her totally "harmless"); horizontal parental (persecutory, insidious and persistent behaviour, of a parent separated, or in the process of separation, towards the other for preventing him from any "interference" in care, assistance and education offspring); vertical parenting (from top to bottom, when a parent, with immature and dependent personality, fearing being placed in a marginal. Finally, it can lead to attempted murder or murder itself).

Given the wide range of types of violence, there is no single form of framing the victims. The question must therefore be observed as announced at the beginning of the chapter from the biological point of view, from the psychological point of view and considering the social implications of all these forms.

"Currently, the existing literature defines intimate partner violence (IPV) as any type of physical or psychic suffered by a person on the part of a family member who, taking advantage of a there, comes to be in a structurally stronger position" (Buchler, 1998) includes threats or acts of physical, psychological or sexual violence carried out within a present or past family or couple relationship (Schwander, 2003) implemented by a partner, a former partner or a relative. This consideration brings us back to the vision of the violent act not as a single moment of loss of control, but as an emotional climate that makes possible an act of this type which is incomprehensible outside this context. Usually, the attackers responsible for IPV are described by acquaintances as mild and unsuspected people of this crime. In the IPV classification, Johnson and Ferraro (2000) propose a system divided into five categories: common couple violence), characterized by sporadic- there episodes of violence without the intention to control and dominate the other. These abusers have a predisposition to physical and psychological violence, especially within the couple; intimate terrorism in which there is a set of manipulatives and controlling behaviours that result in emotional abuse.

While appearing physically stressed during acts of violence, physiologically exhibit no level of activation (arousal). Such conduct was defined by Holtzworth-Munroe and Stuart (1994) as generalized antisocial violence (gen- rally- violent-antisocial) and defined by Jacobson and Gottman (1998) as "cobra" (coldness do you want) which means violent resistance, carried out by the victim, in confronting an over-controlling and intimidating partner. This type of conduct which may not end in a single episode is defined by the law of American self-defence violence; mutual violent control carried out by both parties. It can be considered that other authors underline the presence of alternating phases (Walker, 1979) a sort of "cycle of violence" which have as a precondition a series of well-defined behaviours: induce the other to perceive themselves vulnerable, needy and of little value, through constant criticism, ironic jokes and insults, made even in the presence of strangers (humiliation); isolate the victim from any form of relationship (family, friends, work colleagues etc.) to increase the level of dependence and submission (isolation); harshly punish any form of rebellion with, for example, glaring, insults, gestures of disapproval, vandalism, abuse of pets (intimidation); resorting to the use of blackmail (e.g. slanderous accusations, disclosure of private documents to third parties, compromising photos) to terrify her and make her totally harmless (threats); minimize "one's unforgivable conduct by accusing the other of excessive drama" ("you complain as if I had beaten you": "you look at me as if I were a monster"); justify the aggression by making the other responsible ("if you behaved well, I would not be forced to act in this way") (blaming); making one's "weight" felt within a relationship asymmetric and abusive (domain): For this to happen, no decision can be made without his explicit consent; criticism and/or rebellion against his authority are not allowed; It should be emphasized that violence, particularly domestic violence, has one its cyclical nature (alternating phases) marked by states of tension (psychophysiological activation of anger) to subsequent relaxation (emotional cooling).

Regarding the psychological consequences of the crime, according to the analysis of Fischer and Wertz (1979), affirmed that the victim faces the disruption of his daily life, experiencing dismay and disbelief, anger and desire for revenge towards those responsible. Over time, the victim continues to relive the trauma through the imagination, remaining alert and suspicious of others, as before. She is always ready for new victimization, perceiving herself as helpless, the others as predators and the community as a subject unable to protect her. Parallel to these signs of vulnerability, however, there is also an effort in the victim towards the recovery of independence, security, order and meaning. For a detailed discussion of psychological stress, see the classic study by Lazarus and Folkman (1984). However, they are not enough to integrate the victimization experience. The environment must demonstrate that the constant and extreme vigilance of the victim is no longer necessary, the people around her must pay attention to her and show her respect, to support her in her attempt to make sense of her experience.

The personal effort, the environment and the individuals around the victim are crucial factors, thanks to which deeper victimization, isolation and resignation can be avoided. As Irene Hanson Frieze, Sharon Hymer and Martin S. Greenberg (1987) point out in their systematic review, many authors (e.g. Bard & Sangrey, 1986; Burgess & Holmstrom, 1974, 1979; Caplan, 1964; Forman, 1980; Notman & Nadelson, 1976; Symonds, 1975, 1976, in Frieze et al.) have supported the possibility of identifying some common phases of the psychological reaction to victimization. In particular, Bard and Sangrey (1986) called the phase immediately following victimization, in which the victim experiences a sort of falling asleep, disorientation, together with denial, disbelief and feelings of loneliness, depression, vulnerability, "the impact-disorganization phase" and a sense of helplessness. There is also anxiety, sleep disturbances and nightmares and possible aggravation of pre-existing medical problems (Leymann, 1985). This picture may diminish over time, but if treatment is not ordered or support is not available, these feelings can become chronic. The short-term consequences of victimization (after a few hours or even days) fall into what Bard and Sangrey (1986) called the rejection phase. These consequences can last, approximately, from 3 to 8 months. The victim experiences swings of inexperienced emotions, ranging from anger to fear, from sadness to euphoria, and from self-pity to self-blame. As these emotions fade, the victim enters the final stage, the stage of reorganization. If the victim can cope with and resolve the trauma, victimization can at this point turn into an important moment of personal evolution (Silver & Wortman, 1980). Unfortunately, very often this does not happen. A large number of rape victims interviewed by Burgess and Holmstrom (1975), for example, reported that they never recovered from 4 to 6 years ago and suffered from reduced sexual activity, and flashbacks of trauma with physical pain. During sex and difficulty reaching orgasm. Practitioners who work with victims frequently report low self-esteem, depression, guilt, fear and relationship difficulties, among the most typical long-term consequences of victimization, as reported by the aforementioned Frieze et al. (1987). Hanson et al. (2010), in their systematic review, highlight the negative effects of victimization on the quality of life, identifying, in particular, the problems encountered by the victims on social, occupational and interpersonal functioning, satisfaction and well-being and socio-economic status. Mat Sat proposes a different schematization coming from a sector of trauma research promoted by the APA (American Psychiatric Association). The schematization divides the clinical intervention between the victim at three different times. The first step is to determine the type of violence suffered by the victim. This qualifies and determines the progress of the subsequent phases. In a sufficiently schematic way, we can determine a taxonomy similar to that of other authors (Walker, 1978).

Briefly, Mat Sat identifies the following categories, divided into physical and psychological trauma: Acts of violence (rape, physical abuse, domestic abuse, aggravated assault, attempted murder); Natural disasters (Tsunami, earthquake, floods, typhoons, sinkholes); Crime (Snatch theft, robbery, burglary, retail crime, cybercrime, fraud; Biomedical/physiological (AIDS-HIV, chronic illness, botched operations/corrective surgery); Terrorism (Hostage survivor, kidnapping, war-related terrorism, religious-related terrorism Sexual abuse, physical abuse); Childhood-related trauma (Relatives or friends of sudden death individuals); Accidents and disasters; Witness-based; Death and grief; Relationship failure; Work-life imbalance; Psychological (Betrayal of trust, abuse of power, manipulation of emotions, stress, distress, mental disorders); and Crises (Economic turbulence, property fire or loss, hospitalization of self or family members). The second phase starts by identifying and managing crisis and/or short-term interventions for the survivor's immediate trauma relief. This phase is critical to enable survivors to undergo progressive recovery. The survivor, relatives and professional caregiver are enabled to visualize the direction of psychotherapy and address issues and common reactions after trauma. Psychological assessment is established on the biopsychosocial model. This model is based on an analysis of the individual's heredity, the performance of certain neurotransmitters, psychological symptoms and the impact of trauma upon the person's family and social functioning.

A mental status exam (MSE) emphasizes a survivor's cognitive, emotional and behavioural responses; while paying attention to the survivor's appearance and thinking processes. This in turn indicates intellectual functioning and cognitive capacities. Observing the survivor's mood and affect regulation during the first few client-counsellor sessions helps to determine feelings and emotional responses that are crucial to trauma recovery. In this manner, psychotherapy goes beyond listening to the fears and problems of survivors. Therefore, phase two of the psychological assessment involves the interaction and data compilation from the survivor and the survivor's family members to formulate short-term treatments. Subsequent short-term treatments addressing specific cognitive, behavioural or spiritual concerns accumulate towards long-term trauma recovery. There are common Reactions After Trauma. Following a traumatic event, people typically describe feeling relief to be alive, followed by stress, fear and anger. Having such reactions is what happens to most people and has nothing to do with personal weakness (Allen, 1995; Van der Kolk et al., 1996; Stolorow, 2007).

Common reactions after trauma are divided into three categories: emotive, physiological and relationships. Following the information of the first phase, recovery is an ongoing gradual process. It does not happen through suddenly being "cured" and it does not mean that the survivor will forget what happened. Normally, fear, anxiety, flashbacks, efforts to avoid reminders and arousal symptoms, if present, will gradually decrease over time. It is the task of the professional and those interested in helping survivors to facilitate the recovery process. The subdivision of the CRT is related to the biological, psychological and social axes. Emotive reactions included feeling hopeless about the future, nervous, helpless, fearful, sad, shocked, numb, unable to experience love or joy, being irritable or having outbursts of anger, becoming easily upset, self-blame or negative views of oneself or the world. Physiological dimension includes symptomatic behaviour such as jumpy and startling easily at the sudden noise, staying on guard and constantly alert, stomach upset, trouble eating, trouble sleeping and exhaustion, pounding heart, rapid breathing, edginess, severe headache if thinking of the event, sweating, failure to engage in exercise, diet, safe sex, regular health care Excess smoking, alcohol, drugs, food, worsening of chronic medical problems. The consequences at the social and relationship level take into consideration all those aspects linked to the indicated dimension.

Psychological Tests

Except for some standard batteries, the psychological tests used in the assessment of consequences are usually ad hoc batteries established about the type of trauma suffered. A broad spectrum of tools is identified. The Mental Status Examination (MSE) is a useful tool to assist physicians in differentiating between a variety of systemic conditions, as well as neurologic and psychiatric disorders ranging from delirium and dementia to bipolar disorder and schizophrenia. The examination itself may comprise a few brief observations made during a general patient encounter or a more thorough evaluation by the physician. It also may include the administration of relatively brief standardized tools such as the Mini-Mental State Examination (MMSE) and Mini-Cog. Highly detailed and time-consuming neuropsychological testing is also available, but this is beyond the scope of this chapter. It contains five subdivisions that require clinical judgement on observable behaviour and speech patterns. There are 62 open-ended statements regarding personal image, facial expressions, speech patterns, cognitive dissonance, emotional congruence, personality disorders and perception of reality. Assessment requires between 15 and 30 min. Culture, native language, level of education, literacy, and social factors such as sleep deprivation, hunger, or other stressors must be taken into account when interpreting the examination, because these factors can affect performance. Language skills of the physician and patient are critical; the patient must be able to understand the questions and communicate his or her answers, and the physician must be able to interpret the examination results. If possible, the mental status examination should occur when the physician is alone with the patient and again in the presence of the patient's friends or family members who can provide more longitudinal insight into problems the patient may be having. The physician should maintain a non-judgmental, supportive attitude during the assessment. The examination begins with a general assessment of the patient's level of consciousness, appearance, activity and emotional state. Each of these items may be rapidly assessed by a physician in the initial moments of the encounter through history taking and general observation. These findings, combined with a brief memory test, may be all that is needed to ascertain that no pathology is present. If the general assessment does reveal areas of concern, further in-depth investigation is warranted. When a more thorough examination is indicated, it may be separated into two general portions: observations made by the physician about the patient's physical state, and a cognitive evaluation in which the patient's neurologic and psychological functioning is assessed.

The cognitive portion involves the assessment of 11 different functions: attention, executive functioning, agnosia, language, memory, orientation, praxis, prosody, thought content, thought processes and visuospatial proficiency. The Beck Depression Inventory (BDI, BDI-II) is a 21-question multiple-choice self-report inventory. It is one of the most widely used instruments for measuring the severity of depression. The most current version of the questionnaire is designed for individuals aged 13 and over and is composed of items relating to depression such as hopelessness and irritability, cognitions such as guilt or feelings of being punished, as well as physical symptoms such as fatigue, weight loss and lack of interest in sex (Beck and Beck, 1972). Beck Anxiety Inventory (BAI) is a 21-question self-report inventory used for measuring the severity of an individual's anxiety (Osman et al., 2002). The BAI consists of questions about how the individual has been feeling in the last week. Each question has the same set of four possible answer choices. An initial item pool of 86 items was drawn from three preexisting scales: the Anxiety Checklist, the Physician's Desk Reference Checklist, and the Situational Anxiety Checklist. A series of analyses were used to reduce the item pool. The final scale consists of 21 items, each describing a common symptom of anxiety. The respondent is asked to rate how much he or she has been bothered by each symptom over the past week on a 4-point scale. The BAI showed high internal consistency (alpha = 0.92) and test-retest reliability over 1 week, $r(81) = 0.75$. The BAI discriminated against anxious diagnostic groups (panic disorder, generalized anxiety disorder, etc.) from non-anxious diagnostic groups (major depression, dysthymic disorder, etc). In addition, the BAI was moderately correlated with the revised Hamilton Anxiety Rating Scale, $r(150) = 0.51$, and was only mildly correlated with the revised Hamilton Depression Rating Scale, $r(153) = 0.25$ (APA, 2019).

The Psychopathy Checklist-Revised (PCL-R) is the psycho-diagnostic tool most commonly used to assess psychopathy (Hare & Neumann, 2006). The test should only be considered valid if administered by a suitably qualified and experienced clinician under controlled conditions. In addition to lifestyle and criminal behaviour, the checklist assesses glib and superficial charm, grandiosity, need for stimulation, pathological lying, cunning and manipulating, lack of remorse, callousness, poor behavioural controls, impulsivity, irresponsibility and failure to accept responsibility for one's actions. PCL-R allows us to enormously increase our understanding of the nature and manifestation of psychopathy in a wide range of situations, such as work, family, school, health and relationship with justice. The evaluation process is divided into three phases: administration of a semi-structured interview, to investigate the history of the subject as an adolescent and as an adult, obtain representative examples of his style of interaction and obtain information to compare with the documentation in the possession of the clinician file review procedure, i.e. review of personal documentation for the acquisition of collateral information to the interview, to find credibility in the contents and the interaction style of the subject, and to obtain the main data to assign a score to some items the attribution of the score to the items based on the data collected from the interview and the file review. Fundamental for correct use of the test are the availability of sufficiently solid information to assign the score to the items and the careful examination of any cultural or other differences through which the characteristics measured with the PCL-R could express themselves.

The PCL-R structure consists of 20 items to which a score (0, 1, 2) must be attributed after the file review and the interview. The items are divided into 4 components which converge into 2 factors: Factor 1. Interpersonal/Affective: Describes the interpersonal and affective traits of social interaction, investigating the selfish, callous and remorseless use of others. It is divided into the Interpersonal (Component 1) and Affective (Component 2) components. Factor 2. Social deviance: investigates the unstable and antisocial lifestyle, mainly regarding the aspects of impulsiveness, irresponsibility, and lack of scruples, and measures the aspects related to criminal behaviour. It is divided into the Lifestyle (Component 3) and Antisocial (Component 4) components. Multiple sources of information compete for scoring Evaluation of psychopathic behaviours based on the person's entire life span. PCL-R provides a reliable assessment of the psychopathy construct in a wide range of settings, for clinical and research purposes, but its elective application is in the assessment of psychopathy in criminals and forensic psychiatric patients. The tool is aimed at psychologists and psychiatrists but is also addressed, at least in the main theoretical lines and in the results, to all professionals working in the judicial, penitentiary and forensic fields, who find themselves evaluating, comparing and proposing psychiatric expertise in the field of criminal proceedings.

AQ is a self-report inventory that makes it possible and practical to routinely screen children and adults for aggressive tendencies. The Aggression Questionnaire (AQ) measures an individual's aggressive responses and his or her ability to channel those responses in a safe, constructive manner. This inventory takes 10 min to complete. It consists of 34 items, scored on the following scales: physical aggression, verbal aggression, hostility, anger and indirect aggression. The Bem Sex-Role Inventory (BSRI) provides independent assessments of masculinity and femininity in terms of the respondent's self-reported possession of accept responsibility for one's actions. PCL-R allows us to enormously increase our understanding of the nature and manifestation of psychopathy in a wide range of situations, such as work, family, school, health, relationship with justice, etc. The evaluation process is divided into three phases: administration of a semi-structured interview, to investigate the history of the subject as an adolescent and as an adult, obtain representative examples of his style of interaction and obtain information to compare with the documentation in the possession of the clinician file review procedure, i.e. review of personal documentation for the acquisition of collateral information to the interview, to find credibility in the contents and the interaction style of the subject, and to obtain the main data to assign a score to some items the attribution of the score to the items based on the data collected from the interview and the file review Fundamental for correct use of the test are the availability of sufficiently solid information to assign the score to the items and the careful examination of any cultural or other differences through which the characteristics measured with the PCL-R could express themselves. The PCL-R structure consists of 20 items to which a score (0, 1, 2) must be attributed after the file review and the interview. The items are divided into 4 components which converge into 2 factors: Factor 1. Interpersonal/Affective: Describes the interpersonal and affective traits of social interaction, investigating the selfish, callous and remorseless use of others. It is divided into the Interpersonal (Component 1) and Affective (Component 2) components Factor 2. Social deviance: investigates the unstable and antisocial lifestyle, mainly regarding the aspects of impulsiveness, irresponsibility, and lack of scruples, and measures the aspects related to criminal behaviour. It is divided into the Lifestyle (Component 3) and Antisocial (Component 4) components. Multiple sources of information compete for scoring Evaluation of psychopathic behaviours based on the person's entire life span. PCL-R provides a reliable assessment of the psychopathy construct in a wide range of settings, for clinical and research purposes, but its elective application is in the assessment of psychopathy in criminals and forensic psychiatric patients. The tool is aimed at psychologists and psychiatrists but is also addressed, at least in the main theoretical lines and in the results, to all professionals working in the judicial, penitentiary and forensic fields, who find themselves evaluating, comparing and proposing psychiatric expertise in the field of criminal proceedings.

The structured clinical interview for DSM-5 (SCID-5) is an interview to be used as a guide to formulate the main diagnoses of DSM-5. It is given by clinicians or mental health professionals. It is useful for confirming and documenting one or more hypothesized diagnoses based on the DSM-5 criteria and ensuring that all major DSM-5 diagnoses are systematically evaluated; selecting the population to include in a study; describing a study population in terms of current and past psychiatric diagnoses (The diagnostic data that were obtained using the SCID interview are useful for researchers, trainees, health administrators interested in the incidence of a psychiatric disorder in a specific branch of the population); and improving the style in the clinical interview of those who are not yet familiar with the DSM-5 criteria and increasing the interviewing skills of students of the health professions (psychiatrists, psychologists, social workers and psychiatric nurses).

The Italian edition of the SCID-5 is available in the following versions. SCID-5-CV. It covers the most commonly observed diagnoses in the clinical setting (for example, depressive and bipolar disorders, anxiety disorders, obsessive-compulsive disorder and post-traumatic stress disorder).

SCID-5-PD: It is used to evaluate the ten personality disorders of the DSM-5. It contains the SCID-5-SPQ Questionnaire, an optional short screening tool, lasting 20 min, for reducing the duration of the clinical interview.

SCID-5-AMPD: Guides the clinician in rigorous evaluation of the defining components of the personality pathology presented in the DSM-5 Alternative Model. QuickSCID-5 is taken from the SCID-5-CV. It also includes the diagnoses that are found most frequently in clinical settings but are designed to be more rapid in administration.

The Minnesota Multiphasic Personality Inventory (MMPI) is one of the most frequently used personality tests in mental health. The test is used by trained professionals to assist in identifying personality structure and psychopathology. The current MMPI-2 has 567 items and usually takes between 1 and 2 h to complete. The test assesses the following: hypochondriasis, depression, hysteria, psychopathic deviate, masculinity/femininity, paranoia, psychasthenia, schizophrenia, hypomania and social introversion. The Minnesota Multiphasic Personality Inventory (MMPI) is a psychological test that assesses personality traits and psychopathology. It is primarily intended to test people who are suspected of having mental health or other clinical issues.

Although it was not originally designed to be administered to non-clinical populations, it can be used to assess psychological stability in workers in "high-risk" professions such as airline pilots, police or workers in the nuclear power industry, although using it in this manner is controversial. The MMPI is currently commonly administered in one of two forms — the MMPI-2, which has 567 true/false questions, and the newer MMPI-2-RF, published in 2008 and containing only 338 true/false items. While the MMPI-2-RF takes about half the time to complete (usually about 40–50 min), the MMPI-2 is still the more widely used test because of its existing large research base and familiarity among psychologists (Another version of the test—the MMPI-A—is designed exclusively for teenagers).

The MMPI is not a valid measure of a person's psychopathology or behaviour if the person taking the test does so in a way that is not honest. A person may decide, for whatever reasons, to overreport (exaggerate) or underreport (deny) the behaviour being assessed by the test. The four validity scales are designed to measure a person's test-taking attitude and approach to the test Lie – The Lie scale is intended to identify individuals who are deliberately trying to avoid answering the MMPI honestly and in a frank manner. F – The F scale (the "F" does not stand for anything, although it is mistakenly sometimes referred to as the Infrequency or Frequency scale) is intended to detect unusual or atypical ways of answering the test items, like if a person were to randomly fill out the test. Back F – The Back F scale measures the same issues as the F scale, except only during the last half of the test. K – The K scale is designed to identify psychopathology in people who otherwise would have profiles within the normal range. It measures self-control, and family and interpersonal relationships, and people who score highly on this scale are often seen as being defensive. In this test, "mastery" is defined as the extent to which one regards one's life chances as being under one's control (Pearlin et al., 1981). Mastery is seen as an important intermediary in the transition of life strains, which include trauma. This scale consists of seven items which are answered in a 4-point agree–disagree format.

The Life Satisfaction scales were developed by Neugarten et al. (1961). Scale A measures zest versus apathy, Scale B measures resolution and fortitude and Scale C measures congruence between desired and achieved goals. Scale D measures self-concept, while Scale E measures mood tone. Life Satisfaction Index A contains statements about life in general and Life Satisfaction Index B contains open-end and checklist items regarding living styles. Scales A to E contains 5 statements each. Life Satisfaction Index A contains 20 statements and Life Satisfaction Index B contains 12 questions. Additionally, new validity scales were incorporated into the revised test. MMPI-2: The revised edition of the test was released in 1989 as the MMPI-2. The test received revision again in 2001 and updates in 2003 and 2009, and it is still in use today as the most frequently used clinical assessment test. MMPI-2-RF: Another edition of the test, published in 2008, is known as the Minnesota Multiphasic Personality Inventory-2-Restructured Form (MMPI-2- RF), an alternative to the MMPI-2. MMPI-A: There is also an MMPI, published in 1992, that is geared towards adolescents aged 14–18 years old called MMPI-A. With 478 questions, it takes about an hour to complete. MMPI-A-RF: In 2016, the Minnesota Multiphasic Personality Inventory-Adolescent-Restructure (MMPI-A- RF) was published. Like the MMPI-2-RF, it is shorter, with just 241 questions that take 25–45 min to answer. MMPI-3: The latest version of the instrument, MMPI-3, was released in 2020. The test takes 25–50 min to complete and is available in English, Spanish and French for Canada formats. The Depression, Anxiety, Stress Scales (DASS) is a set of three self-report scales designed to measure the negative emotional states of depression, anxiety and stress (Lovibond & Lovibond, 1995). The Depression scale assesses dysphoria, hopelessness, devaluation of life, self-deprecation, lack of interest/involvement, anhedonia and inertia. The Anxiety scale assesses autonomic arousal, skeletal muscle effects, situational anxiety and subjective experience of anxious affect. The Stress scale assesses difficulty relaxing, nervous arousal and being easily upset/agitated, irritable/over-reactive and impatient.

A comprehensive psychological assessment is required for the victims by a trained psychologist who has expertise in dealing with victims to give a clear picture of the psychological process of the victims.

References

Allen, L. A. (1995). *The effect of future educators' knowledge of child sexual abuse on reporting behavior and attribution of blame*. University of Wyoming.

APA. (2013). *APA 2013 annual convention report. Monitor on Psychology*. Retrieved September 20, 2022, from https://www.apa.org/monitor/2013/09/convention

APA. (2019). *Psychological and neuropsychological testing billing and coding guide*. https://www.apaservices.org. Retrieved September 20, 2022, from https://www.apaservices.org/practice/reimbursement/health-codes/testing/billing-coding

Aupperle, R., Jak, A. J., Jurick, S., Crocker, L. D., et al. (2019). SMART-CPT for veterans with comorbid posttraumatic stress disorder and history of traumatic brain injury: A randomised controlled trial. *Journal of Neurology, Neurosurgery & Psychiatry, 90*(3), 333–341.

Bard, M., & Sangrey, D. (1986). *The crime victim's book* (Vol. 37). Brunner/Mazel.

Beck, A. T., & Beck, R. W. (1972). Screening depressed patients in family practice. A rapid technic. *Postgraduate Med, 52*(6), 81–85. https://doi.org/10.1080/00325481.1972.11713319

Bordeau, J. (2009). *Xenophobia: the violence of fear and hate*. The Rosen Publishing Group, Inc.

Bremner, J. D., Randall, P., Vermetten, E., Staib, L., Bronen, R. A., Mazure, C., Capelli, S., McCarthy, G., Innis, R. B., & Charney, D. S. (1997). Magnetic resonance imaging-based measurement of hippocampal volume in posttraumatic stress disorder related to childhood physical and sexual abuse—A preliminary report. *Biological Psychiatry, 41*(1), 23–32.

Buchler, A. (1998). Domestic violence and state interventions. *Family Matters*, 32–36.

Burgess, A. W., & Holmstrom, L. L. (1974). Rape trauma syndrome. *American Journal of Psychiatry, 131*(9), 981–986.

Burgess, A. W., & Holmstrom, L. L. (1975). Accountability: A right of the rape victim. *Journal of Psychiatric Nursing and Mental Health Services, 13*(3), 11–16.

Burgess, A. W., & Holmstrom, L. L. (1979). Rape: Sexual disruption and recovery. *American Journal of Orthopsychiatry, 49*(4), 648–657.

Cannon, W. B. (1939). *The wisdom of the body*. W.W. Norton.

Cannon, W. B. (1940). The role of chance in discovery. *The Scientific Monthly, 50*(3), 204–209.

Caplan, G. (1964). *Principles of preventive psychiatry*. Basic Books.

Crastnopol, M. (2015). *Micro-trauma: A psychoanalytic understanding of cumulative psychic injury*. Routledge.

Di Blasio, P. (2016). Forms of violence and psychological consequences. *Forms of Violence and Psychological Consequences*, 5–14.

Edwards, K. (1990). The interplay of affect and cognition in attitude formation and change. *Journal of Personality and Social Psychology, 59*(2), 202–216.

Fischer, C. T., & Wertz, F. J. (1979). Empirical phenomenological analyses of being criminally victimized. *Duquesne Studies in Phenomenological Psychology, 3*, 135–158.

Forman, B. D. (1980). Psychotherapy with rape victims. *Psychotherapy: Theory, Research & Practice, 17*(3), 304–311.

Fredrickson, B. L., & Joiner, T. (2002). Positive emotions trigger upward spirals toward emotional well-being. *Psychological Science, 13*(2), 172–175.

Frieze, I. H., Hymer, S., & Greenberg, M. S. (1987). Describing the crime victim: Psychological reactions to victimization. *Professional Psychology: Research and Practice, 18*(4), 299–315.

Gargiullo, B. C., & Damiani, R. (2016). *The stalker, or the persecutor in ambush. Classifications, assessments and psychobehavioral profiles*. FrancoAngeli.

Hanson, R. F., Sawyer, G. K., Begle, A. M., & Hubel, G. S. (2010). The impact of crime victimization on quality of life. *Journal of Traumatic Stress: Official Publication of The International Society for Traumatic Stress Studies, 23*(2), 189–197.

Hare, R. D., & Neumann, C. S. (2006). Psychopathy: Assessment and forensic implications. *The Canadian Journal of Psychiatry, 54*(12), 791–802.

Holtzworth-Munroe, A., & Stuart, G. L. (1994). Typologies of male batterers: Three subtypes and the differences among them. *Psychological Bulletin, 116*(3), 476.

Husum, H., Termeer, E., Mathé, A. A., Bolwig, T. G., & Ellenbroek, B. A. (2002). Early maternal deprivation alters hippocampal levels of neuropeptide Y and calcitonin-gene related peptide in adult rats. *Neuropharmacology, 42*(6), 798–806. https://doi.org/10.1016/S0028-3908(02)00038-2

Issa, G., Wilson, C., Terry, A. V., & Pillai, A. (2010). An inverse relationship between cortisol and BDNF levels in schizophrenia: Data from human postmortem and animal studies. *Neurobiology of Disease, 39*(3), 327–333. https://doi.org/10.1016/j.nbd.2010.04.017

Jacobson, N. S., & Gottman, J. M. (1998). *When men batter women: New insights into ending abusive relationships.* Simon and Schuster.

Jedema, H. P., & Grace, A. A. (2003). Chronic exposure to cold stress alters electrophysiological properties of locus coeruleus neurons recorded in vitro. *Neuropsychopharmacology, 28*(1), 63–72.

Johnson, M. P., & Ferraro, K. J. (2000). Research on domestic violence in the 1990s: Making distinctions. *Journal of Marriage and Family, 62*(4), 948–963.

Karmen, A. (2012). *Crime victims: An introduction to victimology* (8th ed., pp. 122–123). Wadsworth New York.

Lazarus, R. S. (1993). Coping theory and research: Past, present, and future. *Psychosomatic Medicine, 55*(3), 234–247. https://doi.org/10.1097/00006842-199305000-00002

Lazarus, R. S., & Folkman, S. (1984). *Stress, appraisal, and coping.* Springer Publishing company.

Leymann, H. (1985). Somatic and psychological symptoms after the experience of life threatening events: A profile analysis. *Victimology, 10*(1–4), 512–538.

Lovibond, P. F., & Lovibond, S. H. (1995). The structure of negative emotional states: Comparison of the Depression Anxiety Stress Scales (DASS) with the Beck Depression and Anxiety Inventories. *Behaviour Research and Therapy, 33*(3), 335–343.

Markus, C. R. (2002). New insight in the beneficial effects of food on mood and performance: Evidence for interference between stress and brain 5-HT. *Agro Food Industry High Technology, 13*(5), 21–23.

Mason, J. W. (1971). A re-evaluation of the concept of 'non-specificity' in stress theory. *Principles, Practices, and Positions in Neuropsychiatric Research*, 323–333.

McEwen, B. S. (1992a). Steroid hormones: Effect on brain development and function. *Hormone Research in Pædiatrics, 37*(Suppl. 3), 1–10.

McEwen, B. S. (1992b). Re-examination of the glucocorticoid hypothesis of stress and aging. *Progress in Brain Research, 93*, 365–383. https://doi.org/10.1016/s0079-6123(08)64585-9

McEwen, B. S. (2002). The neurobiology and neuroendocrinology of stress: Implications for post-traumatic stress disorder from a basic science perspective. *Psychiatric Clinics, 25*(2), 469–494.

Mondelli, V., Dazzan, P., Hepgul, N., Di Forti, M., Aas, M., D'Albenzio, A., Di Nicola, M., Fisher, H., Handley, R., Marques, T. R., & Morgan, C. (2010). Abnormal cortisol levels during the day and cortisol awakening response in first-episode psychosis: The role of stress and of antipsychotic treatment. *Schizophrenia Research, 116*(2–3), 234–242.

Muratore, M. G., & Tagliacozzo, G. (2008). The Italian national victimization survey. In K. Aromaa, & M. Heiskanen (Eds.), *Victimisation surveys in comparative perspectives*, papers from the Stockholm Criminology Symposium 2007, Publication series European Institute for Crime Prevention and Control, affiliated with the United Nations, 1237-4741; 56 (Helsinki).

Myin-Germeys, I., & van Os, J. (2007). Stress-reactivity in psychosis: Evidence for an affective pathway to psychosis. *Clinical Psychology Review, 27*(4), 409–424.

Neugarten, B. L., Havighurst, R. J., & Tobin, S. S. (1961). The measurement of life satisfaction. *Journal of Gerontology, 16*, 134–143. https://doi.org/10.1093/geronj/16.2.134

Notman, M. T., & Nadelson, C. C. (1976). The rape victim: Psychodynamic considerations. *The American Journal of Psychiatry, 133*(4), 408–413. https://doi.org/10.1176/ajp.133.4.408

O'Brien, J. T., Lloyd, A., McKeith, I., Gholkar, A., & Nicol Ferrier, N. (2004). A longitudinal study of hippocampal volume, cortisol levels, and cognition in older depressed subjects. *American Journal of Psychiatry, 161*(11), 2081–2090.

Osman, A., Hoffman, J., Barrios, F. X., Kopper, B. A., Breitenstein, J. L., & Hahn, S. K. (2002). Factor structure, reliability, and validity of the Beck Anxiety Inventory in adolescent psychiatric inpatients. *Journal of Clinical Psychology, 58*(4), 443–456.

Pearlin, L. I., Menaghan, E. G., Lieberman, M. A., & Mullan, J. T. (1981). The stress process. *Journal of Health and Social Behavior, 22*(4), 337–356. https://doi.org/10.2307/2136676

Sapolsky, R. M. (2003). Stress and plasticity in the limbic system. *Neurochemical Research, 28*(11), 1735–1742. https://doi.org/10.1023/a:1026021307833. PMID: 14584827.

Schwander, M. (2003). *Domestic violence: Legal analysis of cantonal measures.* Federal Office for Gender Equality BFEG.

Selye, H. (1936). Thymus and adrenals in the response of the organism to injuries and intoxications. *British Journal of Experimental Pathology, 17*(3), 234.

Silver, R. L., & Wortman, C. B. (1980). Coping with undesirable life events. In J. Garber & M. E. P. Seligman (Eds.), *Human helplessness: Theory and applications* (pp. 279–340). Academic Press.

Stolorow, R. D. (2007). Anxiety, authenticity, and trauma: The relevance of Heidegger's existential analytic for psychoanalysis. *Psychoanalytic Psychology, 24*(2), 373.

Symonds, M. (1975). Victims of violence: Psychological effects and aftereffects. *American Journal of Psychoanalysis, 35*(1), 19–26.

Symonds, M. (1976). The rape victim: Psychological patterns of response. *American Journal of Psychoanalysis, 36*(1), 27–34.

Ulrich-Lai, Y. M., & Herman, J. P. (2009). Neural regulation of endocrine and autonomic stress responses. *Nature Reviews Neuroscience, 10*, 397–409. https://doi.org/10.1038/nrn2647.

van der Kolk, B. A., Pelcovitz, D., Roth, S., Mandel, F. S., et al. (1996). Dissociation, somatization, and affect dysregulation: The complexity of adaption to trauma. *The American Journal of Psychiatry, 153*(Suppl), 83–93.

Van Dijk, J. J. M. (1999). Introducing victimology. In J. J. M. van Dijk, R. G. H. van Kaam, & J. Wemmers (Eds.), *Symposium on victimology, Amsterdam, August 25-29, 1997* (p. 12). Criminal Justice Press.

Walker, M. A. (1978). Measuring the seriousness of crimes. *The British Journal of Criminology, 18*(4), 348–364.

Walker, L. E. (1979). *Battered woman.* Harper and Row.

Yin, X., Chasalow, S., Dourleijn, C., et al. (2000). Coupling estimated effects of QTLs for physiological traits to a crop growth model: Predicting yield variation among recombinant inbred lines in barley. *Heredity, 85*, 539–549.

Chapter 20
Forensic Investigations and Victims

Rejani Thudalikunnil Gopalan

Forensic investigations are a major part of crime investigation to throw light on the suspect, perpetrator, modus operandi and the conviction of the perpetrator. It involves gathering and analysis of evidence. The area of forensic science is fast growing, and it is defined as the application of scientific principles and techniques to matters of criminal justice especially relating to the collection, examination and analysis of physical evidence (Merriam-Webster, n.d.). In another way, it can be said that forensic science is any science used within the criminal justice system, and forensic investigations are an integral part of it, which involves many techniques. It uses various analyses such as analysis of fingerprint, DNA, bloodstain pattern analysis and digital analysis, and recently it started using the benefits of artificial intelligence for age and gender identification, face recognition, cause of death and various identifications and reasons for crime. Forensic investigation uses various scientific fields such as the medical field, chemistry, zoology, physics and its theory and practical applications to answer the questions related to crimes. Forensic chemistry offers its applications in drug analysis and toxicology, metrology (the science of measurement), combustion chemistry, materials science, and pattern evidence to the needs of both the scientific and the legal communities (Bell, 2009). Forensic entomology, a scientific discipline of zoology that deals with the study of insects are useful in a comprehensive analysis of entomological evidence material and the use of knowledge about insects and other invertebrates to investigate and verify the evidence in civil and criminal law. This branch falls into several categories, including the issue of food pests in industry or agriculture, human and animal parasitology (especially myiasis) and very often the field of criminology and forensic medicine, where the results are mainly applied to determine the length of post-mortem interval (PMI), evidence of manipulation of the corpse, or other forensic facts that result from entomological analysis (Ubomír et al., 2021). Another field which helps

R. T. Gopalan (✉)
Mahatma Gandhi Medical College and Hospital, Jaipur, India

forensic investigation is microbial forensics, which focuses on the characterization of evidence from a bioterrorism act, crime, hoax, or an inadvertent release that involves crime scene(s) investigation, chain of custody practices, evidence collection, handling and preservation, evidence shipping, analysis of evidence, interpretation of results and court presentation in addition to determining the aetiology and identity of the causal agent. Chemical and physical assays may help determine the process used to prepare, store, or disseminate the bioweapon as pathogens and toxins can be converted to bioweapons and used to commit bioterrorism and bio-crime (Budowle et al., 2005). The use of medical knowledge is necessary for the investigation of many types of crimes such as the participation of physicians as specialists in the carrying out of investigative procedures, the physicians' assistance in the form of the re-creation of the deceased person's face with a view to its identification and physicians' consultations in addition to the use of medical knowledge in the form of genotyposcopic and molecular genome research to identify a person during the crime investigations (Yaremchuk, 2019). Reynolds (2010) mentioned that the use of radiography and other medical imaging specialities to aid in investigating civil and criminal matters has increased as investigators realize how radiologic technology can yield information that otherwise is unavailable. Imaging techniques are a powerful tool in forensic science and radiologists are aware of the importance of storing radiographs over prolonged periods and of efficient record-keeping methods, because various legal problems may require the radiographs for additional interpretation or their presentation in court (Kahana & Hiss, 1999).

The forensic investigation uses multi-disciplinary approaches and a wide variety of techniques, and the following section describes briefly the important forensic investigations.

Medical Analysis and Investigations

Forensic medicine belongs to a group of medical specialities. The aim of such studies involves mastering abilities which permit the medical doctor to provide competent opinions for courts and other organs in the administration of justice, consistent with the current medical knowledge, forensic experience and requirements of the law (Berent, 2005). The primary aim of the forensic medical analysis is to provide legal fact-finders with evidence regarding the causal relationship between an alleged action and a harmful outcome. Existing approaches to causation in forensic medicine generally fall into two categories such as intuitive and probabilistic, and the propriety of each approach depends on the individual facts of an investigated injury, disease or death. There is no universally applied systematic methodology for formulating and assessing causality in forensic medical expert opinions (Meilia et al., 2020).

Criminal Profiling

Criminal profiling is a technique to identify the personality and behaviour characteristics to predict the offender which assumes an inherent uniformity among the perpetrator's characters, personality and modus operandi. Criminal profiling usually gives the traits of offenders particularly sexual assault and murder though criminal profiling attempted in all crimes which assist the investigation team and court and it uses both inductive and deductive approaches. Kocsis and Cooksey (2002) analysed serial arson crime and produced a model of offence behaviours that identifies four discrete behaviour patterns which share a constellation of common non-discriminatory behaviours. Galinari and Bazon (2021) studied adolescent offenders to identify the behavioural and psychosocial profiles of 400 male adolescent offenders based on empirical data collected in a Brazilian socio-cultural context, and the they have noticed that profiles indicate differences between the adolescent offenders both in psychological functioning and criminal pattern, as well as the psychosocial risk/protective factors associated with each of the profiles.

According to Verde and Nurra (2010), modern approaches to profiling have been particularly successful in cases of serial homicides and sex crimes, given that compulsive (perverse) acts, because of their ritual nature. Kocsis et al. (2002) did psychological profiling analysis of 62 incidents of serial sexual assault (serial violent crimes) multidimensional scaling which produced a five-cluster model of serial rapist behaviour. The first cluster of behaviours that were identified represent common behaviours to all patterns of serial rape, second demonstrated distinct offence styles under brutality, intercourse, chaotic and ritual and all clusters allowed to identify distinct offender characteristics. Almond et al. (2021) studied a sample of 213 adult male-on-female homicides with sexual or unknown motives from a U.K.-wide database to explore whether homicide offenders' crime scene actions are predictive of their criminal histories. Relationships between 13 preconviction variables and 29 crime scene behaviours were explored using a bivariate statistical approach, and binary logistic regression models were used to predict the presence, or absence, of specific preconvictions based on a combination of offence behaviours. They found 16 statistically significant associations between key offence behaviours and previous convictions, and the results indicate that offenders' criminal histories can be predicted from their offence behaviours, though not all preconvictions may be similarly suited.

Criminal psychological profiling has attained unprecedented recognition despite little empirical evidence to support its validity and the absence of any thorough exposition of the skills involved with the technique. Kocsis (2003) suggested that professional profilers can produce a more accurate prediction of an unknown offender. It required knowledge and skill to produce each offender profiling and to make common characteristics of the offenders committing similar crimes.

Psychological Autopsy

When a death occurs under traumatic, ambiguous, unknown, or uncertain circumstances, death of suicidal origin can be considered psychological autopsy, a method of investigation commonly used to study what leads to suicide identifies aspects of a person's life that explain any lingering mystery that shrouds their death (Acinas et al., 2015; Scott et al., 2006). There are significant differences between a psychological autopsy and the traditional risk assessment of suicide, and the goals of the psychological autopsy are to find out the features of individuality, the patterns of behaviour and the possible motives of suicide methods of psychological autopsy involve investigating, collecting and analysing all related information of the deceased (Tu & Zhao, 2009). Psychological autopsy involves collecting all available information on the deceased via structured interviews of family members, relatives or friends as well as attending health care personnel, and also information is collected from available health care and psychiatric records, other documents and forensic examination which allow a psychological autopsy to synthesize the information from multiple informants and records. The early generation of psychological autopsies established that more than 90% of completed suicides have suffered from usually co-morbid mental disorders, most of the mood disorders and/or substance use disorders which are untreated. More recent psychological autopsy studies have mostly used case-control designs, and thus have been better able to estimate the role of various risk factors for suicide (Isometsä, 2001). On many occasions, a suicide note is found next to the body that helps to clarify certain aspects needed for the investigation to elucidate whether the death is really due to suicide or other causes and there are several types of suicide notes (farewell, instructions, the accusation of others, request for forgiveness, justification of one's suicide) that can contribute to the study of the victims and psychological state and the circumstances that led to death. There is no unanimously approved way to conduct a psychological autopsy, but there are protocols for obtaining relevant information and preparing the report (Acinas et al., 2015).

While doing a psychological autopsy for the cases of youth suicides, it is important to use peer information too. In a study, Looijmans et al. (2021) examined 16 cases to understand the feasibility and added value of including peer informants in a psychological autopsy study of youth suicides. Findings showed that peers added information to parents' narratives in general and particularly on social relationships, bullying, school experiences, social media, and family relations and also the presence of certain issues (such as social media contagion) as well as the emotional impact from certain adverse events that seemed to have functioned as precipitating factors. In a review of 76 studies of suicide, by using the psychological autopsy method, Cavanagh et al. (2003) found that mental disorder was the most strongly associated variable for suicide. Bates et al. (2019) reported psychological adaptation to molecular autopsy (Postmortem genetic testing) findings amongst family members after a young sudden cardiac death and found that 36% reported poor adaptation to genetic information who were more likely to have worse posttraumatic stress symptoms, depression, poor perceived support including poor social and perceived support from significant others family, members, and friends.

Studies based on the psychological autopsy method suffer methodological problems like shortcomings concerning sampling biases in the selection of control subjects, confounding influences of extraneous variables and reliability of the assessment instruments. Also noticed was the absence of homogeneity among studies in the procedure employed, as well as the lack of defined guidelines for performing this type of inquiry and suggested standardization of the procedure (Pouliot & De Leo, 2006). Hawton et al. (1998) reported issues related to psychological autopsy, such as research design, identification of subjects, sources of information and the particular issues concerned with approaching relatives and other informants, choice and recruitment of controls, the difficulties of conducting psychological autopsy interviews with relatives, problems for interviewers, the selection of appropriate measures to obtain information, and achieving valid and reasonably reliable conclusions from diverse information sources. Brent (1989) suggested that the integration of data obtained through psychological autopsies with data obtained through biochemical, toxicological and epidemiological approaches is likely to deepen our understanding of suicide. As suggested by Isometsä (2001) future psychological autopsy studies can be more focused on interactions between risk factors or risk factor domains for a specific suicide populations which would aid for suicide prevention, or use of combined psychological autopsy methodology with biological measurements to enhance the validity (Isometsä, 2001). There is a lack of standard procedures to conduct a psychological autopsy (Tu & Zhao, 2009) but protocols are available for obtaining relevant information and preparing the report (Acinas et al., 2015). Though shortcomings are there, a psychological autopsy has significant implications for the future as the statistics obtained from mortality data affect the course of health care research, the flow of resources, and ultimately public health policy. From a public health perspective, the misclassification of suicides as accidents or deaths from natural causes can negatively affect research funding and policy development related to suicide prevention efforts, making a standardized and accurate procedure imperative, and this procedure has transcended the confines of forensic science and has applications in the many areas of litigation and public health policy (Scott et al., 2006).

Fingerprint Matching

Fingerprints have been used for detecting suspected criminals in a crime and for the identification of offenders, which started to become widely used as an acceptable tool after the first conviction using fingerprints as evidence in 1902. Edward Henry published the Classification and Use of Fingerprints in 1898, and after a century, fingerprints have been used for scene-of-crime investigations and personal identification (Wilshire, 1996; Chen et al., 2021). From 1953-to 2001 it was the usual practice in England and Wales for the police to proffer fingerprint evidence showing

16 common matching characteristics, or features in the agreement or 16-point standard (Leadbetter, 2005). In recent years, age determination techniques based on physical and chemical composition changes in fingerprints have been emphasized and the advanced methods can be classified into two categories including techniques based on the modifications of physical characteristics and chemical composition characteristics and photography, optical, microscopy and electrochemical methods, and also vibrational spectroscopy and mass spectrometry (MS) techniques can be utilized (Chen et al., 2021).

Fingerprint examination and expertise and the conclusions were written in categorical or probabilistic terms. When a crime occurs, the available fingerprint is collected and matched with a stored database for the identification of the offender. Several experiments have now shown that these professional analysts are highly accurate, but not infallible, much like other fields that involve high-stakes decision-making (Tangen et al., 2020). It is was noticed that latent print examinations involve a complex set of psychological and cognitive processes and experience appears to improve the overall accuracy, increase visual working memory and lead to configure processing of upright fingerprints and also show a narrower visual filter and greater consistency when viewing ink prints (Busey & Parada, 2010). Thompson and Tangen (2014) found that experts could match prints accurately when there was reduced visual information, reduced opportunity for direct comparison and reduced time to engage in deliberate reasoning, and opined that non-analytic processing accounts for a substantial portion of the variance in expert fingerprint matching accuracy with general wisdom in fingerprint identification practice and formal training. Less favourable results were also noticed regarding the skill and accuracy of experts. In a signal detection paradigm experiment, Thompson et al. (2014) noticed that experts were even more conservative in their decision-making when dealing with these genuine crime scene prints than when dealing with simulated crime scene prints, and this conservatism made them relatively less accurate overall and also intermediate trainees-despite their lack of qualification and experience performed about as accurately as qualified experts. Tangen et al. (2020) suggested that combining independent judgements from small groups of fingerprint analysts can improve their performance and prevent these mistakes from entering courts.

A more frequently used technique in the analysis of fingerprint is latent fingerprint visualization but fingerprint visualization techniques do not always enable individualization when fingermarks collected in crime scenes are fragmentary, ambiguous or deformed (Chen et al., 2021). Though tremendous progress has been made in plain and rolled fingerprint matching, latent fingerprint matching continues to be a difficult problem, as poor quality of ridge impressions, small finger area and large non-linear distortion cause difficulties and singularity, ridge quality map and ridge flow map are found to be the most effective features in improving the matching accuracy (Jain & Feng, 2011). Cao and Jain (2019) recommended accurate automated latent fingerprint recognition system to make a better prediction of the offenders. Jain and Feng (2009) proposed a latent-to-full palmprint matching system due to reason that evidential value of palmprints in forensic applications is clear as about 30 per cent of the latent recovered from crime scenes are from palms. The biometric systems for palmprint-based personal authentication in access control type of applications mostly deal with low-resolution (about 100 ppi) palmprints and only perform full-to-full palmprint matching.

Though fingerprint examination has a long history, still it is not in an advanced stage and efforts are going on for its full utilization in crime investigation.

Ballistic Analysis

Ballistics refers to the study that deals with the projectile motion in flight, especially in the case of bullets, and the application of ballistics for aiding law and legal agencies to maintain law and order in our society is referred to as forensic ballistics. This field aims to identify the offender and link him/her to the scene of the crime as well as a weapon of offence and collects all the physical evidence at the crime scene, such as fired cartridges, wads, bullets or shots, firearm and clothes of the deceased and accused, to find nature of the crime (homicide, suicide, assault etc.) and to ascertain the number of rounds fired from a single firearm and the total number of shooters, range from which firing took place, crime scene reconstruction, the distance between victim and offender and identification of weapon of offence (aided by analysis of projectile injuries) (https://forensicsdigest.com/forensic-ballistics/). The main issues that can be solved by ballistic legal expertise are related to the weapon (is it a legal one?, type, model and calibre of the firearm, the status of the firearm etc.), firearm use (evidence to prove recent firing, possibilities to fire without pulling the trigger, and to fire a faulty weapon, operating status, calibre and effectiveness of a crafted weapon, the existence of traces of additional factors of firing on the gun barrel, distance and direction of the shot, possibly the victim's and the drawer's positions, if a shot hole is an entry or the exit), ammunition (series, size, model, type of bullet and tube, qualitative state of the shell, made industrially or handcrafted) and the silencer (if a silencer was attached to the gun, the technical features of the silencer, made industrially or handcrafted) (Luca, 2012).

According to Kunz et al. (2013) characteristic bloodstain patterns on the gun and shooting hand, the localization of the entrance wound and the position of the weapon, and additional details such as family background or medical history are important aspects of forensic investigation for determining homicide, suicide or accident. In addition to those secondary changes by relatives at the crime scene, uncommon choice of weaponry and its unusual morphological manifestation often complicate the examination and reconstruction of such cases. Autopsy findings, a careful crime scene investigation and bloodstain pattern analysis, and a ballistic reconstruction can be essential tools to gain knowledge of the shooting distance and position of the gun. Gitto et al. (2021) aimed to provide concrete data to help to discriminate between homicide and suicide based on specific autopsy findings by using a database of the Cook County Medical Examiner's Office from August 2014 through April 2019 and identified 3491 deaths due to gunshot wounds. On bullet trajectory, it was reported that a course leftward-upward-backwards was the most frequent observed trajectory in suicides and a course rightward-upward-frontward was the most frequent observed trajectory in homicides. When the internal trajectory of a bullet is interpreted in the light of all available evidence, it can impeach or corroborate witness statements and highlight consistencies as well inconsistencies in investigative reports and scene examinations. All deaths due to shotguns examined at the Bexar County Medical Examiner's Office between 1988 and 2005 were evaluated by variables like age and sex of the victim, wound location, wound range and manner of death and reported that contact wounds were the most common range in suicides and the head was the most common location, and that for homicides, the most common range of fire was distant, and the most prevalent distributions of wounds were head, chest and multiple wound locations. The study showed significant differences between homicide and suicide wound locations and ranges (Molina et al., 2007). In another study Molina and DiMaio (2008) examined the characteristics of rifle wounds, including both centerfire and rimfire rifles, especially about location and range of the wound and for that all deaths due to rifles examined at the Bexar County Medical Examiner's Office between 1988 and 2004 were reviewed. A total of 509 cases were identified, with 233 suicides and 266 homicides and reported that the average age of suicide victims (41.6 years) tended to be older than that of homicide victims (32.6 years). Suicides tended to be contact wounds to the head, whereas homicides most often had multiple wound locations sustained from a distant range, and the most common location to the head of suicidal wounds was intraoral, whereas homicidal head wounds were more often to the temporoparietal region. Molina et al. (2013) reviewed non-accidental handgun deaths examined at the Bexar County Medical Examiner's Office between 2000 and 2010 and found that the average age of suicide victims (46.7 years) was greater than that of homicides (34.3 years). In suicide, wounds were contact wounds to the head but in homicides the wounds were abdominal, extremity, back and at times, multiple wounds were present. It was also noted that distant and intermediate wounds and handgun wounds to the forehead, side of the head, submental, and intraoral locations were significantly more are common in suicide whereas wounds at face, the apex of the head, and back of the head were more common in homicides.

A common method used to examine lead bullets is a comparison of physical properties such as weight, dimensions, shape and distinctive markings, but ballistic investigations, for example, comparison of characteristic scratches and marks left on fired bullets, do not always give sufficient information because ballistic abrasion patterns can change for a variety of reasons, (e.g., deformation or mechanical strain) and sometimes only particles remain in a victim's body. In such cases, trace-element composition and lead-isotope ratios can be compared with those of controls and the elemental composition of particles and deformed bullets have been compared with the elemental fingerprints and isotope ratios of potential bullet types found on suspects (Ulrich et al., 2004).

Ballistics imaging technology is a potent tool for moving the law enforcement response to violent gun criminals forward by linking multiple crime scenes to one firearm which allowed law enforcement agencies to make hits that would not have been possible using traditional ballistics methods (Braga & Pierce, 2004).

Computer-assisted three-dimensional reconstruction of the crime scene in a homicide by firearm was found to be successful (Kislov et al., 2021).

Molecular ballistics investigates biological evidence that is generated by gunshots at biological targets by using knowledge from molecular biological, forensic ballistic and wound ballistic. Setting out in 2010 with two seminal publications proving the principle that DNA from backscatter collected from inside surfaces of firearms can be retrieved and successfully be analysed, molecular ballistics covered a lot of ground until today (Euteneuer & Courts, 2021). Backscatter traces comprising blood and tissue from the victim are propelled back from the bullet entry site towards the direction of the shooter and can consolidate and persist on the inner and outer surfaces of the firearm, from where they can be collected and analysed. Thus, a link between the weapon and the victim can be established solely by molecular biological trace analysis. Euteneurer et al. (2020) found no meaningful correlation-between backscatter distribution and DNA yields but the shooting distance and the condition of the wound channel could be established. According to Grabmüller et al. (2015) when a firearm projectile hits a biological target a spray of biological material (e.g., blood and tissue fragments) can be propelled from the entrance wound back towards the firearm which is known as "backscatter", and if caused by contact shots or shots from short distances, traces of backscatter may reach the inside surfaces of the firearm. Thus, a comprehensive investigation of firearm-related crimes must comprise wound ballistic assessment and backscatter analysis, and "triple contrast" doped ballistic models were found to be useful for forensic co-analysis of DNA and RNA.

It is well established that estimation of the firing range is often critical for reconstructing gunshot fatalities, where the main measurable evidence is the gunshot residue (GSR). Tuğcu et al. (2005) examined the amount and distribution of gunshot residues (GSRs) of 40 experimental shots which were made to calfskin from distances of 0, 2.5, 5, 10, 20, 30, 45 and 60 cm. Eighty samples were taken from the right and left sides of the wounds, and Alizarin Red S dye staining was performed. The amounts of GSR particles were measured with image analysis and found that as the distance increased, the amount of GSR decreased. A similar finding was noticed in another study. Cecchetto et al. (2011) analysed intermediate-range gunshot wounds through a micro-computed tomography (micro-CT) coupled with an image analysis software to quantify the powder particles and to determine the firing distance for 50 shootings from different distances and found that by increasing the firing distance, micro-CT analysis demonstrated a clear decreasing trend in the mean GSR percentage, particularly for shots fired from more than 15 cm, for distances under 23 cm, the powder particles were concentrated on the epidermis and dermis around the hole, and inside the cavity; while, at greater distances, they were deposited only on the skin surface. The presence of primer-derived GSR on bone provides the potential to differentiate gunshot trauma from blunt trauma when the bone presents an atypical gunshot wound. Berryman et al. (2010) tried to identify bullet wipe on the bone at distances from 1 to 6 feet with 0.45 calibre, full metal jacket ammunition by using Pork ribs with intact muscle tissue and found primer-derived gunshot residue (GSR) deep within the wound tract, and the bone provides the potential to differentiate gunshot trauma from blunt trauma when the bone presents an atypical gunshot wound. Also, the presence of gunshot primer residue at a distance of 6 feet demonstrates the potential for establishing maximum gun-to-target distance for remote shootings.

Clothing can affect the number of gunshot residues (GSR) reaching the body and their distribution as the amount and distribution of the GSR vary according to the distance between the firearm and the target, so it is important to investigate the clothing, as well as the body, to determine the range of fire of entry wounds in firearm injuries. The sodium rhodizonate test provides valuable data when clothing is available for examination, and light microscopic examinations may add additional information regarding the range of fire in the absence of clothing by using the sodium rhodizonate test on 80 garment samples containing the bullet entrance. It was found that gross residues were seen on military camouflage clothing in samples from < or = 45-cm group and white flannel undershirts under the military camouflage contained rhodizonate-positive particles only around the contact wounds. With image analysis, however, the residues could be detected also in the skin samples of the 2.5-cm- and 5-cm-range groups (Tugcu et al., 2006).

The microscopic quantitative method uses sodium rhodizonte to verify the presence of residues and their distribution on the cutis of gunshot wounds. Neri et al., (2007) examined 250 skin samples and evaluation of both macroscopic and microscopic features demonstrated that the amount and the spatial distribution of GSR deposits in the skin surrounding entrance wounds strictly correlated with shooting distance (Neri et al., 2007).

To test the accuracy and repeatability of reconstructing the impact angle of single bullet impacts using the ellipse method, Walters and Liscio (2020) reported that the best performance (accuracy and repeatability) is seen with the measurements of the 0.45 calibre ammunition. They also suggested that ellipse method is useful in providing measurements for most crime scene reconstruction purposes.

Ballistics imaging hits reports rarely contribute to the identification, arrest, charging or sentencing of suspects due to the delay in producing hit reports which require 181.4 days after the focal crime. This causes investigations to proceed without the benefit of information from ballistics analysis (King et al., 2017).

Forensic ballistics is growing in its use and techniques and requires more research in this field regarding its utility and application in crime investigation, especially when crimes related to gun are increasing tremendously.

Report Writing of Forensic Investigations and Court Proceedings

A forensic report is the primary work product of a forensic psychologist, which aims to inform and influence the court, and an effective report is driven by legal evidentiary principles and best practices in assessment. It is advisable that experts are required to integrate both qualitative and quantitative information from a variety of different sources, with varying degrees of reliability and validity and integrate the relevant information to form a conclusion, and that this conclusion is then itself weighted and integrated with other evidence to formulate the final decision in a case (Goodman-Delahunty & Dhami, 2013; Brannick, 2015).

Forensic report writing requires skill, as it influences the outcome of a legal conflict and it is also subject to a high degree of scrutiny from both attorneys and the judge. At least one person is always trying to discredit the evaluator or the report, and the evaluator must write the report in such a way that every word is meaningful, more detailed, precise, clearly written, and substantiated by evidence, structured in a manner that is clear and easily understood by all parties. Report to be self-sufficient that the reader should not need to refer to other documents to understand how the conclusions were reached (Brannick, 2015; Wettstein, 2004; Resnick & Soliman, 2012).

According to Griffith et al. (2010), the major points to be kept in mind while writing the report are the suitability of the information (exclude or include), where and when to give importance to information, appropriateness of vocabulary, and writing style and length of the report. Many make mistakes in terms of not addressing or failing to answer referral questions, language and organization problems, over-emphasizing a single source of data, irrelevant data or mixed data, the wrong choice of psychological test, misinterpretation, not using alternative hypotheses and conclusions or opinions with insufficient explanations (Grisso, 2010). A good report should state facts and information addressing the questions by the court or investigation team; inferences should be stated based on facts and conclusions to be based on scientific background. There are many approaches used for writing a report such as procedure-by-procedure, issue-by-issue and point-by-point. There is no universal format for writing a report, but a robust report is based on evidence and usually the length of reports ranges from 1 to 5 pages. According to Goodman-Delahunty and Dhami (2013) the assumption that the report writer or the trier of fact relatively weights and integrates the relevant information contained in a report to form a conclusion, and that this conclusion is then itself weighted and integrated with other evidence to form the final judgement in a case, is not supported by the extant literature from the field of judgement and decision-making due to the limitations of the human mind and constraints of decision-making, and there is a lot of scope for improving report writing in content and opinion.

Guidelines and Policies for Sexual Abuse Investigation

Sexual assault is a complex situation with medical, psychological and legal aspects and forensic experts play a major role in terms of forensic and gynaecological medical examination and evidence collection to maintain the chain of custody. Victims should be examined by a specially trained medico-legal examiner to avoid multiple examinations in the surroundings that do not meet minimum health standards

(Ludes et al., 2018). There are many protocols available for medical and psychological forensic investigations internationally and country-specific. Many countries have their protocols merged with their specific rules and regulations; however, the core features are similar. While performing the examination, the purpose of forensic medical examination is to form an opinion such as whether a sexual act has been attempted or completed, whether it includes genital, anal or oral penetration by the penis, fingers or other objects as well as any form of non-consensual sexual touching, any harm has been caused to the survivor's body including injuries inflicted on the survivor by the accused and by the survivor on the accused, age of the survivor needs to be verified in the case of adolescent girls/boys and whether alcohol or drugs have been administered to the survivor needs to be ascertained (Ministry of Health, & Family Welfare, Government of India, 2014). As per guidelines for forensic and medico-legal examination of sexually assaulted victims by the Board of the European Council of Legal Medicine (ECLM) (2018), forensic and gynaecological medical examinations must be performed as soon as possible after the sexual assault within 7 days. If the delay is under 48 h, the case must be considered as a forensic emergency because it is within this time limit that HIV post-exposure prophylaxis is indicated, and after a delay of 7 days, the time limit for evidence collection (genetic samples, toxicological samples) has usually been exceeded (Ludes et al., 2018).

There are specifications available for investigation for vulnerable groups like the elderly group and children. Chopin and Beauregard (2020, 2021) reported that sexual crimes against the elderly are more violent and occur more often in the victim's residence, resulting in more severe injuries, motivated by sex, anger and opportunities and are more frequently committed by strangers, making criminal investigations more difficult to solve. Abner et al. (2019) opined that trained investigators are required to handle sexual abuse cases appropriately and that they can investigate the case thoroughly, promptly and with as much information as possible even in a residential care setting. The medico-legal examination for adults, adolescents and children are almost similar, but certain special considerations are given by considering the developmental stages. Consent for examination needs to be sought from the parent or guardian if the child is under 12 years of age. In such situations, history taking can be facilitated by the use of dolls and body charts, and the genital and anal examination should not be conducted mechanically or routinely. The indicators of abuse such as pain on urination and/or defecation, abdominal pain/generalized body ache, inability to sleep, sudden withdrawal from peers/adults, feelings of anxiety, nervousness, helplessness, inability to sleep, weight loss, and feelings of ending one's life to be checked (Ministry of Health, & Family Welfare, Government of India, 2014).

According to Edgardh et al. (1999) non-penetrative sexual acts among adolescent girls leave no lasting genital signs, but that repeated abusive genital penetration significantly more often than non-penetrative abuse leaves deep posterior hymenal clefts and/or vestibular scarring, and a hymenal opening allowing examination with 17–25 mm specula, also in girls without experience of voluntary intercourse. It was noticed that in cases with a confessing perpetrator, no discordance was found between the history of the victim, medico-legal conclusion and the history of the perpetrator. The disclosure of sexual abuse by children also depends on many factors including their age, intelligence, memory and mental status. Keary and Fitzpatrick (1994) have studied the nature of disclosure regarding sexual abuse and they found a strong positive correlation between having previously told someone about sexual abuse and disclosure of such abuse during the formal investigation. Also a strong positive correlation between not having previously told someone and not disclosing during the formal investigation. They have noticed that children under 5 years least likely to disclose of sexual abuse during the investigation was strongly positively correlated with abuse being regarded as confirmed. Katz et al. (2016) explored the emotional language that children within the age group of 3–14 years use during forensic investigations following suspected sexual abuse and found the limited overall presence of emotional language that children hardly used positive emotional language and mainly employed negative emotional language. Suggestibility refers to the susceptibility of memory to distortion or error, and children are not distinct from adults in the sense that adults are also suggestible. The experts recommend establishing ground rules for interviews and emphasize using open-ended questions and prompts and only proceeding to more specific questioning when necessary (Lieb et al., 1997).

Similar care needs to be taken for interviewing a person with a disability for assessing sexual abuse that history must be sought independently, directly from the survivor herself/himself, a person with a disability can decide who can be present in the room while history is being sought and examination conducted, and to make arrangements for interpreters or special educators in case the person has a speech/hearing or cognitive disability (Ministry of Health, & Family Welfare, Government of India, 2014).

In addition to physical injuries caused by abuse, the psychological injuries that occur due to abuse are also to be explored. Psychological impact examination (PIE) evaluates the potential psychological impact of an attack, and it is conducted by highly specialized psychiatrists and psychologists in the medical and legal areas. In many cases, the exact evaluation of the psychological trauma is, however, challenging mainly because of the difficulty in predicting the long-term psychological sequelae, as it varies from person to person depending on many psychosocial factors (Abgrall-Barbry & Dantchev, 2012). The role of a psychologist in the evaluation of sexual abuse cases is very important, especially in making a diagnosis, finding mental capabilities, the strength of coping mechanisms, assessing the impact of abuse, ability to stand for trial, especially giving information related to abuse or as a witness. A comprehensive assessment of cognitive, personality/temperamental psychopathology reports will be more useful rather than addressing a single component. It is the skill and knowledge of the psychologist that affects the assessment and report. In addition to that, the assessment should address the concerns and questions of the court.

Specially trained forensic nurses also play role in the forensic evaluation of assaults and abuses as they provide 24-h-a-day, first-response medical care and crisis intervention to rape survivors in either hospitals or clinic settings, and sexual assault nurse examiner (SANE) programs are very important too which emphasize on promoting the psychological recovery of survivors, providing comprehensive and consistent post-rape medical care (e.g., emergency contraception, sexually transmitted disease [STD] prophylaxis), documenting the forensic evidence of the crime completely and accurately, improving the prosecution of sexual assault cases by providing better forensics and expert testimony, and creating community change by bringing multiple service providers together to provide comprehensive care to rape survivors. Researches showed a positive result on its effectiveness (Campbell et al., 2005). Forensic nursing is an emerging profession in many countries. It plays an important role in the criminal justice system as they are the first person to attend to the victim, and thus able to make remarks on the victim's condition in evaluation and treatment scenarios. They provide direct patient care about violence, abuse, crime, victimization and exploitation and integrate forensic and nursing sciences in their assessment and care of victims and perpetrators and advocate for the collection of evidence and reporting of crimes (Yanai et al., 2012; Kent-Wilkinson, 2010). A study conducted in the Netherlands by de Vries et al. (2019) reported that respondents felt competent in performing forensic nursing tasks, and had a positive outlook on their work as forensic nurses and possibilities for further expansion of their roles. Forty-eight per cent reported that, at times, they experienced resistance to their involvement with forensic matters from other professionals in their work environments (de Vries et al., 2019).

Sexual abuse investigation involves multi-disciplinary inputs to address questions and concerns of the court and to deliver proper treatment. To address the complexities of sexual abuse, professionals involved in the process of forensic investigation and treatment require training, knowledge and skill, with strict adherence to protocols and ethics.

References

Abgrall-Barbry, & Dantchev, N. (2012). Examen de retentissement psychologique après une agression [Psychological assessment of victims]. *La Revue du Praticien, 62*(6), 801–802.

Abner, E. L., Teaster, P. B., Mendiondo, M. S., Ramsey-Klawsnik, H., Marcum, J. L., Crawford, T. N., & Wangmo, T. (2019). Victim, allegation, and investigation characteristics associated with substantiated reports of sexual abuse of adults in residential care settings. *Journal of Interpersonal Violence, 34*(19), 3995–4019. https://doi.org/10.1177/0886260516672051

Acinas, M. P., Robles, J. I., & Peláez-Fernández, M. Á. (2015). Suicide notes and the psychological autopsy: Associated behavioral aspects. *Actas Espanolas de Psiquiatria, 43*(3), 69–79.

Almond, L., Matin, E., & McManus, M. (2021). Predicting the criminal records of male-on-female UK homicide offenders from crime scene behaviors. *Journal of Interpersonal Violence, 36*(21–22), NP11852–NP11876. https://doi.org/10.1177/0886260519888522

Bates, K., Sweeting, J., Yeates, L., McDonald, K., Semsarian, C., & Ingles, J. (2019). Psychological adaptation to molecular autopsy findings following sudden cardiac death in the young. *Genetics in Medicine: Official Journal of the American College of Medical Genetics, 21*(6), 1452–1456. https://doi.org/10.1038/s41436-018-0338-4

Bell, S. (2009). Forensic chemistry. *Annual Review of Analytical Chemistry (Palo Alto Calif), 2,* 297–319. https://doi.org/10.1146/annurev-anchem-060908-155251

Berent, J. (2005). Rola biegłych z zakresu medycyny sadowej w opiniowaniu dla potrzeb sadów i instytucji ubezpieczeniowych [Role of experts in forensic medicine in opinioning for courts and insurance agencies]. *Archiwum medycyny sadowej i kryminologii, 55*(4), 247–250.

Berryman, H. E., Kutyla, A. K., & Russell Davis, J. (2010). Detection of gunshot primer residue on bone in an experimental setting-an unexpected finding. *Journal of Forensic Sciences, 55*(2), 488–491. https://doi.org/10.1111/j.1556-4029.2009.01264.x

Braga, A. A., & Pierce, G. L. (2004). Linking crime guns: The impact of ballistics imaging technology on the productivity of the Boston Police Department's Ballistics Unit. *Journal of Forensic Sciences, 49*(4), 701–706.

Brannick, M. E. (2015). Guidelines for forensic report writing: Helping trainees understand common pitfalls to improve reports. *Graduate School of Professional Psychology: Doctoral Papers and Masters Projects.* 63. https://digitalcommons.du.edu/capstone_masters/63

Brent, D. A. (1989). The psychological autopsy: Methodological considerations for the study of adolescent suicide. *Suicide & Life-Threatening Behavior, 19*(1), 43–57. https://doi.org/10.1111/j.1943-278x.1989.tb00365.x

Budowle, B., Murch, R., & Chakraborty, R. (2005). Microbial forensics: The next forensic challenge. *International Journal of Legal Medicine, 119*(6), 317–330. https://doi.org/10.1007/s00414-005-0535-y

Busey, T. A., & Parada, F. J. (2010). The nature of expertise in fingerprint examiners. *Psychonomic Bulletin & Review, 17*(2), 155–160. https://doi.org/10.3758/PBR.17.2.155

Campbell, R., Patterson, D., & Lichty, L. F. (2005). The effectiveness of sexual assault nurse examiner (SANE) programs: A review of psychological, medical, legal, and community outcomes. *Trauma, Violence & Abuse, 6*(4), 313–329. https://doi.org/10.1177/1524838005280328

Cao, K., & Jain, A. K. (2019). Automated latent fingerprint recognition. *IEEE Transactions on Pattern Analysis and Machine Intelligence, 41*(4), 788–800. https://doi.org/10.1109/TPAMI.2018.2818162

Cavanagh, J. T., Carson, A. J., Sharpe, M., & Lawrie, S. M. (2003). Psychological autopsy studies of suicide: A systematic review. *Psychological Medicine, 33*(3), 395–405. https://doi.org/10.1017/s0033291702006943

Cecchetto, G., Giraudo, C., Amagliani, A., Viel, G., Fais, P., Cavarzeran, F., Feltrin, G., Ferrara, S. D., & Montisci, M. (2011). Estimation of the firing distance through micro-CT analysis of gunshot wounds. *International Journal of Legal Medicine, 125*(2), 245–251. https://doi.org/10.1007/s00414-010-0533-6

Chen, H., Shi, M., Ma, R., & Zhang, M. (2021). Advances in fingermark age determination techniques. *The Analyst, 146*(1), 33–47. https://doi.org/10.1039/d0an01423k

Chopin, J., & Beauregard, E. (2020). Elderly sexual abuse: An examination of the criminal event. *Sexual Abuse: A Journal of Research and Treatment, 32*(6), 706–726. https://doi.org/10.1177/1079063219843899

Chopin, J., & Beauregard, E. (2021). Sexual abuse of elderly victims investigated by the police: From motives to crime characteristics. *Journal of Interpersonal Violence, 36*(13–14), 6722–6744. https://doi.org/10.1177/0886260518821456

de Vries, M. L., Dorn, T., Eppink, M., & Reijnders, U. (2019). Forensic nursing education and practice in the Netherlands: Where are we at? *Journal of Forensic Nursing, 15*(2), 78–83. https://doi.org/10.1097/JFN.0000000000000235

Edgardh, K., von Krogh, G., & Ormstad, K. (1999). Adolescent girls investigated for sexual abuse: History, physical findings and legal outcome. *Forensic Science International, 104*(1), 1–15. https://doi.org/10.1016/s0379-0738(99)00093-6

Euteneuer, J., & Courts, C. (2021). Ten years of molecular ballistics-a review and a field guide. *International Journal of Legal Medicine, 135*(4), 1121–1136. https://doi.org/10.1007/s00414-021-02523-0

Euteneuer, J., Gosch, A., Cachée, P., & Courts, C. (2020). A distant relationship?-investigation of correlations between DNA isolated from backspatter traces recovered from firearms, wound profile characteristics, and shooting distance. *International Journal of Legal Medicine, 134*(5), 1619–1628. https://doi.org/10.1007/s00414-020-02374-1

Galinari, L. S., & Bazon, M. R. (2021). Criminal behavior and psychosocial risk factors in Brazilian adolescent offenders: An exploratory latent class analysis. *International Journal of Environmental Research and Public Health, 18*(19), 10509. https://doi.org/10.3390/ijerph181910509

Gitto, L., Arunkumar, P., Segovia, A., Filkins, J. A., Formica, M. K., & Serinelli, S. (2021). Anatomical distribution and autopsy features of gunshot injuries to support the manner of death. *Journal of Forensic and Legal Medicine, 79*, 102135. https://doi.org/10.1016/j.jflm.2021.102135copyright

Goodman-Delahunty, J., & Dhami, M. K. (2013). A forensic examination of court reports. *Australian Psychologist, 48*, 32–40.

Grabmüller, M., Schyma, C., Euteneuer, J., Madea, B., & Courts, C. (2015). Simultaneous analysis of nuclear and mitochondrial DNA, mRNA and miRNA from backspatter from inside parts of firearms generated by shots at "triple contrast" doped ballistic models. *Forensic Science, Medicine, and Pathology, 11*(3), 365–375. https://doi.org/10.1007/s12024-015-9695-3

Griffith, E., Stankovic, A., & Baranoski, M. (2010). Conceptualizing the forensic psychiatry report as performative narrative. *The Journal of the American Academy of Psychiatry and the Law, 38*, 32–42.

Grisso, T. (2010). Guidance for improving forensic reports: A review of common errors. *Open Access Journal of Forensic Psychology, 2*, 102–115.

Hawton, K., Appleby, L., Platt, S., Foster, T., Cooper, J., Malmberg, A., & Simkin, S. (1998). The psychological autopsy approach to studying suicide: A review of methodological issues. *Journal of Affective Disorders, 50*(2–3), 269–276. https://doi.org/10.1016/s0165-0327(98)00033-0

Isometsä, E. T. (2001). Psychological autopsy studies–A review. *European Psychiatry: The Journal of the Association of European Psychiatrists, 16*(7), 379–385. https://doi.org/10.1016/s0924-9338(01)00594-6. PMID: 11728849.

Jain, A. K., & Feng, J. (2009). Latent palmprint matching. *IEEE Transactions on Pattern Analysis and Machine Intelligence, 31*(6), 1032–1047. https://doi.org/10.1109/TPAMI.2008.242

Jain, A. K., & Feng, J. (2011). Latent fingerprint matching. *IEEE Transactions on Pattern Analysis and Machine Intelligence, 33*(1), 88–100. https://doi.org/10.1109/TPAMI.2010.59

Kahana, T., & Hiss, J. (1999). Forensic radiology. *The British Journal of Radiology, 72*(854), 129–133. https://doi.org/10.1259/bjr.72.854.10365061

Katz, C., Paddon, M. J., & Barnetz, Z. (2016). Emotional language used by victims of alleged sexual abuse during forensic investigation. *Journal of Child Sexual Abuse, 25*(3), 243–261. https://doi.org/10.1080/10538712.2016.1137666

Keary, K., & Fitzpatrick, C. (1994). Children's disclosure of sexual abuse during formal investigation. *Child Abuse & Neglect, 18*(7), 543–548. https://doi.org/10.1016/0145-2134(94)90080-9

Kent-Wilkinson, A. E. (2010). Forensic psychiatric/mental health nursing: Responsive to social need. *Issues in Mental Health Nursing, 31*(6), 425–431. https://doi.org/10.3109/01612840903506444

King, W. R., Campbell, B. A., Matusiak, M. C., & Katz, C. M. (2017). Forensic evidence and criminal investigations: The impact of ballistics information on the investigation of violent crime in nine cities. *Journal of Forensic Sciences, 62*(4), 874–880. https://doi.org/10.1111/1556-4029.13380. PMID: 28111739.

Kislov, M. A., Chauhan, M., Zakharov, S. N., Leonov, S. V., & Shakiryanova, Y. P. (2021). Computer assisted three-dimensional reconstruction of scene in firearm homicide. *The Medico-Legal Journal, 89*(3), 193–198. https://doi.org/10.1177/00258172211018359

Kocsis, R. N. (2003). Criminal psychological profiling: Validities and abilities. *International Journal of Offender Therapy and Comparative Criminology, 47*(2), 126–144. https://doi.org/10.1177/0306624X03251092

Kocsis, R. N., & Cooksey, R. W. (2002). Criminal psychological profiling of serial arson crimes. *International Journal of Offender Therapy and Comparative Criminology, 46*(6), 631–656. https://doi.org/10.1177/0306624X02238159

Kocsis, R. N., Cooksey, R. W., & Irwin, H. J. (2002). Psychological profiling of offender characteristics from crime behaviors in serial rape offences. *International Journal of Offender Therapy and Comparative Criminology, 46*(2), 144–169. https://doi.org/10.1177/0306624X02462003

Kunz, S. N., Meyer, H. J., & Kraus, S. (2013). Gerichtsmedizinische Aspekte suizidaler Schussverletzungen–eine Übersichtsarbeit am Beispiel Deutschlands [Forensic aspects of gunshot suicides in Germany]. *Wiener Medizinische Wochenschrift (1946), 163*(23–24), 541–548. https://doi.org/10.1007/s10354-013-0227-z

Leadbetter, M. J. (2005). Fingerprint evidence in England and Wales–The revised standard. *Medicine, Science, and the Law, 45*(1), 1–6. https://doi.org/10.1258/rsmmsl.45.1.1

Lieb, R., Berliner, L., & Toth, P. (1997). *Protocols and training standards: Investigating allegations of child sexual abuse*. Washington State Institute of Public Policy. 97-01-4101.

Looijmans, M., van Bergen, D., Gilissen, R., Popma, A., Balt, E., Creemers, D., van Domburgh, L., Mulder, W., Rasing, S., & Mérelle, S. (2021). Additional value of peer informants in psychological autopsy studies of youth suicides. *Qualitative Health Research, 31*(11), 2056–2068. https://doi.org/10.1177/10497323211022316

Luca, I. (2012). Technical interpretation of firearms marks problems solved by forensic ballistics. *International Journal of Criminal Investigation, 2*(2), 119–125.

Ludes, B., Geraut, A., Väli, M., Cusack, D., Ferrara, D., Keller, E., Mangin, P., & Vieira, D. N. (2018). Guidelines examination of victims of sexual assault harmonization of forensic and medico-legal examination of persons. *International Journal of Legal Medicine, 132*(6), 1671–1674. https://doi.org/10.1007/s00414-018-1791-y

Meilia, P., Freeman, M. D., & Herkutanto, & Zeegers, M. P. (2020). A review of causal inference in forensic medicine. *Forensic Science, Medicine, and Pathology, 16*(2), 313–320. https://doi.org/10.1007/s12024-020-00220-9

Merriam-Webster. (n.d.). Forensic science. In *Merriam-Webster.com medical dictionary*. Retrieved 28 May 2022, from https://www.merriam-webster.com/medical/forensic%20science

Ministry of Health & Family Welfare, Govorment of India. (2014).

Molina, D. K., & DiMaio, V. J. (2008). Rifle wounds: A review of range and location as pertaining to manner of death. *The American Journal of Forensic Medicine and Pathology, 29*(3), 201–205. https://doi.org/10.1097/PAF.0b013e31818345a5

Molina, D. K., Wood, L. E., & DiMaio, V. J. (2007). Shotgun wounds: A review of range and location as pertaining to manner of death. *The American Journal of Forensic Medicine and Pathology, 28*(2), 99–102. https://doi.org/10.1097/01.paf.0000257415.82728.d7

Molina, D. K., DiMaio, V. J., & Cave, R. (2013). Handgun wounds: A review of range and location as pertaining to manner of death. *The American Journal of Forensic Medicine and Pathology, 34*(4), 342–347. https://doi.org/10.1097/PAF.0000000000000048

Neri, M., Turillazzi, E., Riezzo, I., & Fineschi, V. (2007). The determination of firing distance applying a microscopic quantitative method and confocal laser scanning microscopy for detection of gunshot residue particles. *International Journal of Legal Medicine, 121*(4), 287–292. https://doi.org/10.1007/s00414-006-0110-1

Pouliot, L., & De Leo, D. (2006). Critical issues in psychological autopsy studies. *Suicide & Life-Threatening Behavior, 36*(5), 491–510. https://doi.org/10.1521/suli.2006.36.5.491

Resnick, P. J., & Soliman, S. (2012). Planning, writing, and editing forensic psychiatric reports. *International Journal of Law and Psychiatry, 35*, 412–417.

Reynolds, A. (2010). Forensic radiography: An overview. *Radiologic Technology, 81*(4), 361–379.

Scott, C. L., Swartz, E., & Warburton, K. (2006). The psychological autopsy: Solving the mysteries of death. *The Psychiatric Clinics of North America, 29*(3), 805–822. https://doi.org/10.1016/j.psc.2006.04.003

Tangen, J. M., Kent, K. M., & Searston, R. A. (2020). Collective intelligence in fingerprint analysis. *Cognitive Research: Principles and Implications, 5*(1), 23. https://doi.org/10.1186/s41235-020-00223-8

Thompson, M. B., & Tangen, J. M. (2014). The nature of expertise in fingerprint matching: Experts can do a lot with a little. *PLoS One, 9*(12), e114759. https://doi.org/10.1371/journal.pone.0114759

Thompson, M. B., Tangen, J. M., & McCarthy, D. J. (2014). Human matching performance of genuine crime scene latent fingerprints. *Law and Human Behavior, 38*(1), 84–93. https://doi.org/10.1037/lhb0000051

Tu, W. Q., & Zhao, H. (2009). Psychological autopsy and its limitation in application. *Fa Yi Xue Za Zhi, 25*(5), 380–382.

Tuğcu, H., Yorulmaz, C., Bayraktaroğlu, G., Uner, H. B., Karslioğlu, Y., Koç, S., Ulukan, M. O., & Celasun, B. (2005). Determination of gunshot residues with image analysis: An experimental study. *Military Medicine, 170*(9), 802–805. https://doi.org/10.7205/milmed.170.9.802

Tugcu, H., Yorulmaz, C., Karslioglu, Y., Uner, H. B., Koc, S., Ozdemir, C., Ozaslan, A., & Celasun, B. (2006). Image analysis as an adjunct to sodium rhodizonate test in the evaluation of gunshot residues: An experimental study. *The American Journal of Forensic Medicine and Pathology, 27*(4), 296–299. https://doi.org/10.1097/01.paf.0000248739.79253.25

Ubomír, M., Dana, K., Ján, Š., Roman, K., & Jozef, Š. (2021). Aspects of forensic entomology in forensic medicine. Aspekty forenznej entomológie v súdnom lekárstve. *Soudni Lekarstvi, 66*(3), 39–42.

Ulrich, A., Moor, C., Vonmont, H., Jordi, H. R., & Lory, M. (2004). ICP-MS trace-element analysis as a forensic tool. *Analytical and Bioanalytical Chemistry, 378*(4), 1059–1068. https://doi.org/10.1007/s00216-003-2434-8

Verde, A., & Nurra, A. (2010). Criminal profiling as a plotting activity based on abductive processes. *International Journal of Offender Therapy and Comparative Criminology, 54*(5), 829–849. https://doi.org/10.1177/0306624X09339175

Walters, M., & Liscio, E. (2020). The accuracy and repeatability of reconstructing single bullet impacts using the 2D ellipse method. *Journal of Forensic Sciences, 65*(4), 1120–1127. https://doi.org/10.1111/1556-4029.14309copyright

Wettstein, R. M. (2004). The forensic examination and report. In R. I. Simon & L. H. Gold (Eds.), *Textbook of forensic psychiatry*. American Psychiatric Publishing.

Wilshire, B. (1996). Advances in fingerprint detection. *Endeavour, 20*(1), 12–15. https://doi.org/10.1016/0160-9327(96)10005-3

Yanai, K., Kodama, H., & Tsunematsu, K. (2012). A new role of nursing in violence: A reconsideration of nursing of victims. *Journal of UOEH, 34*(4), 339–351. https://doi.org/10.7888/juoeh.34.339

Yaremchuk, V. O. (2019). The use of medical knowledge in the crime investigation. *Wiadomosci Lekarskie (Warsaw, Poland: 1960), 72*(1), 103–106.

Chapter 21
Medical and Psychological Management of Victimization

Nitha Thomas and Avinash G. Kamath

The scientific study of victims known as 'victimology' was developed as a specialization of criminology. Policymakers and the criminal justice system had traditionally focused on crime- incidence and prevalence of crime, patterns of criminal activity, and profile of offenders. Since the criminal justice system focuses on preventing and responding to crime, early research was on crime and offenders. Victimology is an interdisciplinary field influenced by psychology, law, criminology, sociology, political science, and anthropology. Developments in the field of victimology, delineating themselves from criminology, showcase a radical shift in focus from offender to the victim or survivor (Clevenger et al., 2018).

General victimology focuses on all victims regardless of the causative factors. Victimology studies also can have a narrower focus on victims of crimes or human rights victims. Violent crimes like assault, murder, or rape instil fear and helplessness, are often unpredictable and cause psychological and physical damage to the victims. Victims are often unable to use their existing psychological and physical resources to cope with the impact of crime (Echeburúa et al., 2003; Kilpatrick et al., 1989). The words survivor and victim have different connotations. The word 'victim' is associated with pity and helplessness, while 'survivor' is associated with self-efficacy. Most of the literature from criminology uses the word victim, whereas research literature on mental health usually uses survivor.

This chapter focuses on the psychological consequences of criminal victimization and its management. Criminal victimization is a complex and often traumatic experience of psychological pain, physical harm, and material loss, often because of another's actions. Criminal victimization is associated with short-term and

N. Thomas (✉)
Private Practice, Udupi, Karnataka, India

A. G. Kamath
Department of Psychiatry, KMC Manipal Academy of Higher Education, Manipal, Karnataka, India

© The Author(s), under exclusive license to Springer Nature Switzerland AG 2022
R. T. Gopalan (ed.), *Victimology*, https://doi.org/10.1007/978-3-031-12930-8_21

long-term impacts on physical and mental health. Longitudinal studies show that these effects last for more than a year. Victims of crimes report experiencing frustration, anger, sadness, and fear. Victimization can also change behaviours, for instance, avoiding certain situations and places. Criminal victimization also increases the risk of substance abuse and further victimization (Hanson et al., 2010; Janssen et al., 2021; Rühs et al., 2017).

Types of Crime and Victimization

Victimization can happen in various contexts of gender, socio-ethnic background, living circumstances, confirming or divergent views towards religious practices, and attitudes regarding social environment and peers. These impact the likelihood of victimization or how the individual perceives the event. These subjective factors and contexts can determine attitude toward reporting the crime and the impact of victimization. Conventional criminal victimization can include robbery, vandalism, physical assault, sexual assault, and kidnapping. It is important to understand child victimization in more detail as some of the effects of these adverse childhood experiences (ACE) are associated with long-term adverse physical and psychological outcomes. How children respond to trauma can be different from adults. Severe trauma in children also has a developmental impact. It is also important to remember that in children, victimization occurs by witnessing crime or assault of any kind happening to others or on TV (Monnat & Chandler, 2015; Ruback & Thompson, 2001).

Several terms are used to explain the experience of victimization. Primary victimization results from the direct result of the trauma. There is a higher chance of re-victimization immediate or later in life. This kind of re-victimization can especially be traumatic among victims of sexual abuse. There may be multiple environmental, social, and inter- and intrapersonal factors that can increase the risks of re-victimization. Poly-victimization refers to the experience of multiple types of victimization, such as sexual abuse, physical abuse, neglect, bullying, and exposure to family violence versus multiple episodes of the same kind of victimization (Le et al., 2018; Oram et al., 2017; Ruback & Thompson, 2001).

Victim blaming, inappropriate post-assault behaviour or language by medical personnel, law enforcement professionals, or other organizations with which the victim has contact may further add to the victim's suffering. Victims may also experience secondary victimization by justice system personnel upon entering the criminal justice system. Victims will lose time, suffer reductions in income, and often get ignored by bailiffs and other courthouse staff. They will remain uninformed about updates in the case, such as hearing postponements, to the extent that their frustration and confusion will turn to apathy and a declining willingness to further participate in system proceedings (Ruback & Thompson, 2001).

Most victimization data and its impact come from national crime records and national victimization surveys. The Uniform Crime Reports in the USA and National Crime Records Bureau in India collate reported criminal activities. Crime record data focuses on the offender and crime rather than the victim. On the other hand, victimization surveys are cross-sectional or longitudinal survey research of the general population collecting information about exposure to criminal activities. The victimization surveys attempt to capture the missing data since many victims, especially victims of sexual assault and domestic violence, may not inform law enforcement agencies regarding the crime.

The National Crime Record Bureau, India (NCRB) collates data about reported crimes in India and publishes them yearly. NCRB records show that 66,01,285 cognizable crimes comprising 42,54,356 Indian Penal Code (IPC) crimes and 23,46,929 Special & Local Laws (SLL) crimes got registered in 2020. It shows an increase of 28.0% in the registration of cases over 2019. The crime rate registered per lakh population has increased from 385.5% in 2019 to 487.8% in 2020. A total of 10,47,216 cases of offences affecting the human body got registered, which accounted for 24.6% of total IPC crimes during 2020, out of which 55.3% cases were of hurt (5,78,641 cases), followed by cases of causing death by negligence (1,26,779 cases, 12.1%), and cases of assault on women with intent to outrage their modesty (85,392 cases, 8.2%) (Crime In India, 2020).

Impact of Victimization

Early research on the impact of violence exposure started with the research on the impact of war and later expanded to include the victimization of violent crimes. Victimization impacts the individual, family, and community. The immediate, short-term, and long-term impact of victimization can vary for the individual victim. Victims' thoughts, emotions, and actions can also change as time passes. Friends and family may also respond to the victimization of a loved one in myriad ways, affecting how they interact with the victim. Victimization has both physical and psychological consequences for the victims. One major factor that affects the gravity of the impact of victimization is the type of violent crime. Other factors include gender, age, and sexual orientation of the victim. Precrime functioning of the victim, the relationship between the perpetrator and the victim, and the social support available to the victim are other factors that influence the impact of victimization (Ruback & Thompson, 2014; Sharkey, 2018).

Victims report physical injuries, physical reactions, and sensations during the victimization (e.g. violent assault) or after the realization of victimization (e.g. burglary). Victims may experience shock, disbelief, numbness, depersonalization, or derealization. Fight, flight, or freeze responses are common in victims of violent crime. Autonomic hyperarousal symptoms like increased heart rate, sweating, trembling and hyperventilation, and, at times, losing bowel and bladder control are also reported by victims. Some victims also report difficulties with sleep, headache, loss of appetite, loss of libido, tiredness, nausea, and muscle tension in the immediate aftermath of victimization. These bodily symptoms recur even months after a traumatic event without any obvious cues for many victims (Golding, 1994; Pegram & Abbey, 2019; Tan & Haining, 2016; Ullman & Brecklin, 2003; Young, 1993).

Mental Health Consequences of Victimization

Even though the type of crime can affect the extent of physical and psychological consequences of victimization, victimization can result in various psychological consequences. Some of the common psychiatric diagnoses associated with violent crime victimization are acute stress disorder and post-traumatic stress disorder (PTSD). Research has shown that the prevalence of PTSD is higher among victims of violent crimes than victims of other traumatic events, especially among women victims of violent crime (Guay et al., 2016, 2019; Kilpatrick & Acierno, 2003; Tolin & Foa, 2006). Victimization of violent crimes increases the chances of depression, suicide, anxiety, and psychotic disorders (Fazel et al., 2010, 2014, 2015). A metanalytic study reported that domestic violence victims are seven times more likely to have PTSD, four times more likely to have anxiety, and three times more likely to have depression (Trevillion et al., 2012). Substance use and dependence are also associated with violent offending. Interestingly, both men and women victims of violent crime had increased rates of substance use disorders (Seid et al., 2021).

Another source of evidence for the impact of violent victimization is studies that have looked at exposure to violence among people seeking mental health services. Thirty percent of the 146 women admitted to a psychiatric hospital in India reported experiencing sexual coercion, and half of them had not talked about their experience to anyone (Chandra et al., 2003; Oram et al., 2013, 2017).

Victimization is also associated with cognitive changes in the person and their loved ones. Research has highlighted how exposure to violent crime can alter schemas and core beliefs about self, others, the world, and the future. For instance, the experience of shame and blaming the self is a common reaction to trauma. Children who were victims of bullying, sexual assault, and domestic violence report self-blame The self-blame exists in the context of 'just world belief' that most people hold—'good things happen to good people, and the bad things happen to bad people. When a violent act or crime threatens this belief (Bhuptani & Messman, 2021; Chen & Chen, 2019; Karakurt et al., 2014; Moulding et al., 2015), the individual attempts to protect the same belief by attributing the blame to self—'It happened because "I" was bad or It happened because "I" was alone' (Grove, 2020; Lerner, 2000). Survivors of violent crime also often report an increase in fear of crime (Hale, 1996; Scherg & Ejrnæs, 2021; Sookram et al., 2011). Research has also highlighted that children and women who experience sexual assault are at a higher risk of re-victimization (Walker et al., 2019).

A survey of more than 2500 American participants selected from the general public revealed that 89% of them have experienced traumatic experiences, and the lifetime prevalence of PTSD was 8.3% (Kilpatrick et al., 2013). However, the prevalence rate of PTSD went up to 23% in a study of people who needed medical care for their physical injuries (Zatzick et al., 2007). Research has identified an even higher prevalence of PTSD in victims of violent crime—17.8–38.5% (Guay et al., 2019; Kilpatrick & Acierno, 2003). Victims of violent crime may experience stigma and face victim-blaming, apart from trauma's psychological and physical impact. Such stigma is especially true in the case of survivors of sexual assault and domestic violence. It could be a part of the reason for higher rates of PTSD and other psychiatric morbidities in women who have experienced sexual assault (Tolin & Foa, 2006).

Many victims of violent crime may have experienced another traumatic or abusive event before. Exposure to prolonged or multiple traumatic events is called complex trauma from which there is no escape. Experiencing complex traumas in the past can influence the victim's decision to report the crime or seek help. Complex trauma can also increase the risk for other psychological problems. Victims of violent crime may not always seek help or even inform their mental health care provider about the experience of victimization. Experiencing violent victimization, often at the hands of known perpetrators, might make trusting and seeking help from others and professional help more difficult. Considering the importance of social support in recovery from PTSD, victims' difficulty in trusting and help-seeking can influence how they make sense of the traumatic experience (Chandra et al., 2003; Guay et al., 2006, 2019).

General Guidelines for Working with Victims of Violent Crimes

Medical providers, mental health professionals, and law enforcement agencies should heed the victim's need to feel safe, express feelings and know what comes next. Declaration of Basic Principles of Justice for Victims of Crime and Abuse of Power Adopted by General Assembly resolution 40/34 of November 29, 1985, of the WHO defines a victim and provides provisions for victims and their families irrespective of whether the perpetrator is identified, apprehended, or prosecuted. It clearly states that making these provisions irrespective of race, colour, age, language, religion, nationality, or other differences in beliefs or practices. The resolution speaks about victims of abuse of power needing stringent laws and legislative revisions from time to time. It attempts to keep up with the internationally recognized norms relating to human rights. The resolution highlights the need for medical, psychological, and social support for the victims of violent crime.

1. Access to just and fair treatment: Right to dignity and respect, need for fair, expeditious, fair, inexpensive, and accessible redressal mechanisms for quick and prompt action, access to information about the status of the investigation, and further legal procedures and process. The victim also needs access to informal means to resolve disputes like mediation and arbitration.

2. Restitution: Return of property, payment or satisfactory restoration of damages caused due to victimization, and payment for loss or harm suffered.
3. Compensation: When restitution is not adequate, or compensation by other means is not possible, financial compensation should be endeavoured by the state
4. Assistance: Victims should receive the necessary material, medical, psychological, and social assistance through governmental, voluntary, community-based, and indigenous means. It emphasizes the need for the availability of trained personnel sensitized to the victims' issues and for identifying individuals with special needs (Declaration of Basic Principles of Justice for Victims of Crime and Abuse of Power, 1985).

Mental Health Interventions for Victims of Violent Crime

The Immediate Aftermath of Victimization

The priority in terms of management is to ensure the victim's safety. The first responders should ensure that the victim receives adequate medical attention as soon as possible. Training medical and nursing staff in the emergency department in trauma-informed care can help prevent secondary injury to victims. It can also sensitize the emergency or critical care team to the need to refer victims of violent crime to mental health services.

One of the choices the victim has to make immediately is whether to report to the law enforcement agency or not. Data from the victimization survey indicates that police reports account for only half of the crimes reported. Victims cite many reasons, including crime not completed, lack of proof, fear of media attention, and fear of reliving the experience as reasons for not reporting the crime. Family members' and friends' response also influences the decision to report the crime.

Some studies report that victims may feel good about reporting the crime, especially if the offender is apprehended or if they receive restitution (Frieze et al., 1987, Ruback & Thompson, 2001). On the other hand, reporting can also make the victim feel worse, especially if the law enforcement personnel are harsh and unsympathetic. The fear of this second injury is more apparent in sexual assault and partner violence cases and cases where children or LGBTQ persons are the victims.

A mental health professional can assist survivors and families in a supportive role to facilitate the decision to report the crime. For instance, in our work with sexual assault survivors, we have noticed that the survivors are not in a frame of mind in the immediate aftermath of the assault to decide to report or not. On the other hand, there is a need to collect physical evidence from a legal point of view as soon as possible. Many survivors freeze at the need for a physical examination which they perceive as invasive. The situation is especially tricky as the survivor is in the emergency room, and the land law demands mandatory reporting of crimes. The mental health professional can present the option of reporting the crime to the police and respectfully and non-judgementally listen to the survivor's decision. The mental health professional can inform the survivor of the option of collecting evidence at present and deciding on reporting the crime later. Mental health professionals can support survivors in this turbulent time and remind them that they can make whatever decision they feel is right. Likewise, in our work with children and adolescents, we inform the families of the mandatory reporting of sexual abuse (under the POCSO act*) and help the family and the young person cope with the legal system (Renu & Chopra, 2019). Ensuring client safety and wellbeing while navigating the limitations of client confidentiality and mandatory reporting of crime is an act of delicate balancing for the mental health professional.

Psychological Debriefing

Psychological debriefing interventions usually involve providing emotional and psychological support immediately after the traumatic event. These sessions are usually done in groups and as single sessions of 1–3 h. Debriefing interventions are sometimes called crisis intervention, group debriefing, and process debriefing. The effectiveness of psychological debriefing in preventing PTSD is dubious. The meta-analysis by van Emmerik et al. (2002) and others and the Cochrane reviews (2002) report that debriefing interventions may interfere with natural recovery from trauma and worsen trauma symptoms. The division 12 website of the American Psychological Association considers debriefing as a potentially harmful treatment. NICE guidelines also advocate against psychological debriefing (NICE, 2018; Rose et al., 2002; Society of Clinical Psychology Division 12 American Psychological Association, n.d.; van Emmerik et al., 2002).

Psychological First Aid

Psychological first aid evolved in the aftermath of 9/11 and is now one of the standard services offered to victims of natural disasters, mass violence, and terrorism. There are many models of psychological first aid catering to the needs of different populations, and discussing all of them in-depth is beyond the scope of this chapter. Non-mental health professionals like trained disaster volunteers, teachers, lay counsellors, and first responders deliver PFA. The five common elements of psychological first aid are

1. Safety
2. Calming
3. Connectedness
4. Self- efficacy
5. Hope

Unlike debriefing, psychological first aid does not involve the discussion of traumatic experiences. Instead, PFA involves active listening with compassion, increasing social support, and assistance with coping. PFA is recommended by disaster mental health experts and in many guidelines of PTSD treatments across the globe as an early intervention for survivors. Even though the treatment providers and disaster experts rapidly accept psychological first aid, this needs to be backed by solid research evidence (Dieltjens et al., 2014; Fox et al., 2012; Hobfoll et al., 2007).

Psychological Approaches to Trauma

Cognitive Behavioural Approaches

Cognitive Behaviour Therapy is a kind of psychotherapy that focuses on the relationship between thoughts, emotions, and actions. Variants for CBT for PTSD include primarily behavioural approaches like prolonged exposure therapy, more cognitively oriented approaches like cognitive processing therapy, and adaptations of CBT for youth. Apart from the information processing model and cognitive specificity model of CBT, theoretical models of emotional processing and social cognitive theory also are used to conceptualize PTSD and other responses to trauma in CBT.

In general, CBT for trauma involves helping the person face trauma reminders to decrease distress. CBT approaches generally include psychoeducation, cognitive restructuring, coping skills, and other strategies to manage anxiety. Exposure to traumatic memory usually involves in vivo exposure, imaginal exposure, written accounts of trauma or audiotape, and reading of trauma narrative. Treatment also attempts to help people discriminate between then and now in terms of trauma triggers. Cognitive restructuring techniques focus on the content of cognitions, change in cognitions about the self, world, and others, and guilt. Some variants of CBT also attempt to address comorbid substance use and other problems with PTSD (Ramirez de Arellano et al., 2014; Watkins et al., 2018; Zlotnick et al., 2009).

Prolonged Exposure Therapy

Emotion processing theory posits that fear structure in memory includes information about stimuli causing fear, responses of escape and avoidance, and the meaning of the fear. The usual fear structure is mostly an accurate reflection of reality and is adaptive. Emotional processing theory predicts that emotional processing of traumatic events does not happen at the time of the event. Associations in pathological fear structure often distort reality (association between elements of stimuli is distorted) and may include extreme response elements. Safe elements of stimuli and response may also be associated with meanings of danger. Chronic escape or avoidance also means that the person never learns new information to change the fear structure. Emotional processing theory argues that exposure to feared stimuli can change the relationships in these networks (Foa et al., 2007).

Emotional processing theory offers the rationale for prolonged exposure (PE) treatment for trauma victims as a method to change fear structures. PE theorizes that treatment will work if fear structures in memory are activated, and new information incompatible with pathological fear structure gets incorporated into the fear structure. PE starts with psychoeducation about PTSD and common reactions to trauma. Exposure to PE can be in vivo and imaginal. Breathing retraining is also a component of PE. However, patients are taught not to use the skill during exposure. Homework usually involves listening to the audiotape of the trauma event narrative spoken in the present tense. One crucial treatment aim is habituation (Foa et al., 2007; Watkins et al., 2018).

Cognitive Processing Therapy

People often try to make sense of what happened after a traumatic experience. It is especially true in the case of victims of violent crimes like assault and rape. CPT is based on social cognitive theory, which attempts to explain how people understand and cope with traumatic experiences. Often, traumatic events can change cognitions about oneself, others, and the world, leading to maladaptive cognitive distortions. The CPT approach focuses on the content of cognition rather than emotional responses and behaviour (the result of distorted cognitions). To make sense of a traumatic experience, a survivor may assimilate, accommodate, or over-accommodate trauma information with existing schemas. Assimilation means a person changing new information to match the existing schemas ('Bad things happen to bad people. This happened to me, which means I am bad'). Accommodation involves changing old beliefs to include the new information from a traumatic experience (Even though I was not able to defend myself during the attack, most of the time, I take care of myself). As the name suggests, over-accommodation is changing cognitions to an extreme extent, often to prevent future traumatization (I cannot trust my judgement ever, or I can never trust anyone) (Resick et al., 2006).

In CPT, therapists aim for survivors to balance their beliefs about themselves, the world, and others while considering the traumatic experience. In other words, accommodation of trauma-related cognitions is important. Focus is on effective expression rather than habituation to trauma cues. CPT has both exposure and cognitive therapy components. CPT includes psychoeducation, exploring why the event occurred, and how the event has changed beliefs about self, others, and the world (Resick et al., 2016).

Trauma-Focused CBT

Trauma-focused CBT is an adaptation of CBT for children, adolescents, and their families. TF CBT approach considers the developing nature of emotion regulation and coping skills in children and adolescents. TF CBT also considers the importance of parents and families for children. Like CPT and PE, psychoeducation about the impact of trauma is an integral part of TF CBT. Other strategies include exposure, body safety training, and coping skills. TF CBT also has interventions targeted at the parents (Cohen et al., 2012).

Eye Movement Desensitization and Reprocessing Therapy (EMDR)

EMDR, developed by Francine Shapiro, is a fast-growing approach to trauma and PTSD. The adaptive information processing (AIP) model emphasizes a person's resources and argues that the human brain can usually completely integrate stressful information. When there is an impairment to the information processing system, memory is stored as raw and unprocessed and is often maladaptive. AIP argues that incompletely processed dysfunctional memories are implicated in the aetiology of PTSD. EMDR focuses directly on the memory, attempting to change how the memory is stored rather than focusing on thoughts, emotions, or behavioural responses to traumatic experiences like CBT approaches. There are no prolonged exposure techniques, detailed descriptions of trauma, or cognitive restructuring. Instead, guided visualizations and eye movements facilitate the processing of traumatic memories. Accelerated resolution therapy, a briefer therapy derived from EMDR, also uses guided visualization and eye movements. ART also relies on in vivo exposure and image rescripting. ART, like EMDR, does not give importance to detailed trauma descriptions in recovery (Hase, 2021; Hase et al., 2017; Howe et al., 2018; Kip et al., 2013; Waits et al., 2017).

Other Therapies

TF CBT, CPT, and EMDR are trauma-focused therapies. There is some evidence for non-trauma-focused approaches as well. Person-centred therapy (PCT) is a non-trauma-focused approach that focuses on psychoeducation, problem-solving, and changing maladaptive behavioural patterns. This approach does not use exposure and cognitive restructuring. Brief eclectic therapy for PTSD uses both psychodynamic and cognitive behavioural strategies. This treatment focuses on accepting the emotions and reality of the event and its impact on survivors' lives. Therapy involves clients talking about trauma in the present tense, exploring trauma triggers and practising relaxation. Therapy also focuses on exploring how trauma has changed the survivor. Narrative Exposure Therapy is another brief intervention that helps survivors construct a coherent narrative of their life that helps to place the traumatic event in the context of their life (Belsher et al., 2019; Classen et al., 2011; Gersons et al., 2020; Gersons & Schnyder, 2013; Miller & Davis, 2013).

Pharmacological Intervention for Trauma

Guidelines advocate avoiding medications to prevent PTSD. There is limited evidence for benzodiazepines, and considering the risk for abuse, most guidelines advocate against benzodiazepines. After careful discussion with the clients, clinicians should monitor for trauma symptoms and may start brief symptomatic treatment, especially in flashbacks, autonomic arousal, and nightmares. Medications like a low dose of risperidone and prazosin are used to manage autonomic arousal and nightmares. Some medications like propranolol, clonidine, guanfacine, quetiapine, valproate, and carbamazepine have limited utility, and the level of evidence is Grade IV in most studies (NICE, 2018; Strawn et al., 2010).

Research Evidence and Treatment Guidelines

NICE guidelines advocate monitoring for PTSD symptoms after 1 month of a traumatic incident. Research also advocates monitoring for depression, anxiety, substance use, and suicidal behaviour. Almost all the guidelines advise against debriefing. Research specifically from victims of violent crimes also indicates the futility of debriefing (American Psychological Association, n.d.; Rose et al., 2002; van Emmerik et al., 2002).

In the case of shared trauma, a group trauma-focused CBT can be considered to prevent PTSD. Individual trauma-focused treatment, specifically trauma-focused CBT, is recommended to treat children and adolescents with PTSD. EMDR can be offered to children and adolescents (7–17 years) if they do not respond to or engage with TF-CBT. In the case of adults with acute stress disorder, trauma-focused interventions like cognitive processing therapy, cognitive therapy for PTSD, and prolonged exposure therapy help prevent PTSD. Cochrane reviews also suggest evidence for trauma-focused CBT for people with acute traumatic stress symptoms (Roberts et al., 2010). EMDR is a treatment option for non-combat trauma-related PTSD (Jonathan et al., 2013; NICE, 2018). American psychological association strongly recommends cognitive behavioural therapy, cognitive therapy, cognitive processing therapy, and prolonged exposure therapy to treat PTSD. APA conditionally recommends brief eclectic therapy, eye movement desensitization and reprocessing therapy (EMDR) and narrative exposure therapy (American Psychological Association, 2017).

Conclusion

Violence and crime can impact the physical and psychological health of victims. The criminal justice system and health care system need to address the needs of victims and survivors of violence. It would include policy-level changes, designing of effective services, and research. Most of our knowledge about the impact of violent victimization comes from cross-sectional surveys abroad. The discrepancy between reported crime rates and the crime victimization survey worldwide indicates that many victims find the legal and treatment services difficult and hostile. Whether a universal screening about victimization in mental health and medical health services will help bridge this gap is a matter of future research. There is a definite need to understand the impact of violent victimization, crime victims' felt need, and treatment strategies for crime victims. There is a dearth of literature specifically evaluating the psychological treatment of victimization. However, participants in many trauma treatment research trials are survivors of violent crime. Cognitive behavioural treatments and EMDR seem to be the most widely used treatments for trauma survivors for survivors of violent crime. There is a pressing need to disseminate trauma treatment research. Trauma treatment research and research on psychological management for violent victimization are scant in India. Psychosocial support for victims of violent crime should be accessible and affordable. Another factor to consider is the increased prevalence of victimization among severely mentally ill patients seeking mental health care. Many patients seeking mental healthcare do not inform their providers about violent victimization. There is a need to sensitize medical professionals, mental health professionals, and law enforcement professionals about working with victims. Considering the impact of violent victimization on victims' families, especially in a closely knitted community like India, we need to design programs that will address the needs of victims and their families.

References

American Psychological Association. (2017, July). *PTSD treatments*. https://www.apa.org/ptsd-guideline/treatments/index

American Psychological Association. (n.d.). *Psychological debriefing for post traumatic stress disorder*. Retrieved March 28, 2022, from https://div12.org/treatment/psychological-debriefing-for-post-traumatic-stress-disorder/

Belsher, B. E., Beech, E., Evatt, D., Smolenski, D. J., Shea, M. T., Otto, J. L., Rosen, C. S., & Schnurr, P. P. (2019). Present-centered therapy (PCT) for post-traumatic stress disorder (PTSD) in adults. *Cochrane Database of Systematic Reviews, 2019*(11), CD012898. https://doi.org/10.1002/14651858.CD012898.pub2

Bhuptani, P. H., & Messman, T. L. (2021). Role of blame and rape-related shame in distress among rape victims. *Psychological Trauma: Theory, Research, Practice, and Policy*. https://doi.org/10.1037/tra0001132

Chandra, P. S., Deepthivarma, S., Carey, M. P., Carey, K. B., & Shalinianant, M. P. (2003). A cry from the darkness: Women with severe mental illness in India reveal their experiences with sexual coercion. *Psychiatry, 66*(4), 323–334. https://doi.org/10.1521/psyc.66.4.323.25446

Chen, W. R., & Chen, L. M. (2019). Self-blame tendency of bullied victims in elementary and secondary schools. *Educational Studies, 45*(4), 480–496. https://doi.org/10.1080/03055698.2018.1509772

Classen, C. C., Palesh, O. G., Cavanaugh, C. E., Koopman, C., Kaupp, J. W., Kraemer, H. C., Aggarwal, R., & Spiegel, D. (2011). A comparison of trauma-focused and present-focused group therapy for survivors of childhood sexual abuse: A randomized controlled trial. *Psychological Trauma: Theory, Research, Practice, and Policy, 3*(1), 84. https://doi.org/10.1037/a0020096

Clevenger, S., Navarro, J. N., Marcum, C. D., & Higgins, G. E. (2018). Introduction to victimology. In *Understanding victimology. An active-learning approach* (pp. 1–19). Routledge.

Cohen, J. A., Mannarino, A. P., Kliethermes, M., & Murray, L. A. (2012). Trauma-focused CBT for youth with complex trauma. *Child Abuse & Neglect, 36*(6), 528–541. https://doi.org/10.1016/J.CHIABU.2012.03.007

Crime In India. (2020). *National crime records bureau.* https://ncrb.gov.in/sites/default/files/CII%202020%20Volume%201.pdf

Declaration of Basic Principles of Justice for Victims of Crime and Abuse of Power, General Assembly resolution 40/34. (1985). https://www.ohchr.org/en/instruments-mechanisms/instruments/declaration-basic-principles-justice-victims-crime-and-abuse

Dieltjens, T., Moonens, I., van Praet, K., de Buck, E., & Vekerckhove, P. (2014). A systematic literature search on psychological first aid: Lack of evidence to develop guidelines. *PLoS One, 9*(12), e114714. https://doi.org/10.1371/journal.pone.0114714

Echeburúa, E., de Corral, P., & Amor, P. J. (2003). Evaluation of psychological harm in the victims of violent crime. *Psychology in Spain, 7*(1), 10–18.

Fazel, S., Lichtenstein, P., Frisell, T., Grann, M., Goodwin, G., & Långström, N. (2010). Bipolar disorder and violent crime: Time at risk reanalysis. *Archives of General Psychiatry, 67*(12), 1325–1326. https://doi.org/10.1001/archgenpsychiatry.2010.171

Fazel, S., Wolf, A., Palm, C., & Lichtenstein, P. (2014). Violent crime, suicide, and premature mortality in patients with schizophrenia and related disorders: A 38-year total population study in Sweden. *The Lancet Psychiatry, 1*(1), 44–54. https://doi.org/10.1016/S2215-0366(14)70223-8

Fazel, S., Wolf, A., Chang, Z., Larsson, H., Goodwin, G. M., & Lichtenstein, P. (2015). Depression and violence: A Swedish population study. *The Lancet Psychiatry, 2*(3), 224–232. https://doi.org/10.1016/S2215-0366(14)00128-X

Foa, E., Hembree, E., & Rothbaum, B. O. (2007). *Prolonged exposure therapy for PTSD: Emotional processing of traumatic experiences therapist guide.* Oxford University Press.

Fox, J. H., Burkle, F. M., Bass, J., Pia, F. A., Epstein, J. L., & Markenson, D. (2012). The effectiveness of psychological first aid as a disaster intervention tool: Research analysis of peer-reviewed literature from 1990 to 2010. *Disaster Medicine and Public Health Preparedness, 6*(3), 247–252. https://doi.org/10.1001/dmp.2012.39

Frieze, I. H., Hymer, S., & Greenberg, M. S. (1987). Describing the crime victim: Psychological reactions to victimization. *Professional Psychology: Research and Practice, 18*(4), 299.

Gersons, B. P. R., & Schnyder, U. (2013). Learning from traumatic experiences with brief eclectic psychotherapy for PTSD. *European Journal of Psychotraumatology, 4*(1), 21369. https://doi.org/10.3402/ejpt.v4i0.21369

Gersons, B. P. R., Nijdam, M. J., Smid, G. E., & Meewisse, M.-L. (2020). Brief eclectic psychotherapy for PTSD. In L. F. Bufka, C. V. Wright, & R. W. Halfond (Eds.), *Casebook to the APA Clinical Practice Guideline for the treatment of PTSD* (pp. 139–161). American Psychological Association. https://doi.org/10.1037/0000196-007

Golding, J. M. (1994). Sexual assault history and physical health in randomly selected Los Angeles women. *Health Psychology, 13*(2), 130–138. https://doi.org/10.1037/0278-6133.13.2.130

Grove, L. C. (2020). Managing just world beliefs in an unjust world for victims of sexual violence. *Dissertation Abstracts International Section A: Humanities and Social Sciences, 81*(5-A), 11446. http://ovidsp.ovid.com/ovidweb.cgi?T=JS&PAGE=reference&D=psyc17&NEWS=N&AN=2020-04052-011

Guay, S., Billette, V., & Marchand, A. (2006). Exploring the links between posttraumatic stress disorder and social support: Processes and potential research avenues. *Journal of Traumatic Stress, 19*(3), 327–338. https://doi.org/10.1002/jts.20124

Guay, S., Gravel-Crevier, M., Boyer, R., & Marchand, A. (2016). Acute stress disorder diagnosis, clusters, and symptoms as predictors of posttraumatic stress disorder, and gender differences in victims of violent crimes. In G. El-Baalbaki & C. Fortin (Eds.), *A multidimensional approach to post-traumatic stress disorder – From theory to practice.* Intech open. https://doi.org/10.5772/64900

Guay, S., Beaulieu-Prévost, D., Sader, J., & Marchand, A. (2019). A systematic literature review of early posttraumatic interventions for victims of violent crime. *Aggression and Violent Behavior, 46*, 15–24. https://doi.org/10.1016/j.avb.2019.01.004

Hale, C. (1996). Fear of crime: A review of the literature. *International Review of Victimology, 4*(2), 79–150. https://doi.org/10.1177/026975809600400201

Hanson, R. F., Sawyer, G. K., Begle, A. M., & Hubel, G. S. (2010). The impact of crime victimization on quality of life. *Journal of Traumatic Stress, 23*(2), 189–197. https://doi.org/10.1002/jts.20508

Hase, M. (2021). The structure of EMDR therapy: A guide for the therapist. *Frontiers in Psychology, 12*, 660753. https://doi.org/10.3389/fpsyg.2021.660753

Hase, M., Balmaceda, U. M., Ostacoli, L., Liebermann, P., & Hofmann, A. (2017). The AIP model of EMDR therapy and pathogenic memories. *Frontiers in Psychology, 8*(SEP), 1578. https://doi.org/10.3389/fpsyg.2017.01578

Hobfoll, S. E., Watson, P., Bell, C. C., Bryant, R. A., Brymer, M. J., Friedman, M. J., Friedman, M., Gersons, B. P. R., de Jong, J. T. V. M., Layne, C. M., Maguen, S., Neria, Y., Norwood, A. E., Pynoos, R. S., Reissman, D., Ruzek, J. I., Shalev, A. Y., Solomon, Z., Steinberg, A. M., & Ursano, R. J. (2007). Five essential elements of immediate and mid-term mass trauma intervention: Empirical evidence. *Psychiatry, 70*(4), 283–315. https://doi.org/10.1521/psyc.2007.70.4.283

Howe, E. G., Rosenzweig, L., & Shuman, A. (2018). Ethical reflections on offering patients accelerated resolution therapy (ART). *Innovations in Clinical Neuroscience, 15*(7–8), 32.

Janssen, H. J., Oberwittler, D., & Koeber, G. (2021). Victimization and its consequences for well-being: A between- and within-person analysis. *Journal of Quantitative Criminology, 37*(1), 101–140. https://doi.org/10.1007/s10940-019-09445-6

Jonathan, B., Neil, R., Martin, A., Rosalind, C., & Catrin, L. (2013). Psychological therapies for chronic post-traumatic stress disorder (PTSD) in adults. *Cochrane Database of Systematic Reviews, 2013*(12), CD003388.

Karakurt, G., Smith, D., & Whiting, J. (2014). Impact of intimate partner violence on women's mental health. *Journal of Family Violence, 29*(7), 693–702. https://doi.org/10.1007/s10896-014-9633-2

Kilpatrick, D. G., & Acierno, R. (2003). Mental health needs of crime victims: Epidemiology and outcomes. *Journal of Traumatic Stress, 16*(2), 119–132. https://doi.org/10.1023/A:1022891005388

Kilpatrick, D. G., Saunders, B. E., Amick-McMullan, A., Best, C. L., Veronen, L. J., & Resnick, H. S. (1989). Victim and crime factors associated with the development of crime-related post-traumatic stress disorder. *Behavior Therapy, 20*(2), 199–214. https://doi.org/10.1016/S0005-7894(89)80069-3

Kilpatrick, D. G., Resnick, H. S., Milanak, M. E., Miller, M. W., Keyes, K. M., & Friedman, M. J. (2013). National estimates of exposure to traumatic events and PTSD prevalence using DSM-IV and DSM-5 criteria. *Journal of Traumatic Stress, 26*(5), 537–547. https://doi.org/10.1002/jts.21848

Kip, K. E., Rosenzweig, L., Hernandez, D. F., Shuman, A., Sullivan, K. L., Long, C. J., Taylor, J., McGhee, S., Girling, S. A., Wittenberg, T., Sahebzamani, F. M., Lengacher, C. A., Kadel, R., & Diamond, D. M. (2013). Randomized controlled trial of accelerated resolution therapy (ART) for symptoms of combat-related post-traumatic stress disorder (PTSD). *Military Medicine, 178*(12), 1298–1309. https://doi.org/10.7205/MILMED-D-13-00298

Le, M. T. H., Holton, S., Romero, L., & Fisher, J. (2018). Polyvictimization among children and adolescents in low- and lower-middle-income countries: A systematic review and meta-analysis. *Trauma, Violence, and Abuse, 19*(3), 323–342. https://doi.org/10.1177/1524838016659489

Lerner, M. J. (2000). Just world belief. In A. E. Kazdin (Ed.), *Encyclopedia of psychology* (Vol. 4, pp. 425–427). American Psychological Association.

Miller, K. E., & Davis, J. L. (2013). In M. Schauer, F. Neuner, & T. Elbert (Eds.), *Narrative exposure therapy: A short-term treatment for traumatic stress disorders* (p. 110). Hogrefe Publishing.

Monnat, S. M., & Chandler, R. F. (2015). Long-term physical health consequences of adverse childhood experiences. *The Sociological Quarterly, 56*(4), 723–752.

Moulding, N. T., Buchanan, F., & Wendt, S. (2015). Untangling self-blame and mother-blame in women's and children's perspectives on maternal protectiveness in domestic violence: Implications for practice. *Child Abuse Review, 24*(4), 249–260. https://doi.org/10.1002/car.2389

NICE. (2018, December). *Guidelines for post-traumatic stress disorder. NICE guideline (NG116).* https://www.nice.org.uk/guidance/ng116

Oram, S., Trevillion, K., Feder, G., & Howard, L. M. (2013). Prevalence of experiences of domestic violence among psychiatric patients: Systematic review. *British Journal of Psychiatry, 202*(2), 94–99. https://doi.org/10.1192/bjp.bp.112.109934

Oram, S., Khalifeh, H., & Howard, L. M. (2017). Violence against women and mental health. *The Lancet Psychiatry, 4*(2), 159–170. https://doi.org/10.1016/S2215-0366(16)30261-9

Pegram, S. E., & Abbey, A. (2019). Associations between sexual assault severity and psychological and physical health outcomes: Similarities and differences among African American and Caucasian Survivors. *Journal of Interpersonal Violence, 34*(19), 4020–4040. https://doi.org/10.1177/0886260516673626

Ramirez de Arellano, M. A., Russell Lyman, D., Jobe-Shields, L., George, P., Dougherty, R. H., Daniels, A. S., Shoma Ghose, S., Huang, L., & Delphin-Rittmon, M. E. (2014). Trauma-focused cognitive behavioral therapy: Assessing the evidence. *Psychiatric Services, 65*(5), 591–602.

Renu, R., & Chopra, G. (2019). Child sexual abuse in India and the protection of children from sexual offences (POCSO) act 2012: A research review. *Integrated Journal of Social Sciences, 6*(2), 49–56.

Resick, P., Monson, C., & Chard, K. (2006). Cognitive processing therapy: Veteran/military version. *Clinical Psychology, 74*, 898–907.

Resick, P. A., Monson, C. M., & Chard, K. M. (2016). *Cognitive processing therapy for PTSD: A comprehensive manua.* Guilford Publications.

Roberts, N. P., Kitchiner, N. J., Kenardy, J., & Bisson, J. I. (2010). Early psychological interventions to treat acute traumatic stress symptoms. *Cochrane Database of Systematic Reviews*, (3), CD007944. https://doi.org/10.1002/14651858.cd007944.pub2

Rose, S. C., Bisson, J., Churchill, R., & Wessely, S. (2002). Psychological debriefing for preventing post traumatic stress disorder (PTSD). *Cochrane Database of Systematic Reviews*, (2), CD000560. https://doi.org/10.1002/14651858.cd000560

Ruback, R. B., & Thompson, M. P. (2001). *Social and psychological consequences of violent victimization.* Sage. Page 29–49. https://dx.doi.org/10.4135/9781483345413.n2

Ruback, R., & Thompson, M. (2014). *Social and psychological consequences of violent victimization.* Sage Publications. https://doi.org/10.4135/9781483345413

Rühs, F., Greve, W., & Kappes, C. (2017). Coping with criminal victimization and fear of crime: The protective role of accommodative self-regulation. *Legal and Criminological Psychology, 22*(2), 359–377. https://doi.org/10.1111/lcrp.12106

Scherg, R. H., & Ejrnæs, A. (2021). Heterogeneous impact of victimization on sense of safety: The influence of past victimization. *Victims and Offenders, 17*(3), 395–420. https://doi.org/10.1080/15564886.2021.1943091

Seid, A. K., Hesse, M., Houborg, E., & Thylstrup, B. (2021). Substance use and violent victimization: Evidence from a cohort of >82,000 patients treated for alcohol and drug use disorder in Denmark. *Journal of Interpersonal Violence, 37*(13–14), NP12427–NP12452. https://doi.org/10.1177/0886260521997456

Sharkey, P. (2018). The long reach of violence: A broader perspective on data, theory, and evidence on the prevalence and consequences of exposure to violence. *Annual Review of Criminology, 1*, 85–102. https://doi.org/10.1146/annurev-criminol-032317-092316

Sookram, S., Saridakis, G., & Mohammed, A. M. (2011). Do victims of crime fear crime more? Empirical evidence from the survey of living conditions (2005) of Trinidad and Tobago. *Social and Economic Studies, 60*(2), 127–144.

Strawn, J. R., Keeshin, B. R., DelBello, M. P., Geracioti, T. D., & Putnam, F. W. (2010). Psychopharmacologic treatment of posttraumatic stress disorder in children and adolescents: A review. *The Journal of Clinical Psychiatry, 71*(7), 16144. https://doi.org/10.4088/JCP.09R05446BLU

Tan, S. Y., & Haining, R. (2016). Crime victimization and the implications for individual health and wellbeing: A Sheffield case study. *Social Science and Medicine, 167*, 128–139. https://doi.org/10.1016/j.socscimed.2016.08.018

Tolin, D. F., & Foa, E. B. (2006). Sex differences in trauma and posttraumatic stress disorder: A quantitative review of 25 years of research. *Psychological Bulletin, 132*(6), 37. https://doi.org/10.1037/0033-2909.132.6.959

Trevillion, K., Oram, S., Feder, G., & Howard, L. M. (2012). Experiences of domestic violence and mental disorders: A systematic review and meta-analysis. *PLoS One, 7*(12), e51740. https://doi.org/10.1371/journal.pone.0051740

Ullman, S. E., & Brecklin, L. R. (2003). Sexual assault history and health-related outcomes in a national sample of women. *Psychology of Women Quarterly, 27*(1), 46–57. https://doi.org/10.1111/1471-6402.t01-2-00006

van Emmerik, A. A. P., Kamphuis, J. H., Hulsbosch, A. M., & Emmelkamp, P. M. G. (2002). Single session debriefing after psychological trauma: A meta-analysis. *Lancet, 360*(9335), 766–771. https://doi.org/10.1016/S0140-6736(02)09897-5

Waits, W., Marumoto, M., & Weaver, J. (2017). Accelerated resolution therapy (ART): A review and research to date. *Current Psychiatry Reports, 19*(3), 1–7. https://doi.org/10.1007/s11920-017-0765-y

Walker, H. E., Freud, J. S., Ellis, R. A., Fraine, S. M., & Wilson, L. C. (2019). The prevalence of sexual revictimization: A meta-analytic review. In *Trauma, violence, and abuse* (Vol. 20(1), pp. 67–80). SAGE Publications. https://doi.org/10.1177/1524838017692364

Watkins, L. E., Sprang, K. R., & Rothbaum, B. O. (2018). Treating PTSD: A review of evidence-based psychotherapy interventions. *Frontiers in Behavioral Neuroscience, 12*, 258. https://doi.org/10.3389/fnbeh.2018.00258

Young, M. A. (1993). *Victim assistance: Frontiers and fundamentals.* Kendall/Hunt Publishing Company.

Zatzick, D. F., Rivara, F. P., Nathens, A. B., Jurkovich, G. J., Wang, J., Fan, M. Y., Russo, J., Salkever, D. S., & Mackenzie, E. J. (2007). A nationwide US study of post-traumatic stress after hospitalization for physical injury. *Psychological Medicine, 37*(10), 1469–1480. https://doi.org/10.1017/S0033291707000943

Zlotnick, C., Johnson, J., & Najavits, L. M. (2009). Randomized controlled pilot study of cognitive-behavioral therapy in a sample of incarcerated women with substance use disorder and PTSD. *Behavior Therapy, 40*(4), 325–336. https://doi.org/10.1016/j.beth.2008.09.004

Index

Milton Keynes UK
Ingram Content Group UK Ltd.
UKHW020946071123
432119UK00003B/20